UNIVERSITY OF
GLOUCESTERSHIRE
at Cheltenham and Gloucester

GRAPHIC DESIGN A NEW HISTORY

Graphic Design
A New History

Stephen J. Eskilson

Laurence King Publishing

LAURENCE KING

Published in 2007 by
Laurence King Publishing Ltd
361–373 City Road
London EC1V 1LR
United Kingdom
Tel: + 44 20 7841 6900
Fax: + 44 20 7841 6910
e-mail: enquiries@laurenceking.co.uk
www.laurenceking.co.uk

A catalogue record for this book is
available from the British Library.

ISBN-13: 978-1-85669-512-3 (hb)
ISBN-10: 1 85669 512 3 (hb)
ISBN-13: 978-1-85669-511-5 (pb)
ISBN-10: 1 85669 511 5 (pb)

Designed by Mues Design
Cover design by Pentagram
Edited by Richard Mason
Picture research by Emma Brown
  and Amanda Russell
Set in Garamond Classico
Printed in China

Back cover: Joseph Sattler, *Pan*, 1895.
St Bride Printing Library, London.
Frontispiece: Carlo Carra, *Patriotic
Celebration, Free Word Painting*, 1914.

Contents

6 The Bauhaus and the New Typography 222

Preface

This book emerged in the context of the radical changes that have revolutionized graphic design over the last few years. Digital technology, which had already substantially influenced the field for two decades, has transformed the way in which many designers conceive of and execute their work. Newly established branches of graphic design such as motion graphics and the demand for highly interactive web-based media have spurred a reevaluation of aesthetic principles that had previously gone unquestioned. At the same time, designers have had to cope with an almost constant state of flux in the advertising industry, while at times balancing their commercial work with a broader commitment to shape society in a positive way. These significant developments are discussed at great length in Chapter 10.

Each year, more scholars of the history of art and design devote themselves to interpreting and evaluating the myriad social and aesthetic implications of graphic design. This greater awareness has spawned numerous books grappling with key figures and defining moments in design history. Considering these developments along with the recent transformation in studio practice, it seemed that the time was ripe for a new book that would attempt an overall assessment of the history of graphic design, taking into account this significant new scholarship. It is my hope that this book will provide a sounding board for scholars and students of graphic design who are as devoted to this subject as I am.

It is my belief that graphic design history has too often been presented through a parade of styles and individual achievements devoid of significant social context, and that this tendency has obscured much of the richness and complexity of its development. In contrast, this book is predicated on the idea that graphic design and typography are the most communal of art forms, and I strive to show how deeply they are embedded in the fabric of society in every era. The impact of political movements, economics, military history, nationalism, and gender, as well as other germane topics are treated continually across the breadth of the book. Another important focus of the book is upon the changing roles of graphic designers, an eclectic group of artists whose exact professional status has often been fluid and indeterminate, a situation that persists to this day. A consistent theme in this book is the aesthetic commonality of graphic design with other design practices, a factor that arose as part of the late nineteenth-century quest for a unified style, in both a visual and an ideological sense.

The introduction and ten chapters are organized in a chronological fashion, although there is some overlap with certain topics spanning more than one chapter. For example, several chapters (Chapters 4, 5, 6, and 7) must be read together to achieve a thorough understanding of graphic design in the seminal period of development between World War I and World War II. Also, certain influential movements such as Dadaism are threaded throughout multiple chapters (Chapters 3, 5, and 6) in an attempt

to clarify the web of connections between its many disparate manifestations. The minor difficulties in navigating these disjunctions should be outweighed by the benefits of greater breadth and depth in the narrative.

The introduction traces the history of classical typography from the time of the Renaissance, following through to the dramatic changes wrought by the Industrial Revolution. Chapter 1 examines the revolt against Victorian aesthetics initiated by the Arts and Crafts movement in the late nineteenth century, and tracks the first flowering of Art Nouveau in France, England, and the United States. Chapter 2 completes the story behind this innovative era, considering Art Nouveau and Expressionist artworks from Scotland, Austria, and Germany. Chapter 3 recounts the decline of Art Nouveau in the face of the pioneering Sachplakat style that arose in Germany before World War I, and then shifts gears, tracking two important trends closely tied to that war: propaganda posters and Dada experiments of the 1910s.

In Chapter 4 the focus shifts to the links that were generated between graphic design and emerging modernist art movements, especially Cubism, Futurism, Vorticism, and Purism. The chapter concludes with a thorough consideration of how these influences coalesced to help form the commercial design style now known as Art Deco. Chapter 5 traces the pivotal role that artists of Dutch De Stijl and Russian Constructivism played in formulating a geometric abstract style that would have longstanding and unforeseen consequences for the history of graphic design. In Chapter 6 we consider the complicated origins of the Bauhaus and the New Typography in Germany during the 1920s, which set the stage for Constructivist precepts to subsequently spread across the rest of Europe. Chapter 7 shifts the focus back to the United States, investigating the gradual adoption of Art Deco and Constructivist techniques, the latter promoted in the 1930s mainly by the Museum of Modern Art in New York City. This chapter also delves into the reemergence of strident propaganda imagery in Germany under the National Socialist regime, concluding with propaganda produced by the adversaries in World War II.

Chapter 8 traces the triumph of the International Style through which European and American graphic design was swept up in a newly reinterpreted version of Constructivist aesthetics. In Chapter 9 we explore the first wave of resistance to the International Style that developed in the 1960s, which eventually coalesced into the group of styles and ideologies that formed Postmodernism.

Chapter 10, the last and longest chapter, examines new developments in graphic design and typography, finding both much to celebrate and question in recent years. It covers various eclectic experiments, Web design, motion graphics, global graphics, current typography, viral advertising, customized design, design-it-yourself, and the ethically responsible "citizen designer".

Acknowledgments

Sadly, my onetime graduate advisor at Brown University, Kermit Champa, passed away in 2004. I am sure he would have offered me pithy words of encouragement along the way. Another professor at Brown University, Dietrich Neumann, has for many years served as a role model of all that a professor can accomplish in both research and teaching. At Eastern Illinois University, my chair Glenn Hild was immensely supportive, helping me to receive course relief during the period I was finishing the manuscript. My friend and colleague Robert Petersen was also always on hand for scholarly advice.

This book owes its existence to Publishing Director Lee Ripley at Laurence King Publishing, who first discussed the project with me in 2003 and firmly but graciously kept me on track throughout the long task of writing. It has been a pleasure to work with someone who is such a credit to her profession. Likewise, Senior Managing Editor Richard Mason has assiduously and patiently guided me through the pitfalls of textual revisions, page proofs, and the picture program, encouraging me to write the boxes and to expand Chapter 10 dramatically. At Yale University Press, Patricia Fidler, Publisher of Art and Architecture, has been a welcoming and enthusiastic presence from the very beginning.

The diversity and relative inaccessibility of the images that I sought created a number of problems for the picture researchers Emma Brown and Amanda Russell, and the Picture Manager Sue Bolsom. I enjoyed many months of email correspondence with them as they ably sought out and secured a number of difficult images based on the slimmest of leads. I thank them for their patience. Richard Hollis, Elaine Lustig Cohen, and Emma Gee all graciously helped fill in the gaps. The designer Melanie Mues had an especially delicate assignment in creating the look for a text on the history of graphic design. She has continually astonished me with her exciting ideas and striking graphic solutions.

During the writing process I received indispensable help from the reviewers who helped me to shape the structure of the final text. In the United States these include Carolina de Bartolo of Academy Art University, San Francisco; Rhonda Levy of the School of Visual Arts, New York; and Nancy Stock-Allen of Moore College of Art and Design, Philadelphia. In the United Kingdom Graham Twemlow of the London College of Communication and the Surrey Institute of Art and Design, and Ian Waites of the University of Lincoln, both provided astute comments for which I am grateful. Close to home, Arlene Eskilson read through the entire first draft of the manuscript and made many valuable observations. Some years ago a senior editor at Laurence King Publishing, Kara Hattersley-Smith, instructed me that publishing is the "art of the possible," a sentiment that has helped to get me through many long days of second-guessing and revision.

This book would never have been completed without the joy created at home by my young son David, who brightens every day for me, and without the assistance of his two grandmas, Arlene Eskilson and Gail Friedman. My wife Jordi is the greatest and the underlying inspiration for all my hopes and accomplishments.

Stephen J. Eskilson, March 2007

THE ORIGINS OF
TYPOGRAPHY AND
GRAPHIC DESIGN

1 Johannes Gutenberg, *Gutenberg Bible*, Mainz, Germany, 1455. By permission of The British Library, London.

Many centuries before graphic design was established as a professional practice during the late nineteenth century, typography played a vital role in the culture of Europe. It was the development of movable type during the fifteenth century that allowed the widespread printing of works in the Latin alphabet during the time of the Renaissance in Europe. The name most commonly associated with the invention of mechanically assisted printing is that of Johann Gutenberg (1398–1468), an entrepreneurial-minded man from Mainz, Germany, who had trained as a goldsmith. Although Gutenberg did not himself invent the printing press, oil-based inks, or cast metal type, he seems to have been the first person in Europe successfully to combine these tools in order to publish books. This new technology allowed for the mass production of printed material on a heretofore unheard-of scale, and quickly replaced the agonizingly slow block printing and hand copying that were predominant at the time.

From Gutenberg to Bodoni

In 1455, Gutenberg published his famous Bible, commonly known as the Gutenberg Bible (*fig. 1*). A huge two-volume work comprising 1,282 forty-two-line folio pages, it had been in production in his workshop for almost two years. Gutenberg probably printed fewer than 200 copies of the Bible, which, while printed on a modified wine press using movable type, were subsequently rubricated by hand, greatly increasing the amount of time needed to complete each volume. (**Rubrication** refers to the process whereby words and phrases are highlighted through different colored inks that either underline the text or are used to write the letters themselves.) In later years, the invention of two-color printing would accelerate the printing process because it completely eliminated the need for manual additions to a given book. Eventually, the use of **italics** and **small capitals** would replace the use of color as a way of showing emphasis.

Gutenberg's Bible was set in a typeset variant of **gothic** script called **Textura**, a word that refers to the dense web of spiky letterforms that fill the completed page, giving it a "textured" look. Textura was an example of "**blackletter**" type, meaning the letters strongly resembled the calligraphic writing of medieval scribes. The layout of the Bible is elegant and straightforward, with the text arranged in two columns that are symmetrically balanced. Both columns of text are **justified** left and right, although most copies feature letter illuminations that defy the boundaries that constrain the body text. Just as important as Gutenberg's synthesis of various printing technologies was his commitment to making mechanically printed books that aspired to the same high aesthetic standards as handwritten volumes. It was important that his Bible was beautiful, in order to compete with the richly decorated manuscripts that dominated the market at this time. Books such as those published by Gutenberg were rare, cherished objects and would have been far beyond the means of all but a tiny slice of European society. From the first, Gutenberg's aesthetic feat pushed book printing into becoming a field with a very high standard of typographic quality, a standard that was maintained in subsequent generations. The release of the Gutenberg Bible demonstrated the potential for printing, and over the next few decades the technology spread across most of Europe. By 1500, there were over 1,000 printers in Germany alone.

When Gutenberg defaulted on his business loans in 1455, his workshop was seized by the businessman Johann Fust (?–1466). Fust, along with his assistant Peter Schöffer (1425–1503), published the lavish Mainz Psalter in 1457 (*fig. 2*). The Mainz Psalter represents an important development in that it combines printed type with **woodcut** illustrations, a technique that would become the basis for centuries of **letterpress** printing. Woodcuts and metal type made to the same thickness could be printed together, facilitating a close aesthetic relationship between text and image. Books published before 1501, such as this one, are called **incunabula**, from the Latin word for "cradle." Because of the tremendous expansion of the printing industry in the late 1400s, over 40,000 incunabula were published before the close of the century.

While Gutenberg and Fust had both published their works in blackletter, a competing style, **roman** letters, emerged in Venice in the 1460s in mechanical printing. The development of roman type is directly tied to the central role that printing played in the Renaissance. (The term "Renaissance" is used generically to designate the period from roughly 1300 to 1600, when much of Europe enjoyed a significant economic expansion, but it refers specifically to the rebirth of interest in the Classical culture of ancient Greece and Rome.) Renaissance printing in Italy was influenced by scholars known as humanists, who concentrated their energies on the study of philosophy, literature, the arts, and languages. Italian humanists had adopted a type of handwriting called Carolingian Minuscule that was based on the style of writing used for official documents in the Carolingian empire during the ninth century. Partly derived from ancient Roman cursive, this handwritten script was adopted by Renaissance humanists because of its ties to antiquity. During the late fifteenth century, this style became known as Humanist Minuscule, and it is the basis for roman forms through to the present day. As the printing industry became more respected and commercially viable, there was even greater use of roman letters because it was no longer necessary for printed works to imitate the gothic script of handwritten works in order to be deemed valuable.

Printing was the core technological achievement that made possible the advent of an era of increased scholarship during the Renaissance. While in previous centuries it had taken years for scribes to produce a few hundred copies of a book, with mechanical presses tens of thousands of copies could be made in a matter of months. One of the finest early books printed in Venice using roman type was Eusebius's treatise *De praeparatione evangelica*.

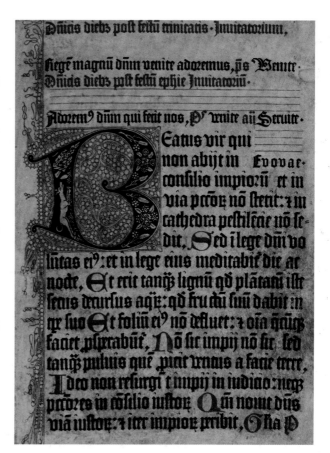

2 Johann Fust and Peter Schöffer, *Mainz Psalter*, 1457.
By permission of The British Library, London.

3 Nicholas Jenson, *Evangelica Praeparatio* from *Veneta in Urbe*, Jenson-Eusebius Typeface, 1470. By permission of The British Library, London.

4 Aldus Manutius, *De Aetna*, Bembo Typeface, 1495. By permission of The British Library, London.

5 Martin Luther, trans., *New Testament*, Schwabacher Typeface, 1522. Woodcuts of the Apocalypse by the Master (sometimes identified as Hans Cranach). By permission of The British Library, London.

ABCDEFGHIJKLM
NOPQRSTVWXYZ
abcdefghijklmnopqrstuv
wxyz1234567890*&!.,?

"With their broad forms and light proportions, Garamond's designs represented a startling change from the rather heavy contemporary French gothics."

6 Claude Garamond, Garamond Typeface, 1540.

Eusebius was a fourth-century Christian theologian who is considered one of the first historians of the church. The treatise was published by a French expatriate, Nicolas Jenson (1420–1480). Jenson had learned the technique of printing in Mainz, where he lived prior to moving to Venice in 1467. Jenson proved to have an excellent eye for forms that were both highly legible and beautiful, and **Jenson-Eusebius**, with its light, open roman letters is much admired to this day (*fig. 3*). The contrast in forms and the sloping **stress** are both derived from writing with a quill pen. Despite the handwritten roots of the typefaces, it is significant that typographers such as Jenson were essentially metalworkers, who designed letters as part of the process of engraving the metal punches—they did not draw their type by hand. This fact makes the smooth, flowing forms and good "color," or overall visual texture, of Jenson's roman that much more remarkable.

Around 1500, Aldus Manutius (1449–1515), a Venetian humanist and printer, published the first work in roman italic type. Based on cursive handwriting, italic was not used as a subset to create emphasis, as it mainly is today, but was its own style— one that proved valuable because more words could fit on each line than with either gothic or roman. In 1501, Manutius, in association with the punch cutter Francesco Griffo, released a volume of poetry by the ancient Latin author Virgil. Manutius's attention to economic issues also led him to become one of the first publishers of small printed books, called octavos because each sheet was folded so as to create eight leaves.

Manutius also produced a number of roman forms, and the one he used in his 1495 volume of *De Aetna*, by Pietro Bembo, proved highly influential (*fig. 4*). This essay tells of the Renaissance author's journey to Mount Etna, the volcano in Sicily that was sacred to the ancient Romans. The type designed for the book, called **Bembo**, was even more readable and harmonious than similar ones produced by Jenson. Its refined proportions allow the eye to flow smoothly across the page. While the individual letters are eminently legible, they are also quite stylish; the midbar of the "F," for example, is elongated for aesthetic purposes. Along with Jenson-Eusebius, Bembo is the basis for the group of roman types called "**Old Style**," which together are distinguished by their understated contrast, bracketed serifs, and oblique stress. Historic typefaces are traditionally grouped into three stylistic and chronological categories: Old Style, followed by Transitional, and then Modern.

Another important contribution to Renaissance typography was made by the French printer and publisher Claude Garamond (1480–1561). One of Garamond's key contributions was an adaptation of Manutius's Bembo that is perhaps more refined than the original (*fig. 6*). With their broad forms and light proportions, Garamond's designs represented a startling change from the rather heavy contemporary French gothics. In absorbing Italian aesthetics, Garamond was following the path paved by his mentor, Geoffroy Tory, a humanist who had journeyed to the Italian peninsula and brought back an enthusiasm for the work of Jenson and Manutius. This was in concert with the strong overall trend in French art and culture during the later Renaissance to admire and absorb Classical forms that were being revived in Italy. While Garamond's roman faces have many Italian characteristics, overall they have somewhat more pronounced contrast and slimmer, mainly horizontal serifs. It is important to be aware that contemporary versions of historic typefaces such as **Garamond** are often not true to the originals.

It was Garamond's promotion of Old Style typefaces that resulted in the gradual disappearance of blackletter in French publishing, as roman faces came to the fore during the sixteenth century. In fact, from that time on, roman type became strongly associated with the French and Italian traditions, while Germany laid claim to the blackletter form. Garamond is also credited with establishing the first type foundry, as he would make copies of his faces and sell them to other printers. He was also the first typographer to use italic as a complement to roman type, and he designed the first italic face that was intended not to stand alone but to serve as a partner to roman letters.

At the time of the invention of mechanical printing, so-called gothic, or blackletter, scripts predominated in Europe. While the older styles called Textura, used by Gutenberg, and Rotunda— which had also been around since the Middle Ages—continued to be used, the new styles called **Schwabacher** and **Fraktur** would prove to be much more influential in future centuries. The reason for this longevity was related to their roots in Germany, through which Schwabacher and Fraktur came to be associated with that region's national identity. Schwabacher appeared in Germany as early as 1480, but its importance was greatly increased in 1522, when it was used for the publication of Martin Luther's (1483–1546) German translation of the New Testament (*fig. 5*). In rejecting the authority of the Pope and the Roman Church, Luther sparked the establishment of Protestantism, a process now referred to as the Reformation. However, Luther's choice of Schwabacher for his text also signaled a rejection of the roman type that prevailed in Italy, giving his seal of approval to the idea that blackletter styles were somehow quintessentially German in character.

Eight years before the publication of Luther's New Testament, in 1514, the printer Anton Schönsperger (?–1520) had developed the type called Fraktur (somewhat confusingly, the term "fraktur" is also used generically to refer to all blackletter scripts created after 1450). Based in Augsburg, Schönsperger relied on that city's long tradition of fine calligraphy in order to design his new type. As suggested by its name, Fraktur features broken curves and oblique strokes that retain the character of the calligrapher's brush that originally inspired the forms. Fraktur first appeared in 1514, when Schönsperger published the *Gebetbuch*, a kind of prayer book, for Kaiser Maximilian I. As would be the case with Luther's book, this event helped to reinforce the concept that blackletter was related to the religion, government, and culture of Germany. By the end of the sixteenth century, roman and blackletter type were both flourishing and were often printed side by side; however, the roots of their future opposition had already been established.

In the seventeenth century, at a time when the roman Old Style faces had become established across much of Europe, there was continuing typographic development, resulting in a new class of typefaces called "**Transitional**." Transitional type gradually arose during the Baroque era, a period that is roughly synonymous with the sixteenth and early seventeenth centuries. While the word "baroque" has stylistic connotations in the fine arts,

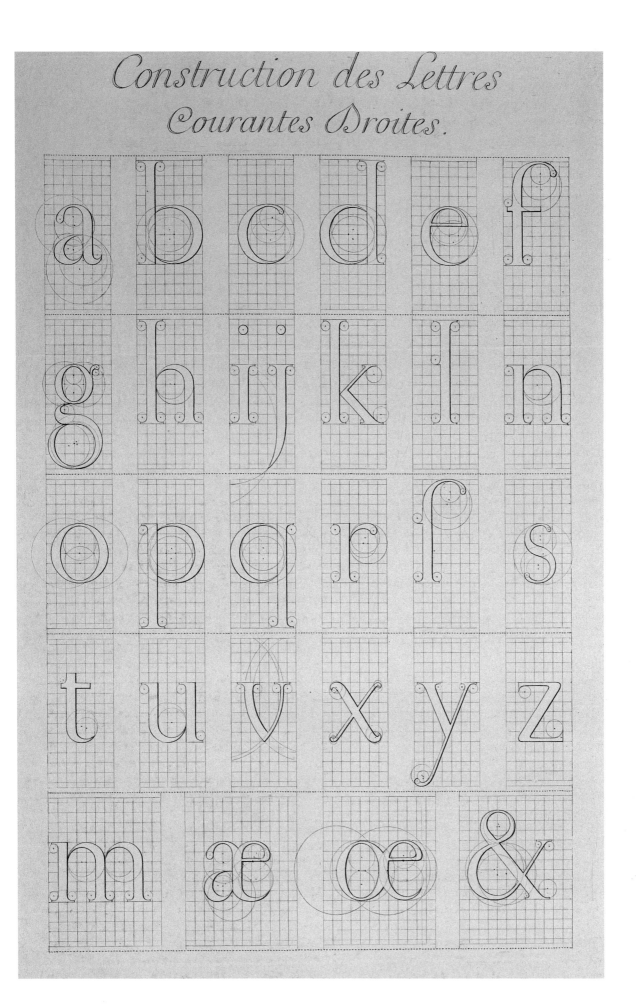

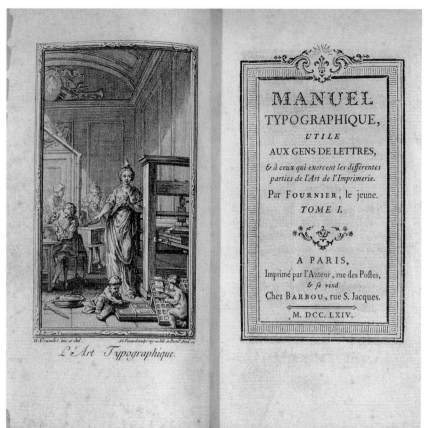

L'Art Typographique.

opposite: **7** Philippe Grandjean,
Romain du Roi Typeface, 1702.
St Bride Printing Library, London.

left: **8** Pierre Simon Fournier, *Manuel
Typographique*, vol. 1, Paris, 1766.
St Bride Printing Library, London.

where it refers to a break with Renaissance harmony in favor of greater expressiveness, in typography the term does not really carry any stylistic meaning. In fact, baroque Transitional faces are very closely connected to the Renaissance aesthetic, emphasizing classical balance over any other attribute.

An important event in typography during the Baroque period was the increasing patronage of the French royal government. This development was part of a broader movement whereby the government under Louis XIV (r. 1643–1715) instituted a state policy through which the arts would be funded and controlled through official institutions. Cardinal Richelieu (1585–1642), a key adviser to the king, had earlier overseen the establishment of an Imprimerie Royale, or "royal printing works." In 1692, the king ordered that a new set of royal typefaces be created for the use of the Imprimerie Royale. After years of research and discussion by a government committee at the Academy of Sciences, Philippe Grandjean de Fouchy (1666–1714) was appointed to cut the new type. The resulting Romain du Roi, "roman of the king," would influence European typography for well over a century (*fig. 7*). The invention of the Romain du Roi represents probably the first time when a horizontal and vertical grid became the basic tool for structuring a typeface. The commission that designed the typeface used a 64-square grid, with each unit further split up into 36 smaller squares, so that the entire system totaled 2,304 tiny squares. This design process gave typography the imprimatur of a scientific pursuit, whereby letter forms are worked out not by intuitive but by rational, logical processes. In a sense, this episode established the final link in the definition of typography that exists unto the present—a field that requires a synthesis of many disparate skills: the practical know-how of the manual worker,

the creativity of the fine artist, and the logic of a scientist. The Romain du Roi established the stylistic principles of the Transitional faces, including more vertical stress, greater contrast in stroke width, wider proportions, and thin, elegant serifs.

Another French typographer, Pierre Simon Fournier (1712–1768), made a major contribution to the field in 1737, when he invented the first point system for measuring type. Fournier's system, a part of the trend toward treating typography with the rational approach of the empirical scientist, used a scale based on inches, which were divisible into 72 points. Fournier also published the first encyclopedic survey of typography, the two-volume *Manuel Typographique* (1766; *fig. 8*). This work represented the first comprehensive overview of type ever published, and it included a discussion of type from across Europe, offering examples of different regional trends. This kind of attention to the classification of a given subject or phenomenon was quite characteristic of the philosophical movement known as the Enlightenment, which began in France in the eighteenth century. Enlightenment thinkers were consumed with the idea of compiling and analyzing human knowledge, and the first universal encyclopedia was published during this era. The scientific approach to typography, whereby it was treated as a field with consistent, mathematically based rules, suggests the application of Enlightenment philosophy to type.

In 1725, William Caslon (1692–1766) set up a type foundry in London that would eventually turn into a family legacy, as future generations of the Caslon family continued to operate it well into the nineteenth century. Before Caslon, English printing, which had been pioneered by William Caxton (c. 1422–c. 1491) in the fifteenth century, had remained a somewhat haphazard

ABCDEFGHIJKLM NOPQRSTUVWXYZ abcdefghijklmnopqrst uvwxyz1234567890.?!*&

"Caslon would in fact become the most influential face ever produced in England."

above, below: **9** William Caslon, Caslon Typeface, 1725.

ABCD
ABCDE
ABCDEFG
ABCDEFGHI
ABCDEFGHIJK
ABCDEFGHIJKL
ABCDEFGHIKLMN

French Cannon.

Quoufque tan-
dem abutere,
Catilina, pati-

Quoufque tandem
abutere, Catilina,
patientia noftra?

DOUBLE PICA ROMAN.
Quoufque tandem abutere, Catilina, patientia noftra ? quamdiu
nos etiam furor ifte tuus cludet ?
quem ad finem fefe effrenata jac-
ABCDEFGHJIKLMNOP

GREAT PRIMER ROMAN.
Quoufque tandem abutere, Catilina, patientia noftra ? quamdiu nos etiam furor ifte tuus cludet ? quem ad finem fefe effrenata jactabit audacia ? nihilne te
nocturnum præfidium palatii, nihil urbis vigiliæ, nihil timor populi, nihil con-
ABCDEFGHIJKLMNOPQRS

ENGLISH ROMAN.
Quoufque tandem abutere, Catilina, patientia
noftra? quamdiu nos etiam furor ifte tuus cludet?
quem ad finem fefe effrenata jactabit audacia ?
nihilne te nocturnum præfidium palatii, nihil
urbis vigiliæ, nihil timor populi, nihil confen-
fus bonorum omnium, nihil hic munitiffimus
ABCDEFGHIJKLMNOPQRSTVUW

PICA ROMAN.
Melium, novis rebus ftudentem, manu fua occidit.
Fuit, fuit ifta quondam in hac repub. virtus, ut viri
fortes acrioribus fuppliciis civem pernicisfum, quam
acerbiffimum hoftem coërcerent. Habemus enim fe-
natufconfulrum in te, Catilina, vehemens, & grave:
non deeft reip. confilium, neque autoritas hujus or-
dinis : nos, nos, dico aperte, confules defumus. De-
ABCDEFGHIJKLMNOPQRSTVUWX

SMALL PICA ROMAN. No1.
At nos vigefimum jam diem patimur hebefcere aciem horum
autoritatis. habemus enim hujufmodi fenatufconfultum, ve-
rumtamen inclufum in tabulis, tanquam gladium in vagina
reconditum ; quo ex fenatufconfulto confeftim interfectum te
effe, Catilina, convenit. Vivis : & vivis non ad deponen-
dam, fed ad confirmandam audaciam. Cupio, P. C., me
effe clementem : cupio in tantis reipub. periculis non dif-
ABCDEFGHIJKLMNOPQRSTVUWXYZ

affair, lacking a clear aesthetic direction. While Caslon designed over 200 typefaces during his career, the type known simply as **Caslon**, which was based on contemporary Dutch models, would always lie at the root of his designs (*fig. 9*). Caslon would in fact become the most influential face ever produced in England. What made the original Caslon so popular was not any dramatic, stylish flair, but rather its solid functionality. The type is eminently legible, meaning that each character can easily be recognized, as well as readable; text set in Caslon seems to flow effortlessly past the reader's eyes. Caslon is a Transitional roman, in that it has more vertically oriented stress, greater contrast, and finer serifs than Old Style faces. In addition, Transitional faces such as Caslon appear overall more fluid than those of the Old Style. In 1734, Caslon issued a broadside specimen detailing thirty-seven typefaces that firmly established his reputation as the premier English typographer of the day.

Caslon became more than just an official type like Grandjean's Romain du Roi; indeed, it became invested with the idea that it encapsulated English national identity. As a national type, Caslon was used in a wide variety of printed matter, from the most exalted government proclamation to the most ephemeral broadside. Caslon made its way across the Atlantic Ocean to the United States, where it was also used as an official type, notably on early printed copies of both the Declaration of Independence and the Constitution. The preeminence of Caslon, which is based more on its overall usefulness than its aesthetic qualities, prefigures the similar widespread use of Helvetica in the second half of the twentieth century.

The other notable English typographer of the eighteenth

ABCDEFGHIJKLM NOPQRSTUVWXYZ abcdefghijklmnopqrst uvwxyz 1234567890.?!*

"... Baskerville had to invent new inks in order to make the slender, delicate shapes of his letters stand out on the page."

10 John Baskerville, Baskerville Roman (great primer), printed by John Baskerville, Birmingham, England, 1772. St Bride Printing Library, London.

century was John Baskerville (1706–1775). In 1750, Baskerville established a foundry in Birmingham and began promoting his eponymous type, which was first used in a volume of Virgil published in 1757 (*fig. 10*). In direct contrast to the stunning success of Caslon, Baskerville's designs were almost universally condemned for what was perceived as their stark, abstract qualities and extreme contrast in stroke widths. In addition, the delicate forms of the letters were criticized as too thin to be read easily. A desire to print his typeface accurately led Baskerville to a number of innovations in the printing process. First, Baskerville had to invent new inks in order to make the slender, delicate shapes of his letters stand out on the page. He also experimented with different paper types, finally settling on wove paper that had a smooth, glossy finish. Baskerville also used a technique called "hot pressing," whereby he would heat newly printed pages between copper plates, a process that smoothed the sheet while also setting the ink more effectively. It is hard for modern eyes jaded by an astonishing range of typeface designs to understand why Caslon could have been viewed as a supreme achievement in type design whereas Baskerville was condemned as an experimental, amateurish product. Today, only committed typographers would be likely to note the differences between these two romans, which share a number of similarities in terms of stress and basic letter shapes. While the lighter proportions of **Baskerville** in comparison with Caslon are quite evident, it is difficult to imagine an age when such apparent subtleties would be recognized and debated outside the profession itself. Furthermore, it may be difficult to conceive of an era when homely appeal won out over stylish experiment.

The second half of the eighteenth century witnessed the continuing evolution of typographic styles, in particular the creation of "**Modern**" typefaces. This term can prove confusing in the context of other usages of the word "modern," which is commonly associated in the history of art with developments in painting from around 1850. Modern typefaces tend toward even greater contrast between thin and thick strokes, so much so that the thin ones are often no more than hairlines. Serifs also are reduced to hairlines. The stress of a Modern face is decidedly vertical, as is the overall geometry of the individual letters, which are more abstract in appearance. The Modern style represents a decisive move through which metal type no longer resembles handwriting but consists of forms built on an armature of horizontal, vertical, and circular elements. In line with the Enlightenment's exaltation of science, it became more common for typographers around this time to use tools such as the compass and ruler in the development of typefaces.

One of the most successful firms in France that pioneered the Modern style was the Didot Foundry, which was originally established in 1713 by François Didot (1689–1757). The founder's son, François Ambroise Didot (1730–1804), was responsible for a number of typographic innovations, including the introduction of smooth wove paper to France. As was the case with Baskerville in England, this achievement allowed for the accurate printing of the hairline strokes that became an important part of the Modern style. The younger Didot also invented a new system of type measurement based on Fournier's original one, but now using the French *pied au roi*, or foot, as the basis. This unit was divided into 12 inches, each consisting of 72 points. Didot also rationalized

OEUVRES

DE

JEAN RACINE.

TOME PREMIER.

À PARIS,

DE L'IMPRIMERIE DE PIERRE DIDOT L'AÎNÉ,

AU PALAIS NATIONAL DES SCIENCES ET ARTS.

AN IX; M. DCCCI.

Imnopqrstu

left: **11** Firmin Didot, *Oeuvres de Jean Racine*, Modern Roman Typeface, Nouvelle Edition, Paris, 1801.
By Permission of The British Library, London.

below: **12** Johann F. Unger and F. Didot, Unger-Fraktur Typeface, 1793.

ABCDEFGHIJKLMNOPQR STUV WXYZabcdefghijkmnopqrstuvwxyz 1234567890.; !?&

"Bodoni, would prove to be more popular than the startlingly original Didot."

13 Giambattista Bodoni, Bodoni Typeface, 1785.

the system of names given to different type sizes, replacing the older, whimsical terms such as "parisienne" with the point system. This radical new system would quickly spread across the whole of Europe, thus creating an international language for classifying type.

François Ambroise Didot's two sons, Pierre and Firmin, were mostly responsible for the final form of the eponymous Modern roman, **Didot**. Around 1783, Firmin Didot refined his family's roman face to help create the new Modern style. Didot would soon become the most influential Modern face, because it set the standard for contrast, stress, and geometric structure. It also introduced the Modern technique of regularizing the width of capitals, so that they do not disrupt the consistency of a line of text with too many disparate sizes. Along these lines, conventionally wide letters such as the "M" are condensed, while narrower ones such as a "T" are expanded, making for a bold block of text. Also, the Modern style eliminated ligatures between letters, such as the "ST," which had been common in the Old Style. Didot represents one of the first instances in which a typographer seemed to be aware of the virtues of white, negative space, as the extreme contrasts of the strokes brought this element to the fore.

Firmin Didot's type was brilliantly employed by his brother Pierre in the latter's acclaimed edition of the works of the foremost French dramatist of his age, Jean Racine (1639–1699). The title page of the first volume shown here (*fig. 11*) displays the great elegance of Didot, its bold contrasts grabbing the eye of the reader. The simple, strong geometric quality of Didot formed a strong parallel with the contemporary painting style called Neoclassicism. As the name suggests, Neoclassical painting revived the linear style of the Renaissance, but it also strove to simplify forms and compositions to reach an almost abstract ideal. Similarly, Didot is a reductive typeface that does away with unnecessary flourishes in order to stress its clear and direct underlying structure.

In 1793, Johann Friedrich Unger (1753–1804), reacting to the increasing dominance of roman forms in Europe as well as to the great expense suffered by German printers who had to work in both blackletter and roman forms, sought to create a variant of Fraktur that would be more universal in appeal. The resulting type, **Unger-Fraktur**, represented an attempt to inject some of the geometric clarity of roman Moderns into the German type (*fig. 12*). Together with Didot, Unger produced a number of variants of his hybrid type, but was unsuccessful in promoting their adoption commercially. Already, the association of roman with the French-Italian tradition and of blackletter with the German tradition had become too deeply entrenched, and European typography would remain split until the mid-twentieth century.

In Italy, Giambattista Bodoni (1740–1830) of Parma introduced the Modern style in the late eighteenth century. Influenced by the work of the Didot foundry, Bodoni created a beautiful roman that further defined the Modern style. Bodoni's roman face adopted many of the innovations of Didot, but is arguably less adventurous, as some of the contrasts, for example, are not as radical as those found in the French typeface (*fig. 13*). As was the case with the typefaces of Caslon and Baskerville, the less extreme example, **Bodoni**, would prove to be more popular than the startlingly original Didot. Five years after Bodoni's death in 1813, his *Manuale Tipografico* was published, which included a comprehensive discussion of over 300 typefaces from across Europe as well as Asia, and which would influence generations of future typographers. This publication in many ways served as a culmination of the classical period of typography, which had begun in the fifteenth century, as changes in society during the nineteenth century fundamentally altered the field. During this era, the element of connoisseurship that had heretofore played such a prominent role in the history of typography would be devalued in favor of the pursuit of commerce. The nineteenth century also witnessed the birth of graphic design.

14 Anonymous, Wood Typeface no. 22, c. 1890.

The Nineteenth Century, an Expanding Field

During the nineteenth century, the continuing Industrial Revolution and the rise of cities stimulated a demand for mass media and advertising on an altogether new scale, while inventions such as the steam press greatly enhanced the possibilities for mass production of printed materials. The German inventors Friedrich Koenig (1774–1833) and Andreas Bauer (1783–1860) sold their new press to the *Times* newspaper of London in 1814. It could produce over 1,000 pages per hour. Koenig and Bauer's flat-bed press was later superseded by the American inventor Richard Hoe's (1812–1886) rotary steam press (1843), which could print literally millions of pages per week. Late in the century, the profession of graphic design was established when the aesthetic dimension of the mass media was separated from its production.

It is possible to understand both the changes wrought in typographic practice and the formation of the graphic design profession only within the context of the Industrial Revolution that had begun in Europe in the eighteenth century and increased in impact throughout the nineteenth. The Industrial Revolution is the name given to the period when European economies shifted from a mainly rural, agricultural base, to one focused on the mass-production of goods in large factories. One direct result of the Industrial Revolution was the increasing concentration of the population in large cities and the consequent rise of mass culture, as merchants of all sorts of products, including artistic ones such as theater and the visual arts, sought to reach out to the millions of inhabitants of the modern metropolis. In this respect, while the

Industrial Revolution is usually defined in terms of the components of industry such as the steam engine, the railroad, coal, iron, and steel, it is important not to overlook how the rise of inexpensive, mass reproduced printed materials contributed to life in the new urban setting. The steam-engine-driven press that was developed in 1814 furthered this phenomenon. The expansion of the printing industry was immense during the nineteenth century, as, for example, the British public witnessed the establishment of over 2,000 periodicals during this period. Some of these inexpensive publications were printed in runs of over 200,000. The situation was similar in other Western locales, especially France, Germany, the Austro-Hungarian Empire, and the United States.

Perhaps the most dramatic transformation in typography during the nineteenth century was the newfound proliferation of a wide variety of innovative typefaces. Responding to the demands of urban culture, printing workshops devised thousands of new typefaces for decorative and display purposes. These typefaces were deployed in a variety of printed media, with the printed broadsheet and its larger and more glamorous cousin the poster being the most ubiquitous.

One class of type invented in the nineteenth century that has remained influential through to the present day is the **sans serif**. The first commercial sans serif was released in 1816 by William Caslon IV (1780–1869), who had taken over the operation of his family's historic type foundry in 1807 (*fig. 15*). Unlike the tremendous contrast visible in contemporary roman Modern faces such as Didot, sans serif type tended toward uniform strokes. However, the vertical stress and strong geometric structure of most sans serifs seem to copy some of the characteristics of Modern romans. This new kind of typeface found a home in advertising, where the letters worked very well in extremely large sizes. The effectiveness

TWO LINES ENGLISH EGYPTIAN.

W CASLON JUNR   LETTERFOUNDER

15 William Caslon IV, Sans-Serif Type, 1816.

16 William Thorowgood, Six-line Pica Egyptian (slab-serif) Typeface, from *New Specimen of Printing Types* by William Thorowgood 1821. St Bride Printing Library, London.

of sans serif type as a vehicle for bold statements is quite evident (*fig. 14*). The type shown here was carved in wood, an economical and flexible technique that arose during the nineteenth century to service the seemingly unquenchable thirst for exciting, inexpensive typefaces. In the 1820s, Darius Wells (1800–1875) had invented the lateral wood router, a machine that allowed for the mass production of wood type. The last decade of the century witnessed the introduction of the first professionally designed sans serif typefaces, such as **Akzidenz Grotesk**, released by the German foundry Berthold in 1896.

Another key typographical innovation of the nineteenth century was the slab serif, which, as the name suggests, denotes typefaces that feature heavy rectangular serifs (*fig. 16*). In direct contrast to the sans serif, the **slab serif** face overemphasizes the serif rather than eliminating it. In some ways, however, the result is the same: slab serif faces appear weighty and grounded, with some of the same uniform strokes common in the sans serifs. The goal, as was the case with so many new typefaces during this era, was to grab the viewer's eye amid a busy urban milieu. Slab serif faces demand to be noticed in a way that was somewhat alien to classical romans; previous successful types such as Caslon had succeeded partly because they were almost invisible in the way they refused to stand out.

In a curious quirk of fate, sans and slab serif faces became known as "Egyptians." There is nothing remotely Egyptian about them; rather, the name arose as a fashionable marketing device, because Europeans were fascinated with Egypt during the early nineteenth century as a result of Napoleon's imperial campaigns. In a period sometimes referred to as an era of "Egyptomania," a myriad products in addition to type sought to capitalize on the fashion for all things Egyptian.

Photography

Photography was an important technological development during the nineteenth century that would later prove crucial to the evolution of graphic design. The ability to make "drawings with light," which is the literal meaning of the word "photography," was discovered simultaneously in the 1830s by a Frenchman, Louis Jacques Mandé Daguerre (1799–1851), and an Englishman, William Henry Fox Talbot (1800–1877). The "daguerreotype" shown here is generally considered to be the first successful photograph ever made, a view of an assortment of objects in Daguerre's studio (fig. 17). Over the next few decades, additional inventors made adjustments to the technology, including the ability to make positive prints on paper, establishing it as a practical way of recording images from life. One of early photography's most reliable markets was the portrait studio, which allowed middle-class people to have inexpensive images made of themselves. The resulting association of photography with low-quality commercial studios created a stigma that lasted for many decades, and it was only in the twentieth century that photography began to be taken seriously by artists and designers.

By the late nineteenth century, technology had improved to the point where photography was a ubiquitous part of life in Europe and the United States. Advancements such as the creation of stop-action photography, as well as the introduction of inexpensive portable cameras, helped establish the medium as a useful component of everyday life. Still, photographs were only rarely mass-produced in magazines and newspapers, mainly because the prevailing letterpress technology prevented the side-by-side reproduction of photo and type. For this reason, when photos were reproduced in the mass media it was through the process of wood engraving, because those images could be printed alongside traditional type. Owing to these printing difficulties, photography did not become an important element of graphic design until the 1920s, many decades after its initial invention (see Chapter 5).

17 Louis Daguerre, *Still Life in Studio,* 1837. Daguerreotype.

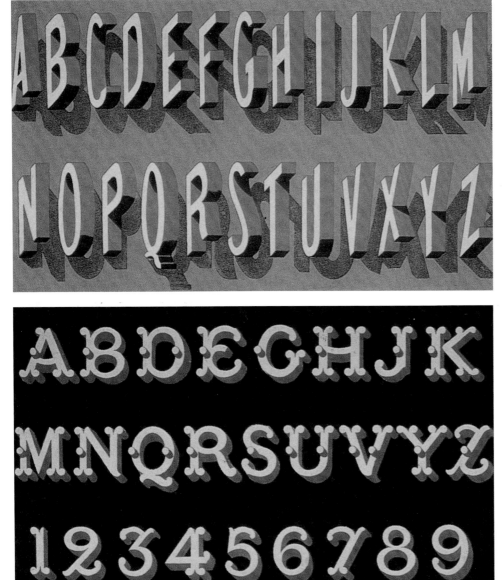

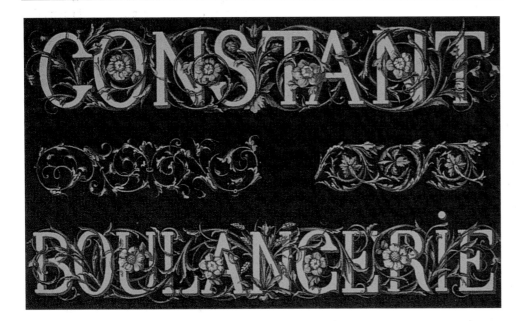

Fat faces, script faces, shaded faces, even three-dimensional ones: a wealth of decorative types made their first appearances during this exciting era (*fig. 18*). The burgeoning markets for the products of foundries in the 1800s vastly expanded as advertisers tried to keep up with the latest trends, while a number of **historicist** design styles also came to the fore. One glance at a type specimen sheet or poster makes it immediately clear how the field of typography experienced an increase in inventiveness and experimentation during this era. One issue that complicates the history of Victorian typography is the fact that the field became overrun not only with the work of knowledgeable professionals but also by a wave of amateur typographers. For this reason, many Victorian typefaces lack any sense of balance or harmony and were clearly the product of untrained printshop workers. This fact cut both ways: on the one hand, a great deal of Victorian type was poorly designed and featured more flash than substance; on the other, the influx of amateur designs enlivened the field with new energy that made nineteenth-century type more exciting than before. This same ambiguous situation has recurred in recent years with the advent of digital technology.

Perhaps the most visible type of inexpensive, mass-printed material in the nineteenth century was the poster. Literally millions of copies of advertising posters were printed on the steam-driven presses of Europe. They were often displayed on every available surface along the streets and avenues of major cities such as London, New York, and Paris. In an attempt to give some semblance of order to this visually chaotic situation, many neighborhoods designated specific kiosks and what were called

"hoardings," where posters could be legally hung by their distributors. Local governments often benefited from the immense number of posters that were pasted on to urban hoardings, as they collected a small tax on each and every image (*fig. 19*). Despite the creation of a number of sophisticated new printing technologies early in the century, most posters from the 1800s were printed with relief type, called letterpress, while the images were printed using inexpensive woodcuts.

One of the most startling aspects of nineteenth-century typography and design—which is often called "Victorian," after the name of the British queen who dominated this era in Europe, reigning from 1837 until 1901—is the manner in which a vast variety of apparently dissonant type styles would be employed together on the same page or poster. The poster illustrated here is a good example of mid-nineteenth-century work (*fig. 20*). The printer has not really attempted to use any clear compositional techniques, but has merely filled in all the available space with either image or text, employing an assortment of type sizes and weights in a manner that creates a chaotic overall effect, like the blaring of a sideshow tout. It seems at times that printers simply grabbed whatever type was at hand and, using eclecticism as the only design criterion, set about finishing the work as soon as possible.

The name "Astley's" at the top of the left column is an excellent example of the "fat faces" that had been invented in the early nineteenth century and were often employed in letterpress posters. Bold fat face type is recognizable by the extreme contrast in width of the strokes, such the "S" or the "Y" in "Astley's." The sheer variety of lettering—roman, italic, silhouette, bold, three-dimensional, etc.—and the tremendous range in "**x height**," or scale, of the letters, is matched by the endless list of spectacles that make up the show being advertised. The nicely **foreshortened** woodcut of the Trojan Horse was probably a stock image that would be reused on successive occasions for a variety of subjects. Interestingly, no attempt is made to knit together the text and image, a design criterion that would subsequently become very important to early graphic artists. One other note on this particular image: it is, unfortunately for the purposes of comparison with later works, undoubtedly one of the finest examples of the work of printers from this era (which is why it has been preserved), and should not be taken as representative of the overall low quality that prevailed at the time.

The Victorian age was one that witnessed the flourishing of a multitude of confusing styles. It was not at all uncommon to find a simple advertisement or magazine cover festooned with a Classical temple and allegorical figures, so that it looked like a page drawn from an illuminated manuscript. A cover from 1874, from *Demorest's Illustrated Monthly*, an American publication, is typical of the genre (*fig. 21*). A bizarre compendium of different type styles was printed so as to appear as if it is written on a magnificent shield, while allegorical figures grace both sides like those in a Renaissance religious painting. With a composition that can only be described as an example of horror vacui (a fear of emptiness), garlands and ribbons were used to fill any available space. Nothing about this illustration would naturally lead the viewer to recognize that they were looking at the cover of "the model parlor magazine of America."

19 John Thomson, Bill Posters, 1876–7, from *Streetlife in London*, 1878. Photograph. V&A Picture Library, Victoria & Albert Museum, London.

20 Anonymous, *The Siege of Troy, or The Giant Horse of Sinon*, Astley's Circus, 1833. Advertisement. Letterpress and woodcut.
V&A Picture Library, Courtesy of the Trustees of the Victoria & Albert Museum, London.

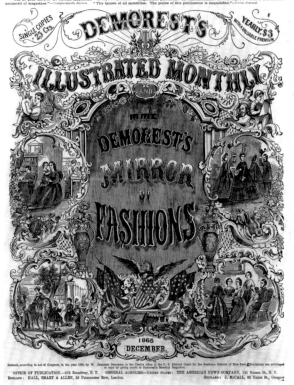

21 Anonymous, *Demorest's Illustrated Monthly*, Dec 1865. Magazine cover. Library of Congress, Washington, DC.

22 Henry Mayhew, ed., *Punch*, p. 10, July 1841, London. By permission of The British Library, London.

It is worth noting that the standard view of Victorian typography—as a sort of dark age characterized by eclecticism, excess, and disorganization waiting for the enlightened reformers of the Arts and Crafts movement to rescue it—is something of a distortion. Plenty of posters, newspapers, and magazines from this era displayed a fundamental commitment to clarity and simplicity. For example, *Punch*, the satirical British periodical known for its irreverent political cartoons, demonstrated an admirable reserve in its pages. The layout of *Punch*, founded in 1841 by Henry Mayhew (1812–1887) and Ebenezer Landells (1808–1860), was actually rather staid. The design featured two columns of justified text separated by thin rules, making it anything other than over-decorative or eclectic (*fig. 22*). Using a harmonious mix of roman and sans serif, the pages are easily readable. This effective layout remained the standard for the magazine for over a century.

The Advent of Graphic Design

The proliferation of the mass media during the nineteenth century came initially without a complementary expansion in the design profession. Rather, the vast majority of printed materials such as posters and books were not "designed," insofar as scant attention was paid to artistic issues of composition, drawing, and color. Instead, most books, posters, and the like were drawn up by the "job printers" who worked on miscellaneous projects with a

vast range in terms of quality. The primary work of a **job printer** was to operate the industrial machinery of publication. The focus of advertisers and the printers who worked for them was on simple functionality—getting a message out to the urban public. In the headlong rush to promote the latest theatrical event, circus, or soap, little attention was paid to the artistic quality of printed posters that were intended to last for only a few days, or perhaps a week, before they would be covered by a new layer of advertising. In fact, one of the major concerns of advertisers during the heyday of the poster in the 1890s was the question of whether an artistically designed image would create more business than a less accomplished one.

Intense competition among the numerous poster publishers, as well as book publishers, of the day caused many to seek cost savings at every turn. Most printed materials offered little in the way of quality typesetting or elegant page layout. This situation allows today's historians, using hindsight, to offer a straightforward answer to one of the most basic questions about the history of graphic design: when did the profession come into existence? The answer is that the profession was established when the task of designing printed material was separated from the task of printing it. Of course, this process did not happen all at once in a single month, year, or even decade, but was the cumulative effect of a number of different market and cultural forces at work. The term "graphic design" itself did not appear until the 1920s, at a time when the profession was still in the process of defining itself. The changing status, generally for the better, of the graphic design profession will be a major theme of this book, and will reappear in a number of later chapters.

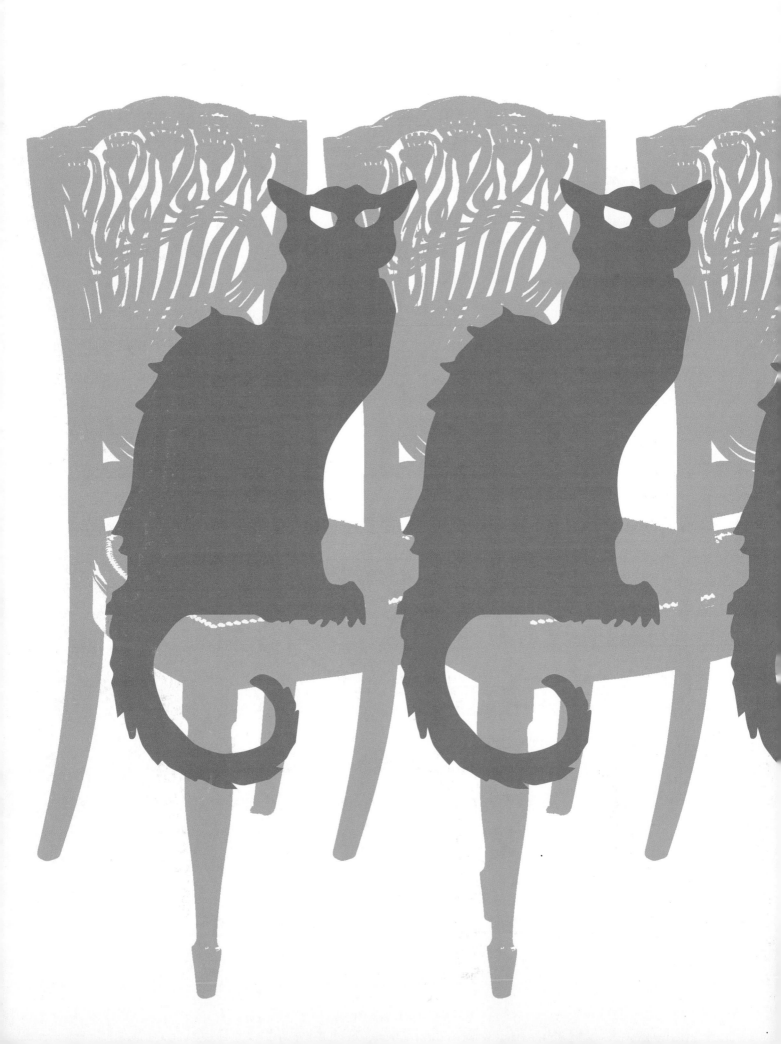

1

Art Nouveau 1:
A New Style for
a New Culture

One person who made a fundamental contribution to the establishment of the graphic design profession was the multi-faceted design theorist and practitioner William Morris (1834–1896). Born to a wealthy British family, Morris was one of the first to recognize that the flood of goods produced because of the advances of the Industrial Revolution all too often lacked artistic merit. From furniture to books, Morris decried the lowly state of the design arts, and contended that the urban environment need not be filled with such downright ugly objects. Propelled by his beliefs, Morris dedicated his life to bettering the quality of British design. Beginning in 1861, he founded the first of a series of firms that would engage a variety of different design problems over the ensuing decades.

An important influence on Morris's attitude toward the arts was the work of the English writer John Ruskin (1819–1900). In two books, The Seven Lamps of Architecture *(1849) and* The Stones of Venice *(1853), Ruskin asserted that industrial society had squelched the independent creativity of workmen. He contrasted this impoverished state with an idealized vision of medieval society, which Ruskin believed had represented a golden age of creative work because skilled design was at that time an integral part of the handcraft production of goods.*

left: **1.1** William Morris, *Sussex Chair*, 1865. William Morris Gallery, The London Borough of Waltham Forest.

below: **1.2** William Morris, *Minstrel with Clarinet*, 1870. Stained glass. William Morris Gallery, The London Borough of Waltham Forest.

The Arts and Crafts Movement

Ruskin also swayed Morris with his assertion that the decorative arts—the name given to objects that may be beautiful but whose primary function is utilitarian, such as furniture or wallpaper— were the most important expression of creative individuals because they affected the mundane visual environment more than the fine arts of painting and sculpture. In addition, Ruskin asserted that architecture was the supreme exemplar of artistic production because it combined many design skills and had an immense effect on the overall human landscape.

In this respect, the decorative arts were credited with not just the ability to "prettify" the urban world but also to lead to an actual transformation of modern society that benefited people's lives in all respects. Ruskin and Morris were especially concerned with the plight of the millions of industrial workers who toiled away their lives in the factories that William Blake famously referred to as "dark satanic mills." It is important to note that many of these ideas about the social utility of good design will be significant not just to an understanding of Morris and his time but to several generations of graphic designers who followed him.

"I do not want ART for a few any more than education for a few, or freedom for a few." With statements such as this, Morris indicated his belief that the design arts had an important role to play in improving the lives of everyday working people. However, this statement is also exemplary of the fundamental disjunction that existed between Morris's published beliefs, and the actual design work with which his firm was engaged for over thirty years. (This theme of the stark contrast between many designers' theories and their practice will reappear several times throughout this text.) While he espoused the beneficial effects of the decorative arts on the lives of working people, Morris almost exclusively made hand-crafted objects that could be afforded only by the very affluent. In the 1880s, his firm even designed interiors for the throne room of St James's Palace in London as well as wallpaper for Queen Victoria's Balmoral estate in Scotland. Morris never

above: **1.3** William Morris,
The Nature of Gothic, pp. iv, 127.
G. Allen: London, printed by William
Morris at the Kelmscott Press, 1892.
By Permission of The British Library,
London.

right: **1.4** William Morris, Golden Roman
Typeface, from *Art & Its Producers*,
1896. St Bride Printing Library, London.

ART AND ITS PRODUCERS. A LEC-
TURE DELIVERED IN LIVERPOOL
IN 1888. BY WILLIAM MORRIS.
I fear what I have to tell you will be looked upon
by you as an often-told tale; but it seems to me
that at the inception of an enterprise for the popu-
larising and furtherance of the arts of life, the sub-
ject-matter of my paper is very necessary to be
considered. I will begin by putting before you a
kind of text, from which I will speak, so that you
may understand from the first the drift of my
paper; a plan which, I hope, will save both your
time and mine.
Whereas the incentive to labour is usually assumed to be the necessity of earning a livelihood,
and whereas in our modern society this is really
the only incentive amongst those of the working-
class who produce wares of which some form of
art is supposed to form a part, it is impossible that
men working in this manner should produce
genuine works of art. Therefore it is desirable
either that all pretence to art should be abandoned
in the wares so made, and that art should be restricted to matters which have no other function
to perform except their existence as works of art,
such as pictures, sculpture, and the like; or else,
that to the incentive of necessity to labour should
be added the incentives of pleasure and interest in
the work itself.
That is my text, and I am quite sure that you will

b   i

really acknowledged the fundamental contradiction of his career, that he was advocating handmade goods as a solution to the ugliness of the design of mass-produced products in an industrial society. In a sense, Morris was the first person to recognize the problems caused by industry, but he was unable to offer a workable solution.

Morris's firm, Morris & Co., first advertised itself in the 1860s as "Fine Art Workmen in Painting, Carving, Furniture and the Metals," and found its greatest success in the manufacture of stained glass, a product that was enjoying newfound popularity partly because of Ruskin's embrace of the medieval period. Morris's *Minstrel with Clarinet* stained glass (1870; *fig. 1.2*) was designed for the home of his friend the painter Edward Burne-Jones (1833–1898). The style of the glass is one that can be termed "historicist," in that it revives a style from the past—in this case, the clear colors, attenuated proportions, and abstract, mannered grace of the medieval period. By using the style of a pre-industrial age, Morris was essentially sidestepping contemporary design problems, and thus had less of a direct stylistic influence on the future.

Morris's design for the Sussex Chair (1875; *fig. 1.1*) exemplifies the focus on a simple, elegant aesthetic, featuring clean lines and well-balanced proportions without indulging in an excess of ornament. This simplicity was a direct response to the contemporary fashion for elaborate ornament in otherwise shoddy mass-produced goods. While some versions of the chair were quite expensive and made of mahogany and other rare and precious woods, other versions were available in a less expensive design, representing the closest that Morris came to a mass-reproduced object. However, it was a design fit for skilled craftsmen, not steam-driven machines, to make. The Sussex chair features uncomplicated shapes and a woven rush seat, which is indicative of its inspiration in country furniture. Around 1890, Morris's type of subdued, harmonious design was termed the "Arts and Crafts" style, a term still used broadly to describe a variety of unadorned, often geometrically structured, decorative art objects and architecture from the late nineteenth century. The term also refers to Ruskin and Morris's idealization of a medieval system of small-scale production whereby the designer of the work was also skilled in its production. Ironically, however, the future of graphic design lay in the exact opposite direction from the one Morris anticipated, as the design process was soon to be separated from the production of printed materials.

William Morris's Kelmscott Press

In 1891, Morris expanded his firm's business to include book design, founding the Kelmscott Press, named after the family estate in Gloucestershire where the business was located. In a parallel to his work in other decorative arts, Morris reacted to the poor design of contemporary mass-produced books by establishing a press that produced limited-run editions featuring handmade paper and expertly tooled leather covers. Morris sought a return to the fifteenth-century book form, which he felt perfectly balanced aesthetic elements with the book's primary functional element: its legibility. In reprinting a chapter from

The Stones of Venice as *The Nature of Gothic* (1892; *fig. 1.3*), Morris chose a text that he admired, and then produced a few hundred copies of a book that features a stunning historicist design, intertwining its ornate, sinuous "dropped capitals," or large capital letters that start a new section or chapter, with the rectangular block of text. At Kelmscott, Morris also worked in the related field of typography, creating a number of historicist typefaces, including Golden (*fig. 1.4*), a roman face based on the Old Style type of Nicolas Jenson.

Predictably, in terms of the fields of typography and book design, Morris's greatest influence lay in his analysis of the contemporary scene, rather than in his reverence for the past, particularly the medieval period. In his preface to *The Nature of Gothic*, Morris reiterated his disdain for industrial mass production: "For the lesson which Ruskin here teaches us is that art is the expression of man's pleasure in labour; that it is possible for man to rejoice in his work, for, strange as it may seem to us today, there have been times when he did rejoice in it; and lastly, that unless man's work once again becomes a pleasure to him, the token of which change will be that beauty is once again a natural and necessary accompaniment of productive labour, all but the worthless must toil in pain, and therefore live in pain." As early as 1893, the Arts and Crafts movement that he helped form was criticized as "the work of a few for the few," because it failed to address the problems of mass production. In the future, designers would not just reject the historical model that Morris embraced, but they would also contend that Morris's use of historicist styles was inappropriate for a new, modern urban society.

French Art Nouveau

Like William Morris, an entire generation of designers in Europe believed that the urban world fostered by the Industrial Revolution lacked beauty. These artists shared Morris's stated desire to make the mundane everyday world a place of aesthetic accomplishment and to unify the different design arts, including graphic design, using a set of basic stylistic principles. However, while Morris looked to the past in his embrace of historicist styles, it was the consensus of other artists that they could, and should, create new styles for the new, industrial world in which they lived. Hence, **Art Nouveau**, or "New Art," became an umbrella term to designate the various design movements of the late nineteenth century in Europe and the United States. Curiously, the French term Art Nouveau, which came into general use around 1885, was most popular with English-speakers, while the French often tended toward the exotic-sounding English translation, "New Art."

Art Nouveau designers sought to devise a range of styles that were not directly based on historical revivals, but rather created a fresh visual vocabulary that celebrated the vibrant pulse of urban life. As we will see, the term Art Nouveau is used to refer broadly to a number of disparate design movements from this era, as well as in a more narrow sense to delineate a specific set of stylistic criteria—meaning that not all Art Nouveau artists, in a chronological sense, display an Art Nouveau style.

1.5 François Boucher, *The Rising of the Sun*, 1753. Canvas, relined,
10 ft 4 in x 8 ft 6 in (3.18 x 2.61 m). Reproduced by permission of the Trustees
of the Wallace Collection, London.

Jules Cheret

The most influential poster designer of the later nineteenth
century was Jules Cheret (1836–1933). A French artist, the son
of a typesetter, Cheret studied in London as a young man before
returning to settle in Paris in the 1850s. Technically innovative
as well as artistically gifted, he is credited with successfully promoting the art of color lithography. **Chromolithography**, through
which a color image is produced using the principle that oil and
water resist one another, had been an established, if underused,
printing process since mid-century. After establishing a firm in
1866 through which to pursue lithographic printing (he was
convinced that color lithography would soon replace letterpress
printing), Cheret worked out a process that allowed him to create
brightly colorful posters with a wide range of hue, value, and
intensity. The secret to his success was what he called the *fond
gradué* ("graduated stone") that he added to the traditional black
and red impressions. Eventually, dramatically colorful images
would be produced by combining as many as fifteen different
colored lithography stones.

There are two major stylistic streams in the poster art of
Cheret; one is the influence of Japanese art (see below), while
the other is the French eighteenth-century style called **Rococo**.
Cheret's use of the Rococo style is quite specific to the condition
of French society in the 1870s. Having suffered a stinging defeat

in the Franco-Prussian War of 1870–71, followed by a precipitous
decline in industrial production relative to other European
powers, the French people felt strongly that their traditional
leadership in the design arts had to be maintained. Cheret accord-
ingly called attention to a style that was uniquely French, and
celebrated the national achievements of a society that was experiencing a wave of self-doubt and introspection. The Rococo style
was famous as the first modern design movement that had unified
all of the decorative as well as the fine arts in dynamic compositions that featured brilliant colorist atmospheres. For example, the
painting *The Rising of the Sun* (1753; *fig. 1.5*), by François Boucher
(1703–1770), shows the French King Louis XV and his mistress,
Madame de Pompadour, amid a swirling atmosphere of color and
light. In addition, Rococo subject matter relied on the same sort
of playful sensuality that was a popular part of the new cabaret
culture in Paris. As Boucher's picture had shocked many people
in 1753 with its nudity, so the frank sexuality of many Art
Nouveau posters scandalized the modern Parisian public.
Cheret's poster *Folies Bergère—Fleur de Lotus* (1893; *fig. 1.6*)
perfectly captures, while updating, the sexual energy of Rococo
art. This poster advertised a ballet and pantomime—popular
entertainment at the Folies Bergère, Paris's most famous cabaret,
founded in 1869. Cheret's use of the Rococo is not historicist
in the manner of William Morris; rather, he has remade the style
by combining it with his own innovations. In addition, Cheret
employed an ephemeral, industrial medium, the mass-produced
chromolithograph—a far cry from Morris's handcrafted use of
age-old materials.

Cheret's poster art rose in prominence at the same time as the
popular theater, which was a source of many designers' commissions. Many of his most famous images feature star performers
from the world of dance, music, and theatrical productions. In
a poster that displays Cheret's dramatic Rococo style, the popular
American dancer Loïe Fuller (1862–1928) spins on the stage as
her silk garments shimmer in a rainbow of color (1893; *fig. 1.7*).
Born in Chicago, Fuller became a dance sensation in Paris in the
1890s through a combination of innovative techniques, such
as the integration of natural movements and improvisation with
more formal dance, as well as her startlingly innovative use of
colorful stage lighting. Here, Cheret has found the performer
whose aesthetic perfectly matches his own dynamic compositions
and profuse colorism.

Cheret's *Les Girard* (1879; *fig. 1.8*), a poster advertising yet
another dance performance at the Folies Bergère, is an excellent
example of his embrace of the Japanese style that had swept
through France. The planes of even color, set apart by crisp contour lines, as well as the two-dimensional character of the overall
work, are all elements derived from the style of *Ukiyo-e* woodblock
prints. In addition to the Japanese influence, *Les Girard* also
demonstrates other stylistic attributes of the new art of graphic
design. Cheret has expertly intertwined the legs of the dancers
with the lettering on the poster. Not only are the text and image
integrated in this spatial sense, but because there is no need to use
pre-designed type in a chromolithograph, Cheret was free to
design his own lettering by hand. Therefore, the exuberant forms
of the letters mimic the frenetic movement of the dancing figures.
The integration of text and image produces a key contrast with

1.6 Jules Cheret, *Folies Bergère—Fleur de Lotus*, 1893. Colored lithograph, 48⅞ x 34⅝ in (124 x 88 cm). Les Arts Décoratifs, Musée de Publicité, Paris.

the older letterpress style, as in figure 20 (p. 28), where the
lettering and the picture of the horse occupy different zones
in the poster and share little in the way of shape or structure.
It is also significant to note how Cheret minimizes the amount
of text in his posters, creating in its place an overall feeling of
jouissance, or joyfulness, which captures the excitement of a
live performance.

The high-profile success of Cheret, a designer who created
over 1,000 original compositions during his career, accounting
for literally millions of mass-produced posters, helped to elevate
the status of the poster designer during the last two decades of
the century. In 1890, Cheret was granted two tributes: first, a solo
exhibition of his posters was arranged in Paris; and second, he
was offered the highest award of the French state, membership in
the Legion of Honor. Coming on the heels of the first group
exhibition of modern posters (in 1884), and the first French book
on poster art (in 1886), Cheret's recognition announced to
Europe that the art of the poster had arrived.

Cheret's entrepreneurial skills were almost as important as
his artistic ones in igniting and feeding the public's appetite for
posters. One of his most significant projects in terms of popularizing the art of the poster was the series of lithographs called *Les
Maîtres de l'Affiche* ("masters of the poster"), which was published
in Paris between 1895 and 1900. *Les Maîtres de l'Affiche* featured
some new work but was focused mainly on small-format reprints
of notable posters designed by ninety-seven artists, for a total
of 256 plates. The plates were published by the printing house
Imprimerie Chaix, which had been allied with Cheret's workshop
since 1881. Each plate bore a special seal based on a design by
Cheret, indicating his central role in the series.

Each month for the five years that the series was in production, subscribers received a set of four reprints, plus an additional
sixteen special plates, made up of brand new images. Cheret, as
director of the project, featured his own work sixty-seven times
in the series, including seven of the sixteen new commissions.
Other artists in the series included Henri de Toulouse-Lautrec,
Alphonse Mucha, Theodore Steinlen, the Beggarstaffs, and
Eugene Grasset—a veritable pantheon of top poster designers.
Les Maîtres de l'Affiche had definite advantages for collectors at the
height of the "poster craze" of the 1890s because they measured
29 x 40cm, a format that was much more easily displayed in a
home than the massive posters used on outdoor hoardings. Also
the series made use of high-quality inks and papers, in contrast to
the cheap newsprint and inferior inks used for the ephemeral
products posted out on the street.

Imprimerie Chaix also published another set of eighty-four
lithographic reprints in a slightly smaller format that was called
Les Affiches Illustrées ("illustrated posters"). Published in two bound
volumes, *Les Affiches Illustrées* featured many of the same posters
from the larger series. Aimed at poster collectors, *Les Affiches
Illustrées* and *Les Maîtres de l'Affiche* also played important roles in
spreading the Art Nouveau style among artists in that these easily
portable plates made their way across Europe and to the United
States. Still, some collectors sought out the large-scale originals,
and for that market dealers such as Edmond Sagot would produce
overruns by popular artists such as Henri de Toulouse-Lautrec
so that they could sell them direct to the collecting public.

above: **1.7** Jules Cheret, *La Loïe Fuller*,
1893. Poster. Lithograph, 48½ x 34½ in
(123.1 x 87.6 cm). St Bride Printing
Library, London.

opposite: **1.8** Jules Cheret, *Les Girard*,
1879. Poster. Lithograph, 22 5/8 x 17 in
(57.6 x 43.1 cm).

Japanese Prints

During the late nineteenth century, the art of Japanese woodblock prints had an enormous impact on European artists, including graphic designers. After Japanese trade with the West increased in the 1850s because of American military threats, an influx of Japanese art, especially a type of mass-produced commercial woodblock print called **Ukiyo-e***, or "floating world," caught the attention of the French art world. The name "floating world" was a euphemism for scenes set in the Yoshiwara district of Tokyo, where many commercial entertainments, including popular theater and dance, as well as prostitution, were allowed to flourish by the authorities.*

Stylistically speaking, the bold passages of flat color arranged in asymmetrical compositions, which lack any three-dimensional perspective spaces, combined with fresh, crisp linear elements, were all adopted by European graphic designers. The manner in which Japanese artists rendered the figure—relying on black contour lines which they combined with short, fluid strokes to produce details in the face—was also widely copied in France. This Asian influence led many European artists to reject the three-dimensional shading with light and dark, called modeling, which had been a fundamental part of European draughtsmanship since the Renaissance.

The print illustrated here of a woman (fig. 1.9) displays many of the attributes of Japanese style, creating an overall sense of flat, decorative beauty. It is important to recognize Japanese influences not just in the style but also in the subject matter of Art Nouveau graphic design.

Many Ukiyo-e *prints highlighted the intoxicating atmosphere of Tokyo's Yoshiwara district and the glamorous women who worked there. The print shown here is an example of* Bijin-ga, *a specialty of Utamaro (1753–1806) that featured idealized pictures of beautiful women. The young beauty here (from the series "Ten Facial Types of Women") is admiring her dyed black teeth; this was a Japanese fashion that had its roots in aristocratic culture and that had become popular among the general population. Posters such as* Fleur de Lotus *or* Loïe Fuller *(see figs. 1.6 and 1.7), which advertise the events held in the pleasure-seeking quarters of Paris, often attempt to emulate the sensual tone of* Bijin-ga *prints.*

Japanese art was widely recognized in France because of its prominent place at three Paris world's fairs—in 1867, 1878, and 1900—and through the efforts of private art dealers such as Siegfried Bing (1836–1905). Beginning in 1875, Bing's succession of decorative arts galleries became an intrinsic part of the frenzied collection of Japanese art, a phenomenon called Japonisme, as well as the Art Nouveau design movement that arose under its influence. In 1895, Bing named his new Parisian gallery the Maison de L'Art Nouveau, creating a showplace where his name became synonymous with the phrase Art Nouveau (fig. 1.10). Bing held a number of exhibitions of Japanese prints during this period, the most notable in 1889 and 1893. The name of Bing's gallery makes it clear that the Japanese influence was one of the fundamental stylistic elements of the Art Nouveau movement.

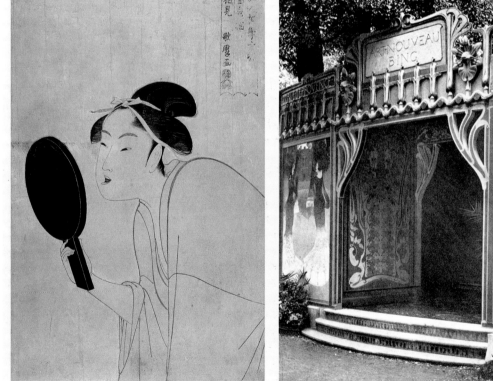

1.9 Kitagawa Utamaro, *Young Woman with Black Teeth Examining her Features in a Mirror,* from the series *Ten Facial Types of Women,* c. 1792–3. Woodblock print, 14⅜ x 9⅝ in (36.5 x 24.6 cm). British Museum, London.

1.10 Siegfried Bing, Maison de L'Art Nouveau, Main Entrance, Paris, 1895. V&A Picture Library, Victoria & Albert Museum, London.

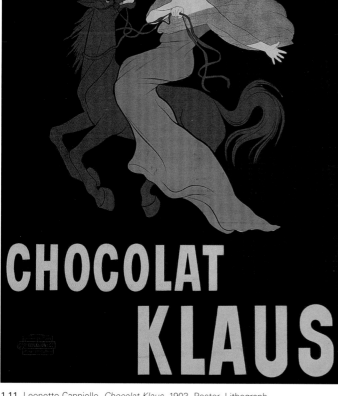

1.11 Leonetto Cappiello, *Chocolat Klaus*, 1903. Poster. Lithograph.
Museum für Gestaltung, Zurich. Poster Collection.

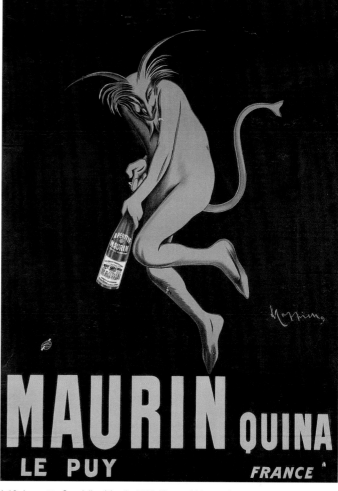

1.12 Leonetto Cappiello, *Maurin*, 1906. Poster. Lithograph.
Museum für Gestaltung, Zurich. Poster Collection.

Leonetto Cappiello

Popular magazines also served a significant role in bringing new graphic art to the attention of the public. One of the most famous, *Le Rire* ("the laugh") was a satirical journal with strong political views, established by Felix Juven in 1894. It also featured thousands of works by key poster designers. The front and back covers as well as an occasional centerpiece, which were printed in color, became important sites for progressive designers to display their work. In its early years, prominent artists including Toulouse-Lautrec contributed several lithographs to the publication. *Le Rire* was also responsible for igniting the careers of young artists, as was the case with the Italian caricaturist Leonetto Cappiello (1875–1942), who moved to Paris from Italy in 1898. Noticing the steady demand for caricatures of famous people at *Le Rire*, Cappiello appealed to a fellow Italian, the celebrity composer Giacomo Puccini (1858–1924), to model for him. The drawing was a success and Cappiello soon found steady work at a variety of publications. He made some of his most popular caricatures for Alexandre Natanson, publisher of the edgy literary journal *La Revue Blanche*, who commissioned Cappiello to draw a series of images of actresses, including the most famous actress in Europe, Sarah Bernhardt (1844–1923). Called *Nos Actrices* ("our actresses")

this enterprising series consolidated the artist's career. Cappiello's work as a caricaturist incidentally led to a request for an advertisement, whereupon he embarked on a new and extremely lucrative career as a designer of commercial posters.

Over four decades, Cappiello produced over a thousand individual designs, rivaling even Cheret in his combination of commercial savvy and memorable aesthetic invention. Cappiello's mature style mixed his own gift for caricature, the influence of Toulouse-Lautrec's love of the bizarre, Japonisme, and a dash of Cheret's kinetic colorism into a striking new synthesis, seen in his 1903 lithograph for a Swiss product, Chocolat Klaus (*fig. 1.11*). The horse and rider are radically simplified, built up only of black contour line and flat fields of color. The palette also shows the influence of Japanese aesthetics, as it is dominated by a juxtaposition of the complementary colors red and green. The dash of yellow in the woman's blond hair ties the image to the name of the company printed below it. Notably, the fact that there is little to tie this equestrian to the product at hand does little to diminish the visual impact of the poster. The relationship, or lack thereof, becomes immaterial in the face of such stunning graphic power.

In 1906, Cappiello produced a lithograph for Maurin absinthe that would soon become iconic of his achievement in the art of the poster (*fig. 1.12*). The image features a dynamically

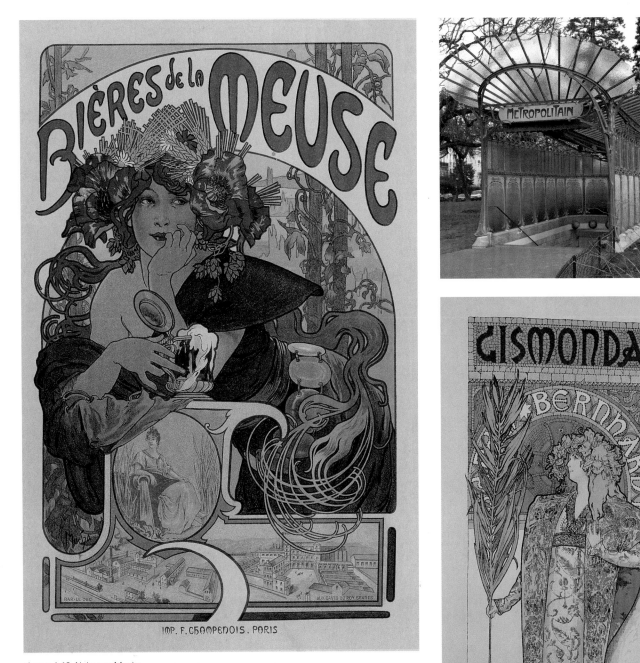

above: **1.13** Alphonse Mucha,
Bières de la Meuse, 1897. Poster,
18⅞ x 13⅜ in (48 x 34 cm).
St Bride Printing Library, London.

above right: **1.14** Hector Guimard,
Métro Entrance, 1899.

right: **1.15** Alphonse Mucha, *Gismonda*
(Sarah Bernhardt), 1894. Poster,
18⅞ x 13⅜ in (48 x 34 cm).
St Bride Printing Library, London.

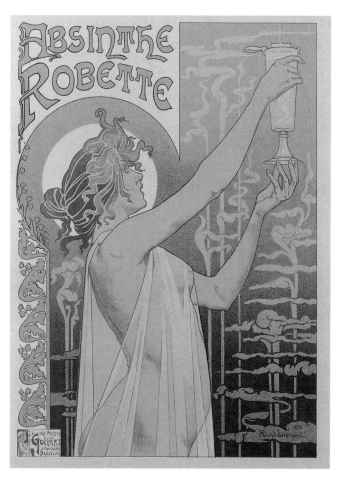

1.16 Privat Livemont, *Absinthe Robette*, 1896. Poster, 18⅞ x 13⅜ in (48 x 34 cm). St Bride Printing Library, London.

moving green devil, which serves as a complement to, or even sardonic commentary on, the ubiquitous, luscious young women posing as "green fairies" that dominated the absinthe poster market. *Maurin Quina* also displays Cappiello's ahead-of-its-time technique of simplifying the commercial message down to its essentials—a single, irresistible image matched only with the name of the product.

Alphonse Mucha

Alphonse Mucha (1860–1939), another expatriate, moved to Paris from Czechoslovakia in 1887, and built his career in posters because of a bit of luck that tied him to a celebrity, Sarah Bernhardt. "The Divine Sarah," as she was called, was renowned for her "golden bell" of a voice, as well as her perfect diction, charisma, and patriotism. By 1880, she had developed an unparalleled international reputation, and she eventually toured the world as a theatrical superstar. On Christmas Eve 1894, Mucha found himself alone as the junior employee of a French print shop, when Bernhardt submitted a rush order for a new poster of herself in the guise of Gismonda, a title role written for her by the dramatist Victorien Sardou (1831–1908). With this first acclaimed poster (*fig. 1.15*), Mucha developed his signature style, that of the elongated figure amid a mesmerizing field of decorative flat patterns. With more muted color than that used by

Cheret, Mucha concentrated on the curvilinear rhythm of contour lines, particularly where they appear in the figure's hair and in the rich floral decoration that fills in Bernhardt's opulent costume as well as any empty space in the composition. The often geometric, repetitive patterns used in posters during the Art Nouveau movement are known as "**arabesques**," although these patterns usually have at best only a distant relationship to the art works of the Arab culture that inspired the term. Bernhardt admired this first poster, and, always aware of the importance of self-promotion, recognized that Mucha's grasp of Art Nouveau decorative glamour, as well as his ability to draw attention to her luxuriant reddish hair, was a perfect vehicle for her public image. After several more successful posters, in 1895 she hired Mucha to design not only more posters but also sets, costumes, and jewelry for her shows.

Mucha's advertisement for *Bières de la Meuse* (1897; *fig. 1.13*) shows a young woman displaying the idealized beauty and open sexuality that became the artist's trademark. An icon of *jouissance*, her image is one of the earliest examples of a favorite theme of advertising: the implicit promise of sexual availability that will be awarded to the male purchaser of a product. As she grasps a frothy glass of beer, the dense floral elements around her are made up of barley and hops. Here Mucha has designed hand-drawn letters whose curving rhythm matches the lines of the figure as well as the overall composition. The young woman's hair depicted in the lower right quadrant has the undulating form that became known as a basic building block of *Le style Mucha*, a synonym for Art Nouveau.

An essential principle of the Art Nouveau movement was the belief that the "new art" must consist of a style that could be applied in all situations, and would not be unique to any one type of art. It was hoped that this type of unifying stylistic coherence would serve to tie together visually an otherwise chaotic urban environment. For this reason, it is important to recognize the ties between Art Nouveau graphics and other art forms, for it is only in this broader context that the aims of the artists involved can be made manifest. Outside the graphic design field, the work of architects provides some of the finest examples of the Art Nouveau movement. Analogous to the lithographic poster in that they were designed as part of a mass-produced series of works that beautified the streets of Paris, the Metro stations created by Hector Guimard (1867–1942) *circa* 1899 provide a stunning example of how the stylistic principles of Art Nouveau could thrive in different media (*fig. 1.14*). The undulating forms, whiplash curves, and exuberant floral motifs of Guimard's underground station entrances exude the same sort of sensuous elegance that Mucha had captured in the medium of the poster. The tendrils of the plants seem to have a life of their own as they wrap themselves around the iron framework, enveloping it in a dense web of abstract design.

Sensuality and Symbolism

An advertisement for an alcoholic drink, the poster *Absinthe Robette* (1896; *fig. 1.16*), by the Belgian artist Privat Livemont (1861–1936), displays the expressive **organic form**, curvilinear

Absinthe, the Green Fairy

The poison that spills from your eyes
Your green eyes
Lakes where my soul trembles
And is turned upside down.

These words by the French poet Charles Baudelaire (1821–1867) celebrate absinthe, the alcoholic drink of choice for many denizens of Paris's café culture. First marketed commercially in 1797 by Henry-Louis Pernod, absinthe combined a high concentration of alcohol with extract of wormwood as well as a variety of other, often aromatic, ingredients. Drinking absinthe was an art in itself, as water was strained into the drink through a sugarcube supported by a spoon. Because of the large, competitive market for serving alcoholic drinks, at a time when there were over 27,000 cafés in Paris alone, many posters of this period served to advertise the liquor, and it was an important element of the glamorous, decadent culture of the "Belle Epoque." By the late nineteenth century, it was apparent that the wormwood in absinthe had a narcotic effect that was highly addictive, and could also lead to seizures, hallucinations, and psychotic episodes. For this reason, absinthe played a role in both the ecstatic highs and the dreary low moments of many people's lives. Artists including Henri de Toulouse-Lautrec and Vincent Van Gogh both became absinthe addicts. Traditional absinthe was banned in most European countries by 1920.

rhythm, and sensual atmosphere that are synonymous with Art Nouveau. Note that Livemont's use of what is essentially an allegorical figure is quite traditional, tying the art of commercial graphic design to the rarefied world of the fine arts while at the same time proffering a powerful sexual fantasy. The color in the poster, a subtle element with slight gradations for which Livemont became justly famous, is derived from the color of the absinthe that it serves to ennoble.

The evocative sensuality and ethereal atmosphere that pervade *Absinthe Robette* show the influence of the French **Symbolist** movement. Centered on a group of poets that included Stéphane Mallarmé (1842–1989), the Symbolists advocated art forms that tantalized the mind and tempted the senses. One of Mallarmé's most famous experimental works, *A Faun's Afternoon*, is loosely based on the amorous adventures of the Greek god Pan. Mallarmé produced a dreamlike work in which it is never quite clear whether events that take place are real or imagined. At one point the lustful god questions, "Was it a dream I loved?" Pan's pursuit of desirable nymphs, minor forest deities, serves as an ambiguous framework for the poem. The many young beauties that appear in contemporary posters wearing revealing, diaphanous drapery are suggestive of the Symbolists' influence on visual culture. These poets theorized an "art for art's sake," in which the aesthetic pleasure of the work is an end in itself, irrespective of any moral lesson or uplifting message. Symbolists also sought inspiration in a veritable smorgasbord of esoteric religious thought, including Theosophy, Rosicrucianism, and other nascent mystical beliefs. In contrast to many artists and designers who found much to celebrate in the new urban spaces of Europe, the Symbolists are seen

by scholars as an example of a flight from modern life, an escape into a dreamy world of visionary nuances.

The Symbolists decried the use of literal description in poetry and, by extension, all of the arts. Mallarmé famously wrote, "To name an object, that is to suppress three-quarters of the enjoyment of the poem … to suggest it, that is the dream." In place of exposition, the Symbolists advocated art works that evoked without describing, replacing clear narrative with subjective feeling and imaginative flights of fancy. It is clear that the unfocused, atmospheric imagery typical of Symbolist poetry has influenced Livemont's poster, in which a fantasy beauty inhabits an undefined space.

Despite the strong currents of nationalism that racked Europe during the Belle Epoque, one of the French Symbolists' great heroes was the German composer Richard Wagner (1813–1883), and in 1885 the Symbolists inaugurated a journal in Paris devoted to his work called the *Revue Wagnerienne*. The Symbolists admired Wagner's musical dramatizations of past worlds full of mythic heroes who confront the mysteries of existence. They also sought to explore Wagner's commitment to a synthesis of the arts, whereby a common aesthetic feeling would unite disparate media. The sinuous designs that pervade Art Nouveau works across many media are indicative of this concern with creating a holistic style for all of the arts.

Théophile Steinlen

The posters of Théophile Steinlen (1859–1923) contrast sharply with the dense, decorative elegance of Livemont or Mucha. Instead, Steinlen's posters, such as *Cabaret du Chat Noir* (1894; *fig. 1.18*) feature the bold simplicity of the Japanese print. Le Chat Noir was one of the first cabarets in Montmartre, the burgeoning entertainment district on the northern outskirts of Paris that became the center of modern social life in the city. Established in

1.17 Théophile Steinlen, *La Rue*
(*Affiches Charles Verneau*), 1896.
Poster for the printer Charles Verneau. V&A Picture Library, Victoria & Albert Museum, London.

1.18 Théophile Steinlen, *Cabaret du Chat Noir*, 1896. Poster. V&A Picture Library, Victoria & Albert Museum, London.

ABCDEFGHIJKLMNOPQRSTUVWXYZ
abcdefghijklmnopqrstuvwxyz1234567890
"The typeface called Auriol was designed in 1901 by Georges
Auriol (1863–1939) for the Deberny & Peignot foundry."

1.19 Georges Auriol, Auriol Typeface, 1902.

1881, Le Chat Noir was also the first establishment to provide its customers with musical entertainment, something that would become a staple of the Parisian nightlife of the 1890s. The rise of popular entertainment of this sort in Paris, often with sexual overtones as well as a great deal of actual prostitution, ties the culture of the city to the one depicted in Japanese prints.

Steinlen's poster advertisement for a printing shop titled *La Rue* (1896; *fig. 1.17*), provides an excellent example of how some artists and critics hoped that the art of the poster would enliven the often grim streets of urban Paris. This movement, called *art à la rue* ("art on the streets"), took up the cause of everyday working people espoused by William Morris, and, like Morris, Steinlen believed that the design arts could have more of an impact on society than simple beautification. The architect Frantz Jourdain (1847–1935), who wrote frequently on the subject, asserted that accessible art works on the street, especially posters, could bring art to ordinary people and help uplift their aesthetic, as well as moral, taste. Like many thinkers of this era, Jourdain thought that a rise in aesthetic knowledge would naturally lead to more important changes in society that would bring about a better life for working people. *La Rue*, an advertisement for the publisher Charles Verneau, a friend of Steinlen's, shows a busy crowd streaming by a wall of colorful posters, which is exemplary of how it was hoped that the urban environment could be shaped so as to make it more livable to the common people. It is apparent that the theory behind *art à la rue* is well intentioned, although it is also somewhat unrealistic in its faith that the design arts can spur dramatic social changes, as well as rather patronizing in its attitude toward working people. However, in later chapters we will see a continuation of this belief in the design arts' ability to act as a catalyst for social change.

The Art Nouveau movement also set the stage for some exciting new advances in typography. The typeface called **Auriol** was designed in 1901 by Georges Auriol (1863–1939) for the Deberny & Peignot foundry (*fig. 1.19*). This type combines elements derived from Asian calligraphic scripts, such as the gestural flourishes and the variable thickness of each line, with the languid elegance of the Art Nouveau.

Henri de Toulouse-Lautrec

The center of Paris's decadent nightlife in the 1890s was the previously rural district of Montmartre. Free of city taxes as well as of the watchful eyes of the authorities, Montmartre became known

above: **1.20** Moulin Rouge, c. 1900. Photo. Rue des Archives, Paris.

opposite: **1.21** Henri de Toulouse-Lautrec, *Divan Japonais*, 1892. Poster. Color lithograph, 18⅞ x 13⅜ in (48 x 34 cm). St Bride Printing Library, London.

for its more than 100 "café concerts," venues combining nightclub, theater, dancehall, and bar, some of the most famous of which were located in former farm buildings. Two of the most notable clubs, the Moulin Rouge, or "Red Mill" (opened 1889), and the Moulin de la Galette, or "Mill of the Pastry" (opened 1874), were distinguished by the renovated windmills that were their most recognizable feature (*fig. 1.20*). At the Moulin Rouge, the artist and designer Henri de Toulouse-Lautrec (1864–1901) became something of a fixture, spending countless evenings drinking absinthe, sketching, and socializing with the rest of the clientele. Lautrec had an unusual background for an artist, as he was a member of the French aristocracy, although he had been excluded from upper-class society because of his stunted legs, the result of a series of accidents he had suffered as a child. Lautrec found comfort in the more marginal social whirl of Montmartre, where bourgeois men consorted with their mistresses and prostitutes.

Each night at the Moulin Rouge, a frisson of sexual excitement was provided by the entertaining spectacles as well as the members of the demimonde, young women who supported themselves by becoming the lovers of wealthy men. Lautrec captured this atmosphere in posters such as *La Goulue at the Moulin Rouge* (1895; *fig. 1.22*), which shows the dancer and performer Louise Weber (1866–1929), who called herself La Goulue ("the

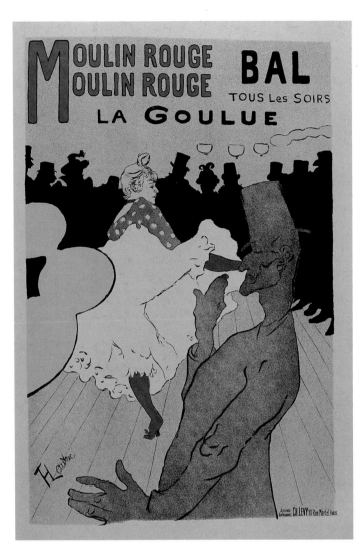

Glutton"), because of her astonishing ability to consume alcohol. Weber was one of the performers who made the "cancan," a dance during which high-kicking women exposed their undergarments (or even more) to the spectators, an enduring motif of Parisian nightlife. In the poster, Weber is dancing with her partner Jacques Renaudin (1843–1907), whose rubbery joints had earned him the nickname "Valentin the Boneless." Lautrec reveled in the odd spectacle of this unmatched pair, which parallels the artist's own life; Lautrec was often accompanied by his unusually tall and gangly friend Gabriel Tapie de Celeyran, who towered above him. Stylistically, this poster shows the artist's expressive style, which is governed by his free-flowing line and decorative sense of color. It is also significant for the technical sophistication of its printing; this was the first time a color lithograph was created using four separate stones (black, red, yellow, and blue). This technique allowed Lautrec's original design to be reproduced without losing any of its splendid colorist effects.

Lautrec's poster for the Montmartre café concert that opened in 1883 called the *Divan Japonais* (*fig. 1.21*) shows the artist working under the influence of the Japanese print aesthetic. The flattened areas of even color, prominent curvilinear black contour lines, and overall simplification are all elements that show a Japanese influence. Here, Lautrec's style matched the interior design of the club, which was an assemblage of Asian motifs. In

this poster, Lautrec represents two of his friends watching a performance of the singer Yvette Guilbert (1867–1944). Guilbert was an important part of the popular music scene, in which over 10,000 new songs were introduced in Paris each year. On the left, the art critic Edouard Dujardin (1861–1949), who had written persuasively on the aesthetic sophistication of Japanese art, seems to be in the middle of making a point, while he is interrupted by the appearance of the singer on the stage in her signature long black gloves. Many of Lautrec's posters suggest a sense of ironic detachment, as the artist distanced himself from the spectacles that were an important part of his daily experience.

A singer who delighted in his rough, outlaw reputation, Aristide Bruant (1851–1925) used his own club, Le Mirliton, as one of several venues where he showed off his rather brutish, satirical lyrics. Famous for verbally abusing his patrons, especially those who were members of the bourgeoisie, Bruant befriended Lautrec in 1885. Lautrec's posters for the singer (1893; *fig. 1.23*), portray Bruant's aggressive personality and stage-dominating charisma. Creating a complex flat pattern of planes that recede or push forward through color, Lautrec again demonstrates his mastery of Japanese style.

Another friend of Lautrec's, the painter Pierre Bonnard (1867–1947), made a number of influential lithographic designs during his career and likely introduced Lautrec to the art of the poster, although Bonnard focused most of his attention on the fine arts. Bonnard's work was heavily indebted to Japanese wood-block prints, as can be seen in this poster advertising the literary journal *La Revue Blanche* (1894; *fig. 1.24*). Demonstrating the asymmetrical composition and diagonal emphasis that could be expected from an artist once called *très japonard*, Bonnard also effectively integrates text and image. Like Cheret before him, he intertwines the figure with the text (note how the "a" grips her leg), and also uses the same unsteady line both to draw the figure and write the words of the banner. Much of the background is made up of a flat, checkerboard pattern. Despite this artistry, Bonnard does not lose sight of the product that he is promoting, as the woman clutches a copy of the journal while the small boy gestures toward it with a satirical sneer.

The participation of artists such as Lautrec and Bonnard in the design of posters had a hugely beneficial effect on the status of graphic design, in that it helped to create the impression that the making of posters was artistically valid and strongly related to the fine arts, not simply a commercial activity. It is possible to date the end of the first great period of French poster design in terms of Lautrec's own life and career. In 1899, he began to decline from the effects of alcohol and absinthe addiction, as well as syphilis. Committed to an asylum, he died in 1901.

The United States

In the nineteenth century, graphic design scarcely existed in the United States. In a parallel to the European situation, most posters and other printed matter were designed by the workmen who ran the industrial printing presses. One significant contrast with the European market was the American use of color posters. In France, bright color became popular in posters through the work of artists such as Cheret, and had not been an important part of the poorly designed woodcuts that his work superseded. In contrast, American printers employed bright, expressive color in their posters from a much earlier date, especially when they were adver-tising popular spectacles such as the circus. The anonymous poster shown here, advertising a part of Barnum & Bailey's extravagant circus, is a good example of the genre (*fig. 1.25*). This poster is a dynamic, exuberant medley of color and potential motion. While the composition is rather chaotic, and every single inch of available space is filled with detail in a cluttered fashion, the overall effect is to recreate the carnival atmosphere, with its abundance of color and light. The performer featured here, Carl Howelsen (1877–1955), pioneered a jump down a 100-foot ramp that was saturated with petroleum jelly, after which he landed 80 feet away on a small platform. Because of his efforts, Howelsen, whom the circus called the "Flying Norseman," is one of the people credited with popularizing snow skiing in the United States. Scholars con-sider it likely that Jules Cheret was influenced by the vivid color and motion of American circus posters like this one.

It is easy to see how the style of Cheret posters, such as *Loie Fuller*, could be partly based on the American circus poster. The difference, of course, lies in the skill with which Cheret created his composition, especially the way he used hand-drawn lettering

opposite left: **1.22** Henri de Toulouse-Lautrec, *La Goulue* (Louise Weber) *at the Moulin Rouge*, 1898. Poster. Color lithograph, 33 x 48 in (83.8 x 122 cm). St Bride Printing Library, London.

opposite right: **1.23** Henri de Toulouse-Lautrec, *Ambassadeurs: Aristide Bruant dans son Cabaret*, c. 1892. Poster. Color lithograph. V&A Picture Library, Victoria & Albert Museum, London.

above: **1.24** Pierre Bonnard, *La Revue Blanche*, 1894. Poster. Color lithograph, 18⅞ x 13⅜ in (48 x 34 cm). St Bride Printing Library, London.

1.25 *The Barnum & Bailey Greatest Show on Earth: Ski Sailing*, Storbridge Lithographing Company, 1907. Color lithograph, 28¾ x 38¹¹⁄₁₆ in (73 x 98 cm). Cincinnati Art Museum. Reproduced by permission of Ringling Bros–Barnum & Bailey Combined Shows, Inc.

to relate the text and image. In comparison, American circus posters appear equally dazzling yet artistically undernourished.

American graphic designers, in the professional sense of artists who do not play a primary role in the actual printing, discovered Art Nouveau in the 1890s. During this period, it had been the strategy of artists of all types in the United States to look to Europe, especially France and Britain, for inspiration. American artists did not generally feel confident enough in their own skills to initiate new styles, and instead sought to reinvent European styles with American subject matter. British magazines such as *The Studio, The Yellow Book,* and *Penrose's Annual* and French poster compilations such as *Les Maîtres de l'Affiche* proved to be significant sources for an aspiring generation of American designers and illustrators. The true European bias existed not among the artists themselves, but among the wealthy Americans—publishers of magazines, for example, who could have offered commissions to their countrymen, but chose not to.

Harper's and Japanese Prints

A key moment in the history of American graphic design came in 1889, when the widely read periodical *Harper's Magazine* published a poster and cover page for its holiday issue (*fig. 1.26*), designed by the Swiss-born French artist Eugène Grasset (1841–1917). Grasset, who would later serve as a major inspiration for Alphonse Mucha, created a poster that used the dense curvilinear ornament emblematic of the Art Nouveau style. The success of this publicity campaign led, during the 1890s, to a fierce competition between established magazines, including *Harper's, Century,* and *Lippincott's.* In fact, there was something of a wave of popularity in the magazine publishing industry at this time, as over 7,000 new periodicals were published in the United States between 1885 and 1905. As the advertising of magazines became more and more important, publishers sought to advertise their holiday issues, although as the competition for readers intensified, other seasonal editions soon featured posters as well. Publishers first relied on European designers such as Grasset because they wanted the most striking, up-to-date styles, including **Japonisme** and Art Nouveau, and there were few Americans able to serve their needs. Furthermore, hiring an expensive European designer had a "snob appeal" that lent a certain cachet to the publisher. However, a clamor quickly arose among American graphic designers, who were aware of the exciting new French styles, and capable of producing posters of the highest quality. In a parallel to the European "poster craze" of the 1890s, American collectors also sought out the finest examples of this new art form, and posters by famous designers often disappeared off the streets immediately after they had been posted.

Edward Penfield (1866–1925), a young American artist who made the expected pilgrimage to Paris in order to study art between 1890 and 1892, was appointed art editor at Harper & Brothers in 1891. In 1893, he became the overall art director at the company, after which he personally designed monthly promotional posters for Harper's various magazines until 1899. Penfield's 1897 poster for *Harper's* February issue shows how far American design had come in embracing the most fashionable

European trends (*fig. 1.27*). Penfield depicts a group of well-dressed Americans on an intercity bus, each and every one of them engrossed in a copy of the new *Harper's* edition. Even the conductor in the background is ignoring his duties because the magazine has proven such a compelling source of entertainment. The style combines the asymmetrical composition, heavy black contour lines, and flat, unmodeled planes of even color characteristic of the Japanese impulse in Art Nouveau. In 1896, a well-publicized exhibition titled "Japanese Color Prints" had been held in New York City.

The pull of Japanese aesthetics for American artists in the late 1890s is obvious from a comparison of Penfield's poster with that of a competing artist for a competing magazine: a poster by J.J. Gould (1876–1933) for *Lippincott's* issue for February 1897 (*fig. 1.28*). Gould's work shows a single figure of a conservatively dressed young woman with a serious mien holding a copy of what

1.26 Eugene Grasset, *Harper's Magazine,*
1892. Colored lithograph,
17⅞ x 14 in (45.5 x 35.5 cm). Les Arts
Décoratifs, Musée de la Publicité, Paris.

1.27 Edward Penfield, *Harper's Magazine*, February, 1897. Poster. V&A Picture Library, Victoria & Albert Museum, London.

must be a serious, significant journal—*Lippincott's*, of course. It is important to recognize that the Japanese style was widely embraced by artists such as Penfield and Gould because it fitted neatly into a longstanding tradition in American art: a commitment to realism. Many Americans prided themselves on being simple and plain-spoken when compared to Europeans— less likely, or so they would have argued, to indulge in artifice or pretension. This cultural value had always informed American art, which favored the simple naturalism of clearly rendered figures. The American version of Japanese Art Nouveau, predictably, emphasizes the clean lines and realistic details of the style, and eschews the more decorative effects, such as the dense, flat patterns of color, that often appear in French works that rely on Japonisme.

The Portrayal of Young Women

Another predictable element of both American and European posters of the late nineteenth century is their tendency to focus on the lives and leisure time of young women. For example, Penfield's poster for Stearns bicycles (1896; *fig. 1.30*), shows an elegant young woman who, to paraphrase the copy writer, is cycling contentedly. The style of the poster is the same mix of fashionable Japanese Art Nouveau with the American penchant for realistic detail (American artists also rarely simplified their forms to the same degree as the Europeans or Japanese).

This poster's subject matter is related to a broad trend in both European and American society at the time: the gradual emergence of women into more fulfilling lives that allowed them to

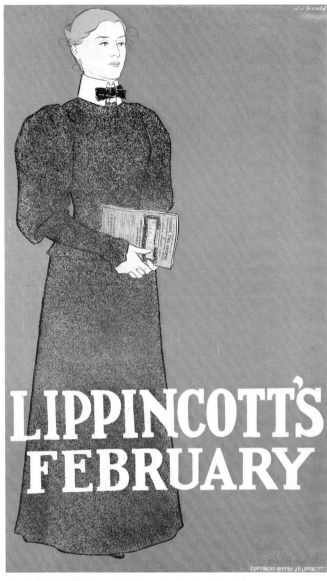

1.28 J. J. Gould, *Lippincott's*, February 1897. Poster. Art & Architecture Collection, Miriam & Ira D. Wallach Division of Art, Prints & Photographs. The New York Public Library. Astor, Lenox & Tilden Foundations.

the dense decorative elements typical of Art Nouveau posters in Europe, the elements from which the arguably less daring American companies kept their distance. Her hair is formed into the intertwining tendrils that are a hallmark of *le style Mucha*, the **curvilinear** lines of which are repeated in the straps of her gown. She seems lost in a dreamy reverie. The American poster, in contrast, features the sort of straightforward realistic style, without the elegant, "artificial" details such as the hair, and combines it with a mundane moment drawn from everyday life. However, the greatest contrast between American and European posters of young women is in their displays of sexuality. The young woman riding the Stearns is modestly dressed, her collar tightly around her neck, and her clothes shielding her body other than a length of her lower leg. In contrast, Mucha's young "spokesmodel" is almost completely falling out of her clothes, providing a provocative view of her breasts. Part of the distinction is that Mucha's young woman is arguably an allegory, which in French tradition would allow the artist more leeway to show idealized nudity, along the lines of the Roman goddess Venus, while Penfield's young woman is intended to represent a customer of the bicycle company. Here, in terms of subject matter, the American penchant for realism, the prosaic moments of everyday life, versus the French love of the dreamlike and the ideal, is made manifest. At the same time, the fact remains that American companies and their customers were simply more prudish than their European counterparts, as well as less adventurous in accepting new stylistic trends.

William Bradley

William Bradley (1868–1962), the most prominent American graphic designer of the 1890s, generated works in a variety of Art Nouveau styles derived from European works. Largely self-taught, his Thanksgiving poster advertising a literary magazine called *The Chap Book* (1895; *fig. 1.31*) displays flat planes of color and the repetition of curvilinear form that integrates Japanese style with the expressive line of Art Nouveau. Note the way in which the "OO"s of the title intertwine, as well as the manner in which the curves of the letters are echoed by the curves in the contours of the figure. Bradley also uses the color red to harmonize the text and image, especially in the way the red word "The" of the title is nestled into the large black "C," in the same way that red and black are balanced in the image of the woman itself. It is important to recognize that at this point in the history of the poster, there was a widely recognized distinction between the thousands of inexpertly designed chromolithographs published each year and the so-called "art poster," such as the ones Bradley produced. "Art posters," with their vaunted artistic pedigrees, initially were only used to publicize avant-garde literary journals, theatrical performances, and the like. Only through a gradual process that lasted well into the twentieth century did such graphic designs become the norm, rather than the exception in the world of advertising.

While Bradley was clearly aware of French Art Nouveau styles, his eclectic work owes more to the British designer Aubrey Beardsley (1872–1898; see below) than anyone else; indeed he was sometimes called "the American Beardsley." Images such as

play larger roles in society. The so-called "safety bicycle" shown in the poster had been invented in 1890, and took its name from the fact that it was much easier to ride and offered less risk than the previous high-wheeled models, which had perched the cyclist high above the ground. With the advent of the pneumatic tire, invented in 1892, bicycling became accessible to more people, but especially to women, who could ride a "safety bicycle" while maintaining the proper decorum expected on public roadways. In fact, the modern bicycle became emblematic of women's newfound freedom and ability to assert themselves as active members of American society. Indeed in 1896, Susan B. Anthony (1820–1906), one of the leaders of the nascent women's movement, declared, "The bicycle has done more for the emancipation of women than anything else in the world."

The poster for Waverley Cycles (*fig. 1.29*), a British company that hired the Paris-based Art Nouveau designer Alphonse Mucha to make this advertisement, provides a fascinating comparison with Penfield's Stearns poster. The Mucha poster displays all of

above: **1.29** Alphonse Mucha, *Waverley
Cycles*, 1898. Poster. Color lithograph.
Copyright © Mucha Trust.

right: **1.30** Edward Penfield, *Ride
a Stearns and Be Content*, 1896.
Color lithograph, 54⅝ x 40 in
(138.7 x 101.6 cm). Library of Congress,
Washington, D.C.

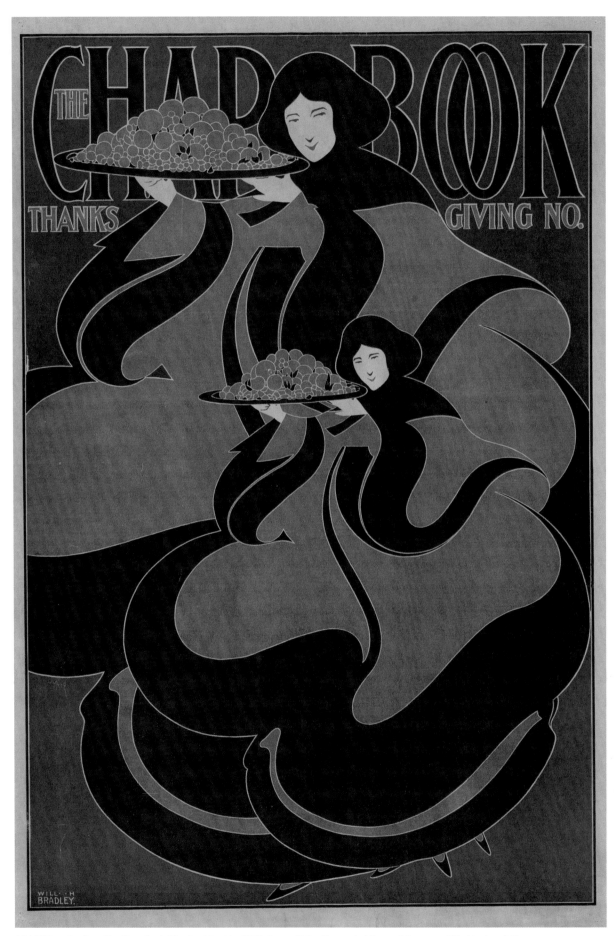

1.31 William Bradley, *The Chap-Book, Thanksgiving No.*, 1895. Poster. Color lithograph. Library of Congress, Washington, D.C.

the cover of the self-promotional magazine *Bradley: His Book*, a zincograph on handwoven paper, are specifically derivative of the British artist's idiosyncratic linear designs (*fig. 1.32*). The sinuous curves of the figure, as well as the elongated proportions, create a vision of languorous elegance that typifies the Art Nouveau. *Bradley: His Book* was published by the artist's own company, the Wayside Press, and served as a publicity tool for this business, which focused on small runs of high-quality output, along the lines advocated by followers of the Arts and Crafts movement.

Bradley also decried the overall low quality of American paper and typesetting. Under the influence of William Morris's critique of the poor quality of modern typography, Bradley became a consultant to the American Type Founders Association (see below), which was dedicated to raising the level of typography in American design. The American Type Founders first noticed Bradley's work in 1894, when they licensed a "blackletter" typeface (one resembling medieval script), which they called Bradley (*fig. 1.33*). The typeface was based on a previous design by the artist for the cover of the Chicago-based journal *The Inland Printer*. Trade publications such as this, despite their narrow, specialized audience, served as important conduits for the publicizing of aesthetic innovations in the nascent design community. Bradley is essentially a historicist style type along the lines favored by Morris, with a clear reference to medieval European styles. In this manner, William Bradley's career was quite eclectic, as he embraced the aims and styles of both Arts and Crafts and Art Nouveau, even though the two were often seen as incompatible.

Typesetting and Competition

One of the most important developments in the history of graphic design was the mechanization of typesetting, which first occurred in the United States during the 1880s. Two industrial machines, the **Linotype** (1886) and the **Monotype** (1889), allowed typesetters to work with a punch keyboard that directly controlled machinery for casting hot-metal type (*fig. 1.34*). The Linotype could produce an entire "line of type" set and justified, while the Monotype used two separate machines to produce hot type character by character. Both had their advantages, as the Monotype's one-by-one compilation of letters allowed for easier corrections. Handset typography was rendered obsolete by these inventions almost overnight, although it was still often used for specialized publications that required the most superior typesetting aesthetic. In fact, the same distinction as that made in reference to posters, between "artistic" and everyday, also existed in typography.

At the same time as these revolutionary inventions, American type producers underwent a series of price wars and consolidations. Eventually, in 1892, twenty-three type foundries joined in a corporate trust called the American Type Founders Association (ATF). ATF sought to set standardized prices for type, as well as control the copyrights for new typefaces, which up to that point had been widely pirated. Among the most famous new faces controlled by ATF was **Franklin Gothic** (*fig. 1.35*), designed by the renowned American type designer Morris Fuller Benton. Franklin Gothic was produced to meet the high demand for "sans serif"

1.32 William Bradley, *The Kiss* from *Bradley: His Book*, November 1896. Color woodcut and lithograph, 39¹⁵⁄₁₆ x 27⁷⁄₁₆ in (35 x 68.7 cm). St Bride Printing Library, London.

faces, faces without serifs, as opposed to traditional "roman" faces, which have serifs (such as Garamond Classico in which this book is set). Sans serif faces were mainly used in large sizes for advertising display purposes, because in most cases they are not very "readable"—meaning they create eye fatigue if set small on a large scale, for example in the body of a text. Franklin Gothic was produced by ATF in a wide variety of sizes and weights to serve the consistently expanding advertising industry in the United States. The term "gothic" can be confusing in its American usage, because it can mean either sans serif type or its exact opposite stylistically—type such as Bradley, which imitates medieval script. In Europe, the term "gothic" has only the latter meaning, but the equally confounding "grotesque" is used to denote sans serif. Additionally, **grotesque** was also used in the United States to denote sans serif faces. The typesetting industry witnessed a rebirth of sorts because of the competition between the makers of the Linotype and Monotype machines, each of which used proprietary faces in order to gain a competitive advantage. In later years, this battle created a situation where almost all standard faces existed in two variants: one initially created for the Linotype, the other for the Monotype machine.

Advertising Agencies

Another important stimulus to the rise of the graphic design field was the establishment of advertising agencies. Volney Palmer of Philadelphia is generally credited with the origination of the industry around 1840, when he began working as a middleman between newspapers, from whom he bought space, and companies, to whom he sold it. The first advertising agency, N. W. Ayer & Sons, was established in Philadelphia in 1869, while prominent New York firms such as J. Walter Thompson formed their businesses in the 1870s. By 1880, there were literally hundred of advertising agencies in all of the major cities of the United States. In 1888, an advertising executive named George Rowell founded the journal *Printer's Ink*, which proved to be the most influential example of a new type of magazine, devoted to tracking the print industry. *Printer's Ink* also acted as an arbiter for the advertising industry and its clients, as it published the first reliable circulation rates for periodicals and newspapers—numbers that were the key to setting consistent rates. Journals such as *Printer's Ink* shone a spotlight on the successes and failures of individual agencies and their campaigns, offering for the first time a way in which the value of certain strategies could be determined. While this evidence was largely anecdotal, it paved the way for a consideration of the value, or lack thereof, in using advanced design aesthetics to lure customers.

By the 1890s, most large firms employed an art director as part of a separate department, which enabled the firms to take over the design of advertisements as well as their marketing. In terms of graphic design, under the American model the "art director," sometimes called an "art editor," was king. Art directors were responsible for the overall design of the advertisements, and devoted much of their energy to finding and hiring the best illustrators, because representational imagery was the cornerstone of the American market. In the United States, a graphic designer was

1.33 William Bradley, Bradley Typeface, *The Inland Printer*, vol. 14, no. 3, December 1894. St Bride Printing Library, London.

just another employee who worked under the art director, and had very little autonomy or control over the final composition of an advertisement. Of course, sometimes the art director was a graphic designer and/or illustrator himself; William Bradley, for example, served as the art director for a number of publications during his career.

England

In England, companies had long displayed the same conservative taste for representational advertisements as their American counterparts. Nevertheless, growing competition for consumer goods created a need for images that stood out on a crowded poster hoarding. That was the motivation behind the industrialist Thomas Barratt's purchase of an oil painting by the artist Sir John Everett Millais (1829–1926). In the 1880s, Millais was perhaps England's most popular and successful artist. His painting *A Child's World*—a sentimental genre scene of a young boy playing—was typical of the artist's late work in both its conventional style and its mawkish subject matter. In 1886, Barratt paid £2,200 for the painting, which had already become well known because it had been exhibited at the Grosvenor Gallery and reproduced in the *Illustrated London News*. In order to advertise Pears' Transparent Soap, Barratt garnered the artist's permission to add the product name plus a bar of soap to the plate used for the painting's reproduction. The resulting lithograph, called *Bubbles*, was printed more than a million times, making it one of the most popular advertisements of the century and one of the most famous lithographs ever made (*fig. 1.36*). One key to this strategy was the fluid relationship that existed between commercial illustration and academic painting during the Victorian age, when both types of art featured naturalistic styles with a high degree of polish. Also, associating Pears' soap with fine art was somewhat akin to hiring an artist such as Toulouse-Lautrec or Bonnard to design an advertising poster, in that it created a certain cachet for an inexpensive mass-marketed product.

English Art Nouveau

One of the most essential stylistic elements of Art Nouveau in Europe was the use of plant tendrils in an asymmetrical, curvilinear design, the first example of which is generally credited to

right: **1.34** Monotype Machine, from
The Lanston Monotype, pp. 4–5, 1903.
St. Bride Printing Library, London.

below: **1.35** Morris Fuller Benton,
Franklin Gothic Typeface, 1902.

ABCDEFGHIJKLMNO PQRSTUVWXYZ abc defghijklmnopqrstvwx yz1234567890?!*&

"Franklin Gothic was produced to meet the high demand for 'sans serif' faces, faces without serifs, as opposed to traditional 'roman' faces [...]"

1.36 Sir John Everett Millais, *Bubbles*, 1886. Pears' Advertisement. Color lithograph. V&A Picture Library, Victoria & Albert Museum, London.

Steinlen, and twenty by Toulouse-Lautrec himself. While the exhibition was a success in terms of attendance, the venue was not exactly the most reputable, as the aquarium was known mainly for lowbrow entertainment and seedy spectacles. It is possible that many of the visitors were less interested in the posters than in various sideshows, which included singing donkeys, a boxing kangaroo, and "Zulima the Female Samson." Several critics cited the dour mood and lack of sophisticated colorism in the English posters, which by all reports paled in comparison with the French works. Nonetheless, this exhibition inaugurated a series of similar shows in England devoted to the art of the poster. Then, in 1898, a new journal called *The Poster* was established in London in order to promote the medium as a new art form. It is important to remember that graphic designers were still struggling for recognition as artists at this time.

below: **1.37** Arthur Mackmurdo, Chair, 1883. Carved and painted mahogany, leather upholstery, 38 x 19 x 18¹¹⁄₁₆ in (97.2 x 49.5 x 47.6 cm). V&A Picture Library, Victoria & Albert Museum, London.

opposite: **1.38** Arthur Mackmurdo, Title Page, *Wren's City Churches*, 1883. Woodcut on paper, 11⅞ x 8 in (29.2 x 22.2 cm). V&A Picture Library, Victoria & Albert Museum, London.

Arthur Mackmurdo (1851–1942). A friend of John Ruskin and William Morris, Mackmurdo helped to found the Century Guild, an association dedicated to the goal of raising the status of British crafts. In 1882, he designed a chair whose back "splat" features this design (*fig. 1.37*). The artist reused the motif in 1883 for the title page of his book *Wren's City Churches* (*fig. 1.38*). In this graphic version, the flowing curves form the tailfeathers of two peacocks, a bird whose ornamental plumage became closely associated with the elegant excess favored by the **Aesthetic movement** (see below). Both of those works were widely exhibited and also reproduced in design magazines, providing a conduit to artists on the European continent.

In England (for Scottish design, see Chapter 2), just as in other European countries, the public's fascination with Art Nouveau posters peaked in the 1890s. In October 1894, a show with the lengthy title "The First International Artistic Periodical Poster Exhibition" opened at the Westminster Aquarium in London. The collector Edward Bella had organized the show, which was dominated by French posters, according to his own taste. Bella had appointed Toulouse-Lautrec to head the French section, which featured nineteen works by Cheret, twenty-one by

Arthur Liberty and Liberty's

English designers had access to Japanese art works through the endeavors of Arthur Liberty, whose shop on Regent Street in London served from 1875 as a major conduit for Japanese art. Like Siegfried Bing's shop in Paris, Liberty's exhibitions brought advanced Asian aesthetics to a generation of British artists. The shop sold original Japanese silks, embroideries, furniture, carpets, and ceramics, and soon added a line of British-made goods in a variety of Asian styles. The Japanese kimono shown here was imported for the shop in the early 1890s, and was later acquired by the Victoria & Albert Museum (*fig. 1.39*). It features a **stylized** abstraction of moving water, complemented by bamboo and small birds, all floating unattached to the flat ground plane. The rich interplay of embroidered textures contrasts with the smooth sheet of silk.

Liberty's shop became a major competitor to William Morris's various Arts and Crafts businesses by offering an alternative to the sometimes stodgy styling favored by Morris. Liberty's embrace of Asian decorative art established his business as the foremost purveyor of Art Nouveau in England. Liberty's British designs, such as the cotton furnishing fabric by Arthur Silver (1853–1896) shown here (1887; *fig. 1.40*), showcase a strong current of Japonisme. Even though it is a roller-printed fabric with no discernible textural element, it is suggestive of the tactile quality of rich embroidered fabrics such as the kimono. Again, the peacock feather design is a favorite motif of the Aesthetic movement, primarily because of its sensuous density of ornament. Silver created a number of designs for Liberty's, although eventually he set up his own shop devoted to Art Nouveau textiles,

called the Silver Studio. Meanwhile, in the 1880s Liberty expanded his business, opening stores in Birmingham and then Paris. By the 1890s, Liberty's Japanese-inspired products had become so successful in Europe that Italians came to call the Art Nouveau style *Stile Liberty*.

Aubrey Beardsley

The career of one of the most influential English designers, Aubrey Beardsley, was ignited in 1893 with the publication of a new art journal called *The Studio*. This innovative periodical, described as "an illustrated magazine of fine and applied art," was the fruit of the collaboration between an established editor, Lewis Hind, and the publisher Charles Holme (1848–1923). Hind sought to find young artists with fresh styles that the journal could champion, thereby helping *The Studio* make a splash in a crowded market. This strategy worked incredibly well because Hind was fortunate enough to make the acquaintance of Beardsley, a 23-year-old unknown. The first issue of *The Studio* featured a cover by the young artist (*fig. 1.41*), as well as a number of other illustrations that supplemented an article on "A New Illustrator: Aubrey Beardsley," by the American art critic Joseph Pennell (1857–1926). Beardsley's cover for the first issue displays how much he had been influenced by the styles of Japanese prints. The scene of a forest is essentially two-dimensional, a series of overlapping flat forms set apart by different types of cross-hatched strokes of the pen. The repeated motif of the flower in the foreground also signals Beardsley's ability to absorb Japanese aesthetics into his own work. He succeeded in

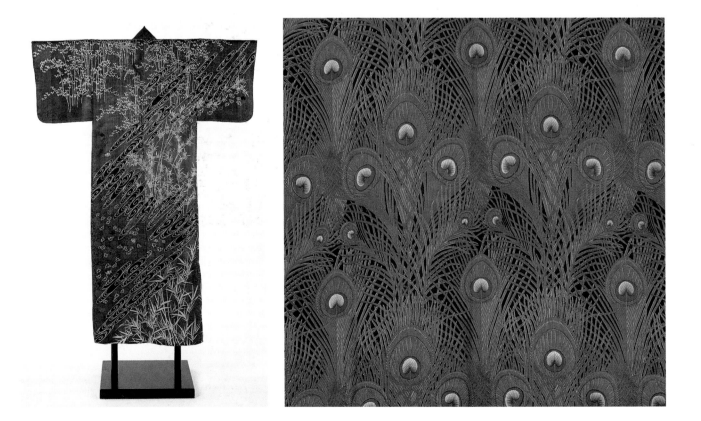

synthesizing an individual style that fused Japanese aesthetics with a graceful curving line as its foremost element. The subject of the cover illustration, a mysterious forest, resonates with the French Symbolists' exaltation of the natural world as an inspiring source of creativity. In fact, Beardsley's original design had included the figure of the Symbolists' favorite sexual persona, the Greek god Pan, but Hind and Holme considered the reference to be too lascivious for the cover.

Beardsley's embrace of French Symbolist principles marks him as part of a parallel movement in England in the later nineteenth century called the Aesthetic movement. Centered on the life and work of the playwright Oscar Wilde (1856–1900), this loosely defined group of authors, artists, and critics rejected the sermonizing morality of Victorian culture. The members of the Aesthetic movement focused on the idea of enjoying the pleasure of art for its own sake, as opposed to seeking out a historical lesson from art's subject matter. Followers of the movement shared the same fascination with provocative images of sexuality, subjective emotional responses, and supernatural mysteries that characterized the Symbolist poets in France. Stylistically, the Aesthetic movement was first inspired by the display of Japanese decorative arts at London's 1862 International Exhibition. In the 1890s, hostile critics labeled the work of the Aesthetic and Symbolist movements "decadent," because it rejected traditional classical styles as well as because of the artists' embrace of overtly sexual themes in their writings and art works. While the term "decadent" was intended as a rebuke, suggestive of the moral weakness of the Aesthetic movement, it was, in turn, adopted by authors such as Wilde as a declaration of their modern taste.

The strangely erotic drawing by Beardsley *I Kissed Your Mouth, Iokanaan* (*fig. 1.42*) was undoubtedly the most striking image included in the first issue of *The Studio*. The imagery is drawn from the play *Salome*, by Wilde, which had been first published in French in 1893. In the play, Wilde had reinvented the biblical narrative of John the Baptist's execution into a story that highlights a phantasmagoria of sexuality and macabre fantasies. This drawing illustrates Beardsley's "hairline" style, as well as his penchant for elongated figures in a vertical format. An alternative version of this drawing, minus the text and some of the decorative linear elements in the background, was published in book form to illustrate the 1894 English translation of *Salome*. Reportedly, Wilde was pleased with the work, although he criticized the license with which Beardsley had chosen to compose his images, many of which did not bear a strong relationship to Wilde's text. In many people's minds, the Art Nouveau style was inherently decadent and erotic, although that connection was rarely as manifest as it was in the composite vision of Wilde's and Beardsley's erotic imaginations.

In direct contradiction of the expensive handmade production techniques used at William Morris's Kelmscott Press, Beardsley's drawings for *The Studio* were created in order to be mass-reproduced by the photomechanical line block process. Because Beardsley worked mainly in black and white, his drawings could be reproduced without losing their visual impact. In this manner, inexpensive industrial techniques enabled Beardsley's designs to be among the most widely circulated of this era, making him perhaps the most influential draughtsman

opposite: **1.42** Aubrey Beardsley, *J'ai Baisé ta Bouche, Iokanaan (I Kissed Your Mouth, Iokanaan)*, from *The Studio*, vol. 1, no. 1, 1893. Illustration to Oscar Wilde's *Salome*. Line block print. V&A Picture Library, Victoria & Albert Museum, London.

above: **1.43** Aubrey Beardsley, *Avenue Theatre*, 1894. Poster. V&A Picture Library, Victoria & Albert Museum, London.

associated with the whole of the Art Nouveau period. Beardsley's influence on advertising imagery was mainly indirect, although he did complete a handful of posters for ostensibly commercial purposes.

In his *Avenue Theatre* poster (1894; *fig. 1.43*), the geometric pattern and attenuated figures characteristic of his work are evident. In one of his few forays into the world of color lithography, Beardsley made this poster to advertise a pair of plays. Note how the transparent screen of circles creates a flat pattern that serves to unify the image with the text. (Beardsley usually kept text and image separate from one another.) Also, the words "Avenue Theatre" have been written in an approximation of Asian calligraphic script. Perhaps the most influential element of Beardsley's style was his tendency to elongate his figures inside a rectangular space. This space generally is proportioned with a narrow width relative to its height, giving the poster a distinct vertical emphasis. This poster, along with the Aesthetic movement in general, was relentlessly mocked by the satirical magazine *Punch*, which referred to it with the phrase "'Ave a new poster."

In 1894, Beardsley and a friend, Henry Harland (1861–1905), decided to embark on their own literary journal, which they called *The Yellow Book: An Illustrated Quarterly*. The chosen title was unabashedly decadent, because plain yellow wrappers were commonly used in the 1890s to cloak "French" novels with sexual themes. Beardsley designed four volumes of *The Yellow Book* at a time when his fame had reached its apogee. The cover for volume 3 shown here (*fig. 1.44*) makes use of Japanese flat, decorative planes and synthesizes them with the exquisite rendering of contour that marked Beardsley's advanced technique. Like many of his works, this one was harshly criticized for what was considered at the time to be a scandalously lascivious subject matter—symbolized by the light from the street lamp shining on the mirror clutched in the woman's left hand. While 1894 found Beardsley at the pinnacle of his celebrity as an artist, the next year would witness a meteoric fall from grace. In 1895, Oscar Wilde pursued a libel suit that ended badly, as he was publicly excoriated and eventually imprisoned for violating laws against homosexuality. Because Beardsley was closely allied with the playwright, his own career rapidly deteriorated in the face of renewed public criticism of his "decadent" drawings. Dismissed by the publisher of *The Yellow Book*, Beardsley went into self-imposed exile in France. In 1898, at the age of twenty-five, Beardsley succumbed to the tuberculosis that he had acquired as a child. Because of his abbreviated life and career, it was other designers, such as William Bradley in the United States, who made Beardsley's style into a profitable, commercially viable enterprise.

opposite: **1.44** Aubrey Beardsley, *The Yellow Book*, vol III, Oct 1894. Black ink on yellow cover. V&A Picture Library, Victoria & Albert Museum, London.

right: **1.45** The Beggarstaff Brothers (William Nicholson and James Pryde), *Harper's*, 1895. Poster, 18⅞ x 13⅜ in (48 x 34 cm). St Bride Printing Library, London.

The Beggarstaff Brothers

The foremost English designers in the Japanese mode were the Beggarstaff Brothers, a name used for the collaborative works made by the artists William Nicholson (1872–1949) and James Pryde (1866–1941). The Beggarstaffs adopted the pseudonym because they did not want their reputations in the fine art world sullied by any association with commercial design. The use of pseudonyms was not uncommon when painters took up commercial graphics—publishers are said to have preferred this arrangement as well, because they could reduce the fee paid to the artist while still receiving a top-quality product. The Beggarstaffs' 1895 poster for *Harper's* displays some of the most aggressive simplification of any work produced in this area (*fig. 1.45*). Clearly indebted to Japanese prints, as well as to Toulouse-Lautrec, the silhouetted figure in this poster is more radically abstract than comparable images of the time, as its contour line disappears in several places so that the figure blends into the background. The flat tones, in stark contrast to contemporary French posters, make the image appear almost completely two-dimensional. Note also how effectively the image is related to the text. Three parts of the figure—its head, waist, and feet—are set off by heavy swaths of black ink. These three highlights are then matched by parallel parts of the text design, as the corresponding words, "Harper's," "Magazine," and "Still One Shilling," are all lettered in boldface black. Curiously, the striking image of a beefeater, a ceremonial royal bodyguard, had been designed for a poster that advertised beef extract, but it was turned down by the original patron. Eventually, it was bought by the American company in order to advertise the European edition of its magazine. It became by far the most successful image that the Beggarstaffs ever produced.

Another Beggarstaff poster, for a performance of *Don Quixote* at the Lyceum Theater (1895; *fig. 1.46*), shows the unusual cropping—note the horses' missing hoofs and the partial view of a windmill—typical of the Japanese style. While the most obvious precedent for the Beggarstaffs' reductive abstraction is Japanese art, it is also apparent that they were making a virtue out of necessity in terms of cost. The simple black and brown scheme of this poster was much less expensive to print than, for example, the polychromed posters of Jules Cheret. Partly because of the challenging nature of their images, the Beggarstaffs did not build the same type of successful practice as other noted designers. In fact, the *Don Quixote* is perhaps the most famous poster never published, as it rose to fame only decades later because of the admiration that a new generation of poster artists had for the rare copies of it. The Beggarstaff collaboration had been one of opportunity, and when the poster craze began to subside around 1900, Nicholson and Pryde, forced to confront the fact that they had not really made much of an income as designers, dissolved their partnership.

right: **1.46** The Beggarstaff Brothers (William Nicholson and James Pryde), *Lyceum Don Quixote*, 1895. Black and brown paper pasted on white, 18⅞ x 13⅜ in (48 x 34 cm). St Bride Printing Library, London. Reproduced by permission of Elizabeth Banks.

ART NOUVEAU:
AUSTRIA, AND GER

SCOTLAND, MANY.

2

Art Nouveau was a major influence on design not only in England and France but also in other parts of Europe. In focusing on artists who worked in Glasgow, Vienna, and various German cities, this chapter traces a number of artists' groups that developed a visual language that was overall more symmetrical, rectilinear, and abstract than that of their French and English contemporaries. Broadly speaking, it also traces a shift from art centered on the evocative potential of line, form, and color to one that eschews ornamental effects in favor of simplicity and clarity.

In addition to providing a survey of major works, this chapter will focus on three recurring themes. First, it explores the continuing attempts by artists to collapse the hierarchical relationship between the "fine arts" of painting, sculpture, and architecture, and the less esteemed "crafts"—a category that included graphic design. Second, the belief in the feasibility of artist-led utopias, or perfect worlds, which served as an escapist alternative to the alienating spaces of the industrial age, is considered. Third, the chapter discusses the use of design styles as a marker of national or regional identity, which celebrated the accomplishments of society under the leadership of bourgeois industrialists.

The Four

Four artists—Margaret Macdonald (1864–1933), Frances Macdonald (1873–1921), Herbert MacNair (1868–1955), and Charles Rennie Mackintosh (1868–1925)—together formed the larger part of the Art Nouveau movement in Scotland. None of these artists worked professionally as a graphic designer; however, the limited works that they did produce were to prove influential, and secured for Scotland a stable niche in the history of the Art Nouveau movement. This partnership, called The Four, consisted of two sisters and their respective husbands-to-be, as Frances Macdonald and Herbert MacNair married in 1899, while Margaret Macdonald and Mackintosh followed suit a year later.

The Glasgow School of Art, Celtic Revival

The city of Glasgow itself is important to an understanding of the Art Nouveau movement centered there. A nineteenth-century "boom town," Glasgow had undergone startling urban growth during the Industrial Revolution. The rapid changes in its economy had created a vast economic chasm between the nascent bourgeoisie with their fortunes and the workers who toiled in the factories. In fact, the city became rather notorious as a vulgar, blighted industrial zone, a reputation that most likely partly reflected English chauvinism. The decorative elegance of Scottish Art Nouveau produced at the Glasgow School of Art (GSA) should be understood in this context, in which art served to provide an alternative world, from which the difficulties of the industrial age could be conveniently banished. At the same time, the art produced at the school also served to reject this caricature of the city and rejoice in the affluence of the Glasgow bourgeoisie, a social class that included the Macdonald sisters. In fact, the sisters' education in the visual arts represented a typical step for young women from the more progressive, affluent families. Finally, the spirit of the Arts and Crafts movement, in which the fine arts and applied arts were equally valued, was intended to act as a democratizing force, one that could in some small way combat the general perception of urban life as rife with social and economic injustices.

2.1 Frances Macdonald,
A Pond, 1894. Watercolor.
Glasgow School of Art Collection.

The collaboration began when the Macdonald sisters enrolled in the Glasgow School of Art in 1893. Once there, the sisters found a supportive group of fellow students determined to engage the newest artistic trends. "The Immortals," as these young women called themselves, were excited by Japonisme as well as by the "decadent" artists gathered around Aubrey Beardsley and Oscar Wilde in England (see Chapter 1). However, the students at the GSA sought to carve out a unique, and specifically Celtic-inspired, visual style and subject matter. In a parallel to French designers' embrace of the Rococo, Scottish artists wanted to establish their art as part of a national tradition. The Four were influenced by the Celtic revival of this era, as evidenced by the continuing fascination with the works of "Ossian," an epic poet whose writings were filled with Celtic symbolism as well as supernatural adventure. ("Ossian" was in fact an invention perpetrated by the author James MacPherson (1736–1796) in 1761—MacPherson is credited with sparking the search for a historically distinct Celtic identity.) The Four were also aware of more recent scholarship, such as *Architecture, Mysticism, and Myth* (1891), a book by W.R. Lethaby (1857–1931) that argued in favor of the prominence of magic, supernatural strivings, and subjective responses in architectural theory. A favorite of the Arts and Crafts Society in London, Lethaby advocated the relationship between architecture and design crafts.

For artists desiring to showcase new work, the importance of publications and willing patrons cannot be underestimated. At the GSA, a group of progressive students organized themselves around a journal they called *The Magazine* (published 1893–6); it was in the November 1894 cover of that periodical that Frances Macdonald published one of the first works, a watercolor, that displays the seeds of mature style. Called *A Pond*, the image combines sinuous, organically shaped figures and water plants with a symmetrical organization (*fig. 2.1*). The attenuated grace of the figures is derivative of a number of other Art Nouveau designs; however, its combination of orthogonal structure and fluid, curvilinear forms, especially at the bottom of the image, as well as its nearly perfect symmetry (the left and right are mirror images outside of the textual elements), suggests the beginnings of a bold new graphic style. The decorative type of the word "November" reverses these two elements, as it combines

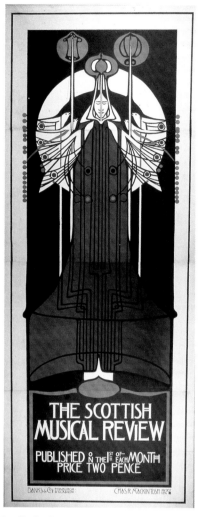

2.2 Frances Macdonald and Margaret Macdonald, *Drooko*, 1895. Poster. Copyright © Hunterian Museum & Art Gallery, University of Glasgow. Mackintosh Collection.

2.3 Frances Macdonald, Margaret Macdonald, and Herbert MacNair, *The Glasgow Institute of Fine Arts*, 1895. Poster. Copyright © Hunterian Museum & Art Gallery, University of Glasgow. Mackintosh Collection.

2.4 Charles Rennie Mackintosh, *The Scottish Musical Review*, 1896. Lithograph, 97 x 39 in (246.3 x 99 cm). Copyright © Hunterian Museum & Art Gallery, University of Glasgow. Mackintosh Collection.

rectilinear letterforms with strong asymmetrical elements. As is the case with many Scottish posters from this era, the palette, featuring a mix of green, purple, and indigo, clearly invokes a set of colors with strong associations to the Scottish identity movement. The subject is evocative and ambiguous, suggestive of mystical creatures who embody the spirit of this watery environment. The female forms decisively reject the prevailing "decadent" images of women as seductive temptresses, as Macdonald's figures exude mystery and ambiguity without defining that mystery in sexual terms.

Early Poster Design

In 1895, the Macdonald sisters received their first graphic design commission, a poster for Drooko Royal Umbrellas (*fig.2.2*). ("Drooko" is Scottish for "drench.") The owner of the company, Joseph Wright, hired the sisters to promote the product, which had inspired the verse, "I walk the world a raintight

fellow/Beneath the Joseph Wright Umbrella." The composition is made up of three vertical bands that are for the most part disconnected from one another. The box of organic elements on the lower left is separate from both the text above it, as well as the attenuated figure in the central space. There has been some attempt to connect the simplified central figure with the flowers on the far right, using the figure's hand, which becomes more plant-like closer to the floral forms, and with the product itself, as the umbrella spans the gap between the center and righthand spaces. The faintly floral-shaped umbrella frames the figure's face, but is not situated in a way that draws attention to the product—which, lost in the background, is the presumed focus of the poster's message.

The first poster by the Macdonald sisters in collaboration with Herbert MacNair displays many of the stylistic devices seen in *A Pond*, albeit in a more staunchly vertical format (*fig.2.3*). Advertising the GSA's 1895 student show, the poster superimposes long, sinewy figures with similarly attenuated plant forms. The most striking element of the symmetrical design is the way the female figure's hair and the male figure's hooded cloak both sweep around behind them and form part of the surrounding abstract design. The hand-drawn lettering of this lithograph has a number of dramatic flairs, despite its overall blocky proportions. For example, the arms of the "F" and "E" both extend out of the **em box** (the implied frame) in a dramatic fashion, while the arm of the "L" in "Glasgow" appropriates the baselines under the "as" as it runs horizontally across the poster. Also, the strong oblique stress of the "S" as well as the merged characters in "the" both create some unique visual emphasis. The text is not directly integrated with the image, but rather formed into a geometric block that creates a plinth on which the figures above are perched as if they are sculpted. The entire composition is made up of a series of boxes that encase more organic forms. The simple, flat forms bounded by bold black contour lines are indicative of the prevailing Japanese influence.

Celtic Manuscripts and The Four

The art of "The Four" was strongly influenced by Celtic art, especially by its celebrated illuminated manuscripts. While Celtic art can be found across much of Europe and even farther afield, its artistic centers were in Ireland, Scotland, and Northumbria in the British Isles. Although the term "Celtic art" can refer as far back as to the ancient works of the La Tène culture (450 B.C.E–600 C.E), it is also used broadly to refer to the medieval art produced in this region between 500–1000 C.E.

A mix of pagan and Christian styles and subject matter, Celtic art represents one of the great examples of cross-cultural ferment that characterized the Middle Ages. Later, in Ireland as well as in Scottish cities such as Glasgow during the mid-nineteenth century, there was a resurgence of interest in Celtic art for nationalistic reasons, and also because of the broader celebration of medieval culture that lay at the heart of the Arts and Crafts movement.

Characteristics of Celtic art include dense interlaced patterns, curvilinear elements, and zoomorphic forms. Although many of the abstract elements were invented by metalworkers working in three dimensions with raised linear elements, a sophisticated knowledge of color allowed artists working in two dimensions to replicate the spirals and flowing, knotted forms. Typically, manuscript illuminators displayed great skill in devising elaborate initial capitals, with letters that transformed themselves into beasts or abstract shapes while maintaining a recognizable typography. These flourishes served as a model for The Four.

A major center of medieval Celtic manuscript production was in a monastery on the island of Iona off the western coast of Scotland. When the monks of Iona fled from marauding Vikings around 800, they settled in Kells on the Irish coast. The resulting Book of Kells *from the early ninth century represents the ultimate achievement of the manuscript tradition. It was published in a facsimile edition in 1892, fueling a burst of creativity during the later stages of the Celtic revival. In the 1890s, the tendency of The Four to mix curvilinear elements with strong geometric structures would have derived from their knowledge of the Celtic manuscript tradition.*

Charles Rennie Mackintosh

Charles Rennie Mackintosh was the last addition to The Four's collaborative group. Trained as an architect, he had met MacNair in 1889, when they both worked at an architectural firm. Between 1889 and 1894, MacNair and Mackintosh both took classes at the GSA. Later, Mackintosh worked as an architectural draftsman for much of the 1890s in the small Glasgow architectural firm of Honeyman & Keppie. By 1895 The Four were complete. Mackintosh's 1896 poster advertising the *Scottish Musical Review*, a periodical, features much of the same mix of curvilinear and rectilinear elements visible in the earlier posters (*fig. 2.4*). It also features the "Scottish" palette of purple, indigo, and green as well as the use of the text box as a pedestal for the centralized image of a figure. However, perhaps because of his architectural training, Mackintosh's style leans more heavily on geometric, **architectonic** elements and so appears weightier than the other works. The *Scottish Musical Review* poster also has a very strong phallic element in the shaping of the figure as well as its erect bulb and stem floral combinations, introducing an element of sexuality that was not apparent in the earlier posters.

The Four exhibited their work outside Glasgow for the first time in 1896. At the fifth exhibition of the Arts and Crafts Society in London, they found their works harshly criticized: one piece by Mackintosh was called "grotesque," by both academic conservatives and members of the society. Followers of William Morris at this time were still wedded to the idea of the preeminence of historicist styles, and they rejected the fluid abstractions of The Four. Only the journal *The Studio* had anything positive to say about the group, recognizing their allegiance to Art Nouveau, which the journal backed. In the same year, a critic at the conservative *Magazine of Art* was to invent a memorable label for the works produced at the GSA, calling the institution the "Spook School" because of the preponderance of wraith-like figures in pieces such as *A Pond*. The Four, particularly, found much greater acclaim in 1900, when the eighth Vienna Secession exhibition featured a Scottish Room (*fig. 2.5*) When Margaret Macdonald and Mackintosh visited the show, they were widely celebrated by the Secession artists, who shared many of their ideals, such as a

2.5 Charles Rennie Mackintosh and Margaret Macdonald-Mackintosh, Room Designed for the Eighth Vienna Secession, 1900. Glasgow School of Art Collection.

rejection of the hierarchical distinction between fine and applied art, as well as their interest in pursuing decorative Art Nouveau graphics (see below).

A compelling parallel to The Four's graphic work can be found in Mackintosh's interior designs for the Glasgow School of Art itself. In 1897, the firm of Honeyman & Keppie, using a project created by Mackintosh, won the competition for the design of a new building for the GSA. The resulting interior spaces, such as the Library (*fig. 2.6*), feature much of the complex mix of symmetry and asymmetry, organic and rectilinear, that characterizes the work of The Four. The coffered grid of the ceiling is balanced with the sometimes irregular curves of the beams and arches to form a composition that has a graceful, linear feel. The library calls to mind the words of the architect Edward Lutyens (1864–1944), who said of another Mackintosh work that it was "all very elaborately simple."

Scottish tearooms provide an excellent example of a new type of establishment that reflected changes in social class as a result of the industrial revolution. Tearooms, sometimes called "Ladies' Luncheon Rooms," provided a new social space where women could socialize in public while avoiding unwanted association with the sordid reputation of the city's pubs and nightclubs. Macdonald and Mackintosh found their most loyal patron in the owner of a number of successful tearooms, Catherine Cranston

(1850–1934). Cranston, a supporter of the temperance movement, wanted her establishments to project a refined elegance, yet also to suggest the excitement of the modern city. Macdonald and Mackintosh eventually produced designs for four of her tearooms, attempting to create an overall vision that would integrate all the different elements of each room, from chairs to wall coverings, in a single aesthetic. The Ingram Street Tearoom was decorated with Macdonald's gesso panel *The May Queen* (*fig. 2.7*), which had already garnered a great deal of praise from the Secession artists when it was shown in Vienna in 1900. Featuring a strong linear element that would appear to have been influenced by Beardsley, the panel harmonizes this curvilinear element with a blocky rectilinear composition. Mackintosh's *Argyle* chair (1897), designed to make a dramatic statement at Cranston's Argyle Street Tearoom, was also exhibited at the Vienna Secession. The oak chair shares the vertical emphasis of the posters made by The Four, and translates the graphic conventions they developed, especially in the shaping of the large ellipse that forms the top rail and the thin posts that support that curving shape.

An important point concerning the historical reputation of The Four is the manner in which their original collaborative ideal, which resonated with the medieval revivalism of the Arts and Crafts movement, was later effaced because of the modern focus on the individual. During their lifetimes, the sense that first the

2.6 Charles Rennie Mackintosh, Library, Glasgow School of Art, 1899.

above: **2.7** Charles Rennie Mackintosh and Margaret Macdonald-Mackintosh, *The May Queen* Panel, Ingram Street Tearoom, 1900. The Burrell Collection, Glasgow, Glasgow City Council (Museums)

opposite left: **2.8** Gustav Klimt, *Secession I*, 1898. Poster. Lithograph, 22⅝ x 17 in (57.4 x 43.1 cm). The Museum of Modern Art, New York.

opposite right: **2.9** Gustav Klimt, *Nuda Veritas*, 1899. Oil on canvas, 99 x 22 in (252 x 56 cm).

Macdonald sisters, and then Margaret Macdonald and Mackintosh, had worked synergistically, was a given, even though they did not receive much acclaim in their native Scotland. In 1900 in Vienna, Macdonald and Macintosh were equally feted as accomplished Scottish artists. In the 1960s, when interest in the Art Nouveau was revived, a new generation of design historians focused on Mackintosh to the almost total exclusion of the other artists. In exhibitions held in Zurich, New York, Paris, and London during the 1960s, Mackintosh was given a progressively greater place, celebrated as an individual genius. Today, he is a cornerstone of design history, while the other three of The Four have been pushed somewhat out of the picture. In particular, Margaret Macdonald's contribution to the couple's work is woefully understated in many design histories.

Vienna Secession

In Vienna, graphic design was an integral part of the Secession movement, led by Gustav Klimt (1862–1918). The artists' group called the **Vienna Secession** was formed in March 1897 by an initial group of eighteen artists who felt that the two artists' organizations in Vienna, the Vienna Academy of the Arts and the Genossenschaft Bildender Künstler Wiens, were out of touch with the newer styles and artistic theories that were spreading across Europe. In the eyes of the Secessionists, the Academy was an aged institution hopelessly wedded to the academic art of the past. The Genossenschaft, a word that refers to its status as an artists' "cooperative," was founded in 1870 and devoted to contemporary art. Sometimes referred to as the Kunstlerhaus, or "artists' house," it

was controlled in the 1890s by men with quite conservative taste. Because the Academy and the Genossenschaft controlled the only public exhibition spaces in Vienna, the Secession artists' first goal was to create an alternative organization with an exhibition venue through which more progressive artists, from both Vienna and abroad, could present their work to the public. The term "secession" means a withdrawal, and it is from the Genossenschaft that the artists originally broke away. Like Art Nouveau artists throughout the rest of Europe, the Secessionists felt that the experience of modern industrial society could be successfully interpreted only by artists open to new aesthetic strategies. And, in fact, the term Secessionstil became yet another synonym for Art Nouveau style.

Gustav Klimt

The first item of business for the Secession artists was to hold an exhibition. This first Secession show met with an indifferent public, and its rented venue, the headquarters of the Viennese Horticultural Society, was unremarkable. Gustav Klimt, who had been elected President of the Secession group, produced a poster for the show that set the tone for much of the art that would follow (fig. 2.8). In terms of style, Klimt adopted the vertical format, asymmetrical design, and empty spaces that had been a key part of Aubrey Beardsley's designs in England. The figure on the righthand edge is Athena, ancient goddess of Wisdom, whose armor references the Secession's struggle to free itself from conservative artistic tradition. In a band across the top of the poster the mythical struggle of Theseus with the Minotaur is played out as yet another allegory of heroic artistic struggle against philistinism.

The monochrome drawing of Theseus is contained in a horizontal band that is balanced at the bottom of the poster by another colorless band, this one containing the text publicizing the exhibition. The sumptuous color of the figure of Athena neatly ties the two elements together. In the upper left of the image, the words "Ver Sacrum" ("Sacred Spring") appear, an oft-repeated slogan of the Secession that refers to yet another mythological story, one in which ancient citizens experience new-found abundance after a calamity. Ver Sacrum was also the title given to an influential journal published by the group, and Klimt reused the image portion of this poster for another one that publicized the journal (see below). The fact that French Symbolist ideas influenced Secession art works is clear in the subject matter of this poster—mainly, the sense that the underlying message is mysterious, ambiguous, and gives priority to the subjective emotional responses of the artist.

It might seem ironic that a Secession artist such as Klimt, who valued his own novelty and avant-gardist views on art and culture highly, would choose to represent the Secessionist struggle in seemingly archaic, mythological terms. However, in 1890s' Vienna, Classical myths were often used to explain quite modern situations, most notably in the work of the Viennese psychoanalyst Sigmund Freud (1856–1939), whose developing theories of sexuality often relied on analogies with Classical mythology as an explanatory tool—as in the "Oedipus complex." The fin de siècle ambience of Vienna was enhanced by a palpable sexual atmos-

phere that informed much of the graphic work done there, as well as the emerging psychoanalytic theories of Freud. It was in fact the strong sexual undercurrent in the poster, manifest in the exposed genitals of Theseus, that caused the authorities to censor it. Klimt then produced a second version, which covered the offending organs with the trunk of a tree.

Nuda Veritas ("Naked Truth"; 1899) is a fine example of Klimt's propensity for combining sumptuous decorative designs with sexually charged, if ambiguous, subjects (fig. 2.9). The painting was exhibited at the fourth Secession exhibition, held in the spring of 1899. There is a strong contrast between the visionary abstraction of the flat, decorative background and the realistically rendered nude woman. This contrast creates a world of allegorical fantasy as well as the suggestion of contemporary sexual intimacy. The Symbolist-inspired figure of truth, presented Eve-like with a serpent coiling around her ankles (and connecting the text of the title with the image), seems to float ethereally in a hazy atmosphere of soft blues. This figure had a longstanding association with alchemy and other esoteric traditions, where she often represented the sexual fusing of male and female as part of a spiritual transformation. Above the figure, text by the German Romantic poet Friedrich von Schiller (1759–1805) reads: "If you cannot please all men by thine actions and by thine art, then please the few; it is bad to please the many"—a reference to the enlightened few, initiates, who appreciated the art of the Secession.

The Secession Building

A key goal for the Secessionists was to control an exhibition space of their own. The young architect Josef Maria Olbrich (1867–1908) was chosen to design the building (fig. 2.10), which was to be located on the Ringstrasse, Vienna's most fashionable avenue. The Ringstrasse had been itself constructed as recently as the 1860s, and the style of its architecture was particularly anathema to the Secessionists. They objected to the fact that it was made up of a series of historicist structures that quoted from all manner of past styles. The Secession artists wanted to make a public statement by locating their innovative exhibition hall and headquarters right in the thick of what they saw as an eclectic mass of tired-looking Neoclassicism. However, because of some official displeasure with Olbrich's design, the building was soon

2.10 Josef Olbrich, Secession Building, 1898.

2.11 Josef Olbrich, *Secession*, 1898. Poster. Lithograph, 30¾ x 20⅜ in (78.1 x 51.8 cm). MAK–Austrian Museum of Applied Arts/Contemporary Art, Vienna.

moved to the less-fashionable Karlsplatz. It is important to note that despite this setback, as well as the artists' antagonistic stance toward official culture, the Secession group generally found the government of the city of Vienna to be willing to help them reach their goals. Additionally, Secession artists quickly found patrons among the wealthy bourgeoisie. These included luminaries such as Karl Wittgenstein (1847–1913), scion of a powerful industrial family, who financed the construction of the Secession building.

Olbrich's design was executed in a matter of months, and it was soon recognized as one of the most notable manifestations of Viennese Art Nouveau architecture. Combining geometric clarity with a garland of gold over the main entrance, Olbrich's creation appeared startlingly severe with its strong axial symmetry. The building creates an unusual contrast between the blank spaces on the cube-shaped walls of the exterior façade and a roof whose elaborate decorations and skylights evoked to its critics both a "gilded cabbage" and a "greenhouse." More notable, in reality, is the way the blank spaces on the façade resonate with the comparable void used in Klimt's poster for the first Secession exhibition. Both artists valued the startling effect of so much emptiness in the midst of a design that is otherwise rich with decoration.

The effort made by Secession artists to unify different media with a holistic aesthetic is an important part of most Art Nouveau movements. The underlying principle at work is that of the *Gesamtkunstwerk*, or "total work of art," a concept originated by the German composer Richard Wagner and made popular by the French Symbolist movement. A *Gesamtkunstwerk* is an art work that encompasses every possible type of aesthetic expression. Wagner felt that he could attain this goal through his operatic compositions, which combined elements drawn from literary, musical, and visual artistic traditions. The French Symbolists,

most of whom revered Wagner and his work, emphasized the mystical and spiritual elements of a unification of the arts. For visual artists, the *Gesamtkunstwerk* was more of a theoretical goal than a concrete reality. Nonetheless, Secession artists and others with their same goals sought to implement the idea of a unification of the arts in as many ways as possible.

While some of the decorative relief panels that edge the blocky mass of the Secession building feature dramatic curvilinear elements, the organic lines are always more tightly controlled by the compositional scheme than they are in, for example, French Art Nouveau. Above the lintel of the main entrance a carving read, "To each age its art. To art its freedom," a credo that resonates with the spirit of revolution and embrace of the modern that was an integral part of Art Nouveau artistic theory. The dome of cascading laurel leaves above this inscription evoked the wreath worn by Apollo, allegorical patron of the arts. Combined with an orthogonal design reminiscent of Egyptian temple architecture, the building was suggestive of the spiritual attitude that the Secessionists had to their work. Inside, the most innovative part of Olbrich's design was immediately evident; the exhibition space featured movable panels, creating an "open plan" that could be rearranged in order to allow the space to take on new forms in short order.

Poster and Journal Design

In November 1898, Olbrich's building was the site of the second Secession exhibition. For both that show and the third, a poster designed by the architect, and featuring his building, publicized the venue as well as its contents (*fig. 2.11*). This vertical-format lithograph depicts the Secession building's front façade centered

2.12 Alfred Roller and Koloman Moser, *Ver Sacrum*, no. 1, 1898. Lithograph, 11⅝ x 11⅛ in (29.5 x 28.2 cm). MAK–Austrian Museum of Applied Arts/Contemporary Art, Vienna.

2.13 Koloman Moser, *Ver Sacrum*, no. 2, 1899. Lithograph, 11⅝ x 11⅛ in (29.5 x 28.2cm). MAK–Austrian Museum of Applied Arts/Contemporary Art, Vienna.

2.14 Koloman Moser, Poster for Secession XIII, 1902. Lithograph, 69 x 23 in (177.2 x 59.7 cm). Private Collection. Museum für Gestaltung, Zurich. Poster Collection.

at the top of the poster, emphasizing its severe geometric scheme. The lower half of the image features hand-drawn text of two distinct, and not particularly harmonious, designs. Other than the centering of the justified text in a rectangular shape, there is no clear relationship between it and the image. It would seem that in this poster Olbrich relied heavily on the "star power" of his building's main entrance, feeling that it alone was enough to make a striking poster.

The Secession journal *Ver Sacrum*, established in 1898, was the locus of a great deal of experimental graphic work. The journal had been proposed at the first general assembly of the Secession artists in June 1897, as an Austrian answer to the popular Art Nouveau periodicals in Germany, *Pan* and *Jugend*. Koloman Moser (1868–1918), one of the founders of the movement, was chosen to organize the journal. The first issue appeared early in 1898, featuring a cover designed by Alfred Roller (1864–1935), the journal's first editor (*fig. 2.12*). An introductory essay in the first issue declared that *Ver Sacrum* "aims to show other countries for the first time that Austria is an independent artistic entity. … [I]t is meant to be a clarion call to the artistic sense of the people, to inspire, promote, and spread artistic life and artistic independence." In this manner, the Secessionists identified their own work as representative of national identity. (Austria was, of course, the dominant part of the larger Austro-Hungarian Empire under Emperor Franz Josef.) Inspired by the theory of the *Gesamtkunstwerk*, the journal was intended to engage with both the performing and literary arts, as well as the visual ones.

The editors of *Ver Sacrum*, especially the graphic designer Roller, sought to integrate typography, ornament, and image into a unified art work on the page, again influenced by the concept of the *Gesamtkunstwerk*. The individual issues generally each sported a single theme (the fourth one, for example, was dedicated to Moser's drawings and other graphics), and the implementation of a unified visual style extended even to the advertisements, which were usually designed by Secession members themselves. A striking example of the type of innovative designs produced for *Ver Sacrum* is Moser's cover for the February 1899 issue, number 2 (*fig. 2.13*), for which he drew an allegorical female figure emerging from lush tendrils that create powerful abstract forms. The flattened planes of her face suggest the influence of Japanese aesthetics, while the subject resonates with the Japanese tradition of *Bijin-ga*. In fact, Japanese art also held a special fascination for the Secession artists, who dedicated their sixth exhibition (in 1900) to it. The decorative lettering features the same sense of flow as is found in Japanese art. The curvilinear details of individual characters, such as the curving "v" and elongated "s" of the title (almost touching the woman's hair), match the overall form of the drawing. The unusual square format of *Ver Sacrum* also garnered attention, and is suggestive of the cubic spaces in Olbrich's building and Klimt's exhibition poster.

Koloman Moser also contributed a poster publicizing one of the Secession exhibitions, this one for the thirteenth show, held in 1902 (*fig. 2.14*). By then, many of the Secession artists had shifted to a decorative scheme built on orthogonal principles. Partly influenced by the Scottish design principles that had made a huge splash at the eighth Secession exhibition in 1900, a subset of the

Secessionists adopted not only a new style but also a new tone, in which subjective, Symbolist-influenced flights of fancy were eschewed in favor of a more straightforward subject matter. At the same time, geometric pattern, which does not lend itself to the sort of sensual atmosphere favored by Klimt, became a more important visual element. In this poster, Moser uses a scheme of three figures arranged symmetrically in a vertical format that is clearly reminiscent of Scottish graphics. The reductive, geometric figures are highly structured; the only curves in their bodies are formed by simple circular and teardrop shapes. The vertical bands that make up their bodies echo the overall shape of the poster. Moser used colors in a similarly subdued fashion, dominated by a flat red and blue that are outlined by hard-edged contour lines. The text is used in the Scottish manner as a plinth for the figures, yet it is better integrated with them by passages of ornament that allow text and image to flow together. In contrast to all of this geometric clarity is the fanciful lettering, which features scarcely legible abstract forms. Some of the letters bulge, some serve as passive foils to the more exuberant letters, while the "R"s in "Österreichs" (fourth line from the bottom) look like deformed "A"s. While replete with curved elements, especially the stems, the curves are not irregular, like the French Art Nouveau, but rather seem to be geometric in their baseline shapes. These dramatic letters are justified, forming a crisp block that belies their exaggerated forms. The geometric pattern and extreme simplification of the figures in this poster are distinctly un-sexual and un-Symbolist, a far cry from the decorative sensuality of Klimt's spiral floral designs, such as the one in *Nuda Veritas*.

Another poster that bridges the curvilinear style of the early Secession with the post-1900 concern with geometry was made by Alfred Roller in 1903 for the sixteenth Secession exhibition (*fig. 2.15*). At the top of the lithograph, the three "S"s in the word "Secession" display short, blunt curves that descend into long sinuous spines, elongated and stylized like the traditional allegorical figure. The field behind them is made up not of lavish floral ornament, but of a reductive geometric pattern. The plinth-like block of text at the bottom features an incredibly dense, bold decorative type, in which the letters expand to fit into every nook and cranny of the box that circumscribes them.

Wiener Werkstätte

Around 1903, Josef Hoffmann (1870–1956), the Viennese architect, designer, and member of the Secession, and Koloman Moser began to develop a new organization that would focus its efforts on promoting high standards of manufacture for Austrian crafts. (The term "crafts" in the early twentieth century denotes the decorative arts associated with architecture such as furniture and textile design, metalwork, as well as bookbinding, graphic design and even the creation of industrial products, and should not be confused with the uniquely American notion of "crafts" as amateurish art projects with ephemeral materials, such as collages made by children.) With the financial support of the industrialist Fritz Wärndorfer, they named their organization the **Wiener Werkstätte**, translatable as the "Viennese Workshops."

2.15 Alfred Roller, *Secession 16 Ausstellung*, 1903. Poster. Color lithograph. V&A Picture Library, Victoria & Albert Museum, London.

Hoffmann and Moser, who were both professors at Vienna's **Kunstgewerbeschule**, or "School of Crafts," wrote in the 1905 manifesto of the Wiener Werkstätte: "So long as our cities, our houses, our rooms, our furniture, our effects, our clothes and our jewelry, so long as our language and feelings fail to reflect the spirit of our times in a plain, simple and beautiful way, we shall be infinitely behind our ancestors." The artists of the Wiener Werkstätte, influenced by William Morris and the principles of the Arts and Crafts movement, as well as by the concept of the *Gesamtkunstwerk*, sought to create works in a variety of media that would beautify modern urban society. Between 1903 and 1905, a schism gradually deepened between artists committed to the collapse of the traditional arts and crafts hierarchy, and those who felt that painting was the most exalted form of art produced at the Secession. (The painter Gustav Klimt was, in fact, part of the former group, devoted to the ideal of the *Gesamtkunstwerk*.) This led to a gradual decline in the cohesiveness of the Secession movement and, after 1905, it was eclipsed by former Secession artists' new commitment to the Werkstätte. While a number of Secession artists had earlier desired to pursue the production of crafts, they had never successfully formed relationships with manufacturers, and so the Werkstätte grew out of the Secession movement's commitment to crafts.

Werkstätte Style

In terms of style, the artists associated with the Werkstätte rejected the irregular, organic curvilinear style of the early Secession and focused their efforts on the geometric clarity of form that had become a major part of *Secessionstil* around 1900. All of the products of the Werkstätte were harmonized to fit this restrained style, a style that was in a way summarized by the two **logotypes** produced to adorn its goods in 1903 (*fig. 2.16*). In tune with the medieval spirit of collaboration that had characterized the Arts and Crafts movement in England, it was never revealed whether Moser or Hoffmann had designed the logos or if they were a communal project. The "rose" logo features the eponymous flower depicted in a severe rectilinear design, its bloom made up of squares within squares, each part of the flower boxed in by a rectangle. The "Twin Ws" logo displays the superimposed letters in a perfectly square shape, essentially an em box around the letters. An important part of the Werkstätte ideology was that the designers, most of whom were graduates of the Kunstgewerbeschule, would be paid royalties from their work, and not have to suffer the lowly status and desperate poverty of wage laborers.

The square shape that is a distinguishing characteristic of many Werkstätte designs was employed equally by Moser and Hoffmann, although the latter used it so prominently that it became known by the nickname the "Quadratl-Hoffmann." For example, in 1905, Hoffmann designed a poster for the Werkstätte that regularly intersperses the "Twin Ws" logo with the words "Wiener Werkstätte" centered and justified into a square block of text (*fig. 2.17*). Here, the use of orthogonal schemes to advertise the elegant functionalism of Werkstätte products is in resounding contrast to the idiosyncratic designs of the Secession—designs

top: **2.16** Josef Hoffmann and Koloman Moser, Werkstätte Logotypes, 1903.

above: **2.17** Josef Hoffmann, *Werkstätte*, 1905. Poster. Offset lithography, 29 ft 6 in x 20 ft (9.05 x 6.18 m). Albertina Museum, Vienna.

right: **2.18** Josef Hoffmann, *Wiener Werkstätte Flatware*, 1904. Silver. MAK–Austrian Museum of Applied Arts/Contemporary Art, Vienna.

below: **2.19** Koloman Moser and Josef Hoffmann, *Floge Reception Room*, 1904. MAK–Austrian Museum of Applied Arts/Contemporary Art, Vienna.

that had effectively signified the Secession artists' interest in Symbolism and mysticism.

In 1904, Hoffmann designed a set of geometrically stylized cutlery for the patron Fritz Wärndorfer (*fig. 2.18*). This flatware was monogrammed in the same manner as the Werkstätte's "Twin Ws" logotype, with boxes circumscribing geometrically shaped letters that have no stresses. The flatware itself was composed of the same type of pure geometric shapes and formal clarity. This place setting was featured along with other tableware at a 1906 exhibition called "The Laid Table," which was held at the Werkstätte's headquarters. It will be important to be able to distinguish between the Werkstätte's rectilinear designs, which have a stylish geometry to them, as evidenced by the sleek shapes and elongated proportions of the fork in this example, and later geometric styles, which are often drier and less decorative in their visual effects. The geometric linear elements in Werkstätte products are essentially decorative, akin to the sinuous lines of Art Nouveau. Just as the curvilinear flourishes of Art Nouveau posters sometimes obscured the legibility of the text, often the stylized geometry of Werkstätte products inhibited their functionality. Without having sampled food with this museum-quality flatware, it would be hard to evaluate this example.

Hoffmann and Moser designed the interior of the fashion house owned by Emilie Floge (1862–1918), an important patron and longtime companion of Klimt. The Schwestern Floge opened in 1904, sporting an interior with a simple orthogonal design. Hoffman contributed the table and chair set seen in this photograph (*fig. 2.19*). The spare, rectilinear simplicity of the chairs, with a strong vertical emphasis, is complemented by the boxy shape of the cubic table. The elongated chairback is reminiscent of Mackintosh's *Argyle* Chair, which had been a part of the Scottish Room at the eighth Secession exhibition of 1900, around the time that Hoffmann shifted his style from one of florid organic forms to this more rectilinear approach. The slight curves in the table's base are positively exuberant by the restrained standards of the Werkstätte. Klimt, in turn, designed a number of textiles for the Werkstätte as well as fashion designs for Floge. Owing partly to its financial success in designing textiles, the Werkstätte opened branches in Zurich, Switzerland, and New York City as well as a new headquarters in a fashionable district of Vienna in 1907.

The Werkstätte artists organized two large-scale exhibitions of their work in the summers of 1908 and 1909, which they called simply "Kunstschau Wien" ("art show in Vienna"). The shows were held in a temporary building designed by Hoffmann. With fifty-four rooms containing the work of over 170 artists, the exhibition presented a wide range of Austrian art, not just that produced at the Werkstätte. However, one of its most notable rooms was devoted to Klimt, another to the products of the Werkstätte itself.

A poster publicizing the show by Berthold Löffler (1874–1960), a professor at the Kunstgewerbeschule and a member of the Werkstätte, features the typical allegorical figure of the arts (*fig. 2.21*). However, in keeping with the tenets of the Werkstätte style, the figure is highly schematic, smooth and sleek in appearance. Her body is punctuated by a handful of symmetrical crosses, each with its corners filled in by black circles. It is

2.20 Rudolph Kalvach, Postcard "name day", 4⅝ x 3½ in (12 x 9 cm). MAK–Austrian Museum of Applied Arts/Contemporary Art, Vienna.

2.21 Berthold Löffler, *Kunstshau*, 1908. Poster. Lithograph, 13⅓ x 18⅝ in (34 x 47.5 cm).

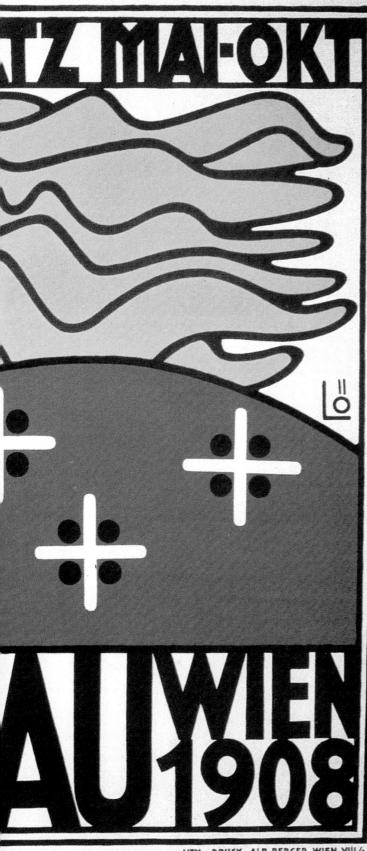

LITH. u. DRUCK ALB. BERGER WIEN VIII/₁

important to remember the ongoing influence of Japonisme in Europe, specifically in the flat areas of color bounded by heavy black contour lines in this poster. Löffler also organized a room at the Kunstschau that was dedicated solely to the art of the advertising poster. A myriad posters featuring rectilinear designs and geometric patterns can be viewed in the photograph. Löffler's show represented the first formal exhibition of the poster to take place in Vienna.

Another type of graphic design widely practiced at the Werkstätte was the creation of postcards; more than a thousand unique postcard designs were printed at the workshop. Because of the inexpensive nature of their production, postcards allowed artists to experiment with a wide range of design styles. For example, a lithographed card designed by Rudolph Kalvach (1883–1932) to celebrate a "name day" is awash with a vivid juxtaposition of the complementary colors blue and orange (*fig. 2.20*). While the reductive drawing and symmetry of the card resonate with the overall Werkstätte style, the ornamental line around the lettering is rather whimsical and idiosyncratic in a manner that is not typical of the workshop. Many of the stems of the letters in the greeting wobble a bit and feature changes in stress, a hint of the *Secessionstil* that contrasts with the firmer geometry and even line of the "Twin Ws" in the lower left.

In book design, the Werkstätte artists displayed a penchant for fine materials much like that of the Kelmscott Press in England. The leather cover of the writing case shown here (*fig. 2.22*) features the same sort of geometric repetition that Hoffmann had used in the poster discussed above (see *fig. 2.17*). The dense, rhythmic pattern was designed by Mathilde Flögl

2.22 Josef Hoffmann, *Writing Case*, 1927–29. Pattern design by Mathilde Flögl. Manufactured by the Wiener Werkstätte. Leather, gilt-stamped, 9¼ x 11⅝ in (23.4 cm x 29.7 cm). MAK–Austrian Museum of Applied Arts/Contemporary Art, Vienna.

(1893–1950). As had been the case with the Kelmscott Press and the broader Arts and Crafts movement in England under Morris, the espoused ideal of making the entire world of mass-produced goods beautiful was fine in theory, but the practice at the Werkstätte was dedicated almost exclusively to the creation of handmade goods such as this for the wealthy bourgeoisie. Other than a few postcards, broadsheets, and children's books, the products of the Werkstätte were accessible only to the moneyed elite. Moser left the Werkstätte in 1907 to pursue a career as a painter. The iconic geometric style that had dominated the organization since 1903 gave way around 1915 to a more eclectic variety of design languages, united only in their continuing goal of beautifying craft production. Hoffmann remained a part of the organization he had co-founded until its dissolution in 1932.

Austrian Expressionism: Oskar Kokoschka, Egon Schiele

Another trend in graphic design that grew out of the Viennese Secession movement was **Expressionism**. Expressionism is neither a defined movement like the Werkstätte, nor is it a unitary style. Instead, it is a mindset whereby the artist seeks not to show what the world looks like, but rather how it feels. Along these lines, many Expressionist artists sought to represent the storm and stress of a tortured soul or a trying situation. Not all Expressionism has a specific, directed feeling in mind; often it articulates a type of generalized anxiety or unease about the world. While Expressionist artists in Vienna were associated with the Werkstätte, their styles stand in stark contrast to the Werkstätte style of geometric clarity and compositional simplicity. In its place, they use distortions of form, color, and space that are designed to increase the emotional impact on the viewer. Viennese Expressionist style has much in common with the expressive power of French Symbolist art as well as Art Nouveau. The art historian Peter Selz recognized this consonance but also elucidated an important distinction, "Symbolism, Art Nouveau, and expressionism share above all their emphasis on form and its evocative potentialities, … Frequently, where symbolism merely suggests and understates, Expressionism exaggerates and overstates." Furthermore, Expressionists eschew the polished finish and ornamental elegance of Symbolism and Art Nouveau.

The foremost Expressionist artists associated with the Werkstätte, Oskar Kokoschka (1886–1980) and Egon Schiele (1890–1918), were both protégés of Gustav Klimt. While Schiele and Kokoschka specialized in painting, they also produced a number of striking posters and other graphics. As a student at the Kunstgewerbeschule, Kokoschka had produced bookbindings and illustrations as well as ceramics for the Werkstätte as early as 1907, some of which were included in the 1908 Kunstschau. Kokoschka also designed a poster, *The Cotton Picker*, publicizing the exhibition (*fig. 2.23*). Certain aspects of the poster show the influence of the *Secessionstil*, particularly the format of a single woman amid an ornamental plant motif. However, nothing about the figure or the cotton displays the decorative fluidity of Art Nouveau. The figure looks rather awkward and disjointed, with an elongated arm hanging at her side that is anything but

2.23 Oskar Kokoschka, *The Cotton Picker*, Kunstschau, 1908. Poster. V&A Picture Library, Victoria & Albert Museum, London.

2.24 Oskar Kokoschka, *Self-Portrait*, from *Der Sturm*, first issue, March 1910. Poster. Lithograph in black, brown, and old rose, 26 x 17 in (66.7 x 44.6 cm).

2.25 Egon Schiele, *Secession 49 Ausstellung*, 1918. Poster. Paper, 26⅝ x 20⅞ in (68 x 53 cm). MAK–Austrian Museum of Applied Arts/Contemporary Art, Vienna.

graceful; her hair seems detached from her head and face; the bold colors of the figure's clothes lack a harmonious sense of balance. Next to the figure, the linear element of the cotton plant appears "clumsily" proportioned and lacks a firm hand. These are all qualities that Kokoschka put into the drawing on purpose in order to increase its expressive power. The chunky proportions of the scarcely legible lettering complement the ungainly shapes in the image portion of the poster. All of the sensuality that Klimt and others put into this type of image has been drained out of *The Cotton Picker*. The subject itself, a worker in a field, is as unsexy as they come, a far cry from the vivid sensuality of *Nuda Veritas*.

Kokoschka takes expressive intensity to a new level with the self-portrait he painted in 1910, which was reproduced as a lithographic poster for *Der Sturm*, a Berlin art journal dedicated to the Expressionist cause (*fig. 2.24*). Kokoschka had shaved his own head that year and reveled in his striking appearance, while also displaying for all to see his almost religious commitment to Expressionist art. Of course, in the poster he has exaggerated the shapes of his features in order to emphasize a sort of misshapen ugliness that exudes emotional intensity, like that of a biblical prophet. The religious motif is continued in his pose, as Kokoschka presents himself in the guise of Jesus, poking at a wound in his chest. He attempted to unify the image and text by placing both his initials, "OK," and the words "Neue Nummer" ("new issue") on his body itself, like a slogan carved into his chest.

Like many Expressionist works, this self-portrait is emotionally raw, reveling in the power of human feeling.

Like that of Kokoschka, Egon Schiele's torturous emotional life is well represented in the art he produced. Schiele had a traditional art education, having studied at both the Kunstgewerbeschule and the Academy of Fine Arts in Vienna. When Schiele was a child, his father degenerated into insanity as a result of a syphilis infection, and Schiele's difficult youth caused him to come into almost constant conflict with authority. Schiele was obsessed with the depiction of sexuality and psychosexual conflict, often mixed together with morbid fantasies of death and decay. He was, of course, a great devotee of Freud's work in this area. Schiele's explicit images of adolescents (the age of sexual consent in Vienna at this time was fourteen) made him notorious, and he was briefly imprisoned in 1912 under an obscenity statute.

The commemorative poster shown here was issued in support of a music festival held in 1912 as a celebration of Austrian composers (*fig. 2.26*). Like Kokoschka in his poster for *Der Sturm*, Schiele used a self-portrait as his Expressionist vehicle. The self-portrait was in many ways the natural subject of these two artists, because their art tends to look inward, at their own minds, as opposed to documenting the outer world. Schiele has distorted his own face into a terrible grimace that is complemented by the blood red color. There is no direct correlation between the image and the traditional event that it promotes, suggesting the

2.26 Egon Schiele, *Musik Festwoche (Music Festival)*, 1912. Poster. 24 x 18⅝ in (61.5 x 47.5 cm). MAK–Austrian Museum of Applied Arts/Contemporary Art, Vienna.

widespread acceptance of the Expressionist idiom as signifying "culture" in its broadest sense.

In 1915, Schiele was granted the first solo exhibition of his paintings and drawings in Vienna, at the Galerie Arnot (*fig. 2.27*). He designed this poster to publicize the show. Displaying his ongoing propensity for narcissism as well as religious imagery, Schiele represented himself pierced by arrows, like the Christian saint Sebastian. While the elongated proportions of the figure have their roots in the Art Nouveau style, here they form part of a disjointed body, an assemblage of distorted parts that do not seem to fit together. This damaged body torn apart by arrows says more about Schiele's internal psychological state than about the actual condition of his corpus. While the image depicts Schiele himself, the viewer is not expected to empathize with the specific facts of his suffering so much as to feel this powerful vision of emotional pain.

The forty-ninth exhibition of the Vienna Secession was held in 1918, even though the organization's best years were behind it.

Schiele contributed a number of works, including a poster (*fig. 2.25*) in which he returned again to religious imagery, which he had so often delved into in the past, in this case the Last Supper. The table has a jagged, angular shape, and the figures seem isolated from one another, two elements that heighten the expressive punch of the work. The text box looks as if it was layered over the image haphazardly, cutting off part of the scene, a compositional technique that suggests a chaotic element in the design. In 1918, the work that Schiele displayed at the Secession exhibition met with considerable acclaim. Three years earlier, Schiele had married Edith Harms (1894–1918), a young woman who lived with her family across the street from the artist, so it appeared that both his personal and professional lives were now finally in place. Tragically, in October 1918 Schiele and his wife, now pregnant, both succumbed to the Spanish influenza that killed many millions of Europeans. Klimt and Moser also died that year, while Kokoschka had long ago settled elsewhere, and an era of Viennese art came to an end.

2.27 Egon Schiele, *Galerie Arnot*, 1915. Wien Museum, Berlin.

2.28 Josef Sattler, *Pan*, 1895. Poster. 18⅞ x 13⅜ in (48 x 34 cm). St Bride Printing Library, London.

Germany

The German Art Nouveau movement, called *Jugendstil*, represents another example of artists' desire to cast off the eclectic historicist styles that had dominated the nineteenth century. Artists in Germany became aware of the French and British movements through publications such as *Das Moderne Plakat* ("The Modern Poster"), a bound volume of fifty-two lithographic reprints of key artists such as Toulouse-Lautrec, Steinlen, and the Beggarstaffs. While *Das Moderne Plakat* was printed in Dresden in 1897 by Gerhard Kuhtmann, German artists also circulated copies of the French series *Les Affiches Illustrée*s and *Les Maîtres de l'Affiche* between 1886 and 1900.

Beginning in 1894, a series of new magazines helped to galvanize a group of young German designers to pursue the new styles that were sweeping across Europe. The issue of national identity played a large part in the public discussion of the new art in Germany, as more conservative artists and intellectuals objected to the international, and especially French, aesthetic innovations that underlay Art Nouveau. As was the case in other countries, Art Nouveau in Germany represented something of a clash of generations. This conflict is indicated by the term *Jugendstil*, which means "Youth Style" and was also the name of one of the new German art periodicals founded by progressive young artists.

Pan and *Jugend* Magazines

The first periodical to promote Art Nouveau in Germany as part of an international phenomenon was *Pan*, launched in Berlin in 1895. Its founders included the 27-year-old art critic Julius Meier-Graefe (1867–1935), who in later decades would become one of the most esteemed historians of modern art in Europe. The title of the journal is suggestive of the international tastes of its editors, as the Greek god Pan, half-man and half-goat, was a familiar reference to followers of the Symbolist and Aesthetic movements in France and England. Pan was associated with creativity, music, and poetry, as well as Dionysian sexuality and visionary nightmares, and therefore encompassed many of the favorite themes of Art Nouveau. Over its five-year run, *Pan* published a wide range of Art Nouveau graphics from France, including works by Toulouse-Lautrec, Theodore Steinlen, and the painter Maurice Denis (1870–1943).

A poster by Josef Sattler (1867–1931) advertising the journal shows the god emerging from an ambiguous watery environment with his characteristic mischievous grin (*fig. 2.28*). At the same time, the stamens of a waterlily spell out "Pan" in a curvilinear fashion, uniting text and image in the fashion of many French posters. This *Jugendstil* image is rife with Japonisme, as both the orange and blue palette, with its juxtaposition of complementary colors, and the flat space made up of two-dimensional planes attest to the Japanese influence. Meier-Graefe, who was serving as both art director and financial manager of the journal, was forced to leave soon after the first issue was published, as the conservative patrons who had financed the venture objected to his French-inflected taste. Meier-Graefe was singled out for criticism partly because of anti-Semitic feelings. After his dismissal, the

2.29 Fritz Erler, *Jugend*, 1898. Printed periodical, 12¼ x 9¼ in (31 x 23.5 cm). Bayerische Staatsbibliotek, Munich.

co-founder Otto Bierbaum (1865–1910) continued at *Pan* and managed to fend off the attempts by his wealthy backers to make the journal beholden to German national identity. It is important to remember that national identity was a prominent issue in Europe at this time, not just in Germany (a useful parallel exists in the French Symbolists' embrace of Richard Wagner, which upset French people who wanted to shut out German aesthetics). Also, the young editors of *Pan* wanted to revive the high standards of German arts and crafts just like their patrons, but they disagreed over the issue of espousing an international trend, as opposed to building a strictly homegrown tradition. Meier-Graefe continued to spread the gospel of Art Nouveau in Berlin, where he founded the influential journal *Dekorative Kunst* in 1898, and in Paris, where he opened a gallery called La Maison Moderne in 1899.

The use of the term *Jugendstil* as a German synonym for Art Nouveau began with a periodical called *Jugend: Illustrierte Wochenschrift fur Kunst und Leben* ("Youth: Illustrated Weekly for Art and Life"), first published in January 1896. The publisher of *Jugend*, Georg Hirth (1841–1916), was committed to modern graphics from the very start. He hired over seventy illustrators to work for the journal, producing a wide variety of Art Nouveau graphics. He employed the Munich-based illustrator Fritz Erler (1868–1940) to create over fifty covers for *Jugend*, including one for the eleventh issue, published in 1898 (*fig. 2.29*). Hirth wanted each cover to reference the theme of youth indicated by the journal's title. Here, Erler has drawn a sinuous figure of a warrior with a sword looking outward toward some confrontation, emblematic of the aggressive persona of young men. Somewhat paradoxically, Erler usually chose to represent "youth" through medieval references, drawing on the longstanding admiration for that period both in Germany in particular and more broadly in Europe in the nineteenth century. The black figure is complemented by the bold red lettering in a **planar** scheme again replete with traces of the Beggarstaffs and Japonisme.

Blackletter

The flowing text that spells out "Jugend" at the top of the image represents an important compromise between *Jugendstil* aesthetics and the traditional German script called "blackletter." Blackletter is a catch-all term for scripted lettering rooted in the Middle Ages "in which the darkness of the characters overpowers the whiteness of the page," according to historian Peter Bain. Blackletter characters strongly resemble the letters formed by the blunt-edged quill pen used to write manuscripts. Because of its roots in the medieval period, blackletter is often called "gothic," a term that was introduced in Chapter 1 as having an alternative definition in the United States, where it referred to sans serif lettering. By the 1890s, much of German printing relied on the variant of blackletter named "fraktur," and this term is sometimes used casually as a synonym for blackletter.

Blackletter is highly ornamental, featuring exaggerated calligraphic flourishes and strong modeling of the stems of the letters. Compared to roman faces, blackletter's narrowly proportioned letters, its stylized ligatures to connect letters, and its small spaces between words and between lines of text, may appear illegible and even unreadable to persons unfamiliar with it. In truth, this is absolutely not the case. Recent studies have shown that readers familiar with blackletter read at the same speed as readers of roman typefaces, while the design of the letters helps to facilitate readability in terms of the specific orthography of the German language (in which, for example, the first letter of every noun is capitalized). The conflicts that arise in Germany during the twentieth century over the use of blackletter versus roman type reappear in several later chapters.

It is very important not to confuse the characteristics of the ornamental, yet highly functional, blackletter script, which was in everyday use in Germany through to the middle of the twentieth century, with the sometimes illegible, unreadable letters of many decorative typefaces. Erler's heading, "Jugend," is typical of German Art Nouveau in that it combines elements of blackletter with curvilinear, decorative elements of modern hand-drawn lettering. These elements can be hard to separate from one another for someone only familiar with roman lettering. However, blackletter generally has spikier, more angular modeling, as opposed to the elongated undulating elements that are dominant in Art Nouveau. Obviously, the synthesizing of new styles had a significant political component because by the twentieth century blackletter had become an important signifier of German national identity, so an artist who merged its forms with script that was

2.30 Otto Eckmann, Eckmann Typeface, from *Schriften und Ornamente*, 1900. From Lewis Blackwell, Twentieth-Century Type, rev ed, 2003. Courtesy Laurence King Publishing.

ABCDEFGHIJKLMNO PQRSTUVWXYZabc defghijklmnopqrstu vwxyz1234567890?& "The curvilinear Art Nouveau style was taken to an extreme in Otto Weisert's typeface called Bocklin"

2.31 Otto Weisert, Bocklin Typeface, 1904.

recognizably influenced by Germany's European rival, France, was sure to offend traditional Germans.

Another excellent example of how young artists sought to merge national tradition and *Jugendstil* aesthetics in typography comes by way of the designer Otto Eckmann (1865–1902). Eckmann was a versatile artist from Hamburg who had academic training in both the fine and applied arts. Knowledgeable regarding everything from French Symbolist aesthetics to Japanese woodcuts, he focused his work after 1894 on decorative graphics. He produced a large number of illustrations, as well as ornamental borders, headings, and the like, for journals including *Pan* and *Jugend*. In 1900, he collaborated with the famous type specialist Karl Klingspor (1868–1950) to create **Eckmann**, an elegant typeface whose styling borrows elements from both the blackletter and Art Nouveau traditions (*fig. 2.30*). While the undulating, swelling shapes of the letters bespeak Otto Eckmann's interest in Art Nouveau, the "open bowls," or incomplete boundaries that circumscribe white space in a letter such as the lower-case "g," reference a calligraphic root in blackletter. The curvilinear Art Nouveau style was taken to an extreme in Otto Weisert's typeface called **Bocklin** (1904; *fig. 2.31*), named after an influential German *Jugendstil* painter. The letters of Bocklin (note the capitals "A" and "B") have the same stylized curves as the hair of a figure drawn by the French poster artist Alphonse Mucha (see Chapter 1).

2.32 Thomas Heine, *Simplicissimus*, 1897. Poster. Lithograph, 30 x 20½ in (76.2 x 52 cm). Museum für Gestaltung, Zurich. Poster Collection.

Simplicissimus Magazine

The same year that *Jugend* was founded in Berlin, 1896, Munich saw the introduction of a satirical magazine called *Simplicissimus*, which would commission some of the most striking images to appear in Germany that decade. *Simplicissimus* was co-founded by the artist Thomas Theodor Heine (1867–1948) and the publisher Albert Langen (1869–1909). Heine's first publicity poster for the journal set a tone, combining art and political satire, that would serve as its editorial direction for years (*fig. 2.33*). In the poster, a young woman typical of Art Nouveau graphics, representing both youth and art, is being abducted by a devil, in a clever play on the well-known mythological story of Hades and Persephone. (Persephone was a young maiden who was kidnapped by the god of the underworld, Hades.) In the poster, the devilish Hades represents satire, which in the journal is mixed with art in equal measure. Art and satire are intertwined, as the young woman writes out the name of the magazine while the devilish figure is too engrossed in its pages to notice her hand on his tail. The bold use of black and red supports a planar design that is indebted to Jules Cheret's dancing women and Toulouse-Lautrec's daring imagery, as well as the Japanese tradition of flat, decorative simplicity.

A second poster by Heine, published in 1897, became the most enduring image associated with *Simplicissimus*, and was revived several times in different ways to promote the journal (*fig. 2.32*). It features a startlingly red bulldog that has broken its chain, and stands confrontationally in an ambiguous field of

black. The sturdy bulldog is neatly complemented by the restrained heading at the top, which stays away from the curvilinear exuberance typical of Art Nouveau. The strength of Heine's balanced use of the blank space between dog and title is particularly notable. This dog served to capture the spirit of sharp, biting commentary that made *Simplicissimus* one of the most famous magazines in Germany. In 1898, Heine was in fact imprisoned for six months because of his work for *Simplicissimus*; the charge was "lese-majesty," indicating that he had offended Germany's imperial government.

Hermann Obrist

The textile designs of Swiss-born Hermann Obrist (1863–1927), a central figure in the *Jugendstil* in Munich, have strong linear elements that were often translated into graphic design. In the 1880s, Obrist traveled extensively through England and Scotland, where he was greatly impressed by the high quality of the crafts produced by members of the Arts and Crafts movement. Following his return to Germany, he enrolled in the Kunstgewerbeschule at Karlsruhe and devoted himself to the decorative arts. In 1894 he moved to Munich, an important center of the "new art" that claimed to have more artists per capita than any other city in Germany.

In 1896, Obrist produced a solo exhibition of textiles based on his designs that were actually crafted by Berthe Ruchet. The fact that Obrist would not embroider the works himself points to a continuing hierarchical view of the crafts as inferior to the fine arts, despite so many designers' claims to the contrary. In past ages such as the Renaissance, artists such as Raphael employed other craft workers to execute their tapestry designs, because learning the necessary skills would have been considered beneath them. That hierarchy often had a gender component, as a male artist such as Obrist considered the execution of needlework to be a manual craft suited to women. While his embrace of the decorative arts made it acceptable for him to design textiles, Obrist would not be comfortable completing the work himself. In contrast, male artists felt that the execution of an oil painting was sufficiently esteemed as a fine art that they would have no such qualms.

One of Obrist's wool and silk embroideries, called *Whiplash*, became a core part of *Jugendstil* aesthetics (*fig. 2.34*). The sinuous curve in this design projects a pent-up energy like the lash of a whip in the pregnant moment when it is suspended in space, about to explode with a mighty crack. The "whiplash" curve is the best expression of Obrist's pursuit of organic abstraction, whereby he molded natural forms so that they became more powerful and expressive. There is clearly a strong undercurrent of Symbolism in Obrist's work, as he often wrote and spoke about the spiritual implications of abstract forms.

In 1902, Obrist, along with the self-taught German artist Wilhelm von Debschitz (1871–1948), founded a private art school named the Munich Teaching and Experimental Studios for Applied and Free Art. This school allowed Obrist to implement some of his ideas about progressive teaching methods while also serving as a forum for his views on the significance of expressive,

2.33 Thomas Theodor Heine, *Simplicissimus*, 1896. Poster. Color lithograph, 30 x 20 in (76.2 x 52 cm). Stadtmuseum, Munich.

2.34 Hermann Obrist, *Whiplash*, 1895. Wool with silk embroidery, 47 x 72 in (119 x 183 cm). Stadtmuseum, Munich.

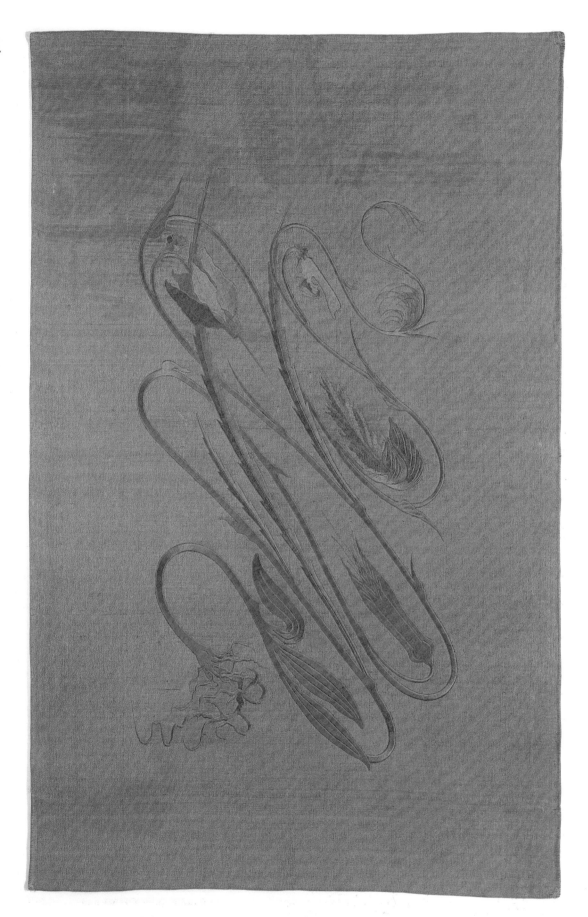

organic abstraction as an artistic approach. The Munich Studios functioned mainly as an "arts and crafts" school, and Obrist continued to work towards collapsing the hierarchy between design work and the fine arts. He also had a significant impact on a number of artists in Munich, most famously the Russian expatriate painter Wasily Kandinsky.

Henry van de Velde

Despite the movement's strong nationalist tradition, one of the most successful *Jugendstil* designers in Germany in the 1890s, Henry van de Velde (1863–1957), was Belgian. Van de Velde began his artistic career as a painter, winning some praise as a Symbolist-inspired member of the Belgian group called Les XX ("The Twenty"). Like many Art Nouveau artists, Van de Velde focused on the decorative arts after a short time spent as a fine artist. Of course, the decorative arts were enjoying a new elevated status and social significance at the time because of the influence of Arts and Crafts theorists. Van de Velde first joined the Art Nouveau movement by way of Paris, where in 1895 he designed three rooms for Siegfried Bing's new gallery L'Art Nouveau (see Chapter 1). Under the tutelage of Bing and Meier-Graefe, who was now living in Paris, Van de Velde embraced the concept of a new art that would represent a synthesis of international, mainly European and Asian, aesthetics. At L'Art Nouveau, Bing commissioned a series of model rooms that were designed to show how interior decoration could serve to beautify the everyday world. The model dining room that Van de Velde designed for Bing's gallery with the help of the progressive French painter Paul Ranson (1868–1909) demonstrated his awareness of the fundamental tenets of Art Nouveau: that all elements of a work must be executed in a unified style, and that decoration was not something applied separately to interiors as an ornament, but rather was the manifestation of sound aesthetic principles. This holistic approach to decoration is visible in all the different objects that Van de Velde designed for the dining room, from ceramic tiles to drawer handles to furniture.

In 1897, Van de Velde's Bing rooms were exhibited at the Arts and Crafts exhibition in Dresden. That exhibition cemented Van de Velde's reputation in Germany, where he was soon receiving commissions for a variety of design projects from patrons in Munich and Berlin. The candelabrum that he created in 1898 is a wonderful example of the spread of Obrist's **whiplash curve** as a fundamental design principle (*fig. 2.35*). The flamboyant arms of the candelabrum, derived from natural forms, exude the dynamic energy of a whip about to strike. "Line is a force," Van de Velde stated, when asked to summarize his aesthetic.

While he on occasion paid lip service to their views, Van de Velde did not share the same commitment to raising the standards of everyday, mass-produced objects through communal workshops professed by Arts and Crafts designers. Instead, he often asserted that his individual talent was paramount, and was best used in the creation of handcrafted objects for the carriage trade. Perhaps because of these beliefs, Van de Velde created only one design for a mass-produced poster during his career. In 1898, he produced an advertisement for the Tropon food company, a European manufacturer of food concentrates based in Cologne. The poster was among the first to be used in different versions in multiple European countries, with the slogan at the bottom translated into the appropriate language (*fig. 2.36*). Here, the familiar plant forms of Art Nouveau actually represent the cracked shells of eggs, the key ingredient in Tropon's signature product, powdered egg whites. While the eggs are still recognizable, the poster comes daringly close to pure graphic abstraction. Van de Velde's curvilinear design maintains the powerful energy of the whiplash, which contrasts with the gentler, less muscular curves seen in other Art Nouveau works such as Guimard's Metro stations.

There is a strong contrast between the decorative flourishes of the eggs or the sinewy letters of the slogan "the most concentrated food" on the one hand, and the rather staid lettering at the top of the poster on the other. Although the letters of the firm's name, "Tropon," feature elongated descenders in the "R" and "P," it is otherwise remarkable for its clean rectilinear design. This brings up two issues that influenced the possible use of *Jugendstil* and its ilk for advertising purposes, and which have substantial implications for the field of graphic design in general. First, does the decreased legibility of the lettering have an impact on the effectiveness of the poster? It is likely that the patrons at Tropon thought so, and instructed Van de Velde to draw their corporate name in a simplified fashion. This question of legibility repeatedly challenged graphic designers throughout the twentieth century. Second, is the investment in an "artistic" poster by a named designer worth the cost: will it be proportionally more effective than an advertisement that does not use a progressive style by a celebrated designer? This second issue is discussed at length in Chapter 3.

Van de Velde's continuing successes in Germany and personal relationships with wealthy patrons precipitated a move to

2.35 Henry van de Velde, *Candelabra*, 1899. Silver. Brohan-Museum, Berlin

2.36 Henry van de Velde, *Tropon*, 1899. Offset lithograph, 31⅝ x 21⅜ in (80.5 x 54.3 cm). Private Collection.

2.37a, b Henry van de Velde, *Also Spoke Zarathustra*, 1908. Book cover. By permission of The British Library, London.

Berlin in 1899, followed by another to the small German city of Weimar in 1902. In Weimar, Van de Velde was appointed the director of a new Kunstgewerbeschule by a powerful local aristocrat, Wilhelm Ernst, the Grand Duke of Saxe-Weimar. The patronage of *Jugendstil* artists by ruling families such as Ernst's was especially important in Germany, where aristocrats had managed to preserve much of their authority over public life. In 1907, Van de Velde also became one of the founding members of the Deutscher Werkbund, an association of designers, architects, and industrial firms based in Munich. The published goal of the Werkbund was based on Arts and Crafts principles learned in England by one of its founders, Hermann Muthesius (1861–1927): "the ennobling of commerce through the collaboration of art, industry, and craftsmanship." The Werkbund nearly split apart in its early years, as members debated the importance of standardized, functional designs, favored by industry, as opposed to the more elitist individual work of artists such as Van de Velde and Obrist.

During his time in Weimar, Van de Velde produced one of his most esteemed graphic works, an edition of *Also Sprach Zarathustra* (1908; *fig. 2.37*) by German philosopher Friedrich Nietzsche (1844–1900). Van de Velde had a personal connection to the philosopher, having befriended one of his siblings, Elisabeth Förster-Nietzsche (1846–1935), who had encouraged the artist's move to Weimar. Van de Velde's edition of *Zarathustra* represents the theory of the *Gesamtkunstwerk*, or total work of art, on a small scale. He attempted to harmonize every aspect of the book, including its ink, illustrations, and typography. The dense patterns on the cover surely must have been influenced by William Morris's designs for the Kelmscott Press, which tended toward similarly tightly-packed compositions. Furthermore, Van de Velde's aesthetic philosophy, emphasizing the powerful vision of an individual creator, was heavily influenced by Nietzsche's own writings on art. When the First World War began in 1914, Van de Velde's status as a foreigner in Germany, which had already complicated a commission he received for the Werkbund, caused him to be dismissed from his post at the Weimar

Kunstgewerbeschule. He recommended that the German architect, and his Werkbund colleague, Walter Gropius (1883–1969), be appointed to replace him (see Chapter 5). Van de Velde left Germany in 1917, and spent the rest of his career in Switzerland and the Netherlands.

Peter Behrens

The art colony established in 1899 at Darmstadt by the Grand Duke of Hesse-Darmstadt, Ernst Ludwig (1868–1937), sought to promote high standards for crafts made in the region. Led by the Viennese Secession architect Josef Olbrich, who designed most of the buildings at the colony's headquarters in Mathildenhöhe Park, the artists at the Darmstadt colony were important promoters of *Jugendstil*. One of the more accomplished designers at the colony was a German architect named Peter Behrens (1868–1940), who had spent the 1890s living in Munich. There, he had pursued both the fine and applied arts while becoming a key player in the Munich Secession (1893), a group like the Viennese equivalent that was dedicated to the spread of new, non-academic styles in the fine arts. Behrens was also well acquainted with the circle of artists around the journal *Pan*, through which he became acquainted with Julius Meier-Graefe and Otto Eckmann. In 1897, as his interest in the applied arts strengthened, Behrens co-founded an Arts and Crafts group in Munich.

2.38 Peter Behrens, *The Kiss*, 1900. Color woodblock print, 10 x 8 in (27.2 x 21.7 cm). Museum für Gestaltung, Zurich.

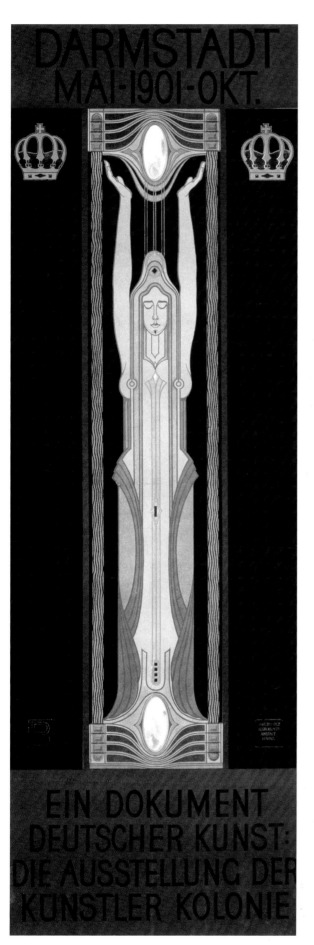

2.39 Peter Behrens, *Darmstadt*, 1901. Poster.

Like so many designers of his generation, Behrens began work in the graphic arts through his love of painting, which he abandoned in the late 1890s in favor of graphic design. A color woodblock print from 1900, *The Kiss* (*fig. 2.38*), combines a softly curving illustration of two lovers' faces with a dense arabesque of hair that approaches pure abstraction. The combination of a sexual theme and a sensually curvilinear style demonstrates how completely Behrens had absorbed the fundamental teachings of Art Nouveau.

The Darmstadt art colony was created as a gathering point for elite artists to pursue the medieval ideal of the workshop. There was a long history in rural, inexpensive areas of Europe, especially Germany, of artists' colonies in which artists could pool their resources while at the same time live amid nature for inspiration. Behrens produced a poster for the Darmstadt colony's first exhibition, held in the summer of 1901 (*fig. 2.39*). The exhibition, also organized by Behrens, represented the first time that the members of the colony presented their work to the public. This poster shows the vertical format typical of Scottish and Viennese work. The rectangular shape of the frame is repeated by the centered box that circumscribes an allegorical figure. This stylized figure's elongated, curving grace is balanced by the stouter proportions of the oval globes above and below her. The symmetrical blue vertical bands are decorated at the top with the Grand Duke's coat of arms. The lettering at top and bottom reverses the color scheme of the image, integrating these two elements despite their clear separation in the overall geometric composition. The essence of this poster is its balance of Art Nouveau flourishes with the more simplified Scottish style.

Behrens and AEG

In 1903, Behrens was appointed the director of the Kunstgewerbeschule in Düsseldorf, a move that coincided with his gradual shift from the organic, curvilinear *Jugendstil* style to one marked by greater simplification and geometric forms. At the school, Behrens restructured the curriculum in order to place

2.40 Peter Behrens, AEG Turbine Factory, Assembly Hall, Berlin, 1908–09.

greater emphasis on design for industry. Three years after his appointment, Behrens was approached by Emil Rathenau (1838–1915), the founder of the electrical utility and industrial producer called Allegemein Elektricitäts Gesellschaft (AEG). In 1881, Rathenau had bought the German rights to the electrical generation system invented by Thomas Edison (1847–1931), and in succeeding decades had developed his company into an industrial giant. Showing considerable foresight, Rathenau wanted his company to be at the vanguard of marketing as well as technology, so he hired Behrens to create a unified design style that would eventually encompass all of AEG's buildings, facilities, and graphic materials.

One of Behrens's first tasks was to design a new building to house the production of electrical generation equipment at the company's headquarters in Berlin (*fig. 2.40*). This turbine building was constructed only of industrial materials—concrete, steel, and glass. Behrens used these to create a balance between classical tradition, seen in the dignified, monumental form of the building, and the new abstract styles. He eschewed almost all ornament for his creation, following the Art Nouveau credo that all beauty must be inherent in the form, not come from applied decorative elements. The shape of the building is exemplary of the reductive geometric style typical of post-1900 *Jugendstil* art. It is nearly impossible for the modern viewer to recognize how startling this type of bold, industrial architecture appeared at the time. It is also notable that three architect–designers who will play prominent roles in later chapters—Charles Edouard Jeanneret, Walter Gropius, and Ludwig Mies van der Rohe—all worked for Behrens during the time that he was developing the AEG style.

The corporate logo that Behrens designed for AEG is visible on the flat plane at one end of the turbine building. This so-called "honeycomb" logotype features three hexagons containing the company's initials. The three geometric shapes are further contained within a larger hexagon. This repetition of form has its roots all the way back in Japonisme, but, eschewing all ornament, the device has here been transformed into a simple, declarative logo that speaks to the seriousness of purpose and power that an electrical company naturally wants to project. The lettering in the logo is derived from a typeface that Behrens created for AEG, the first time that a corporation had ever acquired its own copyrighted lettering. This face was called **Behrens-Antiqua** when it was released to the public by the Klingspor foundry some years later (*fig. 2.41*). As the title suggests, Behrens-Antiqua represents another of Behrens's syntheses of the old and the new, as he attempted to update roman lettering of the modern style with some geometric stylizations.

Through his work for AEG creating mass-produced electrical appliances, Behrens became one of the first "industrial designers,"

2.42 Peter Behrens, *Electric Tea Kettle*, 1909.

a profession that had been acclaimed without many practical results since the onset of Morris's "Arts and Crafts" movement in the 1860s. His *Electric Tea Kettle* (1909; *fig. 2.42*) features the spartan elegance and geometric schemes typical of the Vienna Werkstätte, yet here applied for the first time to an inexpensive, industrially produced item. The octagonal body, reminiscent of the roof of AEG's turbine hall and its logo, and the rectilinear handle of the kettle are balanced by the dramatic curve of the spout. In this kettle, Behrens synthesized a style that combined modern abstract elements with a traditional Prussian classicism.

In 1910, Behrens designed a poster advertising AEG's newest product, a technologically advanced lamp (*fig. 2.43*). The **orthogonal** design is overlaid with an equilateral triangle that contains the lamp and an abstract pattern representing its brilliant output. The lines that make up the poster are a linear variant of the dots that represent light. The text boxes at top and bottom are reminders of past posters, but here the more typical allegorical figure has been replaced by a lamp.

At AEG, Behrens succeeded in creating a unified aesthetic to

Vom Schlechten kann man nie zu wenig und das Gute nie zu oft lefen: fchlechte Bücher find intellektuelles Gift, fie verderben den Geift. Um das Gute zu lefen, ift eine Be–

2.41 Peter Behrens, Behrens-Antiqua Typeface, 1908.

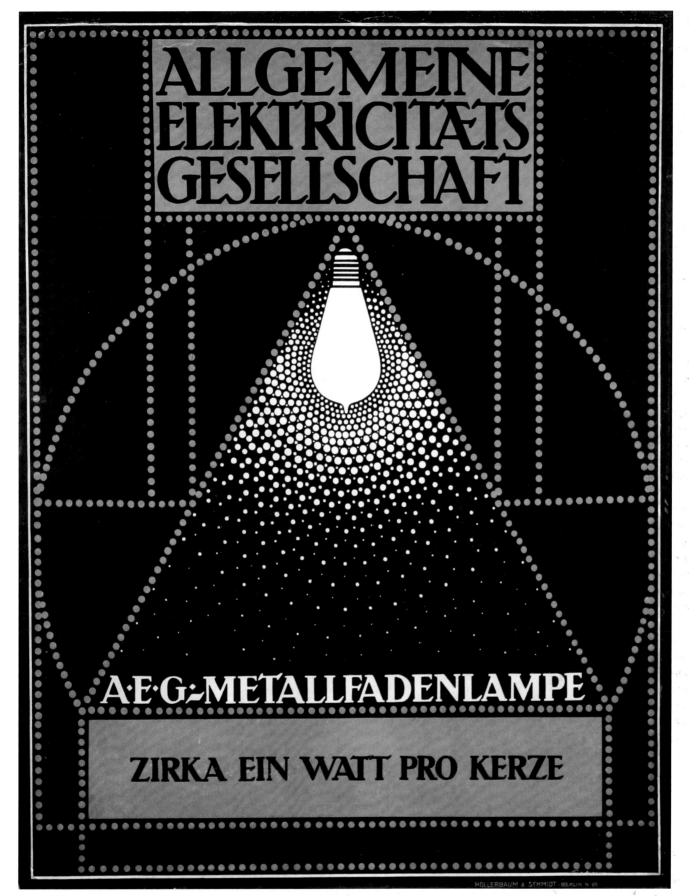

2.43 Peter Behrens, *AEG Lamp*, 1910. Poster. Offset lithograph, 26⅝ x 20 in (67.7 x 52.8 cm).

every aspect of the company's visual environment. This process represents the first sustained example of "corporate identity," a concept that would come to dominate the design professions, especially graphic design, after 1945. It is important to remember that Behrens had been introduced to the concept of the *Gesamtkunstwerk* in Munich as early as the 1890s, and it had also been a founding principle of the Darmstadt colony under Olbrich. At Darmstadt, Behrens himself had designed his own home and its furnishings in a manner consistent with the concept of the "total work of art." However, Behrens's work for AEG represents perhaps the most consistent application of the principles of the *Gesamtkunstwerk*. There is perhaps some irony in that the concept of the *Gesamtkunstwerk* was developed amid the Symbolists' dream of a utopian future, in which all the arts, and even all of humanity, would be unified in aesthetic radiance. However, its greatest deployment turns out to be a commercial project, the corporate identity of an electrical utility. This process of transformation is called "reification" by scholars, meaning that an abstract concept, in this case the *Gesamtkunstwerk*, is made into a concrete reality in such a way that an artistic vision ends up co-opted by commercial interests.

Behrens also made an important contribution to German typography, especially through the three typefaces he designed, Behrens-Antiqua (discussed above), **Behrens-Fraktur**, and Behrens-Schrift (*fig. 2.44*). Behrens-Fraktur is a decorative typeface that combines blackletter with the curvilinear elegance of French Art Nouveau. Behrens-Schrift, which was actually the first typeface designed by Behrens, is a composite of blackletter script modified by roman type's greater clarity. It features calligraphic strokes that have been rationalized in order to create better legibility and readability. Behrens stated that he had hoped to create a typeface that grew organically out of the German blackletter tradition, but would be simultaneously informed by "the new spiritual and material matter of the epoch." Cleverly, Behrens designed a type that balanced German national aspirations with broader appeal, and Behrens-Schrift was widely adopted by the

government for use in international forums, such as the 1904 world's fair held in the United States.

As a leading member of the Deutcher Werkbund—as was AEG—Behrens intended to feature his work at the 1914 exhibition held in Cologne. However, he ran up against the conservative taste of his patrons when he designed a poster advertising the exhibition that was deemed to be too daring for such a staid, international show (*fig. 2.45*). Like his Darmstadt poster, this one features an allegorical figure of leadership in the arts. Here, in a clear sign of Behrens's embrace of classicism, the figure reproduces the grand Roman imperial motif of a mounted rider. Both the rider and horse are simplified to fit into an abstract geometric scheme (note the right angle formed by the horse's head and mane), replicating the box that contains them. The subdued text is separate from the image, and is notable only for its muscular "T," which is compressed by neighboring letters on both sides—an example of spacing between letters done for decorative effect. The bar of the "T" stands out in such a way that it reproduces the right angle of the figure's torch-bearing arm, integrating text and image. The rejection of Behrens's poster is representative of the desire by the industrialists who supported the Werkbund to rid the organization of its more daring styles and their practitioners. The art historian Mark Jazombeck has asserted that the Werkbund after 1910 sought to create a national identity that would conform to the rather conservative tastes of the German bourgeoisie.

As discussed in the next chapter, by 1910 Art Nouveau was in decline. Its demise was ensured by the social changes wrought during the First World War (1914–18). Art Nouveau had really become a widespread style only in the graphic arts, because many of the best works in other media, while intended for mass production, were exorbitantly expensive to produce and therefore unsuited to mass manufacture. Art Nouveau would be rediscovered by collectors in the middle of the twentieth century, with exhibitions held in Zurich in 1952, London in 1952, and New York in 1960.

above: **2.44** Peter Behrens, Behrens-Schrift Typeface, 1901.

opposite: **2.45** Peter Behrens, *Deutscher Werkbund*, 1914. Poster for the Exhibition "Deutscher Werkbund." V&A Picture Library, Victoria & Albert Museum, London.

DEUTSCHE WERKBUND-
AUSSTELLUNG
KUNST IN HANDWERK,
INDUSTRIE UND HANDEL ⋅ ARCHITEKTUR
MAI CÖLN 1914 OCT.

YOU 3

Sachplakat,
The First World War,
and Dada

BRITONS

GO! ENLIST

"Victoire" GFE.

HERAUS!

LIBÉRATION

The Art Nouveau design styles discussed in Chapters 1 and 2 gradually diminished in popularity between 1905 and 1914. This chapter traces three major reasons behind this decline. First, there was an inevitable change in fashion, as the once "New Art" began to look dated. Designers and members of the public who had once been captivated by its dense ornament found themselves wanting less, not more. Second, the expanding customer base for graphic designers included clients with different needs from those of the entertainment industry that dominated the Art Nouveau period. Early in the twentieth century, more and more companies that had previously eschewed graphic design were feeling the need to present a burnished image and attractive products to consumers. Third, the onset of war between the major European powers in 1914 focused designers' work on furthering nationalist causes. The First World War would have a lasting impact on graphic design and its patrons. Later in the chapter, an art movement spawned in reaction to the war, "Dada," introduces a number of new design principles that had broad consequences for graphic design later in the twentieth century.

Sachplakat in Germany

The first decisive blow against the dominant Art Nouveau styles was struck not by an established artist, but by an amateur designer named Lucian Bernhard (1883–1972). While the details of his early life are unclear, it is known that Bernhard was born in Stuttgart to a family that did not support his artistic aspirations. His name at birth was Emil Kahn. In his teens, Bernhard briefly attended art school in Munich, where he also saw an international selection of Art Nouveau posters that included everything from the most ornamental work by Alphonse Mucha to the more simplified posters of the Beggarstaff Brothers. In 1903, Bernhard settled in Berlin, seemingly without any real prospects as an artist—or as a poet, another field that he reportedly dabbled in at this time.

Lucian Bernhard and the Priester Breakthrough

It was at some point while in Berlin that Emil Kahn became Lucian Bernhard, perhaps as a response to conflict with his father, who may have disowned him at this time, or in an attempt to assimilate more effectively into a German society rife with anti-Semitism by effacing the Jewish ancestry recognizable in his surname. Whatever the case, the newly minted Bernhard decided to enter a poster competition for the Priester match company. This type of contest was quite common at the time, as there was no standardized profession of graphic design or established community of professionals to which clients could naturally turn. Bernhard's first draft for his entry showed a smoking cigar astride an ashtray next to a pair of matches. These elements rested on a checkered tablecloth. The most dramatic element of the composition was the smoke from the cigar, which, replicating a *Jugendstil* cliché, transformed midstream into a bevy of beautiful young dancing women. Bernhard used a flat brown background derived from his knowledge of the Beggarstaffs and Japonisme. Floating in the space above the table was the company's name, Priester. Overall, the poster displayed the influence of both the Japanese style and the festive atmosphere favored by many Art Nouveau designers.

As Bernhard later told the story, he next showed the maquette, or model, of the poster to an acquaintance, who mistook it for an advertisement for cigars. This was a natural assumption, because the smoke from the cigar was the only element of the poster that showed a dramatic flourish. Recognizing his mistake,

3.1 Lucian Bernhard, *Priester Matches*, 1905.

Bernhard began a process of "addition by subtraction," gradually removing any element that could possibly "compete" with the matches for the viewer's attention (*fig. 3.1*). For his final draft, Bernhard left only the two red matches, the company name in block letters, and the neutral colored background. It is not clear, although it seems likely considering the harmonious balance of the final image, whether Bernhard rescaled the matches when he created this new, simpler composition, or whether his final draft was strictly a case of the elimination of the superfluous cigar, tablecloth, etc.

The story does not end with Bernhard's submission of the poster to Priester's judges. In an even more dramatic twist, his image was reported to have been immediately thrown in the trash by the judges, only to be rescued by Ernst Growald, an executive for the advertising agency Hollerbaum & Schmidt, which was overseeing the competition. Growald, who would become an important client–patron of Bernhard in subsequent years, is said to have glanced in the garbage can and exclaimed, "This is my first prize! This is genius!" and a new career for Bernhard as well as a revolutionary change in the design of German posters had begun.

Why exactly was the image for Priester matches so extraordinary? Looking back at Chapter 1, it would seem that both Leonetto Cappiello in Paris and the Beggarstaff Brothers in London, to give just two examples, had used similar, simplified designs that drew on Japonisme. While it is arguable that Bernhard has taken these earlier attempts at reductive compositions to a new extreme, the real innovation in the Priester poster lies in its tone. The Beggarstaffs' poster for *Harper's* uses an unrelated image of a Beefeater, one that had actually been intended to publicize a completely different product, in an attempt to add a theatrical flourish to the advertisement. Similarly, Cappiello's poster for Maurin absinthe features a rather bizarre allegorical figure of a green demon in order to enliven its message. Also, both these posters, and especially Cappiello's, are quite lively from a

visual standpoint. In stark contrast, Bernhard's poster displays only the two matches and the company's name, and it does so while completely eschewing any flair, allegorical flourish, or kinetic colorism. It is this simple communication of a declarative message, addressing the viewer forthrightly as if to say, "Here is the product, this is its name," that makes Bernhard's work stand apart. It is this clarity that earned this style of poster the name *Sachplakat*, translatable roughly as "object-poster." In sum, *Sachplakat* designs such as this one looked both to the past, showing a strong Japanese influence, and to the future, because their radical simplification and blunt messages later became a key part of modern advertising.

Because Bernhard was vague, even deliberately obtuse, when it came to divulging the details of his life and career, historians are unsure of the credibility of this famous story of the casual genesis of a poster that revolutionized graphic design. Whether or not the story is apocryphal is in some ways beside the point; what is more important is the fact that the story was considered worth telling at all. Up to this point in history, the artistic decisions that went into the creation of a commercial poster were not really believed to be worth thinking about or telling stories about. The fact that people cared enough to tell and retell this anecdote says more about the rising status of graphic design than do the details of the episode themselves. There is an analogy here with the history of painting and painters' struggle to be taken seriously as an important profession. In the fifteenth and sixteenth centuries, numerous anecdotes of dubious credibility about painters' lives began to be told—that Leonardo da Vinci had died in the arms of the French king, for example—and these narratives represented part of the struggle for painters to be taken seriously, a struggle that graphic designers faced early in the 1900s.

The *Sachplakat* style needs to be understood in terms of the historical dominance of Art Nouveau in 1905. Its radical simplification did not exist in a vacuum, but represents a direct rejection

3.2 Lucian Bernhard, *Bosch*, 1914. Lithograph, 17⅞ x 25 in (45.4 x 64.1 cm).

of the ornamental complexity of Art Nouveau. The relationship between the *Sachplakat* and Art Nouveau is therefore one that scholars call "dialogical," meaning that the style came about as part of a dialogue, in this case with the Art Nouveau style. The *Sachplakat* style offered an alternative to corporate clients such as Priester, who were dismayed by the obvious "artiness" of Art Nouveau graphics, whose complexity of style they felt could obscure their product. It could be argued that an exceedingly decorative poster such as those designed by Mucha actually competed with the product it was supposed to be selling, so that it was unclear what the poster was really about—the product or the poster itself? If the prospective consumer is likely only to glimpse the poster while passing through the city streets, it is necessary that the product's basic function and name be instantly recognizable. In contrast, the product being proffered in many Art Nouveau posters had to be aggressively sought out by the viewer after somewhat longer contemplation. Furthermore, the Art Nouveau style's alliance with the Symbolist and Aesthetic movements of the 1890s could well have tainted the movement with the "decadent" label, something that purveyors of consumer goods wanted to avoid, especially in aesthetically conservative countries such as Germany or the United States.

Bernhard was highly sought after following his success in the Priester competition, and he established himself, and the *Sachplakat* style, as the advertising mainstay for many German companies. In 1906, he opened his own firm, which eventually employed more than twenty graphic designers. In 1907, he became a founding member of the Deutscher Werkbund, an honor indicative of the strength of his reputation. The relationship with Growald and Hollerbaum & Schmidt served as a continuous source of important corporate commissions. Fine examples from the pre-war period include this poster for Bosch sparkplugs from 1913 (*fig. 3.2*), in which a bold juxtaposition of orange and blue creates a striking background for the neutral color of the sparkplug. The rectangular box enclosing the name of the company plays off the irregular starburst that represents the electric spark.

The *Sachplakat* Phenomenon

The owners of the advertising and lithography firm of Hollerbaum & Schmidt immediately attached themselves to both Bernhard and the overall *Sachplakat* phenomenon, signing several

3.3 Julius Klinger, Poster, Möhring Chandelier Factory, 1909. Museum für Kunst und Gewerbe, Hamburg.

3.4 Hans Rudi Erdt, *Opel*, 1911. Poster. Deutsches Historisches Museum, Berlin.

additional designers to exclusive contracts. Included in this grouping, sometimes called "The Six," was the Viennese artist Julius Klinger (1876–1950), whose poster for the Möhring Chandelier Company of 1909 is one of the icons of *Sachplakat* style (*fig. 3.3*). Klinger had trained in Vienna at a technical institute, where he later became a magazine illustrator. His early works show the influence of the curvilinear Art Nouveau promoted by the Vienna Secession movement. After moving to Berlin, he came under the influence of first the Beggarstaffs and then the new style initiated by Bernhard. The Möhring poster displays its product alone and without any setting, eschewing the narrative devices that drive so many advertising messages.

The striking advertisements by Hans Rudi Erdt (1883–1918)

for Hollerbaum & Schmidt include one for Opel cars completed in 1911 (*fig. 3.4*). In a variation on the style, Erdt does not display the product, a type of automobile, but the consumer—in this case, the distinguished-looking face of a man with driving goggles perched on his head. Like the Beefeater from the Beggarstaffs' portfolio, the contour is broken in several places and the man's collar flows into the flat field of green. The closest thing to a representation of a car is the wheel shape of the outlined "O" in Opel, which serves as a metonymic device—that is to say, it stands for the entire car, just as the figure is intended to project the confident feeling of owning one. In the previous year, Opel had introduced its first racing car, in an attempt to add glamour to its stock production line. Erdt's poster captures this element

of prestige associated with the brand, which stands in contrast to the less emotional message of Bernhard's Bosch poster.

Ludwig Hohlwein

Aside from Bernhard, the most successful representative of the *Sachplakat* style was the German designer Ludwig Hohlwein (1874–1949). An architect by training, Hohlwein lived during the 1890s in Munich, where he participated in the Vereinigte Werkstätten für Kunst im Handwerk ("United Workshops for Art and Crafts"). This organization, dedicated to Arts and Crafts principles and the creation of finely crafted goods, also promoted the art of the poster. The United Workshops' output in graphic design tended toward strong figurative elements, which can be seen in Hohlwein's poster publicizing "Richard Strauss-Week" (1910; *fig. 3.5*). Mixing abstraction and three-dimensional modeling, Hohlwein placed a fairly detailed figure in a space that lacks an identifiable horizon line defining it. The design is also abstract in its stark orthogonal framework, through which the vertical figure and her staff are linked together by horizontal lines of text.

In 1911, Hohlwein established himself in Berlin as a graphic designer in the *Sachplakat* mode. In posters for a men's clothing company, Hermann Scherrer, Hohlwein displayed his penchant for Beggarstaff-like reductiveness (*fig. 3.6*). However, Hohlwein has a tendency to maintain more volumetric rendering of form in parts of the image, an element of the style he had practiced in Munich, than Bernhard or the others. Hohlwein's hybrid style mixes the simplicity of the *Sachplakat*, including its restriction in the amount of text to the name of the company, or product, and an occasional short copy line contained a rectangular block, with a projection of upper-class elegance and refinement not typical of the style. Here, the well-bred dog and riding accessories are suggestive of an affluent lifestyle. Additionally, his posters often show a flair for self-conscious design, particularly vivid color and abstract patterning, which distinguishes them from the other artists who pursued the *Sachplakat* style. In this example, the black and white checkered pattern of the man's riding outfit creates a two-dimensional plane that is in tension with the surrounding, more three-dimensional looking, elements.

A poster that Hohlwein produced for the Marco Polo Tee company frames the product in an exotic manner more akin to Art Nouveau posters than to *Sachplakat*. The image works by putting the viewer in the position of an affluent consumer who is being served the product. The poster features a Japanese woman, presumably a geisha, a trained professional who administers to the needs of upper-class men (*fig. 3.7*). Hohlwein has self-consciously imitated the style and subject matter of Japanese woodblock prints of the *Bijin-ga* variety, which display beautiful women, in the manner in which he overlays flat planes with different patterns. The artist's initials, "LH," are inscribed into the yellow pattern that adorns her shoulder. Of course, the yellow rests on a violet field, reproducing a harmonious juxtaposition of complementary colors. Another dramatic passage involves the back of her head, where her black coif blends seamlessly into the abstract background pattern. Other posters for Marco Polo by Hohlwein depicted African servants. For twenty-first-century eyes, it is hard

3.5 Ludwig Hohlwein, *Richard Strauss–Woche (Richard Strauss–Week)*, 1910. Poster.

to view posters such as these outside the context of the brutal European conquest of Africa, which was a major source of Europe's wealth at the time. Coming at the height of Germany's colonial empire, the image of servile foreigners would satisfy the viewer with a reminder that their country's reach stretched around the globe.

Posters and Typography

The most important journal devoted to graphic design in Berlin was founded by a dentist and poster collector named Hans Josef Sachs. In 1905, Sachs had spurred on the creation of the Verein der Plakatfreunde ("Association of Friends of the Poster"), a promotional organization. Sachs recruited Bernhard to act as artistic consultant to the association, and to design its first logotype. In 1910, Sachs desired to publish a journal devoted to his passion, and *Das Plakat* (1910–21) was born. Bernhard designed a poster to publicize the journal in 1916, in which a woman is shown closely examining a poster on exhibition (*fig. 3.8*). The image bears a striking resemblance to the imprimatur that Jules Cheret had created for the *Les Maîtres de l'Affiche* series, an emblem with which Bernhard was surely familiar. In Bernhard's poster, the form of the woman is no more volumetric than the poster

3.6 Ludwig Hohlwein, *Hermann Scherrer*, 1911. Poster. Lithograph, 44¼ x 31½ in (112.3 x 80 cm). Museum of Modern Art, New York.

affixed to the wall. Neither the figure nor the poster is attached to the ground plane. The only indication of a ground is the rectangular bar centered under the figure; it serves a dual purpose, as a ground line and as a visual demarcation between the image and the text under it. Perhaps indicative of his high status as a graphic designer a decade after the Priester contest, is the manner in which Bernhard uses his name as a compositional device to balance the rectangle formed by the poster frame in the upper left. The block-like, symmetrical form and simplified sans serif lettering of the name, "Bernhard," contrast with the flowing *faux* blackletter of the journal's title at the base of the image. In terms of circulation, *Das Plakat* was the most successful poster journal ever produced in Europe, peaking at 5,000 copies for an issue published in 1918, an incredible number for such a specialized magazine.

During the early twentieth century, there was an ongoing dispute as to whether or not Germans should rely on the classic roman types that prevailed in the rest of Europe, or maintain their national tradition of blackletter, especially schwabacher and fraktur, the two sixteenth-century scripts that had Germanic origins. The German authorities seemed to be undecided as to whether or not to maintain a style of type that separated German publications from those of most of the rest of Europe. At the start of the century, newspapers and mainstream literature were all printed in fraktur, while the school system taught young people to write in gothic script. At the same time, a wealth of publications in Germany, especially those that wanted to look modern to the reader, embraced the roman tradition. In 1911, the German parliament had considered forbidding the use of blackletter scripts in state schools and government documents. This "Dispute of the Scripts" had resulted in the defeat of the new legislation, and Germany had continued on a path of dual roman and blackletter writing styles, sometimes representing separate spheres of activity, sometimes published side-by-side in official documents.

3.7 Ludwig Hohlwein, *Marco Polo Tee 2*, 1912. Poster. Yaneff.

3.8 Lucian Bernhard, *Das Plakat*, 1916. Poster.

ABCDEFGHIJKLMNOPQRSTUVWXYZ&

3.9 Lucian Bernhard, Bernhard Antiqua Typeface, 1912.

Several typefaces that attempted to integrate elements of both traditions are symptomatic of this dilemma. In fact, the Art Nouveau types designed by Peter Behrens and discussed in Chapter 2 functioned by transforming the broken curves of fraktur into curvilinear decorative elements. In 1914, Friedrich Bauer (1863–1943) designed an excellent hybrid type called **Hamburger Druckschrift**. Bauer's effort represents an attempt to reconcile this conflict in a visual sense by including formal elements from both traditions. Hamburger Druckschrift has a calligraphic structure that is recognizably tied to blackletter, but all the dramatic flourishes, broken curves, rhomboid and diamond terminals have been suppressed. Also, some of the least legible characters to readers used to roman type have been simplified, such as the "K," "S," and "X." The type appears light in comparison to the dense color of most blackletters, and has taken on the wide proportions and open letter forms of roman type.

The *Sachplakat* poster artists themselves clearly sided with the German industries that wanted a modern look to their advertisements, and so embraced roman lettering. The *Sachplakat* designers contributed to roman typography in Germany, especially after their popularity caused a whole host of designers to copy the plain, block letter style of their hand-drawn posters. In 1912, Frankfurt's Flinsch foundry published **Bernhard Antiqua**, a typeface based on the lettering in Bernhard's original Priester matches poster (*fig. 3.9*). Originally produced for the Linotype machine, this bold roman face preserves some of the idiosyncratic letterforms of Bernhard's hand-drawn work, such as the lower-case "e" that drops below the baseline. After the First World War broke out in August 1914, the pool of *Sachplakat* designers grouped in Berlin around Hollerbaum & Schmidt found new work, as they shifted from the promotion of industry to the needs of the German war machine.

The First World War

On June 28, 1914, the Austrian Archduke Franz Ferdinand, who was visiting Sarajevo, was assassinated by Gavrilo Princip, a Serbian nationalist who resented the Austro-Hungarian Empire's domination of the Balkan states. Because of a series of alliances and security guarantees among the major powers in Europe, the initial conflict between Austria-Hungary and the Serbians precipitated by the assassination quickly led to a much broader conflict. The war pitted the Allies—Britain, France, Russia, Italy, and the United States (after 1917)—against the Central Powers—Austria-Hungary, Germany, and Turkey. One of the most portentous events of the twentieth century, the "Great War" resulted in the collapse of four empires, including those in Austria-Hungary, Germany, and Russia, and set the stage for continuing European conflict throughout the 1920s and 1930s. While the precise number of casualties from the war is even today uncertain, scholars estimate that as many as 20 million people were killed and 33 million wounded. The war's vast scale and use of civilian-soldiers had a greater impact on European populations than earlier European conflicts, which had been fought by small professional armies.

Wartime Propaganda

In terms of the use of graphic design, the First World War created a pressing need to influence the views of potential recruits and financial backers, as well as to garner the general support of the population to maintain backing for a conflict that, when it broke out in the summer of 1914, had been expected to end "by Christmas." It is important to remember that journalists' access to the war was essentially non-existent, so citizens of the belligerent nations were often completely ignorant of the scope of the horror at the front. As the war dragged on and casualties mounted into the many millions, governments became even less forthcoming, refusing to publish statistics detailing the number of missing, dead, and wounded.

The one consistent form of government communication to its citizens was through the posters that were slathered on hoardings across the cities of Europe. Of course, the content and style of these posters were tightly controlled by government agencies, so that the messages therein were just as likely to mislead viewers as to enlighten them. Many of the posters discussed here were in fact collaborations of necessity, not choice, as the government officials in charge of publicity often wrote the text themselves after commissioning the image from an artist. At other times, old images were recycled with new text as the occasion demanded.

Thus, the First World War led to an enormous acceleration in the production of posters as different governments sought to rally their own citizens to support the war effort. When the war began, Britain had the smallest army of all of the European powers, totaling only about 160,000. Because theirs was the only country in the conflict that lacked a military draft, the British authorities had the greatest need to encourage volunteers. While enthusiasm for the war ran high early in the conflict, an initial onslaught of volunteers quickly dried up as casualties mounted. During the eighteen months before a draft was instituted early in 1916, the British government relied heavily on posters to encourage young men to join the fighting. This recruitment need resulted in hundreds of individual posters, with production totals numbering in the millions. The production of posters was centralized in the hands of the Parliamentary Recruiting Committee (PRC), a branch of the War Office. The PRC's campaign was apparently successful, as over 2.5 million British men joined the military between August 1914 and January 1916. However, those numbers were not enough to feed the war machine on the front and so conscription became essential, while poster designers turned to other themes. The precise role that graphic design played in fueling recruitment is essentially unknowable, although anecdotal evidence suggests that many posters strongly resonated with the British citizenry.

Stylistically, there was an abrupt halt to the proliferation of decorative Art Nouveau, Japonisme, and other abstract styles, along with a new commitment to a more conventional type of realistic representation. There are two major reasons for this trend; first, the conservative taste of the members of the PRC, who felt that more traditional, natural styles had a greater appeal for the largest cross-section of the population; and second, the fact that the majority of posters were designed in-house by commercial lithography firms that used their own printers in both design

3.10 Alfred Leete, *Britons, [Lord Kitchener] Wants You*, 1914. Poster. Photolithograph and letterpress. Imperial War Museum, London.

3.11 Alfred Leete, *Who's Absent? Is It <u>You</u>?*, 1914. Poster. Lithograph on paper, 29 x 19⅞ in (74.3 cm x 50 cm). Imperial War Museum, London.

and production roles. Even as styles regressed, designers developed new sophistication in manipulating the population through subject matter. For these reasons, the First World War paradoxically diminished the status of graphic design as an art form. The war poster became in most cases strictly a vehicle for government propaganda, while the three-decades-long effort by designers to enhance the artistic qualities of the poster fell by the wayside.

Among the most influential types of posters designed to bolster British recruitment were those that used a direct appeal, bordering on a command, from a respected military leader. The most memorable of this group was a 1914 poster by Alfred Leete (1882–1933) depicting Lord Kitchener (1850–1916), a national icon and the Secretary of State for War, who oversaw the recruitment drive (*fig. 3.10*). Leete made the original design for the September 1914 cover of the monthly magazine *London Opinion*, then remade it as a poster at the behest of the PRC. While the original version of the poster was drawn by hand, a second poster was unique among British designs in that it used a photograph for its portrait of Lord Kitchener.

Lord Kitchener was so famous that it was unnecessary to record his name; rather, his picture is integrated into the middle of the text, "Britons, [Lord Kitchener] Wants You." Kitchener's dramatically foreshortened right arm ends in his pointed index finger, a finger that complements the semblance of direct eye contact between him and the potential recruit. This dramatic gesture became the cornerstone of an entire genre of appeal, the "pointing poster." The typography in this poster is rather undistinguished, as an eclectic variety of bold display type delivers its message, if nothing more. Leete was not a graphic designer per se, but rather an illustrator and cartoonist for *Punch* magazine. The widespread success of this poster of Kitchener leads invariably to a number of pointed questions. How important is graphic design to the creation of an effective poster? If this rather rudimentary design and typography were successful, is it by definition a "good" poster?

The "pointing" design was widely copied, and variations of it appeared almost immediately. A second poster by Leete features John Bull, a personification of England who had been invented in the early eighteenth century, shown in his typical dress of tailcoat, breeches, and Union Jack vest (*fig. 3.11*). This powerful country squire addresses the viewer with a stern glare and a damning admonition framed as a question, "Is it You?" The moral reproach explicit in the question is as bold as the comportment of Bull himself. Partly because of a long tradition of shielding the general population from the horrors of war, and partly to keep up morale,

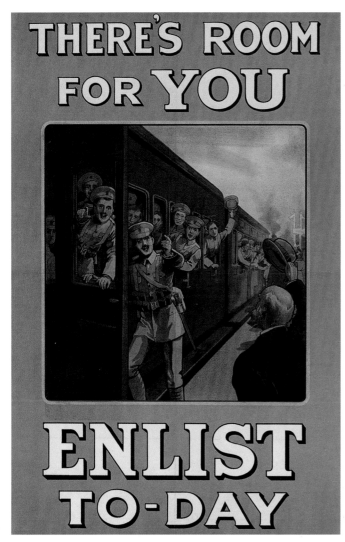

3.12 Anonymous, *There's Room for You. Enlist To-Day*, 1916. Poster. Lithograph on paper, 30 x 20 in (76.4 cm x 51 cm). Imperial War Museum, London.

3.13 Anonymous, *At the Front!*, 1915. Poster. Lithograph on paper, 29⅞ x 20 in (76 x 50.9 cm). Imperial War Museum, London.

there is rarely any actual fighting on display in recruitment posters. The glimpse of a small conflagration behind the line of dutiful soldiers is only minimally suggestive of a conflict that included days such as July 1, 1916, on which 19,000 British soldiers were killed at the Somme. Years such as 1916, when this poster appeared, caused the infantryman and poet Siegfried Sassoon (1886–1967) to write "What in earlier days had been drafts of volunteers were now droves of victims."

A second genre of British war poster stressed the comradeship and excitement of life as a soldier, depicting the war as something akin to a heroic adventure. Confronted in a poster by a train filled with fresh-faced recruits pointing at them in a friendlier fashion than Lord Kitchener or John Bull, young men read, "There's Room for You" and felt that they did not want to miss out on the journey of a lifetime (*fig. 3.12*). Posters such as *At the Front* (1915) display a subsequent moment, when the trip to the front has landed the new recruit into the midst of an adventure; the kinetic action of mounted troops under fire in a blaze of color is truly seductive (*fig. 3.13*). The rearing horse in the foreground is being brought under control by a cavalryman, suggesting the polished professionalism of troops in the army. Inspired perhaps by the scenes of lion hunts made popular by the French Romantic painter Eugène Delacroix (1798–1863), this dramatic image presents the war in the most romantic of terms. Both these posters feature a composition through which the central image functions like a window into another world, an exciting one of color and comradeship. The poster contrasts that romantic vision with the flat, neutral color of the surrounding border and lettering. In this manner, the lack of flair shown in the design of the border and type works to enhance the message, in so much as it stands in for the drab day-to-day existence of young men who resist the call to arms.

Emasculating Messages

For those recruits who proved immune to either the direct appeal of John Bull or the sense of romantic adventure offered by imaginary comrades, British recruiters developed an even more caustic weapon—emasculation. Emasculation, the questioning or weakening of a man's virility, was the most potent psychological attack that any designer could muster. In 1915, Edward Kealey initiated the theme with his poster *Women of Britain Say "Go!"*—which sought to persuade women to pressure their husbands into joining the war effort (*fig. 3.14*). Kealey's message makes use of the traditional Victorian notion of "separate spheres," through which each gender was thought to have its own natural environment— women in the home and men in public life. Kealey displays this concept in a literal fashion, as the mother and children are seemingly embraced by the doorway of their home as the soldiers placed across a balustrade march off as part of their male role. The theme of emasculation centers on the little boy who clutches at his sister's skirt, suggesting that men who stay home are akin to pre-adolescent children clutching their mommies. The illustration is again the heart and soul of the poster, as the lettering does little more than enunciate the theme. This retrograde style has retreated from the advanced composition of sophisticated litho-

3.14 Edward Kealey, *Women of Britain Say "GO!,"* 1915. Poster. Lithograph on paper, 29⅜ x 20 in (74.8 cm x 50.6 cm). Imperial War Museum, London.

graphs from the 1890s by artists such as the Beggarstaffs or Aubrey Beardsley.

The amateur genesis of so many British war posters is exemplified by the story behind the creation of the most famous picture of emasculation ever made, *Daddy, What did you do in the Great War?* (*fig. 3.15*) As his son Paul later recounted, the printer Arthur Gunn asked himself this question one evening in 1915 at home. Recognizing effective emotional blackmail when he saw it, Gunn suggested to his friend, the children's book illustrator Savile Lumley, that it could form the kernel of an effective recruiting poster. In order to heighten the impact of the question, Lumley, author of comics such as *The Boy's Own Paper*, transformed the interlocutor from Paul Gunn into a little girl sitting on her father's lap. In this image the little boy at the man's feet enhances the moral reproach inherent in the scene, as he plays with toy soldiers, signaling that even at such a young age he has more masculine instincts than his father. Lumley's poster, especially the shamefaced visage of the emasculated patriarch, is a masterpiece of bullying propaganda, while its completely uninspiring design does nothing to take away from such blunt condemnation. As stated above, the effectiveness of this imagery is far from certain, and the extreme manipulation of the viewer was greeted cynically by some contemporary viewers. However, it remained the most potent image of the war years in many people's minds. The author George Orwell (1903–1950) mused many years later: "I have often laughed to think of that recruiting poster, 'What did you do in the Great War, Daddy?' … and of all the men who must have been lured into the army by just that poster and afterwards despised by their children."

As the war dragged on year after year with no end in sight, British authorities were compelled to address the civilian population's discontent. A new wave of posters produced after 1916 served to rally the home front, and none performed the feat with more alacrity than the "atrocity" poster. In seeking to unite civilians behind the war, designers turned to images of violence and cruelty that had been avoided in earlier posters. *Red Cross or Iron Cross?*, by David Wilson (1873–1935), is one of the finest examples of this genre, displaying a favorite theme, the paradox of the inhumanly vicious German nurse. This is a rare example of a poster whose effectiveness is driven more by its text than its illustration (*fig. 3.16*). While the image of the nurse and

two German soldiers is adequate, it lacks the gut-wrenching impact of, for example, Lumley's stricken father. However, the last three lines of text, beginning with "The German 'Sister' pours it on the ground before his eyes," together create a staccato rhythm that drives home the brutality of the act. What is most important from a design point of view is the balance of forces—image and text—at play in a poster like this one. Wilson deftly used the inexpensive red and black palette to reinforce the message of the gulf between the conduct of British and German nurses. While there are, of course, no confirmed facts behind this poster or others like it, the theme of the sadistic nurse had particular resonance in England, home to Florence Nightingale (1820–1910). Nightingale, a national hero who died in the years just before the war, had revolutionized the nursing profession, having recognized the role that sanitation played in morbidity and mortality when she had worked at the front during the Crimean War (1854–56). Her story added further resonance to the image, in that it became part of an implicit contrast in the viewer's mind. Wilson, a newspaper cartoonist, became a graphic designer only for the duration of the war.

3.15 Savile Lumley, *Daddy, What Did YOU Do in the Great War?*, 1915. Poster. Lithograph on paper, 29⅜ x 19⅜ in (74.8 cm x 49.4 cm). Imperial War Museum, London.

3.16 David Wilson, *Red Cross or Iron Cross?*, 1917. Poster. Lithograph on paper, 29⅞ x 20 in (75.9 cm x 50.9 cm). Imperial War Museum, London.

Souscrivez à L'Emprunt de la "Victoire"

left: **3.17** Anonymous, *Are You One of Kitchener's Own?*, 1917. Poster. Lithograph on paper, 41⅜ x 27⅜ in (105.2 x 69.4 cm). Imperial War Museum, London.

above: **3.18** Anonymous, *Souscrivez à L'Emprunt de la "Victoire,"* 1917. Poster. Canadian War Museum.

Canadian War Posters

At the time of the First World War, Britain retained its colonial legacy of control over the political and military affairs of Canada. Still a member of the Commonwealth of Nations, Canada in 1914 was a part of the British Empire, a status quo that was maintained until the Statute of Westminster was signed in 1931. Naturally, Canadian recruitment posters featured many of the same manipulative appeals as their British counterparts. Canadian posters also relied on realistic illustration, rather than avant-garde abstraction, in the British manner. The recruiting poster shown here replicates the "pointing" style developed by Alfred Leete, combining the personal appeal of the hand gesture with a rousing quote displayed like a banner at the top of the image (*fig. 3.17*). The question, "Are you one of Kitchener's own?", refers to the specific regiment that is recruiting, in this case the 244th, based in Montreal, which was known as "Kitchener's own." In contrast to the British posters, which made broad national appeals, many of the Canadian designs were aimed at specific populations, such as the men of the city of Montreal. In a literal display of flag-waving patriotism, the majority of the poster is taken up with a Union Jack that appears to be draped from the top, as it would hang at local recruiting stations. The uses of the Union Jack, originally a royal flag, gradually expanded over the centuries and eventually included its status as an insignia of the British Army. St George's emblem, a red cross on a white ground, is the dominant motif of the flag.

Because of Canada's large French-speaking community, many posters produced there, especially in Quebec, were published in both English and French versions. Starting in 1916, all of the belligerents in the war had become reliant on war loans in order to finance their armed forces. One poster shows yet another variation of the pointing style, with this time a harried-looking soldier at the front making the direct appeal (*fig. 3.18*). Instead of instilling guilt for the purposes of recruitment, this soldier is urging French-speaking Canadians to subscribe to a "Victory Loan." The intensity of his gaze is unparalleled in the pointing genre, and considering the millions of war casualties suffered by the time this poster was produced in 1917, this otherworldly soldier would seem to be calling out to his fellow citizens at home from an unmarked battlefield grave.

A fine example of the Canadian penchant for addressing narrow audiences in order to bolster recruitment can be seen in the two versions of this poster aimed at Jewish Canadians, and published in both English and Yiddish (*figs. 3.19, 3.20*). This complex image throws a multiplicity of themes at the viewer. The banner slogan at the top makes a rather universal appeal, invoking a long-standing theme of Judaism that could refer to everything from the biblical Exodus from Egypt to the civil and economic rights garnered during the European Enlightenment in the eighteenth century. One level below that slogan there are three photos of famous Jewish Britons integrated into a collage of Union Jacks, including in the center a picture of Rufus Daniel Isaacs, the Lord Chief Justice of Great Britain, who had joined the peerage in 1914, and become a Viscount in 1916. Other parts of the appeal are suggestive of the adventurous nature of war as well as what is portrayed as a Jewish debt to Great Britain for their emancipation in Europe. The man whose bonds are being severed by a British soldier says, "You have cut my bonds and set me free—now let me help you set others free!"

3.19 and 3.20 Anonymous, *Britain Expects Every Son of Israel to Do His Duty*, 1917. Posters in English and Yiddish. Imperial War Museum, London.

3.21 Frederick Spear, *Enlist*, 1915. Poster. Color lithograph, 32 x 23 in (81.3 x 58.4 cm). National Museum of American History Archives Center, Smithsonian Institution.

The United States

The United States entered the First World War on the side of the Allies in April 1917. In the war's earlier years, the United States had prospered as its industries sold millions of tons of munitions and other goods to the Western Allies. The period between 1915 and 1917 saw increasing tension between the United States and Germany as German submarines attacked merchant ships carrying these exports, killing a number of Americans. The American declaration of war followed on the loss of five vessels early in 1917, after Germany had implemented a new policy of unrestricted submarine warfare. In the ensuing year and a half, the American navy assisted Great Britain in destroying the German submarine threat. In terms of the land war, the greatest American contribution came in the summer and autumn of 1918, when army troops under John Pershing (1860–1948) assisted the Allies in the Meuse-Argonne offensive, which broke through Germany's Hindenburg Line. By the end of the war in November 1918, the United States had deployed nearly 2 million fighting men in France.

German attacks on Allied shipping provoked a number of pre-war contretemps between the United States and Germany. The most fractious dispute involved the sinking by a German submarine of the British luxury liner *Lusitania* on May 7, 1915. One hundred and twenty-eight Americans were killed in the attack, which occurred off the coast of Ireland. A sentimental newspaper report described "a mother with a three-month old child clasped tightly in her arms. Her face wears a half smile. Her baby's head rests against her breast. No one has tried to separate them." In Boston, the American illustrator Frederick Spear produced this image, which became the basis of a recruitment poster (*fig. 3.21*). Perhaps one of the most compelling atrocity images ever published, it shows an ethereal mother and child sinking into the murky depths.

War Posters and James Montgomery Flagg

In the weeks after war was declared on the Central Powers, Americans enthusiastically printed thousands of posters, covering the walls of American cities. In New York City on April 14, hundreds of volunteers pasted over 20,000 posters on every available surface. Despite the United States' late entry into the war, by its end it was the Americans who had produced more posters than any other nation. The majority of posters were made by established magazine illustrators, and, in fact, one of the leaders of the government's publicity campaign was the famous magazine illustrator Charles Dana Gibson (1867–1944). Gibson had established the "Gibson Girl," a refined, fashionable young everywoman, as the most famous character in American illustration. Many of the poster artists had attended or taught at the country's foremost illustration schools, including the Art Students League, Cooper Union, and The New York School of Art in New York City, as well as the School of the Art Institute of Chicago. Several of these schools sponsored contests for the best-designed poster on a given theme, while the military provided props and uniforms for the artists to study. In terms of wartime graphic design, Americans relied on conservative illustration like that practiced in Britain,

3.22 James Flagg, *I Want You for U.S. Army*, 1917. Color lithograph. Library of Congress, Washington, D.C.

3.23 People for the Ethical Treatment of Animals (P.E.T.A) and Lauren Anderson, *I Want YOU to Go Vegetarian*, 2002. Poster. Courtesy of P.E.T.A and Lauren Anderson.

albeit more often employed by top talents with recognized past success.

A number of the earliest American posters were clearly indebted to British works. The most famous Anglo-American connection came via James Montgomery Flagg (1877–1960), who based his most famous poster on the "pointing" style developed by Alfred Leete. In an American take on Lord Kitchener's appeal, Flagg transformed Kitchener into "Uncle Sam," a personification of the United States (*fig. 3.22*). The character Uncle Sam had been invented a century earlier under obscure circumstances. It is believed to be a nickname derived by supply workers in the army, who took the initials "U.S.," which were stamped on every parcel, and expanded upon them to create an imaginary figure who personified the Federal government. Uncle Sam's exact features and clothes proved mutable for decades, although he was usually dressed by illustrators in a star-spangled suit of red, white, and blue. In the later nineteenth century, influenced by President Abraham Lincoln's face, the tradition arose of drawing Uncle Sam

Uncle Sam, an American Icon

After the poster of Uncle Sam was reissued during the Second World War its fame only increased, to the point that it has come to enjoy an iconic status in America society. Later generations have reevaluated "Uncle Sam" as a veritable emblem of American propaganda, expressing the same mistrust of its emotional manipulation that Britons expressed about their own First World War propaganda. In this regard, the slogan "I want you," which is truly unremarkable in the history of wartime appeals, had also become a familiar part of the American lexicon. This situation, in turn, has led to the production of countless knock-offs and parodies of varying charm and intelligence. To cite one recent example, the activist group People for the Ethical Treatment of Animals produced a version in 2002 featuring vegetarian pin-up Lauren Anderson, who modeled nude in an American magazine in order to raise money for stray animal shelters (fig. 3.23).

left: 3.24 James Flagg, First Call, 1917. Library of Congress, Washington, D.C.

opposite left: **3.26** Howard Christy, *Gee!! I Wish I Were a Man*, 1917. Poster. Photolithograph, 40⅞ x 26⅞ in (104 cm x 68.2 cm). Imperial War Museum, London.

opposite right: **3.27** Howard Christy, *I Want You for the Navy*, 1917. Poster. Imperial War Museum, London.

with a white goatee. When Flagg drew Uncle Sam in 1917, he based the image partly on tradition and partly on his own self-portrait. When Flagg completed his image, he had no idea that it was destined to become the most famous American poster ever made, and in so doing fixed his own specific version of Uncle Sam into the popular imagination for generations to come.

Flagg originally created the image for *Leslie* magazine, where he was a longtime illustrator, and it appeared on the cover on July 16, 1917. The rather clumsy title "What are you doing for preparedness?" was replaced when the image was transformed into a recruiting poster the following month. In its place, the simple, declarative appeal, "I want you for U.S. Army" complemented the stern glare and forceful gesture of the no longer kindly Uncle Sam. Between the summer of 1917 and the end of the war, Flagg's poster of Uncle Sam would be printed more than 4 million times. Its great popularity has led over the ensuing years to countless variations. Flagg actually was the first to recycle his drawing, as he made it a part of *First Call*, a recruiting poster for the navy (*fig. 3.24*).

A member of the Committee of Pictorial Publicity, Flagg contributed over forty posters to support the American war effort. He also played a role in one of the government's most unique promotional stunts, the creation of posters in front of crowds on the steps of New York City's landmark library. After each original poster was completed, it was auctioned off in exchange for the purchase of war bonds; such auctions sometimes brought in thousands of dollars. *Tell That to the Marines!* was the result of one such publicity stunt, a poster that displays the strengths of Flagg's ability to match a simple slogan with a compelling illustration (*fig. 3.25*). In a variation on the demonized "Hun" theme developed by British propagandists, Flagg shows an outraged man ready to sign up after learning of German atrocities. It is worthy of note that Flagg had successfully reinvented an adage originally meant to mock the gullibility of young marines—who would apparently believe anything you told them—and turned it into a positive commentary on the soldier's toughness. In addition, the realistic rendering of posters such as this one appealed through its familiarity to a broad swath of the population.

3.25 James Flagg, *Tell That to the Marines!*, 1916. Poster. Lithograph, 39⅝ x 29⅝ in (100.6 x 75.5 cm). Imperial War Museum, London.

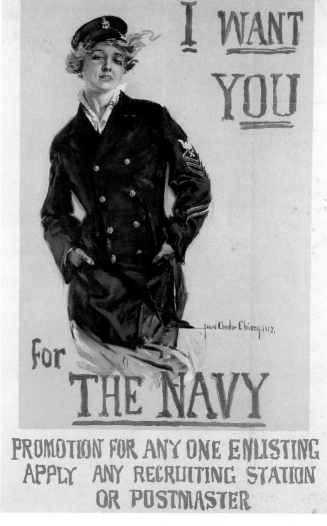

Howard Chandler Christy

In the United States, some of the most successful poster designers used the theme of the war as an adventure "over there," as the lyrics to a popular song put it. Howard Chandler Christy (1873–1952) was perhaps the most famous illustrator who sought to glamorize the military conflict. A popular illustrator for a number of magazines, including *The Century*, *Scribner's*, and *Leslie*, Christy had discovered a gift for wartime illustration when he served as a soldier in the Spanish-American War (1898). His basic device was the "Christy Girl," an American version of the sexualized young women that had populated many European posters beginning in the Art Nouveau era. Christy had drawn his first "Christy Girl" in 1895 for *The Century*, and it had become the fundamental building block of his career as an illustrator. Despite the obvious parallels with European illustration, the pre-war "Christy Girls" tended to be fashionable in a bourgeois manner, rather than overtly sexual.

A more censorious public in the United States than in Europe tempered the use of sexuality in American advertising, but the need for recruitment during the war years facilitated a more progressive stance by artists and the public. In his war posters, Christy was extremely adept at balancing fresh-faced wholesome-ness with just the right amount of giggling sexual availability. A fine example of this balance can be seen in *Gee!! I wish I were a man*, a recruiting poster for the US Navy (*fig. 3.26*). In seeking to join the military services, young women like this simultaneously attracted and emasculated young men of recruiting age. The young woman's plunging neckline and the possibility that she is "playing dress-up" in a navy man's uniform are both sexually suggestive. The poster implies that the sexual availability of young women is part of naval service. At the same time, the suggestion that a girlish young woman is willing to join the navy while men stand aside invokes the manipulative emasculation that was a part of many British posters.

Christy also produced a variation of Uncle Sam's direct appeal using a Christy girl (*fig. 3.27*). In a gesture toward modesty, the Christy girl featured here does not actually point at the recruit, but rather her direct appeal, "I want you," is conveyed solely through the text. Christy's posters, like many of the American images, have quite a bit more flair than those produced by their British counterparts. One obvious reason for this is that, in comparison to British efforts, many American posters were produced by illustrators of consummate skill. Also, as these well-known American artists were more often entrusted with the job of applying text to the poster, they were able to relate the

3.28 Lucien Jonas, *Emprunt de la Libération: Souscrivez* (*Loan for the Liberation: Subscribe*), 1917. Poster. Imperial War Museum, London.

far left: **3.29** Lucien Jonas, *Emprunt National (National Loan)*, 1919. Poster. Lithograph on paper, 47⅞ x 30 in (121 cm x 77.5 cm). Imperial War Museum, London.

left: **3.30** Abel Faivre, *Pour la France Versez Votre Or (For France Pour Forth your Gold)*, 1915. Lithograph on paper, 47⅞ x 31 in (119.8 cm x 79.9 cm). Imperial War Museum, London.

style of text and image in a way that harmonizes the final result. For example, Christy's recruiting poster for the US Navy shown here uses the same breezy line in the rendering of the Christy girl that is visible in the forms of the letters. In the final analysis, however, both countries' artists worked in styles that largely ignored the development of sophisticated graphic design techniques from previous decades.

France

French posters during the First World War tended toward a higher level of aesthetic accomplishment than those produced in Britain or the United States. One of the reasons for this high level of achievement was that the French were generally more appreciative of the poster than their British and American counterparts, so that the art of the poster was more closely allied with the art of painting. For this reason, French images were sometimes designed not by commercial illustrators, printshop workers, or art school students, but rather by top painters with established credentials. Additionally, the close relationship between graphic design and the fine arts led to a greater use of traditional allegorical imagery as well as sophisticated compositional references to the fine art of the past. Still, the French government did not rely on painters or graphic designers with edgy, abstract styles, but turned instead to masters of academic style.

Lucien Jonas (1880–1947) was one of the excellent graphic designers responsible for a number of fine French posters. Mobilized in 1914, by 1915 he had been appointed to the post of "military painter seconded to the Musée de l'Armée." Because of

this role, Jonas produced literally thousands of drawings and sketches based on his experiences at the front. His works were featured in books and magazines throughout the war. His poster publicizing a national war loan (*fig. 3.29*) shows three workers hoisting the French Tricolor atop the spire of a Gothic cathedral. This triumphal scene references the territory won by France in the Alsace region.

His poster publicizing France's sixth War Loan shows a winged "Marianne," the personification of France, flying above the heads of a charging group of soldiers (*fig. 3.28*). The soldiers appear rather rugged and dirty amid a stressful battle, a semblance of the actual conditions at the front that was rarely displayed on posters. The vast majority of wartime publications studiously ignored any imagery that was at all suggestive of the horrors of a conflict in which on a bad day 50,000 men would die in the face of machine guns and artillery barrages. The poses of the soldiers reference the noteworthy Eugène Delacroix painting *Liberty Leading the People* (1830), which shows a powerful figure of Marianne charging into the battle for liberty at the head of a ragtag group of citizens. In the poster, a more graceful and confident Marianne holds a cornucopia in her left hand. Also called the "horn of plenty," the cornucopia is a symbol of an abundant harvest because in Greek mythology it would constantly be refilled with food. Here, Marianne pours out the bounty of the cornucopia on to the French troops. Note how the text at the top of the poster invokes the French revolutionary ideal of "Liberty," as it suggests one should subscribe to the "Loan of the Liberation." An important part of wartime propaganda late in the conflict was the message that the war would indeed end, usually with the additional abstract promise of liberty, freedom, or some other ideal goal.

Another leading graphic artist, Abel Faivre (1867–1945), designed a remarkably inventive image of the symbolic coq d'or, or "golden rooster," attacking a hapless German soldier (*fig. 3.30*). The rooster, used on military escutcheons, symbolized the fighting spirit of France. In this image the rooster has detached itself from a contemporary gold coin that itself depicts the revolutionary slogan "Liberty, Equality, Fraternity." The poster asks that citizens "pour forth their gold" in order to assist the war effort. During World War I, it was highly unusual for enemy combatants to be portrayed in posters—Faivre is quite daring in depicting such an un-demonized German soldier.

The Central Powers

In contrast to the changing conventions among the Allies, the German government did not demand that its poster designers turn away from modern abstract styles. For this reason, the *Sachplakat* manner introduced at the beginning of this chapter, with its startlingly abstract simplifications of form, became a staple of German propaganda. *Sachplakat* artists such as Lucian Bernhard, who reigned at the top of the advertising profession, remained prominent in the creation of war posters.

Bernhard produced a number of compelling designs, including a notable poster publicizing a war loan (*fig. 3.31*). Some elements of the *Sachplakat* style remain, as the armored fist here stands in for the product—German military might. As was the case with the advertising posters, the "product" and its associated text are displayed without any further ornamentation. In addition, the armored fist has been rendered in the simplified form that Bernhard had made famous.

The poster's typography is a far cry from the plain block letter style made popular by the *Sachplakat* movement. First of all, *Sachplakat* lettering is roman and often features small serifs, while Bernhard is here embracing the blackletter tradition. At the time of the outbreak of the First World War, this question of type as a marker of national identity had become an even more inflammatory topic. The outbreak of war with France, Germany's major European rival and a country that had played a large role in the creation of the classic roman tradition, temporarily tilted the balance for German designers in favor of blackletter. During this era it could be identified as a unique national tradition, untainted by "foreign" French aesthetics. This is not to say that all or even most German war posters used blackletter, only that it achieved a resurgence because of militant feelings on the part of designers and the public at large. In Bernhard's poster, the image's reference to medieval German knights and its strident slogan "This is the way

3.31 Lucian Bernhard, *Das ist der Weg zum Frieden (That Is the Way to Peace)*, c. 1917. Poster. Lithograph, 25 x 18⅜ in (65.4 x 46.7 cm). Imperial War Museum, London.

opposite left: 3.32 Hans Rudi Erdt, *UBoote Heraus!*, 1917. Poster. Deutsches Historisches Museum, Berlin.

opposite right: 3.33 Julius Klinger, *8 Kriegsanleihe (8th War Loan)*, 1917. Poster.

to peace—the enemies want it so!" combines with the blackletter script to create a rousing sense of nationalist sentiment.

Other posters designed by *Sachplakat* artists remained closer to the original style. Hans Rudi Erdt's *UBoote Heraus!*, which promoted a government film celebrating submarine warfare, shows a German officer using a periscope to view the sinking of an Allied surface ship (*fig. 3.32*). In this poster, the abstract simplification of the *Sachplakat* style serves to distance the viewer from the grim details of the war, in the same manner that Allied designers avoided undue scenes of carnage. The hand and face of the officer are shown with stylish detachment, his features rendered without any tonal gradation but with the flat planes of the Japanese style. The typography is typical of the *Sachplakat* artists, featuring expanded, bold block letters. The giant "U" encompasses both the U-boat commander and his victim, and appears both as a letter and as a part of the image, its solid form invoking the mass of a submarine itself.

The Austrian designer Julius Klinger (1876–1942), who had returned to Vienna at the onset of war, produced a stunningly original poster publicizing the eighth war loan (*fig. 3.33*). Displaying a close allegiance to *Sachplakat* principles, the poster features a dying serpent, representing the Allies, riddled with eight arrows and entangled in the number itself. The death throes of the serpent and its irregular shape come across as unkempt and

uncivilized when compared to the cleanly delineated number 8 and the simple text, "war loan." It is clear that the public financing is strangling the serpent, its head in a noose formed by the top of the eight. The key element that separates this poster aesthetically from most of the Allied images is the sophisticated way in which Klinger uses the "8" as both a textual and graphical element. Additionally, there is a slight touch of red where the serpent's tongue hangs out that adroitly reinforces the ties between the red text and image. Of course, Klinger is using a palette of complementary colors. This stylish abstraction is a far cry from the literal rendering typical of most Allied war posters.

Realism versus Abstraction

Ludwig Hohlwein's poster shown here features a wounded soldier on crutches, examining tools that could help him rejoin the civilian workforce (*fig. 3.34*). Hohlwein's *Sachplakat* style is still in place, although the simplified forms have been rendered with something of a painterly flair. Still, the central figure and straightforward text look like part of the familiar advertising style. What is unusual about Hohlwein's work is the way in which he is trying to invest a Beggarstaff-like flattened figure with human pathos. The image is straining to create an emotional impact that is per-

haps beyond the means of this type of abstraction. Looking back over the posters surveyed in this chapter, it is easy to find figures done in a realistic style that appear more compelling. Hohlwein's poster suggests that there are limits to the effectiveness of abstraction as a vehicle of emotional manipulation.

While by no means all German propaganda posters were rendered in an abstract, *Sachplakat* style, a large number of the most high-profile designers worked in that manner, and their posters were among the most well-known. An interesting parallel circumstance arose in Britain and Germany after the war; in both countries, there was condemnation of the posters that had been produced. In Britain, much of the criticism focused on the bald-faced emotional manipulation of many of the posters, such as Savile Lumley's *Daddy, What did you do in the Great War?*

In Germany, the inverse of this criticism came to the fore, as later governments criticized the avant-garde stylishness of posters by Bernhard or Hohlwein, which they felt failed to communicate an effective message to a large swath of the population. This idea was particularly attractive to militant German nationalists, many of whom felt that the civilian population had "stabbed them in the back," and hypothesized that better propaganda at home could have won the war. Famously, the Nazi leader Adolf Hitler (1889–1945) rhapsodized about the quality of British emotional manipulation in his book *Mein Kampf*. Referring to British "atrocity" posters, Hitler lauded the posters' ability to connect with "the primitive sentiments of the broad masses." Asserting that British propaganda was "as ruthless as it was brilliant," Hitler's beliefs helped to mold Nazi propaganda of the 1930s. Of course, the two sides would get a chance to revisit wartime propaganda after only two decades, when Europe again embarked on a world war (see Chapter 7).

Hohlwein's poster of a severely injured soldier is particularly poignant in that the millions of badly wounded men who came home after the war ended were often shunned by their fellow citizens. Because of their injuries, these wounded men served as a grim reminder of the slaughter that had taken place between 1914 and 1918, a debacle that their compatriots would sooner forget. Even before the war ended, as early as 1916, a group of artists had joined together to protest a conflict that to them bordered on the absurd.

3.34 Ludwig Hohlwein, *Ludendorff-Spende für Kriegsbeschädigte (The Ludendorff Appeal for the War-Disabled)*, 1918. Poster. Lithograph on paper, 23 x 35⅛ in (59.9 cm x 89.2 cm). Imperial War Museum, London.

Dada

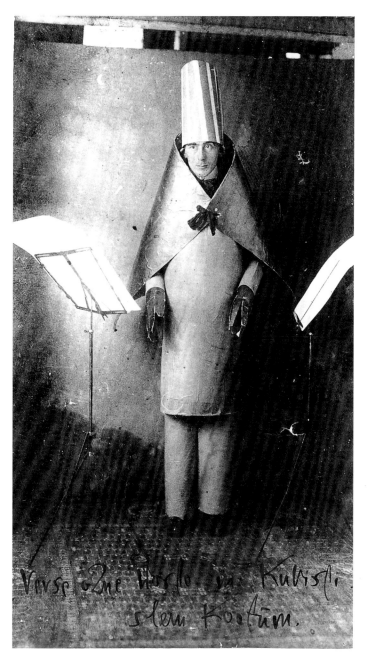

3.35 Hugo Ball reciting 'Verse ohne Worte' (Song without Words), Cabaret Voltaire, Zurich, 1916. Photographic enlargement of a postcard. 28 x 15⅞ in (71.5 x 40 cm). Kunsthaus, Zurich.

A small community of young people opposed to the war gathered in neutral Zurich, Switzerland, from 1914. It was there that German pacifist Hugo Ball (1886–1927) decided to create a gathering place for like-minded artists and activists. Ball had joined the German army after a rush of patriotic feeling (perhaps heightened by war posters) when the war began in 1914, but he soon became disillusioned and fled Germany for Switzerland. His Dada efforts began in February 1916, when he organized the now famous meeting place he called the **Cabaret Voltaire**, which, despite its exalted name, was essentially the back room of a restaurant at No. 1 Spiegelgasse, in a seedy area of Zurich. Partly inspired by the Futurist movement (see Chapter 4), Ball named his establishment in order to honor the French thinker who had attacked the norms of European society in the eighteenth century. Like Voltaire, the members of Zurich Dada (the name of the city is appended to distinguish it from other subsequent incarnations of the Dada spirit) were iconoclasts, or "breakers of icons," meaning that they rejected the ideas and values that other Europeans treasured the most.

The artists who gathered at the Cabaret Voltaire had all come to the conclusion that a collapse of Western culture had occurred amid the barbarism of the First World War. They came from many countries: Ball, Richard Huelsenbeck (1892–1972), and Emmy Hennings (1885–1948) from Germany, Jean Arp (1886–1966) from France, Tristan Tzara (1896–1963) and Marcel Janco (1895–1984) from Romania, all committed to using their creativity in order to protest the war and to draw attention to what they saw as the impoverishment of European middle-class life. They questioned how Europeans could claim to be rational, enlightened, and civilized when they were sending millions to their deaths at the front. For this reason, the Dadaists sought to use irony, satire, and improvisation in their performances in order to shock the public into recognizing the contradictions of European culture. The name itself, Dada, exemplifies the group's iconoclastic spirit, because the word is essentially meaningless. Over the years the members of Dada offered numerous stories about the name's origin, deliberately adding to the confusion while resisting attempts to clarify the origins of a group that had as one of its founding beliefs the negation of clear explanations.

Of the numerous artistic and political strategies pursued by members of the Zurich Dada movement, the most innovative were the chaotic evenings they arranged at the Cabaret Voltaire (*fig. 3.35*). Using random chance while embracing the incoherent effects caused by simultaneous, overlapping elements, Dada evenings featured dance, music, poetry readings, and other hybrid types of performances. Odd costumes, acerbic attacks on traditional culture overlaid with "noise performances," and, of course, inebriated performers and audience members, worked together to create a confounding spectacle. For example, *L'Amiral Cherche une Maison à Louer* ("The admiral looks for a house to rent") by Tzara, Huelsenbeck, and Janco, was performed at the Cabaret Voltaire in 1916. With all three artists speaking at once, and many of their words made up of gibberish and singsong, the final effect depended on the simultaneous contrasts of speech and noise. Much of the ironic strength of the poem lies in its

3.36 Jean Arp, *Collage Arranged According to the Laws of Chance*, 1916–17. Collage, torn and pasted paper, 19 x 14 in (48 x 34 cm). Museum of Modern Art, New York.

found to be stifling. Dada art works are therefore often called "anti-art," because of the Dadaists' contempt for the established order. In place of traditional artistic techniques, the Dadaists displayed a penchant for new media and new stylistic strategies. For example, Arp's witty *Collage Arranged According to the Laws of Chance* was created when the artist dropped small pieces of paper on to a larger sheet of paper and then attached them where they had fallen (*fig. 3.36*). The resulting work embraces chance occurrence not only as an aesthetic itself, but also as a mocking rebuttal to the controlled professionalism of traditional artists. Arp is attempting to enhance his creativity by allowing for a type of free association, rejecting dogmatic techniques in the hope of finding something new and more original. This type of strategy reflects the political strategies of the group, who hoped to use anarchic behavior to open up a route to a new spirit in European society. The Dada thinkers rarely specified, and likely would not have agreed on, the parameters of a new European culture, but they could agree that it would reject the catastrophic destruction of the war.

In terms of graphic design and typography, Dadaists maintained the same contemptuous attitude toward traditional practices, and sought to free the fields from stultifying past standards. The Dadaists eventually had both a direct and an indirect impact on graphic design: direct, in that works by Dada designers created a new visual vocabulary as well as innovative compositional strategies; and indirect, in that the Dadaists' call for freedom from convention diffused into contemporary culture and led designers to have a more open attitude toward non-traditional work. However, it is important to remember that a large part, even the majority, of Dada's impact came to the fore many decades after the movement had ended, when designers in a more progressive age, the 1960s, rediscovered the work of Dada pioneers.

The members of Zurich Dada, like those of many cultural groups, often turned to publishing in order to promulgate their

style, but the absurd and incongruous nature of its imagery complemented the drama of its performance. In addition to the programmed "evenings," art projects by the Dadaists and by people they admired adorned the walls at the Cabaret Voltaire. Jean Arp later recalled:

> Disgusted by the butchery of the 1914 World War, we in Zurich devoted ourselves to the arts. While the guns rumbled in the distance, we sang, painted, made collages and wrote poems with all our might. We were seeking an art based on fundamentals, to cure the madness of the age, and a new order of things that would restore the balance between heaven and hell.

The Cabaret Voltaire was only open for about five months, after which the Dadaists continued their activities at a variety of venues, including theaters and art galleries across Zurich.

Combining an iconoclastic outlook with a love of improvisation and chance, Dada artists sought to pursue social and artistic change through anarchic aesthetic projects. The members of Zurich Dada displayed a range of attitudes toward the visual arts, some seeking mainly the nihilism of the ephemeral transgressive gesture, while others, such as Jean Arp, devoted their efforts to the creation of art works. A central tenet of Zurich Dada was the rejection of antiquated aesthetic rules that Arp and other artists

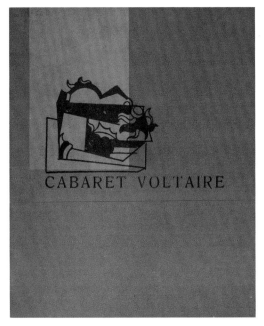

3.37 Hugo Ball, *Cabaret Voltaire*, 1916.

3.38 Tristan Tzara, Contents, *Dada 3*, July 1917. Periodical.

views to a larger audience than could fit in the Cabaret Voltaire. As early as 1916, an early project overseen by Ball, the journal called *Cabaret Voltaire*, was published in Zurich (*fig. 3.37*). In terms of typography and design, *Cabaret Voltaire* was unremarkable, its mission "to clarify the intentions of this cabaret. It is its aim to remind the world that there are people of independent minds—beyond war and nationalism—who live for different ideals." Ball, who wrote the preceding words, broke with other Dada publications in his desire for "clarity" in form and subject, a rational concept that was not a guiding idea Dadaists routinely embraced. The first place in which the word "Dada" appeared in print, only one issue of Cabaret Voltaire appeared but the journal set the stage for a flood of publications still to come.

Tristan Tzara

In 1917, Tristan Tzara, whose name was a pseudonym—he was born Sami Rosenstok—began editing and publishing the journal *Dada*, which was intended to spread word of the movement to like-minded people in Zurich and other European cities. The first issue appeared in July 1917, with a table of contents listing an assortment of poems and articles from a cross section of the European avant-garde. Conventional in format and typography,

the first issue, subtitled *Miscellany of Art and Literature*, was successful in promulgating news of the Dada movement to an international audience. While the second issue of Dada maintained this commitment to clarity and informative content, the third issue marked a dramatic break from both the style and substance of earlier Dada periodicals (*figs. 3.38, 3.39*). Consistent with the transgressive spirit of the movement, the third issue rejected every convention of readable typography and logical composition. A chaotic collection of types often overprinted on one another seemed in some pages to have been scattered across the page without rhyme or reason. Centered, slanted, upside down—words ran up and down and across the page with a spirit of anarchic freedom. It looked as if the designer had sought to fill up the available space, while ignoring the established standards of magazine layouts. This radical design was not, however, merely a puerile joke or nihilist gesture; rather, it sought to disrupt the reader's expectations in a way that signified the revolutionary character of Dada thought—especially its attempt to undermine the rationalist beliefs that underlay European society. Published in both French and German versions on cheap newspaper stock, *Dada* #3 helped to bring international attention to the movement, while solidifying Tzara's leadership role.

Amid the chaotic combination of essays, poems, and advertisements in *Dada* #3 appeared Tzara's own essay explicating the

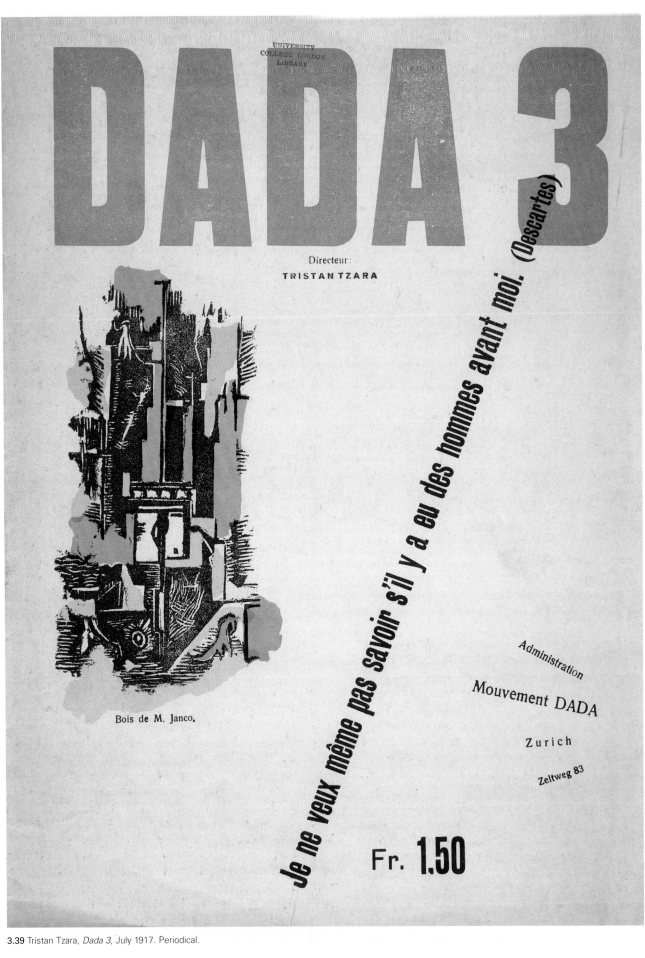

DADA 3

Directeur:
TRISTAN TZARA

Bois de M. Janco.

Je ne veux même pas savoir s'il y a eu des hommes avant moi. (Descartes)

Administration

Mouvement DADA

Z u r i c h

Zeltweg 83

Fr. **1.50**

3.39 Tristan Tzara, *Dada 3*, July 1917. Periodical.

3.40 Tristan Tzara, *25 Poèmes*, 1917. University College London (UCL), Special Collections.

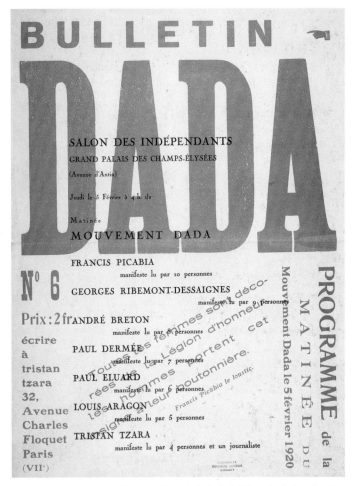

3.41 Tristan Tzara, *Bulletin Dada*, no. 6, 1920. Periodical. University College London (UCL), Special Collections.

Dada spirit. This "Dada Manifesto" is characteristically obtuse, yet the reader can get a general sense of the group's priorities. Tzara wrote: "Dada: the abolition of logic, the dance of the impotents of creation; Dada: abolition of all the social hierarchies and equations set up by our valets to preserve values … Dada: abolition of memory; Dada: abolition of archaeology; Dada: abolition of the prophets; Dada: abolition of the future." Of course, Tzara and other Dadaists would go on to write a series of manifestos and explanations of Dada, often with the deliberate intent of contradicting earlier statements in the hope of keeping the movement forever undefined. Among the admirers of *Dada #3* was the French artist Francis Picabia (1879–1959), who would later join Tzara as a publisher of Dada periodicals. Picabia offered the magazine high praise in his own cynical fashion when he declared that *Dada #3* "is not absolutely stupid." It is important to recognize how expertly the typography and layout of *Dada #3* visually reinforced the underlying message of the essays printed therein.

Another publication overseen by Tzara was a book of his own work called *25 Poèmes*, which was illustrated with ten woodcuts by Jean Arp (*fig. 3.40*). Arp's woodcuts feature what would become his trademark style, one that he reiterated throughout the rest of his career. It is an abstract idiom that consists of organic, fluid forms in an indeterminate space. Arp's forms are suggestive of the improvisational tenets of his work, looking as if he had casually poured pigment on to the page. Still, the elegance of the finished work suggests that Arp never surrendered himself completely to random chance.

Dada in Paris

In 1919, with the First World War recently over, Tzara and Arp moved to France, where they had a formative influence on the establishment of a new branch of Dada in Paris. This move served to raise the profile of the group even more because Paris was arguably the cultural capital of Europe. In Paris, Tzara continued to associate with Dadaists from Zurich while at the same time inspiring a new generation of French writers including André Breton (1896–1966), who later went on to create the Surrealist movement after Paris Dada had run its course.

Tzara's influence was partly maintained by *Dada*, the journal that he had begun in Zurich and kept publishing in Paris until 1922. Issue no. 6, called *Bulletin Dada*, was published in February 1920 (*fig. 3.41*). The cover of this issue, the first one published in Paris, features the familiar use of a bewildering range of typography laid out on several different axes, a jumble of upper- and lower-case letters, and with deliberate overprinting "mistakes" whereby the different blocks of text run into and across one

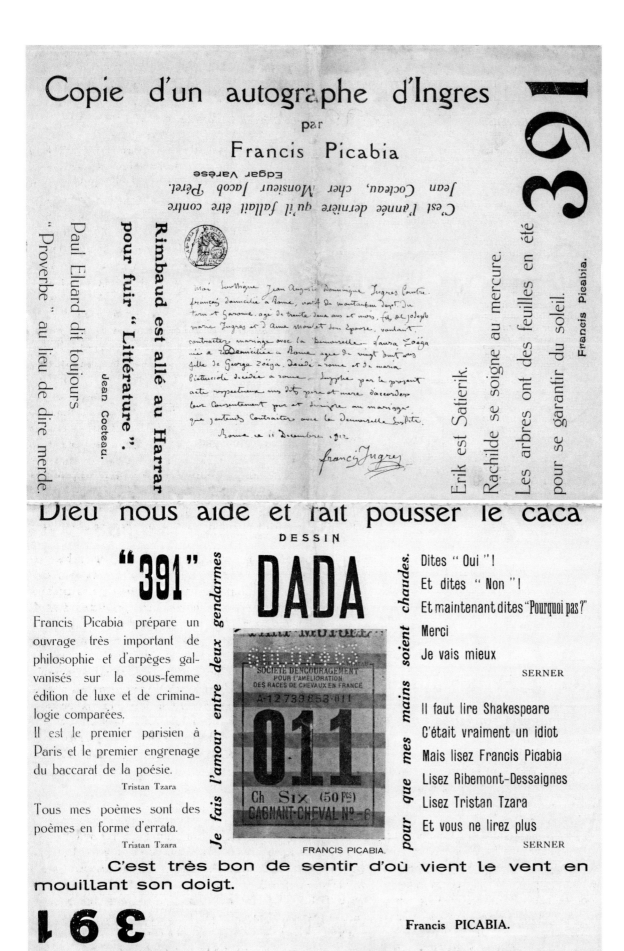

3.42 Francis Picabia, *391*, no. 14, 1920. International Dada Archive, University of Iowa Libraries.

3.43 Tristan Tzara, *Salon Dada*, 1921. Poster. Lithograph.
Merrill C. Berman Collection.

written by the famous French academic artist Jean-Auguste-Dominique Ingres (1780–1867), except that Picabia has overwritten the artist's first initials with his own name, Francis. The resulting "Francis Ingres" is gently satirical in that Picabia exalts himself to a status that he neither seeks nor admires.

In June 1921, Tzara organized an exhibition at the Montaigne gallery. The show consisted of a disparate collection of irreverent projects produced by two dozen artists from across Europe. Tzara designed a poster advertising the exhibition, which he called "Salon Dada" (*fig. 3.43*). The poster features the relevant factual information about the show at the top, including the name of the gallery, its address, and the dates and times of the exhibition. The name and address of the Montaigne gallery are even centered on the page in a gesture toward clear visual communication. The foot of the poster displays a corresponding hand-drawn sans serif display type, with the words "international exhibition" centered. However, the middle of the poster demonstrates the Dada love of chaos and absurdity. A number of ambiguous, even incomprehensible phrases, including "Nobody is supposed to ignore Dada" and "one looks for athletes," have the appearance of having been pasted helter-skelter on the poster, their variable lettering suggestive of a selection of "cuts," reusable stock that any printshop would have in plentiful variety. This is disingenuous, however, as the images refer to Dada and were drawn by Tzara for the lithograph. The largest lettering on the poster forms the words "Salon Dada." The words are presented to the viewer as a jumble of mixed type, the scale and forms of the letters appearing to have been picked out at random. Some seriffed, some sans, some heavy, some light, the nine letters look to be in motion, as if they are rattling against each other, spinning and turning back and forth in a kinetic frenzy.

In October 1924, Picabia published the 16th issue of his journal *391*. The list of the issue's contributors is indicative of the fact that Picabia had become close to the group of French authors centered around the poet André Breton. Between 1920 and 1924, Breton had emerged as a rival of Tzara for leadership of the Dadaists in Paris. Breton and his followers had grown increasingly disillusioned with the extreme iconoclasm of Tzara's work, and wanted to redirect their energies toward more organized political activism. As Tzara and his Zurich circle became increasingly marginalized, partly because they were mainly foreigners competing with a native French group, Breton asserted his intellectual control over the movement he named "**Surrealism**," which eventually replaced Dada as the leading artist-activist group in Europe.

another. The sense of improvisation is boosted by the tremendous use of overlapping text. Still, there is enough clarity to get the message across: in this case, the journal introduced a whole new roster of Dadists who were scheduling a number of new public performances.

Francis Picabia, who had met Tzara in Zurich after sitting out the war in the United States and elsewhere, published his own idiosyncratic Dada journal in Paris in 1920. Called *391*, the title originated in Barcelona, where the first run of the magazine was created by Picabia in 1917. The name 391 gently mocked Picabia's friend Alfred Stieglitz (1864–1946), whose New York City modern art gallery was located at 291 Fifth Avenue, and was nicknamed 291. The cover of issue no. 14 of *391* demonstrates some of the most dynamic Dada graphic design ever produced (*fig. 3.42*). A cacophonous mix of type styles and weights, combined with a dizzying layout that keeps the reader's head spinning in order to view successive blocks of text, makes for a compelling, if disorientating, viewing experience. The text of the cover conveys a suitably ironic message, "A copy of an autograph of Ingres by Francis Picabia." Below this heading there is a copy of a letter

Dada in Berlin

In 1917, Richard Huelsenbeck returned to his native Berlin, where he initiated a new round of Dada provocations with a new group that he called "Club Dada." Huelsenbeck was joined by members of the German avant-garde including Johannes Baader (1875–1955), Helmut Herzfelde, George Grosz, and Raoul Hausmann. With "Club Dada," Huelsenbeck set out to reinvent the Dada movement with a more serious political commitment. Unlike the broadly drawn politics of Zurich Dada, which had located itself against the European bourgeoisie in

3.44 Richard Huelsenbeck, First International Dada Fair, Berlin, June 1920. From left to right: Raoul Hausmann, Hannah Höch, Dr. Burchard, Johannes Baader, Wieland Herzfelde, Mrs. Herzfelde, Otto Schmalhausen (Dadaoz), George Grosz, John Heartfield. Bildarchiv Preussischer Kulturbesitz.

general, the Berlin Dadaists sought to engage more closely with the specific political situation in Germany. German society at the end of the war had in some ways come close to collapse, as competing groups of extremists vied for power. New political groups included fervent communists hoping for a revolution like the one that had occurred in Russia, as well as reactionary fascists seeking a militant imperial government. This polarized and fragmented society proved to be fertile ground for the satirical jabs of the Dadaists.

Typical of Berlin Dada activities was the "Erste Internationale Dada-Messe," or "First International Dada Fair," which Huelsenbeck opened in Berlin in June 1920. Underwritten by a collector of Chinese ceramics named Dr Otto Burchard, who was thereafter christened "Dadafinanz," the exhibition featured over

200 Dada items, most of which were offered for sale to anyone who paid the hefty entrance fee. The most notorious work at the show was made anonymously; it consisted of a dummy with a pig's head dressed in a German military uniform. The dummy can be seen hanging from the ceiling in a photograph of the show (*fig. 3.44*).

Helmut Herzfelde (1891–1968), who had changed his name to the quintessentially English-sounding "John Heartfield" in 1916 as a protest against the German military slogan "May God Punish England," designed the **photomontage** called *Life and Activity in Universal City at 12:05 in the Afternoon* printed on the cover of the fair's catalog (*fig. 3.45*). Heartfield had served in the German military until 1915, when he had faked a nervous collapse in order to be released from service. In 1920 he joined both

Club Dada and the German Communist Party, whose plan for revolutionary social change in Germany represented the main political goal of most Berlin Dadaists. The catalog cover demonstrates Heartfield's mastery of this new type of design, through which fragments of text and image combine to create a new whole. The catalog itself was mainly designed and published by a small firm, Malik-Verlag, run by Wieland Herzfelde (1896–1988), Heartfield's brother. The folio-sized cover featured Heartfield's photomontage, reproduced as a photolithograph, as the background. The image was then itself overprinted with a typically confounding mix of black and red letterforms of various sizes. The "First International Dada Fair" and its catalog were successful in promoting the Berlin movement's visibility across Europe, yet they also resulted in a major financial loss for the group, as two members were fined 900 German Marks for "denigrating the German military."

A German artist recruited for the Berlin movement by Huelsenbeck, Raoul Hausmann (1886–1971), became the most important publisher of German Dada texts when he founded the journal *Der Dada* in 1919. This publication featured the same sorts of "free" typography and layout that characterized other Dada journals. However, where Tzara and Picabia's publications tended toward the whimsical, the fiery politics of the Berlin Dadaists comes across through the aggressive nature of *Der Dada*'s design. The cover of the third issue, published in April of 1920, featured a collage of text and image by Heartfield (*fig. 3.46*). While Heartfield's collage contains the same sort of random, incongruous juxtapositions produced by other Dada artists, it is dominated by a photo of a snarling man on the lower left. This image, a portrait of Hausmann, overwhelms the rest of the collage in that it sets up an aggressive confrontation with the viewer. Heartfield continued to pursue political activism through collages well into the 1930s (his later work is surveyed in Chapter 7). Through *Der Dada*, Hausmann attempted to maintain a connection with other far-flung Dadaists, and the journal at times included contributions from Tzara and Picabia, as well as reports on Dada activity in other European cities. Despite these efforts, the Berlin Dada group began to lose its cohesion as early as 1920, and had faded away completely by 1923, as the artists involved each pursued their own interests.

Kurt Schwitters and *Merz*

The artist and graphic designer Kurt Schwitters (1887–1948) was loosely associated with the Berlin Dadaists during the post-

above: **3.45** John Heartfield, *Erste Internationale Dada–Messe (First International Dada Fair)*, Berlin, June 1920. Catalog cover. Bildarchiv Preussischer Kulturbesitz.

right: **3.46** Raoul Hausmann, *Der Dada 3*, 1920. Collage. University College London, Special Collections.

war years, although he remained something of an independent spirit, partly because he lived off the beaten track in the small German city of Hanover. Schwitters had trained at both the Kunstgewerbeschule in Hanover and at a fine art school, and he served in the German military during the First World War. He first appeared on the avant-garde art scene in 1918, when the Der Sturm gallery established by Herwarth Walden (1878–1941) presented a solo show of his abstract paintings. Walden, who was instrumental in promoting the art of the European avant-garde to the Berlin public, also played a central role in publicizing the work of German Expressionist artists. Schwitters also published a series of essays and poems in the journal *Der Sturm*, including poems that first referenced his imaginary lover, Anna Blume.

For Schwitters, the word fragment "Merz" functioned as a proprietary umbrella label for his work, and its nonsensical relationship to his art was clearly inspired by the Dada spirit. Schwitters came up with the label while making a collage of text in 1919, adopting the term from a fragment of the German word *Kommerz* ("commerce"). While "Merz" is generally associated with Schwitters's Dada-like art, even his commercial design practice used the term, as he called the shop Merz Werbezentrale, which translates loosely as "Merz Advertising Center." The early work *Merzbild 5B (Picture-Red-Heart-Church), April 26, 1919*, a combination of collage scraps of paper, tempera paints, and crayon on a piece of cardboard, is typical of Schwitters's "junk art," a Dadaesque use of the refuse of modern society (*fig. 3.47*). It is hard today to recognize the daring nature of Schwitters's use of bits of paper found on the street to make a work of fine art. A slight reference to contemporary political turmoil, the slaughter of socialist partisans in Bremen by their fascist rivals, is indicated by Schwitter's inclusion of a scrap from a Hanover newspaper that describes the conflict. However, Schwitters's political statements were never as strident as those of the Berlin Dadaists, and he seemed at times to immerse himself in the aesthetic freedom of Merz.

Between 1923 and 1932, Schwitters edited a journal also called *Merz* while maintaining a commercial graphic design practice in Hanover. While most of Schwitters's design work during this decade was guided by his commitment to the Constructivist aesthetic (and will be surveyed in Chapter 5), as indicated by the journal's title, some aspects of Dada aesthetics appeared in the journal too. For example, *Merz* issue no. 11, while using predominantly Constructivist principles, displays text that runs directly across a vertical bar—a framing device usually considered inviolate (*fig. 3.48*). Schwitters's work, like Dada graphic design in general, had relatively little impact at the time of its creation. However, to future generations Dada graphics would prove to be a valuable repository of innovative design ideas.

3.47 Kurt Schwitters, *Merzbild 5B (Picture-Red-Heart-Church), April 26, 1919*. Collage, tempera and crayon on cardboard, 32⅞ x 23 in (83.5 x 60.2 cm). Guggenheim Museum, New York.

90

RED. MERZ, HANNOVER, WALDHAUSENSTR. 5ᴵᴵ.

DIE GUTE REKLAME IST BILLIG.

Ein geringes Maß hochwertiger Reklame, die in jeder
Weise Qualität verrät, übersteigt an Wirkung eine vielfache
Menge ungeeigneter, ungeschickt organisierter Reklame.
Max Burchartz.

MERZ
11

TY PO
RE KLA ME

EINIGE THESEN ZUR GESTALTUNG DER REKLAME VON MAX BURCHARTZ:

Die Reklame ist die Handschrift des Unternehmers. Wie die Handschrift ihren Urheber, so verrät die Reklame Art, Kraft und
Fähigkeit einer Unternehmung. Das Maß der Leistungsfähigkeit, Qualitätspflege, Solidität, Energie und Großzügigkeit eines Unter-
nehmens spiegelt sich in Sachlichkeit, Klarheit, Form und Umfang seiner Reklame. Hochwertige Qualität der Ware ist erste Bedingung
des Erfolges. Die zweite: Geeignete Absatzorganisation; deren unentbehrlicher Faktor ist gute Reklame. Die gute Reklame verwendet
moderne Mittel. Wer reist heute in einer Kutsche? Gute Reklame bedient sich neuester zeitgemäßer Erfindungen als neuer Werkzeuge der Mitteilung. Wesentlich ist die Neuartigkeit der Formengebung. Abgeleierte banale Formen der Sprache und künstlerischen
Gestaltung müssen vermieden werden.   Zitiert aus Gestaltung der Reklame, Bochum, Bongardstrasse 15·

K. SCHWITTERS.
Signetentwurf für Adolf
Rothenberg

DIE GUTE REKLAME
ist sachlich, ist klar und knapp, verwendet moderne Mittel, hat Schlagkraft der Form, ist billig.
MAX BURCHARTZ.

WERBEN SIE BITTE FÜR MERZ.   *Pelikan*-Nummer.

Merzrelief von Kurt Schwitters siehe Seite 91

3.48 Kurt Schwitters, *Merz*, no. 11, 1924. Cambridge University Library, Cambridge, England.

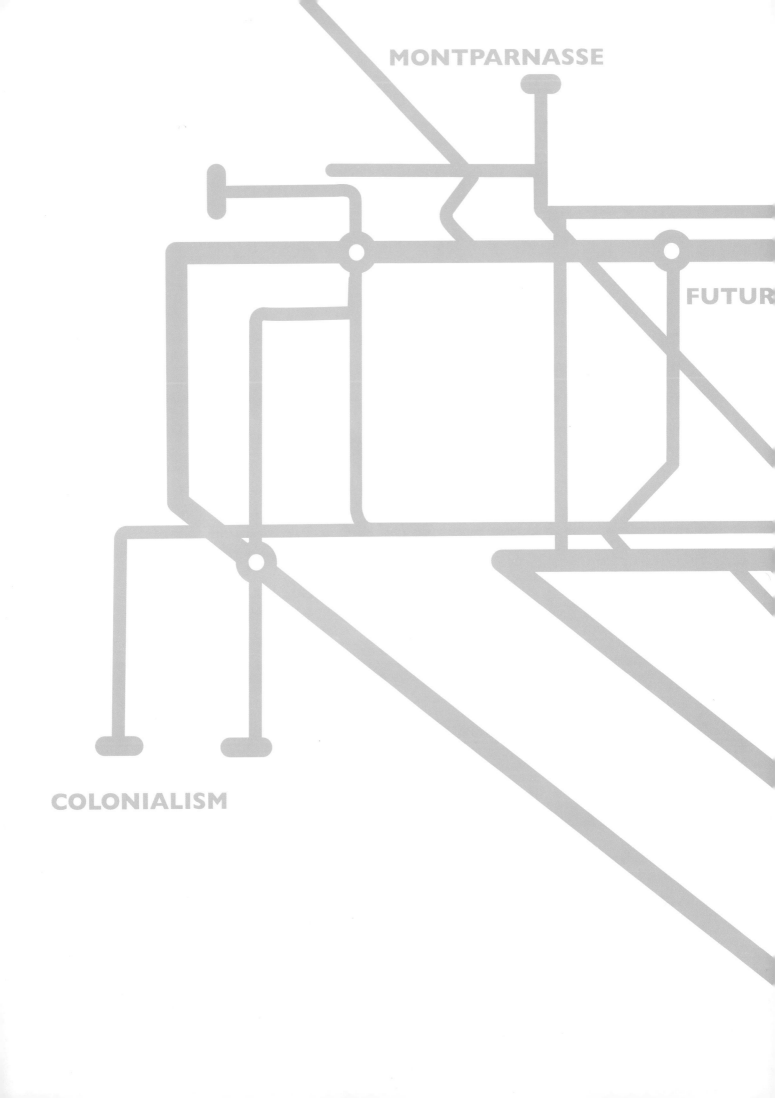

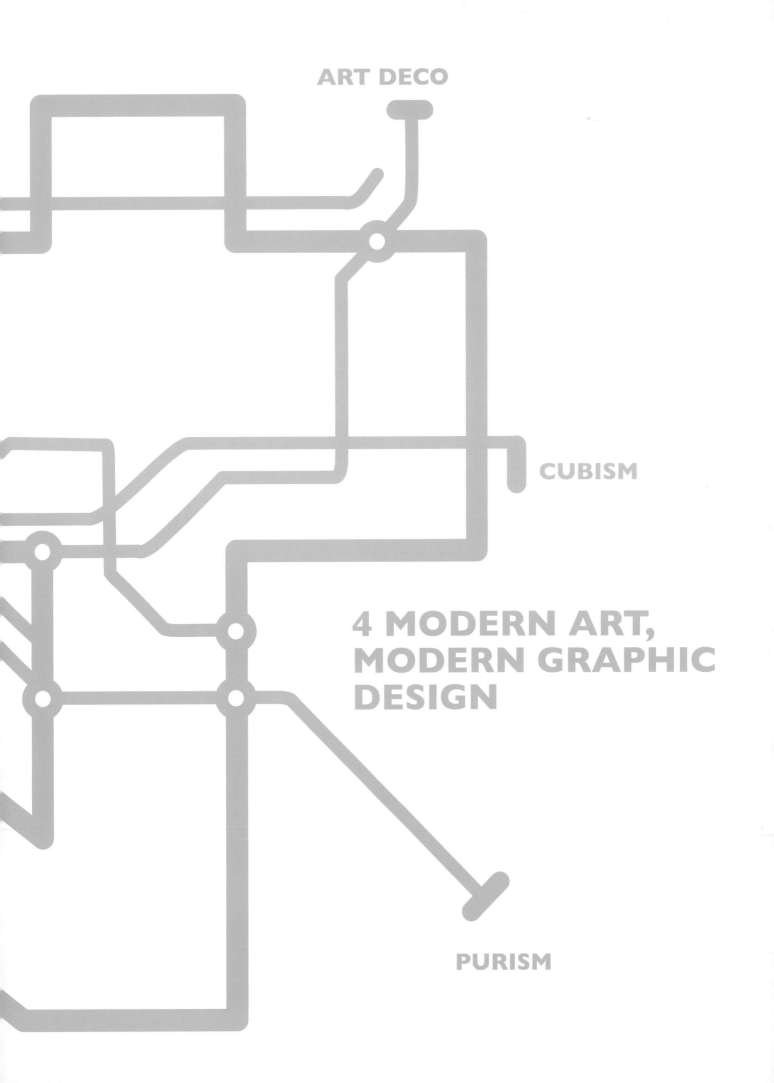

ART DECO

CUBISM

4 MODERN ART,
MODERN GRAPHIC
DESIGN

PURISM

Between 1910 and 1939 a number of modernist art styles were integrated into graphic design. Starting in the 1920s, in particular, a variety of progressive graphic designers in Britain, France, and the United States began absorbing stylistic elements from modern painting movements, especially Cubism and Futurism. Pursuing a number of different formal strategies, almost all of which involved some sort of reductive geometric abstraction, designers such as Edward McKnight Kauffer in England and Cassandre in France sought to integrate advertising design with the sophisticated abstract painting styles of the pre-war years.

Chapter 1 considered the work of a community of artists and designers centered in the Parisian neighborhood called Montmartre. There, artists such as Henri de Toulouse-Lautrec developed professional careers as well as personal relationships that connected poster design and the fine arts. Despite this array of artists and media, the heart of the Montmartre community was devoted to progressive innovation in the art of oil painting. A great deal of painting took place in the artists' residence called the Bâteau-Lavoir (the "Laundry Boat"), so named because of its passing resemblance to the barges used by laundry women on the River Seine. This squalid tenement was the home and workplace of a number of early twentieth-century painters, including Pablo Picasso (1881–1973). Picasso, an expatriate from Spain, was representative of the international character of the art scene that developed in Montmartre after 1900. He lived in the Bâteau-Lavoir from 1904 until 1909, embarking on some of his greatest experimental styles while a resident of Montmartre.

Montparnasse

Beginning early in the 1900s, a second, parallel art scene emerged in another neighborhood on the fringes of Paris, Montparnasse. Between 1900 and 1914, Montparnasse gradually superseded Montmartre as the favored living and working location for avant-garde artists. As was the case in Montmartre, the bohemian community that became entrenched in Montparnasse in the early twentieth century was mainly young and impoverished, so much so that the writer Jean Cocteau (1889–1963) later remarked that "poverty was a luxury" for his fellow artists. In Montparnasse, a residence and studio building called La Ruche ("The Beehive"), located in Passage Danzig, would become famous as the site of three decades of creativity. Originally a wine exhibition building designed by Gustav Eiffel (1832–1923) for the 1900 Universal Exposition, this spiraling structure—hence the name "Beehive"— was relocated to Montparnasse after the exposition closed; there it served as a dormitory for the marginalized young artists who had little money to spend on rent. Montparnasse and La Ruche became a magnet for young artists from across Europe, and folklore developed of youthful foreigners arriving in Paris knowing only two words in French, "Passage Danzig." In 1912, Picasso moved to Montparnasse in search of lower rent, and he remained there until the outbreak of the First World War in 1914. In Montparnasse, Picasso lived near two friends, Georges Braque (1882–1963) and Guillaume Apollinaire (1880–1918), who later would join him in developing the most influential painting style of the twentieth century, **Cubism.**

4.2 Pablo Picasso, *Glass and Bottle of Suze*, 1912. Pasted papers, gouache, and charcoal, 25 x 19¾ in (65.4 x 50.1 cm). Washington University Gallery of Art, St. Louis, MO. University purchase, Kende Sale Fund, 1946.

4.1 Pablo Picasso, *Ma Jolie (Woman with a Zither or Guitar)*, 1911–12. Oil on canvas, 39 x 25 in (100 x 65.4 cm). Museum of Modern Art, New York.

Cubism

The bohemian artists who inhabited Montmartre and Montparnasse early in the twentieth century were, if anything, openly hostile to the creation of commercial art. Part of their self-identification came from the stance that they had rejected mainstream society, and nothing about commercial art, even the outré entertainment posters of Montmartre, appealed to their sensibility. Furthermore, there was no established figure such as Toulouse-Lautrec who could bridge the world of fine art and graphic design. In addition, the special cachet that posters had attained during the "golden age" of the 1880s and 1890s was gone, so young artists had little reason to work in the design fields. Graphic designers were, therefore, not integrated into the prevailing art scene the way they had been in the late nineteenth century. Nonetheless, the fundamental stylistic elements derived for abstract painting by Cubists and others would have a substantial impact on graphic design for decades to come.

The first inkling of the Cubist painting style is visible in works by Picasso and Braque made in 1907, although the term "Cubism" was not invented until the following year. In 1908, the young German émigré art dealer Daniel-Henri Kahnweiler (1884–1979), who consistently sought out new artists from within the Montparnasse circle, staged an exhibition of Braque's abstract paintings. A critic who saw the show disparaged the

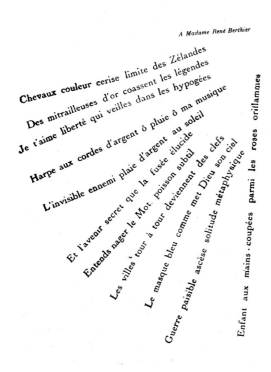

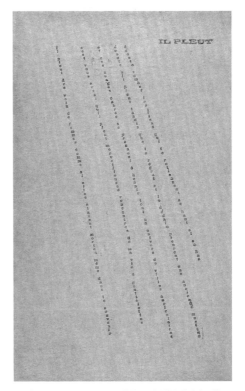

4.3 Guillaume Apollinaire, "Visée" ("Aim") from *Calligrammes*, 1918.

4.4 Guillaume Apollinaire, "Il Pleut" ("It's Raining"), From *Calligrammes*, 1913–16. Private collection.

forms in the paintings as merely "little cubes." From 1908 until 1912, Braque and Picasso worked together to develop the style into its first mature form, now called "Analytic Cubism." In this style, three-dimensional objects are represented on the canvas as two-dimensional abstractions, their rounded forms reduced to hard-edged geometric shapes, called facets. The term "analytic" refers obliquely to this process; the Cubist painter analyzes solid forms and then transfers them to canvas via flat facets that represent the subject from a multiplicity of views.

Picasso's painting *Ma Jolie* (1911; *fig. 4.1*) is an excellent example of fully developed Analytic Cubism. The subject, a portrait of a woman, has been reconfigured as an abstract assortment of overlapping geometric facets. The facets are opaque and blandly colored with a near monochrome effect. In some passages it is hard to distinguish the fragmented figure from the background space, which is also uniformly faceted. The Cubists favored neutral subject matter, mainly still life and portraits, which would not detract from their technical innovations. *Ma Jolie*, which means "My Pretty," could refer to the model herself or to a song that was popular at the time. Analytic Cubist paintings are rife with references to music, which was widely considered by painters to serve as an aesthetic model for abstract painting. Of course, when Analytic Cubism was later used by graphic designers, they had to make adjustments that would allow for the commercial message to be easily grasped by the viewer. Word of the Analytic Cubist style spread quickly in Paris's closely knit art world, and as early as 1912 new groups of Cubist artists had sprung up and started exhibiting to the public.

Around 1912, Picasso and Braque devised a second Cubist technique called Synthetic Cubism. In contrast to the Analytic Cubist penchant for breaking down forms, artists who make

Synthetic Cubist pictures conceive of the image-making progress as flowing in the opposite direction, as the artist "synthesizes" an object out of a mix of abstract parts. Picasso's *Glass and Bottle of Suze* (1912; *fig. 4.2*) is an iconic example of Synthetic Cubism. Here, he has built up a picture of a café table and its associated objects by collaging together scraps of blue and black paper, wallpaper, and newspaper. While the artist has added a touch of shading on the side of the glass, the overall presentation is highly two-dimensional. However, the age-old goal of representational art to reproduce the real world is gently mocked, in that Picasso has pasted an actual label on to his synthesized abstract bottle. In this manner, the Cubist movement was a pioneering force in establishing the significance of the new medium of collage. Synthetic Cubism created a second alternative for artists and designers looking for a structured abstract language with which they could experiment.

Guillaume Apollinaire's *Calligrammes*

As stated above, there was no sustained interest in graphic design among the Cubist painters. However, the poet Guillaume Apollinaire (1880–1918), a friend of many of the Cubist artists, created experimental poetry that would later have a significant impact on graphic design and typography. Apollinaire had been an early champion of the style, and in 1913 he published one of the first critical essays on Cubism, "*Les Peintres Cubists*." Seriously wounded fighting in the First World War, on his return to Paris he published *Calligrammes: Poèmes de la paix et de la guerre 1913–1916*. The term "Calligramme" is a neologism derived from the Greek words for "beautiful writing." Most of Apollinaire's

above: **4.5** Robert Delaunay, *Fenêtres Simultanées sur la Ville (Simultaneous Windows Overlooking the City)*, 1911–12. Oil on canvas and wood, 18 x 23⅝ in (46.3 x 59.9 cm). L&M Services B.V. Amsterdam.

right: **4.6** Sonia Delaunay and Blaise Cendrars, *La Prose du Transsibérien et de la petite Jehanne française (Prose of the Trans-Siberian and of Little Jeanne of France)*, 1913. Musée National d'Art Moderne, Paris.

Calligrammes are a form of "concrete poetry," a type of poem in which the visual structure of the words and the typography are designed to complement the meaning of the text. The materiality of the letters, their graphic shapes, rhythm, and flow all work together to add a visual dimension to the poem.

Abandoning the traditional horizontal flow of text, Apollinaire's *Calligrammes* are clearly influenced by the principles of the Cubist technique. They convey the same sense of fragmented structure and simultaneous experience that can be seen in a Cubist painting. Just as a picture such as *Ma Jolie* appears to show the sitter from multiple angles in one view, so Apollinaire's poems communicate a multitude of feelings and experiences simultaneously. For example, "Visée" ("Aim"), uses a series of autonomous lines to disrupt any linear narrative and replace it with a sense of overlapping verbal images (*fig. 4.3*). These fragmented pieces of the poet's imagination combine to create a meditation on the experience of war. The title refers to a device used to aim artillery shells, and Apollinaire also states ambiguously in the second line that "machine guns of gold are croaking legends." Either of these motifs could be the basis for the structure of the composition, which recalls the raking lines of machine gun fire as well as the triangulation used to mark distant targets for bombardment. The fragmentation implicit in Cubist aesthetics is a perfect vehicle for Apollinaire's ruminations on life and death at the front.

Another *Calligramme*, titled "Il Pleut" ("It's Raining"), proved to be highly influential on later graphic design (*fig. 4.4*). Here, the falling lines appear to represent rain on a window pane, while at the same time reinforcing the rhythmic cadences of the poet's voice. "It's raining women's voices as if they were dead even in memory." This striking first line establishes the lyrical tone of the poem as it evokes the longing implicit in the poet's reminiscences. While the words appear like falling raindrops that are suggestive of Apollinaire's state of mind, they also act as an independent structure that has its own innate beauty separate from its symbolic character. Tragically, Apollinaire died in the Spanish influenza epidemic of 1918, only weeks before the publication of his collection of *Calligrammes*.

Robert and Sonia Terk Delaunay

Apollinaire's association with Cubist painting had developed another dimension in 1913, when he invented the name "**Orphism**" in order to describe the painting of Sonia Terk (1885–1979) and her husband, Robert Delaunay (1885–1941). The Delaunays were at the time experimenting with a synthesis of Analytic Cubist faceting and brilliant color of the sort pioneered in modern painting by French painter Henri Matisse (1869–1954). Apollinaire chose the term "Orphism" in reference to the mythical musician Orpheus, whose music was so beautiful that it could even charm inanimate objects. It was quite common in this era for painters to invoke classical music as a model for abstract painting in an attempt to explain how beauty could exist in a picture that lacked a clear subject matter. Paintings by Robert Delaunay, such as *Simultaneous Windows* (1912; *fig. 4.5*) are almost totally abstract, although a faint hint of the form of the Eiffel

Tower can be made out in the center of the composition. Delaunay attempted to create simultaneous juxtapositions of color, and their prismatic palette positively vibrates with chromatic energy.

In 1913, Sonia Terk Delaunay collaborated with another French poet, Blaise Cendrars (1889–1961), to make one of the most compelling modernist combinations of word and image ever created: their illustrated book *La Prose du Transsibérien et de la petite Jehanne de France* ("Prose of the Trans-Siberian and of Little Jeanne of France"; *fig. 4.6*). On the right side of the nearly 7-foot-long vertically oriented work, Cendrars recounts in a nonlinear fashion two separate train rides he had taken—one through Asia and the other through Europe. Moving backwards and forwards in time, Cendrars's poem evokes the excitement as well as the melancholy nostalgia of travel, as his mistress queries him again and again, "Are we very far from Montmartre?" His thoughts are complemented by the swirling Orphist abstraction that Delaunay painted down the left side of the page. Her passages of brilliant color do not directly illustrate the text, but rather try to complement its feeling in visual terms. The integration of word and image is further accomplished in that Delaunay added patches of color to the right side of the work, so that the words are grouped amid the atmospheric clouds of color. The narrow, elongated format of the work echoes the form of a train or railroad track. The whole being much more than the sum of its parts, word and image combine synergistically to convey great emotion and beauty.

The London Underground

While graphic designers were never integrated into the Cubist movement itself, in later years its formal innovations would open up several exciting new stylistic avenues for commercial art. Designers who used the stylistic elements of Cubism and its related movements are called "modernists," because they integrate modern art into their work. Because of the daring nature of their style, the group of modernist graphic designers in Europe were severely limited in their ability to find consistent, rewarding employment.

One of the first dependable venues where modernist designers could find work was for the London Underground. The first electric underground railway in Europe, the City and South London Railway was completed in London in 1890. Although it was only marginally successful because of its technical limitations, speculators financed several new lines over the following two decades. One of the most successful was the Central London Railway, which opened in 1900 under Oxford Street. Known as the "Twopenny Tube" because of its price, the Central London Railway proved the financial viability of the London Underground. At the same time, technological improvements made the railway safer and cheaper to run. A poster trumpeting the rapid strides made in the first decade of the twentieth century assured passengers that if they rode the Twopenny Tube they would "avoid all anxiety" (*fig. 4.7*). The style of the poster is

eclectic, relying on a framework that separates the space into a series of boxes and rectangles. These spaces were filled with a combination of text and image, with particular emphasis given to five illustrations of decorous passengers making their way through the clean, brightly lit stations and trains. The strong forms of the display type fill out the spaces around the drawings, with the center-left text haphazardly encroaching on the adjacent illustration. Finally, a hand-drawn map of the stations is crammed like an afterthought below the central image.

In 1906, the Central London Railway was consolidated with other underground lines to form the Underground Group, which was administered by a central authority under Deputy Chairman Sir George Gibb (1850–1925). While financial policy was overseen by Sir Albert Stanley (later Baron Ashfield because of his acumen in saving the railway from bankruptcy), Gibb was responsible for overall policy as well as the day-to-day operations of the new conglomerate. Combining a variety of independent railways, each with its own signage and promotional posters, into a distinct new organization proved to be one of the greatest challenges fac-

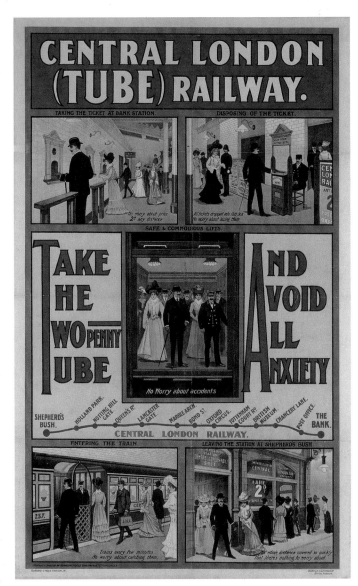

4.7 Anonymous, *Twopenny Tube*, 1901. Poster. London's Transport Museum. © Transport for London.

4.8 Anonymous, Covent Garden roundel, 1907. London's Transport Museum. © Transport for London.

ing the new administration. In 1907, the Underground Group introduced its new trademark, a solid red roundel (*fig. 4.8*). This simple geometric design represented one of the earliest attempts to standardize the signage of the Underground. This example of an original sign marking the Covent Garden station shows how striking the spare geometry and bold red, white, and blue palette appeared to the commuter. However, despite this success in rationalizing the signage, at this early stage little attention was paid to marketing the Underground in a consistent manner.

Frank Pick

Sir George Gibb's assistant Frank Pick (1878–1941), who became the unofficial publicity manager of the Underground Group in 1908, had the vision to become one of the most substantial patrons of modernist posters of the twentieth century. Pick's commitment to bringing new styles to the general public prompted the art historian Nikolas Pevsner to memorialize him in 1942 as the "greatest patron of the arts whom this century has so far produced in England and indeed the ideal patron of our age." While Pevsner's oft repeated comparison to the art patronage of the Medici family of Renaissance Florence is possibly a bit overblown, it is true that Pick recognized the quality of new kinds of graphic design at a time when few others did.

When Pick became the Underground's publicity officer, the Underground Group had not yet devised a consistent promotional strategy. Recognizing that he had a captive audience in the form of hundreds of thousands of commuters every weekday, Pick sought to commission advertising that would convince them to use the Underground for leisure on the weekends. Pick paid special attention to the effective display of these new promotional posters, decreeing that separate hoardings be set up in each station that would only exhibit advertisements for the Underground itself.

Edward McKnight Kauffer

In 1915, Pick made one of his best decisions when he hired Edward McKnight Kauffer (1890–1954) to design posters for the Underground. Born in Montana, Kauffer studied in San Francisco and Chicago before moving to Europe in 1913. In San Francisco, he earned the patronage of an art professor named Joseph McKnight, who financed the young man's initial European sojourn; Kauffer later adopted the middle name McKnight in honor of his patron. In Chicago, Kauffer saw the traveling European art exhibition the "Armory Show," which opened his eyes to the innovative modern abstract styles practiced in Europe. When he left Chicago, Kauffer traveled first to France and Germany, where he was introduced to the *Sachplakat* style while pursuing further training as a fine artist. After the war broke out in 1914, Kauffer planned to return to the United States via England. However, he became enchanted with the city of London and resolved to stay, going so far as to volunteer for the British army—albeit unsuccessfully, because he was a foreign national.

After a series of menial jobs, Kauffer was introduced to Frank Pick by a mutual friend, the English poster designer John Hassall (1868–1948). Pick hired him to promote weekend tourism, and Kauffer's first work for the Underground consisted of posters celebrating the comfort of the train system. *Winter Sales* (*fig. 4.9*) displays how Kauffer integrated provocative Cubist abstraction into his designs. Here, in an image that owes a debt to both Analytic and Synthetic Cubism, Kauffer shows pedestrians battling the inclement London winter. This poster shows unmodeled figures overlaid with no attention to logical three-dimensional space. Their fragmented forms are shaped so as to harmonize with the background. Compare Kauffer's strikingly abstract figures with the conventional drawing in the 1901 Central London (Tube) Railway poster (see fig. 4.7). Kauffer's gift was to know intuitively how to introduce a degree of Cubist abstraction so gradually that it would be accepted by his patrons and viewers.

Kauffer has also done something exciting with the hand-drawn lettering at the bottom of *Winter Sales*, where he has designed the word "Underground" to flicker back and forth in the viewer's eye between two and three dimensions, as the shading momentarily creates a sense of sculptural relief. This type of three-dimensional lettering was quite popular in the nineteenth

century as display type, but Kauffer has here infused it with Cubism so that the shadows sometimes break away from the shape of the letter. It was largely due to Kauffer's own influence that the Tube-riding public of London had by 1924 become accustomed to this type of innovative style in graphic design at a time when the vast majority of the population would have rejected Cubism as an important type of painting. Kauffer remained one of Pick's top designers for decades, and eventually created over 140 posters for the Underground.

Even when he was having more success as a poster artist than as a painter, Kauffer maintained his commitment to the latter vocation. He joined a collection of like-minded modernists called the "London Group," who were dedicated to exploring the Cubist style. Later, he helped to found the "X Group," while also promoting experimental abstract films in London. However, in the 1920s Kauffer decided to give up his work in the fine arts and devote himself to his commercial career. "Gradually I saw the futility of trying to paint and do advertising at the same time," he remembered in 1937. While Kauffer himself was adamant in declaring that graphic design and fine art styles were interchange-

4.9 Edward McKnight Kauffer, *Winter Sales*, 1921. Poster. Lithograph, 39 x 24 in (100.9 x 61.5 cm). Museum of Modern Art, New York

able, he found few people who shared his position. On the one hand, other painters were suspicious of his success with the Underground, mainly because abstract artists at this time sought more than anything else not to be another instrument of industrial capitalism. It was an important part of modern art ideology to separate one's work from the crass realm of commercial culture, as Picasso and Braque had done. At the same time, Kauffer's advertising clients were skeptical of anything that seemed too radical to them, and the artist's association with modern painting groups did not elevate him in their eyes. Throughout his career, Kauffer felt a responsibility to bring gradually more and more edgy modern styles to the British public, and he led a number of advertisers into an embrace of Cubist design.

The modernist influence became gradually more visible in the 1920s, as Pick committed the Underground to a unique and sustainable visual style. He wanted all of the promotional materials overseen by his office to share the startling freshness of Kauffer's Cubist idiom. Posters such as *Move to Edgware* (*fig. 4.10*), by William Kermode, generally do not delve quite so far into abstraction as Kauffer's work does, yet they maintain

something of the spare, unmodeled forms and geometric regularity of his work. Kermode employs Cubist abstraction in the opposite manner of Kauffer—rather than showing a festive crowd, he invokes geometric repetition to symbolize a dismal urban housing block. He juxtaposes this grim scene with a more traditionally illustrated slice of countryside resplendent with color and sunshine. This poster is exemplary of how the English railways promoted suburban living after the First World War, when Britain was facing a tremendous shortage of housing as well as an almost unmanageable density in the city center.

A poster for the Underground designed in 1924 by Austin Cooper (1890–1964), *It Is Warmer Down Below* (*fig. 4.11*), demonstrates the artist's awareness of the Orphist "color cubism" created by Robert and Sonia Terk Delaunay. The central image in the poster is of a roaring fire made up of abstract Cubist facets. Brilliant color makes the square facets seem to dance with energy, shimmering in a range of hues. In an attempt to make a virtue out of necessity, the crowded tunnels of the Tube are trumpeted for their comfortable indoor climate during wintertime.

4.10 William Kermode, *Move to Edgware*, 1925. Poster. London's Transport Museum. © Transport for London.

4.11 Austin Cooper, *It Is Warmer Down Below*, 1924. Poster. London's Transport Museum. © Transport for London.

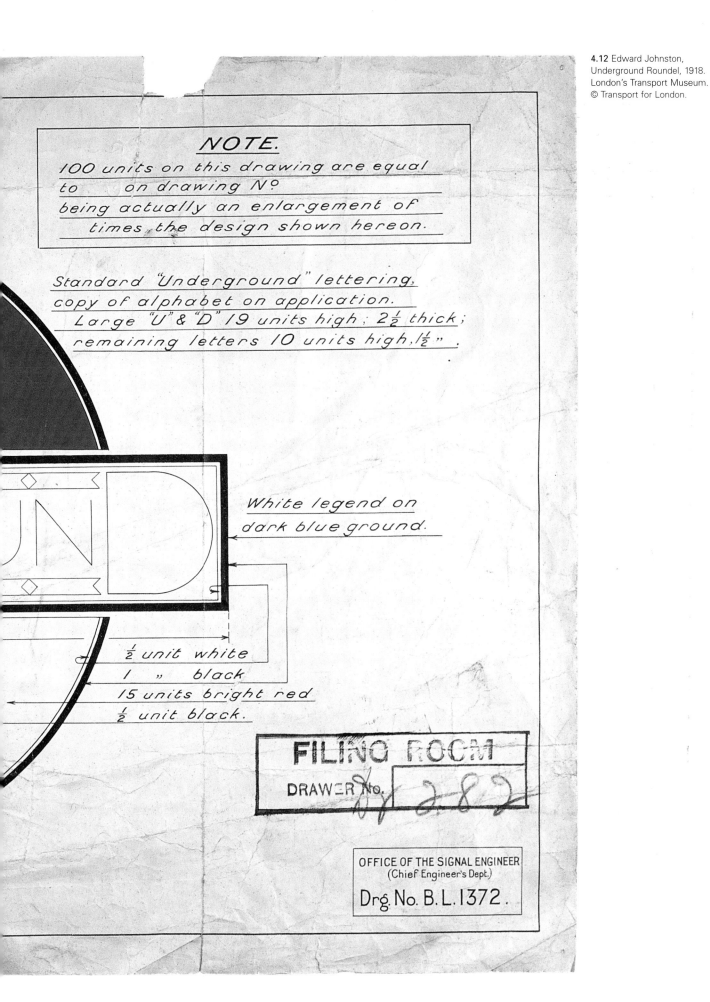

NOTE.

100 units on this drawing are equal to ___ on drawing N°. ___ being actually an enlargement of ___ times, the design shown hereon.

Standard "Underground" lettering, copy of alphabet on application.
Large "U" & "D" 19 units high; $2\frac{1}{2}$ thick; remaining letters 10 units high, $1\frac{1}{2}$".

White legend on dark blue ground.

$\frac{1}{2}$ unit white
1 „ black
15 units bright red
$\frac{1}{2}$ unit black.

FILING ROOM
DRAWER No.

OFFICE OF THE SIGNAL ENGINEER
(Chief Engineer's Dept.)
Drg. No. B.L. 1372.

ABCDEFGHIJ
KLMNOPQRS
TUVWXYZ
abcdefghijk
lmnopqrstuv
wxyz
£1234567890
&,.;:'''""?!-*()

4.13 Edward Johnston, Johnston Sans
Typeface, 1916. London's Transport
Museum. © Transport for London.

Signage and Visual Identity

Pick's second major innovation in managing the visual identity
of the Underground was to complement his promotional posters
with a standardized and easily legible system of signage.
In 1916, he commissioned the typographer Edward Johnston
(1872–1944) to devise a new typeface for the Tube. Johnston
developed an eponymous face (that is, he named it after himself),
Johnston Sans (*fig. 4.13*). As the name suggests, Johnston Sans
uses no serifs, although it does maintain the basic proportions of
seriffed type. The plain block letters demonstrate almost no variation in stroke width. This spare display type is highly geometric,
as Johnston attempted to create lettering that would be legible in
the blink of an eye from a passing train. But the interest in geometry says more about the stylish nature of the type than about its
legibility. The "O," for example, is a perfect circle for design reasons, and could have been easily rendered more legible with some
added stress or adjustment to the shape. However, it was more
important to Johnston and Pick that the lettering provided the
same sense of glamour and modernity that the abstract promotional posters emphasized. A more traditional type of lettering
would have made the posters stand out too much—appearing
somehow radical—from the overall visual style. It is important to

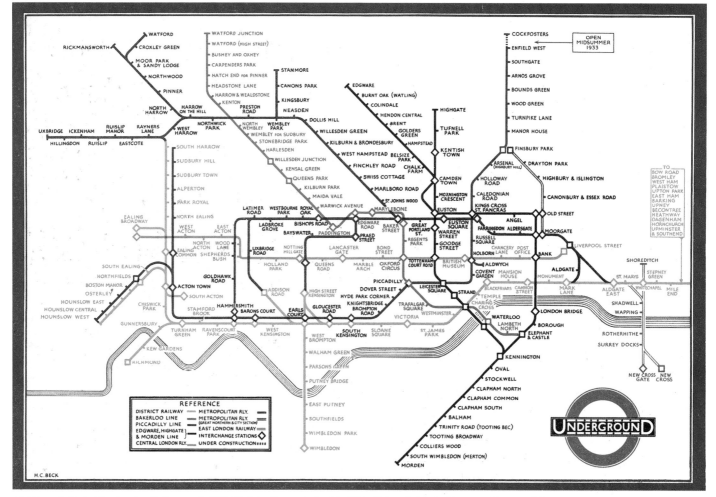

4.14 Harry C. Beck, Map, London Underground, 1931–33. Color lithograph, 6 x 9 in (157 x 226 mm). London Transport Museum. © Transport for London.

note how Pick commissioned works that reinforced the strengths of the Underground—its high technology and status as an exciting modern experience.

The rounded "O" of Johnston Sans also proved to be well matched to the existing trademark of the Underground, the circular roundel. In 1918, Pick commissioned Johnston again, this time to update the roundel and expand on its possibilities as the basis for signage. Johnston updated the design by transforming the solid red circle into a white circle with a red band around it, a bull's eye, and outlining both the red band and the bar that cuts across the roundel with a strong black contour line (*fig. 4.12*). The most important part of this update was a change in the proportions between the bull's eye and the bar, making the former smaller so that it no longer visually overwhelmed the bar and the lettering on it. Johnston kept the palette of white lettering on a blue bar, although he substituted his own typeface for the original one.

The reconfigured bull's eye was to become one of the most recognizable trademarks ever invented, and in the 1930s became the subject of a witty promotional poster. In 1939, when Pick had become the overall head of London Transport, he commissioned the famous expatriate American Surrealist Man Ray (1890–1977) to devise a poster for the Underground. Man Ray played upon the "Surreal" aspects of the bull's eye, likening it to a planet floating in outer space (*fig. 4.15*). At the same time, Pick proved that he had not lost his eye for daring work even as he approached his retirement.

After he became the managing director of London Transport, Pick sought to extend his consistent visual style to all aspects of the system. He oversaw the construction of new stations and the decoration of trains, with a close eye on details. One of the first patrons to implement the theory of a total design style, Pick even hired artists to design the upholstery for the seats in trains and buses. After the Underground network grew in complexity following a massive expansion in the 1920s, Pick commissioned Harry Beck (1903–1974) to devise a simple yet comprehensive map of the different routes. Basing his work on diagrams of electric circuits, which use color and geometry to simplify a more complex and variable system, Beck created a map in between 1931 and 1933 that displayed the tentacles of the system in a logical, predictable diagram (*fig. 4.14*). First introduced as a leaflet, the finished map rapidly became one of the most famous examples of information management ever devised. Beck successfully reduced the irregular layout of the system into a grid-based design that showed each route on a horizontal, vertical, or diagonal axis. Each station and interchange was clearly marked. Beck's innovation has proved to be a lasting one, as similar maps are still used in subway systems around the world.

Beck's design was somewhat anticipated by the route network shown on a 1929 Belgian poster by the Swiss-born artist Leo Marfurt (1894–1977). This image shows a glamorous scene of people boarding a train, conceived in a style that resonates with Synthetic Cubist collage (*fig. 4.16*). Below the image there is a simple map of the major Belgian railway lines. In this manner, Marfurt merged the two major themes of railway marketing: the glamour of the modern city and the efficient rationality that is its greatest claim to fame.

LONDON TRANSPORT-   **-KEEPS LONDON GOING**

4.15a, b Man Ray, *London Transport Keeps London Going*, 1939. Poster. London's Transport Museum. © Transport for London.

4.16 Leo Marfurt, *Chemins de Fer Belges (Belgian Railways)*, 1929. Lithograph. City Archives/Stadsarchief, Ghent.

Futurism

The exciting possibilities of the Cubist style were quickly absorbed by other artists. A group of Italian poets, musicians, and painters led by Filippo Marinetti (1876–1944), who called themselves the **Futurists**, were among the most proficient adopters of the Cubist idiom. Futurism was founded in 1909, when Marinetti, who had spent the years 1893–6 studying in Paris, published his "Futurist Manifesto" in the French newspaper *Le Figaro* (*fig. 4.17*). This essay, which established the philosophical basis for all kinds of Futurist art and activism, was one of the first attempts by an artistic group to explain its own work conceptually before its members had created many concrete examples. Futurism was not intended as an artistic movement like Cubism; rather, Marinetti called for a revolutionary change in Italian society, one that would free the country from its storied Classical history and allow it to compete in the modern industrial world. "It is from Italy that we launch through the world this violently upsetting incendiary manifesto of ours. With it, today, we establish Futurism. … For too long Italy has been a dealer in secondhand clothes. We mean to free her from the numberless museums that cover her like so many graveyards." The "Futurist Manifesto" was followed in succeeding years by a series of additional treatises that explained Futurist concepts of music, painting, and literature. Additionally, in 1911 and 1912, Marinetti made the rounds of European capitals promoting the group and its work, leading to Futurism's high profile among the avant-garde.

In 1910, Marinetti and his associates began organizing riotous Futurist evenings, where the night's entertainment was likely to include a mixture of iconoclastic literary readings, political speeches, "noise" music, and other provocations. One sold-out performance of Futurist music held in Rome in 1914 ended in a violent melee, when the Futurists waded into the disapproving crowd "with blows, slaps, and cudgels." These anarchic performances would, in fact, exercise an enormous influence on the subsequent Zurich Dada movement (see Chapter 3).

Unlike the Cubists, who had isolated themselves from the design arts, the more polemical Futurists wanted to reach the public through a variety of printed works. Partly derived from his knowledge of French Symbolist aesthetics, Marinetti created some of the most daringly experimental typography and graphic design of the early twentieth century. In 1912 he published the first Futurist book, *Zang Tumb Tumb* (*fig. 4.18*). The text is based on Marinetti's experience in the Balkan Wars of 1912–13, when he had served as a soldier. The title words "Zang Tumb Tumb" are an example of Marinetti's use of onomatopoeia, whereby the sound of the word indicates its meaning, in this case the roar of artillery at the Battle of Adrianopolis. Marinetti idealized warfare as a force that could cleanse Italy of its obsession with the past and lead it into a modern industrial future. The cover of *Zang Tumb Tumb* displays a jumble of different typefaces and sizes scattered across the page. There is no clear axis to this non-hierarchical layout; rather, the structure of the composition visually reinforces the dynamism and chaos of war. As was the case with Apollinaire's *Calligrammes*, the text is used as a vehicle for traditional meaning while simultaneously functioning as a graphic signifier.

"Words in Freedom"

In the manifesto titled *Destruction of Syntax/Imagination without Strings/Words in Freedom*, Marinetti espoused his plans for changes in book design. "I initiate a typographical revolution aimed at the bestial, nauseating idea of the book … My revolution is aimed at the so-called typographical harmony of the page, which is contrary to the flux and reflux, the leaps and bursts of style that run through the page." Marinetti felt that traditional literary forms such as the book were dead, that their rigid, static qualities made them unable to express the excitement generated by modern industrial society. He wanted to replace the book with his invention *parole in libertà* (literally, "words in freedom"). Rejecting any and all conventional rules of grammar, punctuation, and syntax, Marinetti wanted typography expressively to reinforce the dynamism of the text—words become images. The inner page from *Zang Tumb Tumb* reproduced here demonstrates Marinetti's call for graphic designs that jump off the page with the same kinetic energy of the experience of war expressed by the text. Like Apollinaire in his *Calligrammes*, here Marinetti is making use of the materiality of the words to reinforce his message in two different ways: first, the text forms the shape of a Turkish balloon like those he saw in the battle; second, the swirling movement of type is suggestive of the soldier–poet's experience of war. Through his extensive publications, Marinetti sought to open up for Futurism a new space for artists that they had never before engaged—the publicity of the mass media.

The Futurist use of a consistent visual style that expressed the group's love of speed and dynamism extended even to their stationery. In 1918, Giacomo Balla's (1871–1958) abstract drawing of a kinetic, abstract "man of the future" became the basis for a dramatic letterhead (*fig. 4.19*), in which the drawing and banner have taken over fully half of the page. While the drawing was made by Balla, the letterhead references the Futurist painter Umberto Boccioni (1882–1916) in the phrase "Il pugno di Boccioni" ("a punch by Boccioni"). By 1918, Boccioni had become a martyr to the Futurist cause when he was killed in the First World War. Each communication written on this stationery, such as the letter by Marinetti reproduced here, served as a strong visual statement of Futurist principles. Because the letterhead overwhelms the available space left for writing, letters from Marinetti could communicate more via the standardized parts of this striking stationery than through the specifics of his written message. Like most of the printed matter produced by the Futurists (as well as other avant-garde groups such as Dada), this stationery was made using letterpress techniques. Having originated in the fifteenth century with Gutenberg, the letterpress technique was inexpensive and accessible, though lacking any ideological connection with the machine world idolized by the Futurists. The late nineteenth century had witnessed the introduction of photomechanical engraving, the technology that allowed hand-drawn illustrations to be reproduced alongside text, as in the Futurist example shown here. While the **halftone** process, which allowed photographs to be reproduced via letterpress, had also been introduced in the late nineteenth century, it was not widely adopted by the avant-garde until the 1920s (see Chapter 5).

55ᵉ Année — 3ᵉ Série — N° 51   Le Numéro avec le Supplément = SEINE & SEINE-ET-OISE : 15 centimes — DÉPARTEMENTS : 20 centimes   Samedi 20 Février 1909

Gaston CALMETTE
Directeur-Gérant

RÉDACTION — ADMINISTRATION
26, rue Drouot, Paris (9ᵉ Arrᵗ)

POUR LA PUBLICITÉ
S'ADRESSER, 26, RUE DROUOT
A L'HÔTEL DU « FIGARO »
ET POUR LES ANNONCES ET RÉCLAMES
Chez MM. LAGRANGE, CERF & Cⁱᵉ
8, place de la Bourse

LE FIGARO

« Loué par ceux-ci, blâmé par ceux-là, me moquant des sots, bravant les méchants, je me hâte
de rire de tout... de peur d'être obligé d'en pleurer. » (BEAUMARCHAIS.)

H. DE VILLEMESSANT
Fondateur

RÉDACTION — ADMINISTRATION
26, rue Drouot, Paris (9ᵉ Arrᵗ)

ABONNEMENT
	Trois mois	Six mois	Un an
Seine et Seine-et-Oise	9 fr.	18 fr.	36 fr.
Départements	13 75	27 50	75
Union postale	21 50	43	85

On s'abonne dans tous les Bureaux de Poste
de France et d'Algérie.

Le Futurisme

M. Marinetti, le jeune poète italien et français, au talent remarquable et fougueux, que de retentissantes manifestations ont fait connaître dans tous les pays latins, vient d'une pléiade d'enthousiastes disciples, vient de fonder l'École du « Futurisme » dont les théories dépassent en hardiesse toutes celles des écoles antérieures ou contemporaines. Le Figaro qui a déjà servi de tribune à plusieurs d'entre elles, et non des moindres, offre aujourd'hui à ses lecteurs le manifeste des « Futuristes ». Est-il besoin de dire que nous laissons au signataire toute la responsabilité de ses idées singulièrement audacieuses et d'une outrance souvent injuste pour des choses éminemment respectables et, heureusement, partout respectées ? Mais il était intéressant de réserver à nos lecteurs la primeur de cette manifestation, quel que soit le jugement qu'on porte sur elle.

Nous avions veillé toute la nuit, mes amis et moi, sous des lampes de mosquée dont les coupoles de cuivre aussi ajourées que notre âme avaient pourtant des cœurs électriques. Et tout en piétinant notre native paresse sur d'opulents tapis persans, nous avions discuté aux frontières extrêmes de la logique et griffé le papier de démentes écritures.

Un immense orgueil gonflait nos poitrines à nous sentir debout tous seuls, comme des phares ou comme des sentinelles avancées, face à l'armée des étoiles ennemies, qui campent dans leurs bivouacs célestes. Seuls avec les mécaniciens dans les infernales chaufferies des grands navires, seuls avec les noirs fantômes qui fourragent dans le ventre rouge des locomotives affolées, seuls avec les ivrognes battant des ailes contre les murs !

Et nous voilà brusquement distraits par le roulement des énormes tramways à double étage, qui passent sursautants, bariolés de lumières, tels des bivouacs en fête que le Pô débordé ébranle tout à coup et déracine, pour les entraîner, sur les cascades et les remous d'un déluge, jusqu'à la mer.

Puis le silence s'aggrava. Comme nous écoutions la prière exténuée du vieux canal et crisser les os des palais moribonds dans leur barbe de verdure, nous entendîmes sous nos fenêtres les automobiles affamées.

— Allons, dis-je, mes amis ! Partons ! Enfin, la Mythologie et l'Idéal mystique sont surpassés. Nous allons assister à la naissance du Centaure et nous verrons bientôt voler les premiers anges ! — Il faudra ébranler les portes de la vie pour en essayer les gonds et les verrous ! Partons ! Voilà bien le premier soleil levant sur la terre !... Rien n'égale la splendeur de son épée rouge qui s'escrime pour la première fois dans nos ténèbres millénaires.

Nous nous approchâmes des trois machines renâclantes pour flatter leur poitrail. Je m'allongeai sur la mienne...

Le grand balai de la folie nous arracha à nous-mêmes et nous poussa à travers les rues escarpées et profondes comme des torrents desséchés. Çà et là, des lampes malheureuses, aux fenêtres, nous enseignaient à mépriser nos yeux mathématiques.

— Le flair, criai-je, le flair suffit aux fauves !...

Sortons de la Sagesse comme d'une gangue hideuse et entrons, comme des fruits pimentés d'orgueil, dans la bouche immense et torse du vent !... Donnons-nous à manger à l'Inconnu, non par désespoir, mais simplement pour enrichir les insondables réservoirs de l'Absurde !

Comme j'avais dit ces mots, je virai brusquement sur moi-même avec l'ivresse folle des caniches qui se mordent la queue, et voilà tout à coup que deux cyclistes me désapprouvèrent, titubant devant moi comme deux raisonnements persuasifs et pourtant contradictoires. Leur ondoiement stupide discutait sur mon terrain... Quel ennui ! Pouah !... Je coupai court et, par dégoût, je me flanquai dans un fossé...

Oh ! maternel fossé, à moitié plein d'une eau vaseuse ! Fossé d'usine ! J'ai savouré à pleine bouche la boue fortifiante !

Le visage masqué de la bonne boue des usines, pleine de scories de métal, de sueurs inutiles et de suie céleste, portant...

Manifeste du Futurisme

1. Nous voulons chanter l'amour du danger, l'habitude de l'énergie et de la témérité.

2. Les éléments essentiels de notre poésie seront le courage, l'audace et la révolte.

3. La littérature ayant jusqu'ici magnifié l'immobilité pensive, l'extase et le sommeil, nous voulons exalter le mouvement agressif, l'insomnie fiévreuse, le pas gymnastique, le saut périlleux, la gifle et le coup de poing.

4. Nous déclarons que la splendeur du monde s'est enrichie d'une beauté nouvelle : la beauté de la vitesse. Une automobile de course avec son coffre orné de gros tuyaux, tels des serpents à l'haleine explosive... une automobile rugissante, qui a l'air de courir sur de la mitraille, est plus belle que la Victoire de Samothrace.

5. Nous voulons chanter l'homme qui tient le volant, dont la tige idéale traverse la Terre, lancée elle-même sur le circuit de son orbite.

6. Il faut que le poète se dépense avec chaleur, éclat et prodigalité, pour augmenter la ferveur enthousiaste des éléments primordiaux.

7. Il n'y a plus de beauté que dans la lutte. Pas de chef-d'œuvre sans un caractère agressif. La poésie doit être un assaut violent contre les forces inconnues, pour les sommer de se coucher devant l'homme.

8. Nous sommes sur le promontoire extrême des siècles !... À quoi bon regarder derrière nous, du moment qu'il nous faut défoncer les vantaux mystérieux de l'Impossible ? Le Temps et l'Espace sont morts hier. Nous vivons déjà dans l'absolu, puisque nous avons déjà créé l'éternelle vitesse omniprésente.

9. Nous voulons glorifier la guerre, — seule hygiène du monde, — le militarisme, le patriotisme, le geste destructeur des anarchistes, les belles Idées qui tuent, et le mépris de la femme.

10. Nous voulons démolir les musées, les bibliothèques, combattre le moralisme, le féminisme et toutes les lâchetés opportunistes et utilitaires.

11. Nous chanterons les grandes foules agitées par le travail, le plaisir ou la révolte ; les ressacs multicolores et polyphoniques des révolutions dans les capitales modernes ; la vibration nocturne des arsenaux et des chantiers sous leurs violentes lunes électriques ; les gares gloutonnes avaleuses de serpents qui fument ; les usines suspendues aux nuages par les ficelles de leurs fumées ; les ponts aux bonds de gymnastes lancés sur la coutellerie diabolique des fleuves ensoleillés ; les paquebots aventureux flairant l'horizon ; les locomotives au grand poitrail qui piaffent sur les rails, tels d'énormes chevaux d'acier bridés de longs tuyaux, et le vol glissant des aéroplanes, dont l'hélice a des claquements de drapeaux et des applaudissements de foule enthousiaste.

C'est en Italie que nous lançons ce manifeste de violence culbutante et incendiaire, par lequel nous fondons aujourd'hui le Futurisme, parce que nous voulons délivrer l'Italie de sa gangrène de professeurs, d'archéologues, de cicérones et d'antiquaires.

L'Italie a été trop longtemps le marché des brocanteurs qui fournissaient au monde le mobilier de nos ancêtres, sans cesse renouvelé et soigneusement mutilé pour simuler le travail des tarés vénérables. Nous voulons débarrasser l'Italie des musées innombrables qui la couvrent d'innombrables cimetières.

Musées, cimetières !... Identiques vraiment dans leur sinistre coudoiement de corps qui ne se connaissent pas. Dortoirs publics où l'on dort à jamais côte à côte avec des êtres haïs ou inconnus. Férocité réciproque des peintres et des sculpteurs s'entre-tuant à coups de lignes et de couleurs dans le même musée.

Qu'on y fasse une visite chaque année comme on va voir ses morts une fois par an !... Nous pouvons bien l'admettre !... Qu'on dépose même des fleurs une fois par an aux pieds de la Joconde, nous le concevons !... Mais que l'on aille promener quotidiennement dans les musées nos tristesses, nos courages fragiles et notre inquiétude, nous ne l'admettons pas !...

Admirer un vieux tableau, c'est verser notre sensibilité dans une urne funéraire au lieu de la lancer en avant par jets violents de création et d'action. Voulez-vous donc gâcher ainsi vos meilleures forces dans une admiration inutile du passé, dont vous sortez forcément épuisés, amoindris, piétinés ?

En vérité, la fréquentation quotidienne des musées, des bibliothèques et des académies (ces cimetières d'efforts perdus, ces calvaires de rêves crucifiés, ces registres d'élans brisés !...) est pour les artistes ce qu'est la tutelle prolongée des parents pour des jeunes gens intelligents, ivres de leur talent et de leur volonté ambitieuse.

Pour les moribonds, les invalides et les prisonniers, passe encore. C'est peut-être un baume à leurs blessures, que l'admirable passé, du moment que l'avenir leur est interdit... Mais nous n'en voulons pas, nous, les jeunes, les forts et les vivants futuristes !

Viennent donc les bons incendiaires aux doigts carbonisés !... Les voici ! Les voici !... Et boutez donc le feu aux rayons des bibliothèques ! Détournez le cours des canaux pour inonder les caveaux des musées !... Oh ! qu'elles nagent à la dérive, les toiles glorieuses ! À vous les pioches et les marteaux !... sapez les fondements des villes vénérables.

Les plus âgés d'entre nous ont trente ans : nous avons donc au moins dix ans pour accomplir notre tâche. Quand nous aurons quarante ans, que de plus jeunes et plus vaillants que nous veuillent bien nous jeter au panier comme des manuscrits inutiles !... Ils viendront contre nous de très loin, de partout, en bondissant sur la cadence légère de leurs premiers poèmes, griffant l'air de leurs doigts crochus, et humant, aux portes des académies, la bonne odeur de nos esprits pourrissants déjà promis aux catacombes des bibliothèques.

Mais nous ne serons pas là. Ils nous trouveront enfin, par une nuit d'hiver, en pleine campagne, sous un triste hangar pianoté par la pluie monotone, accroupis près de nos aéroplanes trépidants, en train de chauffer nos mains sur le misérable feu que feront nos livres d'aujourd'hui flambant gaiement sous le vol étincelant de leurs images.

Ils s'ameuteront autour de nous, haletants d'angoisse et de dépit, et, tous, exaspérés par notre fier courage infatigable, s'élanceront pour nous tuer, avec d'autant plus de haine que leur cœur sera ivre d'amour et d'admiration pour nous. Et la forte et la saine Injustice éclatera radieusement dans leurs yeux. Car l'art ne peut être que violence, cruauté et injustice.

Les plus âgés d'entre nous ont vingt-cinq ans, et pourtant nous avons déjà gaspillé des trésors, des trésors de force, d'amour, de courage et d'âpre volonté, à la hâte, en délire, sans compter, à tour de bras, à perdre haleine.

Regardez-nous ! Nous ne sommes pas essoufflés... Notre cœur n'a pas la moindre fatigue ! Car il s'est nourri de feu, de haine et de vitesse ! Cela vous étonne ? C'est que vous ne vous souvenez même pas d'avoir vécu ! — Debout sur la cime du monde, nous lançons encore une fois le défi aux étoiles !

Vos objections ? Assez ! assez ! Je les connais ! C'est entendu ! Nous savons bien ce que notre belle et fausse intelligence nous affirme. — Nous ne sommes, dit-elle, que le résumé et le prolongement de nos ancêtres. — Peut-être ! soit !... Qu'importe ?... Mais nous ne voulons pas entendre ! Gardez-vous de répéter ces mots infâmes ! Levez plutôt la tête !

Debout sur la cime du monde, nous lançons encore une fois le défi insolent aux étoiles !

F.-T. Marinetti.

4.17 Filippo Marinetti, *The Futurist Manifesto*, 1909.

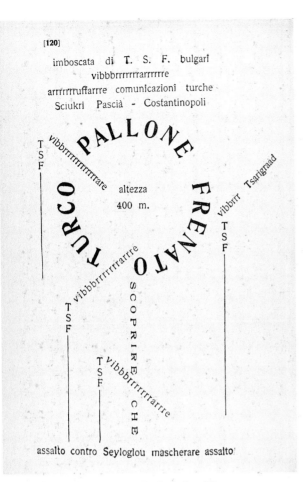

4.18 Filippo Marinetti, *Zang Tumb Tumb*, 1914, p. 120.
Private Collection.

4.19 Giacomo Balla, *Movimento Futurista*, 1918.
Collection Elaine Lustig Cohen.

Lacerba

Another outlet for Futurist typographical experiments came in the form of a collaboration with the editors of the radical newspaper *Lacerba*. Founded in Florence in 1913 by Giovanni Papini (1881–1956) and Ardengo Soffici (1879–1964), *Lacerba* combined political and cultural essays that were designed to shock and provoke: articles such as the one titled "In Praise of Prostitution" almost led to the editors' imprisonment. After Papini and Soffici repeatedly insulted the Milan-based Futurists starting in 1911, in true Futurist style a series of riotous fistfights broke out when the members of the group visited Florence. By 1913, a détente of sorts had been reached, and for almost a year *Lacerba* became closely allied with the Futurist cause. The newspaper was remade in a more aggressive style, complete with a 6-inch-high masthead that blared the name *Lacerba* at the reader (*fig. 4.21*). Inside, the anarchic energy of Futurist typography hit the reader with full force. "Words in freedom" were used to their full effect, as a series of essays were printed with the same spirit of aggressive chaos, mixing sizes and shapes of letters, while lines of text were organized into dramatically kinetic compositions. Just as the colorful abstractions of Sonia Terk Delaunay had complemented the romantic musings of Blaise Cendrars, so here the frenzied typography served to reinforce the Futurists' war-like tone. The Futurists' alliance with *Lacerba* ended in bitter recrimination, and the newspaper continued printing independently until Italy joined the First World War in 1915. Because the war represented the realization of their goal for Italy, Papini and Soffici immediately shut down the newspaper and left to join the Italian army.

Futurist artists made the free typography and energetic wordplay of "words in freedom" a sort of house style, and it was expanded on in other media. A mix of tempera paints and collage on cardboard by Carlo Carra (1881–1966), called *Patriotic Celebration Free Word Painting* (*fig. 4.20*), was designed to recall the sight of leaflets being dropped from a plane. The picture was completed in 1914, at a time when the Futurists were engaged in their "Interventionist" actions designed to foment first revolution, and then the entrance of Italy into the First World War. During this period, Futurist art works were a modest accompaniment to provocative public disturbances, such as the time that the Futurists disrupted a concert by burning an Austrian flag amid the audience. Here, Carra's combination of fragmented words and Italian flags is melded to a kinetic structure, the concentric circles of text pierced repeatedly by powerful diagonal lines, the latter called "lines of force" by the Futurists.

"We declare that the splendor of the world has been enriched by a new beauty: the beauty of speed." When Marinetti wrote these words in the "Futurist Manifesto," he indicated his desire to transform all of the arts into more dynamic forms. The Futurists had their most immediate impact on graphic design through their transformation of Cubist painting into a more vital, energetic style. Umberto Boccioni, perhaps the most important Futurist painter, made works such as *Dynamism of a Football Player* (*fig. 4.22*), which shows how decisively the Futurists were able to remake Cubism to fit their ideological and visual goals. Where Picasso's Cubist works appear static and rigid, Boccioni's painting has a powerful kinetic element. This apparent movement was

4.20 Carlo Carra, *Patriotic Celebration Free Word Painting*, 1914. Collage on cardboard, tempera.

LACERBA

Periodico quindicinale   *Qui non si canta al modo delle rane.*

Anno I, n. 1   *Firenze, 1 gennaio 1913*   Costa 4 soldi

CONTIENE : Introibo — PAPINI, Il giorno e la notte — SOFFICI, Contro i deboli — SOFFICI, Razzi — TAVOLATO, L'anima di Weininger — PALAZZESCHI, Il mendicante — Sciocchezzaio (DE SANCTIS, MAZZONI).

INTROIBO

1.

Le lunghe dimostrazioni razionali non convincono quasi mai quelli che non son convinti prima — per quelli che son d'accordo bastano accenni, tesi, assiomi.

2.

Un pensiero che non può esser detto in poche parole non merita d'esser detto.

3.

Chi non riconosce agli uomini d'ingegno, agli inseguitori, agli artisti il pieno diritto di contraddirsi da un giorno all'altro non è degno di guardarli.

4.

Tutto è nulla, nel mondo, tranne il genio. Le nazioni vadano in isfacelo, crepino di dolore i popoli se ciò è necessario perchè un uomo creatore viva e vinca.

Le religioni, le morali, le leggi hanno la sola scusa nella fiacchezza e canaglieria degli uomini e nel loro desiderio di star più tranquilli e di conservare alla meglio i loro aggruppamenti. Ma c'è un piano superiore — dell'uomo solo, intelligente e spregiudicato — in cui tutto è permesso e tutto è legittimo. Che lo spirito almeno sia libero !

6.

Libertà. Non chiediamo altro ; chiediamo soltanto la condizione elementare perchè l'io spirituale possa vivere. E anche se dovessimo pagarlo coll'imbecillità saremo liberi.

7.

Arte : giustificazione del mondo — contrappeso nella bilancia tragica dell'esistenza. Nostra ragione di essere, di accettar tutto con gioia.

8.

Sappiamo troppo, comprendiamo troppo : siamo a un bivio. O ammazzarsi — o combattere, ridere e cantare. Scegliamo questa via — per ora.

9.

La vita è tremenda, spesso. Viva la vita !

10.

Ogni cosa va chiamata col suo nome. Le cose di cui non si ha il coraggio di parlare francamente dinanzi agli altri sono spesso le più importanti nella vita di tutti.

11.

Noi amiamo la verità fino al paradosso (incluso) — la vita fino al male (incluso) — e l'arte fino alla stranezza (inclusa).

12.

Di serietà e di buon senso si fa oggi un tale spreco nel mondo, che noi siamo costretti a farne una rigorosa economia. In una società di pinzocheri anche il cinico è necessario.

13.

Noi siamo inclinati a stimare il bozzetto più della composizione, il frammento più della statua, l'aforisma più del trattato, e il genio nascosto e disgraziato ai grand'uomini olimpici e perfetti venerati dai professori.

14.

Queste pagine non hanno affatto lo scopo nè di far piacere, nè d'istruire, nè di risolvere con ponderatezza le più gravi questioni del mondo. Sarà questo un foglio stonato, urtante, spiacevole e personale. Sarà uno sfogo per nostro beneficio e per quelli che non sono del tutto rimbecilliti dagli odierni idealismi, riformismi, umanitarismi, cristianismi e moralismi.

15.

Si dirà che siamo ritardatari. Osserveremo soltanto, tanto per fare, che la verità, secondo gli stessi razionalisti, non è soggetta al tempo e aggiungeremo che i Sette Savi, Socrate e Gesù sono ancora un po' più vecchi dei sofisti, di Stendhal, di Nietzsche e di altri " disertori ".

16.

Lasciate ogni paura, o voi ch'entrate !

above: **4.21** Giovanni Papini and Ardengo Soffici, First Page, *Lacerba*, 1913. Newspaper. University College London (UCL), Special Collections.

opposite top: **4.22** Umberto Boccioni, *Dynamism of a Football Player*, 1912. Oil on canvas, 6 ft 4⅛ in x 6 ft 7⅞ in (193.2 x 201 cm). The Sidney and Harriet Janis Collection. Museum of Modern Art, New York.

opposite bottom: **4.23** Fortunato Depero, *Depero Futurista*, 1927. Book. Depero Archive, Rovereto.

Although not all the Futurists survived the First World War, the movement itself was resurrected in the 1920s. One remarkable book design from that second period is worthy of note. A volume published in 1927 by Fortunato Depero (1892–1960) was designed with two enormous bolts holding the covers together (*fig. 4.23*). The title, *Depero Futurista*, ascends diagonally up the frame, while faceted, translucent triangles cut back through the letters creating a sense of dynamism. Inside, the typography again runs riotously across the pages, and it is necessary to turn the book around again and again to follow the text. The additional element of brilliant color enlivens the design and adds a new element that increases the level of chaos, as the variety of typefaces is now matched by a effervescent range of colors. The book itself contained a selection of Depero's Futurist graphic design from the preceding decade. In the 1930s, Depero developed a more mainstream career in New York for clients including *Vanity Fair* and *Vogue* magazine.

Vorticism

Marinetti had visited London in 1911 and again in 1913, and his promotion of Futurist principles had a direct impact on a number of artists there. The painter Wyndham Lewis (1882–1957), who had started working in a Cubist style around 1911, soon adopted some of the kinetic and colorist elements of Futurist painting. After meeting Marinetti in December 1914, Lewis became even more committed to Futurist ideology. He shared a taste for anarchic energy with the Futurists, and the hope that young people could revolutionize art and society for the better. In the summer of 1914, Lewis published the first issue of a new journal devoted to English art, called *Blast*. At the same time, he helped to initiate the formation of a new revolutionary art movement, to be called **Vorticism**. Sometimes viewed as nothing more than a poor

created by a new type of Cubist facet, one that was transparent and brightly colored. Futurist paintings also created movement through the way in which the different facets cut through one another. The Futurists idolized the speed and excitement of modern machines, and here Boccioni transforms an athlete into an abstract, powerful machine, one that disappears in a flurry of motion. The sense of simultaneity evident in the image is an important part of Futurist style, while the man-machine hybrid was one of the most influential Futurist motifs. The color and kineticism of Futurist painting would make it an exciting source for graphic designers who sought to invoke similar themes of the exciting spectacle of modern life.

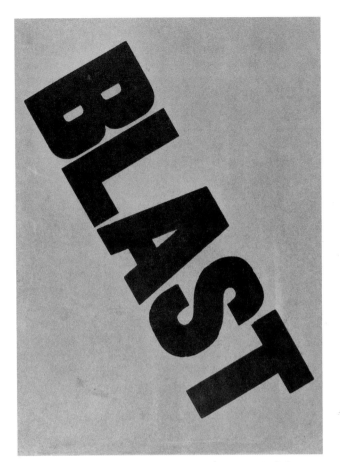

4.24 Wyndham Lewis, *Blast*, no. 1, 1914. Art journal. University College London (UCL), Special Collections.

4.25 Wyndham Lewis, *Blast—War Number*, no. 2, 1915. Art journal. Woodcut. University College London (UCL), Special Collections.

stepchild of Futurism, Vorticism in fact was a complex amalgam of Futurist, Cubist, and Expressionist principles. As the Futurists planned for Italy, so the Vorticists hoped to break the grasp of conservative social institutions in England. Lewis wrote that the Vorticists wanted to "Blast years 1837–1900," invoking the violent imagery favored by Marinetti. The cover of the first issue of *Blast* was awash in a brilliant pink (*fig. 4.24*), while strident bold sans letters that are reminiscent of those used for *Lacerba* cried out from a diagonal axis. Inside, the kinetic typography assaulted the reader's eyes, visually announcing the strength of the new beliefs. The machine idealism expressed in *Blast* had a corollary in Vorticist paintings, which were exhibited in London in 1915 and 1916.

In 1915, Lewis published a second issue of *Blast*, called the "War Number." The cover of this issue (*fig. 4.25*) is dominated by one of Lewis's woodcuts, which displays hybrid man–machine soldiers marching across an urban landscape. In comparison to Futurist compositions such as Boccioni's *Dynamism of a Football Player*, it is clear that Lewis has not adopted the blurred motion used by the Italian artist to depict frenzied movement. Rather, the hard-edged forms suggest movement by their position tilted relative to the background. It is notable that a whirlpool's "vortex," the source of the group's name, does not itself move violently but is instead a repository of pent-up forces. Along these lines, the apparent movement seen in Vorticist works appears clearer and more frozen than in Futurism. Vorticism was short-lived, and

went into decline as early as 1916, when Lewis began serving in the war as an artillery officer.

Edward McKnight Kauffer, already discussed for his Cubist leanings, also used Futurist and Vorticist stylistic elements in his abstract graphic designs. A poster he designed for the London Underground, publicizing a new power station for the railway (*fig. 4.26*), displays the same sort of man–machine hybrid favored by the Futurists. A man's heavily muscled arm represents a conduit for the raw power produced by the station, shown in the upper right. Influenced by Cubist collage, Kauffer has stitched together man and machine. The circle in the center of the image simultaneously forms a vision of a spinning turbine, the wheel of a train, and the bull's eye trademark of the London Underground.

One of the most striking examples of a Vorticist-inspired poster was published in 1919 as an advertisement for the *Daily Herald* newspaper (*fig. 4.27*). Kauffer had originally drawn the image in 1916, and the distinctive clear contours and "frozen movement" of Vorticism are evident in the image. The suggestion of soaring birds is communicated only by the shape of their forms and the angle of their flight relative to the frame. The quiescent yellow-gold background only draws more attention to the speed of the flight. Kauffer's design had languished for three years in 1919, when he submitted it to *Colour* magazine. This journal tried to spur a renewal in the post-war advertising business with a "poster page" that featured the work of young designers. The

4.26 Edward McKnight Kauffer, *Power—The Nerve Centre of London's Underground*, 1925. Poster, 40⅝ x 24 in (103 x 62.9 cm).
Museum of Modern Art, New York.

4.27 Edward McKnight Kauffer, *Soaring to Success! Daily Herald—the Early Bird*, 1919. Poster. Victoria and Albert Museum, London.

4.28 Francis Meynell, *The Iliad* translated by Alexander Pope, Nonesuch Editions, 1931. Book cover. British Library, London.

ABCDEFGHIJKLMNOPQRS TUVWXYZabcdefghijklmnop qrstuvwxyz1234567890?!&*()

"Gill Sans had a fluid character that distinguished it from the more stylized Johnston Sans, [...]"

4.29 Eric Gill, Gill Sans Typeface, 1928.

typographer and publisher Sir Francis Meynell (1891–1975) bought the image to serve as the basis for a poster that advertised a Labour Party newspaper, in the belief that it could serve as an inspiration to rebuild British society after the horrors of the war. Meynell proved to be right about the image's appeal, as the poster was an astonishing success and helped to establish Kauffer's reputation as a top young designer.

Book Design and Typography in Britain

In 1923, Meynell along with David Garnett (1892–1981) established the Nonesuch Press, which produced some of the most gorgeous book designs of the 1920s. With the goal of combining "significance of subject, beauty of format, and moderation of price," Meynell fomented a radical change in the private press movement because he rejected the handmade production techniques that had been its staple since the time of William Morris's Kelmscott Press. Until he founded Nonesuch, high-quality binding and typography had been the province of a rarefied group of specialty publishers who made limited runs of expensive books. Wanting to make quality literature and quality design available to the public at large, Meynell used top designers but had the books typeset by a Monotype machine. While it had taken many decades to come to fruition, the democratic principles espoused by the members of the Arts and Crafts movement (see Chapter 1) were fully realized for the first time in the example of the Nonesuch Press.

While the style of Nonesuch books is not modernist in any way, Meynell's embrace of typesetting technology represents a parallel track to the machine idealism of the Futurists. Nonesuch's 1931 two-volume reprint of Alexander Pope's translations of the Greek classics the *Odyssey* and the *Iliad* is a fine example of Meynell's work (*fig. 4.28*). The English text was set in Monotype's

Cochin, a roman type that had been designed in 1914 by the French typographer and foundry owner Dominique Peignet. The design of this two-volume set represented a collaboration that included some of the best book designers of this era: the Dutchman Jan van Krimpen (1892–1958), who created the open capitals at the head of each book and set the Greek type; Rudolph Koch (1876–1934), a German designer who engraved some of the ornaments; and Koch's assistant Berthold Wolpe (1905–1989), who drew the figure of the Greek warrior for the title pages. Meynell later said, "Our stock in trade has been the theory that mechanical means could be made to serve fine ends," a sentiment that summarizes many different designers' increasing belief in the reproducibility of beauty in a machine age.

In 1922, Meynell also participated in the founding of the Fleuron Society, an alliance of skilled designers who began publishing a periodical, *Fleuron: A Journal of Typography*, the following year. Each of the seven issues of this journal contained articles, facsimiles, and illustrations of innovations in European graphic design and typography. *Fleuron* was instrumental in promoting the use of machine set type as a beautiful and economical publishing tool.

The most successful modernist typeface of the 1920s was designed in 1928 by the British artist and typographer Eric Gill (1889–1940). While Gill's eponymous sans serif typeface was soon to become an icon of modernist graphic design, he actually designed it in an attempt to embrace traditional techniques, not as a celebration of machine innovation. Created for the Monotype Corporation, **Gill Sans** (*fig. 4.29*) resonates with the clear, geometric lines of Johnston's sans face, with which Gill had assisted. Gill Sans had a fluid character that distinguished it from the more stylized Johnston Sans, and it quickly became the type of choice for British publishers seeking a more contemporary look. In 1932, the London and North Eastern Railway adopted Gill Sans for their signage.

4.30 Amedée Ozenfant, *Still Life with Bottles*, 1920. Oil on canvas, 31¹¹⁄₁₆ x 39⁵⁄₁₆ in (80.5 x 99.8 cm) Solomon R. Guggenheim Foundation, Peggy Guggenheim Collection, 1976.

Purism

Near the end of the First World War, two artists, the Frenchman Amedée Ozenfant (1886–1966) and the Swiss-born Charles Edouard Jeanneret (1887–1965), sought to create a new style based on a reinterpretation of Cubist principles. Built on a combination of Analytic Cubist faceting as well as Synthetic Cubist collage, the movement Ozenfant christened "**Purism**" ultimately had a significant impact on graphic design in France. It is impossible to understand the underlying beliefs of Purism outside the context of the First World War. The Purists asserted that the war had been a "great test," a sacrifice that could lead to a more secure and harmonious future for Europe. Because they blamed the breakdown of shared values between European nations for causing the war, Ozenfant and Jeanneret wanted to establish a lyrical, universal aesthetic that could unite the continent.

The Machine Aesthetic

Purist paintings such as Ozenfant's *Still Life with Bottles* (*fig. 4.30*) demonstrate Purist ideas in visual terms. Combining a contemporary machine idealism, visible in the clean geometric shapes and smooth surfaces, with Classical references—note how the objects in the picture resemble monumental architecture—*Still Life with Bottles* represents an attempt to harmonize the past and the future. While some of the objects resemble Classical architecture, others reference the modern world of industry. In reconciling the past and the present, the Purists sought to show how the modern world could contain a Classical aesthetic if designed correctly. Part of Purist thinking was what is called a "**Machine Aesthetic**," an art-historical term that refers to the style of the works, which evoke the smooth, polished shapes of machines, as well as expressing a general high level of admiration for industrial society. The Purists wanted to show that mass-produced goods could be beautiful. This "machine idealism" contrasts sharply with earlier art movements, including Cubism, which tended to ignore or outright reject the modern world of the machine. Ozenfant's colleague Jeanneret had trained as an architect, and there is a clear architectural element in the composition of *Still Life with Bottles*. The clear, strong forms in the painting, as well as the grid-like compositional structure, suggest an architectural influence; art historians call this style "architectonic."

The Purists were heavily influenced by the fashion for **Neoplatonist** philosophy during this era. Neoplatonists asserted that there is an unchanging and eternal reality that is masked by the constant flux of the world perceived by the senses. In paintings such as *Still Life with Bottles*, Ozenfant wanted to portray a modern world that is as timeless and harmonious as the Classical age, at least as the latter was portrayed in European literature. The simple, pure shapes are intended to point the viewer toward a Platonic vision of calm and peace. While the Purists attempted to create an art of universal significance, it is arguable that the resulting synthesis of modern Cubism and a return to classicism speaks more of traditional themes of French art than that of other nations. A shorthand phrase that summarizes the essence of Purist ideals and aesthetics is as follows: "Neoplatonist reductive geometric abstraction."

It is arguable that the Purists took the Cubist style and removed any element that was radical or aggressive, thereby rendering it more palatable to a European public tired of chaos and destruction. Purism completely suppresses individual expression in favor of universal harmony, and wholly rejects the emotional pyrotechnics of artists such as Egon Schiele and the contemporaneous Expressionist movement. It seems natural that a traumatized continent would be ripe for the Purists' Neoplatonist message; the suggestion that a tranquil realm of eternal values existed in a higher plane must have been supremely comforting to a population that was counting war casualties in the tens of millions.

The New Spirit

The Purists were convinced that their ideal of *L'Esprit Nouveau* ("the new spirit") would serve as a visual template for a new society. They shared with a number of modern art movements, such as the Futurists, a desire not only to make compelling art works but also to change society in general. The Purists' sense of responsibility for the rebuilding of post-war Europe is most obvious in the architecture of Jeanneret, who for most of his life used the pseudonym Le Corbusier. In a parallel to the aesthetic developed in 1918 for Purist painting, Le Corbusier felt that modern architecture needed to combine a Classical harmony with modern materials. He felt that this balanced combination of past and present would serve as the basis for a new architecture that could serve the millions of working families that had congregated in major cities, creating housing dilemmas across Europe.

The most high-profile example of Purist architecture ever constructed by Le Corbusier was the Pavillon de l'Esprit Nouveau (*fig. 4.31*), designed for the 1925 exhibition of decorative arts held in Paris. Called the "*Exposition Internationale des Arts Décoratifs et*

4.31 Le Corbusier, Pavillon de l'Esprit Nouveau, 1925.

Industriels Modernes," this European fair brought enormous attention to modern design styles. Le Corbusier's Pavillon de l'Esprit Nouveau shows the same regard for fundamental abstract shapes that characterized Purist painting. He has arranged his modern materials into a reductive abstract design in which ornament has no place. Rather, the interplay of geometric forms is the basis for the aesthetic element. This simple, classical beauty is designed to be at the same time highly functional, establishing an economical modular unit that would become the basis for twentieth-century urban housing.

Art Deco in France and Britain

Purism as a cohesive movement quickly began to decline after the 1925 exposition, and by the following year Ozenfant and Jeanneret had gone on to pursue independent careers. While few people had embraced their ideals, let alone their stark modern aesthetic, later decades would witness the Purist style diffusing into the design arts. In fact, the *Exposition Internationale des Arts Décoratifs et Industriels Modernes*" in Paris proved to be the catalyst for a new wave of attention directed toward the "decorative and industrial arts." The exposition became associated with a drive for a modern, unified design style, such as Art Nouveau of the 1890s. Beginning in 1966, "**Art Deco**," an English term derived from the title of the exposition, became used as a catch-all term for the work of different types of designers pursuing geometric abstraction. Of course, the latter part of the Art Nouveau movement, especially the style promoted by the Wiener Werkstätte (see Chapter 2), in many ways portended the geometric simplicity of Art Deco. While the term "Art Deco" specifically connects the style and the 1925 exposition in Paris, by no means all of the works in that exposition shared an Art Deco style.

The ascendance of Art Deco represents the gradual process whereby modern art styles—especially Cubism, Futurism, Vorticism, and Purism—were turned into trendy fashion so as to

be marketed to a broad public. As this process unfolded, many of the philosophical beliefs and social commitments behind modern art, from Futurism's call for violent revolution in Italy to the Purists' desire to see a new utopian age of harmony, were separated from the artistic styles allied with them. In place of these varied philosophies there arose a commercial message that celebrated the glamour and excitement of affluent modern lifestyles. Some aspects of modern art ideology, such as its machine idealism, remained, but in general the commercial message behind Art Deco was as sleek and smooth as the developing style. The basic elements of the Art Deco style—simplicity, symmetry, planarity, geometry—formed a visual language that was applied across a tremendous range of art and design products. Using the same basic vocabulary of rectilinear and orthogonal elements, the Machine Aesthetic, and reductive geometric abstraction, a cross section of young architects and designers devised new visual forms for the commercial market. While the stylistic elements of the Art Deco style eventually filtered down to the world of mass production, the majority of Art Deco work was expensive and handmade, as had been the case with Art Nouveau.

The English china manufacturer Shelley Potteries produced a tea service in the 1930s called "Vogue" that featured startlingly modern forms (*fig. 4.32*). Conceived by Eric Slater, the radically tapered shape of the cup combined with a boldly triangular handle to create a thoroughly unconventional design. The reductive geometric sunrise pattern, a favorite element of British Art Deco, asymmetrically folds itself over the lip of each cup and saucer. On the edge of each saucer, the flat, stylized beams of light, reminiscent of elements in Vorticist paintings, cut across the band that delineates the basic shape of the saucer. The vocabulary of forms that make up this tea set is consonant with the use of geometric abstraction in British Art Deco graphics such as the Underground posters of Edward McKnight Kauffer seen earlier (see fig. 4.9), whose earliest work displays an Art Deco synthesis of modern art *avant la lettre*.

Another elegant household object, in this case a cocktail shaker by the Frenchman Jean Puiforcat (1887–1945), was executed *circa* 1926 (*fig. 4.33*). Here, the sleek form of the shaker is topped by a succession of curves, the dominant one of which

4.32 Eric Slater, All bone china "Vogue Shape" with sunrise pattern. Shelley Potteries, 1930–1. Victoria and Albert Museum, London.

4.33 Jean Puiforcat, *Cocktail Shaker*,
c. 1926. Sterling silver, 11 in (27.9 cm) high
x 4 in (12.1 cm) wide x 3 in (9.5 cm) deep.
The Minneapolis Institute of Arts,
The Modernism Collection. Gift of Norwest
Bank Minnesota.

4.34 A.M. Cassandre, *Wagon-Bar*, 1932. Poster. Lithograph, 39⅜ x 24⅜ in (99.8 x 61.7 cm).
Museum of Modern Art, New York.

creates a perfect semicircle. Like most Art Deco objects, this shaker was made in limited quantities for wealthy members of the bourgeoisie. Its expensive material, sterling silver, is indicative of the exclusive nature of Puiforcat's clientele.

Poster Art: Cassandre and Carlu

Perhaps the most well-known Art Deco graphic designer in Paris was a Ukrainian immigrant named Adolphe Jean-Marie Mouron (1901–1968), who used the pseudonym Cassandre. Cassandre was well acquainted with the members of the Purist group, and counted Le Corbusier as one of his closest friends. The architectonic structures and clearly delineated forms of Purist painting are evident in his posters. While Le Corbusier's architecture had been harshly condemned at the 1925 exposition, Cassandre won an award for one of his Purist-inspired lithographs. Cassandre's new style is evident in posters such as one from 1932 advertising the café cars of the French railways (*fig. 4.34*). The sleek, pure shapes of the bottles and the perfect circle that underlies the shape of the wine glass are reminiscent of Ozenfant's painting. The architectonic structure is clear by the way the crisp forms stand out like the skyline of a city. The bottles and glasses that signify the café car are collaged, like in a Cubist work, on to a fragment of a train's undercarriage. The shape and direction of the bold words "Wagon-Bar" connect visually to the black rail and the whole mass of the train undercarriage. The pristine clarity of the forms is matched by the simple palette of primary colors: red, blue, and yellow.

In 1926, Cassandre published an essay on poster design in *Revue de l'Union de l'Affiche Française*. In this text, he invoked the medieval tradition of communicating meaning through images alone, a strategy he hoped to emulate in his own work. But while he was committed to the traditions of graphic design, Cassandre—and artists like him—was not an ideologically committed member of any modern avant-garde movement. Rather, he was one of many artists who poached stylistic elements from a variety of different, contrasting modernist groups and remade them to serve as signifiers of glamour and affluence. In Cassandre's case, the ideological underpinnings of Purism, its belief in the creation of a wholly new utopian society, were transformed into a decorative style that reinforced the status quo. If there is any utopian element in Cassandre's posters, it is a resplendent capitalist utopia of unbridled wealth. Unlike Kauffer, who worked mostly in the fine arts and who hoped to collapse the distinction between fine and commercial work, Cassandre saw his own work as distinct from the art of painting, and this belief in "separate spheres" obviously informs the way in which he dismantles modern art into useful stylistic elements devoid of their original meaning.

An advertisement for Dubonnet liquor (*fig. 4.36*) proved to be one of Cassandre's most memorable posters because of the way he used the images to convey meaning. The three successive panels show a man drinking Dubonnet, which gradually flows through his body, symbolically fulfilling him as his form is filled in with color. With this poster, Cassandre invented the idea of the serial poster, whereby successive images expand on a concept.

4.35 Jean Carlu, *Au Bon Marché,* 1928. Advertisement and poster. Lithograph. Bibliothèque Forney, France.

4.36 A.M. Cassandre, *Dubo Dubon Dubonnet*, 1932. Color lithograph, 17½ x 45 in (44.5 x 115.6 cm). Museum of Modern Art, New York.

The repetition of the image is itself suggestive of the modern world of standardized mass production. As a parallel to the successive images, the text first spells out "Dubo," which sounds to a French speaker like "some beautiful," then "Dubon," which sounds like "some good," and finally the full name of the brand itself.

Cassandre had succeeded in the Dubonnet poster in achieving his goal of designing a work that had an instantaneous visual impact, and therefore could be grasped when glanced briefly from a moving vehicle on a city street. The man's body has the same sort of smoothly abstract form that characterizes Cassandre's images of inanimate objects, his torso a crisp rectangle while his head forms a semicircular dome that is as smooth as the product of a machine. In this poster, Cassandre effectively presents the product in the language of desire that structures modern advertising, so that the viewer connects the product to an intangible, satisfying experience—the sense of being filled up—rather than to a mundane, mass-produced beverage.

Jean Carlu (1900–1997) produced a magnificent lithograph in the Art Deco style for the department store Au Bon Marché in 1928 (*fig. 4.35*). The image shows a doorman, styled in a reductive geometric fashion, holding an umbrella over a pert bourgeois child. While the doorman's body is structured orthogonally with a dominant rectangular shape, the little girl is framed by an equilateral triangle. Considering that Carlu had trained originally as an architect, the use of architectonic forms probably came naturally to him. The two erect figures with their tightly delineated, sleek shapes contrast with the chaotic jumble of toys and stuffed animals held by the doorman. The poster is aimed broadly at the middle class, as it is advertising "toys and New Year's gifts" for children at a store whose name emphasizes economical prices. As was the case with Art Nouveau, lithographs represent some of the only Art Deco works that were intended for the general urban public, and this populist element contrasts with the majority of Art Deco products, which were especially commissioned for the carriage trade.

Carlu and Cassandre were both founding members in 1925 of the Union des Artistes Modernes (UAM), a trade group of modern architects and designers that also included Le Corbusier, Sonia Terk Delaunay, and the influential French typographer and art director Maximilien Vox (1894–1974). The UAM was formed of a group of like-minded artists and designers who together sought to advance the modernist style as a unified design language appropriate for the modern world. They explicitly rejected pre-war design in an attempt to erase the war's memory. In place of pre-war styles, they advocated the cheerful and ebullient spirit and machine idealism of the Art Deco. In both their membership and their ideology, UAM came the closest to establishing a bridge between the commercial design movements and the fine art groups like the Purists who had inspired them.

The *Normandie*

If any one object symbolized the glamour and wealth of the consumers of Art Deco, it was the ill-fated French ship *Normandie*, designed by Vladimir Yourkevitch (1885–1964) and launched in

Art Deco in Asia

During the Art Nouveau era in the late nineteenth century, the influence of Asian aesthetics, particularly Japanese woodblock prints, was paramount to the development of that key commercial style. Inverting the original cross-cultural exchange, the European Art Deco movement had a substantial impact on commercial graphics in Asia during the 1920s and 1930s. For an Asian audience, Art Deco graphics were suggestive of the same themes of affluence and modernity that they invoked in Europe, but with an additional, exotic element because of their Western, non-Asian style. Since Art Deco is in many ways yet another manifestation of the decorative line and flat forms that Western artists had adopted from Asia since the nineteenth century, there is a certain circularity in the way that the style was passed back to Japan and China decades later.

An anonymous 1925 advertisement for Shiseido cosmetics (fig. 4.37) displays a clearly Western-looking woman on the left side of the frame. Her elongated torso has a distinct rectangularity that is indicative of Art Deco. In addition, her simple, elegant clothes and casual manner are an outgrowth of European Deco graphics. The landscape along the bottom of the image is a common element in posters by Edward McKnight Kauffer and others; it is similarly made up of slices of form that demonstrate the influence of Analytic Cubist abstraction.

In China, the port city of Shanghai, known in the early twentieth century as the "Paris of the East," had become a major commercial and banking center mainly because of its extensive trade ties with the West. Shanghai's cosmopolitan citizens heartily embraced the Art Deco style in many media, including a number of high-profile architectural projects. Because of its commercial significance, Shanghai was also the first Chinese city to sustain a substantial graphic design industry. Called Meinu Yuefenpai *in Mandarin, advertising posters made in Shanghai generally featured images of beautiful young women. Most of the women represented were inventions of the artists, although famous actresses and other modern women were also portrayed on occasion. The true novelty of* Meinu Yuefenpai *was the use of realistic Western drawing styles and figure compositions, so that Shanghai Art Deco posters display more modeling of the figure and more traditional poses than is common in contemporary European graphics. The basic elements of the images, however—fashionable young women rendered in a combination of realistic and abstract modern styles—are fundamentally the same in both cultures.*

4.37 Mitsugu Maeda, Skin Lotion Advertisement, 1925. Poster. Shiseido Corporate Museum, Tokyo.

4.38 Vladimir Yourkevitch (designer), *SS. Normandie*, 1932. Photograph.

1932 (*fig. 4.38*). The *Normandie* was the first French ship of over 1,000 feet in length that had the speed to match the great British liners and contend for the cherished Blue Ribbon that was awarded to the fastest Transatlantic crossing. Built in the Penhoët shipyards of Saint Nazaire, France, the *Normandie* swept across the Atlantic on her maiden voyage from Le Havre to New York City at a crusing speed of 29 knots. The *Normandie* was designed to serve a narrow slice of European society, with the majority of its interior spaces given over to first-class lounges and a magnificent dining room. But its glamorous image was publicized to a larger swath of society as a symbol of the wealth, technological prowess, and aesthetic sophistication of the French nation.

Yourkevitch, a Russian immigrant to France, created a vessel with the sleek lines and smooth surfaces of the Art Deco style. The *Normandie* is a fine example of another Art Deco stylistic mainstay, **streamlining**. This strategy used clean, sweeping curves to create a sense of movement. While a fast ship such as the *Normandie* represented streamlining that was functional in that it reduced wind resistance while in motion, the use of streamlined forms became less a functional element than a decorative gesture when it was later applied to stationary objects such as refrigerators. Just as Art Deco separated modern art styles from their ideological underpinnings, so it separated streamlining from its functional aspect and made it nothing more than a sleek, decorative design element.

Cassandre's poster publicizing the *Normandie* (*fig. 4.39*) features the prow of the ocean liner looming over the text. The sleek lines of the ship are evident, although Cassandre has treated the mass of the ship reductively, like a bottle in a Purist still life. The smooth, planar body of the hull stands erect on the water without cutting into it. The word "Normandie" sits symmetrically right below the hull and is of the same width, serving as a pedestal for the liner as well as providing a transition from image to text. In August 1939, the *Normandie* made her last westbound voyage, as she was held in New York after the outbreak of the Second World War. Tragically, fire broke out in 1942 during the ship's conversion to military use, and an inexperienced firefighting team flooded the ship, causing it to roll on to its side in New York harbor. Hopelessly damaged, the *Normandie* was sold for scrap in 1945.

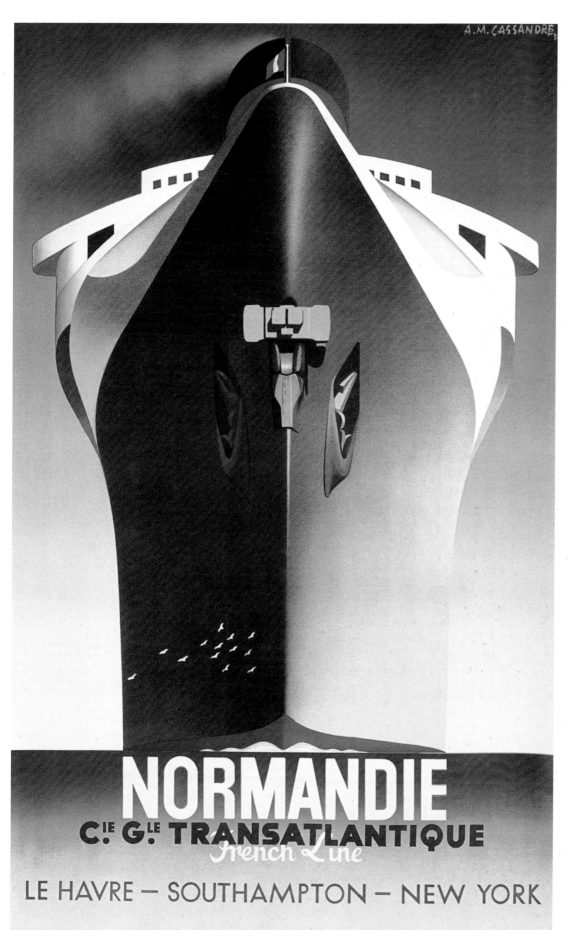

4.39 A.M. Cassandre, *Normandie*,
1935. Poster. Colored lithograph,
39½ x 24⅜ in (100 x 62 cm).
Les Arts Décoratifs, Musée
de la Publicité, Paris.
Photo: Laurent Sully Jaulmes.

4.40 Morris Fuller Benton, Broadway Typeface, American Type Founders, 1929. Cover. St Bride Printing Library, London.

Typography

Cassandre designed a number of display typefaces throughout his career, beginning with **Bifur**, introduced in 1929 by the influential French foundry Deberny & Peignot (*fig. 4.41*). Bifur is another example of the stylized reductive geometric abstraction characteristic of Art Deco, as the letters have been reduced to their most fundamental geometric shapes, with smaller details indicated by shaded areas. While geometric Art Deco types such as Bifur are never austere in their geometry, Cassandre designed the sweeping streamlined curves of the letters with attention to decorative flourishes. Type such as Bifur is conceptually tied to Cassandre's poster aesthetic, inasmuch as it uses strikingly stylized shapes in order to grab the viewer in the blink of an eye. While ostensibly not a display face according to Cassandre, Bifur, like many Art Deco faces, makes such a strong visual statement that it was very seldom used for unassuming general purpose text. Broadly speaking, most Art Deco types are so easily associated with the look of this era that they did not develop longstanding or universal appeal.

While American Art Deco is discussed at length in Chapter 7, it is notable that one of the most familiar typefaces of this era was designed by the esteemed American typographer Morris Fuller Benton (1872–1948) of American Type Founders. His 1929 **Broadway** (*fig. 4.40*) is titled to suggest the connection between the stylized letters and New York City's famous entertainment district. Essentially a revival of the early nineteenth-century "fat faces" fused with a sleek geometric sense of form, Broadway became instantly indicative of the glamour of the ultimate modern city, New York. During this period, European graphic designers idealized New York City as the pinnacle of urban modernism. While clearly not intended for general use because of its low readability and precarious legibility, Benton's type uses dramatic contrasts in order to call immediate attention to itself. In

one of the few instances in which an Art Deco typeface has been able to transcend its dated style, Broadway has become established in a niche of its own as the preferred lettering for twenty-first-century nightclubs and restaurants that want to project an aura of sophistication.

Cassandre had his greatest success as a type designer with the introduction in 1937 of the all-purpose face **Peignot**, which was destined to become an icon of the Art Deco era (*fig. 4.42*). Named after Georges Peignot (1872–1915) of the foundry that had supported his works for years, Peignot made a huge splash at the 1937 exhibition in Paris, the last great world's fair to be held before the Second World War. Carved into the side of the fair's major architectural landmark, the Palais de Chaillot, Peignot was the most unique visual identifier of the Art Deco style that still predominated twelve years after its introduction in Paris. This sans serif alphabet was intended by Cassandre to be both legible and readable while retaining some of the unique geometric styling of Art Deco. In the lower-case alphabet, which is actually made up of small capitals, Peignot extends the idea of elegant, attenuated form to a radical extreme. For example, the "l" is almost a pure vertical, while the lower case "h" features an asymmetrical ascender on its left half.

The Deberny & Peignot foundry was also responsible for the publication of two influential periodicals in the 1920s. Its trade journal *Les Divertissements Typographiques* was given away to people in the publishing industry as a way of marketing Deberny & Peignot's aggressively modernist house style. The cover for the first volume of *Divertissements Typographiques* was designed by the French typographer and Deberny & Peignot consultant Maximilien Vox, and shows his ready adaptation of modernist abstraction to graphic design (*fig. 4.43*). The orthogonal composition that is structured by the vertical bars on each side is nicely complemented—in the manner of a Purist still life—by the centered black circle, the latter made more dynamic by the diagonal

above: **4.41** A.M. Cassandre, Bifur Typeface, 1932.

right: **4.42** A.M. Cassandre, Peignot Typeface, Deberny & Peignot, 1937. St Bride Printing Library, London.

far right: **4.43** A.M. Cassandre and Maximilien Vox, *Divertissements Typographiques*, 1927. Journal cover. Cary Graphic Arts Collection, RIT, Rochester, New York.

ALPHABET
MEDIUM 72 POINT

A A B b C c D d E E F f G G
H H I i J j K k L l M M N N
O O P p Q Q R R S S T T U U
V V W W X X Y y Z Z
1234567890
1234567890

TOME 1

DIVERTISSEMENTS TYPOGRAPHIQUES

TRAVAUX DE VILLE

hand that cuts across it from lower left to upper right. Issues of *Les Divertissements Typographiques* were used to introduce new products, such as Cassandre's Bifur, which nonetheless never recouped the initial high investment in engraving the type. Maximilien Vox secured a noteworthy place for himself in design history when he created a new and influential system of typeface classification called ATypI-Vox that is still in use today.

Deberny & Peignot's second publication was not a trade periodical, but was rather aimed at wealthy consumers of Art Deco products. Called *Arts et Métiers Graphiques*, this magazine was started in 1927 as a forum for articles on modern art and culture as well as fine printing. Like *The Fleuron* in London, this journal served as a key source for designers interested in the newest trends and design philosophies. Journals such as this were necessary in carving out a rationale for modernist design because of the divorce of Art Deco design from the fine art philosophies that had inspired it. But beneath this surface subject matter, the true raison d'être of the journal was to publicize the fine printing and typography of the firm.

Bookbinding

Some of the most truly stunning bookbindings of the twentieth century were designed as part of the Art Deco movement. One notable artist, Pierre Legrain (1889–1929), returned to Paris from the war after a medical discharge in 1916, and soon found work there with Jacques Doucet (1853–1929), a major collector of modern art. Throughout the 1920s Legrain went on to design bindings for over 1,000 books, many of them one-of-a-kind covers for works from Doucet's own library. Legrain's cover for Doucet's copy of Paul Morand's *Les Amis Nouveaux* (*fig. 4.44*) consists of a soft blue calf leather binding attached to steel plates. This material, which was at the height of fashion during the 1920s, tied the book directly to the modern world of the machine. The plates themselves are pierced by holes in a symmetrical geometric design, each hole adorned with a gold dot. The restrained elegance of this design, combined with precious materials that are beautiful in themselves, is a testament to the beauty of Art Deco luxury goods.

A bookbinding by Paul Bonet (1889–1971) unites Art Deco aesthetics with one of the early leaders of the modern movement, Guillaume Apollinaire. In 1932, Bonet created a new edition of Apollinaire's *Calligrammes* (*fig. 4.45*) that featured a Cubist-inspired design. The lettering shifts back and forth between positive and negative forms while the kinetic rhythm of the rectangular facets is enhanced by their overlapping, textured, and three-dimensional qualities.

4.44 Pierre Legrain, *Les Amis Nouveaux*, 1927. Illustrated by Jean Hugo, 1924. Bibliothèque Littéraire Jacques Doucet, Paris.

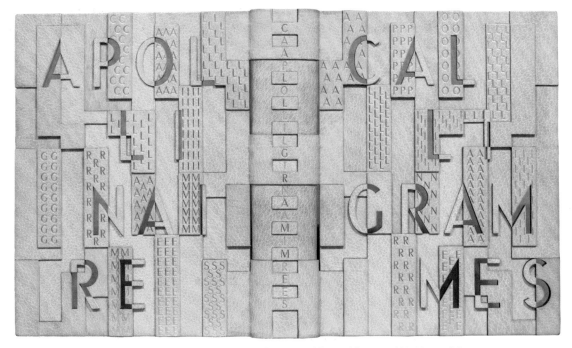

4.45 Paul Bonet, *Calligrammes* by Guillaume Apollinaire, 1932. Book cover. Library of Congress, Washington, DC.

EAST-AFRICAN TRANSPORT~OLD STYLE

4.46 Adrian Allinson, *East African Transport—Old Style*, 1931. Poster, 60 x 40 in (152.4 x 101.6 cm). National Archives Picture Library.

Art Deco and Colonialism

Most Art Deco graphic design was concerned with publicizing products, from travel to beverages, that were a part of the affluent urban lifestyle. However, in an interesting aside, a number of Art Deco graphic works were commissioned to advertise the colonial empires that were a huge part of the European economy. In the face of criticism at home regarding the economic and moral issues of colonialism, both Britain and France sought to convince their own citizens of the virtues of empire.

In 1926, the British government established the Empire Marketing Board, in order to persuade its citizens to do business with British colonies. After its success in the First World War, the British Empire had increased to its greatest size, encompassing 25 per cent of the world's population. Britain oversaw colonies in Africa, the Middle East, Asia, the Pacific Islands, and the Americas. The Board's assignment included a variety of duties, such as overseeing agricultural research, but its most high-profile activity was the mounting of publicity campaigns. The Board spent over £1 million to increase the importation of foodstuffs from around the Empire. It was hoped that, as colonial economies found new markets for their export foodstuffs, they would increase the amount of finished goods purchased from Britain.

The publicity section of the Empire Marketing Board, which included among its members figures such as Frank Pick, of London Underground fame, commissioned over 800 lithographic posters between 1927 and 1933, when the Board was dissolved. Pick brought to the Board the conviction that modern abstract styles were more effective at catching the eye of the viewer than traditional illustration, and this view held sway with the other members. At the same time, the Board maintained authority over the designs, as artists were forced to submit them for approval on completion; in a number of instances, designers were forced to remake an image that did not pass muster with Pick and the other Board members. The posters produced for the Board varied greatly in size; the first major commission went to MacDonald Gill (1884–1947), whose *Highways of the Empire* was reproduced at the huge scale of 10 by 20 feet. However, most of the graphic production of the Empire Marketing Board was much more modest in size, no more than 20 by 30 inches, and was intended to be displayed in stores, schools, and government buildings around the country.

Empire Buying Makes Busy Factories (*fig. 4.48*), by Clive Gardiner (1891–1960), is an example of an image from one of these installations. It shows the familiar Futurist man–machine theme that was reproduced in a style based on Cubist geometric

EAST·AFRICAN TRANSPORT

above: **4.47** Adrian Allinson, *East African Transport—New Style*, 1931. Poster, 60 x 40 in (152.4 x 101.6 cm). National Archives Picture Library.

opposite: **4.48** Clive Gardiner, *Empire Buying Makes Busy Factories*, 1928. 60 x 40 in (152.4 x 101.6 cm). National Archives, Surrey, England.

abstraction. The men in the image are just as anonymous as the machines, even though they have slightly more irregular contours. This futuristic glorification of industry refers to the idea that strong colonies will buy more and more manufactured goods from Britain.

In January 1927, Pick initiated the idea of building special hoardings for the Board's posters, as he had in the London Underground. Pick's idea was that each hoarding could serve as the site for an ensemble of similarly themed posters, all 40 inches high but with varying widths. There is no more dramatic example of the theme of a white Briton bringing "civilization" to the primitive cultures of the Empire than the pair of posters by Adrian Allinson (1890–1959) on the theme of "East African Transport" (*figs. 4.46, 4.47*). Paired as part of one of Pick's five-poster ensembles, the two images do not communicate an economic theme, but rather are intended to convey the message that the Empire has improved life in the colonies while at the same time assuring the public of the benevolent control exercised by the white man. In this case, the British overseer in one poster is compositionally paired with the fierce-looking African woman on the other, adding a sexist patriarchal theme as part of this portrayal of East African society as needful of European assistance.

The 1931 International Colonial Exposition

During the first half of the twentieth century, the French nation several times addressed its own citizens as well as those of the rest of Europe through the medium of the World's Fair. The 1931 International Colonial Exposition held in Paris sought to show the success of France's huge empire, much of it acquired as a result of the First World War, after which France counted over forty-five nations under its control. The goal of the Exposition was to create a sense of community among the different colonial peoples represented by exhibits spread out over 500 acres in the forest of Vincennes, just outside the city. While the North African Arabic lands under French control were familiar to visitors, there was tremendous fascination with objects and people from the new Central African and West Indian possessions. Over 34 million visitors went to the Exposition, making it one of the most popular international exhibitions ever mounted.

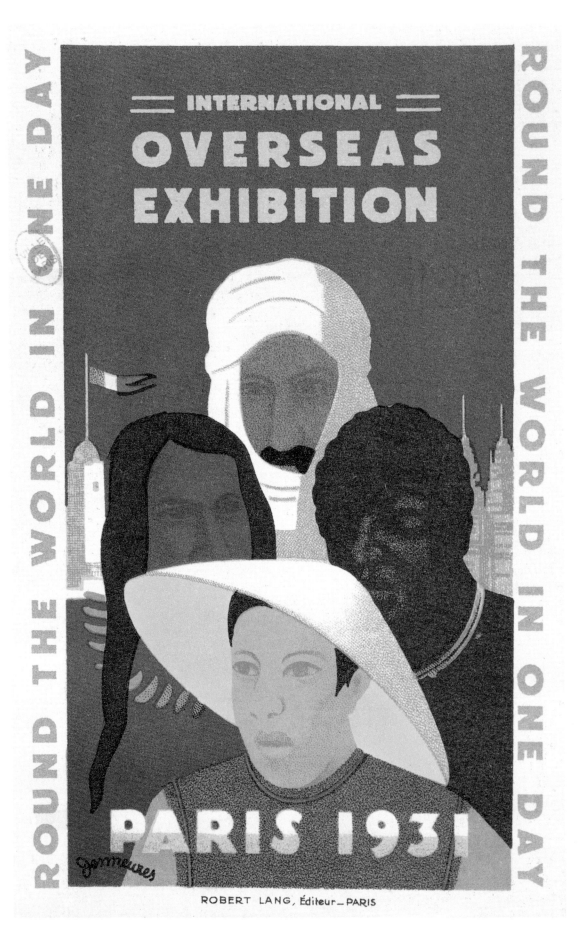

4.49 Victor-Jean Desmeures, *International Overseas Exhibition*, Paris, 1931.
Poster. Color lithograph. Bibliothèque Historique de la Ville de Paris.

The Art Deco style predominated at the exposition. For example, the only permanent building, an art gallery designed by Léon Jaussely (1875–1932) and Albert Laprade (1883–1978), has the sleek, elegant lines and simplified geometric forms of Purism (*fig. 4.50*). Alfred Janniot (1889–1969) contributed an immense relief sculpture illustrating the connections between Paris and the overseas colonies, again in a style informed by reductive geometric antecedents. The building likewise visually demonstrates the strong connections between Art Deco and the French classical tradition, as both have roots in elegant materials, balanced proportions, and a sturdy sense of geometric form. The gallery was later transformed into the Museum of African and Oceanic Art.

Echoing the colonial sensibility of British posters, the French painter Victor-Jean Desmeures's poster publicizing the exhibition (*fig. 4.49*), captioned "all the world in one day," displays caricatured stereotypes of non-Europeans, most prominently in the face of the Asian in the foreground. His furtive glance is suggestive of Europeans' view of Asians as "inscrutable." Desmeures has used a basic palette of bold flat colors to differentiate between the citizens of different parts of the French empire in a schematic and ornamental way. Again, the Art Deco tendency to emphasize decorative form at the expense of substance is evident here.

A poster by Jules Isnard Dransy (1883–1945) aimed at promoting Italian tourism attempts to make a connection between the Exposition and a more traditional Art Deco theme, entertainment (*fig. 4.51*), but nonetheless reiterates a racist mindset. Paris at the time was famous for its African American singers, especially the American expatriate Josephine Baker (1906–1975), and this poster shows a woman of color seductively pulling aside a curtain. Obviously, the sexual availability and imagined exoticism of women from the colonies was a major undercurrent in European culture during the colonial period.

Art Deco represents only one of the main routes whereby modern art movements were transformed into stylish commercial messages. The next chapter will grapple with a second route, showing how Dutch De Stijl and Russian Constructivism also served as springboards for graphic design.

4.51 Jules Isnard Dransy, *Visitate l'Esposizione Coloniale Internazionale (Visit the International Colonial Exhibition)*, Paris, 1931. Poster. Colored lithograph, 39⅓ x 24⅜ in (100 x 62 cm). Les Arts Décoratifs, Musée de la Publicité, Paris. Photo: Laurent Sully Jaulmes.

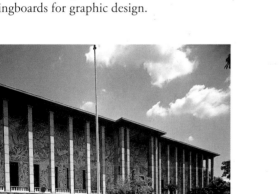

4.50 Léon Jaussely and Pierre Laprade, South Façade of the Colonial Exposition Gallery (now the Musée des Arts d'Afrique et d'Oceanie), 1931.

5 REVOLUTIONS IN DESIGN

DE STIJL
REVOLUTION IN RUSSIA
THE RUSSIAN REVOLUTION
AND THE BOLSHEVIK POSTER
RUSSIAN SUPREMATISM
AND CONSTRUCTIVISM

Britain, France, Italy, and the United States were not the only countries in which avant-garde art movements had a major influence on graphic design in the period after the First World War. The two major developments introduced here, Dutch De Stijl and Russian Constructivism, had a long-lasting impact on graphic design. Both these artistic trends were indebted to Cubism and emphasized geometric abstraction. For this reason, they also had an indirect impact on the Art Deco style discussed in Chapter 4. However, De Stijl and Russian Constructivism were less closely tied to the Paris art scene, which included Cubism, Futurism, and Purism; and Art Deco was by no means the most far-reaching consequence of De Stijl and Russian Constructivism in terms of graphic design. Some special circumstances informing the creation and dissemination of De Stijl and Russian Constructivism, especially considering the latter's revolutionary context, merit that they be considered separately.

The work of both groups can only be understood in the context of the conclusion and aftermath of the First World War. Out of that conflict arose new trends that established a visual language that would eventually come to dominate the graphic design field for decades to come.

5.1 Piet Mondrian, *Tableau 2, with Yellow, Black, Blue, Red, and Gray*, 1922. Oil on canvas, 21⅞ x 21⅛ in (55.6 x 53.4 cm). Guggenheim Museum, New York. © 2007 Mondrian/Holtzman Trust c/o HCR International, Warrenton, VA.

5.2a Theo van Doesburg, Study 1,
Composition (The Cow), 1916.
Pencil on paper, 4⅝ x 6 in (11.7 x 15.9 cm).
Museum of Modern Art, New York. Purchase.

5.2b Theo van Doesburg, Study 2,
Composition (The Cow), 1917. Pencil on paper,
4⅝ x 6 in (11.7 x 15.9 cm).
Museum of Modern Art, New York. Purchase.

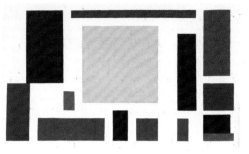

5.2c Theo van Doesburg, Study 3,
Composition (The Cow), c. 1917.
Oil on canvas, 14¾ x 25 in (37.5 x 63.5 cm).
Museum of Modern Art, New York. Purchase.

De Stijl

The post-war **De Stijl** movement in the Netherlands embraced a sense of order that was in many ways a response to the trauma of the First World War. "De Stijl" means "The Style," and the sense of impersonal, universal principles conveyed by that bland name was an important part of the group's ideology. Founded in the city of Leiden in 1917 by a group of artists and architects that included Theo van Doesburg (1883–1931), Piet Mondrian (1872–1944), Bart van der Leck (1876–1958), and Gerrit Rietveld (1888–1964), De Stijl mixed admiration for the modern machine world with an at times mystical asceticism. Van Doesburg, in many ways the driving theoretical force behind De Stijl, had returned to Leiden after serving in the Dutch army for three years. The artists of De Stijl felt that rampant individualism as well as nationalist egotism was responsible for the savagery of the conflict that began in 1914, and they offered a universal language of geometric abstraction as a salve for Europe's wounded psyche. Van Doesburg wrote, "The old is connected with the individual. The new is connected with the universal." In their view, reductive geometric abstraction could not be identified with any one country or individual and therefore stood as the most suitable universal style for the new post-war era. The Dutch words *nieuwe beelding* ("new imagery") served as a sort of catch-all term, indicating the group's desire to spur on a fresh start in the visual arts as well as in society in general.

Seeking Universal Harmony

The De Stijl artists shared with the Purists and others a strong Neoplatonist bias: their art was guided by the concept of an abstract ideal of universal harmony. By limiting the number of expressive elements in their work, they believed that they could effectively represent their communal, abstract ideals in material terms. De Stijl features a strong utopian theme, as its members purified art of representation and emotion in the hope of effecting broader social change. As was the case with a number of modern art movements, the messy details of social change were brushed over, and outside vague notions of universal peace and harmony, it was never clear what specific utopia the De Stijl artists hoped to gain. It should be noted that the puritanical attitude toward art promulgated by De Stijl as a universal doctrine resonates, in fact, with a Dutch national tradition that values sobriety and Calvinist discipline. As was the case with the French Purist movement, it proved impossible for De Stijl artists fully to embrace universalism in a way that shed their national identity. Furthermore, it should be noted that the various artists who founded or later passed through the group did not all share one homogeneous vision of art or of society.

Piet Mondrian used the term "**neo-plasticism**" to refer to his aesthetic, one that rejected the decorative excesses of pre-war art as well as the emotionally laden complexity of contemporary Expressionism. While Mondrian had progressed through a Cubist phase after moving to Paris in 1911, in De Stijl, although still clearly influenced by Analytic Cubist strategies, he advocated a more radical type of simplification than that of Pablo Picasso or George Braque. A mature work from 1922 by Mondrian, *Tableau 2*, is completely "non-objective," meaning that it does not represent anything from the natural world, only Mondrian's abstract ideals (*fig. 5.1*). For Mondrian, a painting such as this demonstrates a series of balanced forms suggestive of the inherent harmony of the universe. He has limited his use of formal elements to straight lines, orthogonal compositions, and an austere palette of primary colors along with white, black, and gray. Despite its **non-objective** quality, *Tableau 2* displays the precision and hard-edged geometric shapes consonant with a commitment to the machine aesthetic.

A series of three images by Theo van Doesburg indicates how an apparently non-objective painting can be derived from the artist's study of nature (*fig. 5.2a,b,c*). Through the systematic process of simplification and the gradual introduction of geometric structure, van Doesburg manages to transform a drawing of a cow into a total abstraction. This process indicates how De Stijl artists felt that natural forms contain the essence of universal harmony, so that even as mundane a creature as a cow is representative of a higher plane of Neoplatonist transcendence. It should also be noted how this series of images betrays De Stijl's roots in Analytic Cubist faceting, as the image of the cow passes through a Cubist phase before it is further simplified. Van Doesburg explicitly endorsed this Cubist connection, although he asserted that De Stijl artists had gone farther in considering the formal implications of the style that had originated with Picasso and Braque. Of course, De Stijl was created as a universal design style that was not to be limited to the fine art realm; rather it was to unify all types of visual culture under one set of harmonious principles. It is important to remember that De Stijl was not simply an art movement, but comprised a group of people who wanted to act as agents of social change.

Typography and Journal Design

Of all of the post-war avant-garde art movements, De Stijl had one of the most immediate impacts on graphic design and typography in Europe. In October 1917, the same year that the group was first established, van Doesburg began publishing a journal also called *De Stijl*. In many ways *De Stijl* was at the core of the movement, because it allowed the members to promote their art

5.5 Theo van Doesburg, *NB De Stijl*, 1921. Art journal. Letterpress. University College London (UCL), Special Collections.

above: **5.3** Theo van Doesburg (logotype) and Vilmos Huszar (woodcut), *De Stijl*, 1919. Art journal. Letterpress. University College London (UCL), Special Collections.

below: **5.4** Theo van Doesburg, *Alphabet*, 1917.

and ideology to a wider public. During the years 1917–32, *De Stijl* established itself as a consistent vehicle wherein the ideas of the European avant-garde could be discussed and critiqued. At the same time, the journal served as a visual example of the group's aesthetic principles in the realm of typography and graphic design.

During its first three years, van Doesburg published thirty-six issues of *De Stijl*, featuring a series of articles about the movement's philosophy and aesthetics. The overwhelming majority of these essays were written in Dutch. These early essays mainly concerned the aesthetic and quasi-philosophical principles espoused by Mondrian, who it is estimated wrote over 70 per cent of *De Stijl*'s content before 1920. In a letter to another founding member of De Stijl, Bart van der Leck, van Doesburg outlined his plans for the journal: "The magazine will only concern itself with the modern style … Typographically and aesthetically it will be austere, without any trappings." Van Doesburg followed through with this plan, and the resulting journal was for the most part nondescript from the standpoint of graphic design. However, a cover page combining a logotype at the top by van Doesburg with a woodcut design by Vilmos Huszar (1884–1960) is more aggressive in asserting the artistic principles of De Stijl (*fig. 5.3*). Reproduced via letterpress, van Doesburg's logotype features

letters that are made up of squares and rectangles, each letter's horizontal and vertical elements separated into discrete units. While each letter is itself defined by its rectilinear and orthogonal elements, the overall word also forms a tight rectangular block. The logotype produced for the journal did not have legibility as its prime feature, but rather represented an attempt to establish a dramatic form with immediate impact on the viewer. Note that the explanatory text at the bottom is composed of more legible letterforms, declaring De Stijl a "monthly journal of the expressive professions."

In 1919, van Doesburg completed an experimental alphabet in which the letters were similarly determined by an underlying geometric scheme, in this case the shape of a square box—like an em box—that had been divided into twenty-five equal parts, five

5.6 Piet Zwart, *Jan Wils* Logo, 1920. Letterpress. Collection Elaine Lustig Cohen.

5.7 El Lissitzky, *"Of Two Squares"* from *De Stijl*, 1922. Book frontcover and backcover. Private collection.

rows of five (*fig. 5.4*). In designing this alphabet, van Doesburg took exceptional liberties with the rules of proportion that govern traditional typography. In this upper-case alphabet he distorted letters on both the horizontal and vertical axes in order to make them fill out the shape of the square. This investigational endeavor demonstrates how an imaginary grid underlies much of De Stijl's graphic design and typography. For most of the avant-garde artists discussed in this chapter, the grid was a fundamental underlying structure, serving both as a representative of pure, Neoplatonic forms and as a key design element.

Huszar's abstract design is centered on the cover along with the logotype, although the fundamental aesthetic principle it illustrates is asymmetry. Here, Huszar shows how simple geometric elements can create expressive tension when they are composed with an exquisite sense of contrast. This fundamental element of modern graphic design and typography is manifest not only in the differing shapes and their alignment on the horizontal and

vertical axes, but also in the drama created between solid and void. The startling asymmetry of the design makes a perfect counterpoint with the tight rectangular block of text—a rectangle that itself plays off the proportions of the overall page and the surrounding empty space. For the artists of De Stijl, the aesthetic principle of contrast, visible in terms of composition as well as color, was suggestive of the elemental forces of the universe. In accordance with the ideas of the Dutch spiritual philosopher M. H. J. Schoenmaekers (1875–1944), members of De Stijl believed that they could express universal truths through the employment of contrasting elements.

De Stijl Redesigned

Early in 1921, van Doesburg along with Mondrian completely redesigned the journal *De Stijl* as part of a new effort to appeal to a broader European audience. The subtitle was changed to include the words "International Monthly," and the publication sites, now including Paris and Rome as well as the original Leiden, were listed on the cover. Articles were to be published in more widely known languages than Dutch, especially French. Despite Mondrian's participation in the initial makeover—which had actually been spurred by his visit to Paris and surprise at *De Stijl*'s limited penetration into the art world there—the new *De Stijl* was primarily a mouthpiece for van Doesburg.

The new design for the cover featured the title, *De Stijl*, printed in black on top of the red letters "NB," an acronym for the slogan *nieuwe beelding* (*fig. 5.5*). The most noticeable break with the earlier design resides in the asymmetry of the composition, which deviates from the axial centering of the first three volumes. There is a broad, blank space in the center of the cover, which for De Stijl artists did not represent "absence" of design, but was an intrinsic element that was balanced with the filled-in parts of the composition. The typeface is fairly nondescript, a rather bold grotesque of nineteenth-century origin with the proportions of roman capitals. The overprinted black letters seem to float on top of the larger "NB," creating a slight illusion of three-dimensional space. This use of color as a structural element in design was another important contribution of De Stijl to modern design. While in the current example Mondrian and van Doesburg were limited to red and black, they are able to get the most out of even this inexpensive palette through careful juxtapositions. The design of *De Stijl* is also representative of one type of avant-garde letterpress printing, the use of standard types, ornaments, and rules in new dramatic combinations. Some contemporary designers were dogmatic in wanting to develop their new, abstract language out of the everyday elements of an average printer's typecase, thus showing how beauty can be found in the most mundane aspects of the modern world. Van Doesburg had first used this technique in the third volume of *De Stijl*, when he had published an article that mixed different type sizes in order to create visual and conceptual emphasis.

The new phase of *De Stijl* prospered under van Doesburg's editorial guidance, mainly because of his openness to emerging artistic trends that shared many of the same interests as those of De Stijl's membership. For example, in 1922, he published a Dutch version of the children's poem "Of Two Squares" (*fig. 5.7*), by the Russian artist El Lissitzky (1890–1941). Informed by both the Suprematist and Russian Constructivist movements (see below), Lissitzky's design showcases an experiment in the same fundamentally reductive abstract language as that used by the artists of De Stijl. In addition, he displays an inventive use of typography as a signifier of meaning that demonstrates awareness of Apollinaire's "Cubist" *Calligrammes*. Lissitzky demonstrated a much more sophisticated use of existing type, transforming it into a breathtakingly novel and dynamic composition. In the page reproduced here Lissitzky does not limit himself, as De Stijl artists did, to the horizontal and vertical axes, but includes asymmetrical, diagonal elements as well. It is arguable that De Stijl's greatest contribution to graphic design lay in the popularization of Lissitzky's graphic work.

Oblique designs such as Lissitzky's were eventually adopted by van Doesburg in 1924, when he made a series of paintings in which the familiar rectangular blocks have been turned 45 degrees. Van Doesburg called these new, more dynamic forms "Contra compositions," and argued that they increased the vitality of the overall composition while still maintaining the rigorous geometry of De Stijl. The oblique allowed for van Doesburg to explore new relationships while continuing to abide by the founding principles of asymmetry and contrast. Mondrian staunchly disagreed with van Doesburg's new strategy, as he felt that diagonal compositions introduced an element of personal expression that violated the universal precepts of De Stijl. This dispute led to the break-up of De Stijl as a unified group, resulting in van Doesburg's ascendance to a position of unqualified control. As editor of *De Stijl*, he was the most well-known figure in the movement and the one most able to dictate in print where it was headed in the future.

A few of the members of De Stijl quickly adopted its principles for the purpose of completing advertising commissions. It is significant to note that despite its utopian aspirations, the members of De Stijl were not antagonistic toward modern society, and in fact hoped to promulgate De Stijl principles as much as possible through a variety of fine art as well as commercial projects. In 1919, Piet Zwart (1885–1977) became acquainted with De Stijl ideas when he joined the architectural firm of Jan Wils (1891–1972), a founding member of the movement. In 1921, Zwart designed a letterhead for Wils's firm that demonstrates all of the qualities of De Stijl design: orthogonal structure; contrasts of solid and void, horizontal and vertical; dynamic asymmetry; and sans serif lettering composed into block-like rectangles (*fig. 5.6*). Zwart further refined his use of this basic design language in a series of logos for the Ioco Corporation beginning in 1922. In this design, the monumental quality of the shapes, as well as their architectonic relationships, shows Zwart's grounding in the practice of architecture.

De Stijl Architecture

The exploration of architectonic form was in many ways at the heart of the De Stijl enterprise. Architecture's centrality came about partly because of the abstract geometry that underlies most architectural projects. However, its central role was mainly based on the fact that it represented the most complete opportunity for an artist to synthesize many arts into a unitary whole. This relates again to the concept of the *Gesamtkunstwerk*, or "total work of art," first discussed in Chapter 2. Modern artists with a utopian bent had long sought to build a complete environment, one that in De Stijl's case would serve as a visual manifestation of the "new harmony" in art and society that was the ultimate goal of the group. Van Doesburg had become interested in color in architecture as early as 1917, when he began a series of studies that demonstrated how color contrast could be used in building design. Beginning in 1922, he started to collaborate with the architect Cornelis van Esteren (1897–1988) on a model house called the Maison Particulière. The "axonometric" drawing, a type of three-dimensional projection (1923; *fig. 5.8*), displays the De Stijl principles of contrast and asymmetry in both the overall composition as well as in the color relationships.

For the most part, van Doesburg's architectural work remained speculative, and it was another De Stijl architect, Gerrit Rietveld, who was first commissioned to make the neo-plastic style into an architectural reality. Rietveld's Schröder House, the fruit of a collaboration with his patron, Mrs Truus Schröder-Schräder of Utrecht, shows the potential of De Stijl design to serve as the basis for a dynamic new architecture (*fig. 5.9*). The Schröder House appears less like a series of solid volumes than as a conglomeration of individual planes that pass through one another. The brightly colored planes of the building interpenetrate in a manner indebted to Cubism and Futurism, seemingly unattached to a solid volume. Rather, a sense of weightless openness pervades the structure. The contrasting bold primary colors also add to this effect, as certain details, such as the yellow steel post that supports one corner of the front balcony, seem almost detached from the overall building. In some important ways, the extravagant stylization of Rietveld's work can be compared to the

above: **5.8** C. Esteren and Theo van
Doesburg, Axonometric drawing,
Maison Particulièro, 1923. Pencil and
watercolor on tracing paper. Netherlands
Architecture Institute.

left: **5.9** Gerrit Rietveld, Schröder House,
Utrecht, 1924–5. Het Utrechts Archief.

illegibility of van Doesburg's original De Stijl logotype. It is the case with both these works that an attempt to convey universal principles of harmony was essentially overshadowed by the startlingly idiosyncratic nature of the finished work. Rather than appearing as the anonymous harbingers of a new, international style, they both come across as radically unique, paradoxically the product of a startling, individual vision that fundamentally contradicts the core beliefs of the whole group.

De Stijl Poster Design

The graphic designer Bart van der Leck's commercial work and painting both served as an important precursor of De Stijl around the time of its creation. His 1915 poster for the Müller shipping line, one of a variety of design projects he completed for the powerful Kröller-Müller family, features a highly structured geometric clarity that was soon integrated into the broader De Stijl vocabulary (*fig. 5.10*). While the illustration of the ship is conventional in many details, its overall effect is one of horizontal mass. Its black shape is reinforced by the bold horizontal and vertical rules, which introduce an element of contrast. The lettering that Van der Leck devised for this lithograph shows some of the tendency to "find the frame" in the way in which the letters are distorted horizontally so that their widths will all be equal. Finally, his uncomplicated palette of mainly primary colors shows his embrace of simplicity at a time before it had been allied with De Stijl's sometimes obscurantist ideology.

As much as his work and friendship with Mondrian made Van der Leck a key figure in De Stijl, he soon tired of the dogmatic assertions of van Doesburg and Mondrian, and by 1919 was already starting to separate himself somewhat from the group.

It was in 1919 that Van der Leck made his most overt De Stijl commercial poster, a design for the Delft Salad Oil Factories (*fig. 5.11*). The Delft factories had a long history of commissioning edgy new designs for their advertisements, most famously an 1894 Art Nouveau poster by Jan Toorop (1858–1928). That poster had been such a stunning success that the phrase "Salad-Oil Style" became a Dutch synonym for Art Nouveau. To produce his design, Van der Leck passed through a series of twelve graduated images, each one showing more of a transformation from illustration to geometric abstraction. Beginning with a drawing that shows the strong black outlines he had long favored, Van der Leck sequentially removed the outlines and filled in the former empty spaces with primary colors. In the final maquette, the figure has been reduced to a series of discrete geometric shapes, including squares, rectangles, and trapezoids. While a human shape has been maintained, the body of the figure has been transformed into a solid block. As in the first cover of the journal *De Stijl*, Van der Leck has created a letterset made up of separate geometric shapes, sacrificing much in the way of legibility.

Unfortunately, Van der Leck's final design was rejected by the Delft Salad Oil Factories' leadership, and therefore it was never reproduced. This fact points to the difficulty that De Stijl designers had in convincing the general public at large that their elemental vocabulary was a viable form of commercial communication. In contrast to Art Nouveau, for example, overt De Stijl works never made the transition that had made the former style an accepted part of the graphic design industry. However, De Stijl designers and their work did form part of a constellation of avant-garde art groups devoted to geometric abstraction that together would have a decisive impact on commercial graphics later in the twentieth century.

5.10 Bart van der Leck, *Rotterdam–London*, 1915. Poster. Merrill C. Berman Collection.

left: **5.11** Bart van der Leck, *Delft Salad Dressing*, 1919. Gouache, 34 x 23⅛ in (87 x 58.7 cm). Merrill C. Berman Collection.

left: **5.11** Bart van der Leck, *Delft Salad Dressing*, 1919. Gouache, 34 x 23⅛ in (87 x 58.7 cm). Merrill C. Berman Collection.

below: **5.12** Constructivist Congress, Weimar, Sept 1922. Photograph.

De Stijl and Dada

While it may seem that De Stijl and Dada artists would have very little in common—the Dadaists' embrace of absurdity and random chance would seem to stand in direct opposition to the De Stijl commitment to rational structure—there were some interesting collaborations in the 1920s involving members of the two groups. The most important collaboration grew out of the visit that the Dada artists Tristan Tzara, Kurt Schwitters, and Jean Arp made to the Kongress der Konstructivisten, or **Constructivist Congress**, held in Weimar Germany in 1922 (*fig. 5.12*). The term "Constructivist" can refer broadly to avant-garde artists who pursued geometric abstraction as a means to a utopian end, including the artists of De Stijl and Russian Constructivism. At the Congress, the Dadaists met their host van Doesburg (Schwitters

5.13 Theo van Doesburg and Kurt Schwitters, *Kleine Dada Soirée (Small Dada Evening)*, 1922. Lithograph, 11⅞ x 11 in (30.2 x 28.5 cm). Gift of Philip Johnson. Jan Tschichold Collection.

and van Doesburg had been acquainted the previous year), who had organized the gathering in the small German city of Weimar, where he lived from 1921 to 1923. Importantly, Weimar was the home of the German art school known as the **Bauhaus** (see Chapter 6). Van Doesburg, who had strong interests in Dada aesthetics himself, had organized the Congress in order to explore possible synergistic connections between Dada and Constructivist principles. A number of the Constructivist participants were initially scandalized by the arrival of the Dada artists, but van Doesburg managed to negotiate a détente of sorts. De Stijl principles subsequently influenced Schwitters's adoption of a Constructivist style in the 1920s.

It is important to realize that Dada after 1918 had in some ways lost its original raison d'être—protesting the First World War—and Dada artists had become more invested in pursuing art

and design professionally. While still vaguely anti-authoritarian in outlook, Dada as practiced by Schwitters or van Doesburg in 1922 had been transformed into a recognizable set of aesthetic principles. With less emphasis on the nihilistic politics of the war years, Dada ideas of unfettered creativity and artistic rule-breaking could be broadly infused into avant-garde art. Also, both Dadaists and Constructivists shared a disdain for past tradition, the "old" forms that lacked a creative spirit and were representative of the authorities that led European civilization into war. Both groups also tended to submerge the individual artistic personality into a depersonalized matrix, Dada celebrating the irrational while De Stijl and Constructivism sought to build a new rationality.

In several issues of his publication *Merz*, Schwitters developed a unique hybrid style that successfully reconciled Dada rule-breaking with the geometric abstraction favored by De Stijl and

5.14 Theo van Doesburg, *Mécano*, no. 3, 1923. Magazine cover. Letterpress on paper, 6 x 5 in (16.5 x 12.7 cm). International Dada Archive, University of Iowa Libraries.

the Russian Constructivists (see below). In 1923, Schwitters and van Doesburg traveled around the Netherlands promoting "Dada-Merz Evenings," a return to the Dada tradition of provocative performances. At the first evening, Schwitters interrupted van Doesburg's introductory lecture by letting loose with a series of barks—and then the absurdity and iconoclasm really got started. The two Dadaists created a poster (*fig. 5.13*) to advertise their performances. It displays recognizable Dada elements of chaos, and it is hard to reconcile the promoter of the "new harmony" taking part in such a disharmonious endeavor. Mixing type styles and scale, overprinting on a variety of axes, the red word "Dada" repeatedly cropped where it runs off the page—all these elements complement the confusing text, which itself combines quotes from Tristan Tzara and Francis Picabia with the nonsense sayings favored by Schwitters.

Despite the sense of communality engendered by the Weimar Congress, the distance separating De Stijl and Dada strategies is manifest in the fact that van Doesburg used a pseudonym, I.K. Bonset, when he was working in a Dada idiom. The name is in fact a phonetic joke, because to a Dutch speaker it sounds like the phrase "I'm crazy." Between 1922 and 1923, van Doesburg, or "Bonset," briefly published a new journal devoted to his Dada work. Called *Mécano*, the journal featured the same sort of topsy-turvy Dada designs that were featured in other similar publications. The cover of the third issue (out of a total of four) of *Mécano* appears to be a hybrid of De Stijl-type orthogonal structure and a whimsical use of letters rotated on to different axes, forcing the reader to rotate the page in order to make sense of the words (*fig. 5.14*). The saw blade in the center served as an emblem of *Mécano*, representing the destructive force of Dada satire. This "red" issue—the second one had been the "blue" issue—was published in both Dutch and French in an attempt to attract a broad international audience. Of course, the penchant for primary colors speaks to the aesthetic of the De Stijl movement.

Revolution in Russia

Perhaps the most spectacular outcome of the First World War was the collapse of four imperial governments: those of the Ottomans, Germany, Austria-Hungary, and Russia. In terms of impact on the visual arts, it was the disintegration of imperial Russia that proved to have the most lasting effects. When the war began in 1914, Russia was ruled by an autocratic monarch, Tsar Nicholas II (1868–1919). Unpopular because of widespread corruption and inefficiency in the government, as well as a failing economy, Nicholas further eroded his credibility when he sent Russia's unprepared and ill-supplied army to fight against the Central Powers, with disastrous results. The war made the Tsar's rule increasingly untenable as the economy collapsed and the military weakness of Russia became more apparent as its losses mounted. When riots broke out in the capital city of Petrograd (now St Petersburg) early in 1917, the Tsar was forced to abdicate.

After the dissolution of the Romanov government in the so-called February Revolution, two competing groups of citizens tried to take control of Russia. Members of the Duma, a parliamentary body, established a Provisional Government while other groups banded together to establish the Petrograd Soviet of Workers' and Soldiers' Deputies. Additional Soviets, or workers' councils, were soon established in other Russian cities, although those in Petrograd and later Moscow took the lead in civil affairs. Throughout 1917 the Provisional Government and the Petrograd Soviet clashed repeatedly over the conduct of the war (the Soviets wanted an immediate end to Russia's role in the conflict) and the form of Russia's next government. This period of near anarchy ended in the fall of 1917, when one of the constituent parties of the Soviet, the Bolsheviks under Vladimir Lenin (1870–1924), managed to seize control of the country. This second revolution, called the **Bolshevik** (or October) Revolution, was followed quickly by a peace treaty with the Central Powers, as the Bolsheviks were willing to make large territorial concessions to the west in order to focus on the consolidation of power in Russia itself.

Soon after the Bolsheviks' formation of a new government, anti-Bolshevik forces began organizing in an attempt to displace the regime. The subsequent Russian Civil War of 1918–20 was fought between the Red Army, representing the Bolsheviks, and a loose coalition of forces led by ex-imperial military officers collectively known as the "Whites." The anti-Soviet Whites were assisted by Allied governments, including Britain and the United States, in a bloody yet unsuccessful attempt to forestall the Bolsheviks' establishment of a Communist state. For this reason, the civil war led to increasing hostility between Russia and Western democratic states.

In January 1918, Lenin had overseen the writing of a new constitution that explicitly voided the property rights of those he called "exploiters"—Russia's nobility, capitalist bourgeoisie, and clergy. The Bolsheviks claimed that they would replace these oppressive ruling classes with a new form of government that would privilege the rights of urban workers and landless peasants. Based loosely on the theories of the German philosopher and social activist Karl Marx (1818–1883), the Bolshevik government espoused Communism—a doctrine whereby private property was abolished and the "means of production," which encompassed all aspects of economic life, were held communally by all citizens—as a panacea for all of Russia's social problems. Under the Bolsheviks, Communism was essentially a utopian promise, because as early as 1918 the Bolsheviks had begun centralizing state power in the hands of a small group of party leaders. While offering a greater voice in political affairs to formerly dispossessed groups of workers and peasants, the promise of a classless society of plenty proved to be always just around the corner, tantalizingly out of reach. Partly in response to the civil war of 1918–20, the Bolsheviks quickly began relying on a state apparatus of powerful domestic security forces that used violence and intimidation to suppress dissent.

The Russian Revolution and the Bolshevik Poster

In order to explain Russian graphic design in the twentieth century, it is necessary to introduce two important traditions that played a part in the country's popular visual culture. Beginning as early as the seventeenth century, a type of inexpensive illustrated woodcut called a *lubok* (plural: *lubki*) become a pervasive part of Russian life. The mechanical production of *lubki* gradually advanced, shifting from woodcut to copper engraving and, in the nineteenth century, lithography. With tremendous variations in quality, *lubki* artists combined text and image to convey religious parables, folklore, and even political satire to a wide audience. Stylistically, the exuberant use of color and horror vacui compositions—allowing little or no empty space—became an influential force in Russian art. In the twentieth century, *lubki* also served as symbols of patriotic sentiment because they invoked a unique national tradition. The *lubok Give Me the Bucket* displays the quintessential characteristic of the genre, making up for its lack of polish with an overall high-spirited vitality (*fig. 5.15*).

Another important influence for Russian graphic design was the Orthodox Church's promulgation of religious icons. These tempera and gold leaf paintings generally feature figures from the history of Christianity, especially Mary and Jesus, surrounded by a field of gold. These images were designed to promote religious piety in a largely illiterate population, facilitating each figure's identification with consistent color and stock poses and facial features. Icons were important in terms of familiarizing the population with the techniques of symbolism and allegory. Under the Bolsheviks, there would be a similar need for images that conveyed strong messages through color and simple actions so that they were understandable to the broadest swath of the population.

After the revolution, Malevich also garnered new status as well as a new position in 1919 as head of a teaching studio at the State Art School led by the Expressionist painter Marc Chagall (1887–1985) in Vitebsk. There he continued to promulgate the Suprematist aesthetic, while having a significant impact on a number of students and colleagues, including El Lissitzky. Malevich and Lissitzky were both important members of UNO-VIS, a group of Suprematist artists dedicated to the Bolshevik cause whose name roughly translates as "Affirmers of the New Art." From the outset of the revolution, it became clear that Suprematist principles were less directly transferable than Constructivism to the service of revolutionary propaganda. The metaphysical realm of Suprematist "pure feeling," as well as Malevich's commitment to the autonomy of art from everyday life, made it difficult to envision Suprematism as an effective tool of agitation and propaganda.

By 1922, Malevich was forced to keep his continuing work on Suprematist paintings secret from his colleagues because they were considered to be at best a waste of valuable time and energy that would be better spent on utilitarian works. Nevertheless,

Lissitzky's famous poster from the civil war years *Beat the Whites with the Red Wedge* (1920; *fig. 5.25*) demonstrates how Suprematist principles were at times successfully employed as propaganda in service of the revolution. This two-colored lithograph was published by a military printing house in a run of 2,000. Despite the reductive geometric abstract forms, it is clear that Lissitzky is employing the same type of simple color symbolism and dynamic movement that more realistically inclined poster designers were using in their works. In a parallel to Zvorykin's *The Struggle of the Red Knight with the Dark Force*, the Red Army is shown here in the form of a wedge piercing the soft circular form of the Whites' counterrevolutionary forces. While the imagery is clearly indebted to Malevich, Lissitzky has added elements of texture and three-dimensional shading that significantly enhance the potential range of both formal experiments and expression of Suprematist abstraction. Indirectly invoking the *lubok* tradition, Lissitzky makes a simple, direct emotional appeal to the viewer. Lissitzky believed that the universal language of abstract Suprematism could convey meaning to both learned intellectuals and the illiterate peasants who were the main focus of the agitprop campaign.

below: **5.23** Vladimir Tatlin, *Monument to the Third International*, 1920. Painted wood, iron, and glass, 20 ft (6.1 m) high. Russian State Museum, St Petersburg.

right: **5.24** Vladimir Tatlin, *Monument to the Third International by Nikolaj Punin*, 1920. Cover with letterpress illustration on front, 11 x 8⅝ in (28 x 21.9 cm). Gift of the Judith Rothschild Foundation, 215.2001.1-2. Museum of Modern Art, New York.

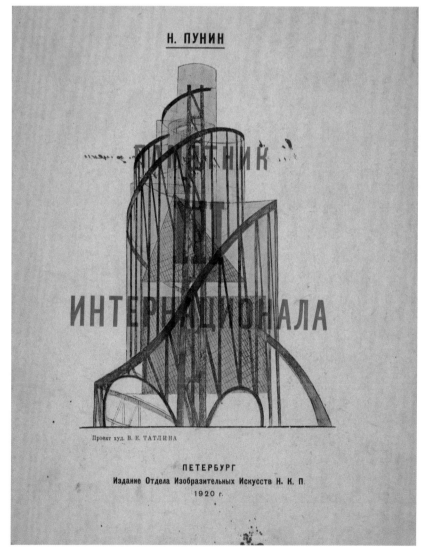

5.25 El Lissitzky, *Beat the Whites with the Red Wedge*, 1919–20. Offset lithograph, 19½ x 28 in (49.5 x 71.4 cm). Van Abbemuseum, Eindhoven, The Netherlands.

Constructivism and Alexander Rodchenko

While the Suprematists found continuing difficulty trying to reconcile their aesthetic beliefs with service to the Communist cause, the Constructivists, led by the versatile artist and designer Varvara Stepanova (1894–1958) and her husband Rodchenko, chose to renounce fine art completely. While Rodchenko had risen to prominence as an abstract avant-gardist, in 1921 he came to the conclusion that in order truly to serve the revolution it was necessary to end his career as a painter and sculptor. Constructivists coined the term "Productivism" to indicate their desire to make works that served a practical purpose within the context of the Communist cause. The central role of art formulated by the Constructivists was as a complement to the new workers' state. For this reason, they sought to ally their art with industrial production, and worked to design practical goods such as propaganda posters, workers' clothes, and government buildings. With the fine art approach of Suprematism gradually suppressed, the aesthetic formulations of Malevich and others were partly absorbed into the Constructivist aesthetic, so that after 1921 the two movements are largely woven together.

Under the influence of the Constructivists, graphic designers found an exalted status in society unlike any they had enjoyed before. Because the new regime was skeptical of the bourgeois decadence of the fine arts, graphic designers, who had participated fully in the agitprop campaigns of Communism, took their place as ideologically pure artistic leaders. Designers such as Rodchenko rejected the term "artist" in favor of more practical words such as "engineer" or "constructor," both of which suggested a more pragmatic social role as well as an awareness and integration of industrial technology.

Soon after the Bolsheviks prevailed in the civil war and the consolidation of the Communist-led regime (the Bolsheviks changed their name to the Communist Party in 1918), Lenin introduced the New Economic Policy (NEP). A response to the industrial decline that had resulted from the revolution and civil war, the NEP allowed for some new private enterprises to develop in competition with state-owned companies. This quasi-capitalist situation led to the need for increased advertising by state-owned firms, several of which turned to Constructivist artists for their design projects. Enthusiastically asserting himself in this new arena, Rodchenko worked on a number of publicity campaigns for state companies. In 1922–3, he designed the first comprehensive corporate identity ever seen in Russia for the Dobrolet State Merchant Air Service. Rodchenko's designs included posters as well as logos and letterheads for its corporate communication.

The basic image in all of Rodchenko's design work for Dobrolet is a drawing of a Junkers aircraft, the mainstay of the airline's fleet. Sometimes Rodchenko used a realistically rendered image of the plane, while in other instances he used a reductive geometric abstraction. Whatever its form, the aircraft is generally portrayed tilted as if in a climb, lending an element of dynamic energy to the image (*fig. 5.26*). In many graphic works from this period, Rodchenko is making a virtue out of economic necessity; the spare use of color and basic letterpress typography (the latter most likely chosen by the printer) are symptomatic of the general lack of resources that plagued Russia in the early 1920s. It is important not to overlook the continuing color symbolism of Constructivist designs that use only red, the color of the Communist Revolution. In addition, the spare Constructivist style served as a direct rejoinder to the gaudy ornament employed by the defeated imperial government.

Rodchenko's posters for Dobrolet combined Constructivist design with slogans exhorting the viewer to invest in the airline for patriotic reasons. "Shame on you, your name is not yet on the list of Dobrolet stockholders. The whole country follows this list," reads the text in this poster. This type of slogan marks an important contrast between Russian and Western advertising techniques; Rodchenko is not trying to create desire for a product, but is basing his appeal on the propagandistic themes of guilt and duty more often seen in war recruitment posters. The Russian government maintained at this time that an imminent world revolution would spread Communism throughout the West, and the urgent, militant tone of Rodchenko's ad copy sounds the same themes as Russia's agitation and propaganda campaigns.

Alexander Rodchenko, Vladimir Mayakovsky

In 1923, Rodchenko joined with the avant-garde poet activist Vladimir Mayakovsky (1893–1930) in order to form an advertising firm that they called Ad-Constructor. Rodchenko's striking graphic style was combined with Mayakovsky's clever turns of phrase to create many advertisements for state industries, including Mosselprom, a state-owned chain of food stores based in Moscow. The foods sold at Mosselprom were generic government products, lacking specific brand names or labels, so Rodchenko and Mayakovsky had to create an identity for the goods through the poster designs themselves. The texts on the posters were complicated by the need to maintain a tone of agitation, educating consumers on how a product serves the revolution just as much as it fulfills an individual's day-to-day needs.

A fine example of one of Ad-Constructor's images is an advertisement for cocoa, displaying one of Rodchenko's favorite compositional devices, the triangle, in this case formed by two arrows at the base pointing toward the product itself (*fig. 5.27*). The label of the cocoa looks archaic in comparison with Rodchenko's bold Constructivist design. The huge sans serif letters spell out the text in the Cyrillic alphabet with a variety of styles. Some of the letters are outlines; some are carved out of negative space; others run on the diagonal. All of this creates a tremendous sense of dynamism. Mayakovsky's text urges the viewer to buy the product by invoking the vigorous health of the new Russian citizen. "Comrades, don't argue! Soviet citizens will become stronger in sport. In our might is our right. And where is strength? In this cocoa." The text makes use of many of Mayakovsky's typical rhetorical devices: assonance, alliteration, and exclamation points. This use of repetition and aggressive emphasis neatly parallels the bold color and strong forms of Rodchenko's design.

5.26 Alexander Rodchenko, Dobrolet, 1923.
Poster. Offset color lithograph,
13 x 17⅞ in (34.9 x 45.4 cm).
Museum of Modern Art, New York.

5.27 Alexander Rodchenko, *Kakao (Cocoa)*, 1923–4. Poster. Pencil, gouache, 33⅛ x 23 in (84 x 59.6 cm). Text by Vladimir Mayakovsky. Rodchenko Archives.

Photomontage and Film

Soviet graphic designers were perhaps the most technically innovative and original artists of their generation. They were among the first groups of artists to make sustained use of photography and to develop ways in which text and photography could be integrated into a successful composition. While photography had been mass-reproduced in newspapers and magazines through the use of the halftone process for over two decades, its ubiquity did not garner it a very significant role in graphic design until the 1920s. In Russia, the camera was idolized because of its apparent ability to produce depersonalized photographs that spoke to collective ideals more than to the individual vision of a creator. Also, the camera represented an excellent opportunity for many artists to synthesize their love of modern machinery with Constructivist aesthetics.

While straightforward photographs were sometimes integrated with text in a conventional manner, as would be seen in a magazine, more often **Russian Constructivists** turned to the technique called photomontage. A photomontage is a composite image made up of a variety of photographic source materials. These might include original artwork, but most often artists liked to use images culled from popular newspapers and magazines.

The composites were generally formed through a positive process, whereby images are cut and pasted together to form a collage, which itself is then subsequently mass-produced by letterpress or lithographic processes. Photomontages could also be made in the darkroom using photographic negatives, which could be sandwiched into an enlarger. Alternatively, the photographic paper could be masked as it was exposed to successive images in different areas.

In Russia, it was hoped that the startling juxtapositions of photomontage could result in works that disrupted the conven-

Photomontage

The invention of photomontage remains something of a contentious issue in the history of the avant-garde. The Berlin Dadaist Raoul Hausmann has established perhaps the most compelling case for claiming the credit for himself, mainly because he is able to tie the invention to a specific trip he made to the Baltic coast in 1918. Hausmann recounted that he was struck by a military memento that showed a photo of the head of a specific soldier pasted on to a generic image of a soldier's body. "It was like a flash; I saw instantly that one could make pictures composed entirely of cut-up photos." Hausmann conveniently left out of this recollection the fact that his colleague and romantic partner Hannah Höch (1889–1978) had accompanied him on the trip and played an equal role in the development of photomontage as a visual strategy. Höch and Hausmann quickly assimilated this technique into their Dada experiments, allowing them to open up a new source of raw materials for a satirical eye to contemplate.

Höch's montage features a title that says it all—Cut with a Kitchen Knife Dada through the Last Weimar Beer-Belly Cultural Epoch of Germany (fig. 5.28). Her montage exudes contempt for the bourgeois materialism and official culture that were constant targets of Dada. She has created an impulsive, spontaneous satire of contemporary Germany out of a mass of fragmented images drawn from popular magazines and newspapers. There is a strong kinetic element produced by the multiple diagonal lines that crisscross the page. The absurd juxtapositions of incongruous images seem on the one hand to lack any specific insights about Weimar culture. Most of the images were derived from commercial publications, although personal touches, such as the photo of Hausmann screaming that was featured in Der Dada #3 *(see fig. 3.47) were also included. Additionally, a closer look at some of the fragments shows Höch's affinity for Communist politics, as both Karl Marx and Vladimir Lenin are recognizable. Also, several other images are portraits of accomplished women, such as the German Expressionist painter Käthe Kollwitz (1867–1945); these photos are pasted close to a map of Europe that shows the gradual spread of women's suffrage. Clearly, Höch is commenting on the societal turmoil taking place in Germany over the "New Woman" movement, a loose term for the cultural drive toward greater emancipation and civil rights for women that took place after the end of the First World War. Tellingly, Höch includes a small portrait of herself adjacent to the map that depicts women's increasing voting rights in Europe. Photomontage, which began in Germany as a Dadaist anti-art strategy, quickly became recognized as having opened up new, fertile aesthetic territory.*

5.28 Hannah Höch, *Cut with a Kitchen Knife Dada through the last Weimar Beer-Belly Cultural Epoch of Germany*, 1919.

5.29 Alexander Rodchenko, Photomontage accompanying Vladimir Mayakovsky's poem "About This," 1923. State Mayakovsky Museum, Moscow. Rodchenko Archives.

tional passive reception of photographs and unleashed the
revolutionary potential of modern images. This general goal of
transforming the consciousness of the viewer to a more enlightened state was behind many of the Constructivists' formal
experiments. Rodchenko made some of his first photomontages in
1923, when he collaborated with Mayakovsky on the publication
of a book of the writer's poems, called *Pro Eto* ("About This").
The poems relate Mayakovsky's distress at his separation from his
lover Lili Brik (1891–1978), distress that he connects to their
shared fervor for Communist revolution. In the pages of the
book, Rodchenko's montages alternate with pages of text. The
fact that he was illustrating abstract poetry gave Rodchenko
almost free rein to design images that feature only distant relationships to the printed text. Most of his montages combine
figures with the elements of modern industrial life; thus it is not
the subject matter that illustrates the verses of *Pro Eto*, it is
Rodchenko's style. Just as he and Mayakovsky matched text and
image in their advertising posters, so here Rodchenko's abrupt
shifts in scale and dramatic compositions are perfectly matched
to the intangible feelings expressed in the poem. The page
illustrated here is unique in that Rodchenko has eschewed the
typical horror vacui style used by many early photomontage
artists. Instead, Rodchenko's composition is based on a strong
diagonal element, using a lot of empty space to draw the eye in
to the central mass (*fig. 5.29*).

Filmic Vision

Rodchenko was equally enchanted by "filmic" vision, and he
collaborated often with the Russian filmmaker Dziga Vertov
(1896–1954), first designing film titles for his documentaries in
1922. Vertov was one of a new generation of Soviet filmmakers
who rejected the "bourgeois" tradition of storytelling in film
because it encouraged passivity and dampened the revolutionary
potential of the viewer. In place of narrative, Vertov sought to
energize the viewer with a camera that records the moments of
everyday life in modern, industrial Russia. Using jump cuts,
montaged juxtapositions, abstract patterns, kinesthetic interpene-
trations of machine and people, and a Constructivist framework
emphasizing orthogonal elements, Vertov tried to create a new
aesthetic for cinema that was tied to that art's specific medium.

The 1924 film *Kino Glanz* ("Film Eye") consists mainly of
a montage of newsreel footage celebrating post-revolutionary
Russia (*fig. 5.30*). Rodchenko created a poster advertising the film
that makes use of his favored triangular composition, the triangle
formed by two faces that lead on diagonals through two motion
picture cameras directly into the center of an eye. Vertov had
written in a manifesto that the human eye and the dispassionate
camera eye—the subject of the film's title—could be merged:
"I am kino-eye, I am mechanical eye, I, a machine." Rodchenko's
poster shows two repeated images of a boy (the base of the

5.30 Alexander Rodchenko, *Kino Glanz (Film Eye)*, 1924. Lithograph, 27½ x
36 in (69.9 x 92.7 cm). Museum of Modern Art, New York.

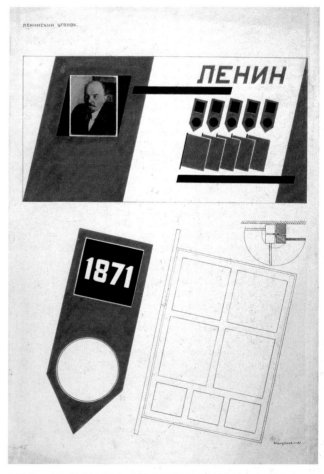

5.31 Alexander Rodchenko, Lenin Corner. Fragment of the interior of the
Worker's Club. Soviet section, Exposition Internationale des Arts Décoratifs et
Industriels Modernes, Paris, 1925. Private Collection. Rodchenko Archives.

triangle) in extreme close-up at an oblique angle, an element clearly taken from his study of current cinematic techniques. The boys stare at the cameras, which in turn lead upward to the powerful eye at the top of the pyramid, as they seem to confront this new technology. The gigantic sans serif letters gracefully harmonize with the images. Paradoxically, Rodchenko produced this homage to the machine entirely by hand. The "photographs" are all in fact hand-drawn, and the large block letters are similarly rendered. What appears to be a letterpress poster incorporating halftone reproductions of photographs is in fact a lithograph no more technologically advanced than the earliest poster by Jules Cheret. As was the case with Tatlin's *Monument to the Third International*, Russian technology was not always up to the task of fulfilling artistic visions.

Rodchenko rarely traveled outside Russia, so his works were not well known in Europe. However, he did provide a design for a Workers' Club that was part of the Russian display at the 1925 "Exposition Internationale des Arts Décoratifs et Industriels Modernes" in Paris (*fig. 5.31*). The *Workers' Club* was exhibited in order to contrast the active, participatory role of the industrial proletariat in communal life in Russia with the passive, decadent individual leisure of the European bourgeoisie. Rodchenko took as his theme the recent death of Lenin in 1924, and created a "Lenin Corner" in the club. This type of memorial was quite fashionable after the leader's death, and in fact invoked the Russian tradition of having a corner of the household set aside for the family's religious icon. Rodchenko sought not only to memorialize Lenin but also to promote his policy of increased education for working people. The design for the Lenin Corner shows the standard tropes of Constructivism: a photo of Lenin floating amid a dynamic geometric design of red and black.

Gustav Klutsis

Gustav Klutsis (1895–1944) was one of several Constructivist artists who worked not only to create new graphics but also to design dynamic display signs. Klutsis had impressive credentials; he had fought in both revolutions, defended Moscow during the civil war, joined Malevich's Suprematist organization UNOVIS, and later made important contributions to the Russian intellectual organizations known as "LEF" and "October," which included many Constructivists. As part of the agitprop campaign, Klutsis designed a rotating sign that featured revolutionary slogans (*fig. 5.32*). Using geometric shapes, bright colors, and outdoor illumination, this propaganda sign helped show the connection between new technology and the new consciousness of the proletariat. These types of structure, like Tatlin's *Monument to the Third International*, remained essentially theoretical, as few were actually ever constructed.

The manner in which the chaotic energy of Dada was subsumed into Constructivism is clear in Klutsis's poster publicizing the Spartakiada Moscow athletic games of 1928 (*fig. 5.33*). While the overall design is an orthogonal one, there is a contrapuntal rhythm to the image that is more spirited than the majority of austere Constructivist graphics. *Spartakiada Moscow* has the feel of one of Hannah Höch's Dadaist photomontages, rationalized

5.32 Gustav Klutsis, *Fundamentals*, Agitprop design, c. 1926. Pencil, ink, gouache, 7⅟₁₆ x 4¹³⁄₁₆ in (18.1 x 11.9 cm). Merrill C. Berman Collection.

and made to conform to a grid, yet it still projects the pent-up chaotic energy of Dada. In collaging together different types of photographs with lettering cut out of construction paper, Klutsis created an epic image that encapsulates the vitality of athletic competition. Athletes were often used as emblems of the new Soviet citizen, and the equality of women under the Communist regime relative to their ancillary role in Western European society—represented by the prominent photo of a female athlete in the upper right corner—was a major selling point of Russian propaganda.

Constructivists under Stalin

After Josef Stalin (1879–1953) came to power in the mid-1920s, there was increasing political pressure on artists to make works that presented Russian leaders in heroic terms. Klutsis was the most effective of the Constructivists at using photomontage to glorify the Communist leadership. This theme in Soviet propaganda had started after the death of Lenin in 1924, when a huge number of public memorials were built across the USSR. This memorial cult was engineered by Stalin, as General Secretary of

5.33 Gustav Klutsis, *Spartakiada Moscow*, 1928. Halftone photographs, gelatin silver prints, colored paper, paste, 23¾ x 27 in (60.3 x 69.8 cm). Merrill C. Berman Collection.

the Communist Party's Central Committee, who seized control of the Soviet state after Lenin's death. Stalin would prove to be much more hostile toward avant-garde art than his predecessors, and it was necessary for an artist such as Klutsis who worked in the Constructivist idiom to position himself strategically in terms of subject matter—honoring the great heroism of Lenin and Stalin at every turn—so as to assure the leadership of his ideological purity in the face of an abstract style.

In 1928 Stalin instituted the first of his "Five Year Plans," a program of crash industrialization that helped to bring Soviet society closer to its economic goals. The two themes of the heroism of Lenin and Stalin and the triumphs of "socialist industry" under the Five Year Plans, are woven together in a number of Klutsis's photomontages from the early 1930s. Klutsis felt strongly that only radical new art forms such as photomontage were fit to convey the themes of revolutionary Communism:

> The old disciplines in the visual arts (drawing, painting, graphic art), with their obsolete techniques and working methods, are insufficient to satisfy the demands of the Revolution as concerns the tasks of agitation and propaganda on a massive scale … Art must be on the same high level as socialist industry.

5.34 Gustav Klutsis, *Under the Banner of Lenin for Socialist Construction*, published by the State Publishing House, USSR, 1930. Victoria and Albert Museum, London.

A poster published by the state publishing house in 1930, *Under the Banner of Lenin for Socialist Construction* (*fig. 5.34*), demonstrates how effectively Stalin, whom Lenin had distrusted and attempted to undermine before his death, created overlapping cults of personality that tied his own rule to that of the original Bolshevik hero. In this photomontage, Lenin and Stalin's eyes have been merged into one, suggesting the former's approval and authorization of his successor. Klutsis fills out the image with a montage of scenes that showcase Russian industry under the first Five Year Plan. The strong diagonals that structure the composition capture the excitement and inherent drama of massive factories and machines.

Film Posters: the Stenbergs

The witty and whimsical film posters of the brothers Georgii Stenberg (1900–1933) and Vladimir Stenberg (1899–1982) provide an interesting alternative to the generally severe work of the Constructivists. The Stenberg brothers completely revolutionized the aesthetics of film posters during the 1920s, using exciting compositional techniques that reproduced filmic vision, including the close-up and freeze-frame. Their expressive posters also make use of implied movement and vertiginous shifts in scale and perspective that leave the viewer dizzy while powerfully evoking the intensity of the cinematic experience.

The film industry in Russia had gone into severe decline because of the First World War and subsequent revolution. Many prominent producers and directors had allied themselves with the Whites, and a number of them eventually emigrated after the Bolsheviks gained power. Moscow, home before the war to over 125 movie theaters, including a number of palatial landmarks, had no functioning cinemas whatsoever by 1920. However, by 1922 there was the beginning of a resurgence in the industry, and after 1923 movies once again became an important part of Russian popular culture. The attitude of the Communist Party to the cinema was complex; while it hoped to build a new Soviet film industry that could become an important part of the agitprop campaign, at the same time the relative openness of the New Economic Policy allowed for the distribution of foreign films, especially from Germany and, later in the 1920s, the United States. The government was badly in need of funds after the destruction of the civil war, and the popular cinema proved to be a ready source of income for the state.

The genius of the Stenberg brothers was their ability to montage elements from a film in such a way as to produce an overall sense of the excitement of the drama. Their posters are not simply out-takes from the films themselves, or images of the stars. Rather, they are wholly original compositions that capture the mood of the film at hand. In order to replicate the effect of an artist masking different parts of photographic paper to form a montage, the Stenbergs designed and built a projection apparatus that allowed them to copy images from a movie frame by frame. Faced with the dearth of quality printing equipment in the USSR, the Stenbergs, like Rodchenko, had to copy the images by hand, resulting in posters that appear to contain photo reproductions but are in fact hand-drawn lithographs. For example, *High Society*

5.35 Georgii and Vladimir Stenberg, *High Society Wager*, 1923. Poster. Merrill C. Berman Collection.

5.36 Georgii and Vladimir Stenberg, *The Man with the Movie Camera*, 1929. Poster. Lithograph.

Wager, publicizing a German film of 1923, shows the characters in the film climbing a staircase (*fig. 5.35*). The movie recounts the story of the downfall of a wealthy couple who become involved in gambling. The Stenbergs' poster does not show a specific scene from the movie, but instead bases a montage on some of its elements. The spiral stair that structures the composition is on the one hand a geometric Constructivist device, yet on the other hand it projects danger and adventure in a way that contrasts greatly with the austere works of Tatlin or Rodchenko. The stairway also serves as a metaphor for the "social climbing" that leads to the downfall of the protagonists.

The 1920s was a golden age for the experimental Soviet cinema, and the Stenberg brothers often made posters for avant-garde filmmakers such as Dziga Vertov. Vertov's 1929 film *The Man with the Movie Camera* is the story of a day in the life of the city of Moscow. Reflecting Vertov's theory of the plotless film sustained by the "Kino-Eye," the movie uses a number of experimental techniques—montage, jump cuts, extreme close-ups—to create an abstract work that pulses with the life of socialist industry. The Stenbergs' poster publicizing the film shows the fragmented form of a woman rotating in a cityscape of towering skyscrapers (*fig. 5.36*). A spiral of text echoes her motion while providing some details about the film. The image in the poster appears to be taken from *The Man with the Movie Camera*, but it is in fact a total reinvention of how the movie feels. Nothing in the image comes from the actual film other than the woman's face and the spiral, which in this case evokes the lens of a camera.

El Lissitzky

As noted above, El Lissitzky—real name Lazar' Markovich Lisitskii—joined the art school at Vitebsk in 1919. There he worked in a Suprematist idiom, enchanted by the intuitive aesthetic style championed by Malevich. Lissitzky soon devised his own manner of abstraction based on Suprematist principles, adding elements of three-dimensionality, rotation, texture, and even realistic rendering to his repertoire, in contrast to Malevich's more reductive approach. Lissitzky called this work Proun, or "Project for the Affirmation of the New Art," a name that resonates alongside UNOVIS in suggesting a role for Suprematism in building a new society. Examples of Proun graphics include the poster *Beat the Whites with the Red Wedge* (see fig. 5.25) and the children's book *Of Two Squares* that Lissitzky published in the Dutch journal *De Stijl* (see fig. 5.7). The original title for the children's book in its Russian edition was *Suprematist Story of Two Squares in Six Constructions*, and it featured a red square and a black square, which unite to join the revolutionary cause.

Despite his early commitment to Suprematism, Lissitzky also collaborated with the Constructivists, so that his work after 1921 represents an amalgam of the Suprematist exaltation of intuition and abstract ideals with the Constructivists' belief that utilitarian work was morally superior to fine art. A photomontage from 1924 called *The Constructor* (*fig. 5.37*) demonstrates how Lissitzky adopted the Constructivist theme of "artist as engineer," superimposing a hand holding a compass across a self-portrait. The combination of eye and hand, uniting intellectual and manual

work, was an important part of the new identity sought by Russian artists in the 1920s. The photographic elements are particularly well integrated with the geometric design of the background, for example in the way a smooth circle is juxtaposed with the compass that could have produced it. *The Constructor* also shows evidence of Lissitzky's experimentation with camera-less photography, as some of the background elements were made through direct exposure of photographic paper.

El Lissitzky in Germany

Despite his strong desire to support the Soviet state, Lissitzky differed from his colleagues in that throughout the 1920s he traveled widely outside the USSR. Fluent in German, he was largely responsible through his lectures, publications, and participation in conferences, for fueling the interest in Russian avant-garde art among Europeans. He spent most of the years 1922–5 in Germany, where he had numerous contacts with members of De Stijl, Dada, and the Bauhaus. Lissitzky continually networked with other artists, attending events such as the Constructivist Conference organized in Weimar by Theo van Doesburg in 1922. The German state was a natural fit for Lissitzky, because it had longstanding trade ties with Russia, was considered a pariah state after the First World War (like the USSR), and hosted a diverse community of artists interested in pursuing new abstract styles. Lissitzky's belief that Constructivist aesthetics could be separated from their political origins in Communism was in staunch opposition to the view of many other artists, such as Klutsis or Rodchenko, who felt that ideology, not art, was at the heart of the project. Scholars now generally separate Russian Constructivism, with its strong ideological bent, from "International Constructivism," as practiced in diverse ways by European artists devoted to geometric abstraction.

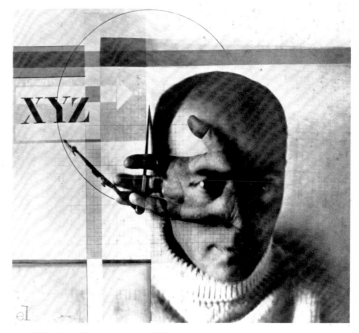

5.37 El Lissitzky, *The Constructor*, 1924.

left: **5.38** El Lissitzky and Kurt Schwitters, *Merz* 8/9, 1924. Journal. Victoria and Albert Museum, London.

below: **5.39** El Lissitzky, "Our March" from *For the Voice*, poems by Vladimir Mayakovsky, 1923. Book. Letterpress, 7⁷⁄₁₆ x 10¼ in (19.5 x 26 cm), open. Merrill C. Berman Collection.

In 1924, Lissitzky collaborated in Hanover with Kurt Schwitters on a copy of the latter's *Merz* journal (*fig. 5.38*). The resulting issue #8/9, nicknamed "Nature," encouraged artists to incorporate natural forms in their work. The cover illustrated here displays a startlingly asymmetrical design, the horizontal lines of red text resting on a blue grid that appears to be cantilevered from the left margin. This dynamic asymmetry is balanced by the centered banner at the top of the cover. Later installments of *Merz*, such as issue #11, discussed in Chapter 3 (see fig. 3.49), show Schwitters integrating Constructivist principles with his Dadaist inclinations.

Schwitters helped Lissitzky, who was suffering from tuberculosis, find work designing graphics for the Pelikan Ink Company, based in Hanover. One of the resulting advertisements shows how Lissitzky borrowed a motif from Constructivism, draining it of its revolutionary ideology in the process. The ad employs the compass-wielding hand from his photomontage *The Constructor*, now transformed from the hand of a revolutionary artist into the hand of a Western consumer (*fig. 5.40*). The original had featured the artist's commanding eye, which has here been replaced by a bottle of ink. The cuff on the arm in the advertisement has also been changed from something plain into the French cuffs, complete with cufflinks, of a well-manicured member of the bourgeoisie.

One important advantage for Lissitzky during his German sojourn was the ready availability of up-to-date printing equipment, so that he was never forced to "fake" his typographic experiments by using hand-drawn lettering that pretended to be mechanical type, something Rodchenko had had to do on several occasions. In 1923, in Berlin, Lissitzky actually published one of his most important works for a Russian audience, a collection of poems by Mayakovsky called *For the Voice* (*fig. 5.39*). Using only the standard elements of letterpress available in any printer's typecase—letters, rules, symbols—Lissitzky created one of the most inventive series of layouts ever seen. The book was indexed with tabs so that each individual poem could be readily found by someone reciting the poems for an audience, as indicated by the Russian title, which can also be translated as "Poems for Reading Out Loud." Lissitzky's designs to illustrate the poems bear a closer relationship to the text than the series of photomontages that Rodchenko made for another of Maykovsky's books. For example, the poem entitled "Our March" features letters that seem literally to march across the page. Most of the elements in *For the Voice*—the mixing of differently scaled type, the diagonal axes, even the overall sense of kineticism—had already appeared in Dada and Futurist publications. But, like Klutsis in his photomontage *Spartakiada Moscow*, here Lissitzky manages to assert some sort of control over the Dadaist chaos, creating a hybrid work that combines the frenetic energy of Dada with the discipline of Constructivism.

Lissitzky returned to Russia in 1925, although he continued to travel and maintain his contacts among the European avant-garde. In a photomontage of 1926, he took up the theme of the athlete as hero in a dynamic work that combines a hurdler with a double exposure of Times Square in New York City (*fig. 5.41*). That American city, a continual source of inspiration for the avant-garde who romanticized its brilliant displays of night-time illumination and its iconic status, was at the heart of the most

5.40 El Lissitzky, *Pelican Drawing Ink*,
1925. Advertisement. Color lithograph,
12 x 17⅜ in (32.3 x 44.1 cm).
Merrill C. Berman Collection.

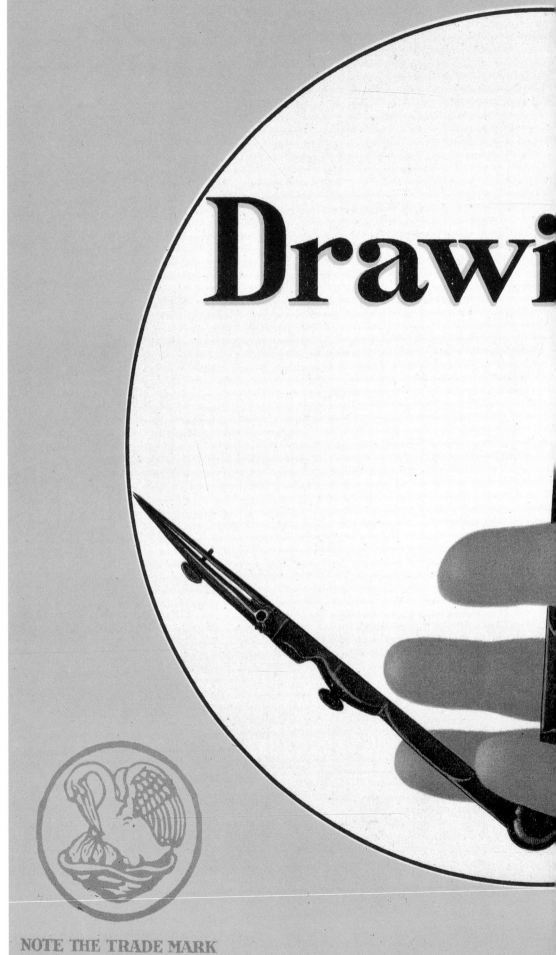

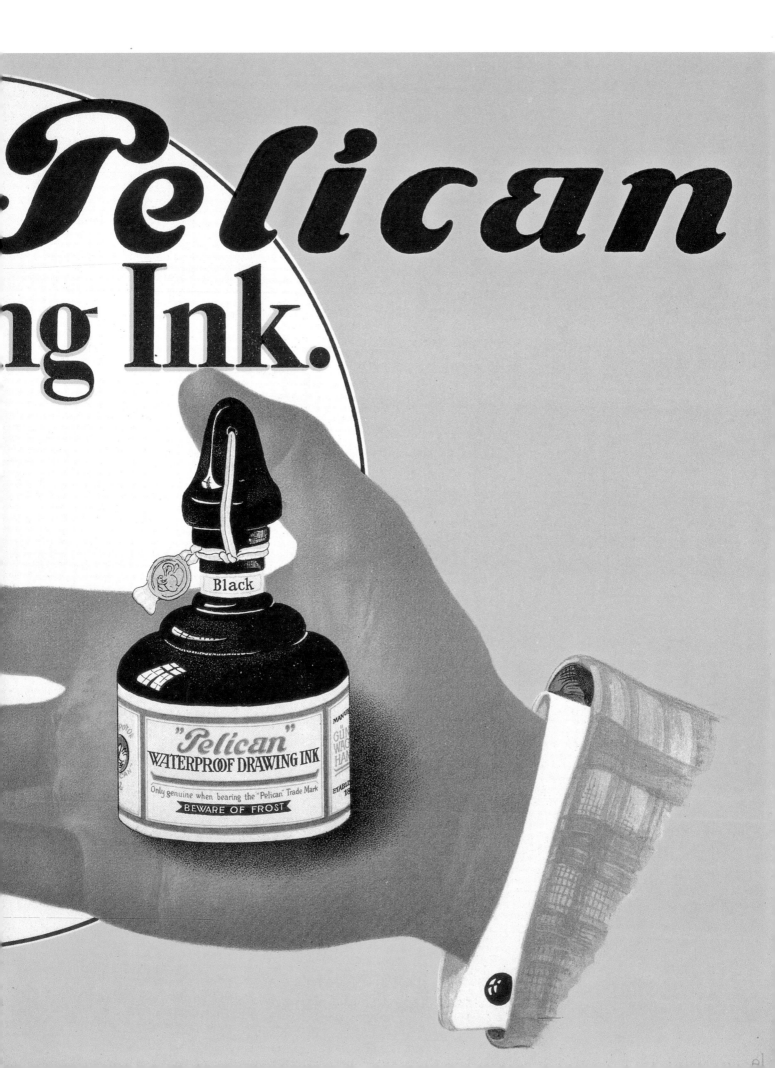

technologically sophisticated nation in the world. Lissitzky has stretched the image on the horizontal axis by cutting the montage into strips and pasting them down with slight spaces in between each column. Showing a concern with the speed of the modern city that matches Vertov's, Lissitzky created an image that captures the simultaneity favored by Futurism.

On his return to the USSR, Lissitzky was instrumental in the production of Russian exhibitions in Europe. In 1929, he designed a poster advertising an exhibition of Russian applied arts to be held at the Kunstgewerbemuseum in Zurich, Switzerland (*fig. 5.42*). The image displays Lissitzky's continuing commitment to the Soviet cause, despite his international interests. It shows two robust young Russians, male and female, merged to symbolize the state's gender equality, staring out into a hopeful future. Below them, the words "Russian Exhibition" have been neatly integrated with a photograph of the exhibition building (also designed by Lissitzky) so that the letters form a banner that recedes into space in the same perspective. These words and the building itself appear to be cantilevered off the red band that runs vertically up the left margin.

In Russia itself, the Constructivist artists faced increasing political pressure throughout the 1930s to conform to Stalin's call for greater realism in the arts. It is obvious in the photomontages of Klutsis, for example, that he is attempting to temper his Constructivist aesthetic with heroic images in the style of "**Socialist Realism.**" While Russian Constructivism was gradually suppressed by the increasingly totalitarian government in the USSR, the "**International Constructivism**" of Europe was only just beginning to flex its muscles. International Constructivism was especially powerful in Germany, a cultural base for many expatriates such as Van Doesburg and Lissitzky. In addition, a number of native German artists dedicated themselves to an exploration of the potential of universal abstract form. The next chapter will consider the Constructivist movement in Germany.

5.41 El Lissitzky, *Runner in the City*, 1926. Gelatin silver print, 5³⁄₁₆ x 5¹⁄₁₆ in (13.1 x 12.8 cm). Metropolitan Museum of Art. Gift of Ford Motor Company and John C. Waddell, 1987.

5.42 El Lissitzky, *Russian Exhibition*, 1929. Poster. Gravure, 49 x 35 in (124 x 89.5 cm). Museum of Modern Art, New York.

6 typography the bauhaus and the new

bauhaus

Chapter 3 discussed the unstable situation in German society after the disastrous defeat of the German military in the First World War. Reflecting the polarized political situation of that era, the members of Berlin Dada had thrust themselves into the fray, making political works that excoriated the foibles of the Weimar Republic (1919–33) as well as the violent nationalism of the nascent Nazi movement in Germany. The "Weimar Republic" denotes the democratic government based in the small city of Weimar that led Germany between 1919 and 1933. It oversaw an era marked by artistic ferment as well as social instability that was aggravated by periodic economic crises. It was into this volatile climate that Russian Constructivism was first introduced to Europe around 1920. Notably, one the most significant early routes whereby Russian Constructivism was brought to the attention of artists in Germany was through the efforts of the Berlin Dadaists. Several members of the group had joined the German Communist Party, and they hoped that a Communist revolution could rise from the ashes of the war in their own nation.

Dada and Russian Constructivism

In 1920, at the Berlin Dada exhibition called the "First International Dada Fair," the slogan "Art is Dead! Long Live the Machine Art of Tatlin!" was displayed prominently on the wall of the main gallery. Serving as a sort of unofficial theme for the exhibition, this idealization of Tatlin's Constructivist art had more to do with the Berlin Dadaists' embrace of utopian Communism than with their employment of Russian Constructivist aesthetic strategies. In a similar vein, in 1920, Raoul Hausmann made a photomontage called *Tatlin at Home* (*fig. 6.1*). This work shows a man–machine hybrid, his brain made up of various industrial parts, including an automobile steering column. The figure's left eye is merged with a wheel from a car, suggesting that Tatlin's artistic vision is dispassionate and clinical, the vision of an engineer. In the upper right corner, a photograph of a ship's propeller seems to spring from the man's brain, like a thought bubble in a comic book. The photo is not an actual portrait of Tatlin, but a found image that is just as anonymous and impersonal as any of the other photographic elements. Hausmann later stated that he had only a vague notion of the guiding principles of Russian Constructivism in 1920, and had derived the idea of a machine–man representing Tatlin through an almost random process. At

this time, the members of Berlin Dada were especially disgusted with the prominence in Germany of Expressionist art, which they believed was hopelessly subjective and romantic in outlook. Dadaists argued, somewhat inaccurately, that Expressionist artists loved to wallow in their own emotional tribulations while ignoring the reality of post-war society.

An influx of Russian émigrés in the early 1920s, including El Lissitzky, Naum Gabo (1890–1977), and Antoine Pevsner (1884–1962), created a critical mass of artists interested in exploring Constructivist principles. Gabo and Pevsner were brothers who had left Russia for Germany in 1922 because their views on Constructivism, which stressed its aesthetic dimension, were not considered sufficiently orthodox by more politically minded Soviet artists. Combined with the high quality of the German printing industry, this influence made Germany the center of Constructivist thought. Theo van Doesburg's Constructivist Congress of 1922 served as an important touchstone for this community of artists. Under the influence of Kurt Schwitters and Theo van Doesburg, Germany remained the focus for artists who sought to explore the connections between the Dada and Constructivist modes of making art. It should be noted that by 1922 the De Stijl movement led by Van Doesburg (see Chapter 5) had been essentially folded into the general concern for geometric form in the 1920s that goes under the name "International Constructivism." International Constructivism, often called just "Constructivism," is distinct from the Russian movement of the

6.1 Raoul Haussmann, *Tatlin at Home*, 1920.

same name in that it was not always associated with revolutionary Communist ideology. While it may seem difficult to tease out the two related strands of the Constructivist movement—and they often overlap—designs made in Europe including those by Russian artists such as Lissitzky (see fig. 5.38) are classified as International Constructivism.

The Constructivists' concept of the artist as engineer had a number of parallels in Dada, whose members also rejected taking on the role of the fine artist because of its association with conventional aesthetics. The term "photomontage" in fact originated with Berlin Dada, who thought of themselves as "assemblers" (in German, a *montage* is an assembly). An interest in the potential of photomontage to serve as a tool of social activism united Dadaists and Russian Constructivists. It was important to Dada artists who wanted to make works that engaged with society to find a strategy that allowed them to represent the modern world in a novel way, without recourse to conventional realistic painting techniques. The Dadaists shared with the Russian Constructivists a sense that abstraction, by definition, could only communicate ideas in a limited fashion, and that it was necessary to reference the real world in order to convey their polemical beliefs.

6.2 Robert Wiene, *The Cabinet of Dr. Caligari*, 1919. Film still.

6.3 Erich Ludwig Stahl and Otto Arpke, *The Cabinet of Dr. Caligari*, 1919. Poster. Institut Collectie Nederland, Rijswijk, Amsterdam.

German Expressionism

Despite the inroads made by Dada and Constructivist artists early in the 1920s, it is important to remember that Expressionism remained a dominant force in German post-war culture. Before the outbreak of war in 1914, Germany had been perhaps the most important locus for Expressionists such as Oscar Kokoschka. The gallery owner Herwarth Walden had helped to create a thriving scene for artists who portrayed subjective, emotional states of mind. His Berlin gallery Der Sturm and the journal of the same name were essential purveyors of Expressionist aesthetics in cities such as Berlin.

Expressionist Film

The turmoil after the war naturally led to a situation where artists sought to use a language of feeling, creating a subjective sense of

mood and atmosphere through their work. Some of the most stunning Expressionist projects in the post-war era were produced by German filmmakers. The government-subsidized film studio called Universum Film Aktiengesellschaft (UFA) oversaw a "golden age" of German cinema during the years of the **Weimar Republic**. The largest film studio in Europe, UFA became internationally renowned for its Expressionist dramas and spectacular sets and special effects.

The breakthrough film for UFA was made by the director Robert Wiene (1881–1938) immediately after the First World War ended in 1918. Called *The Cabinet of Dr Caligari*, this movie recounts the story of a gruesome series of murders in a small German town. Narrated in flashback by a young man who recounts how a hypnotist, the Dr Caligari of the title, and his zombie-like assistant come to his town and wreak havoc on the local citizenry. *The Cabinet of Dr Caligari* ends with what the film industry calls a "reveal," a dramatic new revelation that completely changes the viewer's interpretation of what has gone on before in the story. In this case, the "reveal" is the fact that the narrator is really an inmate in an insane asylum and the story is nothing more than a demented fantasy based on the doctors and patients where he lives. This story of a madman had particular resonance in post-war European society, where so many young men had returned from the trenches suffering from "shell shock," the term given at that time to sufferers of post-traumatic stress disorder.

The set designers of *The Cabinet of Dr Caligari* created dramatic Expressionist scenery, complete with distorted, illogical spaces and exaggerated, spiky forms (*fig. 6.2*) in order to express the tortured psyche of the narrator. Walter Reimann (1887–1936), Walter Röhrig (1897–1945), and Hermann Warm (1889–1976), the Expressionist artists in charge of the design, also devised fantastical lighting techniques that gave the film a forbidding atmosphere of mystery and violence. The highly subjective mood of the story is greatly enhanced by the compelling nature of their achievement.

Posters advertising the release of *The Cabinet of Dr Caligari* share the aura of emotional distress that was depicted in the film's story, sets, and lighting. One striking poster was designed by Erich Ludwig Stahl (b. 1887) and Otto Arpke (1886–1943), collectively known as Stahl-Arpke. Their 1920 poster shows an empty room, the "cabinet," or office, of the title, with a lone chair before a desk with one burning candle (*fig. 6.3*). In traditional art, an empty chair often symbolizes a dead person, which adds to the poster's projection of unease. The chair and desk, as well as the walls and window in the background, are oddly shaped, their distorted forms suggestive of a world gone mad. The candle projects just enough light to make out the misshapen room, while dark shadows coat the edges of the floor and mask the ceiling completely. Stahl-Arpke had one advantage over the film's set designers, whose works were filmed in black and white; the poster artist is able to introduce a fiery palette of reds and oranges that complements the distorted space and eerie lighting. At the top of the poster, an odd assortment of hand-drawn letters, some nearly sans serif while others echo the blackletter tradition, sprawl topsy-turvy across the image in a shape that mimics the floor design.

Metropolis

In 1927, UFA released its much-anticipated blockbuster science-fiction film *Metropolis*. Directed by Fritz Lang (1890–1976), *Metropolis* featured what at the time were the most expensive sets ever built for a film. The dramatic Expressionist scenery was populated by over 30,000 extras, to create one of the most spectacular film sets in cinema history (*fig. 6.4*). *Metropolis* relates a convoluted story about the social injustices of a large modern city, where a small elite live high in the skies in beautiful sky-scrapers while the masses of nameless and faceless workers toil underground in hellish industrial plants. This underground world of deep shadows projects a pervasive Expressionist theme of anxiety and alienation. Lang combined the basic theme of injustice with a love story as well as an Oedipal drama that features tension between a father and son.

In the film's semi-coherent narrative, the administrator of Metropolis concocts a plan to defeat the leader of the rebellious workers by replacing her with a robot. This female robot is fash-ioned by a diabolical scientist in a frightening laboratory space that combines high-tech machinery with spiky, medieval architec-ture. In this way, *Metropolis* combined two themes that are pervasive in German Expressionism after the war; the fear of machines and the fear of women. In contrast to the technological utopianism embraced by artists of De Stijl and the Russian Constructivists, Expressionists offered an alternative view heavily influenced by the destruction wrought by machines during the First World War. For these artists, modern industrial society was a nightmarish place that portended a coming "dystopia," or anti-utopia, in this case a vision of a soulless, corrupt, and alienating future. While Lang shared the Constructivists' fascination with machines, he interpreted their effects on society in an almost dia-metrically opposed manner. The workers whose repetitive drudgery is a central visual motif of *Metropolis* perform their tasks in a mechanical way that resonates with the man–machine hybrids of the technological utopians. Yet, their labor is destroying their

6.5 Heinz Schulz-Neudamm, *Metropolis*, 1927. Poster.

6.4 Fritz Lang, *Metropolis*, 1927. Film still.

individuality, transforming them into soulless automatons. Additionally, many male Expressionists such as Lang made works that project a distinct unease with respect to assertive women. It would seem that the "New Woman" movement in Germany (see Chapter 5), with its call for greater social and economic justice for women, was perceived by some as a threat to traditional, patriarchal society. The emotionally laden language of Expressionism proved to be a perfect vehicle to convey these anxiety-provoking themes.

A poster by Heinz Schulz-Neudamm (1898–1969) for *Metropolis* uses an Expressionist idiom to suggest some of the major themes of the film (*fig. 6.5*). The angular, attenuated shapes of the letters at the top of the poster perfectly mesh with the visionary architecture and powerful beams of light depicted below it. This stylized, Expressionist title lettering sets the emotional tone for the poster, while the more pedestrian factual information at the bottom of the image is drawn with an anonymous bold sans serif. The robot woman that is at the center of Lang's narrative hovers in the foreground, confronting the viewer with a steady gaze. However, the chilling Expressionist vision of the future in a technologically advanced society was contested in Germany by artists committed to the belief that the machine would help Europe build a more just and equitable society.

The Arbeitsrat für Kunst

The political and artistic activist group named the **Arbeitsrat für Kunst** ("Workers' Council for Art") played an important role in articulating the role of artists and designers in rebuilding German society after the First World War. Founded in December 1918 by the Expressionist architect Bruno Taut (1880–1938), the group was designed to serve as a think-tank where artists could help plan the new direction for post-war Germany. The founders of the Arbeitsrat, which included the art critic Julius Meier-Graefe (see Chapter 2), held strong utopian beliefs, and many hoped that a new society would be built on Marxist principles of equality and justice. Taut, in composing the group's manifesto, asserted that artists would play a central role in terms of molding public opinion through the employment of the visual arts. He wrote, "Art and the people must form a unity. … From now on the artist alone will be responsible for the visible fabric of the new state." This suggestion that artists were destined to play a leadership role in the political arena had often been theorized by Expressionist avant-garde artists; the dreams of the Arbeitsrat met the same fate as those of their predecessors, as the group never succeeded in making its vision into a reality.

A woodcut attributed to Max Pechstein (1881–1955) serves as a sort of visual manifesto of the Arbeitsrat (*fig. 6.6*). Designed as the cover for an essay outlining the group's beliefs, the image shows three people holding the tools of an engineer and a construction worker. Together, these figures appear to have crafted the words "Arbeitsrat für Kunst Berlin," which soar outward from them. The spiky, abstract drawing forming a vision of stars and beams of light in the background is typical of Expressionist art. The subset of Expressionists with utopian aspirations in particular

often envisioned crystal cathedrals as a metaphor of spiritual transformation. Similarly, the oblique reference to non-Western art in the use of the "primitive" mask on the face of the figure to the left represents another key element from the repertoire of Expressionism. The use of the woodcut medium itself harks back to the medieval prints that were an important source of inspiration for German Expressionist artists. One element of the Arbeitsrat's vision for the future, its call for more collaboration in the arts that are to be the product of a close-knit community, was in fact rooted in an idealized vision of the past. Many Expressionists from the early twentieth century asserted that the medieval period had been a golden age of fraternal collaboration, when artists and craftsmen had worked side by side anonymously in pursuit of a common goal.

The membership of the Arbeitsrat was made up of artists and critics from a variety of fields, although architects in some ways dominated the group. When Taut dispiritedly resigned in 1919 because of the failure to achieve any significant political impact, leadership of the group was transferred to Walter Gropius, an architect who had worked before the war in the studio of Peter Behrens (see Chapter 2). Gropius eschewed direct political action on the part of the Arbeitsrat, instead refocusing the group on a visionary architectural plan he called the *Bauprojekt* ("building project"). This imaginary building was to serve as a center for the social and cultural regeneration of Germany. Again, the utopian nature of the plan bears witness to the Expressionist roots of the Arbeitsrat—there was a pervasive belief in the group that Germany could be the site of a dramatic, if unspecified, social and even spiritual transformation. The Arbeitsrat soon folded as the violence and turmoil of the immediate post-war era did much to undermine people's faith in speculative, utopian projects. However, two important themes devised at the Arbeitsrat would reappear in Gropius's later work: first, that the visual arts could play an instrumental role in the building of a new society; and, second, that architecture must assume a leadership role in the arts because it afforded the opportunity for the greatest aesthetic and social impact. Gropius's view of architecture was, of course, influenced by the concept of the *Gesamtkunstwerk*, or "total work of art." He believed that the practice of architecture could serve as a centralized locus whereby all of the arts could be fused together into a new whole.

6.6 Max Pechstein, *Arbeitsrat für Kunst Berlin*, 1919.
Research Library, The Getty Research Institute, Los Angeles, CA.

6.7 Lyonel Feininger, *Cathedral*, 1919. Woodcut, 12 x 7 in (30.5 x 19 cm). Staatliches Bauhaus, Weimar. Museum of Modern Art, New York.

Weimar Bauhaus

In April 1919 in the German town of Weimar, Gropius established an educational institution that brought to fruition some of the ideas that had originated with the nineteenth-century Arts and Crafts movement as well as those of the Arbeitsrat. In merging Saxony's school of the fine arts, the **Kunstschule**, with its school of the applied arts, the Kunstgewerbeschule, Gropius was able to pursue a curriculum that collapsed the conventional hierarchy between fine and applied arts (see Chapters 1 and 2). The Kunstgewerbeschule was at that time run by the Belgian designer Henry van de Velde, who recommended Gropius for the job when he was himself dismissed because of his foreign nationality. Gropius hoped that the new combined schools would complement each other, with the aesthetic theory of the fine arts dialectically interwoven with the empirical knowledge of the practitioners of the applied arts. The majority of the students at the school were men, and Gropius actively sought to exclude women from most media and especially the exalted practice of architecture, generally restricting them to the weaving, pottery, and bookbinding workshops.

In naming his new institution the Staatliches Bauhaus ("National House of Building") Gropius indicated his conviction that the arts and crafts could best be synthesized thorough the example of architecture, the *Gesamtkunstwerk*. The neologism "Bauhaus" was intended to call to mind the medieval guilds of

craftsmen that served as an inspiration for the school at the time of its founding. Before the First World War, Gropius had been a member of the Deutscher Werkbund and had wanted to design new, functional architecture for the modern industrial world. However, the trauma of the war drove him as well as many other members of the Werkbund to hunger for what they felt was a more spiritually authentic medieval past, in which artists had collaborated for the greater good. Fairly quickly Gropius would revert to his pre-war faith in the machine aesthetic and drop this utopian nostalgia for the Middle Ages, but by that time the faculty at the Bauhaus had already been filled out with a number of spiritually minded Expressionists.

Expressionism at the Bauhaus

The Bauhaus was initially under the sway of Expressionist precepts brought to the curriculum by Gropius and two of his first faculty members, Lyonel Feininger (1871–1956) and Johannes Itten (1888–1967). Feininger, a German-American with experience as a cartoonist, was given direction of the printmaking workshop by Gropius. One of his first works as a faculty member at the Bauhaus, the woodcut *Cathedral* (*fig. 6.7*), shows the strong influence of Expressionism in his work, as it is reminiscent of Max Pechstein's design for the Arbeitsrat, of which Feininger also was a member. Used as the title page for the *Programm des Staatlichen Bauhauses im Weimar*, the first publication that outlined the vision for the new school, Feininger's work portrays the institution in starkly Expressionist terms. Here, the Bauhaus is portrayed as something akin to the Arbeitsrat's *Bauprojekt*, a visionary building shining such as a cathedral on a hill. Combined with the additional religious imagery of the brightly shining stars, this cathedral symbolizes the quasi-spiritual sense of mission that characterized the Bauhaus in its first years and which was drawn from Expressionist doctrine. The text of the *Programm* reinforced the theme of Expressionist spirituality that guided the new institution's faculty.

> Let us create a new guild of craftsmen without the class distinctions that raise an arrogant barrier between craftsman and artist! Together let us desire, conceive, and create a new building of the future, which will embrace architecture and sculpture and painting into one unity and which will one day rise toward heaven from the hands of a million workers like the crystal symbol of a new faith.

Clearly, Feininger's woodcut was intended to put into visual terms this concept of the Bauhaus as a "crystal symbol of a new faith." It is also notable that Gropius in the text touches on both the intended erasure of the arts and crafts hierarchy as well as the "new building," which will unify the arts in an architectural *Gesamtkunstwerk*.

An acquaintance of Oskar Kokoschka, Gustav Klimt, and Herwarth Walden, Johannes Itten already had a long-established career as an Expressionist painter and printmaker when he joined the Bauhaus in 1919. His initial assignment at the school was to

6.8 Oskar Schlemmer, *Utopia*, 1921. Watercolor, silver, gold, bronze over drawing in ink, 12 x 9 in (31 x 24 cm). Oskar Schlemmer Theater Estate. C. Raman Schlemmer Collection.

6.9 Johannes Itten, *Self-Portrait*, 1920. Photograph. Bauhaus-Archiv, Berlin.

typographic elements drawn from Cubism and Futurism. The dramatic letterforms, an odd mix of outlined letters, expanded bolds, and attenuated sans serifs, are suffused with vibrant colors that appear to be derived from the palette of the Expressionist painter Paul Klee (1879–1940), another faculty member at the Bauhaus. Itten believed that form must always express content, and here his design is fully evocative of the romantic aspirations espoused by much of the faculty and many of its students in the early years.

At the time of the Bauhaus's founding, the institution was forced to confront the dispute in Germany over the relative merits of blackletter versus roman lettering. As part of their utopian belief in a universal design style, Bauhaus graphic artists focused on the latter, as they did not want to associate the school with German nationalist sentiment. Under the influence of the avant-garde, artists such as Schlemmer began experimenting with sans serifs from the time of the school's founding in 1919.

The continuing dominance of Expressionist aesthetics is evident in a lithograph by Lyonel Feininger, director of the print-making workshop that was established in 1921. The lithograph was created as the cover of *New European Graphics*, a collection of Bauhaus prints published late in 1922 (*fig. 6.10*). The spiky letter-ing displays a strong calligraphic character, as the elongated legs of the letters seem to drip down on to the row of text beneath them. The form of the letter "M," in particular, resonates with the crystal-like forms of Expressionist graphics. The horizontal rows of

oversee the sculpture, metalwork, and glass painting studios, as well as to design and implement an introductory course for all students. This six-month-long foundation course included practical training, such as an introduction to different media and basic design principles, but it emphasized the more diffuse goal of setting free the innate creativity of students. Using unconventional teaching techniques, such as breathing exercises, Itten soon became a favorite of the Bauhaus's student body. Yet, more than an administrator or teacher, he was a presence that resonated throughout the institution. Usually garbed in monk's robes, his head shaved like a Buddhist holy man, he was a literal embodiment of the Expressionist view of art as an essentially spiritual activity (*fig. 6.9*). In the early 1920s, when Itten's student followers took to fasting and self-mutilation at their leader's behest, his colleagues became more and more uncomfortable with him. He resigned from the Bauhaus early in 1923.

In 1921, Itten oversaw the publication of a yearbook featuring Bauhaus works that he called *Utopia* and subtitled *Documents of Reality* (*fig. 6.8*). This idiosyncratic title is indicative of the hazy Bauhaus goal of making utopian speculation into a social reality. The typography of the lithographed cover, by Oskar Schlemmer (1888–1943), complements Itten's conceptual speculation with its whimsical, intuitive design, which features an assortment of

6.10 Lyonel Feininger, *New European Graphics*, 1922. Poster. Lithograph. Bauhaus-Archiv, Berlin.

text are decidedly uneven, as if they had been scrawled as part of a passionate frenzy of artistic inspiration. It was precisely this type of emotional impact that so disgusted the Dadaists and Constructivists who were beginning to congregate in Germany at this time.

By 1922, the overarching Bauhaus emphasis on intuition and Expressionism evidenced by the prominent roles of faculty members such as Itten, Klee, and Wassily Kandinsky (1866–1944) led to criticism by other members of the progressive avant-garde, especially followers of De Stijl. It is notable that Kandinsky, a Russian émigré, had joined the faculty in 1922, following an attempt to establish himself in post-revolutionary Russia. Unable to reconcile his Expressionist and spiritual beliefs with the nascent Constructivist movement and its reverence for political activism, Kandinsky had returned to Germany, where he found a refuge at the early Bauhaus.

Constructivism and the Bauhaus

When the De Stijl leader Theo van Doesburg settled in Weimar late in 1921, he provided young artists with an alternative vision to that espoused by faculty members such as Kandinsky. Van Doesburg had numerous contacts with the Bauhaus professors and students during 1922, when he offered a series of lectures explaining the rational, geometric principles behind De Stijl and Constructivism. He also organized the Constructivist Congress in Weimar in 1922, which was attended by Lissitzky (see above). Van Doesburg found a receptive audience among the Bauhaus student body as well as members of the faculty who were not comfortable with the prevailing Expressionist ethos. Oskar Schlemmer, who had joined the faculty in 1920 and soon became the head of sculpture in stone and wood, wrote about his concerns in March of 1922: "Turning away from Utopia! We must be realistic, and strive for the realization of ideas. Not cathedrals but machines to live in." Two exhibitions held in Weimar during 1922 that featured a preponderance of works by Itten's followers further reinforced the opinion that the Bauhaus was failing in its mandate to advance the development of German art and architecture.

László Moholy-Nagy

In 1923, under the influence of De Stijl and Russian Constructivism, the Bauhaus moved toward a curriculum that emphasized functionalism and a machine aesthetic based on reductive geometric abstraction. In the spring of that year, Gropius responded to the increasing pressure on him from van Doesburg and the Constructivists by appointing to the faculty László Moholy-Nagy (1895–1946), a Hungarian artist who had moved to Berlin in 1921. In Germany, Moholy-Nagy had become acquainted with both van Doesburg and Lissitzky, and he had quickly absorbed their knowledge of Constructivist aesthetics. Moholy-Nagy arrived at the Bauhaus during the same term that Itten resigned, and the young Hungarian quickly assumed control over both the metals workshop and the preliminary course that

Women at the Bauhaus

When the Bauhaus was established in 1919, Germany was in the throes of reconstruction and dramatic social change following its defeat in World War I. The 1919 Weimar Constitution had stipulated an end to gender discrimination in many aspects of German life including education, so women were no longer to be excluded from publicly funded institutions such as the Bauhaus. Director Walter Gropius initially embraced this doctrine, telling a gathering of students in 1919 that women students should expect "absolute equality of status, and therefore absolute equality of responsibility." However, in practice Gropius and other Bauhaus teachers pursued a policy that channeled female students into craft-oriented workshops, mainly those teaching weaving, bookbinding, and pottery.

The relegation of women students to such workshops only reinforced the stereotype that certain artistic practices were innately "feminine" while others were uniquely "masculine." Such a traditional approach was somewhat surprising in an institution dedicated to breaking the age-old distinctions between fine arts and crafts.

The weaving workshop—which became the textile department after the move to Dessau in 1925—played the largest role in women's careers at the Bauhaus, mainly because the bookbinding workshop was closed in 1922 and the professors in the pottery workshop proved resistant to accepting female students. After completing the preliminary course in the weaving workshop, students were taught by George Muche with the technical assistance of Helene Börner, who had previously worked for Henry van de Velde at the Weimar Kunstgewerbeschule. Students of weaving were inspired by the paintings of Paul Klee and Johannes Itten, and they worked towards making textile design a respected form of non-functional artistic expression.

After 1925, former student Gunta Stölzl (1897–1983) was appointed technical instructor of the textile department, and she assumed the role of artistic director in 1927, a position she held until 1931. Stölzl became the first female artistic leader of a Bauhaus workshop. Embracing the machine aesthetic wholeheartedly, Stölzl introduced new modern materials to the students, including rayon and cellophane. She also established some of the strongest links between a Bauhaus workshop and industry, an original goal of the school that had proved to be little more than a pipe dream in many of the other workshops.

Despite the entrenched attitudes that prevented women from working in a full range of workshops, a few artists such as Marianne Brandt (1893–1983) managed to overcome these barriers and succeed outside the weaving milieu. In 1923 she matriculated from the metal workshop, which had moved away from the Expressionist, fine-art interests championed by Itten to the Constructivist functionalism of László Moholy-Nagy. Brandt was part of a collaborative team that designed one of the Bauhaus's most successful products, the Kandem Lamp that remains ubiquitous to this day. With the departure of Moholy-Nagy in 1928, Brandt became artistic director of the metal workshop and, like Stölzl, proved to be one of the school's most effective negotiators, establishing a number of contracts with local industries. She is also remembered as a pioneering photographer.

6.11 Lewis W. Hine, *Mechanic at a Steam Pump in an Electric Power House*, 1920. Gelatin silver print, 6 x 4 in (16.4 x 11.3 cm). George Eastman House, Rochester, New York. Gift of the Photo League.

had been Itten's province. The appointment of Moholy-Nagy allowed Gropius to avoid feeling compelled to hire van Doesburg, whose strong personality and somewhat dogmatic beliefs threatened Gropius's own authority. The new direction at the Bauhaus also represented another response to the trauma of the First World War, as the leaders of the school emphasized the rebuilding of society at every turn.

Moholy-Nagy's influence was immediately apparent in the way in which he reorganized the preliminary course that served as the foundation of the Bauhaus curriculum. Assisted by Josef Albers (1888–1976), Moholy-Nagy moved quickly to rationalize the teaching of elementary design principles so that the focus shifted away from idiosyncratic spiritual values and toward the logical analysis of form. Promoting Constructivist principles, Albers and Moholy-Nagy made an understanding of new materials such as Plexiglas and steel one of the centerpieces of the course. The exercises that Moholy-Nagy designed for the three-dimensional section of the preliminary course became legendary for the way in which they enabled students to master the fundamentals of Constructivist technique. Students were taught to use the tools of the engineer, the compass and the straight-edged ruler, in place of freehand drawing techniques. It is important to realize how these tools serve to distance the hand of the artist in a literal as well as a conceptual sense from the resulting work —a direct rejection of the Expressionist ethos that privileges both the artist's subjective sensibility and his or her masterly touch of the brush.

The concept of the artist turned engineer also resonates with the widespread adoption in Germany after the war of the principles of scientific management of industrial processes. The American theorist Frederick W. Taylor (1865–1933) had advocated the rationalization of labor in order to advance the effectiveness of mass production. After watching workers on the assembly line and analyzing the specifics of each movement and the time taken to perform each task, Taylor was able to suggest ways in which industrial workers could improve their efficiency. Taylor's principles thematically connect with the idea of the man–machine hybrid, enforcing strict rules whereby each worker performed a mechanical, repetitive task as quickly as possible. While critics saw "Taylorism" as another factor that made industrial work soulless and alienating, most people in the 1920s embraced Taylor's theories as another positive step down the road to a machine-driven utopia. Just as workers must become machines, as reflected in a famous photograph (*fig. 6.11*) by Lewis Hine (1874–1940), so artists would become engineers in the coming industrial utopia. The romantic view of technology espoused at the Bauhaus viewed Taylorism in this positive sense, and hoped to put its principles into effect in the cause of advancing German industry.

The 1923 Exhibition

Moholy-Nagy arrived at the Bauhaus at a critical time in the school's history, because the Thuringian state government, which had provided financing since 1919, was demanding that the institution hold an exhibition in the summer of 1923 to justify

left: **6.12** László Moholy-Nagy, Logo for Bauhaus Press, 1923. Bauhaus-Archiv, Berlin.

below: **6.13** Herbert Bayer, Thuringian Banknotes, 1923. Bauhaus-Archiv, Berlin.

the past four years of work. The relationship between the Bauhaus and the state government had been a tumultuous one, and it appeared that the exhibition was required in the hope that it would result in the public humiliation of the school. The government demand resulted in the "Bauhaus Austellung 1923," at which Gropius had an opportunity to display the institution's new, post-Expressionist, functionalist identity. Taking the theme "Art and technology, a new unity: technology does not need art, but art does need technology," Gropius used the exhibition as a platform from which he could turn the Bauhaus back to the machine aesthetic and the Deutscher Werkbund goal of providing high-quality designs for the modern world.

During the months leading up to the exhibition, Moholy-Nagy was instrumental in overseeing the design of publicity materials for the exhibition as well as any other Bauhaus graphics. In 1923, he devised a new logo for the Bauhaus Press, consisting of an interlocked square and equilateral triangle tightly circumscribed by a circle (*fig. 6.12*). Functioning visually as an arrow in some instances, this composition displays the elementary geometry and dynamic asymmetry that are at the heart of the Constructivist aesthetic. Moholy-Nagy also quickly established an expanded sans serif as the typographic standard at the school. He was adamant that all typography must emphasize clarity over any other element, rejecting the whimsical Expressionism of Feininger and Itten. The issue of clarity is just one example of the overall "functionalist" principles that Moholy-Nagy established as the focus of the curriculum; each and every art form was to be evaluated primarily on its ability to perform its most basic task effectively. There was no room for decorative effects that jeopardized the core principles of a book, or a poster, chair, teapot, or building.

The Bauhaus's promulgation of sans serif typography proved to be one of the successes of the 1923 exhibition, as the

Thuringian government hired a Bauhaus student, Herbert Bayer (1900–1985), to design new paper currency (during this period each German state government issued its own currency). The resulting bills were a model of sans serif typography, the letters and numbers set off by rectangular blocks of color to enhance their readability (*fig. 6.13*). Because of the rampant inflation that was destabilizing the German economy at that time, the bills quickly became worthless, as even their high denominations could not match the astounding rise in prices of that summer and fall. By November 1923, a newspaper in Germany cost 50 billion Marks, and Bayer's 2 and 3 million denominations seemed quaint.

The dramatic shift in the style of Bauhaus graphics during the spring of 1923 shows how swiftly the students and faculty shifted gears to embrace the Constructivist trend. Of course, professors such as Schlemmer had been longing for just this sort of opportunity. Schlemmer's 1922 design of a man in profile, clearly influenced by the reductive geometric abstraction of De Stijl, became an important motif at the Bauhaus after 1923. Besides serving as the new Bauhaus official seal, replacing an Expressionist design, it was included in a variety of graphics including a lithographed poster (*fig. 6.14*) by Fritz Schleifer (1903–1977). An advertisement for the 1923 exhibition, Schleifer's poster shows a simplified design in which the profile of the face consists solely of four rectangles, with a red square indicating the all-important eye. Schlemmer's original had featured hairline serifs leading off the geometric shapes at right angles.

Another Bauhaus student, Joost Schmidt (1893–1948), designed an exhibition poster that is clearly indebted to Russian Constructivism (*fig. 6.15*). A tight oval shape structures the composition along a dynamic diagonal axis; all the other elements of the poster respond in some way to this oval form. On the upper end, a circle filled with Schlemmer's man in profile is embedded in a circle that is itself embedded in the curve of the oval. Lettering that spells out "State Bauhaus" wraps itself around the circle forming the contour of the oval, yet the word "Staatliches" breaks away from the dominant shape, its form falling outside the original contour. In the middle of the poster, the word "Ausstellung" ("exhibition") cuts into the side of the oval, bisecting it. The simple red and black palette enhances the design, as it creates the same sort of point-counterpoint that governs the balancing of the geometric forms. Schmidt's functionalist design anticipates the dominant style at the Bauhaus after 1923, and he in fact went on to become a member of the faculty, leading the advertising workshop between 1928 and 1930.

Perhaps the most important graphic design to come out of the 1923 exhibition was the exhibition catalog *Staatliches Bauhaus im Weimar, 1919–1923*. Moholy-Nagy himself created the layout, while Bayer was appointed to design the binding. The cover page represents perhaps the best use of the book's unusual square format (*fig. 6.16*). All of the text is structured based on its relationship to this frame, and each row and column of this orthogonal design calls attention to the upper left corner of the page. The expanded bold sans serif type features dramatic contrasts, because some of the words are made up of letters divided into horizontal bars. The overprinting of the "B" in Bauhaus is unorthodox and seems to introduce a Dada element into the rigidly structured composition. It is notable that, despite the dogmatic assertions

6.14 Fritz Schleifer, *Bauhaus Ausstellung*, July-Sept 1923. Poster. Lithograph, 39 x 28 in (101.1 x 73 cm). Bauhaus-Archiv, Berlin.

6.15 Joost Schmidt, Exhibition Poster, 1923. Lithograph, 27 x 19 in (68.6 x 48.3 cm). Bauhaus-Archiv, Berlin.

6.16 László Moholy-Nagy, Exhibition Catalog *Staatliches Bauhaus im Weimar, 1919–1923*, 1923. Cover.

of Constructivists such as Moholy-Nagy, who would define his aesthetic as something diametrically opposed to Expressionist whimsy, elements such as the square format and the overprinted "B" are arguably expressive and idiosyncratic in a manner akin to the style of Itten.

The center of the 1923 exhibition was, of course, architecture. Despite its proposed role at the Bauhaus as the overarching *Gesamtkunstwerk*, there was in fact no department of architecture at the school by 1923. Furthermore, most of the workshops operated as discrete units and there had been little opportunity to explore a grand synthesis of the arts. While Gropius had not had any opportunity to build a monument of lasting significance, the collection of models and drawings grouped around the theme "International Architecture" served to explain the Bauhaus director's plans for a new architecture based on geometric abstract design. Including designs by Le Corbusier, the De Stijl architect J.J.P. Oud (1890–1963), and Gropius, the survey sought to place the work of the Bauhaus in a broader European context.

Political Problems

It was very important to the future of the school in the face of government hostility to portray geometric abstraction, either in architecture or any other medium, as devoid of political content. Considering the Bauhaus's ideological roots in the Arbeitsrat für Kunst, it was especially important to separate the Bauhaus from the polemical Communism of that group and from the revolutionary politics of Russian Constructivism. Hence, the idea that Constructivist aesthetics were apolitical and universal, or at least pan-European, was at the heart of the conceptual framework of the exhibition. This concern went a long way in terms of divorcing Russian Constructivism from the "International Constructivism" practiced at the Bauhaus. The entire enterprise was somewhat disingenuous, because it was true that a significant number of students and faculty at the Bauhaus had contempt for the bourgeois-dominated Weimar Republic, and in fact hoped that their abstract work could help bring about some sort of revolution in Germany.

Despite some success in the summer of 1923, the Bauhaus's future in Weimar was still imperiled during the winter of 1923–4. While Gropius and the faculty worked to implement the new curriculum and to create more commercial relationships with local industry, changes in the Thuringian Landtag, a type of parliamentary body, sealed its fate. New elections had resulted in the defeat of a socialist majority in favor of a new assembly dominated by conservatives and right-wing reactionaries. Because the Bauhaus was viewed as inextricably tied to the socialists who had overseen its first charter, the new ministers sought to dismantle the school as quickly as possible. Gropius's championing of the International Constructivist style greatly upset right-wing politicians, who wanted the Bauhaus to have a more overt German nationalist profile. The hostility of the right-wing government caused the Bauhaus's former enemies in progressive circles, such as Van Doesburg (who felt that the remaining "older" faculty continued to taint Moholy-Nagy's new Constructivist approach), to rally around the school. The new parliament moved quickly, sharply cutting the state's financial support. Reading the writing on the wall, Gropius abruptly announced the closure of the Weimar Bauhaus in December of 1924.

Dessau Bauhaus

Fortunately for the students and faculty of the Bauhaus, the school was not without options, as a number of less conservative German states proved eager to host the institution. Eventually Gropius negotiated a new set of contracts with the mayor of the industrial city of Dessau, and the process of moving commenced in the spring of 1925. For the first twenty months the Bauhaus operated out of temporary quarters, while Gropius directed the design and construction of a new complex of buildings financed by the Dessau government.

New Buildings

The main structure completed at Dessau late in 1926 featured three wings: one devoted to the workshops, another to the administrative offices, and a third to serve as a student dormitory

(*fig. 6.17*). These three rectangular blocks, two with a horizontal emphasis in their mass and one, the dormitory, taller and more vertically proportioned, were stitched together by three corresponding hallways that intersected in the middle. The hallway that connected the administration wing with the other areas was constructed as a bridge, and hovers a full story above the ground. From the air, the building looks like an asymmetrical airplane propeller, a feature that was in part an homage to the Junkers company, an aircraft manufacturer that was among the most important industries in Dessau. However, asymmetry was also a key aesthetic component of Gropius's plan for the Bauhaus building. He believed that conventional architecture was essentially two-dimensional, the buildings' symmetrical façades flat and static in appearance. In contrast, the Bauhaus buildings were intended to be experienced in three dimensions, their geometric shapes interacting in a dynamic fashion. Gropius wrote that it was necessary for the viewer to walk around the complex in order to grasp the inherent harmony of its different parts.

Conforming to the principles espoused by Moholy-Nagy's preliminary course, the Bauhaus building is constructed of the most modern industrial materials—steel, reinforced concrete, and glass. While these materials had been used for decades in architecture, in conventional buildings they would be cloaked under a skin of stone or terra cotta. Gropius, in contrast, boldly

6.17 Walter Gropius, Bauhaus Buildings (front), Dessau, 1925–6. Bauhaus-Archiv, Berlin.

6.18 Marcel Breuer, "Wassily" Chair, 1925. Photograph.

left these materials exposed, demonstrating the beauty of the machine aesthetic. The most dramatic element of the structure is the "curtain wall" of glass that encases the wing housing the work-shops. Treating a wall as only a barrier against the weather, Gropius demonstrated how modern materials allowed for new forms, as the glass walls of the Bauhaus are possible because they are not functioning as part of the load-bearing structure. Only the steel frame of the building is necessary to support its own weight.

Like Le Corbusier's Pavillon de l'Esprit Nouveau, also from 1925 (see Chapter 3), the Bauhaus does not feature decorative elements that are superfluous to the function of the building. Instead, the geometric abstraction of the composition serves as both the functional and the main visual element. This austere aesthetic, in which each element is simultaneously functional and aesthetically pleasing, is clearly related to Constructivist princi-ples. Constructivist graphic designers tried not to add anything to their compositions that would take away from a given work's clar-ity and readability. In architectural parlance, there are two axioms that can help illuminate the modern style of the Bauhaus: "form follows function," which refers to the integrated nature of the aesthetic and functional elements; and, "less is more," which is illustrated by the Bauhaus building's spartan negation of ornament. The conventional wisdom asserts that the Bauhaus buildings in Dessau represent the polar opposite of the Expressionist style in their logical order and dry functionalism. However, it is also possible that the curtain wall of glass, a mate-rial whose ostensible spiritual qualities—witness the stained glass in medieval cathedrals—made it a favorite metaphor of Expressionism, gives the building a residual Expressionist flavor.

Gropius's building program represented his first opportunity to pursue architecture under the rubric of the *Gesamtkunstwerk*. The majority of the light fixtures, furnishings, equipment, and even the blankets on the student's beds, were designed to comple-ment the reductive geometric abstraction and modern industrial materials of the building itself. For example, Marcel Breuer (1902–1981) designed chairs for the building that for the first time employed unadorned tubular steel for the frame. A fine example of Breuer's work at the Dessau Bauhaus is the *Wassily*

chair, named for his colleague Wassily Kandinsky (*fig. 6.18*). Its spare steel frame forms cubic shapes that seem to pass through each other, its beauty resting in proportion and the balance of simple geometric forms. Eschewing the springs and wood frames of conventional furniture, Breuer designed this chair and others like it with unadorned pieces of canvas fabric. Some later versions of the *Wassily* chair featured more luxurious materials, the steel now chrome plated and the seat and arms made of strips of leather.

After the Bauhaus moved to Dessau, the Constructivist curriculum championed by Moholy-Nagy was strengthened, with more resources devoted to art forms that could serve a modern industrial society. The pottery workshop, for example, was abolished while technological processes such as photography were given added emphasis. Additionally, the preliminary course, which was devoted to the machine aesthetic, was expanded to encompass twelve months of work.

Herbert Bayer

The printing workshop that had been led at Weimar by Lyonel Feininger, an unrepentant Expressionist, was transformed at Dessau into a new area that focused on commercial, as opposed to fine art, graphics. Herbert Bayer was appointed the head of this revamped workshop devoted to typography and advertising, allowing graphic design to become more central to the curricu-lum. Bayer, like Marcel Breuer, was one of a new type of teacher called a *Jungmeister* ("young master") who had himself completed the Bauhaus curriculum as a student and was subsequently hired as a member of the faculty. Along with Albers and Moholy-Nagy, Bayer worked assiduously at the Dessau Bauhaus to improve the quality of modern graphics.

Bayer's mature Constructivist style is evident in a poster he designed in 1926 to publicize an exhibition and birthday celebra-tion for Kandinsky (*fig. 6.19*). The basic orthogonal composition of the poster is equivalent, in its dynamic asymmetry, to the overall plan of the Bauhaus buildings. Squares and rectangles are connected to one another by bold rules much like the wings of

6.19 Herbert Bayer, *Kandinsky*, 1926. Poster. Bauhaus-Archiv, Berlin.

6.20 Herbert Bayer, *Bauhaus*, 1928. Magazine. Bauhaus-Archiv, Berlin.

the building and their respective hallways. The viewer's eye must travel around the composition in much the same way that Gropius intended the viewer to walk around his building in order to grasp its overarching harmony. Bayer has added an additional element, however, in the way in which he skews the whole geometric structure on to a slight diagonal, creating a kinetic element. A principal concern of graphic designers at the Bauhaus was the integration of typography with photographs. Here, Bayer has used the rectangular frame of a photo to form a discrete geometric unit, which is balanced by the text directly across the page. The black and white photograph also meshes nicely with the subdued black and red color of the typography.

In 1928, Bayer designed a cover for a journal called simply *bauhaus* that featured the simple geometric solids and engineer's tools that are fundamental to the machine aesthetic (*fig. 6.20*). In particular, the transparent plastic triangle represents both a tool of the engineer as well as a commitment to exciting industrial materials. The geometric forms recall the Neoplatonist philosophy that was the conceptual basis for so much geometric abstraction during this era. In this cover photograph, Bayer also made use of a favorite design trick from this era: using the subject of the picture to perform double duty as the banner of the journal itself. In this case, the image consists of what looks like a folded architectural drawing on a desk, with the fold artfully placed so that the word "Bauhaus" on it serves also as the title of the journal.

"Typophoto"

As part of his work at the Dessau Bauhaus, Moholy-Nagy made significant progress in terms of integrating photography into the design arts. While he was untrained as a photographer and most of his work in this vein was highly experimental, some aspects of his photographic practice were absorbed into functionalist projects. In 1925, Moholy-Nagy coined the term "**typophoto**," stating as his goal a set of aesthetic principles that would govern the integration of typography and photography in graphic work. He was able to put his principles into practice in the *Bauhausbücher* ("Bauhaus Books"), a series of volumes devoted to international developments in modern art. Edited by Moholy-Nagy and Gropius beginning in 1925, the Bauhaus books covered topics that included works from the school itself as well as related movements such as De Stijl and even Cubism.

Moholy-Nagy published his own essays in *Malerei Photographie Film* ("Painting Photography Film"), the eighth book in the series (*fig. 6.21*). The cover combines an orthogonal structure for the text with a startlingly abstract background photograph. Moholy-Nagy was at this time experimenting with a number of "cameraless" photographic techniques, and the result shown here is an atmospheric overview of unidentifiable geometric shapes. Cast on a diagonal axis, the scaled gray tones and murky forms strongly contrast with the bold, clearly delineated

6.21 László Moholy-Nagy, *Malerei Fotografie Film (Painting Photography Film)*, 1927. Book jacket.

6.22 László Moholy-Nagy, *Bauhaus Books*, 1927.

character of the text. Note especially how the number "8" is played off a series of concentric circles in the photograph that themselves resemble an "8" perched on its side. Additionally, the photographic background lends the image a sense of three-dimensional depth that is lacking in most non-photographic Constructivist work.

Amid the varied writings that made up *Malerei Photographie Film*, Moholy included a discussion of typophoto that would prove to be hugely influential on the practice of graphic design. "What is Typophoto? Typography is communication composed of type. Photography is the visual representation of what can be optically apprehended. Typophoto is the visually most exact rendering of communication." For Moholy-Nagy, the synthesis of these two iconic industrial technologies was the key to revolutionizing graphic design so that it could convey with clarity the modern spirit. Taking his cue from the Futurists, Moholy-Nagy asserted in the book that "simultaneity," as displayed by film and neon signs, was the optical focus of the modern age. This kinetic model, he believed, would replace the "Gutenberg" model for

typography, which was static and rigidly linear. Moholy-Nagy's publicity leaflet from 1927 promoting the Bauhaus books wittily referenced letterpress and photographic printing technologies (*fig. 6.22*). Anticipating the design of Bayer's 1928 cover for the journal *bauhaus*, here Moholy-Nagy used a photograph of metal type as the subject—that same metal type of course also conveying the message of the work. His photograph is in fact a montage, as he has combined a reverse view of the type with a positive one. Compositionally, the two rows of type create competing perspective devices, leading the eye of the viewer back into space at oblique, contradictory angles.

Depoliticization at the Bauhaus

It is very important to recognize how Constructivist principles, most of which had arisen in Russia in the service of a specific political vision, were largely "depoliticized" during the period 1925–8 at the Bauhaus. As mentioned above, it was necessary for the school's own survival that it de-emphasize the radical politics that had played a role in the adoption of Russian Constructivism. In later decades, the political commitments of many members of the faculty and student body would be written out of art history. The period 1928–30, when Hannes Meyer (1889–1954)—promoted from head of the architecture workshop to overall director—attempted to bring revolutionary Communist politics to the fore at the school, is often completely omitted from histories of the institution. Similarly, the root of the Bauhaus in Arbeitsrat für Kunst is often ignored in design histories.

For example, Moholy-Nagy's often repeated quote "To be a user of machines is to be of the spirit of this century. It has replaced the transcendent spiritualism of past eras," from 1922, can be seen as exemplary of the functionalist vision of technological advancement that he put into place at the Bauhaus in 1923. However, the context of the quote and others like it is often disregarded. The statement in fact comes from an article called "Constructivism and the Proletariat" that Moholy-Nagy published in the revolutionary left-wing Hungarian periodical *Ma*. At this point in his career, Moholy-Nagy was upset that the new Communist regime in his native Hungary had refused to accept non-representational art as a propaganda tool, as the Bolsheviks had initially done in Russia. Disgusted with a party that he condemned as "bourgeois," Moholy-Nagy exiled himself in 1920 to Austria, before eventually ending up in Germany. It is crucial to keep in mind that Moholy-Nagy viewed Constructivism as indivisible from its revolutionary context, and it was this commitment to radical social change that drove his work, as well as that of many other Bauhaus participants.

Scholars today view the political climate at the Bauhaus as harboring one central contradiction: the simultaneous embrace of Communist ideology and an adoration of the capitalist industries that stood as icons of the modern machine age. This situation would seem to provoke the strongest possible cognitive dissonance, as the two ideologies were diametrically opposed to one another. What did unite Russian Communism and European capitalism in the 1920s was a shared vision of technological utopia, and it was this theme that allowed members of the Bauhaus to reconcile these seemingly disparate trends in political and economic thought.

Typography at the Bauhaus

An essential component of modern graphic design espoused at the Bauhaus was the use of rational, geometric letterforms. Bauhaus typographers believed that sans serif type was indispensable for three reasons: first, it was the only type capable of expressing the spirit of the machine age (geometric forms were increasingly viewed more as an instrument of logical planning than as representative of Platonic beauty); second, sans serif lacked any nationalist associations (unlike blackletter), so it could serve as a unifying force in the post-war era; and, third, its simple clarity and impersonal character were the best match for photography—hence typophoto.

An example of a geometric sans serif developed at the Bauhaus can be seen in Josef Albers's Stencil, developed in 1925

(*fig. 6.23*). In this type each letter has been built up out of a set of simple geometric forms—mainly semicircles, rectangles, and triangles—that are intended to remove any subjective, Expressionist, or decorative elements from the letters. Stencil is unusual among the Bauhaus sans serifs in that it appears highly stylized, calling attention to itself along the lines of Art Deco designs such as Broadway or Peignot. Stencil also exemplifies the most obvious flaw in the reasoning that justified the widespread use of sans serifs: it is scarcely legible and exceedingly difficult to read. While this is an extreme case, it is true that the supposed "clarity" of geometric sans serifs was at the very least widely overstated by their more zealous partisans. The nineteenth-century view of sans serifs, that they were effective as a highly legible display type but unreadable in body text, represents a more balanced view, unbiased by the technological utopianism of the Bauhaus.

The most famous sans serif experiment to come out of the Bauhaus was Bayer's **Universal**, which he began work on in 1923 and revised several times over the years (*fig. 6.24*). Universal differs from Stencil in that its geometric forms are made up of strokes of uniform thickness, obviating the calligraphic element of most type. Bayer intended his new type to be printed by machines, so he felt that conventional type designers' nostalgic use of forms that had been developed in the age of the chisel and the quill pen was anachronistic. Like Stencil, the forms of Universal are made up of geometrically perfect circles and orthogonal horizontal and vertical lines. Some letters, such as the "m" and the "w," are standardized so that they are simply inverted versions of one another. Bayer chose a set of three angles with which he structured the armature of each letter. Universal's stark forms reject any sense of eclecticism or illusionism that could mar its perfect clarity. Like an engineer, he developed the type using only the compass, T-square, and triangle.

Bayer did not feel that he was inventing new letterforms for Universal, but rather that he was completing a logical progression that resulted in rationalized shapes for each letter. This process of refinement was based on historical roman letters, not on the German blackletter tradition. While Bayer intended Universal to stand alone as an international typeface, conservative Germans argued that its basis in roman, as opposed to blackletter, type, represented a snub to German tradition. Essentially, it was impossible completely to avoid a political reading of typography amid the overheated discourse of post-war Europe. Bayer's theory of type also echoes Taylor's principles of scientific management, whereby each action on an assembly line is designed to demonstrate the utmost economy and efficiency.

Another significant aspect of Universal is the fact that it was designed as a single-case alphabet. Bayer asserted that upper-case letters were superfluous in the age of scientific management, 1and a single-case letterset would be both easier to learn and read, as well as providing substantial savings for the printing industry. There were a number of precedents for Bayer's single-case strategy in the world of display type, where all-upper-case alphabets had been common since the nineteenth century. In the contemporary era, Art Deco letters such as those in Cassandre's Peignot were only designed in upper case. After 1925, when Bayer joined the faculty of the Bauhaus, all of the school's publications were printed solely in lower case, along the lines advocated by Bayer.

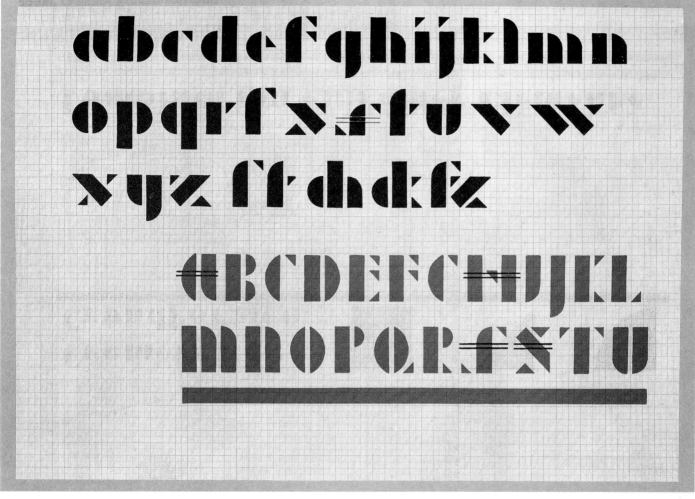

6.23 Josef Albers, Stencil Typeface, 1925, from *Offset Buch und Werbekunst*, July 1926, p. 397. Bauhaus-Archiv, Berlin. St Bride Printing Library, London.

abcdefghijklmnopqrstu

6.24 TYPE

vwxyzl234567890O?!*[]%

"universal differs from stencil in that its geometric forms are made up of strokes of uniform thickness, obviating the calligraphic element of most type"

6.24 Herbert Bayer, Universal Typeface, 1923–5. Courtesy of P22 Type Foundry.

ABCDEFGHIJKLMNOP QRSTUVWXYZabcdefg hijklmnopqrstvwxyz 1234567890?!*%

"Futura (1927), by Paul Renner (1878–1956), would prove to be the sans serif with the most long-lasting impact on modern typography."

6.25 Paul Renner, Futura Typeface, 1927. St Bride Printing Library, London.

In contrast to the illusory clarity of sans serif text, Bayer's claim that the single-case alphabet would not harm the readability of text was apparently true, as most readers never even notice the shift that occurred in Bauhaus publications. However, by advocating an alphabet that was strictly lower-case, Bayer again walked into a uniquely German political quagmire. In the orthography of the German language, the rules of capitalization play a more prominent role than in other native European tongues. For example, all nouns have an initial capital in German, regardless of their place in a sentence. By eliminating all upper-case forms, Bayer inadvertently found yet another way to aggravate German conservatives, who argued that his Universal was not only "unGerman," but also that its roman lineage associated it with the tradition of France, Germany's sworn enemy. It proved impossible for Bayer to control the reception of his work, and Universal became iconic of all that was wrong with the Bauhaus in the minds of right-wing politicians.

Paul Renner and Futura

While not designed at the Bauhaus, **Futura** (1927; *fig. 6.25*), by Paul Renner (1878–1956), would prove to be the sans serif with the most long-lasting impact on modern typography. The director of the typography department at the Frankfurter Kunstschule, Renner had originally trained as an architect. His work in many

ways parallels the formal and ideological concerns of the "functionalists" at the Bauhaus. Like Bayer, he advocated the use of a single-case alphabet while trumpeting the clarity and the clean, logical forms of geometric sans serifs. However, Futura is also a perfect example of a designer forced to confront the difficulties of putting theory into practice; while developing Futura, Renner recognized that the most pure geometric forms neither appeared beautiful as individual shapes nor connected fluidly with one another. For these practical reasons, the final version of Futura departs from the pure geometry of the earliest prototypes, and Renner introduced a weighted, slightly calligraphic stroke in many of the letters.

Produced by Bauer, a prominent commercial foundry, Futura quickly gained fame and was adopted by Renner's colleagues in the avant-garde. Kurt Schwitters was among its more enthusiastic practitioners, and he made Futura the typographical basis for the stationery that he designed in a Constructivist style for his home city of Hanover in 1929. Schwitters succeeded in making Futura the "official typeface" of Hanover, while establishing a consistent visual identity for the city. However, in 1933, under the new Nazi government, Futura was officially banned in Hanover and government offices were forbidden to use it ever again.

The year 1928 marks the end of the "golden age" of the Dessau Bauhaus. By the end of it, Gropius, Moholy-Nagy, Albers, and Marcel Breuer had left the school to pursue other opportunities. Schlemmer resigned in 1929. Hannes Meyer, the previous head of the architecture workshop (which had finally been established in 1927), took over as director and helped to expand the Bauhaus's engagement with German industry. While a proponent of the machine aesthetic, however, Meyer was also a committed socialist, and his overt political stance further angered conservative forces in the German government. He was replaced for political reasons in 1930, after which the less ideologically inclined architect Ludwig Mies van der Rohe (1886–1969) assumed the directorship. Under Meyer and Mies van der Rohe, the Bauhaus became increasingly a school of architecture, and work in the other design arts as well as the fine arts was increasingly sidelined.

In 1932, the Dessau Bauhaus was closed because of pressure from newly elected members of the extreme right-wing National Socialist (or Nazi) Party. While the school was briefly reopened in Berlin, it was shut down for ever in 1933 by the Nazis, who gained control of all of Germany that year (*fig. 6.26*). Eventually, most of the major artists fled Germany for countries that were less hostile to modern art. By 1939, the year of the outbreak of the Second World War, Gropius, Albers, Moholy-Nagy, Bayer, and Mies van der Rohe had all immigrated to the United States, where they would have an enormous impact on the way in which the design arts would be practiced in that country after the war.

6.26 Anonymous, Closing of the Bauhaus, 1933. Newspaper photograph.

The New Typography

The catch-all term for the modern progressive movement in typography of the 1920s, the **New Typography**, was first used by Moholy-Nagy in 1923. He included the phrase in a catalog essay that accompanied the Bauhaus exhibition held in Weimar in the summer of that year. Both the phrase and the machine aesthetic on display at the exhibition caught the eye of a young German from Leipzig named Jan Tschichold (1902–1974). The son of a lettering artist and sign painter, Tschichold had worked for several years as a calligrapher while becoming gradually more involved in the field of typography. Profoundly moved by what he saw at the Weimar Bauhaus exhibition, and energized by his acquaintances Moholy-Nagy and Lissitzky, Tschichold soon established himself as a leading voice in the promulgation of the New Typography.

Perhaps the most significant contribution that Tschichold made to the New Typography was the creation of two seminal publications outlining the theory and practice of a wide range of avant-garde designers. The first appeared in 1925, when Tschichold edited a special issue of the Leipzig journal *Typographische Mitteilungen* ("Typographic News"; *fig. 6.27*). Christening the issue *Elementary Typography*, Tschichold set out to establish a standardized set of principles for the New Typography that could be easily grasped by printers unfamiliar with modern art and design. For this journal, Tschichold took on the Slavic-sounding nom de plume Ivan Tschichold, showing his desire to emulate the work of the Russian Constructivists.

The names of the contributors to *Elementary Typography* were listed on the cover, and included Moholy-Nagy and Bayer of the Bauhaus, Lissitzky, and Schwitters, as well as Tschichold himself. The texts in this anthology of writings included the Russian Constructivist manifesto of 1920 as well as a number of excerpts from Bauhaus publications. The cover demonstrates many of the most important formal principles of the New Typography: orthogonal design, bold rules, positive use of negative space, asymmetry, and sans serif lettering. While on the one hand Tschichold's work seems exemplary of the most extreme machine functionalism, it is notable that Constructivist principles had been increasingly integrated with the exuberant experimentation of Dada and Futurist design.

Tschichold was adamant in adapting sans serif lettering as representative of the machine age, although he tended to favor the less stylized "grotesques" by anonymous designers of the nineteenth century that were widely available and inexpensive. He disdained the assertiveness of Bauhaus type such as Stencil or Bayer's Universal, which he felt called too much attention to their individual "artistic" aspects in their extreme abstract structure. In a sense, he felt that conventional grotesques were more functionally "universal" in their anonymity than the artist-designed equivalents. Tschichold was also a strong proponent of the abolition of upper-case letters, thereby aligning himself with Bauhaus designers such as Bayer. The cover of *Elementary Typography* is a fine example of a design that eliminates capital letters without sacrificing clarity. It is essential to remember the continuing controversy provoked by this issue in Germany; it is never a wholly aesthetic decision for a German designer to eschew blackletter. Overall, Tschichold worked to "rationalize" typography into a

zeitschrift des bildungsverbandes der deutschen buchdrucker leipzig ● oktoberheft 1925

mitteilungen

typographische

sonderheft

elementare
typographie

natan altman
otto baumberger
herbert bayer
max burchartz
el lissitzky
ladislaus moholy-nagy
molnár f. farkas
johannes molzahn
kurt schwitters
mart stam
ivan tschichold

6.27 Jan Tschichold, *Typographische Mitteilungen: Elementare Typographie (Typographic News: Elementary Typography)*, October 1925. Journal cover. Dada Archive.

6.28 and 6.29 Jan Tschichold, *Die Neue Typographie (The New Typography)*, 1928. International Dada Archive, University of Iowa Libraries.

functional science, emphasizing simple sans serif letterforms that resulted in the utmost legibility.

Die Neue Typographie

"The essence of the New Typography is clarity. This puts it into direct opposition to the old typography, whose aim was 'beauty' and whose clarity did not attain the high level we require today." In 1928, Tschichold published in Berlin *Die Neue Typographie*. This book, subtitled *Ein Handbuch für zeitgemäss. Schaffende* ("Handbook for the Contemporary Designer"), was intended further to codify his avowed set of design principles (*fig. 6.28*). As a handbook published by the educational department of a printer's union, *Die Neue Typographie* was intended to set out in clear terms the history, theory, and practice of the New Typography. The design of the book itself, a sober black volume with silver lettering and rounded corners so that it could be slipped into the working designer's pocket, bespeaks Tschichold's adoption of the artist-as-engineer paradigm favored by the Constructivists. While one might expect that a book like this that extolled the virtues of the machine age would be typeset using the mechanical hot-metal systems, it was in fact set by hand. This anomaly was probably a result of Tschichold's publisher, a labor union consisting of "old school" printers.

Many of the themes sounded in *Die Neue Typographie*—such as the significance of speed and simultaneity in modern life, the need to work collectively as opposed to individually, the new role of the engineer replacing that of the artist, the absolute goal of clear communication, and the need to integrate typography and photography as the quintessential modern media—had all appeared in earlier essays by modern designers such as Moholy-Nagy or El Lissitzky. What Tschichold accomplished was to

provide a text replete with examples that could serve as a fundamental reference for graphic designers both inside and outside the major modern groups.

One of the most famous sets of illustrations from *Die Neue Typographie* shows how asymmetry functions to enliven the page (*fig. 6.29*). Tschichold renounced axial symmetry as one of the most deadening elements of what he generically called "old typography." He felt that axial symmetry was a dishonest, decorative strategy that negatively impacted the clarity of the text. Tschichold wrote:

> The liveliness of asymmetry is also an expression of our own movement and that of modern life; it is a symbol of the changing forms of life in general when aymmetrical movement in typography takes the place of symmetrical repose. This movement must not however degenerate into unrest or chaos.

The last part of the quoted text demonstrates how Tschichold, while citing Dada and Futurist designers such as Tzara and Marinetti as pioneers of the New Typography, also sought to bring the "chaos" of those revolutionary movements under control. Compared to his more expansive stance in the 1925 *Elementary Typography* issue, in *Die Neue Typographie* Tschichold seems dogmatic in asserting that the new styles must demonstrate the artist's firm control at every turn. For Tschichold, the impulsive play and rulebreaking spirit of Dada were yet further examples of a superfluous element—like older decorative, seriffed letters—that must be ruthlessly eliminated so as not to compromise the plainness and clarity that are the goal of all typography. For Tschichold, asymmetry represented a sort of "controlled Dadaism," expressive of the new freedoms of the modern industrial world while remaining a supportive part of the

6.30 Jan Tschichold, *Die Frau ohne Namen, Zweiter Teil (The Woman without a Name, Part II)*, 1927. Offset lithograph, 48 x 34 in (123.8 x 86.3 cm). Museum of Modern Art, New York. Peter Stone Poster Fund.

underlying order manifest in the orthogonal grid. In *Die Neue Typographie*, Tschichold heartily embraced Moholy-Nagy's concept of typophoto, arguing that the integration of typography and photography best expressed the modern spirit. Visually speaking, he called for graphic designers to focus on the dynamic contrasts made available by juxtaposing photography's three-dimensional element with typography's inherently two-dimensional character.

An example of Tschichold's own work in this vein can be seen in the movie poster he made in 1927 for the Phoebus-Palast in Munich (*fig. 6.30*). Advertising a film called *The Woman without a Name, Part II*, the lithograph artfully synthesizes photos of people that have a clear sculptural mass with linear geometric elements that playfully suggest three-dimensional space without providing the weighted forms that would make it convincing. The photographic elements are arranged on an asymmetrical, diagonal axis formed by a schematic linear perspective drawing; the title-words seem to soar on another diagonal out of the same illusory vanishing point.

An important part of Tschichold's conception of typophoto was the use of sans serif text only. While in other situations Tschichold had suggested that simple roman forms were acceptable, he felt that the modern photograph could only be complemented by sans serif block. The key to the relationship between photography and sans serif lettering was their shared objective and impersonal form, which was the most suitable rejoinder to the individuality expressed by the decorative old typography. For the text of *Die Neue Typographie*, Tschichold employed Akzidenz Grotesk, an anonymous sans serif that was widely available at the time. While he had intended the book to rebut claims that sans serif was unfit for long, continuous passages of text because of its readability issues, a number of commentators pointed out that reading the book through was "hardly the pleasant exercise that Tschichold assumes it will be."

Like the other members of the avant-garde, Tschichold considered the New Typography to be exemplary of the merging of art and life that was a fundamental tenet of modern design movements such as De Stijl, Constructivism, and the Bauhaus. Rather than simply a visual style, the New Typography was to serve as the basis for a more just and equitable society administered according to socialist principles. However, it is unclear whether Tschichold was a "true believer" in the Soviet state or whether he was simply going through the motions of associating Constructivism and socialism. While *Die Neue Typographie* makes continual reference to socialist thought, more ideologically committed designers criticized Tschichold for what they considered to be his lack of political fervor. For example, a review in the journal *bauhaus*, written at the time when Hannes Meyer was director and the institution was at its most overtly political, sharply attacked Tschichold for being nothing more than a dogmatic formalist, questioning his ideological purity in the same manner in which the Russian Constructivists were attacked by promoters of Socialist Realism under Stalin. On the other hand, Tschichold's book later became known as the bible of modern "functionalism," and, like the parallel writings by Moholy-Nagy at the Bauhaus, was often misrepresented as completely rejecting political activism, and intended only as a scientific discussion of typography, no more politicized than an introductory physics

textbook. It would seem likely that the truth lies somewhere outside these two polarized distortions of Tschichold's work. In a fascinating development, Tschichold drastically altered his own perspective on the New Typography in later decades (see Chapter 8).

Ring Neue Werbegestalter

In 1928, Kurt Schwitters was instrumental in the establishment of a loose group of graphic designers who called themselves the **Ring Neue Werbegestalter** ("Circle of New Advertising Designers"). Sometimes nicknamed the "Ring," and not to be confused with a contemporary association of German architects that had inspired Schwitters, this group of typographers and graphic designers used exhibitions to promote the Constructivist aesthetic in the commercial realm. Between 1928 and 1930, members of the Ring displayed their work in cities across Germany and the Netherlands via two traveling exhibitions. While Schwitters was himself based in Hanover, the Ring existed mainly in epistolary form, as the different members and invited guests, who included Tschichold, Moholy-Nagy, Bayer, Gropius, John Heartfield, and Piet Zwart (formerly of De Stijl), organized the group's

6.31 George Trump, *NWG ring "neue werbegestalter,"* c. 1928. Letterhead. Letterpress. Collection Elaine Lustig Cohen.

6.32 Paul Schuitema, *Toledo-Berkel*, 1930s. Berkel advertisement. Bookprint. Research Library, Getty Research Institute, Los Angeles, CA.

exhibitions through the mail. The German typographer Georg
Trump (1896–1985) designed the letterhead that was used by
Schwitters when he circulated new designs for the members of
the Ring to peruse and judge (*fig. 6.31*). Trump's asymmetrical
composition, sans serif lettering, and use of rectangular elements
to organize information are all typical of the Constructivist style
favored in the Ring. The one dramatic element of this design is
the way in which the acronym NWG has been pushed into the
upper right corner of the page, creating an element of tension in
the way it crowds the margin. Compare the overall "feel" of those
letters with the more austere and spacious character of the rest
of the letterhead.

The members of the Ring faced the same dilemma as the
Bauhaus artists, with whom they were closely associated: how to
reconcile left-wing political ideology with the service of clients
from the capitalist countries of Europe. No one artist resolved this
conflict in a simple manner; rather, it was something that each
struggled with, perhaps bolstered by the belief that a new and
more just society was in the making. This new society would be
somehow made possible by the modern technology exemplified
by the typophoto style. The overarching style of most of the Ring
designers was drawn from the standards of the New Typography,
featuring sans serif type organized by an underlying grid and integrated with elements of photomontage. While photomontage had
earlier been perceived as a vehicle of strict revolutionary sentiment, by the late 1920s it was just another formal device in the
modernist designer's repertoire, and could be employed outside
its original ideological context.

A fine representative of the many contradictions implicit in
the work of the Ring can be seen in the writings and designs of
the Dutch artist Paul Schuitema (1897–1973). At the same time
that he was writing articles such as "Photography as a Weapon in
the Class War" for Dutch left-wing periodicals (in this case *Links
Richten*, literally "Left Aiming," February 1933), he was happily
working on commercial graphics in a Constructivist style. For
example, Schuitema designed a series of advertisements for the
Dutch scale manufacturer Berkel, combining montaged photos
of their product with sans serif lettering (*fig. 6.32*). Berkel was a
major industrial conglomerate in the Netherlands, and throughout his career Schuitema worked on their advertising posters,
stationery, exhibition booths and other printed ephemera. In this
advertisement, a vertical bar on the left margin serves to anchor
both the text, which is ranged off it horizontally, and the photomontage, in which the repeated curves of the scales contrast
with the geometric clarity of the grid. The photomontage seems
to compete with the text, at times managing to subdue it, as when
the edge of a scale bites into the top of the letter "e" in "Toledo."

During the time he was associated with the Ring, Tschichold
designed the cover of a portfolio of photos by reusing Lissitzky's
famous photomontage self-portrait originally called *The
Constructor* (*fig. 6.33*). Lissitzky himself had previously recycled the
image in a lithograph for Pelikan Ink (see fig. 5.44). Tschichold's
catalog, titled *Foto-Auge* ("Photo Eye"), was intended to invoke
the work and theory of the Soviet filmmaker Dziga Vertov,
who had romanticized the eye of the camera as the perfect,
dispassionate symbol of modern vision. Again, at the same time
that he was promulgating the depoliticized functionalism of the

New Typography, Tschichold still recognized his debt to
Constructivism's Russian, Communist roots. A survey of modern
photographic techniques, *Foto-Auge* was condemned by the Nazis
in 1933, and Tschichold's co-editor Franz Roh (1911–1965), an
art historian, was arrested and imprisoned for having published
the book. In fact, the Nazi seizure of power in 1933 immediately
halted almost all of the work of the German avant-garde—be they
at the Bauhaus, members of the Ring, or individuals committed
to the New Typography. Chapter 7 will trace the dramatic
evolution of graphic design in Germany at the time when it was
dominated by the National Socialists, or Nazis.

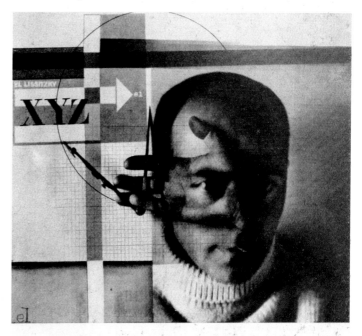

6.33 Franz Roh and Jan Tschichold, eds. *Foto-Auge*, 1929.
Photomontage by El Lissitzky. Merrill C. Berman Collection.

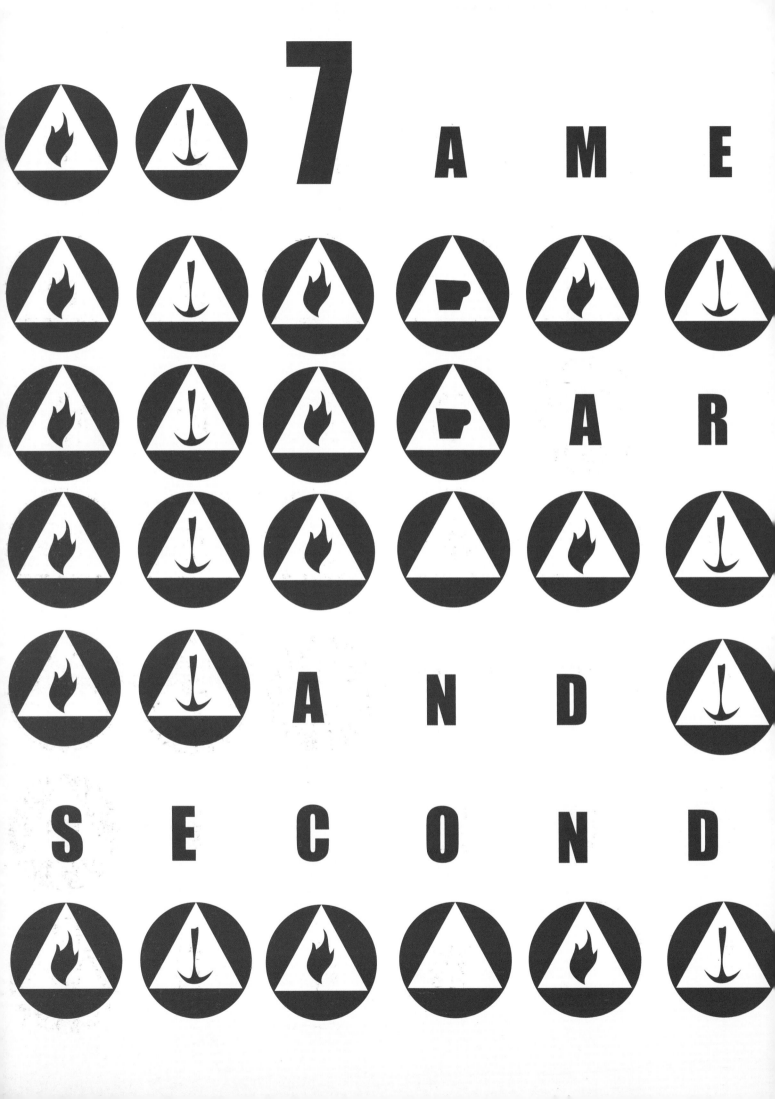

During the 1920s, the professions of graphic designer and art director gradually increased their visibility in the United States. Someone with the title "art director," often a graphic designer, had general responsibility for the design and typography of a given publication, although they might not always do the actual work themselves. In the 1920s, a number of organizations were founded in the United States that provided lectures, exhibitions, and conferences that helped support and define the field. In 1920, the Art Directors' Club of New York was established, and 1927 saw the creation of the Society of Typographic Artists in Chicago. While the American Institute of Graphic Arts had been founded in 1914 with a focus on fine art printing, it gradually shifted its activities into the commercial design fields. Through a diffuse process, there was also increasing recognition that individuals proficient in the manipulation of text and image were central to all types of printed media.

Advertising agencies and publishers, especially in the mass media, became more cognizant in the 1920s of the unique set of skills possessed by art directors. There was a concomitant expansion of the advertising industry in the United States during this period that created new opportunities for graphic designers. Between 1914 and 1929, the annual dollar volume of advertising rose from $600,000 to nearly 3 billion dollars. New advertising agencies appeared almost monthly, while older operations doubled and trebled their staffs. Newspapers alone carried 2.25 million dollars' worth of advertisements in the year 1927. The advertising "game" acquired a new sense of professionalism as it became gradually more economically important to the country.

7.1 Joseph Binder, *Skyscraper Christmas Tree, Fortune Magazine*, Dec 1937. Magazine cover, 11 x 13 in (27.9 x 34.9 cm).

7.2 T. M. Cleland, Contents Page, *Fortune* magazine, Feb 1930, p. 53.

7.3 Margaret Bourke-White, "In mammoth dust-heaps ends the pig, completely disassembled, his remains ground to pungent dust, he fulfils his final function as good food for animals. In this storeroom are 1500 tons of rich pig-dust, macabre mountains of meal." Photograph, *Fortune* magazine, Feb 1930, p. 61.

7.4 Wurlitzer Advertisement, *Fortune* magazine, Feb 1930, p. 33.

The American Magazine

While the 1920s in Europe were marked by the development of modern, abstract styles, in the United States the decade saw the continued dominance of conventional design and typography. While there were isolated instances of experimental modern graphics reaching mainstream publications, conservative American advertisers favored traditional illustration and rather unadventurous photography over more progressive styles.

However, as early as 1925, the year of the influential *"Exposition Internationale des Arts Décoratifs et Industriels Modernes"* in Paris, a gradual trickle of European and European-inspired designs made its first appearance on the American scene. The United States had earlier rejected sponsoring a pavilion at the exposition because of a disdain for the modern styles to be exhibited there. However, in 1925, exhibits from that summer's exposition were featured at New York City's Metropolitan Museum of Art's annual "Industrial art" exhibit, signaling very strongly for the first time a mainstream interest in the Art Deco style. Department stores in a number of major American cities across the country soon followed the museum's lead, and 1926 witnessed a further expansion of interest in Art Deco, at least among sophisticated urban consumers.

It is important to be able to identify the two separate streams that made up modern European design during this era; the first, discussed in Chapter 4, consisted of designers such as Edward McKnight Kauffer and Cassandre who used formal devices derived from modern art movements, including Cubism, Futurism, Orphism, and Purism, in order to create striking graphics. This first stream culminated in the Art Deco style, and is sometimes referred to by scholars as "**commercial modern**." The second stream of European design, discussed mainly in Chapters 5 and 6, consisted of Dada as well as the various "functionalist" oriented groups, including De Stijl, Russian Constructivism, International Constructivism, Bauhaus, and the New Typography. This second stream can be differentiated from the first by the member artists' deep commitment to political change. More importantly, the second, Constructivist stream emphasized graphic design and typography over fine art, so that its work directly speaks to the graphic design profession. Of course, there is substantial overlap between the Art Deco and Constructivist projects, and a movement such as Futurism, for example, inspired artists in both camps. However, it is useful to be able to recognize the different historical roots in the work of a designer who employs functionalist typography versus a designer who draws in a Cubist-inspired decorative idiom.

During the 1930s, the vast majority of modern design works in America and Europe proudly displayed the Art Deco, or commercial modern, style. Promoters of the austere Constructivism of the Bauhaus and the like were rare, small voices crying in the wilderness.

In order to give some sense of the development of American graphic design during the 1930s, it is helpful to undertake a selective survey of the contents of two mainstream magazines from February 1930, *Fortune* and *Vanity Fair*. While the overwhelming majority of advertisements published in these magazines, as well as the design of the publications themselves, feature conventional graphics and typography, much of the most exciting work during the 1930s was published in publications such as these. Periodicals would evolve more quickly than other media and present one of

7.5 IMM Advertisement, *Fortune* magazine, Feb 1930, p. 17.

7.6 Carrier Advertisement, *Fortune* magazine, Feb 1930, p. 5.

7.7 Carrier Advertisement, *Fortune* magazine, March 1930, p. 5.

the best sources of commissions for expatriate European designers as well as Americans with a contemporary sensibility.

Fortune

The first issue of *Fortune* magazine appeared in February 1930. A product of the large media corporation Time, the new periodical was aimed at the affluent urban businessman. Published and edited by Henry Luce (1898–1967), *Fortune* contained critical analyses and feature articles on major American industries. For example, the inaugural issue presented commentary on the financial markets as well as articles on a variety of business-related subjects, from the use of color in consumer goods to a profile of the Rothschild banking family in England. It also promised that March's issue would cover subjects including aluminum, railroads, and jewels.

Fortune's first art director was T.M. Cleland (1880–1964), who chose a characteristically conservative design, the most prominent element of which was the bold, three-dimensional seriffed lettering used as the masthead. For the most part, the text and images were set apart as discrete units, with headings placed symmetrically at the top of the page (*fig. 7.2*). The only daring element in the magazine's early stages was the employment of photographer Margaret Bourke-White (1904–1971). Bourke-White had initially established herself as a photographer of industrial landscapes in Cleveland, Ohio, where she ran a small independent photography studio. Discovered by Henry Luce in 1929, she set to work that autumn on a series of photographs of Swift and Co.'s Chicago hog processing plant, which illustrated

the first issue of *Fortune*. While her editor at *Fortune*, Parker Lloyd-Smith, had to quit the scene when he was overcome by the stench of the slaughter, Bourke-White persevered through the assignment, reportedly abandoning all her photographic equipment to be burned when she was finished. Her photo series included the strikingly modernist image shown here of a mountain containing 1,500 tons of "pig-dust," ground remains that would be turned into animal feed (*fig. 7.3*). The abstract geometry of the piles provides a perfect counterpoint to the organic shape of the lone worker shoveling remains. The cropping of this macabre image makes it more unsettling, as the piles of remains and the figure are not securely anchored to the ground line. While Bourke-White's photos were often composed with sophisticated Constructivist elements, their layout in *Fortune* was quite conventional. The frame around the image separates it from the page, for example, while the centered caption detracts from the asymmetry of the photo.

The first fifty-two pages of *Fortune*'s inaugural issue were made up of advertisements that ranged widely in design. However, the majority of the ads featured quite conventional typography matched with realistic illustration or photography. A fine example of a typical American advertisement from this period appeared on page 33 (*fig. 7.4*). It is useful to analyze this advertisement so as to establish a baseline of typical advertising fare from the beginning of the decade. Promoting the "Wurlitzer Reproducing Organ," a self-playing device, the most striking part of the ad's typography is the letter "E" in the word "Entertaining." Serving as a kind of dropped capital, this letter is monstrously proportioned and clashes with the rest of the tag line, which is printed in a seriffed italic. This boxy, plaid "E" is just one part of an overall chaotic exercise in typography, as throughout the ad a number of inelegant faces compete for the reader's attention. This typography lacks both the stylized grace and elegance of Art Deco and the functional clarity of Constructivism.

There are two illustrations in the advertisement, the most prominent of which is centered at the top. Here, a pedestrian representational style has been used to showcase a wealthy family listening to the organ in their elegant salon. The image and text are aligned symmetrically, but there is little else connecting them. It is obvious from advertisements such as this that the copywriter was the most prominent part of any advertising team as the 1930s began. The Wurlitzer organ is described in three columns of text that exalt "the pleasure it gives your guests and your family, the cultural development it affords your children, the distinction it adds to your home." Indeed, this ad is actually relatively concise by the standards of the day, at a time when companies expected their publicity materials to set out fully in writing the basis for the product.

In the staid pages of *Fortune*, the vast majority of the illustrations, such as those in the Wurlitzer ad, were devoid of modern tendencies. American corporations had a fundamentally conservative outlook, and more than anything else they sought out art directors who would avoid offending middle-class taste. The few instances of more progressive design techniques tended to occur when the advertised company itself was European or featured a product directly related to Europe. For example, the combined White Star, Red Star, and Atlantic Transport Lines, owned by the International Mercantile Marine Company (IMM), paid for an ad trumpeting their passenger and freight services. IMM was in fact an American company, part of J.P. Morgan's financial empire, but it had maintained a European flavor in acquiring a number of British shipping interests in 1910. The illustration for this ad makes for a dramatic contrast with the representational style of the Wurlitzer designer; the bow and side of a ship shown here are pure Art Deco: simplified forms, a powerful diagonal axis, cropping, and extreme foreshortening (*fig. 7.5*). As in the ad for the organ, there is a great deal of text, and the image is seemingly a secondary concern. Both ads feature a prosaic design that places headline text in large scale sandwiched between an image above and body text below. The typography is a mix of sans serif headings and seriffed text, arranged in an asymmetrical block that is rather daring for the pages of *Fortune*. Presumably, someone preparing a business trip to Europe would be familiar with modernism and more open to this sort of stylish rendering.

In the advertisements published in *Fortune*, illustration and photography seem almost interchangeable. Like the image used for the Wurlitzer ad, the majority of the photos are completely nondescript in both style and subject matter. One advertisement from the air-conditioner company Carrier in the February issue, however, stood out for its striking modernist photographic composition (*fig. 7.6*). The ad, featuring the tag line "Are these tallest office buildings already obsolete?" is, like so many others, heavily dependent on expository text. Promoting the new technology of "manufactured weather," or air conditioning, the copywriter has explained in great detail the advantages of this "healthful comfort." The roman type makes a number of seemingly eclectic shifts between italic and bold, although some attempt is made

to indicate emphasis, as in the words "already obsolete." While many elements of the typography appear to us reserved and conventional, this photograph of New York skyscrapers is so startlingly modern in appearance that it could almost have been shot by László Moholy-Nagy. The three buildings are shown from a radically oblique angle, hovering over the viewer. An essentially abstract composition, three gray geometric masses appear to float in the air, as the photo is cropped so that none of the buildings appears anchored to the ground. The ambient light has created a range of tones that emphasize the blocky shapes of the structures.

Carrier's advertisement for the March issue of *Fortune* displayed a similar concept, combining conventional design with stunningly modern photography, in this case a photomontage that could have been taken from the work of Berlin Dada (*fig. 7.7*). Presenting a dynamic overview of a modern city, the image combines skyscrapers, monumental neon signs, and even the US Capitol. Despite the photo's striking style, it is still part of a conventional layout that separates the image from the text with framing devices. It is essential to remember that the use of photography in the Carrier ads was extremely anomalous in 1930, as the overwhelming majority of advertisements avoided progressive design techniques at all costs.

In 1937, *Fortune* featured one of the most famous Art Deco designs of all time when the cover revealed a work by the Austrian expatriate artist Joseph Binder (1898–1972). Binder, who had studied in Vienna under Alfred Roller (see Chapter 2), moved to the United States in 1934. His cover for *Fortune*, published in December 1937, uses the basic shape of a Christmas tree to structure a tower of skyscrapers, a major symbol of American corporate power (*fig. 7.1*). The buildings display the stepped-pyramid form that is typical of Art Deco architecture forced to conform to zoning laws regulating the amount of shadow produced by a building on city streets. Binder successfully contested the strong symmetry of the triangular frame with a high contrast deployment of black and white blocks that form the sides of the skyscrapers. A comparison of this image with Lyonel Feininger's *Cathedral* (see fig. 6.7) shows how Art Deco artists successfully assimilated Expressionist devices such as the crystalline forms and starry sky shown here in order to convey the magnificence of an urban, capitalist utopia. Overall, *Fortune* remained quite reserved in its design until 1945, when the German designer Will Burtin (1909–1972), who had fled Nazi Germany because his wife was Jewish, took over as art director and introduced a new modern style.

Mehemed Agha and *Vanity Fair*

One would expect that the editors of *Vanity Fair* magazine, the fashionable periodical devoted to the arts and culture edited by Frank Crowninshield (1872–1947) and published by Condé Nast (1873–1942), would be more open to progressive design than the editors of *Fortune*. *Vanity Fair* was the premier periodical of this era to focus on modern art, often publishing reproductions of Cubist, Futurist, and Expressionist works. Nast's stable of publications included a number of European editions of his magazines, *Vogue* being the most prominent example.

7.8 Georges Lepape, *Vanity Fair*, Feb 1930. Magazine cover. Original artwork by Georges Lepape. Copyright © 1930, Condé Nast Publications Inc. Reprinted by permission.

Condé Nast, *Vogue*, and Fashion Photography

Although the magazines that Condé Nast oversaw until his death in 1942 included such notable publications as Vanity Fair, House and Garden, *and* Glamour, *it was his original effort,* Vogue, *which secured his place in fashion history. Nast bought* Vogue *in 1909 and took what was then a small niche publication aimed at New York society and transformed it into a fashion publication with a powerful American and European following; by 1920, Nast had established British and French editions.*

As one of the leading fashion magazines in the United States (along with its rival Harper's Bazaar*),* Vogue *was positioned to have an enormous influence on the industry. More than any other publication,* Vogue *engineered the rise of fashion photography in the 1920s and 1930s. Nast's first major coup was to sign Edward Steichen (1879–1973) in 1923 as principal photographer. Steichen quickly established a reputation as a stylish innovator with artificial lighting. His commercial style was a variant of the "straight photography" that he had pioneered in the 1910s with Alfred Stieglitz, whereby the model was shot with a view towards eliminating obvious artifice, such as soft focus, and any overwhelming sentiment. Steichen also established the precedent that fashion photography had to be technically perfect and display the highest possible production values.*

In the 1930s Vogue *and Steichen were joined by luminaries including Baron George Hoyningen-Huene, Cecil Beaton, Horst P. Horst, and André Durst. Their photographic work was furthered by talented models such as Lisa Fonssagrives, who would appear on hundreds of* Vogue *covers.*

Fashion photographers faced an uneasy reputation during their heyday. With its unseemly ties to commerce, fashion photography was deemed beneath consideration as an art form (even among its practitioners and patrons). Many fashion photographers displayed a non-commercial "art" portfolio to potential clients to convince them of their artistic pedigree.

However, photography's artistic reputation shifted dramatically after the Second World War, when Steichen became the Director of Photography at the Museum of Modern Art. In this position that he held for fifteen years, Steichen helped to secure photography's place in the canon of modern art. Yet, to this day fashion photography remains on the outside looking in, never having quite achieved the status of an art form.

In 1929, Nast had hired the art director of the German edition of *Vogue* magazine, Mehemed Agha (1896–1978), to take over the design of his flagship publications, first the American *Vogue*, and immediately thereafter *Vanity Fair* and *House and Garden*. At *Vanity Fair*, Agha worked quickly to install a new style that used elements drawn from both the Art Deco and Constructivist streams of European modernism. Art Deco had in fact already been highly visible in the pages of *Vanity Fair*, especially its cover art. The February 1930 issue is typical of this trend; the cover was drawn by Georges Lepape (1887–1971), a famed Art Deco illustrator (*fig. 7.8*). Lepape was French, and this cover shows his usual whimsical assortment of characters drawn from folklore and the **Commedia dell'Arte**, which was a type of popular, improvisational theater that utilized stock characters. The stylized simplification of forms and strong geometric elements reminiscent of Cubism demonstrate how Lepape, like Cassandre and others, transformed modernist painting into a sleek, glamorous form of commercial illustration.

The more dramatic initial change that Agha instituted at *Vanity Fair* concerned the magazine's typography. A devotee of sans serif letters, Agha redesigned the contents page using Paul Renner's Futura type as well as the bold rules and positive use of negative space typical of Constructivist aesthetics (*fig. 7.9*). However, Agha's design does not display the austere functional-

ism typical of European Constructivist designs. Rather, the attenuated proportions and wide spacing between the letters that spell out "*Vanity Fair*" and "in this number" are replete with the decorative elegance of the Art Deco style. In this way Agha has successfully synthesized a new layout and typography from the two main trends of European design, combining the clarity of Constructivism with the sinuous grace of Art Deco. International Constructivism and the New Typography had made very few inroads into American design culture at this point.

As early as 1930, Agha, who had already been the first art director to use double-paged photo spreads and color cover photography, became the first designer to make use of the "full bleed," allowing photographs to expand to all four margins and

FEBRUARY, 1930   25

V A N I T Y   F A I R

FRANK CROWNINSHIELD—editor   DONALD FREEMAN—managing editor

COPYRIGHT, 1930, BY THE CONDÉ NAST PUBLICATIONS, INC.

i n   t h i s   n u m b e r

complete contents of this issue—february 1930

Subscribers are notified that no change of address can be effected in less than one month

Published monthly by The Condé Nast Publications, Inc., Boston Post Road, Greenwich, Conn. Executive and publishing offices at Greenwich, Conn. Editorial offices, Graybar Building, Lexington at 43rd Street, New York. Cable address Vanseit, French office, 65 avenue des Champs-Élysées, Paris. Condé Nast, President; Francis L. Wurzburg, Vice-President; W. E. Beckerle, Treasurer; M. E. Moore, Secretary. Subscription $4.00 a year in the United States and Colonies, Mexico and Canada. $5.00 in foreign countries. Single copies 35c. Address all correspondence relating to subscriptions to Vanity Fair, Greenwich, Connecticut. Entered as second class matter at Greenwich, Conn., under the act of March 3, 1879. Printed in the U. S. A. by The Condé Nast Press. Title Vanity Fair Reg. U. S. Patent Office. Manuscripts must be accompanied by postage for their return if unavailable. Vanity Fair assumes no responsibility for unsolicited contributions except to accord them courteous attention and ordinary care. The entire contents of Vanity Fair—text and illustrations—are protected by copyright in the following countries and must not be reproduced in any manner without written permission: United States, Austria, Brazil, Canada, France, Germany, Great Britain, Hungary, Italy, and all other countries which are members of the International Copyright Union.

VOL. 33 No. 6   35 CENTS A COPY $4.00 A YEAR

7.9 Mehemed Agha, *Vanity Fair*, Feb 1930. Contents page. Copyright © 1930, Condé Nast Publications Inc. Reprinted by permission.

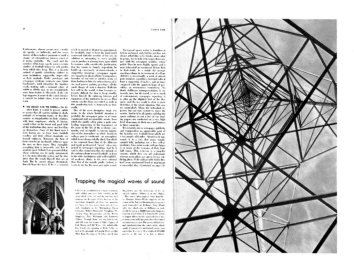

Trapping the magical waves of sound

7.10 Margaret Bourke-White et al, "Trapping the Magical Waves of Sound", *Vanity Fair*, May 1934, pp. 26–7. Copyright © 1934, Condé Nast Publications Inc. Reprinted by permission.

completely cover the page. This allowed for dramatic contrasts of form and texture that created more sophisticated relationships between text and image. In an example from *Vanity Fair* for May 1934, an exceptional photograph by Bourke-White of a radio transmission tower taken from an extremely oblique perspective has completely suffused the right page (*fig. 7.10*). In contrast to the use of Bourke-White's photographs in *Fortune*, here there is no rule or frame to separate the image from the page itself. This **"full bleed"** allows the asymmetrical, geometric complexity of the tower's composition to play off the solid blocks of text to the left. The title "Trapping the magical waves of sound" serves to connect text and image in the way it replicates a horizontal element in the photograph. Note also how the heading is located asymmetrically two-thirds of the way down the page, again in contrast to the conventional, symmetrical layout in *Fortune*.

In 1931, Condé Nast acknowledged Agha's importance to his magazine empire when he included the art director's name on the masthead of the contents page of *Vanity Fair*, alongside those of the editor, Frank Crowninshield, and Nast himself. Agha's significance to American magazine design was further recognized in the mainstream press as early as 1939, when a brief article in *Time* made note of his accomplishments. Significantly, this unattributed piece appeared in the "Art" section of *Time*, which was an accomplishment in itself. While heralding the art director as a pioneer in the use of typography and photography, the article still manages to be snide when it comes to modern design, suggesting that Agha's use of blank spaces leaves "room for your laundry list" while noting that the photography he uses features "cock-eyed" perspectives. Agha is quoted to the effect that his success has already started to dilute the effectiveness of his designs because they are so widely copied.

Cipe Pineles

Agha enhanced his influence on American graphic design through the significant number of young protégés he groomed at Condé Nast. This group included Alex Liberman and Cipe Pineles (1910–1991), both of whom enjoyed considerable success long after Agha left Condé Nast in 1943. Pineles, a woman of Austrian ancestry who had emigrated to New York in 1923, was hired by Agha in 1933 to work at *Vanity Fair* and *Vogue* (the former was absorbed into *Vogue* in 1936). A fine example of Pineles's work at Condé Nast is the April 1, 1939 cover of *Vogue* (fig. 7.11), which features a full color image of two women's faces by renowned photographer Horst P. Horst (1906–1999). The dramatically cropped photo is off center to the right and tilted clockwise about 20 degrees so that the upper left corner points at the magazine's name. The text and image in this manner form a diagonal compositional line that cuts across the page. The letters that spell out "*Vogue*," in addition, are written in a decorous script, an example of how Agha never established a fixed set of principles for the cover, but rather allowed artists such as Pineles the freedom to design entire covers from scratch.

Pineles eventually moved on in 1942, to become the art director of *Glamour* magazine, where she would introduce many of the modern design techniques she had learned while working

above: **7.11** Cipe Pineles, *Vogue* Cover,
April 1, 1939.

right: **7.12** Cipe Pineles, *Seventeen*
Cover, July 1949.

for Agha. Pineles was a pioneer in that she was the first woman art director of a mass-market periodical, and her success at *Glamour* led to subsequent positions as art director at *Seventeen*, *Charm*, and *Mademoiselle*. Her work at *Seventeen* in the late 1940s truly established her independent reputation as a talented modern designer. In contrast to *Vogue*, where the cover logo changed constantly to fit that issue's image, at *Seventeen* Pineles employed a standardized type, lower-case Bodoni in its bold, condensed italic form. The cover photo generally featured a young woman, naturally posed, as can be seen in the July 1949 cover (*fig. 7.12*). On this cover, photographs by one of Pineles's own favorites, Francesco Scavullo (1921–2004), have been montaged so that at first glance the viewer perceives a reflected image. Only when one studies how the hand in the top image appears almost to grasp the umbrella in the lower photo does the true nature of the cover become clear. The red, white, and blue palette connects the cover to the 4th of July holiday. In the 1950s, outside the purview of this chapter, Pineles became famous for her innovative strategy of employing established artists such as Ben Shahn (1898–1969) as

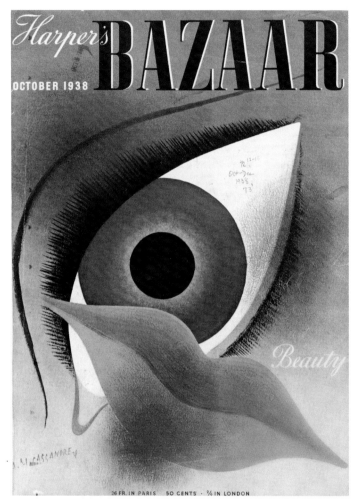

7.13 A.M. Cassandre, *Harper's Bazaar* Cover, Oct 1938.

magazine illustrators. In 1948, she became the first woman granted membership in the prestigious New York Art Directors' Club, a heretofore all-male bastion of design professionals.

Alexey Brodovitch

Alexey Brodovitch (1898–1971), another European immigrant who became an influential art director in America during the 1930s, was hired by Carmel Snow (1887–1961), the editor of *Harper's Bazaar*, in 1934. Brodovitch worked on a parallel track to that of Agha, introducing modern design elements over a period of years. While working in Paris during the 1920s, Brodovitch had become acquainted with the work of Art Deco illustrators such as Cassandre, whom he hired in 1938 to create a series of dramatic covers for *Harper's Bazaar*. The cover from October 1938 features an illustration by Cassandre of a disembodied eye and pair of lips (*fig. 7.13*). The rich red color and sinuous shape of the lips as well as the obvious care with which the eyelashes have been shaped suggests that these are parts of a glamorous woman's face. The shape of both the iris and pupil of the eye is perfectly round and suggestive of Cassandre's early adoption of a style influenced by Purism (see Chapter 4). However, the use of fragments of a woman's body is evidence of the fact that Cassandre had absorbed some of the principles of the French Surrealist movement. Surrealist artists of the 1920s and 1930s such as Joan Miró (1893–1983)and Salvador Dalí (1904–1989) often painted images that contained disembodied pieces of human anatomy; these fragmented bodies were a vehicle that allowed artists to convey their dreams and fantasies. A great deal of Surrealist work

7.14 Alexey Brodovitch, *Harper's Bazaar* Spread, March 15, 1938.

dealt with sexual fantasies, and the eye and lips shown in Cassandre's cover design are emblematic of male desire.

Brodovitch also oversaw the design of some of the most compelling double-page spreads of photography and text ever seen. Like Agha, he employed a series of prominent photographers, including Horst P. Horst, Cecil Beaton (1904–1980), and George Hoyningen-Huené (1900–1968), to create startling photographs that served as the basis for the overall design of the spread. Hoyningen-Huené shot the photo shown here, repeating the stylish curve of the model's left hip with a shadow that drapes across the right side of her form (*fig. 7.14*). Brodovitch bled this photo across the **gutter**, where he formed a column of type into another smooth curve that echoed the contour in the photograph. The use of bold lettering to start each line of text further emphasizes the sweeping line that structures the entire spread. Brodovitch used the eminently functional modern seriffed typeface called Bodoni for most of the text in *Harper's Bazaar*, showing that sans serif type was not essential to the creation of a harmonious modern design.

PM Magazine

While mainstream magazines such as *Harper's Bazaar* and *Vanity Fair* brought new modern styles to the attention of the mainstream, smaller trade publications that served design professionals had an important role in educating a generation of young American art directors. Among the most prominent examples of this type of periodical was called *PM Magazine*, the initials standing for "production manager," which first appeared in 1934 as a

mouthpiece of the typography firm called The Composing Room. This firm had been founded in 1927 by Sol Cantor (?–1965) and Dr Robert L. Leslie (1885–1987), who sought to join in the print advertising boom of the 1920s. The early issues of *PM Magazine*, edited by Percy Seitlin, focused mainly on practical issues related to the printing and typesetting businesses. However, Leslie's interest in European design soon came to the fore as the monthly magazine focused more and more on bringing European styles to the attention of American art directors.

In 1936 the magazine began publishing overviews of individual European artists such as Lucian Bernhard, whose *Sachplakat* style was the major topic of the March edition (see Chapter 3). Bernhard had immigrated to the United States in 1923 and had established a successful freelance design firm there. He kept up with innovations in graphic design and typography, and in 1929 he designed Bernhard Gothic (*fig. 7.15*) for the American Type Foundry, a "functionalist" sans serif type intended to rival Paul Renner's ubiquitous Futura. Bernhard served as the guest art director for the March issue of *PM Magazine*, so he was able to design the layout of articles celebrating himself. The double page spread shown here juxtaposes the almost mythical Priester poster

ABCDEFGHIJKLMNOPQRSTUVW
XYZ abcdefghijklmnopqrstuvwxyz
1234567890

7.15 Lucian Bernhard, Bernhard Gothic Typeface, 1929.

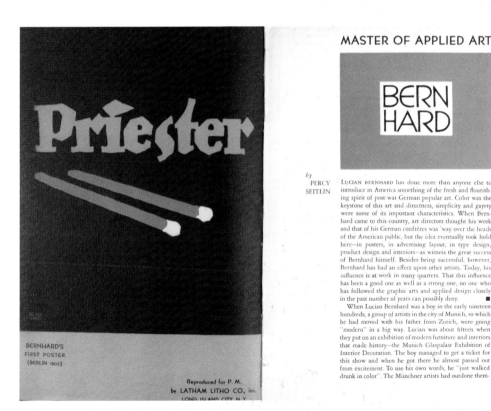

7.16 Lucian Bernhard, *PM Magazine*, 1936. Archives & Special Collections, RIT Library, Rochester Institute of Technology, Rochester, New York.

The Bauhaus Tradition and the New Typography

7.17 Lester Beall, *PM Magazine*, Nov 1937. Archives & Special Collections, RIT Library, Rochester Institute of Technology, Rochester, New York.

7.18 Lester Beall, *PM Magazine*, June/July 1938. Archives & Special Collections, RIT Library, Rochester Institute of Technology, Rochester, New York.

with a laudatory overview of Bernhard's work written by Seitlin (*fig. 7.16*). Bernhard adopted many of the principles of Constructivism in his new job, using asymmetry as well as a red geometric block in this composition.

The November 1937 issue devoted similar attention to an American artist, Lester Beall (1903–1969), suggesting that the influx of European émigrés was having an impact on homegrown graphic designers. Beall created the cover image for the issue, which wittily mocks the decorative excesses of conventional typography by juxtaposing an elaborate Victorian "P" with a slab seriffed "M" composed in a bold geometric fashion (*fig. 7.17*). Two red rules seem to reach out and pull the asymmetrical letter "M" into the future, away from the ornamental past symbolized by the "P." The dramatic use of negative white space also indicated Beall's knowledge of the Constructivist style. The article on Beall's work was written by the advertising executive Charles Coiner (1898–1989), one of the only non-artists involved in the industry to recognize the potential for modern design at an early date.

Leslie and Seitlin were, of course, committed to Bauhaus ideals of the integration of the design arts and architecture, and numerous articles covered this subject over the magazine's eight-

year run, including Gropius's "Essentials for Architectural Education" in the February/March 1938 issue. For the June/July 1938 edition, Beall oversaw the design of an issue devoted to "The Bauhaus Tradition and the New Typography." The cover page for that article, shown here, floats two lines of text so that they offer the sparest indication of the underlying orthogonal grid (*fig. 7.18*). Aside from the Bauhaus, subsequent issues dealt with other modern manifestations, such as the 1939 issue that declared the 1930s to be "Agha's American Decade."

The magazine's focus on graphic design was finally indicated by a title change in June of 1940, when *PM Magazine* became *AD, An Intimate Journal for Production Managers, Art Directors, and their Associates*, further highlighting the artistic interests of the editors. During this period, Leslie also operated a small exhibition space devoted to progressive graphic design in the offices of his firm. Called the "AD Gallery," it became an important meeting place for like-minded young designers. The inaugural show at the gallery featured the work of the then unknown Swiss émigré Herbert Matter (1907–1984), who had recently arrived in New York and was working as a photographer for *Vogue* and *Vanity Fair*. Matter soon established a stellar career as a designer of corporate identity as well as an educator at Yale University's influential design program (see Chapter 8).

Government Patrons

The Great Depression

Amid all the glamour and affluence portrayed in magazines such as *Vanity Fair* during the 1930s, it easy to lose sight of the fact that most of the decade was spent in the grip of the Great Depression. This severe economic downturn began in October 1929, when "Black Monday" initiated a stunning pullback in the American equities markets. The decline in prices was exacerbated by the fact that many Americans had bought stock using loans, or margin, and were unable to pay off their newly acquired debts. The stock market crash alone did not cause the Great Depression, but it set off a chain of financial calamities that resonated throughout the United States and Europe.

By 1933, unemployment in the United States surpassed 30 per cent. Because of the continuing effects of the Great Depression, some graphic designers were forced to turn to the government for work as the commercial segment of the market contracted. The new administration elected in 1932 under President Franklin D. Roosevelt (1882–1945) sought to alleviate the crisis by hugely increasing the federal workforce. Roosevelt established the Works Project Administration (WPA), whose most visible work involved the construction of hundreds of public projects, mainly roads, dams, and government buildings. However, one branch of the WPA, called the Federal Art Project (FAP), was given the responsibility of providing government work for artists in a variety of fields. Much of the work sponsored by the FAP consisted of fine art, especially murals to decorate the hundreds of new public buildings, but a small subset was devoted to poster design. During an eight-year period, the FAP commissioned over 35,000 unique designs, resulting in 2 million published posters.

FAP Posters

The FAP viewed the poster as a democratic art form, one that could reach out to people from all walks of life, especially those not of the elite, who were for the most part excluded from the study and appreciation of fine art. Stylistically speaking, this government patronage had the opposite effect from what one might expect, as it led to a more open environment in which the introduction of sophisticated Art Deco styles became widespread for the first time. Under the FAP, American artists were free to pursue the modernist styles that corporate advertisers in the United States had largely shunned.

As many as one third of the FAP posters were produced in New York City. Richard Floethe (1901–1988), the German-born director of the New York poster division of the FAP from 1936 until 1939, had trained as a student at the Bauhaus in the 1920s. As a poster designer in the United States, he favored Art Deco over more austere Constructivist styles, although the influence of

the Bauhaus is also visible in his frequent use of Josef Albers's Stencil lettering. Floethe's 1936 poster publicizing an FAP art exhibition displays the rounded curves and elegant, idiosyncratic sans serif lettering typical of Art Deco (*fig. 7.19*). Like the majority of the graphic works produced by the FAP, this poster is a small (14 by 22 inches) silkscreen that uses a restricted palette. The silkscreen process, whereby ink is pushed through a taut screen of fabric, was first introduced in the New York division by Anthony Velonis (1911–1997), who adapted it from his knowledge of commercial printing techniques. **Silkscreening**, which was most often used for graphic ephemera, was much less expensive than lithography, and after an eight-color process was developed it allowed for almost as much range of color. After the FAP artists shifted to silkscreening, their output increased tremendously. For example, the New York shop often printed over 500 posters in a single day.

The FAP posters were viewed by a dramatically larger audience than the educated elite who read *Fortune, Vogue,* or *Vanity Fair.* Despite their banal subject matter and obviously inexpensive production values, these posters functioned to awaken the broader American public to the beauty of Art Deco abstraction in a way that no magazine would have been able to. Like the posters of Edward McKnight Kauffer designed for the London Underground, images such as *Foreign Trade Zone* No. 1, by Martin Weitzman, appeared normative and non-threatening (*fig. 7.21*). Weitzman's poster uses a style based on Cassandre's Purist work (see fig. 4.39), which reduces the bow of the ship to a flat plane that runs off of the frame on three sides. The vertically proportioned lettering complements the towering height of the ship's prow. This striking style had a real potential to offend conservative American viewers; but this potential was nullified by the official, government-sanctioned nature of the message, complete with the name of the Mayor of New York. How could a poster that is signed by the Commissioner of the Department of Docks seem too radical?

One of the most visually strong posters to come out of the FAP was printed under the aegis of the Chicago division. This silkscreen by an artist named Carken suggests familiarity with the *Sachplakat* style, as the illustration of the powerful panther has been joined with simple, declarative text (*fig. 7.20*). The flatly

7.19 Richard Floethe, *Oils and Watercolors Exhibition*, 1938, Works Progress Administration. Poster. Silkscreen, 14 x 22 in (36 x 56 cm). Library of Congress, Washington, D.C.

7.20 Carken, *Brookside Zoo*, 1936. Color silkscreen, 14 x 22 in (35.6 x 56 cm). Library of Congress, Washington, D.C.

attached to the surface confirming its two-dimensionality. The white arrows are balanced by the red contour line that runs from the middle to the lower right corner of the page. What so distinguishes Beall's work from that of his contemporaries is the manner in which he eschews most of the decorative excesses of Art Deco in favor of a more radically simplified Constructivist style. The lack of "styling" in the arrows or the lettering is evidence of his penchant for clear, functional design solutions.

Beall's 1937 work for the Department of Agriculture effectively integrates black and white photography with an abstract geometric background (*fig. 7.23*). The horizontal bars of the fence echo the red and white striped background, while the grinning children convey an upbeat message that is reinforced by the patriotic use of color. In a nice touch, the stenciled lettering appears to be printed on the fence itself, although the shadow on the diagonal crosspiece reduces the legibility of some of the letters. The stenciling in Beall's poster represents not a sophisticated "universal" alphabet, but rather the prosaic look of everyday official writing on crates. Finally, the slightly off-kilter angle of the photograph vis à vis the background creates a shallow space while also breaking the photograph out of the strict orthogonal grid.

In 1937, Beall received a huge honor when his work was featured in a solo exhibition of graphic design at New York's Museum of Modern Art. As discussed below, Beall's embrace of

7.21 Martin Weitzman, *Foreign Trade Zone No. 1*, Feb 1937. Poster. Silkscreen, Library of Congress, Washington, D.C.

rendered panther crouches in the ambiguous space created by the words "Brookside" and "Zoo," tying text and image together with its tail. This connection is reinforced by the way in which the animal's tongue picks up the orange color of the lettering. The wide block of letters spelling out "Brookside" complements the panther's torso and tail just as the compact mass of the letters in the word "Zoo" echoes the coiled muscles of his chest and head. In 1942, after the United States had entered the Second World War, the FAP poster division was transferred to the Defense Department Graphic Section, through which graphic designers continued to serve the government.

Lester Beall

Lester Beall, born in Missouri, moved in 1935 to New York City, where he opened a freelance graphic design business. During the 1930s, Beall was one of the most important homegrown American designers to adopt sophisticated European styles. Among his important early works are a series of posters designed for the Rural Electrification Administration, a government body that promoted the use of electricity in the countryside. A 1937 poster trumpeting the relatively new technology of radio (which was made possible by electricity) uses a simple abstract scheme to convey its message (*fig. 7.22*). The three white arrows are obliquely positioned so that they create a modicum of space in what is an otherwise completely flat plane, the single word "radio"

7.22 Lester Beall, *Rural Electrification–Radio*, 1937–41. Archives & Special Collections, RIT Library, Rochester Institute of Technology, Rochester, New York.

7.23 Lester Beall, *Rural Electrification Administration*, 1937. Silkscreen, 40 x 30 in (101.6 x 76.2 cm). Library of Congress, Washington, DC.

Constructivism perfectly complemented the interests of the museum's curators, who sought to promulgate the more severe Constructivist style in the face of an overwhelming attachment to the stylish Art Deco preferred in the United States.

The Museum of Modern Art

The Museum of Modern Art (MoMA), which was established in New York City in 1929, soon became an important champion of modern design in the United States. On November 8, 1929, the MoMA opened officially to the public. In *The Nation*, Lloyd Goodrich observed, "The foundation of the new museum marks the final apotheosis of modernism and its acceptance into respectable society." While Goodrich was, of course, mainly referring to painting and sculpture, from an early point the MoMA also devoted resources to the display of architecture and other related design materials. The founding trustees of the museum included many prominent industrialists such as A. Conger Goodyear (1877–1964), but Frank Crowninshield, the editor of *Vanity Fair*, also made the list. Throughout the 1930s, the Rockefeller family and other wealthy philanthropists provided considerable financial support and status to the museum, securing for it a significant role in American cultural life. This section surveys four exhibitions held at the MoMA during the 1930s that had a considerable impact on the way in which Americans perceived modern graphic design.

The International Style

At the MoMA, there was a decided emphasis on Constructivist functionalism, which was considered to be a much more significant development than the "modernistic" Art Deco. The first show at the MoMA that advocated a Constructivist aesthetic was focused exclusively on architecture. "Modern Architecture: International Exhibition," curated by Philip Johnson (1906–2005) and Henry-Russell Hitchcock (1903–1987), opened in 1931 (*fig. 7.24*), providing a survey of modern architecture that the organizers grouped under a new term, the "**International Style**." A book that was authored by the curators, called *The International Style: Architecture since 1922*, was published in 1932 as an accompaniment to the exhibition. In this book, Johnson and Hitchcock celebrated the abstract geometric architecture of great architects such as Le Corbusier, Walter Gropius, Mies van der Rohe, and the De Stijl architect J. J. P. Oud as exemplary of the rising new trend in building.

The authors identified three main aesthetic principles that define the International Style in architecture. While they did not originally intend to prescribe the rules for architecture, but rather to describe them, the book became enormously influential for modern architects. Additionally, these principles of the International Style would prove to be equally important to the subsequent development of graphic design in the United States. The first principle submitted by Hitchcock and Johnson stated that modern architecture emphasized volume—the enclosure of space by planar elements—over mass. While difficult to translate into two-dimensional media, this rule resonates with the flat, geometric planes of a lot of Constructivist graphic design. For Hitchcock and Johnson, the three-dimensional orthogonal skeletons of steel beams that form the basic structure of a building are essential to determining its form. Similarly, the grid is the underlying element in Constructivist graphic designs.

Their second principle called for "regularity as opposed to symmetry," a rule whose application in graphic design was a major tenet of Laszlo Moholy-Nagy and Jan Tschichold's New Typography. The "regularity" invoked here refers to the same type of machine standardization that is a prominent part of Constructivism. The third element of the International Style was its dependence on proportion, not applied ornament, as the basis for its aesthetic achievement. This is, of course, a central tenet of graphic design of the 1920s.

The promulgation of the International Style in architecture by the MoMA was based solely on aesthetic principles. Hitchcock and Johnson deliberately ignored what they called the "sociological aspects" of modern architecture in their exhibition and book. In this manner, the design principles of Russian Constructivism, De Stijl, and the Bauhaus were introduced to an American audience completely devoid of political context. This gradual depoliticization of Constructivism was already traced in the context of the Bauhaus (see Chapter 6). It is striking how quickly modern design, whose post-war roots were so closely tied to political events in Russia and Germany, became completely detached from its political history.

In regard to lettering on the sides of buildings, which Hitchcock and Johnson considered to be suitably functional as opposed to ornamental, they wrote, "Clear unseriffed letter forms are most legible at a good scale and conform most harmoniously to the geometrical character of contemporary design." Invoking the principle of regularity, they called for lettering to respect the underlying geometric composition of the building. A good example of this type of lettering existed at the Bauhaus, where the name of the institution was incorporated into the structure using Herbert Bayer's all-lower-case Universal. Like most Constructivists, Hitchcock and Johnson were under the misapprehension that sans serif lettering was more legible and functionalist than traditional seriffed forms, while in reality the serifs on letters serve to increase their legibility and especially their readability (the body text of *The International Style* was set in roman). In this case as in many others, sans serif lettering is preferred for its perceived, rather than empirically deduced, functional qualities in typography.

While this theme will be developed in greater depth in Chapter 8, it is crucial to note how Constructivist graphic design was aided by its perceived aesthetic closeness to International Style architecture. This alliance, which has its roots mainly in the *Gesamtkunstwerk* pursued at the Bauhaus, would become very important in establishing the intellectual and stylistic credibility of functionalist graphics. Anecdotally speaking, this analogy was expressed best by the art director Charles Coiner when he called the designer "the architect of the printed page." This is not to say that graphic designers sought to connect their work to architecture for the cynical purpose of gaining professional status, since the stylistic parallels between the two arts had naturally developed as part of the modern movement.

7.24 Philip Johnson and Henry-Russell Hitchcock (curators), "Modern Architecture: International Exhibition," Museum of Modern Art, New York, 1931.

During the period covered by the exhibition at MoMA, the radical simplification of form espoused by modern architects such as Corbusier and Gropius was almost completely absent from the American scene. Corporations in the United States were only just beginning to accept the "modernistic" Art Deco style, which often featured elaborate ornament that violated one of the core tenets of the International Style. For example, the same year of Hitchcock and Russell's exhibition, New York City residents witnessed the completion of the Art Deco Chrysler building (*fig. 7.25*), by William Van Alen (1883–1954). Designed as the tallest manmade structure in the world, the Chrysler building soared 1,046 feet from Lexington Avenue to the top of its stainless steel spire. The summit of the building is composed of an eccentric series of seven parabolic curves clad in stainless steel, punctuated by triangular windows that radiate upward. In addition, Van Alen placed steel gargoyles at the corners of the major setback, a medieval device that, like the wheel-shaped carvings near them, indicated the building's ties to the automobile industry. An iconic example of the opulent use of geometric ornament characteristic of Art Deco,

left: **7.25** William van Alen, Chrysler Building, New York, 1928–30.

opposite bottom left: **7.26** Josef Albers, *Machine Art* Exhibition Catalog, Museum of Modern Art, New York, 1934.

the flamboyant decorative scheme is completely at odds with the austere functionalism of the International Style. The Chrysler building celebrates mass, symmetry, and applied ornament, and is indicative of how completely marginalized the Constructivist style was in the United States at this time.

The "Machine Art" Exhibition

In March 1934, MoMA opened its "Machine Art" exhibition, the second to assert the primacy of the machine aesthetic in modern life. This unique exhibition focused on objects that were traditionally excluded from the museum realm, such as industrial products, mass-produced furniture, and even scientific instruments. The conceptual basis of the "Machine Art" show was set out in the introduction to the catalog, which opened with an excerpt from the writings of Plato. "By beauty of shapes ... I mean straight lines and circles, and shapes, plane or solid, made from them by lathe, ruler, and square. These are not, like other things, beautiful relatively, but always and absolutely." The Neoplatonist basis for the beauty of geometric abstraction had, of course, been asserted for years by the artists of De Stijl, Purism, and the Bauhaus. The catalog further draws a series of parallels between the "pure shapes" of machine-made objects and Plato's Classical aesthetic, celebrating the objects' kinetic rhythms, simplified surfaces, visual complexity, and functional beauty.

The catalog that accompanied the exhibition was notable for its striking cover, designed by Josef Albers (*fig. 7.26*). One of the many former Bauhaus professors who had emigrated from Germany some time after the Bauhaus was closed by the Nazis in 1933, Albers had a significant impact on American graphic design. The cover is starkly simplistic, combining a photograph of one of the objects in the show, SKF Industries' "Self-Aligning Ball Bearing," with all-capital sans serif letters. There is a strong contrast created between the extreme close-up image of the circular ball bearing and the architectonic structure of the typography.

In his essay in the "Machine Art" catalog, Philip Johnson, the director of the MoMA's Department of Architecture and Industrial Art, sketched the last eighty years of industrial design in terms of the reconciliation of handcrafted quality with mechanical reproducibility. Using architecture as an analogy, he asserted that design had developed separately but toward the same end—showing sturdy simplicity and the elimination of superfluous ornament. The exhibition at the MoMA was based on Bauhaus principles of Constructivist functionalism, and the curators rejected the opulent ornament of Art Deco. Citing an American need to resist the "'modernistic' French machine-age aesthetic," Johnson reminded his readers that in America the machine tradi-

7.27 Kem Weber, *Zephyr Clock*, 1933. Brass, copper, 3½ x 8 x 3⅛ in (8.89 x 20.32 x 7.94 cm). The Minneapolis Institute of Arts, Minneapolis, MN. The Modernism Collection. Gift of Norwest Bank.

tion is "purer and stronger." He also took a swipe at "styling" firms, which Johnson felt were responsible for the overzealous use of streamlining as ornament. This use of a machine element as a decorative device was abhorrent to functionalist artists because it subverted the underlying principles of machine art.

At the time of the "Machine Art" exhibition, the American market for luxury goods was saturated with Art Deco objects. American Art Deco often stressed the streamlined look whereby ornamental geometric lines determined the form of the composition. A good example of this type of work can be seen in the *Zephyr Clock* from 1933 (*fig. 7.27*) by Karl Emanuel Weber (Kem) (1889–1963). Manufactured by Lawson Time Inc. in a combination of brass and copper with celluloid numerals, the clock features two rounded curves, one on the vertical axis and one on the horizontal. Born in Berlin, Weber had been working in San Francisco on behalf of the German government in 1915, when he was stranded by the First World War. He set up shop in the United States, and established a thriving design practice in Los Angeles. The *Desk Clock* is exemplary of the sort of object that Philip Johnson disliked because it uses streamlining "dishonestly,"

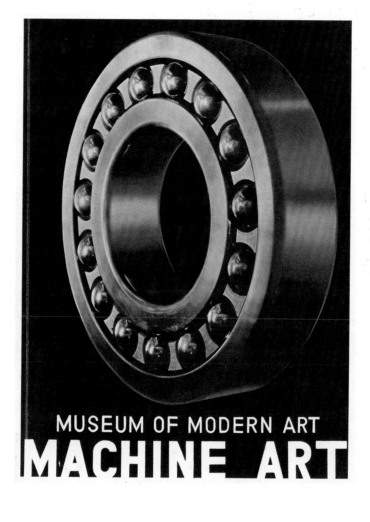

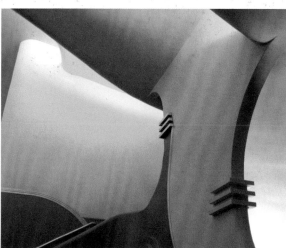

7.28 John Eberson, *Colony Theater*, originally designed 1930, renovation in 1990. Mesbur & Smith Architects, Ontario & Process Creative Studios Inc, Cleveland, OH.

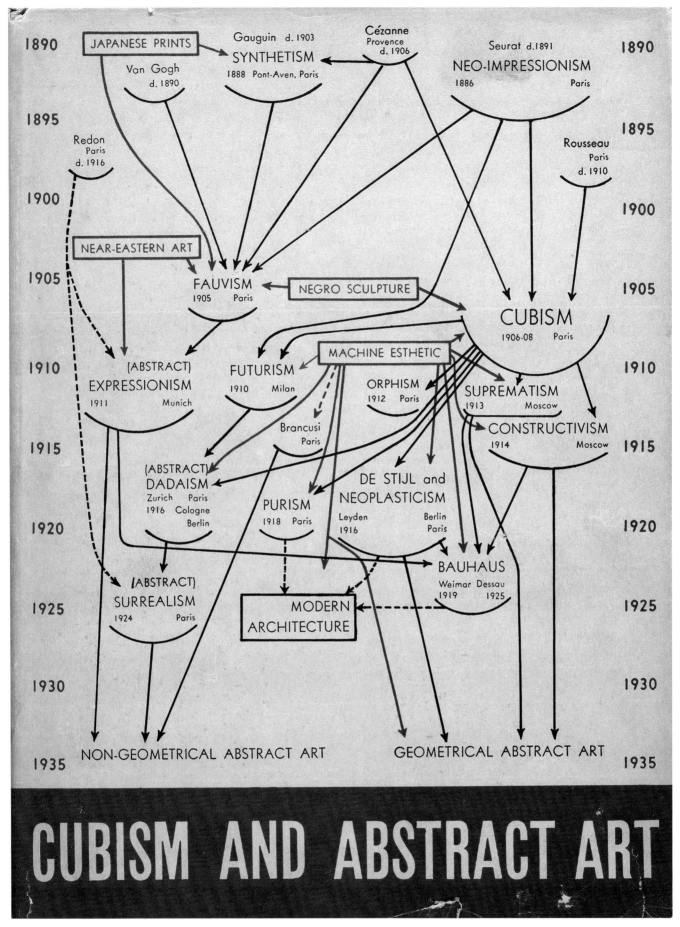

7.29 Alfred H. Barr, *Cubism and Abstract Art* Exhibition Catalog, Museum of Modern Art, New York, 1936.

its form being essentially decorative as opposed to functional.

Art Deco designers shared the same love of decorative elegance as their counterparts in Art Nouveau. A stunning stylistic comparison can be made between Hector Guimard's Paris Metro from Chapter 1 (see fig. 1.15) and an Art Deco interior space designed by John Eberson (1875–1964) for the Colony Theater in 1930 (*fig. 7.28*). The sinuous curves of Art Nouveau have been replaced by the planar geometric abstraction of Art Deco. Of course, the work of the Art Nouveau designer Henry van de Velde seemed to anticipate the geometric stylization of Art Deco in many ways (see Chapter 2). It is also important to recognize how the MoMA's embrace of strict machine functionalism was not widespread in the 1930s, when Art Deco took precedence in American industrial and graphic design.

The "Cubism and Abstract Art" Exhibition

The influential exhibition "Cubism and Abstract Art," curated by MoMA director, Alfred H. Barr, Jr (1902–1981), opened in April 1936. This show represented the first historical survey in the United States of abstract art, mainly painting, dating from 1890 to 1935. While "Cubism and Abstract Art" focused primarily on painting, a variety of related manifestations in industrial design, the theater, and even abstract film were also included. Although only brief mention was made of graphic design and typography, the accompanying catalog, written by Barr, made clear that these were important parts of the Russian Constructivist and De Stijl movements.

In a startlingly innovative employment of graphic design outside its usual context, the jacket of the *Cubism and Abstract Art* catalog displayed the history of modern painting in diagrammatic fashion (*fig. 7.29*). This illustration, designed by Barr himself, applied the emerging discipline of "information design" to the history of art. Like Harry Beck's map of the London Underground, also designed in the 1930s (see fig. 4.15), this diagram was intended to render complex information and interrelationships schematically, in a clear and logical manner. Using the simple red and black color scheme favored by Constructivists and championed at the MoMA, Barr attempted to show that modern art had formed two streams—a geometric one encompassing Art Deco and Constructivism, and a non-geometric, Expressionist one. Barr's diagram became more controversial than most examples of information design, because later art historians felt that the reductive nature of the exercise tended to oversimplify a vast and often contradictory subject.

7.30a, b (left) H. Nöckur, *Pressa, Köln 1928*, 1928. Poster. (right) Fritz Ehmcke, *Köln, Pressa 1928*, 1928. Poster. Museum für Gesltatung, Zurich. Poster Collection.

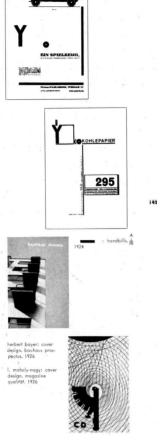

7.31 Herbert Bayer, Bauhaus Catalog, 1938.

The "Bauhaus 1919–1928" Exhibition

The MoMA made a further commitment to the machine aesthetic and Constructivism when it brought the art of the Bauhaus to the public in 1938, the year that the exhibition "Bauhaus 1919–1928" opened. Over the previous two years, numerous faculty members from the Bauhaus, including Herbert Bayer, Walter Gropius, Ludwig Mies van der Rohe, Josef Albers, László Moholy-Nagy, and Marcel Breuer, had all immigrated to the United States. This is not to give the impression that the entire faculty fled Germany the moment that the Nazis came to power; on the contrary, Bayer pursued a private practice in Berlin for several years, accepting numerous government-sponsored commissions, including some that made clear references to the Nazis' perverse ideological concerns. MoMA's show featured a unique installation designed by Bayer that highlighted the leadership of Gropius in formulating the new school's aesthetic principles. The accompanying catalog, edited by Bayer as well as Gropius and his wife, Ise, served as a sourcebook of primary materials related to the Bauhaus. Bayer designed the typography and layout of the accompanying catalog, using a sans serif characteristic of the New Typography throughout the text. In order to illustrate the post-1925 introduction of all lower-case lettering at the Bauhaus, Bayer eliminated capitalization from the concluding sections of the catalog (*fig. 7.31*). He also structured the text and images with regularity, not symmetry, while making use of Constructivist devices such as the bold arrow in the lower left margin. As was the case with the "International Style" and "Machine Art" exhibitions before it, here again the MoMA asserts the significance of Constructivism over the ornamental decadence of the Art Deco.

Pulp Magazines

In striking contrast to the elite styles both of Art Deco and Constructivism, which advanced in the United States during the 1930s, are the thousands of covers made for pulp magazines. In many ways a response to the misery of the Great Depression, pulp fiction flourished in the United States during this period, offering people an escape through stories of mystery, adventure, and sexuality. Millions of "pulp" magazines—so-called because the paper used to print them was of the lowest possible quality—formed a thriving popular culture industry that provided work for thousands of artists.

The vast majority of pulp magazine covers were created by artists trained in the traditional skills of representation, making their work appear quite retrograde by the standards of Agha or Beall. In fact, pulp covers served those artists as a foil, exemplary of everything that modern design rejected, including realism and Expressionist displays of emotion. Most pulp covers were originated as oil paintings that measured roughly 20 by 30 inches, with the artist often having only a vague notion of the text that served as the images' complement.

Designed to catch a passer-by's attention from the shelves of a newsstand, pulp covers usually featured brilliant colors and bold design elements. One popular pulp genre during the 1930s was

As was typical of modern art exhibitions at the MoMA, "Cubism and Abstract Art" emphasized stylistic development over a consideration of subject matter; the political ramifications of Constructivism, in particular, were largely glossed over. However, the rise of Nazism in Germany and the Nazis' hostility to abstract art was the subject of an introductory paragraph in the catalog. In this statement, titled "Contrast—and Condescension," Barr called attention to the transformation that was occurring in German versus American aesthetic taste. Illustrated with two posters advertising the "Köln Pressa," a printing exhibition held in Cologne in 1928 (*fig. 7.30*), Barr sought to make the point that abstraction was being suppressed in Germany just as it was gaining a foothold in the United States. The poster on the left, by H. Nockür, was illustrated to serve as a foil to the one on the right, because for Barr the former, aimed at English-speakers, represented "the fairly realistic poster style common to mediocre travel posters the world over." Of course, Barr and other MoMA curators' hostility toward Art Deco was well established at this point. Further on, Barr praises the highly abstract Constructivist style of the other poster, by Fritz Ehmcke (1878–1965). While condemning the Nazis, Barr also used this comparison in order to make a backhanded criticism of the philistine taste of most American commercial artists and their patrons.

the science fiction magazine, which focused on adventures in outer space. One of the foremost designers of pulp science fiction covers was Frank R. Paul (1884–1963), an Austrian immigrant who had a background in architecture. Starting in 1926, Paul created a plethora of covers for the Hugo Gernsback science fiction empire, which included Amazing Stories, Science Wonder, and Wonder Stories. Paul's most famous works consist of architectural fantasies that run the gamut of his imagination. The back cover of one of the Amazing Stories called *Quartz City on Mercury*, for example, shows otherworldly creatures inhabiting a tower made up of hexagons (*fig. 7.32*). The jewel-like brilliance of the predominantly red and green palette calls attention to itself, as do the crystalline shapes of the structures.

Most pulp magazines trod very close to the edge of contemporary decency codes, and some featured explicit themes of sexual violence that were taboo for the respectable mainstream. The most overtly obscene pulp publishing house was formed by Harry Donenfeld (1926–1965) and Frank Armer in 1934. Their company, named Culture Productions presumably out of a sense of irony, commissioned covers that displayed explicit scenes of sex and violence. For example, the 1936 cover for *Spicy Mystery Stories*, by H.J. Ward (1909–1945), is a paean to voyeurism (*fig. 7.33*). The beautiful young assistant of a humpback archer has been brutally bound to a target; her eyes well with tears as she tries to ignore the leering menace beside her. While her pink clothes suggest innocence, her bare torso and jutting breasts are provocatively posed. In typical pulp fashion, the evildoer holds a phallic arrow close to her pelvic region. The misogyny in images such as this one is as palpable as the bold color. Despite their myriad faults, the visceral energy of this type of representational drawing with its heavy

above: **7.32** Frank R. Paul,
Amazing Stories, 1941. Copyright ©
Forest J Ackerman.

right: **7.33** H.J. Ward, *Spicy Mystery
Stories*, 1936. Magazine cover.

7.34 Anonymous, Poster and Crowd, Germany, 1932.
Photograph.

chiaroscuro and bright palette appears more vital in some holistic way than contemporary abstract designs. Ward was also responsible for the cover that eventually put Culture Productions out of business. In 1942, the mayor of New York, Fiorello Laguardia, walked by a newsstand and a copy of Spicy Mysteries caught his eye, exactly as it was intended to. Laguardia started an assault on the Spicy empire, which was soon forced to close.

Germany in the 1930s

While the 1930s in the United States was a time during which a critical mass of modern artists was coming together to forge new styles, America's gains came largely at the expense of continental Europe—particularly Germany, which had been the leading site for International Constructivism in the 1920s. The situation in Germany had changed swiftly and dramatically in the spring of 1933, when the Nazis successfully consolidated their power. The Nazi government immediately implemented two of its core governing strategies: the use of violence and intimidation, complemented by aggressive control of the mass media and related culture.

The Nazis and the Mass Media

Scholars consider the Nazi regime to be one of the most media-aware governments of the twentieth century. Before 1933, Nazis used the mass media in order to sway popular opinion. The photo illustrated here (*fig. 7.34*) shows some people in Berlin circulating around a 1932 election poster. Under the direction of Josef Goebbels (1897–1945), Reichsminister für Volksaufklärung und Propaganda (Minister of National Enlightenment and Propaganda), there was an officially sanctioned effort to control most aspects of German culture. Illustration and graphic design, for example, were overseen by "Department V," a part of the 6th division of Goebbel's ministry, which oversaw the wide range of visual arts. Other divisions set standards for the press, broadcasting, theater, music, and literature. Goebbels and the rest of the Nazi leadership, minds twisted by delusions of national and racial superiority, desperately desired to define German culture in terms that fitted their ideological beliefs. Anything that shied away from their reactionary conservative sensibility was suppressed. Typographers and graphic designers were expected to reject modern styles, and artists of all types were compelled to use regressive representational styles in works that idealized the leadership of the Nazi party.

Typical of Nazi arts policy was the closure of the Berlin Bauhaus in 1933. As previously discussed (see Chapter 6), the Dessau Bauhaus had been shut down in 1932, when the Nazis had taken over the regional government, but a group of professors and students had reopened the school in modest quarters located on the outskirts of Berlin. A photomontage by student Iwao Yamawaki (1898–1987), *The Assault on the Bauhaus*, shows Nazi officials marching back and forth across the buildings, which have been turned on their sides at an oblique angle so that they form

below: **7.35** Hans Schweitzer, *Unsere letzte Hoffnung: Hitler (Our Last Hope: Hitler)*, 1932. Poster, 34 x 24 in (86.3 x 60.9 cm). Hoover Institution Archives, Stanford University, CA. Poster Collection.

right: **7.36** Iwao Yamawaki, *Der Schlag gegen das Bauhaus (The Assault on the Bauhaus)*, 1932. Photomontage. Copyright © VG Bild Kunst Bonn, Germany. Bauhaus-Archive, Berlin.

ramps (*fig. 7.36*). In a prescient foreshadowing of the terrors yet to come, Yamawaki has strewn his composition with screaming figures and bodies lying on the ground.

On April 11, 1933, police and paramilitaries raided the Berlin Bauhaus, and closed it after claiming to have found "illegal propaganda material of the German Communist Party." An article from the next day in a Berlin newspaper reinforced this assertion that the Bauhaus was a hotbed of Communist revolutionaries, claiming that Gropius had removed himself to Russia. As the closing indicated, the attempts by Mies van der Rohe and others to depoliticize the Constructivist style practiced there had not been successful. Clearly, while no one in 1933 on the faculty and staff of the Bauhaus was actively working against the Nazi government on behalf of Communism, few people at the institution supported the new regime. In the context of the Nazi belief that all culture is inherently political, the Bauhaus style was allied both with Communism and with a commitment to universalism that contradicted the government's desire to promulgate strong nationalist ideology. Amid the obsession with so-called "Aryan" German culture that characterized the regime's propaganda,

the Bauhaus was considered not sufficiently German enough.

The cultural program overseen by Goebbels was not strictly one of suppression, as many graphic designers were employed by the government in order to promote its policies as well as the general reputation of the Nazis. Even before Hitler gained power in 1933, Hans Schweitzer (1901–1980) had allied himself with the Nazis, becoming a party member in 1926. A close friend of Goebbels, Schweitzer took on the pseudonym "Mjölnir," a reference to the hammer of Thor, a Norse god of thunder. The poster *Our Last Hope: Hitler* dates from Hitler's unsuccessful presidential campaign of the spring of 1932 (*fig. 7.35*). Schweitzer had been trained in an academic style, and he used the type of conventional plain drawing techniques that were favored by the Nazi leadership. In this image the letters are made up of negative space, and the bold all-capitalized "Hitler" appears as a banner being carried by the figures in a march. Schweitzer later achieved his greatest success with posters that showed idealized paramilitary "stormtroopers," and in 1937 Goebbels appointed him the director of the Hilfwerk für Deutsche Bildende Kunst, an administrative body.

The graphic designer known by the single name Leonid produced a poster in 1936 that stated *All of Germany Listens to the Leader with the People's Receiver* (*fig. 7.37*). Scholars often cite this image as evidence of the centralized control of the press and mass media that was such a fundamental part of Nazi ideology, and which contrasted with the commercial media dominant in the rest of Europe. This image creates an odd juxtaposition in that it combines a truly modern element, the photomontage, with fraktur lettering. (Nazi typography is discussed below.) According to modern design principles, nothing clashes more than a mix of ornamental script with a photo. Leonid attempts to have it both ways, referencing the modern technology of the radio by putting it into the context of traditional German nationalism.

The graphic work of Richard Klein (1890–1967) is exemplary of one specific trend in Nazi design: the embrace of classical idealism. Hitler himself greatly favored this ancient imperial style, and it was employed prominently in government buildings designed by Albert Speer (1905–1981). Klein's poster for the "Great German Art Exhibition" held in 1937 and 1938 displays centered lettering that is intended to remind the viewer of the carved inscriptions on monuments of the ancient Roman Empire (*fig. 7.38*). The emblem above the text is made up of swastika, eagle, torch, and helmeted allegory—a motley assortment of items, most with an imperial pedigree. Klein's classical design has been influenced by Art Deco style, particularly in the smooth geometric shapes of the figure's head.

Most Nazi propaganda posters used traditional illustration combined with personal appeals to the viewer. The image shown here reads, "Hitler constructs, help him by buying German goods." It features a typical "Aryan" idealized man working with

opposite: **7.37** Leonid, *Ganz Deutschland hört den Führer mit dem Volksempfänger* (*All of Germany Listens to the Führer with the People's Receiver*), 1936. Poster.

above: **7.38** Richard Klein, *Grosse Deutsche Kunstausstellung (Great German Art Exhibition)*, 1938. Poster, 8 x 8⅛ in (21 x 20.8 cm). Copyright © VG Bild Kunst Bonn, Germany. Bauhaus-Archive, Berlin.

right: **7.39** Anonymous, *Hitler Baut auf (Hitler Is Building)*, 1940. Library of Congress, Washington, D.C.

his hands (*fig. 7.39*). The image suggests a return to German tradition in that there is no sign of modern life in the poster, a theme reinforced by the fraktur lettering and the crude construction techniques shown in the image. This poster illustrates the Nazi commitment to *Heimatschutz*, the "preservation of regional tradition," through which the party set itself up as the heroic protector of German identity in the face of corrupt, urban-based, universal concepts such as those promoted at the Bauhaus.

While most of the designers employed by the Nazis had never been involved in modern design movements, one, Ludwig Hohlwein, had established himself in the early 1900s as an innovative artist. A pioneer of the *Sachplakat* style, one of the first modern design movements (see Chapter 3), Hohlwein continued to employ it on behalf of his new masters. The poster shown here publicizes a girls' sports festival held in 1934 (*fig. 7.40*). Hohlwein has posed the figure of a young athlete so that her limbs replicate the shape of the swastika on the flag behind her, while the color of her shorts reinforces the connection. The flat areas of color in her torso as well as the lack of a horizon line and cropping all hark back to the roots of *Sachplakat* in Japanese woodblock prints.

Some government-sponsored publications, such as *Deutschland Ausstellung*, the catalog for an exhibition celebrating German culture under the Nazi regime, were produced in an up-to-date Constructivist style. Herbert Bayer, who worked in Berlin in private practice during the 1930s, was the designer of the catalog shown here, which surveyed radio broadcasting in Berlin, the

new capital city under the Nazis (*fig. 7.41*). The roman type at the top forms a solid block of text, while the illustration is suggestive of the elegant Art Deco work of Cassandre. This publication was clearly aimed at a sophisticated urban audience, not inspired by *Heimatschutz*, one to whom conventional illustration would have looked retrograde. The previous four examples—one classical, one conventional illustration, one *Sachplakat*, and one modern—are indicative of the precarious balancing act of the Nazi regime as it selectively, and pragmatically, mixed styles and ideologies to reach different constituencies.

"Degenerate Art"

As early as 1933, the Nazis had appropriated the scientific term "degenerate," meaning "to have declined to a subnormal state," as part of its attack on modern art. The most notorious use of the term "degenerate" occurred in 1937, when the government organized an enormous show of so-called *Entartete Kunst* ("degenerate art"). This exhibition was conceived of as a broad indictment of all forms of modern art and design, including just about everything that has been covered in the previous few chapters: Expressionism, Cubism, Futurism, Dada, Purism, De Stijl, Art Deco, and Constructivism. Organized by Adolf Ziegler and Schweitzer, the "*Entartete Kunst*" exhibition opened in July 1937 in Munich; it consisted of a hastily assembled survey of modern art from German public collections (*fig. 7.42*). The art works were installed in a cavernous space broken up by temporary partitions. The works were deliberately displayed in a helter-skelter fashion, mixing disparate trends in the art of the twentieth century. The walls of the show were festooned with slogans decrying the supposed "degenerate" character of the art and artists who made it. For example, a number of works by Kandinsky were juxtaposed with the words "Crazy at any price," while additional text noted that the artist was a "teacher at the Communist Bauhaus at Dessau until 1933."

The *Entartete Kunst* catalog also displays an attempt by the Nazis to distort the tradition of modern art. The cover shows a full-bleed photo of an Expressionist sculpture, *The New Man*

opposite: **7.40** Ludwig Hohlwein, *The Reich Sports Day of the Association of German Girls*, 1934. Poster.

above: **7.41** Herbert Bayer, *Deutschland Ausstellung (German Exhibition)*, July – Aug 1936. Catalog cover, 8 x 8⅕ in (21 x 20.8 cm). Copyright © VG Bild Kunst Bonn, Germany. Bauhaus-Archiv, Berlin.

7.42 Anonymous, *Entartete Kunst (Degenerate Art) Exhibition*, 1937.

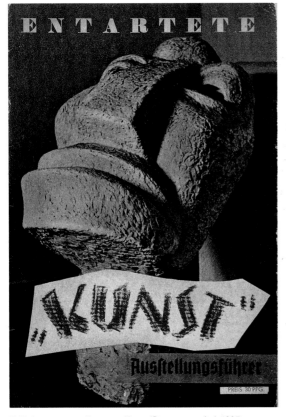

7.43 Anonymous, *Entartete Kunst (Degenerate Art)*, 1937, an exhibition that opened in Munich July 19, 1937, and toured Germany 1937. Catalog cover. The cover shows Otto Freundlich's sculpture *Der Neue Mensch (The New Man)*, 1912. Plaster cast, height 54 in (139 cm). Location unknown.

7.44 Anonymous, *Entartete Kunst (Degenerate Art) Exhibition*, 1936–7. Poster. Lithographic print, 47 x 33 in (120 x 84 cm).

(1912), by Otto Freundlich (1878–1943), in extreme close-up (*fig. 7.43*). One of the main themes of the exhibition was that Expressionist distortions of form were the result of diseased, "unGerman," and, of course, "Jewish" art practices. The typography on the cover is an artful mix of letters. The top spells out the word "Entartete" with neutral type, a bold, condensed roman. Below the sculpture, the word "'Kunst'" appears to be scribbled on to a piece of paper; the word means "art" and was placed in quotation marks in order to question whether the works are indeed art. The letters feature the spiky, angular forms seen in Expressionist graphics. Farther down, the word "Ausstellungsführer," meaning "exhibition guide," is composed in a new type of fraktur (see below). Finally, the price is displayed in plain sans serif letters at the bottom. All these different type styles are used in order to reinforce the different message carried by each word or phrase. As opposed to a unified design, the artists chose to treat each bit of text as a discrete unit; of course, the overall chaotic effect was also intended to replicate the supposed irrational disorder of modern art.

Most of the posters produced to publicize the 1937 show and its smaller-scale predecessors mined the Expressionist vein featured on the cover of the guide. However, one poster from 1936 was created in a Constructivist style in order to mock the practices of modern design pursued at the Bauhaus (*fig. 7.44*). The text refers to the exhibition as featuring work that is both "Bolshevik" and "Jewish," two terms often applied to progressive modern artists regardless of their political sympathies or religious identity. Naturally, the poster makes use of geometric abstraction and the familiar red and black of Constructivism without any attention to compositional balance or aesthetic achievement. Compare this last work with Klein's poster for the "Great German Art Exhibition"; the latter was installed in a new classically inspired building in 1937 and was intended to serve as a foil to "*Entartete Kunst.*" However, the juxtaposition of these two exhibitions generally failed in the attempt to convince the German people that art and design under the Nazis had reached new heights of aesthetic achievement.

Typography under the Nazis

The ongoing debate in Germany over the appropriateness of roman versus fraktur lettering also gained new impetus under the Nazis. While this debate had long been rife with political overtones, it is notable that a majority of the German public probably did not care one way or another. While in *The New Typography* Tschichold had asserted that fraktur was a dangerously nationalist form of lettering, many progressive typographers before 1933 had worked in both styles without asserting a specific political viewpoint. Likewise, the Constructivist designer of Futura, Paul Renner, sometimes produced texts using fraktur. While Renner worked briefly for the Nazi government, and was head of design for an international exhibition in Milan, his 1933 article "Kulturbolschewismus?" ("Cultural Bolshevism?") led to his arrest. In this article, Renner challenged the Nazi claim that modern, urban culture was somehow "Bolshevik," a theme often repeated in government publications. The Nazis were able to gain considerable support from German industrialists by invoking the specter of Communism and suggesting that private enterprises were in danger of being made into communal property. Despite his opposition to Nazi policies, Renner was one of the only modern designers who never fled Germany.

After the Nazis seized power, they quickly instituted a policy whereby all official government publications had to be printed in fraktur. Because they considered blackletter script to convey a strictly German national identity, children's textbooks and curricula were overhauled to stress this new national style. While this policy was never totally implemented, and exceptions were made for the *faux* classicism exemplified by Klein's work, the overt use of either seriffed lettering or sans serif forms as well as the geometric principles of the New Typography became quite rare. Under this state ideology, the New Typography became known as *Schriftentartung* ("degenerate writing"), a corollary to the concept of *Entartete Kunst.* The Nazis were obsessed with the idea of cultural decline, which they believed they would forestall through the implementation of conservative typographic principles. Significantly, the strict cultural policies of the Nazi government were not always enforced to the letter, and plentiful examples

of sans serif type and ranged left designs exist from this period.

While there were already a number of useful fraktur scripts in circulation in the 1930s, the Nazis oversaw the creation of a number of new alphabets, most with staunchly ideological names such as **Deutschland** or National (*fig. 7.45*). These 1930s' scripts are referred to by typographers with some irony as *Schaftstiefelgrotesk,* which means roughly "jackboot grotesques." The stylistic reference in the name points to the schematic shapes of many of the letters in these new alphabets, which tended to favor long black vertical elements reminiscent of the long black boots worn by Nazi paramilitary forces. Undoubtedly unbeknown to the Nazi patrons of the *Schaftstiefelgrotesk* forms, they actually represent a hybrid type of blackletter that merges the fraktur tradition with some of the abstract geometric principles of contemporary sans serif.

In a stunning reversal to this policy that often goes unremarked today, in 1941 the Nazis abruptly instituted a total elimination of fraktur in favor of roman type. The reason for this shift was not immediately clear, as the official communiqué made use of the Nazi's catch-all theme of the "Jewishness" of fraktur (*fig. 7.46*). While no scholar would attempt to explain Nazi policy in entirely rational, human terms, the notion that blackletter script represents a tradition of *Judenletter* (literally "Jewish letters")

»Deutfchland«
marfchiert!

7.45 Anonymous, Deutschland Typeface, 1934.

7.46 M. Bormann, A Letter Against Fraktur, 1941.

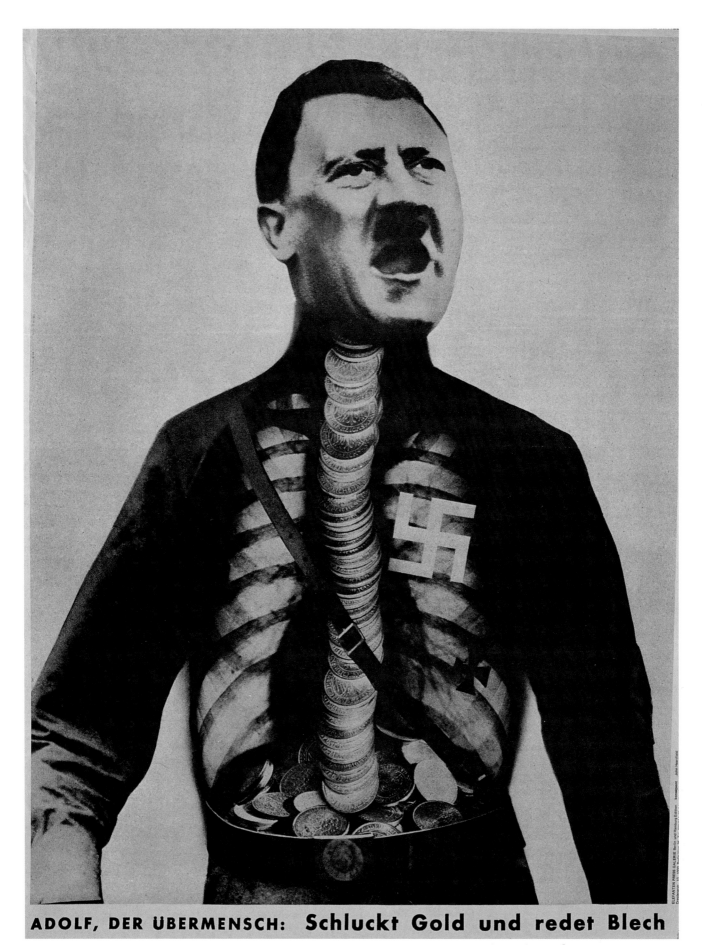

ADOLF, DER ÜBERMENSCH: Schluckt Gold und redet Blech

7.47 John Heartfield, *Adolf, der Übermensch: Schluckt Gold und redet Blech* (*Adolf the Superman: Swallows Gold and Spouts Junk*), July 17, 1932. Photomontage.

is an especially bizarre fabrication even for a regime led by anti-Semitic monsters. The historian Hans Peter Willberg has pointed out that the shift to roman probably represents the German government's belief in 1941, the year of its greatest military successes in the Second World War, that it would inevitably dominate the entire globe. Taking a page from the Bauhaus ideology of universalism, it probably seemed apropos for the regime to adopt a more "global" style of roman typography. In addition, civilians in many countries under German occupation were unable to read fraktur. Ironically, this late shift in style went largely unrecognized by later generations, and in the post-war years fraktur was hopelessly tainted by its perceived function as "Nazi writing."

John Heartfield's Photomontages

An interesting counterpoint to Nazi propaganda emerged in the case of John Heartfield, a Berlin Dada artist (see Chapter 3) who used photomontage to subvert the propaganda images of the Third Reich. Heartfield had joined Berlin Club Dada in 1918 following his discharge from the German military. Along with

7.48 John Heartfield, *Das Spiel der Nazis mit dem Feuer (The Nazis Play with Fire)*, 1933. Poster. Rotogravure print, rephotographed montage with typography, 15⅛ x 10⅜ in (38.5 x 26.5 cm). Courtesy George Eastman House.

Hannah Höch, Raoul Hausmann, and George Grosz, Heartfield endeavored to make some of the first Dada photomontages at this time. He also enthusiastically embraced the German Communist Party, with which he remained involved well into the 1930s.

Heartfield's 1932 photomontage *Adolf the Superman: Swallows Gold and Spouts Junk* was created as a political poster for use in the 1932 elections (*fig. 7.47*). Its artful combination of a photo of Hitler, an X-rayed torso, and a cascade of gold coins was used to undermine the politician's vaunted public speaking ability through caricature. By calling attention to the wealthy industrialists who bankrolled the Nazi party, Heartfield sought to discredit the idea of the Nazis as representative of everyday working people—an idea shown in Schweitzer's poster from the same election (see fig. 7.35).

After working for a number of publications, in 1930 Heartfield joined the staff of the Communist-inclined *Arbeiter-Illustrierte-Zeitung (AIZ)*, or "Worker's Illustrated Newspaper," for which he made some of his most daring photomontages. A February 1935 cover for *AIZ*, captioned at the top "Nazis Playing with Fire," used montage to depict the Nazi Hermann Goering (1893–1946) as a crazed arsonist (*fig. 7.48*). Goering is shown using a flaming torch to set fire to the Earth, a reference to the second anniversary of the notorious Reichstag fire of 1933. Goering was a Nazi deputy and President of the Reichstag in 1933, and played a significant role in the Nazi crackdown following the fire. Most historians believe that the fire was started by the Nazis themselves in order to provide a pretext to round up, imprison, and kill a number of their political enemies in what would become the first of many extrajudicial actions by the government. Soon after Hitler consolidated his power in 1933, Heartfield fled to Czechoslovakia and eventually settled in Britain. Heartfield's image of Goering as a violent monster is actually not too far off the mark, as in 1941 Goering initiated the plan for the complete elimination of European Jewry now known as the Holocaust.

The Second World War

The Second World War began on September 1, 1939, when Nazi Germany and the Soviet Union invaded Poland, triggering that country's defensive alliance with France and Great Britain. Prior to the invasion of Poland, Britain and France had sought to appease Hitler in the vain hope of avoiding armed conflict. The first two years of the war saw a series of spectacular successes by the German military, which came to control most of continental Europe. By 1941, swelled by the army's achievements and convinced of Germany's inevitable global domination, Hitler commenced "Operation Barbarossa," opening a second, Eastern front against his former ally Russia. In December of that year the United States joined the Allied cause, having previously provided Britain with a lifeline of military supplies. During 1942, the Nazis established the "final solution" as secret state policy, committing substantial resources to the mass murder and elimination of all European Jews. The two European fronts, Western and Eastern, eventually proved impossible for Germany to sustain, and Nazi

forces suffered their first major defeat against Russia in 1943 at Stalingrad. After that loss, Germany was gradually overcome by the Allies, and ultimately surrendered after Hitler's suicide in his bunker on May 7, 1945. The survey of Second World War propaganda posters here is not as detailed as the section on those of the First World War, and is intended solely to point out new trends during the second conflict; it should be noted that most propaganda of the second conflict repeated techniques and themes from the first.

Germany

When the Second World War began in 1939, the German government continued its substantial output of propaganda. The Nazis favored the new media of radio and newsreel, but still relied on posters as well. Chapter 3 made note of Hitler's disdain for Germany's emotionally flat propaganda posters from the First World War and his admiration for the British effort; before and during the Second World War Nazi poster artists used emotionally laden themes of guilt that British designers had deployed over two decades earlier.

While propaganda artists worked in a variety of styles, illustration was the mainstay of the German war poster. Early in 1939, Goebbels initiated a new poster campaign called the "Message of the Week." The resulting images were among the most emotionally manipulative produced during the war. For example, a poster from September 19 that year, produced just two weeks after the invasion of Poland, juxtaposes a photograph of dead civilians with a photo of the British Prime Minister, Neville Chamberlain (1869–1940), and the slogan "Chamberlain's Work!" (*fig. 7.49*). The reference is to the murder of a group of German civilians by Polish partisans; the poster echoes the ridiculous Nazi claim that the attack was planned by the British. In fact, the Nazis had conceived the attack in order to provide a pretext for their invasion. The photo of the bodies of what are clearly civilians combined with the blood-red, dripping letters create a prime example of an "atrocity" image intended to inflame public opinion.

Ludwig Hohlwein continued to serve the Nazi cause during the war, producing a number of posters in his familiar *Sachplakat* style. An example from 1942 calls for German civilians to obey the blackout rules established to hinder allied bombing campaigns (*fig. 7.50*). The elegant skyline is formed from a series of overlapping flat blue fields, punctuated by the bright yellow windows.

opposite: **7.49** Anonymous, *Chamberlain's Work!*, 1939. Poster, 34 x 47 in (86.3 x 119.3 cm). Hoover Institution Archives, Stanford University, CA. Poster Collection.

below: **7.50** Ludwig Hohlwein, *Blackout*, 1942. Poster. 33 x 23 in (83.8 x 58.4 cm). Hoover Institution Archives, Stanford University, CA. Poster Collection.

below right: **7.51** Anonymous, *Mightier Yet!*, 1942.

Boxes for text add energy to the image in that they seem to have been hurled in the air by an explosion. The scripted letters read, "Can you be responsible for this? You are helping the enemy!" This poster sounds the note of betrayal that Hitler had first invoked following the First World War, in which he argued that German civilians had treacherously undermined the war effort.

Britain

In a telling contrast to German propaganda, British designers tended to tone down their posters during the Second World War, as there had been substantial criticism by English pundits of the extremely manipulative nature of First World War posters. Most of the new British posters returned to familiar themes of heroism and adventure (*fig. 7.51*), without resorting to explicit themes of guilt, as in the first war's *Daddy What did you do during the Great War?* In this example the text attempts to lift morale on the home front through a wholly positive message that is reinforced by the image of soaring Spitfires. In addition, there was a much more widespread use of photography in posters during the Second World War.

The British poster captioned "Never was so much owed by so many to so few" celebrated the heroism of the Royal Air Force

7.52 Anonymous, "Never was so much owed by so many to so few" (Winston Churchill), 1940. Poster. Imperial War Museum, London.

7.53 Ivanov and Burova, *Our Hope Is in You, Red Warrior!*, 1943. Poster, 34 x 23 in (86.3 x 58.4 cm). Hoover Institution Archives, Stanford University, CA. Poster Collection.

(RAF) in the Battle of Britain, when the RAF managed to hold German forces at bay during the summer of 1940 (*fig. 7.52*). By maintaining air superiority, Britain was able to forestall Hitler's planned invasion of the isles indefinitely. The text of a famous quote about the battle, spoken by Prime Minister Winston Churchill (1874–1965) in a speech in the House of Commons on August 20, 1940, appears to float in the sky on top of a full-bleed photograph (actually a photomontage) of British pilots. The white lettering is placed so that it looks like "skywriting" on the blue sky. The all-capital sans serif lettering emphasizes Churchill's inspiring words while seamlessly meshing with the modern photographic image. The pilots are framed so that they seem to look into the distance over the head of the viewer, a vantage point seen previously in El Lissitzky's Russian exhibition poster of 1928 (see fig. 5.42) as well as Lester Beall's poster for the US Department of Agriculture (see fig. 7.23).

Russia and France

After the German invasion of Russia in 1941, artists in that country ramped up their production of propaganda posters. There is

some irony in that, under Josef Stalin, the Constructivist style that the Nazis claimed exemplified "Bolshevism" had been completely suppressed in the Soviet Union itself. In fact, Stalin insisted on the same type of idealized naturalism in the arts that Hitler admired; for both countries it was imperative that pro-government propaganda be intelligible to the broadest number of people. For these reasons, Russian posters from the Second World War use the techniques of illustration combined with strong emotional appeals. The example shown here, *Our Hope is in You, Red Warrior!*, shows a tearful young woman in a German prison camp (*fig. 7.53*). In the background, a Nazi soldier is shooting through the barbed wire at helpless civilians. After the invasion, millions of Russians had been trapped behind the advancing German forces.

In contrast to German and Russian realism, a French poster from 1944 is in line with Art Deco style. This poster celebrates the courage of the "Legion of French Volunteers" who fought the Nazi occupation of France (*fig. 7.54*). The sleek, geometrically stylized wedge of the soldier's body rises up at an angle like the prow of a ship, a subject seen in so many Art Deco travel posters. Invoking the machine aesthetic, the figure's body has the same smooth texture as the steel of his machine gun.

7.54 Anonymous, *Legion of French Volunteers*, 1944. Poster, 43 x 31 in (109.2 x 78.7 cm). Hoover Institution Archives, Stanford University, CA. Poster Collection.

7.55 J. Howard Miller, *We Can Do It!*, 1942, Poster. Photolithograph, 22 x 17 in (55.9 x 43.2 cm). National Archives, Washington, DC.

7.56 Jean Carlu, *America's Answer! Production*, 1942. Poster. Offset lithograph, 29⅞ x 39⅝ in (75.9 x 100.5 cm). Museum of Modern Art, New York.

DIVISION OF INFORMATION
OFFICE FOR EMERGENCY MANAGEMENT
WASHINGTON, D. C.

The United States

In the United States, the Second World War witnessed a continuation of the Art Deco styles made popular by the Federal Art Project, a trend that was reinforced by the assistance of several European expatriate artists, such as the French graphic designer Jean Carlu. Carlu's poster *Production: America's Answer!* was created in response to a contest organized by the Museum of Modern Art in April of 1941 (*fig. 7.56*). Later printed by the Office of Emergency Management, the image shows a gloved hand turning a hexagonal nut that also forms the letter "O." While the sleek machine forms are pure Art Deco, the rather plain-looking lettering lacks the stylish shapes typical of the style. Carlu uses this nondescript lettering in order to convey the simple, unadorned strength of American industry in a manner that is visually striking without appearing affected and elitist. Cognizant that the poster was intended for the walls of factory lunch rooms, Carlu found just the right balance of artifice and naturalism.

Charles Coiner, who served as an art director for the Office of Emergency Management during the war, oversaw the production of Carlu's poster. He also worked in the field of information design, which had taken on a new urgency because of the need to train millions of unskilled soldiers in the use of complex weaponry. Coiner's most famous foray into information design was a set of symbols for the Citizens' Defense Corps which were to be used if the United States itself was invaded (*fig. 7.57*). The symbols made use of simple iconic drawings each of which indicated a different role, such as fireman or policeman. Anticipating later integrated information design systems, Coiner's work used "universal" geometric shapes such as the triangle.

During the war years, traditional realistic representation also thrived, as iconic figures such as "Uncle Sam" were rolled out again, matched now with "Rosie the Riveter," a figure that personified the millions of American women who worked in factories in support of war production. The legend of Rosie arose partly out of the verses of a popular song written in 1943 by Redd Evans and John Loeb:

> All the day long,
> Whether rain or shine,
> She's a part of the assembly line.
> She's making history,
> Working for victory,
> Rosie the Riveter.

But it was not until the famed illustrator Norman Rockwell featured "Rosie" on the cover of the Saturday Evening Post in May 1943 that the character became well known. Because Rockwell's work was copyrighted, the poster captioned *We Can Do It!* by J. Howard Miller, an illustrator for the Westinghouse Corporation, became the most recognizable image of "Rosie" (*fig. 7.55*). Miller's image was widely accepted as representing "Rosie" even though it was an anachronism, having predated the song by almost a year. It is interesting to compare the muscular, commanding figure of "Rosie" with the lithe, feminine "Christy Girls" of the First World War. While the Christy Girls were intended to appeal seductively to an audience of men, the image of Rosie was used to encourage thousands of women to join the war effort.

Norman Rockwell

While American propaganda posters of the 1940s toned down the "atrocity" themes, like their British counterparts, many images sought to contrast American society with that of Nazi Germany. Perhaps the greatest examples of this theme were the images of the "Four Freedoms," produced by Norman Rockwell (1894–1978), based on a speech by Franklin Roosevelt. On January 6, 1941, President Roosevelt spoke before Congress, implicitly decrying the lack of civil rights in Germany. He listed "four freedoms." "The first is freedom of speech and expression—everywhere in the world. The second is freedom of every person to worship God in his own way—everywhere in the world. The third is freedom from want … The fourth is freedom from fear."

Rockwell, America's most renowned illustrator at the time, made four original paintings for the *Saturday Evening Post* based on the speech. Later, these illustrations were turned into posters advertising war bonds. The *Freedom of Speech* poster features a working man who looks suspiciously like former President Abraham Lincoln at a town meeting (*fig. 7.58*). Rockwell's idealized portrayals of American life earned him a popular following, although progressive artists disdained his representational style.

In many ways, the Second World War marked the end of an era in American graphic design, as realistic illustrations such as Rockwell's, which had dominated American graphic media for decades, had one final hurrah. After the war, the modern abstract styles championed by Condé Nast and the Museum of Modern Art came to dominate the mass media. One reason for this development was that idealized naturalism became tainted in many people's minds by its association with the manipulative propaganda of Nazi Germany. The triumph of International Constructivism is discussed in Chapter 8.

left: **7.57** Charles Coiner, Citizens'
Defense Corps Symbols, 1942.
Collection of Merril C. Berman.

opposite: **7.58** Norman Rockwell,
Save Freedom of Speech, 1943.
Poster. Color lithograph, 40 x 28 in
(101.6 x 72.39 cm).

8

The Triumph of the International Style

In the post-war period, the graphic design profession was transformed by the rise of the Swiss style (also called the International Style, a term this author prefers), which, despite its name, found its greatest success under the patronage of corporations in the United States. The rise of the International Style directly parallels the development of "corporate identity," the process whereby graphic designers created logos and other devices that established a set visual theme for a company. This chapter, along with Chapters 9 and 10, can be distinguished from the preceding ones because the material and concepts considered herein are still viable parts of the contemporary design world.

With the establishment of the International Style in the 1950s, the formerly radical, politically engaged works of Dada, De Stijl, Russian Constructivism, and the Bauhaus were remade into a neutral discourse of commercial communication. The still current concept of the graphic designer as someone who rationally approaches a design problem on behalf of a corporate client and produces a functional solution arose as part of the International Style. Essentially, that style comprises the visual elements of Constructivist graphic design and the New Typography, stripped of their historical context—the Russian Revolution, for example. There was a parallel development in architecture during the second half of the century, as the architectural "International Style" introduced at the Museum of Modern Art in the 1930s gained a greater foothold in the mainstream.

Jan Tschichold:

Typographische Gestaltung

Benno Schwabe & Co . Basel 1935

8.1 Jan Tschichold, *Typographische Gestaltung (Typographic Design)*, 1935. Book title page. Museum Gestaltung, Zurich.

"Swiss Style"

Jan Tschichold

In the post-war period, Switzerland, a country renowned for its banking industry as much as its political neutrality, became the perfect site in which the International Style could gain traction. In fact, it was in the 1930s that a small cadre of dedicated designers had first begun exploring the New Typography and Constructivism. Swiss artists such as Max Bill (1908–1994) and Theo Ballmer (1902–1965), returning to their country after training in Germany at the Bauhaus, sought to introduce geometric abstraction to the design community. In addition, Jan Tschichold, the most famous proponent of the New Typography, was forced to emigrate from Germany in 1933; he chose to settle in Basel, Switzerland. Because of the Nazis' contempt for the "Bolshevik" Constructivist style, Tschichold had previously been arrested and fired from his teaching position in Munich soon after the Nazi takeover. At this point in his career, Tschichold was already broadening his views on typography to include an admiration for traditional typography and layouts, and the book he published in Switzerland in 1935, *Typographic Design*, was set mainly in the modern roman face Bodoni (*fig. 8.1*). In this new book, Tschichold reiterated his support for the New Typography but also suggested that the asymmetric, flush left layout was not the only suitable design formula. At the same time, it is possible that Tschichold's new, more moderate tone was influenced by his personal situation; his residency in Switzerland was quite tenuous, and Tschichold feared expulsion if he were to upset the authorities. Although there was a small community of graphic designers who valued his work, Swiss culture was quite conservative during the 1930s, and he may have feared being branded a "decadent Bolshevik," as had happened in Germany. While the Constructivist style made its first inroads in Switzerland during the 1930s, between 1936 and 1945 it almost completely disappeared in the face of a resurgent Swiss nationalism that was expressed in Neoclassical, representational forms.

The story of Tschichold's Swiss sojourn took an unexpected turn immediately after the war. Around 1946, he began publicly repudiating the principles of the New Typography that were so closely attached to his name. In an odd paradox, just as the International Style was finally gaining a solid reputation in the mainstream, Tschichold suggested that the absolutist terms in which he and others had formulated the style paralleled the dictates of the Nazis. He wrote of the New Typography in the journal *Schweizer Graphische Mitteilungen* that "Its intolerant attitude certainly corresponds in particular to the German inclination to the absolute." This interpretation put Tschichold at odds with other designers and critics; the common wisdom after the war was that since the Nazis had suppressed geometric abstraction in favor of first blackletter, then roman, type, it was the perfect vehicle with which to convey "anti-Nazi" modern sophistication. It was this latter interpretation that made the country of Switzerland and International Style graphic design appear to be such a perfect fit—both had essentially sat out the war and were untainted by any associations with fascism. The Swiss designer Richard Paul Lohse (1902–1988), for example,

advocated the International Style as representative of anti-fascism. In recent years, scholars have attacked what they now call the myth of "Swiss neutrality," and pointed to a number of instances in which Switzerland was a complicit partner in financial schemes that kept the Nazi regime afloat. Nonetheless, during the 1950s and 1960s, the height of the identification of the International Style with Switzerland, there was a sense that Swiss culture perfectly embodied the rationalism and logic conveyed by geometric abstraction.

Tschichold had also portrayed the New Typography as aesthetically inferior to older typographic styles. When he gave a speech in Zurich in 1946 to the Association of Swiss Graphic Designers, Tschichold in fact proclaimed a preference for symmetrical, centered layouts. In the 1940s, he would begin a new career as a designer of roman type while also pursuing an interest in classical Chinese manuscripts. His change of heart, for both aesthetic and ideological reasons, angered a number of young designers who felt that their icon had betrayed them. In Zurich, Max Bill, the most theoretically minded of the "Swiss style" artists, rebuked Tschichold for having betrayed the principles of the New Typography. The International Style in Switzerland also benefited from the arrival of additional German émigrés who had not repudiated the New Typography; designers such as Anton Stankowski (1906–1998), who moved to Zurich for a time in the early 1930s after studying photomontage in Essen, Germany. Bill, Stankowski, and a critical mass of like-minded artists eventually came to ignore Tschichold's new pronouncements and established a thriving community of designers dedicated to the Constructivist principles established in Germany in the 1920s.

The Predominance of Akzidenz Grotesk

Following the 1920s practices of Jan Tschichold, the practitioners of the International Style in Switzerland consistently relied on the late nineteenth-century sans serif type called Akzidenz Grotesk (*fig. 8.2*). First introduced by the German foundry Berthold in 1896, this type combined the dramatic modern look that they were seeking—it was, for example, well matched to photography—with less rigidly geometric forms that positively impacted its readability. Akzidenz Grotesk represented the perfect compromise for Swiss designers, in that it conveyed the functionalist ethos without appearing too stylized, as Herbert Bayer's Universal did. Its dry, mundane feel did not draw attention to itself in the manner of the more geometrically pure types. Max Bill employed Akzidenz Grotesk for the exhibition "Die gute Form" ("The Good Form"). This exhibition surveyed industrial design with an attention to functionalist aesthetics much like that of the previous decade's "Machine Art" show at New York's Museum of Modern Art (*fig. 8.3*). The Swiss Werkbund later named their annual design award after the exhibition, calling it the "Good Form" prize.

Bill, who had worked as an industrial designer, used Akzidenz Grotesk for the exhibition's wall stencils and labels. This lettering was the ideal choice to serve as the typographic paradigm of the post-war International Style; while it looks clear and functional, it carries none of the political baggage associated with Russian Constructivism or the Bauhaus. Rather, it is the

ABCDEFGHIJKLMNOP QRSTUVWXYZabcdef ghijklmnopqrstuvwxyz 1234567890?!*&£()%

"Akzidenz Grotesk represented the perfect compromise for Swiss designers, in that it conveyed the functionalist ethos without appearing too stylized, as Herbert Bayer's Universal did."

8.2 Berthold Staff, Akzidenz Grotesk Typeface, Berthold Foundry, 1896.

«Kontinuität» Plastik von Max Bill SWB, Zürich

Unsere Ausstellung zeigt Spitzenleistungen aus verschiedensten Gebieten menschlicher Tätigkeit, von der reinen Feststellung besonders vollkommener Naturgebilde über die Entdeckung wissenschaftlicher Wahrheiten bis zu Ergebnissen, die aus dem schöpferischen Trieb der künstlerischen Intuition entstehen und die dann ihre Parallele finden in der Anwendung der Naturgesetze in der Technik, vom Bestandteil einer Maschine bis zum Apparat und den oft umfänglichen Gebilden, die dem Menschen heute als Werkzeuge dienen. Alle diese Formen entspringen mehr oder weniger exakten Überlegungen. Sie basieren meist auf reicher Erfahrung und sind die Ergebnisse langjähriger Entwicklung. Dies ist nicht mit allen Gegenständen, die uns umgeben, so. Manche erhalten durch vollständig andersartige Beweggründe ihre Form. Die Entwicklung verläuft nicht gradlinig. So ent-

8.3 Max Bill, *Die Gute Forme (The Good Form)*, 1949. Book page. Museum für Gestaltung, Zurich. Graphic Collection.

ultimate depoliticized type, which matches the theme of Bill's show in that it views Constructivist functionalism in strictly formal terms, as exemplary of "good form," and devoid of political meaning. Of course, this process of "depoliticization" had begun as early as the 1920s, when prominent Constructivists such as Ludwig Mies van der Rohe, Kurt Schwitters, and El Lissitzky pursued commercial work in Germany that sidestepped their political commitments. This depoliticization was the key to the renewal of Constructivism as a universal, but not Communist, style after the war. "Swiss Style" was a neutral style based in a neutral, capitalist country. In the 1940s in Switzerland, Akzidenz Grotesk and the International Style first attained the "timeless" aura that would serve them well for decades.

Josef Müller-Brockmann

Josef Müller-Brockmann (1914–1996), an illustrator who became a convert to the International Style in the 1950s, also made excellent use of Akzidenz Grotesk throughout his career. In 1952 he used it for public signage that he designed for the Swiss Automobile Club (*fig. 8.4*). This "Accident Gauge" was installed on the Paradeplatz in Zurich, where it warned of the hazards of driving by presenting a numerical summary that highlighted each week's total automobile-related accidents and deaths. The

8.4 Josef Müller-Brockmann, *Accident Gauge*, Paradeplatz, Zurich, 1952.

understated forms of the letters and numbers in Akzidenz Grotesk are a superb match for this type of dry, statistical information which is nonetheless loaded with an emotional undercurrent. The numerical statistics are supplemented visually by actual gauges on the vertical axis that show yearly totals. The gauge was constructed according to an abstract three-dimensional design reminiscent of the information kiosks planned by several Russian Constructivists in the 1920s.

Müller-Brockmann's 1955 *Beethoven* poster for the Zurich Tonhalle represents the epitome of the Swiss style: carefully regulated curves sweep around an asymmetrically positioned block of text (*fig. 8.5*). The lower-case subhead "beethoven" is ranged left in a void on the lower half of the poster—just far enough below the midline to disrupt any semblance of ordered symmetry. Sketches made by the designer show how he took a symmetrical circular design and rescaled it while cropping it asymmetrically to come up with the final composition. By 1955, Müller-Brockmann had already developed a taste for "musical" compositions. In this example, the smooth curves that make up the abstract image were intended to be suggestive of Beethoven's powerful music. Müller-

Brockmann was invoking, perhaps unintentionally, one of the decades-old explanations of abstract art: that its aesthetic structure is comparable to the non-representational structures of musical composition. Max Bill also invoked a "music model" for abstraction, writing in a 1936 exhibition catalog, "Just as clear, clean musical forms are pleasant to the listener, and give joy to the knowledgeable in their structure, so clear, pure form and color should give visual pleasure to the viewer." In terms of the International Style, this "music model" represents yet another interpretation of Constructivism that steers the conversation away from the utopian Communism of the 1920s.

While many International Style poster designers used hand-drawn elements, other artists pursued Constructivist typophoto solutions. A poster by Hans Neuburg (1904–1983) advertising Liebig Bouillon combines sans serif letters with an obliquely shot and cropped photo by his colleague Anton Stankowski (*fig. 8.6*). The catchphrase "Super Bouillon" overlaps the scripted letters of the company name, which, in turn, overlaps the image of a container of the product, linking them together. There is a slight tilt to the text and photo that contests the rigid rectangle of the

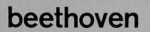

beethoven

tonhalle grosser saal
dienstag, den 22. februar 1955,
20.15 uhr
4. extrakonzert
der tonhalle-gesellschaft

leitung carl schuricht
solist wolfgang schneiderhan

beethoven ouverture zu «coriolan», op. 62
violinkonzert in d-dur, op. 61
siebente sinfonie in a-dur, op. 92

vorverkauf tonhalle-kasse, hug, jecklin,
kuoni
karten zu fr. 3.50 bis 9.50

8.5 Josef-Müller Brockmann, *Beethoven*, 1955. Poster. Offset lithograph, 50 x 35 in (127.5 x 90.3 cm).

8.6 Hans Neuburg, *Liebig Super Bouillon*, n.d. Museum für Gestaltung, Zurich. Graphic Collection.

frame, producing an asymmetrical kinetic element. Notably, the image of the smiling young woman recalls many Constructivist works all the way back to El Lissitzky's Russian Exhibition poster from the late 1920s (see fig. 5.42). This fact makes Neuburg's poster a great example of an icon of utopian Communist workers being transformed into smiling consumers in a capitalist society.

New Typefaces

While Akzidenz Grotesk remained the type of choice for Bill and Müller-Brockmann throughout their careers, Paul Renner's Futura also persisted as a popular choice for Swiss designers. However, during the 1950s three new typefaces were introduced that would become mainstays of the graphic design profession and are still widely used today. The first typeface, now known as Helvetica, was created in 1953 for Eduard Hoffman of the Haas foundry in Zurich. Hoffman had noted the exceptional popularity of Akzidenz Grotesk and desired a proprietary alternative for his own business. In 1951 he commissioned Max Meidinger (1910–1980) to create a new sans serif based on Akzidenz Grotesk, and Neue Haas Grotesk was born (*fig. 8.7*). The new typeface synthesized the bland flavor yet exceptional legibility (for a sans serif) of Akzidenz Grotesk with a slightly more regular structure that referenced the Purist geometric sans faces such as the Universal that Herbert Bayer had devised at the Bauhaus.

In 1957, Neue Haas Grotesk was sold by Haas to a German foundry, Stempel. In Germany the typeface was renamed Helvetica, the original Latin name for Switzerland. In the early 1960s, Helvetica was licensed for the Linotype machine, making it more readily obtainable. Soon, Helvetica was to become an icon of the International Style as its functional legibility and widespread availability—as well as the cachet of its "Swiss" name—combined to make it the sans serif choice of a generation of typographers and graphic designers.

The Swiss typographer Adrian Frutiger (b. 1928) moved to Paris in 1952 in order to accept a position at the celebrated French foundry Deberny & Peignot. Once there, he set to work on a number of new typefaces, including **Univers**, which was released in 1957 (*fig. 8.8*). A follower of the functional, logical precepts of the International Style, Frutiger attempted to rationalize the categories that were used to describe type. As he saw it, the problem lay in the fact that while different typographers and foundries used the same common terms—bold, extended, etc.— they never meant quite the same thing from usage to usage. In pursuit of a new more logical system, Univers was released along with a color-coded diagram that displayed numbered weights on the vertical axis and different widths (condensed versus extended) on the horizontal one. In an innovative move, all of the various weights of the typeface were released at once. This exercise in information design did away with indeterminate terminology in favor of a visual tool that illustrated the different variants and their relationship to one another.

In 1950, a few years before Frutiger joined Deberny & Peignot, the firm had developed the "Lumitype Photon" **photo-typesetting** system. Eight years later Berthold introduced the Diatype, which was sold around the world. Offering the promise

8.7 Max Meidinger, Neue Haas Grotesk Helvetica Typeface, 1951. St. Bride Printing Library, London.

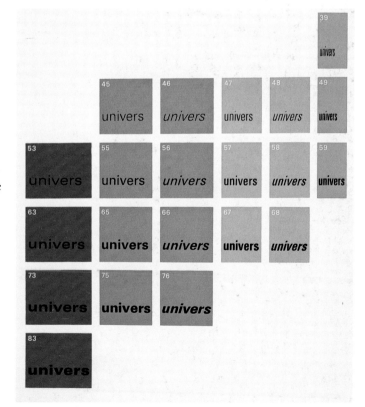

8.8 Adrian Frutiger, Univers Typeface, Deberny & Peignot Foundry, 1954–7. St. Bride Printing Library, London.

ABCDEFGHIJKLMN OPQRSTUVWXYZ abcdefghijklmnop qrstuvwxyz12345 67890 ?!*&

"Zapf had sought to make a sans serif that included some of the structural characteristics of seriffed letters, particularly those of ancient Roman carvings."

8.9 Hermann Zapf, Optima Typeface, 1952–8.

of flexibility combined with economy, reliable phototypesetting had been sought after by type foundries for decades. As the name suggests, with these systems the type is reproduced from photographic negatives instead of metal type like that used in the Linotype and Monotype machines. Univers became one of the first faces produced for use with phototypesetting systems. As phototypesetting made inroads into the typography business in the 1960s and 1970s, it had a detrimental impact on the appearance of much of the mass media. The problem resulted from the system's flexibility; type of one scale could be rescaled larger or smaller quite easily. However, for a good result, different sizes of type need to be subtly reproportioned at different sizes, and phototypesetting made it possible for printers inexpensively to sidestep this important element of good typography. A gradual decline in the quality of mass-produced media ensued, further conditioning an already indifferent public to ignore the qualitative differences in typesetting. This problem has become even more of an issue in the digital age, when phototypesetting has been superseded by even more flexible and economical equipment (see Chapter 10).

The third new 1950s sans serif discussed here was designed in Germany by the legendary typographer Hermann Zapf (b. 1918). Called **Optima**, this conservative typeface was released for the Linotype in 1958 (*fig. 8.9*). Zapf had sought to make a sans serif that included some of the structural characteristics of seriffed letters, particularly those of ancient Roman carvings. Zapf also admired the typography of the Renaissance, and there are variations in stroke width in Optima that recall the calligraphic strokes of Modern styles. Typefaces that add less rigid, non-geometric design elements to an essentially sans serif design are sometimes called "Humanist sans serif."

Journal and Advertising Design

Richard Paul Lohse began editing the magazine *Bauen und Wohnen* ("Building and Living") in 1948. Published in Zurich, the center of the Swiss style in the 1940s, the magazine cover shown here (*fig. 8.10*) combines sans serif lettering with the orthogonal grid characteristic of the style. Two innovative devices were employed for the cover of issue #4. First, there are dramatic contrasts in the scale of the various photographs, giving the page an evocative rhythmic element. This device also has a function, as the scale of the pictures is both aesthetic and hierarchical, indicating the key topics inside the journal. Second, the overlapping colors, which bridge voids and photographs, create interesting interconnections between the different parts of the composition. In the lower left, an abstract circular shape cuts into the corner of a rectangle of photographs, producing a muted diagonal axis that nicely complements the strong vertical and horizontal organization.

Müller-Brockmann made use of the same sort of colorful overlap in his typophoto design for VOLG brand grape juice (*fig. 8.11*). Here, the grid has been reductively split into just two wide verticals, one red and one yellow. While the text, in Akzidenz Grotesk, of course, is restricted to just the left half of the page, the artfully cropped, full-bleed photo underlies both colors. The yellow half of the image frames the man's face, which is balanced by a red void across the page. In an example of a

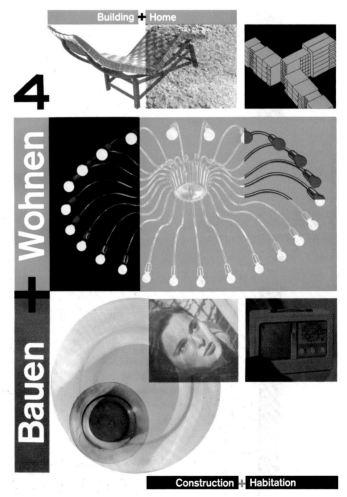

8.10 Richard Paul Lohse, *Bauen und Wohnen*, 1948. Magazine cover.

8.11 Josef-Müller Brockmann, *Volg Traubensaft*, 1962. Poster.

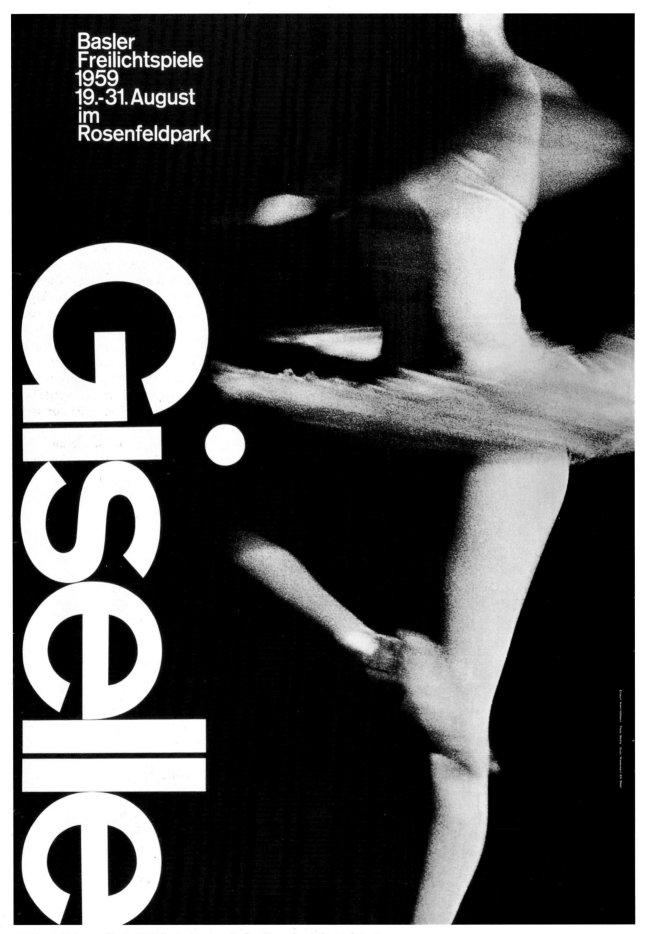

8.12 Armin Hofmann, *Giselle*, 1959. Poster. Museum für Gestaltung, Zurich. Poster Collection.

functionalist design that conveys an extremely irrational message to the consumer, this advertisement is promoting "natural grape juice" with the vision of a handsome model driving a car. The tagline "Konzentration" suggests that imbibing the product will give one the steely focus of the man in the photo. It is fairly unusual for the "clear and logical" Swiss style to be used in order to impact the viewer with an emotional, intangible message.

Basel Type

A poster designed by Armin Hofmann (b. 1920) in 1959 for a theater in Basel, Switzerland, is more daring than those of many of his Zurich-based contemporaries (*fig. 8.12*). Hofmann, who had trained in Zurich with the influential teacher Ernst Keller, had moved to Basel in 1946 in order to accept a position as a professor of graphic design at the Allgemeine Gewerbeschule (later Schule für Gestaltung). In the 1950s, he and his students, a group that included notable artists such as Karl Gerstner (b. 1930) and Max Schmid, made Basel an alternative Swiss style "scene." In broad terms, the artists based in Basel were less doctrinaire than their Zurich counterparts, and were more likely to disregard the unofficial "rules" of the International Style. Compared to the austere works of Zurich artists such as Bill or Müller-Brockmann, graphics produced in Basel can appear downright whimsical. For example, Hofmann's ballet poster *Giselle* features text that runs downwards on a vertical axis, violating the rule that text must always run horizontal. The expanded bold letters that spell out

"Giselle"—the name of the ballet, which was conceived by Théophile Gautier (1811–1872) in the 1840s—curve in a way that mimics the dancer's body, calling attention to themselves in a way that is uncharacteristic of the Swiss style. Also, there is a very small space between the letters and the photograph, causing the text and image to come dangerously close to interfering with one another.

Neue Grafik

In Zurich in 1958, Müller-Brockmann, Lohse, Neuburg, and Carlo Vivarelli (1919–1986) together founded the influential journal *Neue Grafik* ("New Graphic Design"). Subtitled *International Review of Graphic Design and Related Subjects Issues in German, English and French Language* and replete with articles that summarized the major tenets of the Swiss style, *Neue Grafik* was responsible for establishing Switzerland's reputation as the key center of the International Style (*fig. 8.13*). In a gesture to the universalism of the 1920s, numerous essays were written collaboratively by the four editor–designers, who signed them with the acronym "LMNV." Müller-Brockmann and his colleagues limited their design to the reticent Akzidenz Grotesk, which appears in only two sizes. One tenet of the Swiss style was that the designer should never mix typefaces—a belief that the apostate Tschichold had embraced in the 1930s—and additionally must use only one or two weights. The weights, in turn, should provide a functionalist hierarchy to the viewer, showing by

8.13 LMNV, *Neue Grafik (New Graphic Design)*, 1958. Journal cover. Museum für Gestaltung, Zurich.

8.14 Josef-Müller Brockmann, *SBB*, 1972. Museum für Gestaltung, Zurich. Poster Collection.

scale what are the most important parts of the text. The cover of the first issue of *Neue Grafik* is a fine example of the modular grid that underlies the compositions of almost all International Style works. Müller-Brockmann later titled his penultimate publication, a manual of graphic design, *Raster Systeme* ("Grid Systems"). On the cover of *Neue Grafik,* there are four narrow vertical elements that traverse the void in the middle of the cover. The title, repeated in three languages, acts as a horizontal block that establishes the orthogonal grid. The double-page spread recapitulates the grid, as the four columns of ranged left, ragged right text continue to structure the page, with artfully placed voids indirectly creating a horizontal element. Of course, this type of positive use of negative space is another key stylistic element of the International Style.

While *Neue Grafik* was exceptionally successful during its seven years of publication, it also became "exhibit A" to critics who felt that the Swiss style, especially in Zurich, had become inflexible and dogmatic as its international reputation grew. The extremely limited range of graphic design "solutions" presented by the more rigid proponents of the style grew repetitious over time (see Chapter 9). It can be argued that many practitioners of the Swiss style lacked the dynamic, even chaotic thread that tied Russian Constructivist design to the innovations of Dada and Futurism. Defenders of the International Style are more apt to portray it as a responsible set of professional and even moral principles, not simple a "style" that has gone out of fashion. By the 1970s, the scope of available European patrons for Swiss style designers had narrowed considerably. The style had become emblematic of a type of cold, institutional communication that offered little in the way of variety. Müller-Brockmann's information design of 1972 for SBB, the Swiss railway consortium, is exemplary of how International Style "functionalism" became identified with pallid, very functional, graphic projects (*fig. 8.14*). A comparison of these pages from his design manual and Edward Johnston's signage for the London Underground of the 1910s shows how the earlier design embodied the fashionable glamour of the train while the SBB signage is constrained by its austere anti-expressionism.

England and the International Style

Stanley Morison

In the United Kingdom, typography and graphic design professionals of the 1930s through the 1960s were generally reluctant to adopt the International Style. Stanley Morison (1889–1967), the most well-known typographer and typographical historian in England during this period, in many ways dominated the scene with his commitment to finely crafted traditional typefaces as well as his numerous publications. His book *First Principles of Typography*, originally an essay in *The Fleuron*, became a sort of bible for British typographers after its publication in 1936. In the 1920s, Morison engineered the revival of a number of classic typefaces, including Bembo (*fig. 8.15*), Baskerville, and Fournier.

ABCDEFGHIJKLMNO
PQRSTUVWXYZabc
defghijklmnopqrstuvw
xyz1234567890?!★&%
"In the 1920s, Morison engineered the revival of a number of classic typefaces, including Bembo, Baskerville, and Fournier."

8.15 Stanley Morison, Bembo Typeface, 1929.

8.16 Stanley Morison, Times New Roman Typeface, 1932.

As the main typographic consultant to the Monotype Corporation, Morison was well positioned to promote the use of conventional modern faces in the machine age. This is not to imply that he rejected modern sans serifs completely, as he was instrumental in arranging the production of Gill Sans. In many ways, Morison's influence and good judgment helped make Monotype the dominant mechanical typesetting system in Britain.

Morison also held two other key positions during his career, as the chief book designer for Cambridge University Press and as a consultant to *The Times* of London. In 1932, he introduced an exceptional new typeface for the newspaper, **Times New Roman**, as a part of a general redesign (*fig. 8.16*). An extremely narrowly proportioned seriffed face, designed to save space and enhance legibility, Times New Roman was produced by Monotype, and was made available to the wider printing industry a few years after it was introduced at *The Times*.

Jan Tschichold at Penguin

Having himself rejected the dogmatic assertions of the New Typography, Jan Tschichold accepted a position at Penguin Books of London in 1947. Penguin, founded in 1935, was the first commercially successful paperback book company in Britain. Paperback books had quickly established themselves as a hot commodity before the war, allowing a huge segment of the population for whom hardcover tomes were offputtingly expensive to read literature and popular fiction. During the conflict, Penguin paperbacks, which were not designed with any particular aesthetic qualities in mind, proved to be the perfect portable, functional companion for soldiers.

Tschichold inherited a chaotic situation when he moved to London in 1947. Up to that point, Penguin editions, which numbered in the hundreds, had been typeset and designed by a huge range of people, mainly the job printers who ran the machinery. It was immediately clear to Tschichold that, apart from Morison's work for Monotype, little in British publishing rose to the level of German or Swiss standards. While working at Penguin, Tschichold did not put in place a dogmatic set of rules regarding book layout or type, rather, and according to his new, broad taste in typography, allowed book designers to use a wide variety of faces. What he did insist on was that each run of books follow general principles of good design, be they conventional or modern in origin. His most enduring contribution to Penguin was a leaflet called *Penguin Composition Rules*. In this four-page essay, Tschichold demanded that Penguin's designers follow standardized rules for all aspects of layout and typography. A typical dictum includes simple rules and the explanation for them: "All text composition should be as closely word-spaced as possible … Wide spaces should be strictly avoided. Words may be freely broken whenever necessary to avoid wide spacing, as breaking words is less harmful to the appearance of the page than too much space between words."

Tschichold also took time out to design many covers himself, such as one for the Penguin edition of Dante's *The Divine Comedy*, released in 1947 (*fig. 8.17*). While quite conventional in design, combining a small woodcut with typography by Tschichold, it is a

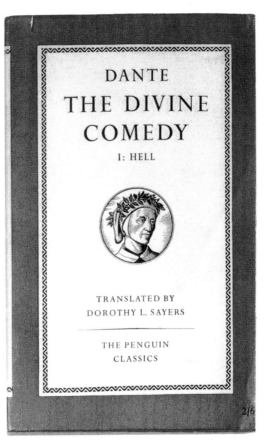

8.17 Jan Tschichold, Dante's *Divine Comedy*, 1947. Penguin Books.

clear and well-balanced composition that is immediately legible to the viewer. The solid blue border is reinforced by a geometric rule that provides a strong frame for the centered lettering set in Monotype's Perpetua. During his tenure, Tschichold standardized the design for Penguin's various book series, and *The Divine Comedy* is a fine example of the basic elements he devised for Penguin Classics, making them instantly recognizable to the consumer. In raising the aesthetic level of a mass-market distributor of paperback books, Tschichold brought to fruition the vision that had been espoused, but never acted upon, by William Morris in the nineteenth century (see Chapter 1). Tschichold later wrote, "We do not need pretentious books for the wealthy, we need more really well-made ordinary books."

While Penguin had used only a limited variety of types in its early years, under Tschichold the publisher employed a wide range of elegant faces made available because of Morison's work at Monotype. Morison's and Tschichold's work in England during the mid-twentieth century raises the question of what is the most functional typography. At a time when "functionalism" was the credo of the followers of the International Style, it is arguable that the quieter, conventional designs that predominated in England best fulfilled that mission.

Herbert Spencer

During this period, England had one great champion of the International Style, the typographer Herbert Spencer

315

(1924–2002). Through his own work, much of it for the publisher Lund Humphries, and the journal *Typographica*, which he edited and designed from 1949 until 1967, Spencer unflaggingly sought to promote the geometric abstract style in England. Spencer also authored and designed an influential book that summarized his beliefs, *Design in Business Printing*, in 1952. Acquainted at an early age with both Max Bill and Rudolf Hostettler (1928–), the editor of *Schweizer Graphische Mitteilungen*, Spencer promoted the Swiss point of view well into the 1990s.

In France, there was even greater resistance to the establishment of the International Style, and the corporate identity movement that energized graphic designers in the United States did not play a large role in French commerce until the 1980s. In its place, the art of the poster retained its status, and designers such as Pierre Fix-Masseau (1869–1937) continued to make advertisements in an Art Deco vein.

American Innovators

In the decades immediately following the war, the United States witnessed an economic expansion that paralleled the dramatic increase in its status on the world's stage. With its military triumphant, its industries intact, its cities spared from bombardment, the country was ideally situated to experience an era of welcome prosperity. The 1940s, 1950s, and 1960s would prove to be a boom time for American industries as well as for the graphic designers that served them. In the United States, the International Style had barely scratched the surface of the nation's consciousness prior to the war; institutions such as the Museum of Modern Art has been like voices crying in the wilderness, touting a set of principles on which a new art of design could be based. After the war, this message would gradually break through, and the United States would become second only to Switzerland as a site for the

8.18 Alvin Lustig, *Fortune* magazine, Dec 1946.

exploration of geometric styles. However, with a few notable exceptions, the majority of American designers never became doctrinaire in their adoption of the style, but remained open to an eclectic range of influences.

Among the most talented American book and magazine cover designers of this period was a Los Angeles native named Alvin Lustig (1915–1955). Lustig worked in a variety of media during his brief career, splitting his time between New York and Los Angeles. In 1946, he was hired by Will Burtin, Art Director of *Fortune*, to produce a cover for the magazine. Burtin had assumed the position at *Fortune* in 1945, and he was successful in updating its typography and introducing modern design principles (see Chapter 7). Lustig's cover image features a full bleed rainbow of colors; it is traditional in American art history to associate such an exuberant polychrome tendency with the state of California, which may well have been the explanation in this case (*fig. 8.18*). On top of the color field Lustig has placed a number of two- and three-dimensional elements, ranging from a completely flat, hand-drawn curlicue that bumps into the "e" to

a photo of a pin cushion that seems to project aggressively into the viewer's space. A line leading from this latter object enters an area of negative color, almost like an X-ray, before meandering off the page.

The idiosyncratic nature of Lustig's cover for *Fortune*, especially the way in which the different elements of the design seem almost whimsically derived, exemplifies the "Americanization" of the International Style that occurred in the United States during this period. While some American graphic designers accepted the rigid ideology prevalent in Zurich, many more saw the International Style as just that—a style, which should be flexibly employed as the occasion demanded. For this reason, it is common to see elements of the Art Deco or other, eclectic styles intrude into an otherwise geometrically structured image. For example, Lustig's 1948 book jacket for *Anatomy for Interior Designers* has a firm orthogonal design underlying it (*fig. 8.20*). The right angles of the body parts are reinforced by lines of hyphens which appear to perform some measuring function. However, this clear structure and asymmetrical, cropped layout

left: **8.19** Alvin Lustig, Exhibition Catalog *The New Decade*, 1955, Museum of Modern Art, New York. Collection Elaine Lustig Cohen.

opposite below: **8.20** Alvin Lustig, *Anatomy for Interior Designers*, 1948. Book jacket. Collection Elaine Lustig Cohen.

The New Decade:
European Painters
and Sculptors
22

are overlaid with flat, organic shapes that contest the profundity of the grid. Lustig loved the flowing line created by shapes such as these, and he integrated them into many of his works.

In 1954, Lustig designed a cover for an exhibition catalog published by the Museum of Modern Art (*fig. 8.19*). The eclectic nature of Lustig's work is obvious when compared with the previous examples, as here he has eliminated any superfluous element in favor of a design that consists only of typography. Taking a cue from German work of the 1920s, Lustig has created a striking geometric abstraction that makes ample use of the grid and of negative space. However, his employment of seriffed modern type deviates from the standards set by the Swiss school. In addition, the overprinting of the "2" on top of the word "European" suggests a Dada element, generating a deliberate "error" that disrupts the simple harmony of the composition.

Saul Bass

Saul Bass (1920–1996) was another influential American designer who practiced in Los Angeles. Born in New York, he moved after the war to California, where he set up his own independent design practice. In 1954, he was hired by the movie director Otto Preminger (1905–1986) to create film posters. The following year, he completed his poster for *The Man with the Golden Arm*, Preminger's newest picture, which dealt with the gritty, urban theme of drug addiction (*fig. 8.21*). Bass's poster was composed of a geometric grid made up of flat rectangular planes of bold color. The basic grid of the image is not a fixed structure, as the slightly irregular shapes from which it is built up—some encasing still photos of the actors—seem to wobble within the frame; this device creates a slight kinetic force that is not found in most Swiss

8.21 Saul Bass, *The Man with the Golden Arm*, 1955. Poster. Museum für Gestaltung, Zurich. Poster Collection.

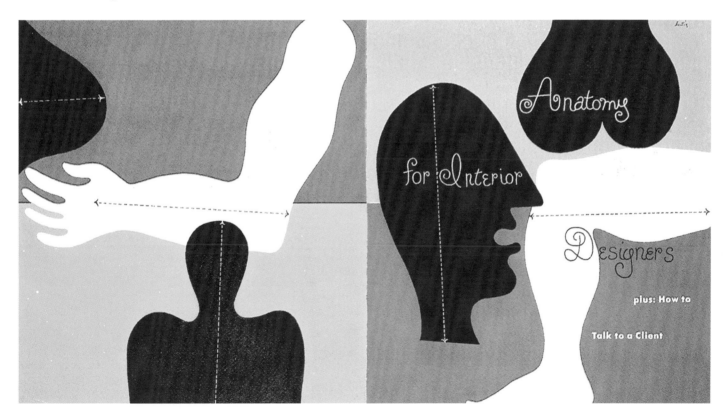

8.22 Saul Bass, *Vertigo*, 1958. Poster. Lithograph, 10⅝ x 41 in (27 x 104.1 cm).

8.23 Saul Bass, *Exodus*, 1961. Poster. Lithograph. Museum für Gestaltung, Zurich. Poster Collection.

style compositions. It is apparent that many American designers were impressed by the raw energy of pulp fiction covers, and one can sense that Bass did not want to constrain his images with the grid. The most striking element in the poster is a man's jagged arm, which dangles in the center of the image. This image on the one hand clearly recalls the drooping arm of Jesus in the series of *Pietàs* that Michelangelo produced in the early sixteenth century—sculptures that had been copied many times over the centuries. In a contemporary sense, the arm stands as the symbol of the protagonist's heroin addiction. Bass's greatest gift was the ability to create a single strong motif that would stick in the viewer's mind and serve to summarize a whole complex of ideas and feelings.

Preminger was so taken by the "jagged arm" symbol that he asked Bass to design titles for the film using the same motif. Bass created an animated title sequence in which white bars coalesce on a black field background, ultimately morphing into the jagged arm, which this time briefly stands alone, dominating the frame with its stark impact. At the end of the title sequence, the director's credit appears, with the horizontal text broken by the fingers of the hand. When *The Man with the Golden Arm* was sent out to theaters, a note on the film canisters requested that projectionists open the stage curtains before the titles. Previously, film titles had been essentially ignored by the audience, and were often not even projected on to the screen at all. But because Bass's jagged arm was so successful at summarizing the themes of drug addiction and degradation that drove the story, Preminger considered them to be an essential element to his film.

In 1958, Bass began working with the celebrated director of thrillers, Alfred Hitchcock (1899–1980). For Hitchcock's *Vertigo*, Bass designed a poster that shows a man and a woman's silhouette captured in a spiraling vortex (*fig. 8.22*). The black lettering, which looks as if it were drawn with a trembling hand, is representative of the anxious, agitated state of mind of the protagonist in the film, who faces his fear of heights as well as an unnerving set of circumstances that may be rooted in his psychological afflictions. The field of red in the background aggressively jumps out at the viewer, creating a strong contrast with the energy of the vortex that seems to draw the viewer into the poster. For this film, Bass, who hoped to become a director in his own right, was allowed to direct a dream sequence that is at the core of the film's narrative. It shows the actor Jimmy Stewart's crazed expression superimposed on an abstract spiral akin to the one in the film's poster.

Another astonishing example of Bass's use of the human arm as a powerful symbol was created in 1961 for Preminger's film *Exodus* (*fig. 8.23*). Based on the novel by Leon Uris, *Exodus* tells the story of the struggle to found the state of Israel in the years after the Holocaust. In a sort of inversion of the jagged arm used in *The Man with the Golden Arm*, here Bass shows an arm rising up from some flames at the bottom of the image. Without becoming too literal in its description, the image suggests the themes of struggle, destruction, and heroism. The blue background and white lettering do provide a more hopeful color scheme than the red of the poster for *Vertigo*. It is essential to remember that Bass was largely responsible for the "professionalization" of the film poster artist in the United States. Before he started collaborating with Preminger, film posters were generally produced by publicity firms that had very little stake in the aesthetic quality of the result. Rather, like pulp fiction covers, movie posters had been designed to catch the viewer's eye with photos of the stars or suggestions of salacious content. In contrast to Bass's spare style, most posters of the day were cluttered with a melange of text and image. Both in introducing a high aesthetic standard and in signing his posters, Bass changed the common practices in Hollywood, as the effect of good design on a film's success became apparent.

that had been the bedrock of the advertising industry began to look obsolete and also seemed somehow too close to the idealized fantasies promoted by fascist governments during the war. Because the International Style had been so thoroughly depoliticized by its Swiss practitioners, it ironically became the style of choice for large companies and corporations that wanted to promote their products "universally" without raising the specter of nationalism.

For many scholars, the corporate identity logos that were devised starting in the 1950s—many of which are still in use today—represent the apotheosis of the International Style. Multinational corporations reinvented the "universal" ideology of utopian Communism as expressed by geometric abstraction in order to convey the authority and stability of dominant capitalist enterprises. This period witnessed the golden age of the corporate logo, when designers such as Paul Rand (1914–1996) created some of the most familiar trademarks of the century. This section will concentrate on a group of examples of the corporate identity movement that demonstrate this reconfiguration of avant-garde art.

Design at Ulm

Of course the idea of corporate identity, meaning a unified look that encompasses everything from logo, to stationery, to architecture, did not first develop in the 1950s. Among its antecedents was the work in Germany for AEG that Peter Behrens performed during the 1910s (see Chapter 2). However, Behrens's work was essentially anomalous during the early part of the century, and it was only in the post-war period that the majority of large, multinational corporations felt the need to present a unified design front to the consumer. In Germany, a center for post-war graphic design arose in the city of Ulm. There, Max Bill, Otl Aicher (1922–1991), and Inge Scholl (1917–1998) founded the Hochschule für Gestaltung ("University of Design") in 1951. With a curriculum based largely on Bauhaus principles, the HfG represented a German corollary to the austere Swiss style as it was practiced in Zurich. Scholl brought anti-fascist credentials to the International Style, as her parents had been executed by the Nazis in 1943. Bill, the first Director of the school (1951–7), was of

Corporate Identity in Germany and America

During the 1950s, the profession of graphic designer finally came into its own. The International Style took hold in the United States after the Second World War, mainly because it found a group of willing corporate patrons who became convinced that it provided a politically neutral style that appeared efficient and professional. By the late 1940s, geometric abstraction had gained a new cachet because of the way it was suppressed by Hitler and Stalin, who had both embraced representational styles for their propaganda campaigns. To Americans, the realistic illustrations

8.24 Otl Aicher, Lufthansa Logo, 1969.

Deutsche Bank

8.25 Anton Stankowski, Deutsche Bank Logo, 1974.

8.26 Otl Aicher, Munich Olympics Pictograms, 1972.

convey meaning—such as the words of a language or the abstract shapes of the International Style—focuses on how ideas are constructed in society. Taking note of the way that language functions through a system of differences, so that the word "sofa," for example, partly derives its meaning by the fact that the speaker did not choose the word "couch," the professors at Ulm attempted to establish a credible academic theory for their design practice.

As the industrial powerhouse of Europe got back on its feet, German graphic designers found numerous opportunities to design corporate logos. In 1969, Aicher devised a new logo for Lufthansa, the preeminent German airline (*fig. 8.24*). Aicher installed a new, softer version of the blue and yellow color scheme that had been developed in the 1920s, and devised a sleeker version of the crane that had been originally drawn by Otto Firle in 1918, circumscribing it in a circle in the Bauhaus manner. Aicher also made **Helvetica** the standard face for the airline's name. Provocatively, Aicher's redesigned livery is essentially indistinguishable from the work of less scholarly designers such as Paul Rand, bringing up the question of what role the theory of graphic design can play in the actual practice of the profession.

Anton Stankowski, who taught at the HfG during the 1950s, designed a new corporate identity for Deutsche Bank in 1974 (*fig. 8.25*). This slash and square emblem displays the formal rigor of 1920s Constructivism, and successfully resists any obvious display of contemporary "trendiness." Rather, it attempts to create an abstract vision of timeless strength and security. Like many designers of corporate identity, Stankowski needed to devise new colors for Deutsche Bank, eventually leading to the development of "Deutsche Bank Blue." During the post-war era, financial institutions largely turned away from the Neoclassical styles that had been their design mainstay for centuries, styles that had suggested permanence and stability. Instead, banks invoked the "new timeless," the International Style.

Both Stankowski and Aicher played important roles in the design of the 1972 Munich Olympics. Stankowski worked mainly as an administrator, serving as Chair of the Committee for Visual Design that oversaw every aspect of the extravaganza. Aicher, in turn, made his most significant contribution in the area of information design, creating a system of pictograms that were intended to be understandable despite the polyglot nature of the athletes and guests at the games. Aicher approached this project with the 1920s work of Otto Neurath (1882–1945) as a precedent. Neurath, an Austrian sociologist, had developed the visual classification system he called the "**Isotype**," an acronym for "International System of Typographic Picture Education." With the help of the illustrator Gerd Arntz (1901–1988), Neurath had invented a set of bold symbols that conveyed simple, factual information without resorting to text. Like Neurath's prototypes, Aicher's Olympic symbols were made up of simple lines and circles superimposed on a grid. The resulting icons are easily identifiable: swimming, cycling, and soccer (*fig. 8.26*). These symbols work even better than a common verbal language, as witnessed by the soccer/football confusion possible in English. Putting the universal themes of avant-garde modernism into practice, Aicher's signage proved clear and effective, and set a precedent for the creation of universal symbols that are now widespread around the world.

course himself Swiss and had played a large role in originating the Swiss style. Precisely measured axial grids, crisp geometric forms, sans serif type, and a minimal use of text characterized the products of the Ulm school.

What truly separated the professors and students at the HfG from their contemporaries was their concern for the theoretical dimension of graphic design. At a time when many American designers, in contrast, were largely self-taught and gave very little thought to the intellectual structures behind their work, the faculty at Ulm was consistently bringing the most advanced sort of philosophical issues into the classroom. Aicher and Scholl pioneered the semiotic analysis of graphic design at a time when few outside the HfG were operating at such a high intellectual level. **Semiotics**, the academic study of signs and symbols that

Container Corporation of America

In the United States, the original visionary behind the corporate identity movement was the owner of Container Corporation of America (CCA), Walter Paepcke (1896–1960). In 1934, Paepcke realized that CCA, which made cardboard boxes on a vast industrial scale, could benefit from a redesign of its packaging and promotional materials. Paepcke hired Egbert Jacobson (b. 1890) to formulate the new look for the company. Jacobson devised a modernist solution for CCA, placing the company's initials in a grotesque face inside an elongated hexagon (*fig. 8.27*). Paepcke's embrace of an overall corporate identity program, at the core of which was a new logo, established a precedent that would be widely embraced in the 1950s and 1960s.

The most daring move made by Paepcke at CCA came after 1936, when he was convinced by Charles Coiner, art director of his account at the N.W. Ayer agency, to initiate the Great Ideas advertising campaign. Between 1936 and 1960, CCA commissioned progressive European and American artists and designers to create posters that related to famous quotes from the Western tradition. In this manner, the posters seemed to transcend the vulgar economic messages of most advertising, and instead promulgated the idea of CCA as a patron of culture. Viewers were not supposed to think of the product, cardboard boxes, when they viewed these ads, but to see the company as a responsible corporate citizen; in the post-war era, corporations soon recognized the value of creating an "individual" personality for their company,

one that consumers could relate to on a more personal level. This advertising trend paralleled developments in the American legal system, whereby corporations more and more were treated like individual citizens, complete with "inalienable rights" to property, expression, and the like.

The Swiss designer Josef Müller-Brockmann was one of many partisans of the International Style who created a poster for the Great Ideas campaign in the 1950s (*fig. 8.28*). Like all the commissioned artists, he was given a quote and asked to base his image on it without dramatically referencing CCA. It is not clear how the quote from the British philosopher John Stuart Mill (1806–1873), which advocates freedom of speech for individuals, bears any explicit relationship to Müller-Brockmann's design. Nor need it; by the 1950s, modern abstract art, such as the De Stijl-influenced blocks of primary color located on an asymmetrical orthogonal grid used by Müller-Brockmann, itself represented resistance to tyranny and the primacy of individual expression in a broad sense. This interpretation was harnessed by institutions such as the Museum of Modern Art, which made a determined effort to explain the significance of abstraction to the mainstream public in the 1940s and 1950s—in a way, this became the museum's core mission (see below). In contrast to most commercial design, the Great Ideas posters all featured the artist's name or signature, in order to capitalize on their reputation. The corporate identity of the patron of this poster, CCA, is only barely indicated, appearing in the lower left corner along with a small cardboard box logo.

above: **8.27** Egbert Jacobson, CCA Logo, 1937.

right: **8.28** Josef-Müller Brockmann, *Container Corporation of America (CCA)*, 1957. Poster.

8.29 Paul Rand, *Modern Art in Your Life*, 1949. Book cover, 7 x 9 in (18 x 23 cm).

Paul Rand

The graphic designer whose name most became equated with corporate identity and the International Style in the United States was Paul Rand. Trained in New York City at the Pratt Institute, Rand became the art director of *Esquire* magazine in 1935. While there was little in the way of formal training in modern graphic design styles available at that time in New York—oddly enough, Rand once took a class in the 1930s with the Dada artist and German émigré George Grosz—Rand later related that he scoured the pages of European journals such as *Gebrauchsgraphik* for information about the newest styles. He became a part of the circle centered on the Composing Room (see Chapter 7), and

served as guest artist for three issues of *PM Magazine* between 1938 and 1941.

The February/March 1941 issue of *PM Magazine* featured a prominent article on Rand written by none other than Laszlo Moholy-Nagy. In the piece, Moholy-Nagy wrote that he and other young Europeans had envisioned the United States as a technological utopia, an icon of the modern world, when they worked on devising the Constructivist style in the 1920s. He went on to write that he had been bewildered by the "old-fashioned advertising" that he discovered when he moved to Chicago in 1937. "I was greatly surprised to find that we Europeans were, to a certain extent, more American than the Americans." The country that had inspired Constructivism in many ways had failed

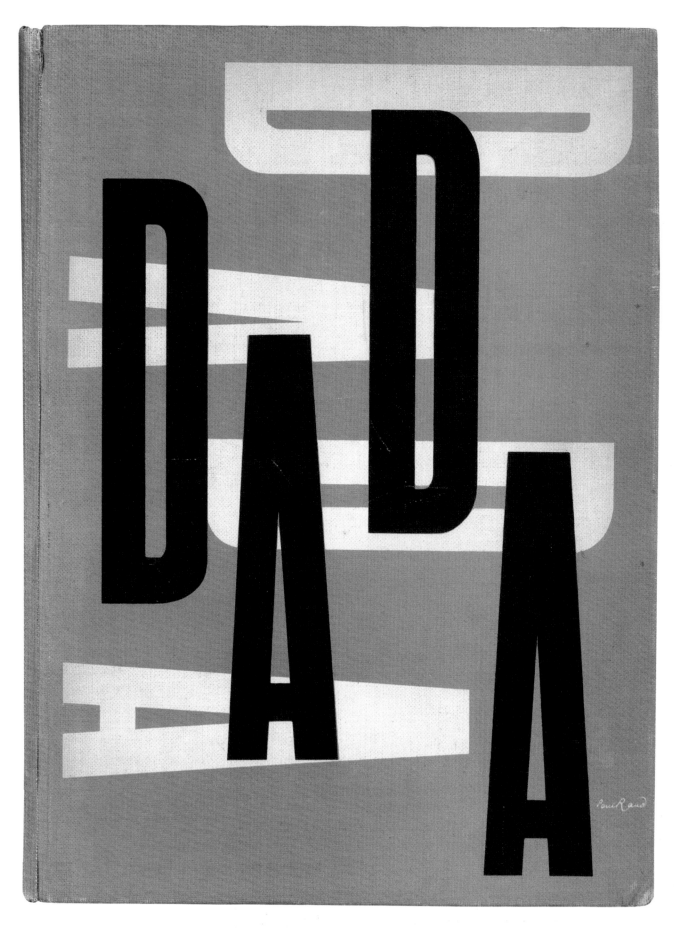

8.30 Paul Rand, *The Dada Painters and Poets*, 1951. Book cover, 7⅝ x 10 in (19.3 x 26 cm).

to live up to his expectations. The short article is matched with ten pages illustrating Rand's designs for everything from furniture to posters.

The insert in *PM Magazine* on Rand that included Moholy-Nagy's essay was, according to the editor's custom, designed by Rand himself. In deference to the Bauhaus style of typography, Rand set his own name in lower-case type, while Moholy-Nagy's signature is reproduced much larger. This element effectively projects a spirit of humility on Rand's part, as he cleverly deemphasizes himself in favor of the celebrity, Moholy-Nagy, who had founded the "NewBauhaus" in Chicago in 1937 and was at that time directing the Chicago School of Design founded by Walter Paepcke. The blank space at the top of the page is broken only on the right margin, where a cropped photo of a few fingers points at the title and text below. The large space after the colon in the title as well as the ragged word "The," which breaks up the block of otherwise justified text, both seem out of sync, as if Rand was experimenting with the International Style without fully converting to it.

In 1949, the Museum of Modern Art produced an exhibition accompanied by a catalog designed by Rand, called *Modern Art in Your Life*. In an attempt to contest the idea that abstraction was politically radical and visually obtuse, MoMA sought to redefine modern art as something respectable and safe. One of the ways in which the museum sought to show that abstract art played a role in mainstream culture was by convincing the American public that abstract art played an important role in mass culture. Along these lines, juxtapositions in the catalog matched abstract fine art with commercial works. This type of comparison cut both ways, of course, because it also served to bestow the cachet of a Pablo Picasso or a Joan Miró on the design arts.

The cover of the catalog itself demonstrated this strategy, as Rand gestured toward a number of different abstract styles in creating his design (*fig. 8.29*). While orthogonals dictate the composition, the smeared areas of color and "*faux* childlike" drawing of objects contest the rigid structure of the grid. The quirky symbolism of the dinner setting with the plate replaced by an artist's palette shows how well Rand understood the importance of making designs that translated ideas into visual terms, rather than simply decorating a surface. His cover conveys the message that abstract art is as friendly as a meal at home with simplified precision akin to that employed by Bass in his film posters.

During the post-war era in the United States, even the revolutionary art of the Dadaists was domesticated, its political message deflated in favor of a newfound concern with its formal, fine art characteristics. Another book design by Rand in 1951 indicates this reevaluation, although in this instance the message is somewhat inadvertent. Rand's cover for Robert Motherwell's anthology *The Dada Painters and Poets* is made up only of typography; an extremely narrow bold grotesque repeats the word "Dada" twice on the page (*fig. 8.30*). While there is overprinting and the letters seem to bounce kinetically, two elements drawn from Dada itself, the overall simplicity and respect for the grid go against everything anarchic and chaotic that the Dada movement stood for. Rand has created a look that perfectly encapsulates the new, safe Dada—more about bouncy fun than revolutionary politics.

Paul Rand and IBM

After thirteen years working for the Weintraub Advertising Agency, in 1955 Rand embarked on a freelance career. Over the next four decades he established himself as the top purveyor of corporate identity in the United States, with his initial success concentrated around the year 1960. Rand's new focus on corporate logos began when he was employed in 1956 by Eliot Noyes (1910–1977) to work as a consultant for International Business Machines (IBM), the makers of typewriter and, later, computer systems. Executives at the company had become aware that their sprawling business lacked a consistent style, and, spurred on by the dramatic modernist work of Leo Lionni (1910–1999) for a competitor, Italy's Olivetti Corporation, they decided to pay more attention to IBM's visual identity. This new project did not involve only graphic design, as Noyes hired Marcel Breuer, formerly of the Bauhaus, to work on the firm's architecture, and the industrial designer Charles Eames (1907–1978) to help with some product designs.

While corporate identity comprises the overall design of packaging, stationery, architecture, and printed ephemera, designers have always seen the logo as the heart of the enterprise. A logo needs to distill the identity of a corporation while at the same time remaining flexible in its different applications. In designing the logo for IBM, Rand used only typography, and relied somewhat on the existing acronym, which was then rendered in a condensed Beton Bold that had a slight Art Deco flair. He also based the new type on nineteenth-century "Egyptian" letters, which featured heavy slab serifs, while at the same time referencing George Trump's City Medium grotesque face. (Trump had replaced Paul Renner at the Munich Meisterschule für Deutschlands Buchdrucker after Renner was arrested by the

8.31 Paul Rand, IBM Logos, 1956–90. Reproduced by permission of IBM Corporation.

far left: **8.32** Paul Rand, Westinghouse Logo, 1956. Yale University Library.

left: **8.33** William Golden, CBS Logo, 1951.

Nazis, and later went on to design a Schaftstiefelgrotesk called Trump Deutsch in 1935.) The resulting logo was similar to but much crisper-looking than the older one, with more elegantly proportioned lettering (*fig. 8.31*). Shortly afterwards, Rand reconfigured his original logo, adding an outline version in two weights. The problem with the original logo was that it appeared too heavy in a visual sense, unbalancing some documents, for example, while also appearing "heavy-handed' in an ideological sense. In 1962, Rand added the "8 bar" and "13 bar" versions, which split the type into horizontal bands of even weight. Rand also introduced the German idea of the "design manual" at IBM, including the aptly named 1990 pamphlet *Use of the Logo/Abuse of the Logo*. These sourcebooks directed employees worldwide how and when to use IBM's corporate identity. In Europe, Josef Müller-Brockmann was hired as a consultant in order to oversee the use of the logo on the continent.

Rand's work at IBM led to several subsequent high profile commissions, including those for Westinghouse, the American Broadcasting Corporation (ABC), and United Parcel Service (UPS). At Westinghouse, a multinational maker of electrical products that employed Noyes as a design consultant beginning in 1959, Rand again relied on elements from a previous design, in this case a "W" with a line underscoring it, to create a new logo (*fig. 8.32*). This logo featured the letter "W" made up of three dots and four lines that form a letter with the suggestion of the format of an electrical circuit board. It is notable that the logo, which seems rather unadventurous when compared to its contemporaries—especially with the holdover lozenge under the letter W—was deemed too strikingly abstract by many Westinghouse executives, and almost never made it into production. Regardless of the variations in letterforms in examples such as IBM and Westinghouse, throughout Rand's work, the simplified clarity, sans serif lettering, and bold geometric shapes of the International Style reign supreme.

In 1968, Rand redesigned the packaging for Westinghouse's Lamp Division, mainly by taking an "addition through subtraction" approach and eliminating a lot of unnecessary graphics (*fig. 8.34*). He used a Helvetica-like grotesque, called simply **Westinghouse Gothic**, to fashion numbers that for the first time told the consumer the wattage of the bulbs. The design creates a contrapuntal rhythm between the circular Westinghouse logo and the diagonal blocks of text. This type of effective design, which is much clearer than the older packaging and which also highlights the salient fact of the wattage in large numerals,

lends sans serif lettering the aura of "functionalism" even though the design would be just as legible if seriffed letters were used. Also, an orange and "Westinghouse electric blue" juxtaposition of complementary colors added a slightly decorative element to the design.

In his logo for ABC, Rand refashioned a combination of Renner's Futura and Herbert Bayer's Universal into a new gothic. He also borrowed Bayer's predilection for lower-case letters to make an acronym that is enclosed, like many similar Bauhaus designs, by a perfect circle. ABC had been forced, like many media companies, to refine its visual identity after the success of the in-house work done by William Golden (1911–1959) at the Columbia Broadcasting System (CBS) in the 1950s (*fig. 8.33*). In 1951, Golden had invented CBS's "eye" logo, which quickly established itself as a versatile emblem that resonated with the eye of the television camera. Of course, this celebration of the "Kino-Eye" harks back to the anti-capitalist film projects of the Russian Constructivists, who glorified the objective eye of the camera as a symbol of Communism's fair and balanced social policies. While the eye logo was sometimes embellished with the CBS acronym in grotesque letters, Golden also established the redrawn version of a modern roman face, Didot Bodoni, as the house typeface for the network.

Rand's use of Universal for ABC's logo represents perhaps the best example of this unexpected culmination of the International Style in the service of corporate design. Bayer's typeface was named Universal for a reason: his belief, formed at the Bauhaus, that simplified geometric forms could serve as the visual basis for a new style that would unite all people in a utopian future. Of course, this unification came about in a perverse way in that the mass media, of which ABC is a prominent member, have become "universal' in global culture, but a culture that is relentlessly commercialized, in which ABC unifies people by selling to them. When ABC was sold in the late 1980s, the new owners planned to update Rand's design but were unable to decide on a suitable replacement.

Rand's reinvention of the UPS logo in 1961 paired unstressed bold sans serif lettering with a holdover device from the old logo, a shield (*fig. 8.35*). Above the shield he added a whimsical touch, a schematic rendering of a wrapped gift. Rand was never as austere in his designs as were his Swiss and German colleagues, and while he adopted many of the stylistic precepts of European design he never absorbed the complicated terminology or the theoretical dimension of design that were paramount in Ulm and Zurich.

8.34 Paul Rand, Westinghouse Light-Bulbs, 1968. Yale University Archives.

A key aspect of corporate logos is their proposed longevity versus other more ephemeral types of graphic design. Because companies strongly desire to establish a mark that will last for generations, most designers of corporate identity projects strive to avoid short-lived trends. This factor was important in the adoption of avant-garde modernism by post-war graphic designers. The "universal" nature of simple geometric designs makes them much more adaptable and able to function over several decades without looking obsolete. When a modern design has been retired, it has often been the case that a whimsical touch, such as the UPS gift-wrapped present, has begun to look "dated" even though the overall abstraction is still sound.

In 2003, Rand's UPS logo was updated with a new look by the corporate design firm FutureBrand (*fig. 8.36*). The twenty-first-century UPS logo has jettisoned the gift-wrapped box while maintaining the look of a shield. The new logo has been criticized for combining three clichés of contemporary corporate identity: first, *faux* three-dimensionality created by shading, the antithesis of modernism's "honest" two-dimensional aesthetic; second, a "swoosh" of sorts, a device that has become ubiquitous ever since its invention for Nike by a graphic design student at Portland State University named Caroline Davidson; and, third, a redrawn version of Hans Reichel's **FF Dax** typeface, which features a stylized transition between the vertical and curved strokes of the letters U and the P. On the other hand, Rand himself had often quibbled over his UPS logo, and it is arguable whether the new update fulfills his oft-quoted principles, "The ideal logo is simple, elegant, economical, flexible, practical, and unforgettable."

One of the most important graphic design programs in the United States was established at Yale University in 1951. At that point, Yale's art department was chaired by the Bauhaus professor and German émigré Josef Albers. Albers played a pivotal role in making Yale into an institution where the International Style would thrive in the fine arts, including architecture, as well as in the design areas. Along with Herbert Bayer, Walter Gropius, László Moholy-Nagy, Marcel Breuer, and Ludwig Mies van der Rohe, all of whom were employed by American universities in

Bauhaus Masters at American Universities

Having left Germany for England in 1934, Walter Gropius later settled in Cambridge, Massachusetts, in 1937, where he became a professor at Harvard University's Graduate School of Design, later Chair of the Department of Architecture. Gropius retired in 1952 but continued to work in private practice. Curiously, despite his accomplishments during his pre-war career, Gropius had less impact in the United States, even though his stature as an icon of modern style subtly influenced American architecture and design culture.

Gropius was joined at Harvard in 1937 by his Bauhaus colleague Marcel Breuer, who remained at the university until 1946; the two men often collaborated on projects. Breuer's students included a number of people who would have a profound effect on American architecture in the ensuing decades, including Philip Johnson, I.M. Pei, and Paul Rudolph.

While several former Bauhaus professors worked on the East coast, two others, László Moholy-Nagy and Ludwig Mies van der Rohe, eventually settled in the midwestern city of Chicago. Moholy-Nagy was committed to continuing the educational mission of the former German art school, as evidenced by his choice of the name "New Bauhaus" for the institution he led in Chicago, beginning in 1937 under the aegis of the American Association of Arts and Industries. The New Bauhaus quickly ran into financial difficulties, as Moholy-Nagy's original supporters, a conservative trade group, found themselves uncomfortable with its progressive goals and withdrew their financial support. Moholy-Nagy persevered by reopening the newly renamed Chicago School of Design in 1939 with a commitment to the same ideals he had espoused in the 1920s, including functionalist design and a machine aesthetic. The school was renamed yet again in 1944 as the Institute of Design. Moholy-Nagy died in 1946. The Institute of Design was absorbed by the Illinois Institute of Technology in 1949.

Ludwig Mies van der Rohe, who as the last Director of the Bauhaus had presided over its closure in 1933, emigrated to Chicago in 1938 where he took a position as Director of the Department of Architecture at the Armour Institute, an engineering college. In 1940 the institute merged with another technical college to form the Illinois Institute of Technology (IIT). As Director of the College of Architecture, Planning, and Design at IIT, Mies van der Rohe gained both a forum for his views on architecture and major commissions. In the 1940s and 1950s he designed a series of buildings as well as a master plan for the university's campus.

Mies van der Rohe believed strongly that architecture must both respect universal aesthetic laws of harmonious proportion and respond to the cultural epoch from whence it derived, and his convictions earned him legions of followers across the country. In a collaborative effort with the developer Herbert Greenwald, Mies van der Rohe transferred his architectural vision to the design of skyscrapers, where his leadership was so ubiquitous as to become almost invisible. Headquartered in his adopted city of Chicago, the architectural firm of Skidmore, Owings, and Merrill—home to many architects who trained under Mies van der Rohe—has spread a Miesian aesthetic throughout the world.

the 1950s, Albers was an influential proponent of the "Bauhaus approach to problem solving." This concept collapsed and depoliticized the different currents that made up the Bauhaus into one rational, logical stream that could provide efficient "solutions" for American industry. Rand was perhaps the most influential professor of graphic design at Yale University, where he taught from 1956 until 1993 while also contributing to Yale's summer program in Brissago, Switzerland, beginning in 1977. While Rand was mainly self-taught—he once remarked about his class with George Grosz, "You wondered what he was driving at. I am still wondering"— he played an important role in instituting study of the International Style that dominated the graphic design curriculum at Yale for many years. Rand contributed the logo for Yale University Press in 1985, stitching together the serifs of the letters to form a web of linear elements (*fig. 8.37*). Other Yale professors in the 1950s and 1960s included Lustig, the Swiss émigré Herbert Matter, Leo Lionni, Alexey Brodovitch, Bradbury Thompson (1911–1995), and Armin Hofmann.

The Golden Age of Logos

In the 1960s, both Lester Beall and Saul Bass joined the rush to create new modern corporate logos. Beall created a new corporate identity for the International Paper company. The new logo both referenced the source of IP's products, trees, while also acting as an homage to Moholy-Nagy's design for the Bauhaus Press of 1923 (*fig. 8.38*). The equilateral triangle ensconced within a circle is typical of the type of reductive geometry that is the mainstay of most contemporary corporate design. Like Beall's logo, Bass's 1969 logo for Bell Telephone circumscribes his design, in this case an abstract bell that relates to the older logo, inside a pure circle (*fig. 8.39*).

A firm that claimed a large role in the booming corporate identity movement of the 1960s, Brownjohn, Chermayeff & Geismar, was first established in New York in 1957, soon after the latter two partners had graduated from the graphic design program at Yale. Robert Brownjohn (1929–1970) had left the firm and moved in 1960 to London, where he had a significant impact on British graphic design. Building on the reputation established by its work for Chase Manhattan Bank of 1959, the renamed firm of Chermayeff & Geismar took on a number of high-profile clients in the 1960s.

The redesign by Tom Geismar (b. 1931) of the logo of Mobil Oil, a collaboration with Eliot Noyes, made use of a customized version of Futura, the perfect circle of the "O" now representing petroleum products (*fig. 8.40*). In discussing the logo, Geismar does not relate the use of the perfect "O" from Futura to the history of the avant-garde. "The idea of the red O came about partly to reinforce a design concept to use circular canopies, circular pumps, circular display elements, etc. for a distinctive look." Noyes, in turn, designed the famous cylindrical pump for Mobil's retail outlets. It is clear from this unified design program how corporate identity projects are in a way the impoverished descendents of the *Gesamtkunstwerk* that captured so many artists' imaginations in earlier decades. Futura remains a reliable standard that is still widely used by graphic designers in the corporate

8.35 Paul Rand, UPS Logo, 1961.
Reproduced by permission of UPS.

8.38 Lester Beall, International Paper
Logo, 1972.

8.39 Saul Bass, Bell Telephone Logo,
1969. Reproduced by permission
of Bell South.

8.36 FutureBrand, UPS Logo, 2003.
Reproduced by permission of UPS.

8.40 Tom Geismar and Eliot Noyes,
Mobil Logo, 1965.

8.37 Paul Rand, Yale Logo,
Yale University Press, 1985.

8.41 Lindon Leader and Landor
Associates, FedEx Logo, 1994.

8.42 Ludwig Mies van der Rohe and Philip Johnson, Seagram Building, New York, 1957.

realm. For example, when Lindon Leader (b. 1950) of Landor Associates in San Francisco invented the new Fedex logo in 1994, he used a customized combination of Univers 67 (bold condensed) and Futura (*fig. 8.41*). In order to fit an arrow into the design of the logo, Leader customized his lettering with a higher x-height and ligatures. The resulting arrow, which is formed by the negative space in between the "e" and the "x," is often overlooked by viewers and users, so that it operates almost on a subliminal level.

The International Style in Corporate Architecture

The field of architecture presented an important parallel to the International Style in graphic design. During the time when the International Style of design and typography rose to the top, the same abstract design principles were also applied to corporate architecture in the United States. Of course, the term "International Style" was originally applied to architecture; it had first been employed by Philip Johnson and Henry-Russell Hitchcock for their 1932 exhibition of avant-garde architecture at the Museum of Modern Art. Bauhaus architects including Gropius, Mies van der Rohe, and Breuer had all settled in the

United States during the 1930s, and after the war they popularized the reductive geometric style. In 1947, Johnson curated an exhibition of Mies's work titled "The Architecture of Mies van der Rohe," which brought great public renown to the German architect. As was the case with graphic design, the employment of avant-garde architecture for corporate headquarters buildings constituted a process whereby formerly radical, utopian—even Communist—styles were remade into a visual signifier of triumphant capitalism.

During the 1950s, Mies van der Rohe became the preeminent skyscraper architect in the United States, basing his work on the principles of the International Style that had been formulated at the Bauhaus in the 1920s. Mies van der Rohe, director of the Bauhaus from 1930 until 1933, lived in Chicago beginning in 1938, when he became director of the Architecture Department

8.43 Ludwig Mies van der Rohe, IBM Building, Chicago, IL, 1971.

8.44 Anonymous, IBM Selectric II Typewriter, 1971. Manual cover.

1996 | **Enron Annual Report** *to Shareholders and Customers*

8.45 Paul Rand, Enron Logo, 1996. Yale University Library.

of the Armour Institute, which was later absorbed into the Illinois Institute of Technology. Built in collaboration with Johnson, Mies van der Rohe's first high-profile skyscraper was the Seagram Building on Park Avenue in New York City (*fig. 8.42*). This corporate headquarters was to become an iconic example of how companies and their architects reinterpreted the revolutionary geometric abstractions of the 1920s as language that spoke of stability, efficiency, power, and sophistication—all qualities that companies wanted to project to the public. This thirty-nine-story tower shimmers in shades of brass and brown, standing as if on a pedestal because of the pylons that separate the main volume from the plaza under it. The "glass box" structure seems to be a pure Neoplatonist solid, a universal shape of harmony and balance. Of course, this type of building conveys the functionalism of the International Style, its undecorated steel and glass form enclosing open interior spaces that could be easily altered to fit the changing needs of workers. Notably, Mies van der Rohe himself was not fond of the concept that his buildings were purely "functional," and he resisted that nomenclature, preferring to see his buildings as elegant design solutions that transcended simple functionality.

IBM's corporate architecture program represents an example where the stylistic and ideological impact of architectural, industrial, and graphic design styles can be investigated side by side. Eliot Noyes, the director of design and all-around corporate identity guru at IBM starting in the 1950s, was trained as an architect, and was a former student of Breuer, who had taught in the architecture program at Harvard University between 1937 and 1947. During the 1960s, Noyes and Breuer each designed multiple buildings for IBM, which was in the middle of an era of expansion. Perhaps the most stunning IBM building from this era was in fact designed by Mies van der Rohe, who was hired to design a skyscraper to house the corporation's Chicago headquarters (*fig. 8.43*). Not completed until 1971, two years after Mies van der Rohe's death, the Chicago IBM building displays all of the imposing grandeur of his other works. A glass box of black steel and tinted windows, it arises at a bend of the Chicago River, dominating a notable vista of the city. Like the IBM logo designed by Rand, the building projects logic and rationality, its crisp geometric form not simply functional but beautiful as well. The question brought up by Mies vander Rohe's architecture as well as Rand's logos is: was the International Style in the post-war age reduced to just that, a style, or does it still manage to convey some of the universal moral philosophy that was a part of its birth?

In 1971, the year in which Mies van der Rohe's classic Chicago IBM building was completed, Noyes introduced his redesign of one the company's key products, the Selectric II typewriter. The advertisement shown here features the new design, which involved establishing a sleeker shape and smoothly contoured body for the machine (*fig. 8.44*). The Selectric II also boasted new functional elements, especially the ability to switch between ten- and twelve-point type at the pull of a lever. The modern style of this manual integrates the cropped photo of the typewriter with Rand's 8-bar logo. The underlying grid, asymmetry, and prodigious negative space all reflect the updated corporate identity program overseen by Noyes.

The Tilted E

In a sort of cosmic irony, the last corporate logo designed by Paul Rand before his death in 1996 was for the Enron Corporation of Houston, Texas. Originally called the "multicolored, tilted E," Rand's logo took the form of a square balanced on one corner at a 45-degree angle (*fig. 8.45*). Simple and bold, like so much of Rand's work, the logo presents a successful design solution, combining the company's name with a huge sans serif "E" that has a high visual impact. At a 1997 party to unveil the new corporate identity, Kenneth Lay (1942 – 2006), Chairman and CEO of Enron, said "This new advertising campaign and logo will begin to inform people around the world of who Enron is, and how we can help them make decisions to improve their businesses and their lives." After the 2002 collapse of the company under the weight of its fraudulent business practices, Rand's "E" took on a whole new meaning; rechristened the "crooked E," it inadvertently became the most powerful anti-logo of its time. No parodist of corporate identity could have devised a more startling outcome.

The Enron debacle created much soul-searching among the graphic design community, as artists pondered the ethical dimensions of their power to shape people's perceptions. A few years ago Milton Glaser (b. 1929), a prominent **postmodern** graphic designer discussed in the next chapter, devised a list of hypothetical dilemmas that could arise in the career of a contemporary graphic designer:

1. Designing a package to look bigger on the shelf.
2. Designing an ad for a slow, boring film to make it seem like a light-hearted comedy.
3. Designing a crest for a new vineyard to suggest that it has been in business for a long time.
4. Designing a jacket for a book whose sexual content you find personally repellent.
5. Designing a medal using steel from the World Trade Center to be sold as a profit-making souvenir of September 11.
6. Designing an advertising campaign for a company with a history of known discrimination in minority hiring.
7. Designing a package for children whose contents you know are low in nutrition value and high in sugar content.
8. Designing a line of T-shirts for a manufacturer that employs child labor.
9. Designing a promotion for a diet product that you know doesn't work.
10. Designing an ad for a political candidate whose policies you believe would be harmful to the general public.
11. Designing a brochure for an SUV that turned over frequently in emergency conditions and was known to have killed 150 people.
12. Designing an ad for a product whose frequent use could result in the user's death.

While corporate identity based on the International Style continues to thrive, from the 1960s a number of new styles and design philosophies arose that contested its dominant position.

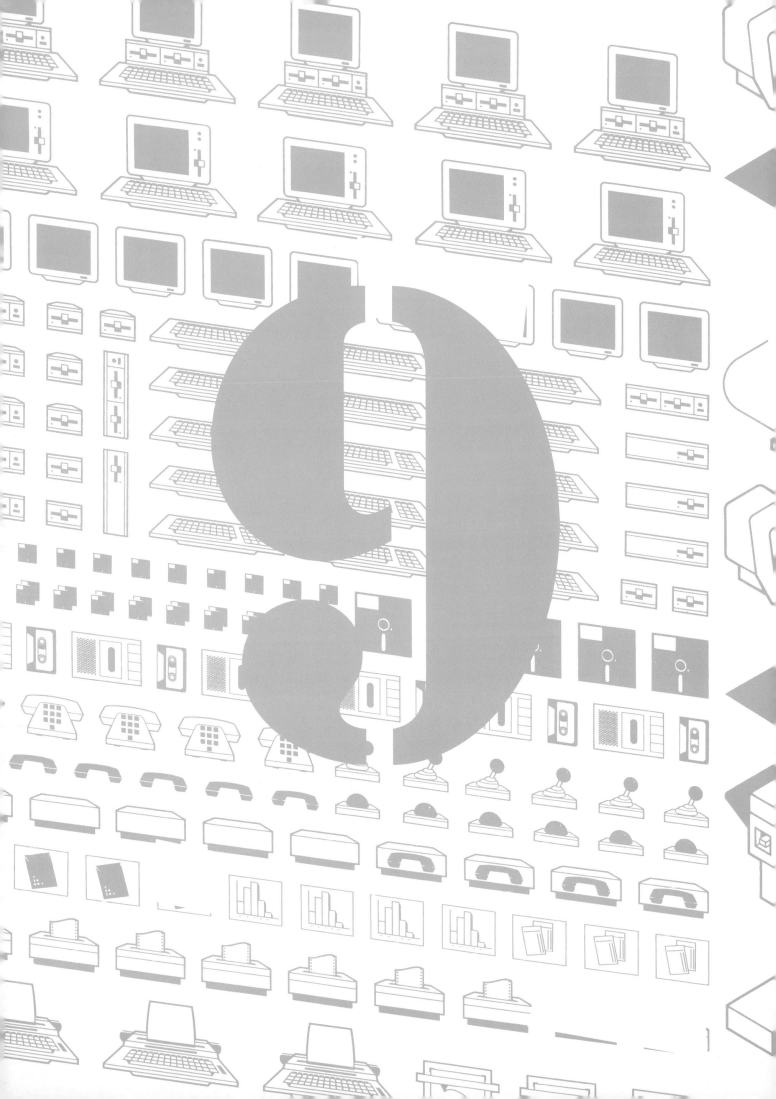

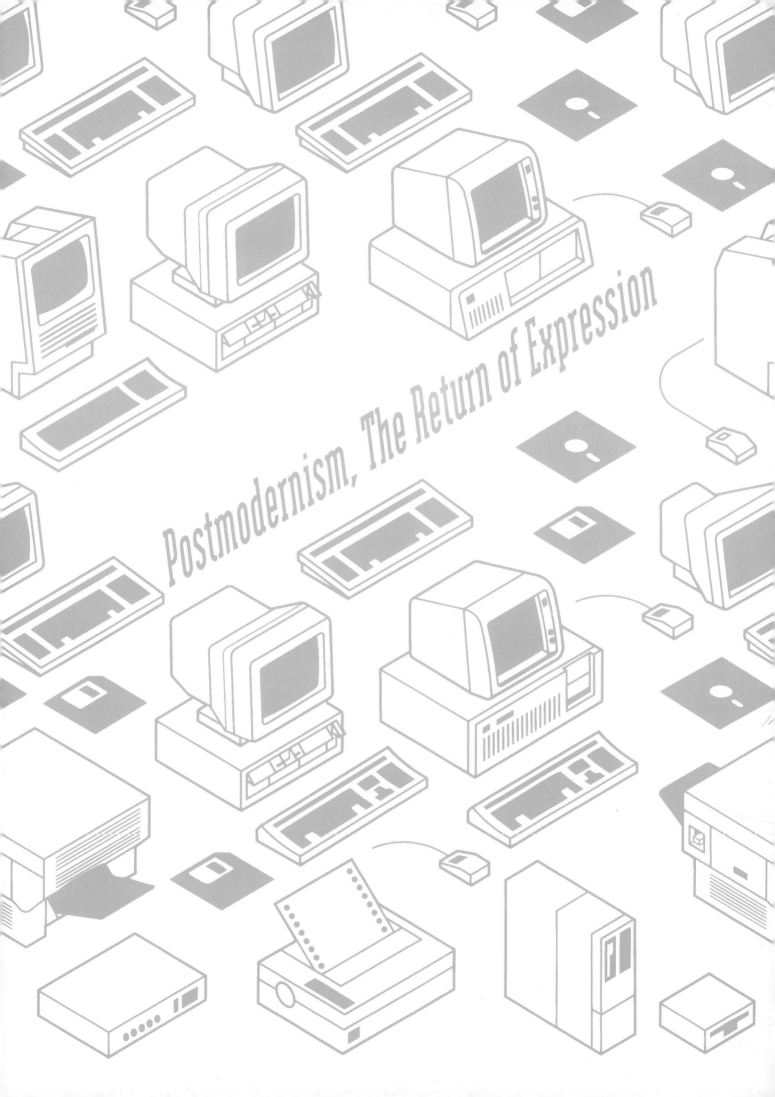

Postmodernism, The Return of Expression

The end of the twentieth century saw the gradual breakdown of the hegemony of the International Style in the face of challenges that arose as part of the "postmodern" movement. The term "postmodern" is at its heart a chronological term that means simply "after-modern." However, the term has been complicated by a variety of different and overlapping definitions that were devised to fit certain situations. One overarching idea of what constitutes the "postmodern" is that it rejects that which is "modern." For the purposes of graphic design, modern refers to the International Style, so one should expect postmodern design neither to look like nor to have the same conceptual basis as the work discussed in the previous chapter. The stylistic conventions of postmodern graphic design include mixing diverse type sizes and weights, overprinting, cluttered pages, deliberate "mistakes," unpredictable historicist references, blurred photographs, and even in some cases an embrace of general messiness—all elements that reject the dogmatic rules of the International Style. However, most scholars feel that the modern movement did not end with the beginning of postmodernism, so that modernism and postmodernism actually have existed side by side, with the former losing ground to the latter over the years. While postmodernism cannot be confined to any one specific country or even continent, this chapter and the next will focus mainly on the American and British works that are considered to be at the heart of the movement.

9.1 Wes Wilson, *Captain Beefhart & His Magic Band,* 1966. Poster. Color lithograph, 19 x 13¼ in (48.3 x 34.9 cm).

Psychedelic Posters

Despite decades of dominance, the International Style was being undermined as early as the 1960s. At that time a variety of young designers began experimenting with an eclectic variety of styles. Some graphic designers created work that was a self-conscious reaction to the International Style, while other projects seem to have grown organically out of the social circumstances of the 1960s and beyond. An example of the latter phenomenon arose around 1965 in San Francisco, where a critical mass of young people focused their energies on the burgeoning music scene in California.

This group of poster designers, many of them without any formal art training, developed an exuberant, expressionist visual language that neatly complemented the counterculture that was developing among young people during that decade. As the name implies, the "counterculture" refers to the overwhelming rejection, or "countering" of conventional mores and social norms that characterized many young people's beliefs in the 1960s. There was a prevailing sense among young people that their parents' lifestyles were stifling and outdated, and that it was necessary to resist mainstream middle-class values that would lead to an inauthentic existence. Profoundly idealistic, young people in Europe and the United States nonetheless succeeded in forcing dramatic changes in the way many people viewed the world.

Psychedelic drugs, particularly LSD, played a significant role in the formation of the counterculture. LSD had a profound effect on the user's brain, causing visual and auditory hallucinations that resulted in a dream-like "trip," which in turn was believed to lead to more enlightened thinking and an expanded consciousness. Especially in California, where drugs were legal until 1966, it quickly became fashionable for artists and designers to adopt a facsimile of a "psychedelic trip" in order to appeal to young consumers. The resulting posters, many of which advertised rock concerts, dramatically contrast with the clarity and legibility that were the norm for graphic designs of all types.

A fine example of a psychedelic poster was created by Wes Wilson (b. 1937) in 1966 (*fig. 9.1*). This lithograph seemingly contradicts its own reason for existing; why even make a poster if the resulting text and image are so illegible as to be unreadable? The flame-like red lettering seems to zigzag back and forth across the page, with the shape of each letter changing in order to fit into the available space. The red letters seem to project from the cool green background; this use of brilliant complementary colors is a hallmark of the 1960s rock poster. In response to this sacrifice of legibility in the name of expressiveness, the concert promoter Bill Graham (b. 1931) resorted to using asterisks that referred the viewer of the poster to the bottom margin, where the specifics of the concert were rewritten in legible type.

The psychedelic poster movement in San Francisco manifested another key aspect of postmodernism: the embrace of historicist styles. In 1965, the University of California at Berkeley had hosted exhibitions that highlighted early twentieth-century Expressionist and Art Nouveau styles, and these shows had a clear impact on posters from the following years. For example, Wilson's *Captain Beefheart* lithograph borrows the vertical format and flat stylized ornament of Art Nouveau and combines it with the

9.2 Victor Moscoso, *Youngbloods*, 1967. Poster. Museum für Gestaltung, Zurich. Poster Collection.

undulating letters of the psychedelic. This sort of borrowing need not be so direct, as, for example, the Expressionist element in general of the psychedelic movement probably was influenced by historical posters. Postmodernists borrowed indiscriminately from past styles without adopting the ideology or full aesthetic principles of any given historical movement. Also, postmodernists often mixed together historical references that did not necessarily fit with one another.

Victor Moscoso (b. 1936), who taught at the San Francisco Institute of Arts beginning in 1966, was one of the only psychedelic designers with formal training in the visual arts, having studied at Cooper Union and then at Yale with Josef Albers. In the psychedelic poster scene of the 1960s, formal art training was not necessarily considered something to be proud of, as it contradicted the "underground," anti-establishment vibe that dominated the counterculture. Moscoso combined the exuberant hand-drawn lettering of his psychedelic peers with more sophisticated techniques such as photocollage in order to make images of breathtaking originality. His 1967 *Youngbloods* integrates the lettering into the forms of a pair of dancing, naked hippies, whose gyrations mimic the kinetic force of the abstract patterns that fill out the image (*fig. 9.2*). Note how the words "Avalon Ballroom," which caption the image, seem to be expanding and flowing off

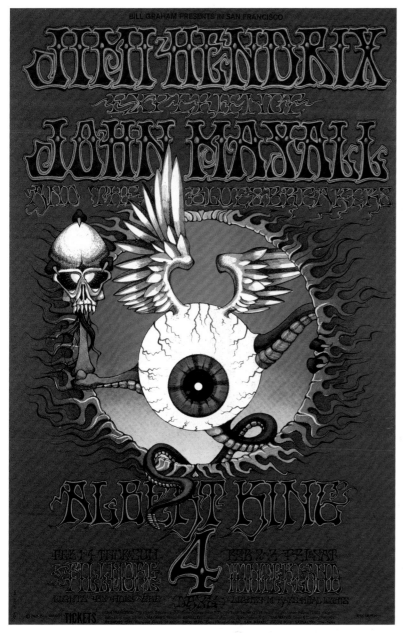

9.3 Richard Griffin, *Flying Eyeball*, 1968.

9.4 Hapshash and the Coloured Coat (Michael English and Nigel Waymouth), *Pink Floyd, "CIA-UFO,"* designed and printed for Osiris Agency Ltd., London, 1967. Poster. Screenprint. © Michael English, V&A Images.

the bottom of the poster, a technique that recalls the visual hallucinations of LSD users. The vivid palette adds to the sense of unreality, giving the image the aura of a spectral vision.

Wilson and Moscoso, along with Alton Kelly, Stanley Mouse (b. 1940), and Richard Griffin, became known as the "Big Five" of psychedelia. In 1967, they founded the Berkeley-Bonaparte agency to market poster art, as they profited from yet another "golden age" of the poster. Griffin's *Flying Eyeball* poster of 1968 remains one of the most famous works produced by Berkeley-Bonaparte (*fig. 9.3*). Publicizing a concert headlined by Jimi Hendrix, it shows a monstrous image of a creature climbing through a flaming hole burned into the poster. The ligatures that connect the lettering make them almost illegible. This type of strange, inventive supernatural imagery would become a mainstay for rock posters and record album covers in the 1960s and 1970s.

British Psychedelics

The psychedelic movement was not confined to San Francisco, as artists adopted the style elsewhere in the United States and in Europe. In the United Kingdom, Michael English (b. 1940) and Nigel Waymouth (b. 1941) pursued psychedelic graphics under the name Hapshash and the Coloured Coat. A central aspect of these designs is that psychedelic posters for rock bands, such as one for the British group Pink Floyd (*fig. 9.4*), sought to express the same sense of drug-induced dreamy reverie that was implicit in the bands' music. This poster combines the fantastical elements typical of the genre, seen in the castle-like structure floating on an island in the sky surrounded by flying saucers, with salacious details such as the nude woman/angel who floats toward the viewer. The curvilinear rhythm of her tendrils of hair suggests

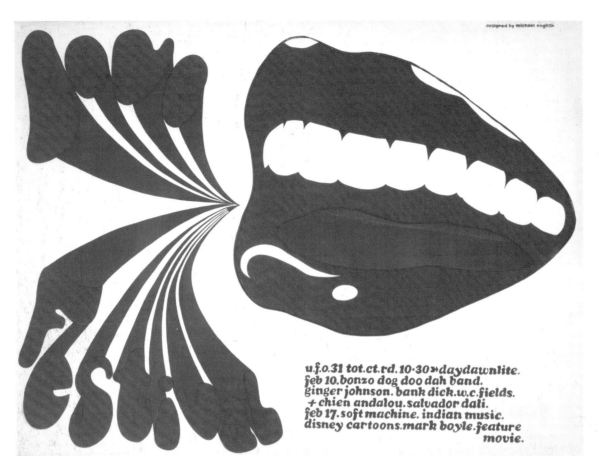

designed by michael english

u.f.o.31 tot.ct.rd.10·30»daydawnlite.
feb 10.bonzo dog doo dah band.
ginger johnson. bank dick.w.c.fields.
+ chien andalou.salvador dali.
feb 17.soft machine. indian music.
disney cartoons.mark boyle.feature
movie.

left: **9.5** Michael English,
Love Festival, 1967.
Poster. Color screenprint.

below: **9.6** Jann Wenner,
Rolling Stone, July 17,
1975. Magazine cover.

opposite: **9.7** Jon
Goodchild and Virginia
Clive-Smith, *Oz*, no. 8,
Jan 1968. Magazine cover.

a knowledge of the Art Nouveau posters produced by Alphonse Mucha (see Chapter 1). In fact, the overall tone of the poster, particularly the ethereal dreamlike quality of the landscape and the nude, harks back to the Symbolist themes of the late nineteenth century. Of course, both Art Nouveau and psychedelic posters mainly served to publicize entertainment aimed at the young and daring—whether they were the denizens of Montmartre's nightclubs or followers of the London counterculture is almost beside the point.

One of the climactic events of the British psychedelic scene was 1967's Love Festival. Michael English created a tantalizing image to publicize the festival, and the poster was destined to become one of the icons of the psychedelic era in Britain (*fig. 9.5*). The dazzling palette combines with letters that seem to stream out of the suggestive red lips, enticing the viewer with its aura of sensuality and chaotic joy.

Magazine and Album Design

Another high-profile publisher of rock graphics beginning in the 1960s was *Rolling Stone* magazine. Founded by Jann Wenner (b. 1946) in San Francisco's warehouse district in 1967, *Rolling Stone* was the first publication to focus on the music industry as a core part of modern culture. Before the magazine started publication, rock music was still viewed as somewhat out of the mainstream and not necessarily worthy of such detailed explications as appeared in the pages of *Rolling Stone*. Wenner was also one of the

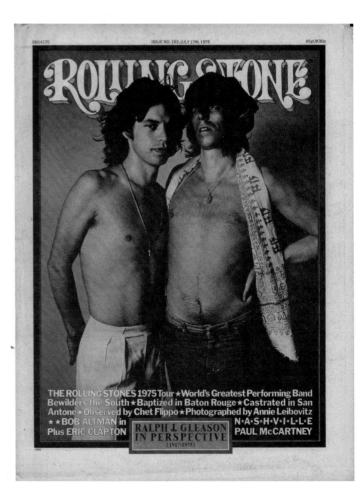

first people to recognize that rock music intersected with broader themes of social and political values, and these subjects were often given significant space in the magazine, which became well known for its investigative reporting on a variety of issues. At the same time, *Rolling Stone* greatly amplified the burgeoning culture of celebrity that surrounded young musicians, and its artful photography had a huge impact in creating the aura of glamour that still surrounds popular musicians, or rock stars, to this day.

The original *Rolling Stone* logo was itself a product of the San Francisco psychedelic music scene, as it was drawn by the poster artist Richard Griffin (1944–1991). The fundamental shapes of Griffin's letters are still used at *Rolling Stone* to this day, although the aggressively illegible letterspacing and elaborate ornamental curlicues were toned down in later years. While the logo is instantly recognizable, the most striking aspect of *Rolling Stone*'s design has always been the photography, which during the 1970s was mainly the work of the famed artist Annie Leibovitz (b. 1949). Leibovitz's captivating images of musicians, such as the July 17, 1975, cover featuring Mick Jagger and Keith Richards of the *Rolling Stone*s (*fig. 9.6*), imbued her subjects with a poise and gravitas that belied their years and reputations. Under art director Tony Lane, the covers had been simplified in the 1970s, with large single photos often bleeding over the logo, so that the entire composition resembled a contemporary rock poster. It was not until 1981 that *Rolling Stone* covers started to appear without the insistent framing device shown here, as the photos were finally reproduced in full-bleed style on glossier paper.

In England, *Oz* magazine, first published in January 1967, featured a wide range of graphic experiments that challenged the notion that clarity must be a designer's primary concern. Edited by Richard Neville (b. 1941) and Martin Sharp (b. 1942), both originally from Australia, where *Oz* had its first incarnation, the magazine featured social and political satire. Not just a lifestyle magazine, *Oz* took unpopular positions characteristic of the counterculture, including opposition to the war then raging in Vietnam. A staunch promoter of anti-establishment values, *Oz* was the most recognized product of the so-called "underground press." While Sharp was responsible for the magazine's overall design, the cover of issue no. 8 (January 1968; *fig. 9.7*) was devised by John Goodchild and Virginia Clive-Smith. The cover is a compendium of mismatched type and image overprinted one upon another. The topless young woman in the background, presumably representative of "*Playboy*'s dirty flics," seems to bear no direct relationship to the war cartoon in the foreground. The cartoon itself was reproduced in brilliant fluorescent inks so that it appears to almost jump right off of the page. This use of fragments of popular culture outside their original context—in this case, a cartoon from a newspaper—is clearly part of the phenomenon that the art critic Lawrence Alloway termed "pop art." Pop artists often used the strategy shown here, reproducing an emotionally charged image from popular culture without commenting on it, allowing viewers to come to their own conclusions. In 1971, the editors of *Oz* were brought up on obscenity charges, and their trial became a *cause célèbre* for proponents of the counterculture

left: **9.8** Peter Blake and Janna Haworth, *Sergeant Pepper's Lonely Hearts Club Band*, 1967. Album cover.

opposite left: **9.9** Seymour Chwast, *The Push Pin Monthly Graphic*, no. 24, 1959. Cover.

opposite right: **9.10** Seymour Chwast, *The Push Pin Monthly Graphic*, no. 24, 1959. Interior.

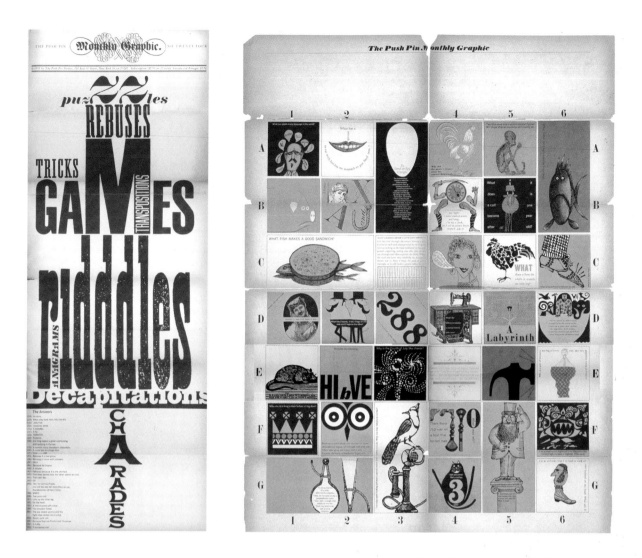

including John Lennon. Accused of "conspiracy to corrupt public morals," the three defendants were eventually acquitted.

The connection between graphic design and rock music also played a significant role in **pop art** graphics, as the artists Peter Blake (b. 1932) and Richard Hamilton (1922–2005) both designed album covers for the Beatles. Blake's cover for the 1967 album *Sergeant Pepper's Lonely Hearts Club Band*, perhaps one of the most famous and influential rock albums ever recorded, shows the band posed in uniforms made up of psychedelic colored fabric (*fig. 9.8*). In an example of the postmodern love of pastiche, the actual members of the band are shown surrounded both by a set of wax figures of themselves borrowed from Madame Tussaud's famous museum and a disparate group of celebrities that includes both Marlene Dietrich and Edgar Allan Poe. The whole ensemble is posed as if in a park, with the band's name spelled out in topiary. At the time he made this design, Blake was a well-known painter in the pop art movement. Once again, pop art ideology sought to erase the distinction between fine and commercial art, so Blake considered his album covers, for example, to be just as significant as his paintings. This battle to collapse the hierarchy between the fine and applied arts had been fought intermittently since the late nineteenth century. Despite the efforts of generations of artists, there is still some semblance of this hierarchical belief in place today, in the twenty-first century.

Early Postmodernism

Push Pin Studio

The music industry was not the only patron of new graphic design styles during the 1960s. A number of independent graphic design firms came to the fore in New York City during this period, some of which sought out alternatives to the International Style. Perhaps the most influential of these firms was Push Pin Studio, originally founded in the mid-1950s by Seymour Chwast (b. 1931), Reynold Ruffins, Edward Sorel (b. 1929), and Milton Glaser (b. 1929). Chwast and Glaser, who provided much of the artistic direction at the firm, channeled their energies into the exploration of a wide variety of visual artifacts. The sheer diversity of their work, which embraced various styles and was imbued with popular culture and the fine arts, marks it as an alternative vision to the rigid principles of the International Style.

One of the main strategies pursued by Glaser and Chwast was to embrace styles that were seen as obsolete, even passé, such as eclectic Victorian typography, and to cause people to look at them in a new light. For example, the cover from *The Push Pin Monthly Graphic* #24 (1959) makes use of old wooden type available from the Morgan Press, a typography outfit that owned a varied collection of what were at the time considered museum pieces (*fig. 9.9*).

9.11 Seymour Chwast, *The Push Pin Monthly Graphic*, no. 54, 1959. Interior.

The oddly shaped letters that clash up and down this cover, including everything from shadow letters to strangely proportioned grotesques, seemingly violate every rule of modern typography while indirectly recalling the zany absurdity of many Dada publications. *The Push Pin Monthly Graphic* was not a true journal, but rather a trade publication that the firm used in order to drum up business and as a space where they could explore new styles. Its content was as idiosyncratic as its graphic design, and rarely commented directly on the field in the manner of most other publications of this type. Even the name was rather off kilter, as the *Monthly Graphic* appeared on an irregular schedule, never monthly, and was eventually renamed simply *Push Pin Graphic*. However, this type of work does not equal a Victorian revival, as the artists and Push Pin never made any sort of determined commitment to one artistic period or another; rather, they simply chose to work with whatever caught their eye at the time.

On the inside pages of *Monthly Graphic* issue #24, an almost random sampling of new illustrations, clip art, and lettering are arrayed in a boxed grid (*fig. 9.10*). This particular design seems almost like a parody of the International Style grid, as it fills the spaces with quirky images that scarcely relate to one another. Whimsically applied color adds to the cheery absurdity of the whole ensemble. This image is a good example of another aspect of the work created by artists at the Push Pin Studio, its humor. At a time when the International Style represented the utmost in seriousness, designers such as Chwast reveled in silly visual puns and caricatured drawings.

In 1967, Chwast published issue #54 of the *Monthly Graphic*, which used the same sort of surreal combinations that the studio was later known for in its commercial work, but this time in the service of a political statement (*fig. 9.11*). Using both text and image, Chwast sought to point out the endemic racism of the United States by juxtaposing images of victims of white racial

violence, such as Emmit Till, a fifteen-year-old who had been murdered in Mississippi in 1955, with idealized images of the American South drawn from everyday culture. Chwast overlaid black and white photos that carried the weight of objective reality, on brightly colored reproductions that showed a view of the region favored by white Southerners. Likewise, he juxtaposed factual texts relating the details of racial murders with snippets of songs and poems praising the beauty of the Southern landscape and people. While the *Monthly Graphic* was not a mainstream publication and issue #54 appeared and disappeared without sparking much comment, Chwast's use of his skills as a graphic designer to make a political statement anticipates another trend in postmodernism, the employment of graphic design and the mass media as a tool of social protest (see below).

It was not only the raw material that influenced their work that seemed unfashionable, because the members of Push Pin also favored illustration as the basis for everything from record covers to corporate identity programs. At a time when unmanipulated drawings looked hopelessly out of date, Push Pin artists devised a number of refreshing individual styles that soon gained in popularity. For example, Glaser's 1966 poster of the young Bob Dylan

9.12 Milton Glaser, *Bob Dylan*, 1966. Poster. Museum für Gestaltung, Zurich. Poster Collection.

9.13 Milton Glaser, *Valentine Olivetti*, 1968. Poster.

9.14 Milton Glaser, *I "Love" NY*, 1975.

9.15 Paula Scher and Roger Huyssen, *Boston*, 1985. Airbrush album cover.

is truly no more than an inventive drawing (*fig. 9.12*), able to capture the essence of how people felt about Dylan and his music. In typical Push Pin fashion, Glaser had based the image on two disparate sources, a classical Persian miniature painting and a twentieth-century collaged self-portrait by the French Dadaist Marcel Duchamp (1887–1968). The artist later noted how poignant it was that this drawing, with its exotic pedigree, came to be viewed as an example of a quintessentially American style of graphic design.

The Dylan poster, which became an icon of the rock scene in the 1960s, eventually sold over 6 million copies. The poster revival of the 1960s and 1970s was predicated on a new use for these images that was pioneered by young people—as decorations on the walls of bedrooms across the country. Before this era, posters had never made it inside people's homes on a large scale, but it soon became common for walls to be plastered with posters celebrating stars from television and the rock industry.

An image for the Olivetti Corporation is a wonderful example of the Push Pin style applied to advertising (*fig. 9.13*). Glaser created this pastiche of Italian Renaissance painting, stencil lettering, and a dog—the latter an icon of American culture—in order to advertise a shiny new red typewriter. It is this type of illustration, capriciously devoid of any recognizable internal logic, that brought the fanciful vision of Push Pin into the mainstream. The faithful dog, rendered in three dimensions, guards the typewriter, while a flat pattern background contests the illusion of space. Right above the typewriter, itself an Italian product, there is a winding river that is a cliché of classical Italian painting. It is important to note that this poster suggests a narrative, something that did not play a part in the International Style. While the "story" is ambiguous, the surreal combination of dog, typewriter, and sandaled feet suggests that something is going on, as opposed to the anti-narrative strategy that characterized contemporaneous

abstract works. This sort of graphic design privileges the vision of the individual who created it—in this case, Glaser—who seemed not to work with any systematic principles but only according to the dictates of his skill and imagination. Since Glaser liked Italian classicism and stencil lettering, he found a way to bring them together.

In 1975, Glaser created one of the most familiar American logos of the twentieth century, the *I 'love' NY* **rebus** (*fig. 9.14*). A rebus is made by combining pictures of objects that viewers interpret as sounds or words—such as the red heart—thus adding an element of whimsy to an otherwise unspectacular phrase. Designed for free by Glaser at the behest of the New York Commerce Commission, the rebus formed part of a publicity campaign that was needed to shore up New York City's reputation as a tourist destination at a time when many people associated the city with violent crime and urban decay. The situation in the city was summed up best by a now notorious newspaper headline of a story about President Gerald Ford's refusal to offer more federal assistance, "Ford to City: Drop Dead." Although Glaser had left Push Pin to establish his own firm in the early 1970s, the studio's light-hearted, quirky spirit and embrace of illustration underlay his rebus.

With the new logo, the Commerce Commission accomplished something that had never before been achieved in the history of modern cities; it had used graphic design to "rebrand" New York's image. Reproduced tens of millions of times on every available surface, from coffee mugs to billboards, the rebus, which had come to Glaser while he was riding in a taxicab, inspired a flood of like-minded designs over the next decade, including Paul Rand's new take on his original IBM logo. The success of the city's campaign also led to many similar attempts by city and state governments to establish identity programs, hoping to mold people's perceptions of their own metropolises.

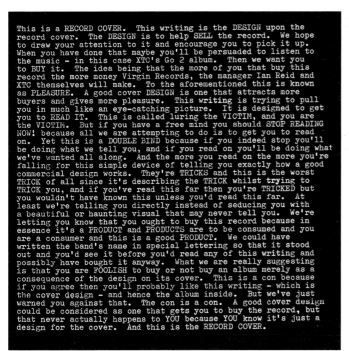

This is a RECORD COVER. This writing is the DESIGN upon the
record cover. The DESIGN is to help SELL the record. We hope
to draw your attention to it and encourage you to pick it up.
When you have done that maybe you'll be persuaded to listen to
the music - in this case XTC's Go 2 album. Then we want you
to BUY it. The idea being that the more of you that buy this
record the more money Virgin Records, the manager Ian Reid and
XTC themselves will make. To the aforementioned this is known
as PLEASURE. A good cover DESIGN is one that attracts more
buyers and gives more pleasure. This writing is trying to pull
you in much like an eye-catching picture. It is designed to get
you to READ IT. This is called luring the VICTIM, and you are
the VICTIM. But if you have a free mind you should STOP READING
NOW! because all we are attempting to do is to get you to read
on. Yet this is a DOUBLE BIND because if you indeed stop you'll
be doing what we tell you, and if you read on you'll be doing what
we've wanted all along. And the more you read on the more you're
falling for this simple device of telling you exactly how a good
commercial design works. They're TRICKS and this is the worst
TRICK of all since it's describing the TRICK whilst trying to
TRICK you, and if you've read this far then you're TRICKED but
you wouldn't have known this unless you'd read this far. At
least we're telling you directly instead of seducing you with
a beautiful or haunting visual that may never tell you. We're
letting you know that you ought to buy this record because in
essence it's a PRODUCT and PRODUCTS are to be consumed and you
are a consumer and this is a good PRODUCT. We could have
written the band's name in special lettering so that it stood
out and you'd see it before you'd read any of this writing and
possibly have bought it anyway. What we are really suggesting
is that you are FOOLISH to buy or not buy an album merely as a
consequence of the design on its cover. This is a con because
if you agree then you'll probably like this writing - which is
the cover design - and hence the album inside. But we've just
warned you against that. The con is a con. A good cover design
could be considered as one that gets you to buy the record, but
that never actually happens to YOU because YOU know it's just a
design for the cover. And this is the RECORD COVER.

9.16 Hipgnosis, *Go 2* by XTC, 1978. Album cover. Virgin.

9.17 Paula Scher, *Sakura: Japanese Melodies for Flute and Harp*, 1978.
Album cover.

In the late 1970s, Chwast was hired by *Forbes* magazine to
design a series of print ads. It is somehow disconcerting to see a
drawing style that had been associated with progressive politics
and an anti-authoritarian, countercultural outlook matched with
the bold lettering that spells out, "Forbes, Capitalist Tool." The
Forbes illustrations show how the Push Pin style, like many other
edgy, alternative graphic visions, gradually became more acceptable in the mainstream. However, this was about the closest that
the Push Pin style came to success with mainstream advertisers, as
the majority of its work had been executed for small-scale businesses and progressive organizations. As Glaser later stated, "You
can take intellectual risks on book jackets."

Album, Poster, and Magazine Design

Another designer associated with the Push Pin Studio, Paula
Scher (b. 1948), enjoyed a stellar run between 1974 and 1982
as an art director for CBS records. During this era, record album
covers helped drive sales in many instances, and were considered
absolutely paramount to the success of a given project. Paralleling
the new poster craze that started in the 1960s, music fans
collected certain albums because of their highly regarded covers.
The bands themselves were often involved in selecting designs,
as the imagery on the album cover served as a sort of mini-poster
that "branded" the musical group. The band's input was often
unwelcome, however, as the players' design ideas were often
puerile at best.

One cover overseen by Scher, which was for the inaugural
album by the band Boston, was destined to become one of the
most recognizable images of the 1970s (*fig. 9.15*). The illustration
by airbrush artist Roger Huyssen (1946–) shows the Earth
exploding in a fiery ball while a fleet of guitar-shaped spaceships

flees the catastrophe. The lead ship in the foreground sports the
vaguely psychedelic "Boston" logo that had been designed by
Gerard Huerta (b. 1952), while smaller ships featured the names
of other, apparently lesser, cities such as Paris and Rome. The
science fiction fantasy element of the illustration was to become
a mainstay of 1970s' graphics, suggestive of rock music's ability
to transport the listener into another world far from workaday
reality. At the same time, this cover resonates with the rich color
and kinetic froth of the pulp fiction covers of the 1940s (see
Chapter 7). *Boston* became one of the most successful albums
of the 1970s, selling over 6 million copies, despite the fact that
many critics consider neither the cover nor the music to be
particularly good. Scher later joked that she is "absolutely
horrified" at the thought that her epitaph will read "art director
of the original Boston album."

The small British firm Hipgnosis, founded by Aubrey Powell
(b. 1946) and Storm Thorgerson (b. 1944) in 1968, also produced
a number of striking album covers during the 1970s. Their 1978
design of the album *Go 2* for the band XTC stunningly rejected
the dependence on dramatic images that was *de rigueur* in the
music industry (*fig. 9.16*). In their place, the cover consisted only
of a ranged left block of white type on a black background; for
this reason, the lettering is being used as a graphic as well as a textual element. The declarative nature of the text, which states
"The DESIGN is to help SELL the record," partakes of the "New
Advertising" technique of engaging the reader with ironic humor
aimed at the act of marketing itself. Another clever satirical element is the use of all capitalized letters sporadically throughout
the text in order to emphasize the obvious: "This is a RECORD
COVER." The reliance on text in the *Go 2* cover also had a strong
parallel in the art scene of that period, in this case the "conceptual
art" movement, which had emerged and developed in the late
1960s and early 1970s.

Conceptual art, in which the idea for the work is more important than the object itself—and there might not even be an object itself—often was text-based, and it led to a great deal of artistic work that explored the potential of language to be used in the aesthetic realm. A number of high-profile conceptual works in fact consisted solely of letters on a blank background, like the record cover by Hipgnosis.

In 1978, Scher designed the cover for an album of Japanese music performed by the flautist Jean-Pierre Rampal (1922–2000; *fig. 9.17*). In a maneuver typical of postmodern artists, Scher collaged together a few passages from some copies of *Ukiyo-e* prints (see Chapter 1) in order to create a new composition. The resulting work is exemplary of the trend by which graphic artists appropriated at will, without following a specific set of principles. The typography on the cover is on the one hand reminiscent of vertically composed Japanese text, while on the other hand it looks like the signage of American commercial streets, with its shadowed capitals enclosed in ruled boxes. "Vernacular art" refers to that part of visual culture that is commonplace and taken for granted, the sort of everyday graphics that people view many times a day without giving the matter any thought. Most of the graphic design discussed in this book is not vernacular, but rather the product of highly trained artists, for whom elements of style are at the center of their work. The reassessment of vernacular sources by postmodernists was influenced by the work of Andy Warhol (1928–1987), an artist who found great fame starting in the 1960s as a leader of the pop art movement. Trained as a commercial illustrator, Warhol asserted that vernacular, "popular" culture—hence the term "pop art"—was a legitimate basis for fine art. This trend, in turn, helped to spur on commercial artists to reassess their own view of vernacular sources.

Postmodern graphic designers such as Scher began looking outside the fine arts for their design sources, and opened up the field to include everyday objects such as cheap commercial signs that had previously been scorned by practicing artists and designers. The back of the Rampal album is unusual in that its design relied solely on typography, at a time when record covers tended to be image saturated on both sides. On the back, a variety of disparate shaped and brightly colored boxes seem to hang from the top margin of the cover, with each frame enclosing a different type of informative text. The funky mix of historical and vernacular American references that Scher used in this cover is emblematic of the open-ended design strategies originally devised at the Push Pin Studios.

Richard Hollis is an influential English graphic designer who explored his own eclectic vision in a manner similar to that of the Push Pin Studio artists. In his work for the Whitechapel Art Gallery between 1970 and 1983, Hollis devised a wide range of posters, catalogs and other graphic ephemera to publicize a variety of modern art exhibitions. The flyer-cum-poster shown here displays many elements typical of the International Style: for example, an orthogonal structure—here reinforced by the folds in the paper—hierarchy of typesize, and overall good legibility (*fig. 9.18*). However, the word "open" at the lower left appears to be falling out of its assigned line of text, and the blocky letters all feature contours that waver ever so slightly, making them appear somewhat organic and irregular. Additionally, Hollis made use of the sequential opening of the folded paper—a friend of his christened these works "unfolders"—so that intriguing fragments of text gradually led to a final, complete poster. A notably postmodern aspect of Hollis's work from this era is its adaptability, the way in which he was willing to pursue unconventional, even idiosyncratic, combinations of type, layout, and color that fit his concept of each individual project.

In the postmodern age, it is not unusual for images to contain inside jokes that only aficionados of graphic design would under-

9.18 Richard Hollis, *Whitechapel*, 1970. Whitechapel Open Exhibition, 1980. Two-color poster.

9.19 Paula Scher, *Swatch*, 1985. Poster. Museum für Gestaltung, Zurich. Poster Collection.

9.20 Herbert Matter, *Pontresina Engadin*, 1935. Gravure, 41 x 25 1/8 in (104.1 x 63.7 cm).

stand. For example, Scher's 1985 magazine advertisement for the Swatch company (*fig. 9.19*) was devised as an almost exact recreation of a famous travel poster of 1935 by the Swiss designer Herbert Matter (*fig. 9.20*). After working with Le Corbusier and Cassandre in France in the early 1930s, Matter had immigrated to the United States in 1936. He had quickly become an influential force in American graphic design, and served as a professor in Yale University's program beginning in 1952. Matter's poster demonstrates the Constructivist "typophoto" technique of positioning a photo of a person floating at the top of the image and looking into the distance. While experienced graphic designers undoubtedly recognized the playful irony of Scher's **appropriation** of the Swiss poster, the average reader of *Mademoiselle* magazine, where it briefly appeared, would be unlikely to be aware of the image's antecedents. For the lay person, the ad works almost conversely, as they view it as a startling "original" and "novel" image. Scher was later publicly criticized for taking the image out of context and parodying it, as some designers saw this type of close-copying of an original as close to constituting plagiarism—it is quite possible that Scher's critics simply lack a sense of humor.

Postmodern Typography

In the 1960s and 1970s, a number of new typefaces were designed as alternatives to the popular Helvetica and the conventional seriffed typefaces then in wide use. In 1967, Herb Lubalin (1918–1981) was asked by Ralph Ginzburg (b. 1936) to design the logo for his new magazine *Avant Garde*. Ginzburg wanted an updated sans serif that would express a knowledge of the modern tradition without slavishly imitating the typefaces of the past. The resulting logo featured evenly weighted capital letters, with an innovative flair created by the sharply angled stems of the "A" and the "V." Some of the letters, such as the "G," are reminiscent of the Purist geometric sans serifs of the 1920s, while the "R" is quite conventional and legible. The popular acclaim accorded this magazine heading led Lubalin to devise a full typeface in three weights out of his original logo, which was released by Lubalin Burns, and later expanded in a subsequent release by the International Typeface Corporation (ITC) that Lubalin had founded with Aaron Burns (1922–1991). Called **Avant-Garde Gothic** (*fig. 9.21*), this face was fabulously popular during the

ABCDFGHIJKLMNOP QRSTUVWXYZabcdef ghijklmnopqrstuvwxyz 1234567890?!*&%

"Called Avant Garde Gothic, this face was fabulously popular during the 1970s, when it appeared on every imaginable sort of publication."

9.21 Herb Lubalin, Avant-Garde Gothic, 1967.

ABCDFGHIJKLMNOP QRSTUVWXYZabcdefg hijklmnopqrstuvwxyz 1234567890?!*&

"Like many typefaces from this era, the letters of Souvenir were designed to be tightly spaced, forming a clump of text [...]"

9.22 Ed Benguiat, Souvenir Typeface, 1970.

1970s, when it increasingly appeared on every imaginable sort of publication.

ITC was to become one of the first type publishing companies, one that licensed typefaces to publishers without taking part in the printing process itself. The company in effect acted as a middleman between typographers and phototypesetting firms, a business model that has come to dominate the industry in the digital era. Another ubiquitous typeface of the 1970s released by ITC was **Souvenir**, designed by Ed Benguiat (b. 1927) in 1970 (*fig. 9.22*). The soft, fluid shapes of Souvenir, as well as its rounded corners, can be seen as a rejection of the straight lines and sharp corners of Helvetica and other typefaces favored by practitioners of the International Style. Like many typefaces from this era, the letters of Souvenir were designed to be tightly spaced, forming a clump of text, a factor that helps distinguish 1970s fashion from the more widely spaced designs of the 1980s.

Robert Venturi and *Learning from Las Vegas*

There are a number of important parallels between early postmodern graphic design and postmodern architecture. Two of the most obvious issues that united the fields were their embrace of both historicist and vernacular sources, strategies that completely went against the prescriptions of the International Style. Just as artists such as Glaser and Scher made use of a bewildering array of seemingly unrelated sources and included vernacular passages such as the dog in Glaser's Olivetti advertisement or the signage on Scher's Rampal cover, architects began looking at ways in which they could mix historical styles and also use commonplace "not-designed" architectural works in their practice. One of the most high profile proponents of architectural postmodernism, Robert Venturi (b. 1925), demonstrated the virtues of these two strategies in both his works and his published writings.

The house that Venturi built in 1962 for his mother is a wonderful example of how the first idea, the mixing of styles, could be explored in architecture (*fig. 9.23*). The house combines Renaissance, Baroque, and modern stylistic elements into a new formal vocabulary, so that these disparate styles flow together seamlessly. The conventional view would be that each of these styles has its own internal logic and set of principles so that it would be impossible, and even irresponsible, to mix them together. In addition, modern architects considered the erasure of historical references to be a fundamental precept of their art, so that Venturi's combination of modern ribbon windows with a Baroque pediment essentially subverts the whole basis of the International Style.

The influential book *Learning from Las Vegas*, which Venturi co-published with Denise Scott Brown (b. 1931) and Steven Izenour (b. 1940) in 1972, made the case that architects should pay attention to the ordinary buildings—the vernacular architecture—that surrounded them in everyday life. Venturi called attention to the less than celebrated gas stations and fast food restaurants of Las Vegas, a city that for many was symbolic of all that was plain and vulgar in American culture. He did not advocate the idea that architects should build crummy, unattractive structures, but suggested that they should be able to learn from the way in which vernacular architecture solved certain aesthetic or functional problems on its own terms. This argument essentially collapses the distinction between "fine art" architecture and the vernacular variety, asserting that the two forms are equally valid as visual references in the contemporary age. This is a more dramatic development than the nineteenth-century attempt to merge the fine and applied arts, because Venturi is arguing that artists can look for sources outside the art world altogether. As was the case with graphic design, this idea resulted in postmodern architecture being much more eclectic and open-ended in outlook than its predecessor, the "modern" International Style.

9.23 Robert Venturi, *Vanna Venturi House*, 1964. Photograph. Courtesy Rollin La France

Mature Postmodernism

Wolfgang Weingart

The "official" postmodern movement, in the sense of professional graphic designers who self-consciously rejected the International Style, arose in Basel, Switzerland, during the early 1970s, among a group of students and their inspirational teacher Wolfgang Weingart (b. 1941). Weingart had been born and raised in Germany, where he received no academic training in the design arts, but found work as a hot metal typesetter for a number of years. As a typesetter, Weingart came to the practice of graphic design from the production side of things, a background that influenced his work in a number of ways. In 1968 Weingart moved to Basel, where he accepted a position at the same *Kunstgewerbeschule* where Armin Hofmann taught. Chapter 8 noted that the circle of designers around Hofmann were much less doctrinaire than their colleagues in Zurich in terms of their application of the principles of the Swiss style. This stylistic open-mindedness proved to be an important influence on Weingart, who was one of the first designers to abandon the strict aesthetic principles that had governed Swiss design for decades. It is likely that the fact that Weingart was self-taught allowed him to break free of academic dogma more decisively than graphic designers who had been "indoctrinated" in the precepts of the International Style.

Looking back on his teaching in 1985, Weingart stated:

I try to teach students to view typography from all angles: type must not always be set flush left/ragged right, nor in only two type sizes, nor in necessarily right-angle arrangements, nor printed in either black or red. Typography must not be dry, tightly ordered or rigid. Type may be set center axis, ragged left/ragged right, perhaps sometimes in chaos.

While his rejection of the International Style is obvious, it is important to remember that Weingart's work is still largely informed by the style, in that he is deliberately situating his work against that of the Swiss designers who still revered the grid. Also, Weingart felt that it was important that any design feature a strong structure and logical composition, a point of view that is clearly derived from his experience with the International Style. In this manner, Weingart could be viewed as someone who did not make a definitive break with the style, but rather pushed its aesthetic limits in such a way that it forms a natural progression, continuous with the Hofmann circle's earlier, somewhat experimental works. If one accepts this interpretation, then Weingart's work could perhaps better be called "late modern," rather than "postmodern." However, as most scholars feel that the break Weingart made with the Swiss style created a significant rupture, the latter term is generally preferred. It is important to remember that postmodern design is an eclectic and diverse phenomenon that shows considerable range in how closely it approaches, or how far it strays from, the International Style. Of course, the International Style itself did not end with the onset of postmodernism, and it is still a vital part of contemporary graphic design.

A poster for a calligraphy exhibition at the Basel Kunstgewerbeschule shows many of the basic elements of Weingart's work (*fig. 9.24*). While there is an obvious underlying grid to the design, it is being buffeted by a variety of forces. To start with, the rectangular frame itself seems to be overlaid on another rectangle that peers out from around the edges. This outer band has a syncopated placement of triangles and stripes that create a kinetic element. Some of the stripes seem to cross under the main image, even under some of the lettering, while others are blocked as if the middle of the poster is opaque. While all of the elements of the International Style are there, including grids, sans serif lettering, and geometric shapes, the overall composition has become unhinged, allowing different disparate forms seemingly to move around the poster at will.

Technology had an obvious effect on Weingart's graphic designs, as new techniques allowed for a greater stylistic variety; in this case, the introduction of transparent films in the 1970s allowed him to experiment with overlapping forms and collage in a fundamentally new way. In this poster, there are a variety of jagged geometric shapes that lay claim to different parts of the composition, complicating the viewer's task of decoding what it conveys. Furthermore, the sans serif type consists of multiple sizes, while there is a striking range in both the letterspacing and the gaps between entire words. The black letters that spell out "Kunstgewerbe" feature two different types of white marks running off the letters and unbalancing their forms. And the word "Schreibkunst" has to contend with a number of distractions: everything from a lightning bolt to a series of underlying shapes of different color. Two lines down, the word "in" is much smaller than it should be according to the conventions of the International Style, and, of course, Weingart uses more than just one or two sizes of type. Somewhat confusingly, Weingart's work has at times been called the "new typography," a reference to the revolutionary nature of his attacks on the sanctity of the International Style.

Another poster by Weingart, one publicizing a 1984 exhibition of Swiss posters at the Gewerbemuseum (*fig. 9.25*), shares a number of stylistic devices with the first poster. For example, there is the same sense of overlapping planes that shift between being transparent and being opaque. In both works, Weingart has enlarged the dots from a halftone screen so that they are readily visible, and in *Das Schweizer Plakat* the field of dots cuts into the lettering in an unpredictable fashion, in one case forming the simple cross that is a Swiss emblem. This poster has a hazy red background, where clouds seem to be forming irregular shapes that contest the rigid structure of the grid. It is helpful to compare these two posters because the consistent stylistic elements exemplify how most postmodern work, such as Weingart's, despite its apparent rejection of dogmatic aesthetic principles, is not some sort of free-for-all. While it is true that the 1960s experienced a resurgence of interest in Dadaist artistic ideas, such as random chance and the celebration of the irrational, Weingart's work is restrained in its employment of Dada chaos. Rather, he and other postmodernists operated according to highly developed principles that they apply consistently to all manner of work. Despite all the innovations that increase the two images' overall dynamism, it is hard to see these posters as displaying "chaos," because in

9.24 Wolfgang Weingart, *Schreibkunst*, 1984. Museum für Gestaltung, Zürich. Poster Collection.

9.25 Wolfgang Weingart, *Das Schweizer Plakat (The Swiss Poster)*, 1984. Offset lithograph, 47 x 33⅛ in (120 x 84.3 cm).

a holistic sense they still manifest a sense of control akin to that expressed by works in the International Style. Clearly, Weingart is open to the idea of using "intuition" as well as analytic skills to create a composition, an individualistic, unpredictable strategy that was anathema to practitioners of the Swiss style.

Dan Friedman and April Greiman

During his tenure at Basel, a number of American students traveled to Switzerland in order to study with Weingart, which created intense interest in his work among American designers. Weingart's open-mindedness, more than any specific stylistic gambit of his, had a large impact on designers such as Dan Friedman (1945–1995), who was trying to create a new individual style. Friedman was a student in the inaugural year of the postgraduate program at Basel that was held in 1968, Weingart's first year as an instructor. After he returned to the United States in 1969, he taught at a number of places, including Yale and the Philadelphia College of Art (PCA). At PCA in 1971, he met April Greiman (b. 1948), who had just returned from a year in Switzerland studying with Weingart. Together they popularized the Swiss designer's approach in the United States, with Friedman helping to plan a lecture tour for Weingart in America.

Despite the manner in which Friedman's and Weingart's names are often linked in critical studies of graphic design, Friedman stated that he never adopted Weingart's intuitive approach, but rather was enchanted by the theoretical sophistication of the other professors and his fellow students in Basel. During the 1970s, Friedman influentially rejected the absolutism of "legibility" as the core criterion for judging graphic design, replacing it with the more open-ended term "readability," which in his mind allowed for a more multivalent creative process. He also remained more open to the International Style, as he felt that it was never such an overwhelming part of American design so there was no need to reject it in its totality. Friedman, who called himself a "radical modernist," sought to recover the progressive attitude that had marked the birth of the modern movement in the 1910s and 1920s.

In 1975, Friedman became a designer of corporate identity, creating a visual program that included a new trademark for Citibank. In a way, by using two contradictory modes, the International Style and the postmodern style, he exemplified the postmodern embrace of eclecticism, not making a firm ideological commitment to any one style. Along these lines, his heterogeneous approach, including continued employment of the modern style, is in some ways Friedman's most postmodern act as a graphic designer. The postmodern spirit is supposed to reject dogmatic rules in favor of a "pluralistic" approach, meaning that there are many different, even contradictory, approaches available to the designer, and no one style is favored over another.

In 1973, Friedman collaborated with Greiman on a silkscreen poster publicizing a concert at Yale University (*fig. 9.26*). This poster displays a number of postmodern elements, including the quirky mix of lettering in a wide variety of weights and sizes, whimsical overprinting that distracts the viewer from the core of the design, and multiple axes that create a kinetic effect. Note the

9.26 Dan Friedman and April Greiman, Yale Symphony Orchestra Concert, 1973. Poster. Lithograph.

way in which the red accents on "Janacek," normally minor diacritical elements, jump out at the viewer. In compositions such as this, Friedman and Greiman, like Weingart and other postmodernists, maintained an allegiance to the International Style concept that graphic design involves finding abstract solutions to design "problems."

In 1976, Greiman opened her own design firm in Los Angeles. Once established, she began to experiment with "hybrid imagery," a term referring to the synthesis of digital technology with traditional hand-drawn practices. Greiman wanted to produce work that clearly advertised its technological sophistication—graphics that were not just made with a computer but had a "digital aesthetic" analogous to the machine aesthetic of the 1920s (see Chapter 4). For example, a five-color offset lithograph from 1985 publicizing a poster show at the Museum of Modern Art in New York (*fig. 9.27*) features several strikingly futuristic passages created through the manipulation of imported video. Although some aspects of this poster show the residual influence of Weingart—overlapping planes with various levels of transparency, visible halftone dots, jagged geometric forms, and a deconstructed grid—the powerful three-dimensional illusion created by the overlaid drawing of a vortex, the digital layering, and the steeply foreshortened polychrome grids demonstrate how Greiman had successfully developed her own personal digital style. The bright color and kinetic energy of designs such as this were sometimes referred to as part of the "New Wave" movement. In the context of graphic design history, "new wave" was used both as a synonym for "postmodern" and as a reference to a specific sort of softer, commercialized punk culture popular in the 1970s. This latter usage aligned graphics with broader cultural phenomena that included music, fashion, and interior design.

Early Desktop Publishing

Greiman was one of the first graphic designers to make use of the new powerful tools that would eventually transform the profession completely. In 1984, she bought a Macintosh personal computer and immediately set out to explore its potential to facilitate her creative work. Like many artists in the 1980s, Greiman saw the computer in a utopian light, believing that it would lead to an age of expanded creativity that would permeate human consciousness. Along these lines, she did not view the computer as simply a functional tool with which to execute a preconceived idea, but as something that had led her to experiment in a way that opened up new avenues of serendipitous design. A superb example of one of her first-generation digital experiments is the composition she created for *Design Quarterly* in 1986, in which she deconstructed the thirty-two-page magazine into one horizontal poster (*fig. 9.28*). Created with a Macvision image digitizer and Macpaint, the 2 by 6 foot poster combines a self-portrait with a timeline showing a history of technology that ends in the invention of the Macintosh computer. On the one hand, this poster seems to trace facts in a straightforward manner: nothing could be more objective than a timeline. However, the dense collage of photographs and drawings that overlays the self-

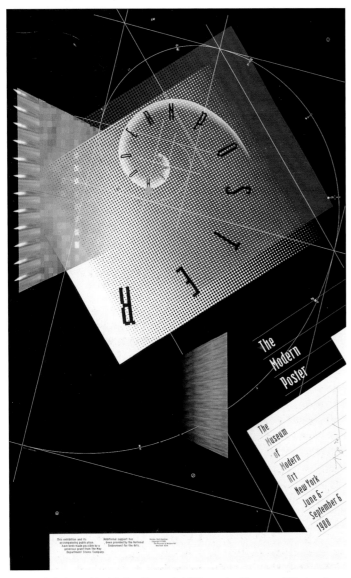

9.27 April Greiman, *The Modern Poster*, Exhibition at the Museum of Modern Art, New York, 1988. Poster. Color offset lithograph.

portrait, the visible pixels, reverse printing, as well as the subtle dislocations that occur—with part of the center of her body detached from the surrounding form, for example—all combine to create a self-consciously chaotic impact. The image deliberately looks like it contains "mistakes" in its composition, lending it an energy that is often lacking in the products of the International Style. As in many postmodern designs, clarity and legibility have been sacrificed in order to enhance the expressive aspects of the work; "less is more" has been abandoned in favor of a celebration of sensual excess. Another impact of the desktop computer was the way in which it lowered the overhead for designers who were just starting out, allowing them to establish small businesses that could produce professional results without needing large professional staffs.

Eventually, the products of three corporations—Apple Computer, Adobe, and Aldus—came together in the mid-1980s in such a way that they established a totally new system for graphic designers and typographers. By combining the Apple Macintosh's "what you see is what you get" format, commonly referred to by the acronym WYSIWYG, and its new laser printer with Adobe's Postscript printer language and Aldus's PageMaker software, any designer could produce camera-ready, typeset-quality work without having to leave their studio or employ a typesetting firm. While crude by today's standards, PageMaker was the first program that allowed graphic designers effectively to reproduce on the computer what they had formerly drawn by hand; desktop publishing, a term coined by Aldus founder Paul Brainerd (b. 1947), quickly became a reality.

Cranbrook Academy of Art

Weingart also had a significant impact on the work of students at the Cranbrook Academy of Art in Michigan, one of the first schools to embrace the postmodern movement wholeheartedly. Even to this day, many graphic design programs in American universities feature curricula that are more focused on the International Style and its aura of professionalism than on the more progressive, eclectic postmodern work of the last three decades. However, Katherine McCoy (b. 1945), co-chair of the graphic design program at Cranbrook, had a more daring outlook than most academics, and invited her students to explore new trends. Weingart lectured often at Cranbrook during the 1970s. It is essential to note how the modern International Style can be distinguished from the postmodern style by the amount of expression permitted on the artist's part. Staunch modernists usually suppress any quirky or whimsical element in their designs, while postmodernists welcome idiosyncratic displays of personal style like those present in the work of Cranbrook designers such as Edward Fella (b. 1938).

At Cranbrook, McCoy espoused the idea that the reading of text and the viewing of image should not be conceived of as discrete practices. Rather, reading and viewing overlap and interact synergistically in order to create a holistic effect that features both modes of interpretation. McCoy called this theory "typography as discourse," the term "discourse" connoting the idea that the meaning of a work is part of a conversation between text and image that "runs around," and cannot be fixed to form one stable result. A poster from 1989 publicizing a lecture on the topic of "typography as discourse" illustrates the impact of these theories on the Cranbrook style (*fig. 9.29*). Designed by Allen Hori (b. 1960), this splendidly cluttered image has a number of clear references to Weingart's work, including the reversed text and playful abstract composition that simultaneously creates and deconstructs a grid. However, compared with Weingart's *Das Schweizer Plakat*, Hori's design is much more focused on using letters as a visual element than as text, so that many of the abstract shapes that make up the image are crafted from letters. And Hori's choices have an impact on the legibility of the poster; while the meaning of Weingart's design can be immediately identified, the Cranbrook image forces the viewer to hunt for the necessary

The Postmodern Book and Richard Eckersley

Most of the earliest experiments in postmodern design involved ephemeral, consumable media such as posters and magazines. Because of prevailing conventions and the desire of book publishers not to endanger their often substantial investments in new texts, their book designers were slower to adopt the postmodern strategies of illegibility, pastiche, and deconstruction. However, in the 1980s a small cadre of pioneering book designers collaborated with authors and publishers to create new ways of presenting text.

One of the most influential book designers of this era, Richard Eckersley (1941–2006) was born in England but emigrated to the United States in 1981 when he took up a position as senior designer at the University of Nebraska Press. At Nebraska, Eckersley gradually began to experiment with what was perhaps the most conventional graphic product, the academic book. Beginning in 1986 with his design for a translated edition of Jacques Derrida's Glas, *Eckersley subverted the staid format used at Nebraska in an attempt to bring new life to the genre; he used mainly typographic means, including a mixture of type sizes, the insertion of startling breaks within sentences and between paragraphs, negative line spacing that caused overlap, and the creation of pictures out of text—as in Apollinaire's* Calligrammes *(see figs. 4.3 and 4.4).*

Eckersley's typographic decisions were probably influenced by the content of the academic texts he was designing, as most of them dealt with topics drawn from advanced literary theory and he himself was an avid reader. There is in fact a parallel between the deconstructive arguments of the authors, who were dedicated to a radical revision and even dismantling of the traditional humanities, and the dislocations that defined Eckersley's designs. For example, in his most famous work, the 1989 design of Avital Ronell's Telephone Book: Technology, Schizophrenia, Electric Speech—*a book that delved deeply into deconstructive theory—Eckersley devised dramatic "rivers," sinuous white spaces that meander down the page, brilliantly reinforcing the fluidity of Ronell's postmodern ideas. It was only natural that postmodern theory be presented through postmodern design strategies.*

At this time Eckersley also began using computers to design books, and while his adoption of digital technology is not readily apparent in his book designs—in contrast to the work of April Greiman (see figs. 9.27 and 9.28) or Rudy VanderLans (see figs. 9.38–9.40), two other digital pioneers—this strategy serves as yet another example of how new technology and postmodern design were linked in a conceptual manner.

9.28 April Greiman, *Design Quarterly*, 1986.
Poster, 2 ft x 6 ft (0.6 x 1.82 m).

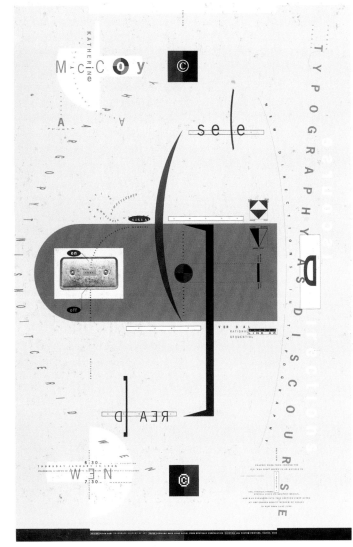

above: **9.29** Allen Hori, *Typography as Discourse*, 1989.

opposite left: **9.30** Katherine McCoy, *The Graduate Program in Design*, Cranbrook Academy of Art, MI, 1988. Poster. Color offset lithograph, 27 x 22 in (69.9 x 55.9 cm). Museum für Gestaltung, Zürich. Poster Collection.

opposite right: **9.31** Gert Dumbar, Holland Festival, The Netherlands, 1987. Poster. Studio Dumbar, The Netherlands.

information in an effect close to that of the psychedelic style. Hori's aesthetic is also relatable to the concrete poetry that Guillaume Apollinaire produced in the 1910s (see Chapter 4), except that the poet used letters to create shapes that had a direct tie to the content of the text, while Hori turned loose his letters to create unrelated forms.

Another Cranbrook poster, this one by McCoy herself, was created in order to promote the design program at the school, which was for post-Baccalaureate students only (*fig. 9.30*). This poster looks at first glance like the sort of information design seen at airports or in the London Underground, as dotted lines seem to connect the words "read," "see," "text," and "image," while color seems to create a strong vertical axis down the middle of the poster. However, the more the viewer looks the more disjointed the connection appears, as the lines are forced to traverse a chaotic mass of random, found images that could have come from a Dada collage. Overprinted on this image the viewer finds a series of paired terms that are hard to read, and which point to abstract concepts—how does one resolve "mathematicpoetic"?—that serve to signify the emphasis on critical thinking that was a profound part of the curriculum at Cranbrook. Note how the paired terms do not respect the axial symmetry created by the color, but instead add to the sense of chaotic energy.

The Netherlands and Britain

Another highly fashionable and influential designer of the 1980s was Gert Dumbar (b. 1940), whose studio was based in The Hague, although he soon developed an international following. Studio Dumbar became an important conduit through which postmodern tendencies that had been mainly the province of experimental, academic design communities became an important part of the mainstream. Many of Dumbar's works, such as a poster for the Holland Festival (1987; *fig. 9.31*), feature dramatic three-dimensional elements, at times almost creating an imaginary world through which the viewer's eye can roam as if it is real space. Most of the widely spaced letters of the word "festival" seem to be marching across a bridge, for example, while colorful beams of light turn and twist in the distant background. In another postmodern swipe at legibility, the "F" in "festival" has been almost completely obliterated by other forms, and exists mainly in the viewer's mind. The kinetic energy of the type layout, which has a strong circular flow to it, is matched by the exuberant colorism pervading the entire image.

In the 1980s, Neville Brody (b. 1957) became one of the most sought after graphic artists in Europe, as his work in record album and magazine design had a startling impact on what had been a moribund art scene. Based in London, Brody studied at the London College of Printing and then started working for the independent record label Fetish. His covers for Fetish Records, included one from 1983 for a compilation album of various artists (*fig. 9.32*). Budgets at Fetish were generally low, and this represented one of only two times that Brody got his work printed with a four-color process. Brody has written that the hand grasping the fish is a symbolic reference to the demise of the independent music scene, "Really, it's not even about losing your innocence—you're fished out and eaten before you get to reach that point." The irregularly shaped images of hand and fish are in stark contrast to the strong geometric grid formed by the type. The blurred shapes are filled in with collaged photos, and on the back cover there is an additional layer as drawing, photos, and type fight for position. It is fascinating to realize that this cover is completely handmade, even though its cluttered look anticipates much of the digital design from later in the decade. Brody was in fact one of the earliest adopters of Macintosh technology when it came on the scene in 1985.

From 1981 until 1986, Brody worked as the art director for *The Face*, a London-based lifestyle magazine. There, he often explored the limits of legibility while devising new ways of signaling the beginning and end of a feature, redefining the relationship of text to photography, and continually experimenting with new typographic styles. For example, in issue no. 30 (October 1982; *fig. 9.34*), he laid out an article called "Workwear" with exceedingly widely spaced type that forms a visual unit structuring the placement of the photographs. Everything in the design is integrated so that spaces between photographs deftly balance spaces between type. The dramatically varied scale of the lettering and the fact that some of it reads upside down or from the side make the reader into an active viewer, one who has to interpret the article not just through its content but through its design. Brody's focused attention to typography is, unfortunately, all too rare among people trained as graphic designers, many of whom seem to treat type as an afterthought.

Brody's dynamic covers for *The Face* were often destabilized

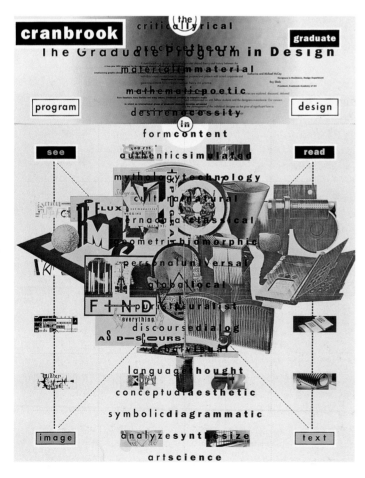

further by the way in which photographs bled off the page. For example, the July 1983 cover (*fig. 9.33*) shows only a fraction of the face of a member of the band New Order. While Brody overturned a wide variety of magazine layout conventions, he always kept in mind the fact that his design had to remain functional and must always enhance, rather than hinder, the reader's experience of a given article. He was not just following his impulses, but questioning how to integrate his work with the magazine's editorial content. In this example, Brody was working from the idea that Stephen Morris, one of the members of New Order, was not sufficiently well known to grace the cover of the magazine. Hence, the resulting cover design features a slice of his face that demonstrates the magazine's quandary in visual terms.

More than any other British designer, it was Brody who made postmodern design visible to the public, and sparked a whole generation of graphic artists to reject the conventions of traditional typography and the International Style. After the publication of *The Graphic Language of Neville Brody* as well as an exhibition of his work at the Victoria and Albert Museum in 1988, he became the first of what would prove to be a series of "celebrity designers." This term refers to a group of artists whose work won them large followings and high status among their peers as well as attention from the mainstream media. (This phenomenon is discussed at length in Chapter 10.)

9.32 Neville Brody, *The Last Testament,* 1983. Record cover. Fetish Records.

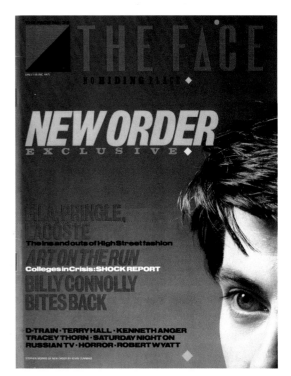

9.33 Neville Brody, *The Face,* no. 34, July 1983. Cover.

9.34 Neville Brody, *Workwear*, *The Face*, no. 30, October 1982.

Tibor Kalman

Tibor Kalman (1949–1999), the founder of the New York firm M&Co., became well known during the 1980s for his witty explorations of the vernacular culture of the United States. Originally born in Hungary, Kalman's family had moved to the United States when he was only age seven. One of the most influential self-taught designers of the postmodern era, Kalman studied journalism and became a political activist in the late 1960s. Kalman's career is exemplary of two major trends in contemporary graphic design; the embrace of political activism and the rise of the self-taught designer. While politics and graphic design are discussed below, it is important to note here that the postmodern resistance to the rigid aesthetic principles that were promulgated at most design schools led to a reappraisal of the virtues of amateurism. A number of successful contemporary graphic designers, including Kalman, David Carson (b. 1956), Edward Fella, and Art Chantry (b. 1954), have all made the point that their "outsider" status has allowed them the freedom to explore unusual, alternative design concepts. However, while valuing amateurism, each has also noted that the vast majority of untrained graphic designers are simply very bad at what they do.

M&Co. rose to prominence partly through a number of high-profile designs for record covers during the 1980s, especially a series of covers for the band Talking Heads. For the 1983 album *Speaking in Tongues* (*fig. 9.35*), Kalman collaborated with the band's leader, David Byrne. The resulting cover mixed a reference to the abstract decorative Tantric paintings derived from Hindu and Buddhist scripture with photos of a chair turned in various positions. Byrne favored the Tantric angle, while Kalman favored the quirky photographs; the achievement lies in Kalman's ability to put the two disparate sources together in a harmonious fashion. The lettering on the cover splits up the words into unintelligible syllables, an allusion to the garbled religious speech mentioned in the album's title.

In a spirit close to that of Robert Venturi, Kalman appropriated the look of the typical signage in a modest American diner for an advertisement for the hip eatery called the Restaurant Florent (*fig. 9.36*). The letters appear as if they were casually applied to the sign, while the text mixes subtle references to the restaurant with a seemingly out of place synopsis of the weather. In many of Kalman's works, the quality of the design in a technical sense is not really at issue, because the piece is intended to function on a conceptual level, if anything gently mocking the precision and rigor of the International Style. In other words, it's not about the finely tuned typographic details, but about the holistic impact of seeing a sign such as this one in such an unusual context.

Kalman's espousal of progressive politics—his political activism expressed, for example, in his 1988 election posters—made him one of the first graphic designers who seemed to be self-consciously ambivalent about the work of the profession. Kalman in many ways attempted to have it both ways, simultaneously heading a thriving firm that executed a great deal of work for corporate entities while maintaining a public persona that was positively anti-establishment. When he combined the two, for example in his extensive work for the magazine *Colors*, which was sponsored by Benetton, a maker of clothes, there was widespread outcry that the company was cynically profiting from the exploitation of emotionally charged, even tragic, issues such as racial politics and the AIDS epidemic. Like Neville Brody, Kalman enjoyed an almost cult-like status during the 1990s, as many designers sought to emulate his clever conceptual strategy. Kalman's work was compiled in a 1998 book, *Tibor Kalman Perverse Optimist*.

9.35 Tibor Kalman, *Speaking in Tongues*, 1983. Album cover.

NOVEMBER

SOUP   BOUDIN & WARM TARTS

GUSTY WINDS

HIGH S UPPER 40S TO MID 50S

LOWS UPPER 30S TO MID 40S

FLORENT

OPEN 24 HOURS 989 5779

WATCH FOR HEAVY RAINS

WEAR YOUR GALOSHES

MNCO

9.36 Tibor Kalman, Restaurant Florent, 1987. Poster.

Postmodern Architecture

In the 1980s, there arose a number of new parallels between postmodern graphic design and postmodern architecture, as a new generation of architects adopted the same pluralistic, expressive principles as graphic artists. It is difficult to say when precisely the postmodern era of architecture began, but there are a number of important historical signposts that are suggestive of a gradual change in how both professionals and lay people viewed the modern International Style. One eloquent example involves Minoru Yamasaki's (1912–1986) Pruitt-Igoe Public Housing project, built in St Louis in 1953. This type of urban housing for the poor had been designed on the principles of International Style architects such as Le Corbusier, who believed that modern abstract styles carried with them a moral force that could help people improve their circumstances. As part of the utopian vision of modern architecture, housing projects such as this were built with the belief that the architecture could serve to bring members of impoverished communities into the mainstream.

In 1972, the Pruitt-Igoe housing was demolished, as the utopian vision of modern skyscrapers serving as a launching pad for new lives had collided violently with the reality of urban poverty. Instead of functioning as an exemplar of moral authority and progress, the buildings had concentrated disadvantaged citizens in densely populated buildings cut off from the rest of society. The open areas around the buildings, which had been intended to serve as welcome green spaces, had become dangerously empty lots ruled by violent young people. Essentially, with the destruction of Pruitt-Igoe the utopian dream and moral authority of the International Style were completely undermined, as the theories of 1920s architects proved untenable in modern urban societies.

In 1981, Thomas Wolfe (b. 1931) published the book *From Bauhaus to Our House*, a polemic that attacked what he saw as the cold and unfriendly effect of the pervasive International Style.

> Has there ever been another place on earth where so many people of wealth and power have paid for and put up with so much architecture they detested? … Every child goes to school in a building that looks like a duplicating-machine replacement-parts wholesale distribution warehouse … Every new $900,000 summer house in the north woods of Michigan or on the shore of Long Island has so many pipe railings, ramps, hob-tread metal spiral stairways, sheets of industrial plate glass, banks of tungsten-halogen lamps, and white cylindrical shapes, it looks like an insecticide refinery.

Wolfe's exaggerated characterization of the International Style in architecture as a starkly abstract, incomprehensible, and impracticable language that was unpleasant to live in struck a chord with a number of people.

The notion that the International Style lacked zest, vitality, and human scale had an impact on a number of high-profile architects and their work. Philip Johnson, formerly a disciple of Mies van der Rohe, displayed his own rejection of the International Style in the early 1980s, when he designed the AT&T Headquarters in New York City (*fig. 9.37*). The design of this corporate headquarters building comprised an eclectic mix of historical references to older styles of architecture, including the Renaissance. These gestures to the past were combined with an entirely novel top to the structure, which seemingly replicates the shape of American Chippendale furniture. This subtle witticism on Johnson's part, conflating the shape of a skyscraper with the shape of a dresser, would have had no place in the International Style. Also, the building is clad with a pinkish granite that has no clear relationship to the other design elements. In sum, the building is a pastiche, combining many different styles in an unlikely fashion.

In order to make the AT&T building function on a human scale, Johnson designed the ground floor arcade to be integrated with the surrounding streets, allowing pedestrians easily to enter and cross through the building. In a holistic sense, the warm colored stone, decorative flourishes, and ground floor arcade contrast greatly with the steel and glass, reductive geometry, and separation from the surrounding space of Johnson and Mies van der Rohe's Seagram Building, an icon of the International Style. The postmodern AT&T building is overall friendlier; it is less austere and serious in its expression, drawing people in rather than repelling them with its abstract grandeur.

9.37 Philip Johnson, AT&T Headquarters, New York, 1984.

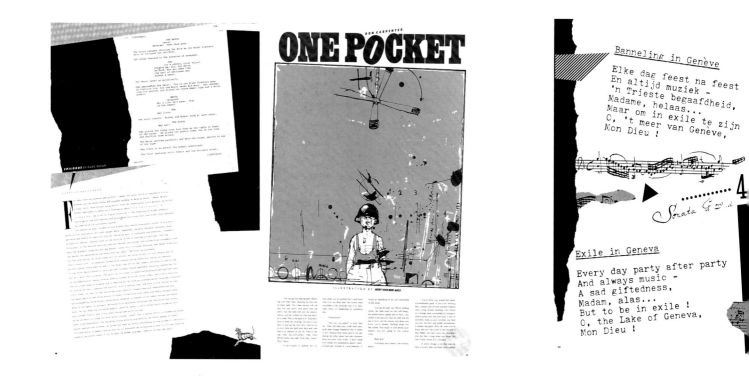

Postmodern Typography

Nowhere was the introduction of digital technology more rapidly integrated into practice than in the typography community. It is absolutely correct to refer to a revolution in typography having occurred in the 1980s, as the introduction of computer systems changed almost every aspect of type design over the course of a little more than a decade. In just a few short years, all of the older systems for setting type began to vanish, as it became possible for typefaces to be created, produced, and distributed without ever leaving the virtual environment.

Emigre Graphics

The California design team of Zuzana Licko (b. 1961) and Rudy VanderLans (b. 1955) founded Emigre Graphics in Oakland, California, in 1984. VanderLans, originally from the Netherlands, where he studied graphic design under teachers devoted to the International Style, immigrated to the San Francisco area in 1980. Newly ensconced in the Bay area, he entered graduate studies at Berkeley in photography while pursuing his interest in graphic design on the side. In 1981, he also found work as a designer for a local newspaper, *The San Francisco Chronicle*. There, VanderLans was shocked by the disregard that the editors had for good design.

> In Holland, graphic design is well integrated into society. Everything from postage stamps to money to telephone books is produced with a great deal of respect for design. … Therefore, when I came to the United States and started working at a newspaper, of all places, I was just stunned. … All the things that they taught me at art school [in the Netherlands] about legibility and good type and bad type were swept aside.

At the *Chronicle*, editors controlled the design of the newspaper, and VanderLans realized that, although the paper was not beautiful, it successfully served its purpose of distributing the news. Instead of simply rejecting this American disregard for design as an example of provincialism, VanderLans was inspired by the idea that "people read best what they read most," and the design of the paper was perfectly legible to its daily readers. This concept opened up his eyes to the vernacular culture of the world around him, as he realized that there was much more room for experimentation outside the strictures of the International Style.

In 1983, VanderLans founded *Emigre* magazine, along with two other Dutch expatriates he had met in San Francisco. The name, of course, referred to their status as migrants, and in fact the original vision for this large-format magazine was as a showcase for Dutch artists who had moved to the United States. The first issue of *Emigre* shows VanderLans's reaction against the International Style, as he laid out torn, collaged photographs in a disorienting fashion alongside typewriter type (*figs. 9.38, 9.39*). The historian Rick Poynor has pointed out that while the digital revolution in graphic design is widely recognized, what could be called the "Xerox revolution" that began in the 1960s has been largely ignored. The widespread availability of the photocopier in the pre-digital age allowed artists such as VanderLans to appropriate fragments of popular culture and use them to create radically unconventional new designs. While the use of the photocopier and the typewriter partly reflected the low budget for *Emigre*, it also displayed VanderLans's penchant for using vernacular sources; like many postmodernists, VanderLans wanted to use these simple elements not for their own sake, but as a jumping-off

point for experiments in graphic design. He also wanted to make graphic design a medium that allowed for the intuitive expression of the artist. This desire is part of the general postmodern trend whereby designers rejected the model of "artist as engineer"—a concept that arose in the 1920s and become part of the fabric of the International Style—in favor of the idea of the designer as a creative, artistic individual who puts his or her own stamp on each project.

Digital Typefaces and Zuzana Licko

Zuzana Licko, VanderLans's eventual partner at Emigre, had been born in Czechoslovakia but immigrated to the United States as a young girl. She met VanderLans while studying first architecture, and then visual studies, at Berkeley in the early 1980s. In 1984, she became one of the first typographers to work with the newly released Macintosh computer. Using a rudimentary program called FontEditor, Licko was immediately attracted to the idea that this new technology could be the basis for a new aesthetic. In other words, she did not want to use computer technology simply to facilitate the creation of old styles; rather, she felt that it was essential that the new technology be allowed to lead to the invention of new forms. The most obvious limitation of the technology of 1984 was the fact that both the screen, and more importantly the then cutting-edge dot matrix printer, could only display 72 dots per inch (dpi). Given this constraint, Licko set about developing **bit-mapped** typefaces using the Macintosh. ("Bit-mapped" means that the individual letters are made up of an array of pixels, tiny dots, and do not have the smooth, unbroken contours of earlier type. For this reason, 1980s bit-mapped type had very low resolution, and the coarse letterforms could not be scaled outside

Emperor 8
Emperor 10
Emperor 15
Emperor 19

top row from left:
9.38 and 9.39 Rudy VanderLans,
Emigre no. 1, 1983.
Collage and typography.

9.40 Rudy VanderLans,
Emigre no. 3, 1985.
Collage and typography.

above: **9.41** Zuzana Licko,
Emperor 8 Typeface, 1984.
Bitmap font.

ABCDEFGHIJKLMNOPQRSTUVW XYZ abcdefghijklmnopqrst uvwxyz 1234567890?!*&

"For example, in 1986 she released Modula, a face that consists of Emperor type that has been automatically smoothed in order to be printable at 300 dpi"

9.42 Zuzano Licko, *Modula*, 1986. Bitmap font.

ABCDEFGHIJKLMNOPQRST UVWXYZabcdefghijklmnopqr stuvwxyz1234567890?!*&%

"Ed Fella, created in Template Gothic a sort of hybrid that mixes the wavering line of hand-drawn letters with the firm structure of a sans serif such as Helvetica."

9.43 Barry Deck, Template Gothic Typeface, Emigre, 1989.

ABCDEFGHIJKLMNOPQRSTUVWXYZ abcdefghijklmnopqrstuvwxyz 1234567890?!*&%£

"Brody had designed Arcadia in 1986 as a banner for Arena magazine"

9.44 Neville Brody, Arcadia Typeface, 1986.

of a limited range.) Bit-mapped typefaces such as Licko's **Emperor 8** are characteristic of the genre; Licko established a ratio based on using a two-pixel stem to a one-pixel counter (*fig. 9.41*). Emperor 8 is dramatically minimalist in its form as it uses the absolute minimum number of pixels necessary to complete the alphabet. The Emperor family of typefaces each feature a number, in this case "eight," which specifies the height in pixels of capital letters. Because of the coarse resolution, a designer cannot simply rescale Emperor 8 into a larger size, but must turn to another typeface, say Emperor 15, which has the same proportional scheme as its sister face.

In this pre-internet decade, the main route through which Licko's digital typefaces garnered popular attention was through the journal *Emigre*, which gradually became more and more focused on experimental graphic design. *Emigre* no. 3 was the first issue in which Licko's typefaces were used instead of the type-writer type of the first two issues (*fig. 9.40*). In *Emigre* no. 3 Licko's and VanderLans's experiments in digital design melded together, as he used MacWrite and MacPaint to plan the unconventional layouts of text before printing them on a dot matrix device. In order to make the type look less coarse, the galleys were further scaled down in the printing process. The contents page of *Emigre* no. 3 shows how effectively the two designers collaborated, as Licko's bit-mapped fonts and VanderLans's quirky layout coexist without one drowning the other out. *Emigre*'s typefaces were also used by technology-savvy designers such as April Greiman in order to indicate the excitement of the digital age even at a time when the resulting work was limited by the constraints of early technology. Licko and Vanderlans recognized the technological limitations on their work, and embraced the role of digital pioneers, referring to themselves as "new primitives" who would be among the first to explore this new territory.

By far the most successful firm to come out of the digital revolution in type was Adobe Systems. With the introduction of its Postscript language in 1985, Adobe was situated to play a significant role in the design and distribution of type in the digital age. Postscript, which was soon almost universally adopted by typographers, established a standard for saving information about type in a digital format. Postscript was "device independent," meaning it allowed a designer to command just about any sort of output device, including 3,000dpi professional image setters of all sorts, to print type exactly as it was intended. It also eliminated the need for designers to deal with bit-maps, because it could render type in more sophisticated terms using outlining techniques based on Bezier curves, a type of cubic equation that underlies a great deal of computer graphics software. Postscript allowed Adobe to dominate the font business for a number of years, causing Apple and Microsoft eventually to join forces and establish the TrueType language as a competitive alternative.

As digital typography quickly evolved during the 1980s, especially following the release of Postscript, Licko continued to produce fonts that expressed the fundamental parameters of the technology with which they were produced. For example, in 1986 she released **Modula**, a face that consists of Emperor type that has been automatically smoothed in order to be printable at 300 dpi (*fig. 9.42*). In this manner, Licko's high-resolution Postscript fonts have the same underlying structures as her earlier bit-mapped

work; in the example of Modula, she has completely removed her own hand from the work, allowing the automated processes of a software program to become part of the creative process.

By 1989, the success of Licko's designs both as type and in calling attention to the broader work of the Emigre studio, caused the partners to open up an independent type-licensing business. Their digital foundry grew throughout the 1990s, distributing a wide variety of progressive, edgy designs from around the world. As even the most staid corporations adopted novel design programs during the ensuing years, Emigre's fonts went from being alternative and idiosyncratic to becoming an important part of the mainstream of graphic design. One of the most successful releases by Emigre during the 1990s was **Template Gothic**, which was designed by Barry Deck (b. 1962) and licensed by Emigre (*fig. 9.43*). Deck, who studied under the legendary self-taught designer Ed Fella, created in Template Gothic a sort of hybrid that mixes the wavering line of hand-drawn letters with the firm structure of a sans serif such as Helvetica. Another influence on Deck's design was a set of stencils he had seen at a local laundromat, making Template Gothic another example of the appropriation of vernacular culture into the art of design. Template Gothic was a great commercial success, perhaps because it displayed exciting, novel characteristics without looking so radical as to appear illegible or anti-authoritarian. Template Gothic is sometimes referred to as an early example of "grunge typography," a term that refers to the ragged, unkempt look of the letters; this term also connects the type with the graphic design of artists such as David Carson (see Chapter 10). In many ways, Template Gothic was for the 1990s what Lubalin's Avant Garde had been for the 1970s—a type that somehow caught the spirit of the time and subsequently developed a broad appeal across many segments of the design world.

The computer revolution in type led to new businesses set up in order to serve the needs of new technology. Bitstream, founded in 1981 by Mike Parker (b. 1929), Matthew Carter (b. 1937), Cherie Cone, and Rob Friedman, was one of the first firms to develop a library of digital fonts. While the company released a number of new creations over the years, its core business was the creation and sale of digital versions of typefaces with long established credentials—everything from Bodoni to Helvetica. Bitstream and other firms like it liberated type from being the exclusive property of production companies, so that the whole history of typography was available to anyone who bought a license and had the means to reproduce it. Now, typefaces could be shared among hundreds of firms, and the problem of proprietary equipment that could not communicate with other systems was eliminated.

While it was common during this period for foundries such as Bitstream to release digital versions of historic typefaces such as Garamond, there was a similar move to release digital adaptations of more recently designed fonts. At this point, typefaces that were only a few years old had not been created on computers. For example, the postmodern typefaces originally designed by Brody for *The Face* and *Arena* had been drawn in the conventional manner, so in 1990 Linotype produced a digital version of a few of the most well-known faces, including **Arcadia** (*fig. 9.44*). Brody had designed Arcadia in 1986 as a banner for *Arena* magazine; it has a

9.45 Peter Gee, *Dr. Martin Luther King*, 1968. Black photo silkscreen on black gloss paper, 30 x 19 in (76.2 x 48.3 cm).
Collection of Olga Gee.

strong vertical emphasis, hairline cross bars, and an overall stylized geometry that is reminiscent of Art Deco fonts such as Morris Fuller Benton's Broadway of 1929. The new digital libraries created during this era vastly opened up the field of typography, so that novel, "experimental" types which had formerly been confined to niche markets could quickly find a huge commercial audience.

Postmodernism of Resistance

A signature facet of postmodern graphic design is the fact that it is often joined with social activism on the part of the artists. This represented a rejection less of modern style, than of the manner in which the design profession had become completely subsumed by conservative corporate interests, losing its roots in the radical politics of the 1910s and 1920s. This trend draws a stark contrast with the "depoliticization" that was characteristic of the International Style overall, and represents essentially a "repoliticization" of graphic design. This type of postmodern work is

also another historicist impulse, as artists sought to intervene in political discourse in the same way that earlier generations (the avant-garde of the 1920s) had involved their profession in social action.

Starting in the 1960s, a number of professional designers sought to reestablish the mass media of the poster as a vehicle for protest. This facet of postmodernism is sometimes referred to as the "postmodernism of resistance," meaning that the message presented in the work resists, or attempts to undermine, aspects of society that the artist wants to change. The revival of the protest poster came out of the politicization of European and American young people in the 1960s, especially university students, who were outraged by what they saw as racist, sexist, and class-based discrimination in their societies. Events such as the Vietnam War (1965–74), the student uprisings of May 1968, and the civil rights movement, galvanized an entire generation to work for social change.

In April of 1968, the civil rights leader Dr Martin Luther King, Jr (1929–1968), was assassinated in Memphis, Tennessee. The death of Dr King, a charismatic speaker who had established the viability of non-violent protest as an agent of social change, both horrified and energized his followers. A poster by Peter Gee (b. 1932) (*fig. 9.45*) consists of four repetitions of a photograph of

9.46 Ron Haeberle (photographer), Peter Brandt (caption writer), *Q. And babies? A. And babies*, 1970. Poster. Offset lithograph, 25 x 38 in (63.5 x 96.5 cm). V&A Picture Library, Victoria & Albert Museum, London.

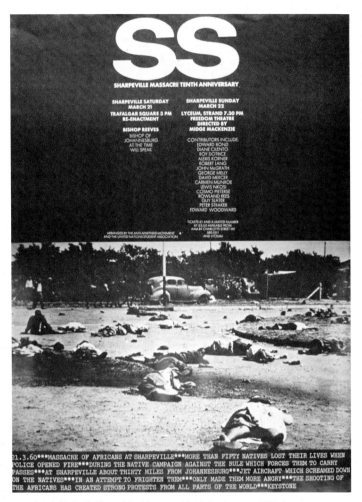

9.47 Derek Birdsall, *Sharpeville Massacre Tenth Anniversary*, 1970. Poster.
Courtesy Derek Birdsal.

order to protest the exhibition policies of the Museum of Modern Art. In the poster, the horrific scene reproduced in the photograph stands out all the more because of the cold, clinical feel of the brief question and answer. The transparent, blood-red lettering hovers above the bodies. Posters like this one played an important role in the counterculture, as they galvanized young people who hoped to change society for the better.

A number of British graphic designers in the 1970s took up the anti-apartheid cause, calling for an end to the profound racial discrimination practiced by the South African government. For example, the *Sharpeville Massacre Tenth Anniversary* poster (*fig. 9.47*), by Derek Birdsall (b. 1934), publicizing a weekend of public rallies in London, used a stark image of the slaughter in the same manner as Peter Brandt. The text at the top of the poster is made up of smooth sans serif letters arranged according to the dictates of the International Style, so it is more the intent of the poster rather than its aesthetic that distinguishes it from the modern movement. Both Birdsall and Brandt effectively revived the "atrocity image" as a tool of the counterculture, borrowing a strategy that had played such an important role in the government-sanctioned propaganda of the First World War (see Chapter 3).

Perhaps the most well-known graphic designer to take up social activist themes in the 1980s was Barbara Kruger (b. 1945). In the 1980s, after spells working as an art director and graphic designer for Condé Nast publications *Mademoiselle* and *House & Garden*, Kruger left the commercial design field in order to pursue her interest in art. She quickly developed a signature style that converted the language of advertising—dramatic photographs melded to strong declarative slogans—into a language of art and protest. In combining black and white photography with red and black rules and Futura bold italic lettering, Kruger found a means by which she could explore the dynamics of gender and social power in American society. Her chosen format mixes the tropes of print advertising with a color scheme—red and black—and a use of photography that immediately call to mind the avant-garde work of the Russian Constructivists. In that sense, Kruger's style is partly a postmodern appropriation of found photography and partly a historicist revival of the avant-garde. One of her most famous images, *Your Body is a Battleground*, uses a positive–negative dichotomy akin to that in Peter Gee's poster of Dr King to establish a central axis. The work was converted in 1989 into a poster publicizing a protest march in Washington DC (*fig. 9.48*). Previous chapters showed how established fine artists such as Henri de Toulouse-Lautrec had ventured into the graphic design field; Kruger is exemplary of the postmodern trend whereby the process was reversed and graphic designers could successfully cross over into the realm of fine art. Her work managed to bring graphic design as well as political protest into the mainstream in the 1980s, establishing a new role for graphic designers in both the art world and in the field of social activism.

Dr King in prison after he had been jailed for leading public protests. On the left side the photograph is printed as a positive image, while on the right side it is shown as a negative image, which creates the effect that Dr King is looking at himself. Additionally, the use of positive and negative images is suggestive of life and death. It was through the efforts of designers such as Gee that the photomechanical silkscreen process used here made the transition from being a strictly commercial process to one that was employed by artists as well. The text of the poster, with its repeated invocation of a drum major, is taken from a sermon that Dr King gave two months before he died, in which he expressed the wish that his eulogizer would "say that I was a drum major for justice."

Like the Dadaists of the 1910s, young people in the early 1970s felt that the ongoing Vietnam War had proved once and for all that Western society was immoral and illogical. One of the most shocking protest posters to come out of the antiwar movement was Peter Brandt's 1970 *Q: And babies?* (*fig. 9.46*). Brandt, a member of the Art Workers' Coalition, captioned this photo by Ronald Haeberle, which shows the aftermath of the My Lai massacre of Vietnamese civilians by American forces in 1968. The Art Workers' Coalition was a loosely organized quasi-Communist protest group based in New York City that had been formed in

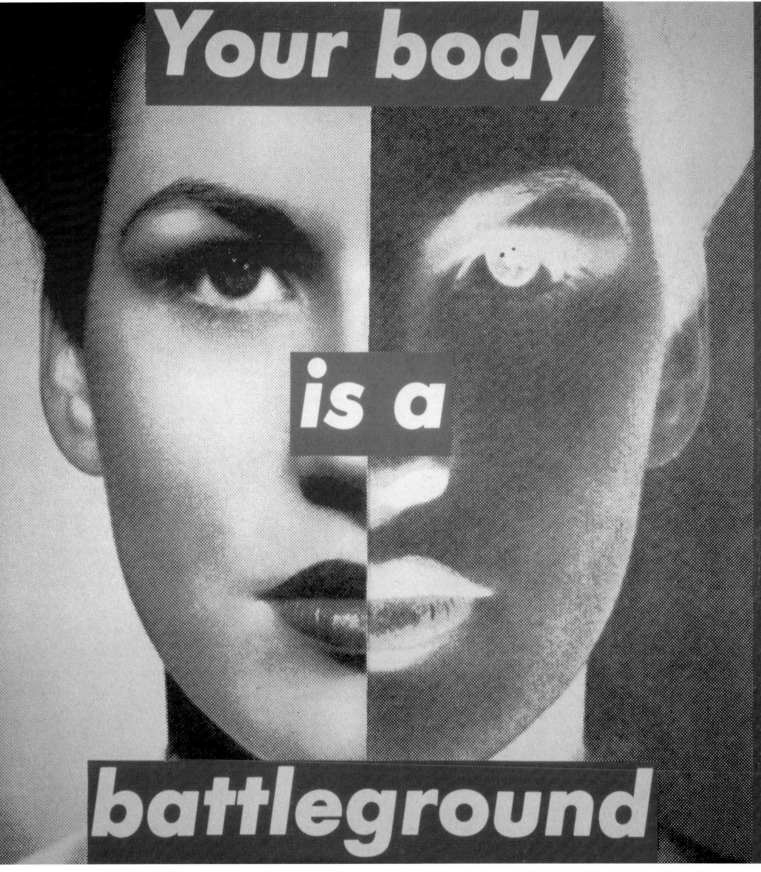

9.48 Barbara Kruger, *Your Body Is a Battleground*, 1989. Poster. Photographic silkscreen on vinyl, 112 x 112 in (2.84 x 2.84 m). The Broad Art Foundation, Santa Monica, CA.

10

ECLECTIC EXPERIMENTS

THE TECHNOLOGY AESTHETIC

WEB DESIGN

MOTION GRAPHICS

CONTEMPORARY TYPOGRAPHY

GLOBAL GRAPHICS?

DESIGN IT YOURSELF

THE "CITIZEN DESIGNER"

CONCLUSION

CONTEMPORARY

GRAPHIC

DESIGN

Since 1990, Western designers have been open to an eclectic range of postmodern styles. There has also been a greater acceptance of the use of vernacular material such as "street art," comics, and other non-traditional graphic media. Because graphic design successfully established itself as an artistic profession during the modern period, postmodern designers now feel comfortable referencing the popular culture that designers hitherto had rejected. Also, as large corporations attempt to develop corporate identities that transcend political and ethnic boundaries, there have been serious efforts to create globally effective design campaigns. Together with the rapid development in new technology, these changes amount to a revolution in the graphic design industry.

10.1 Tomato, *Dubnobasswithmyheadman* by Underworld, 1993. Album cover.

Eclectic Experiments

"Grunge" Designs

In the 1990s new and innovative styles proliferated, and graphic designers continued to experiment with the limits of legibility. One powerful trend in popular culture that influenced graphic design was an interest in celebrating the unkempt, the ragged, and the disheveled. The term "**grunge**," most often associated with the music scene that sprang up in Seattle during these years, is an apt term for the overall effect of many designs of the 1990s. At this time, the Southern California-based designer David Carson (b. 1956) came to the fore through his work for a number of niche magazines, especially *Ray Gun* between 1992 and 1994. Carson's style can be summed up by the phrase "expressive deconstruction," meaning that he broke just about every standard rule regarding composition and legibility in pursuit of expressive effect; his works (not illustrated here) look as if they are in the process of being dismantled. While many of the elements that make up Carson's work—overprinting, chaotic typography, disorder, deliberate "errors," blurred photographs—had precedents elsewhere, both in earlier movements such as Dada and in contemporaneous designs, he put them together in a novel way that brought a new level of decorative energy to postmodernism. On the other hand, critics have repeatedly raised the issue of whether Carson's designs exist only on a surface level, lacking a thorough conceptual basis. According to their analysis, the word "decorative" takes on a negative tenor, suggesting ephemeral pleasure at the expense of serious thought.

Other noteworthy examples of expressive, chaotic graphics were produced in the 1990s by the British firm Tomato. Founded in 1991 by a collaborative group that included people with backgrounds in visual art, writing, illustrating, and design, Tomato created a number of dramatic record covers including one for Underworld (*fig. 10.1*). Although the band's name and the name of the album are quite legible near the top of the front cover, the rest of the text, some of which is reversed, is so overprinted with other letters and fragments of abstract designs as to be nearly impossible to read. Despite this unruly clutter, a bold symbol consisting of a fractured handprint inside a broken circle stands out clearly. This strong abstract mark looks somewhat like a sinister corporate trademark, its geometric clarity disrupted by the handprint, which could remind the viewer of a crime scene. Overall, there are a number of deliberate "mistakes" in alignment and so forth that give the image a powerful kinetic energy, while the layering of type suggests a three-dimensional sculptural element that belies the flat surface of the cover.

The expressive, illegible aesthetic still represents a significant force in graphic design in the twenty-first century. New young artists are exploring its potential, while basking in the aura of radical chic that surrounds it. For example, the French designer Benjamin Savignac, art director and one of the founders of *DEdiCate*, a very hip fashion magazine based in Paris, has made a name for himself mining the sort of expressive visual chaos that arose in the 1990s. The page shown here displays a glossy frontal bust-length view of a model typical of the fashion genre, yet the photo has been transformed in myriad ways (*fig. 10.2*). First, a hairline horizontal rule about three-quarters of the way down the page calls attention to a shift in tone and color intensity, as the lower portion of the photo is overall lighter than the upper sections. Second, the shoulders of the model feature ghost images that make it appear as if she was moving during the exposure, even though the lower part of her body is frozen. Third, and most dramatically, the model's face has been shifted horizontally out of the central axis. The type on the page further masks her face, while a giant "X" seems to cross out the whole cover. A touch of humor is added by the grayed-out vision of a hairdresser at the upper right, who seems to be overwhelmed by her flowing tendrils. Savignac's synthesis of hip design and the fashion industry, which also relies on glamour and spectacle, points to the high profile that graphic design has attained as an indicator of coolness.

Depoliticized Design

Grunge designs have also run into criticism for their apparent lack of interest in considering graphic design an important part of social activism. Carson's oft-quoted remark, "graphic design will save the world right after rock & roll does," suggests a depoliticized sensibility that rubs more politically committed designers the wrong way. In an era when a vocal minority of working professionals have explicitly questioned the morality of fueling capitalist consumer culture, there has often been criticism of graphic designers who do not actively question the corporate dominance of graphic design. Because many elements of grunge design, and especially the overall impact it has of appearing radical and anti-establishment, are related to the strategies developed by the most political design movement of all time, Dada, some practitioners have been criticized for not sharing Dada's oppositional attitude toward the mainstream. As a consequence, the "citizen designer" movement (see p. 417) has risen to the fore.

10.2 Benjamin Savignac, *DEdiCate*, Paris, 2003.

Part of this mini-controversy over grunge design came about because of the penchant over the last two decades for corporations to try to appear hip and trendy in order to appeal to young consumers. This phenomenon actually began as early as the 1970s, when the "new advertising" swept through Europe and the United States, and companies began proffering an often ironic, playful sensibility to the customer. While it had taken decades for the work of the historical avant-garde of the 1910s and 1920s to be absorbed into commercial culture, in the 1990s advertising agencies proved adept at identifying and exploiting elements of youth culture only months after trends appeared.

Along with Neville Brody and Tibor Kalman, David Carson achieved a near-celebrity status in the mid-1990s that represents a new trend in the graphic design profession, as earlier artists, no matter how great their professional reputation, never received the sort of adulation these designers garnered. One aspect that has helped to fuel the emergence of the graphic-designer-as-celebrity phenomenon has been the publication of monographs that enhance the visibility of designers even when they are still quite young. Whether graphic designers will continue to enjoy this sort of attention from the mainstream, or whether the era of celebrity designers will seem quaint in a few years, is unknowable.

Art Chantry

A number of artists with a wide variety of experimental, idiosyncratic styles have been able to find niches in today's design scene.

10.3 Art Chantry, *Kustom Kulture*, 1994. Poster. Serigraph, 33 x 22⅜ in (85.7 x 56.8 cm). © Art Chantry.

10.4 Art Chantry, *Urban Outfitters*, 1994. Brochure, non-heatset newsprint, web offset, 9 x 12 in (22.8 x 30.4 cm).

Art Chantry first emerged in the 1980s in Seattle, where he found work publicizing concerts and bands that were a part of the thriving independent music scene developing there. Chantry is exemplary of the "contrarian" designer, who is on the one hand a part of the anti-establishment subculture while on the other working selectively for mainstream commercial clients. Part of Chantry's reputation comes from the fact that he has resisted the use of digital technology, which a number of designers feel has led to repetitive, homogeneous graphics in recent years. Chantry's idiosyncratic, expressive style makes use of lettering and images appropriated from the vernacular world to create compositions with a forceful kinetic energy that draw the viewer in. The poster *Kustom Kulture* (1994; *fig. 10.3*) publicized a local art exhibition and shows Chantry's unique blend of found photographs, chaotic varied lettering, vivid colors, and fanciful doodles. Chantry usually works to achieve a horror vacui effect, whereby every available square inch of the page is covered. The tongue-in-cheek tone of this work, featuring photographs of people with absurdly serious expressions, appealed to young people who cultivated an ironic, detached attitude toward the world.

Throughout the history of graphic design there are examples of progressive trends later being accepted by, or arguably exploited by, corporate advertisers. As it turns out, Chantry's style was a perfect fit for advertisers who sought to appear hip to young consumers. Chantry, helped out by Hank Trotter, devised a sale flier for Urban Outfitters, an American retailer of clothing (*fig.*

10.4). Featuring a mix of Futura, Franklin Gothic, Trade Gothic, and Rockwell, the flier is an ironic recreation of the cluttered, poorly designed advertisements of years past; it gently mocks the culture of the young consumer's parents. Flashy detail, such as the ridiculous Urban Outfitters mascot at the lower right, reinforce the satire. The text complements this design, as it features silly, old-fashioned-sounding phrases such as "A Fine Value!!" While fliers like this are of course quite ephemeral, they also give designers the satisfaction of seeing their work reproduced in enormous print runs; this flier was reproduced in a run of 1 million. The argument can be made that this sort of commercialized counterculture is in some ways more insidious than straightforward corporate identity, inasmuch as it co-opts anti-authoritarianism in pursuit of commerce.

Historicism and Appropriation

David Lance Goines (b. 1945), a graphic designer based in San Francisco, has developed a historicist style that contains elements of both Art Nouveau and the *Sachplakat* approach of the early twentieth century (see Chapters 2 and 3). Historicist design differs from the appropriation of the vernacular insofar as the artist borrows solely from artistic movements throughout history, and not from common signage or the like. A poster for the Berkeley Conference Center (*fig. 10.5*) revives the flat pattern of Japonisme as it was practiced by artists such as Edward Penfield in the 1890s (see fig. 1.30). Nineteenth century advertisements often showed people absorbed in reading, like the figure in Goines's poster. The sensuous curve of the figure's back resonates with the curvilinear rhythm of Art Nouveau. Of course, the dense block of background text further flattens the image while creating a swath of overprinting that would never have been seen in the 1890s.

In June 2005, Nike found out the limits of historicist appropriation as a marketing device when it borrowed from the graphics of the punk band Minor Threat. In order to create a promotional poster publicizing Nike's line of skateboarding shoes, the company almost exactly reproduced a famous cover from an album that the band released in 1981. Followers of the anti-consumerist independent record label Dischord Records reacted immediately in calling attention to Nike's appropriation. The shoe company quickly backtracked, issuing a press release that stated, "Minor Threat's music and iconographic album cover have been an inspiration to countless skateboarders since the album came out in 1984 [*sic*] … for the members of the Nike Skateboarding staff, this is no different." Nike also assured the public that it would destroy all copies of the image.

Nowhere has postmodern nostalgia for styles of the past appeared more startlingly strange than in Russia. After the collapse of the Soviet Union in 1989, the now faded empire has gone through an identity crisis of sorts, and it is still not quite clear today what the future holds; will Russia become fully integrated with the predominantly capitalist countries of Western Europe, or will it remain somewhat separate from the West and continue to maintain social and economic policies derived from its Communist past? Whatever the case, there has been a pronounced thirst in Russian society in recent years for images that

10.5 David Lance Goines, *Berkeley*, 1993. Poster. © David Goines.

10.6 Russky Khit, *Russian Dumplings*, 2002.

invoke the grandeur of either the former Soviet Union or even the Tsarist regime that the Bolsheviks overthrew in 1917 (see Chapter 5). Take, for example, the package of dumplings shown here; it features an image of what any Russian would immediately recognize as a remnant of the Soviet era, a "heroic worker" shown with a hammer and anvil (*fig. 10.6*). The triangles that fly through the air because of the force of the hammer blows, as well as the forthright lettering at the top of the image, are reminiscent of the geometric style favored by 1920s Russian Constructivists such as Alexander Rodchenko. Other contemporary packages feature symbols of the tsars, including crowns and the double-headed eagle of their insignia. In a statement published in *Print*, the Russian graphic designer Yevgeny Dobrovinsky made light of the contradictory situation in Russia's graphic design community, suggesting that the perfect symbol of today's Russia could be "a double-headed eagle with a hammer in one claw and a sickle in the other." Russian designers have yet to establish a new style that will signify to people the changes that have taken place politically

and socially in Russia. Just as Constructivist graphics were evidence of a strong vision for a new society in the 1920s, so the historicism and chaos that characterize today's Russian graphic design are evidence of a society that is not sure what it stands for.

By the 1990s, the ironic appropriation of "retro" visual culture had become a staple of the graphic design profession. A cover of *Rolling Stone* magazine from 1997 is a fine example, slyly sending up the pulp fiction covers of the 1940s (see Chapter 7) with a photograph of the actress Gillian Anderson in the grasp of a hokey-looking monster (*fig. 10.7*). The hand-drawn lettering shows many of the same overwrought devices, such as the steeply foreshortened words "Beast Within!" which had been used by illustrators in the 1940s. Of course, Fred Woodward (b. 1953), the art director at *Rolling Stone*, is able to have it both ways, as he mocks the salacious themes of pulp fiction while simultaneously featuring a scantily clad young woman prominently on the cover. This sort of work is emblematic of postmodern artists' embrace of "kitsch," popular visual culture that is so awful as to be good.

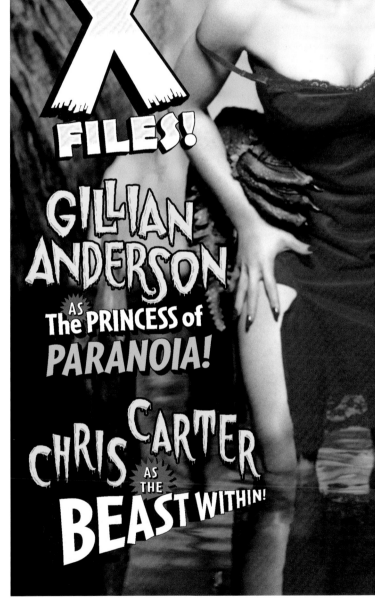

DAVID BOWIE! PAVEMENT! SILVERCHAIR! MOBY!

Rolling Stone

ISSUE 754 • FEBRUARY 20, 1997

The **X** FILES!

GILLIAN ANDERSON
AS
The PRINCESS of
PARANOIA!

CHRIS CARTER
AS THE
BEAST WITHIN!

PHISH
AMERICA'S
BIGGEST
JAM BAND!

10.7 Fred Woodward, *Rolling Stone*, Feb 20, 1997. Magazine cover.

PLAY MORE

WWW.PLAYMORE.COM

XBOX

10.8 Fuel, *Play More*, 2000. Poster.

Fuel

The London-based studio Fuel, formed by Stephen Sorrell (b. 1967), Damon Murray (b. 1967), and Peter Miles, came to the fore in the 1990s with a style that was much more understated than the prevailing taste for densely ornamental graphics. The members of Fuel are exemplary of the contemporary trend for young designers to coalesce into a firm through which they do not stress their individual contribution but rather the synergy created by their collaboration. Design firms' promotional materials these days are filled with references to "cross-pollination," "teams," and the "studio approach," whereby a diversity of viewpoints is integrated into each project. This trend partly represents the diffusion of postmodern theories regarding what some consider to be an over-emphasis on the individual that has characterized modern Western society; a point of view that has been especially evident in the way in which the history of art has been conventionally written. Collaborative design studios seek to reject the individual celebrity of a Carson or a Brody in favor of a collective reputation. Many of these new firms tend toward "hipper-than-thou" names as well as a rejection of traditional specializations, in tune with their unorthodox approach to the design industry.

One of Fuel's most inventive conceptual campaigns was produced for Microsoft's Xbox game console. In a series of print images, the slogan "play more" is written across witty photographs that appear to be culled completely from outside the realm of electronic games. In one image, there is an absurd picture of a set of false teeth soaking in a drinking glass complete with straw (*fig. 10.8*). The glass is perched on a prosaic-looking table in a modest room, an image that contrasts sharply with the excitement normally used to market video games. The ironic message is that people are becoming absent-minded as they delve more into the virtual world of the Xbox. The use of such plain-looking photos and simple text separates this advertisement from the chaos of grunge or the horror vacui style of Chantry and others.

Elliott Earls

In recent years, it has become harder and harder for graphic designers to create something that will get them quickly noticed. In an era when iconoclasm reigns, it is often necessary to stake out new territory in order to garner attention. Elliott Earls (b. 1966), who received his Master of Fine Arts from the Cranbrook Academy of Art in 1995 after several years working in various design firms, has been an influential figure over the last decade with his striking designs for clients including Nonesuch Records. Now the designer in residence and head of 2D design at Cranbrook, Earls has been widely acclaimed in the design community because of his visionary experimental projects, including work on films, poetry, music, and performance art. The sense that Earls has pushed graphic design into an expanded field encompassing many disparate aesthetic realms has added to his high

10.9 Elliott Earls, Elliott's Blue Eyeshadow Typeface, 2000.

profile. In addition, he has assertively stressed his own reputation as an iconoclast, famously including on his resumé the note that in 1988 he was "fired from Deharak and Poulin Associates NYC for 'general incompetence,'" and in 1995 he was again "fired from Elektra Records for 'general incompetence.'" In the 1980s, the firm of Deharak and Poulin was a staunch defender of the International Style, so being rejected by them serves as a young radical's badge of honor. Earls's popularity with young designers has garnered him the sort of rock star status associated with Carson and Brody.

Earls calls his studio the Apollo Program, a retro reference to the sense of optimism that pervaded the exploration of space in the 1970s. His first success in typography came in the mid-1990s, when a number of his custom typefaces were published by *Emigre*. The *Emigre* collection now includes typefaces such as **Elliott's Blue Eyeshadow**, part of the Apollo Program Font Set (*fig. 10.9*). Elliott's Blue Eyeshadow features organic forms and long, winding serifs that sometimes seem to turn back and attack or embrace the letter itself. In other letters, such as the "W," a sans serif form is shadowed by a calligraphic doppelganger. Some of the letters are so irregular in form that they appear to be falling apart in a quite literal demonstration of the theory of deconstruction. What is unique about Earls's typefaces is the way in which the overall work seems to have a strong sense of internal logic, despite the wide variation in individual letter forms. Without being too reductive, it is fair to say that Earls's typefaces feature the unkempt expressiveness that is associated with the ascendance of a grunge aesthetic.

It is always fascinating to gauge how designers such as Earls with aggressively illegible tendencies put together publications that need to stress information as well as visual impact. Earls's pamphlet *Presenting Cranbrook* is a fine example, as a series of rules and color shifts create structure, impinging on the text at the same time that it sets it apart (*fig. 10.10*). A repeated abstract floral drawing appears and reappears across the pages, sometimes confined-looking as if it has gravitated to a corner of the design, and in other instances roaming free of the grid, blocking parts of the illustrated works.

Stefan Sagmeister

One of the most recent new celebrity designers is Stefan Sagmeister (b. 1962), who grew up in Austria but moved to New York City in the 1980s, when he attended the Pratt Institute on a Fulbright scholarship. He later worked at Tibor Kalman's studio, M&Co. (see Chapter 9). Like Kalman, Sagmeister yearns for design that means something, that connects to people at a human level. In 1996, he pioneered a unique stylistic device, a tattooed look, for a poster publicizing a new album by Lou Reed called *Set the Twilight Reeling* (*fig. 10.11*). In a technique somewhat similar to that used by the makers of psychedelic posters as well as Tomato's record cover for Underworld, here Sagmeister sets the basic factual information in the lower right against a black background so that it is easy to pick out. While the recording's title also appears at the top of the poster, it is much harder to see because it seems to be drawn across Reed's forehead. This device extends across the musician's entire face, as the lyrics to a song are tattooed across Reed's skin. The image also looks as if a close-up headshot of Reed has been attacked by a graffiti artist; the expressive strokes of the hand-drawn lettering disfigure a pristine image. Reed's tormented lyrics are perfectly matched by this writing on his face, as if his powerful emotions are bursting out of his head.

Sagmeister took this eye-catching technique to a new extreme in 1999, when he produced a poster publicizing a lecture sponsored by the Cranbrook Academy and the Detroit branch of AIGA (*fig. 10.12*). In this image, rather than digitally adding the letters to a photo, as he had done in the Lou Reed poster, Sagmeister instead had an assistant carve the letters into his own

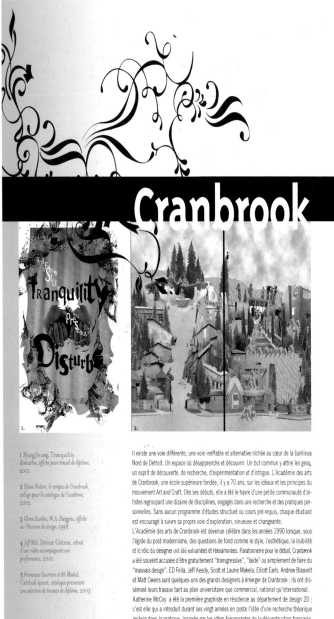

1 *Myung Jin song*, Tranquility disturbs, *affiche pour travail de diplôme, 2001.*

2 *Dylan Nelson, le campus de Cranbrook, collage pour le catalogue de l'académie, 2002.*

3 *Glenn Suokko, W.A. Dwiggins, affiche sur l'histoire du design, 1998.*

4 *Jeff Mill, Divine Citizen, extrait d'une vidéo accompagnant une performance, 2001.*

5 *Francesca Guerrero et Ali Madad, Critical space, catalogue présentant une sélection de travaux de diplôme, 2003.*

Il existe une voie différente, une voie ineffable et alternative nichée au cœur de la banlieue Nord de Detroit. Un espace où désapprendre et découvrir. Un but commun y attire les gens, un esprit de découverte, de recherche, d'expérimentation et d'intrigue. L'Académie des arts de Cranbrook, une école supérieure fondée, il y a 70 ans, sur les idéaux et les principes du mouvement Art and Craft. Dès ses débuts, elle a été le havre d'une petite communauté d'artistes regroupant une dizaine de disciplines, engagés dans une recherche et des pratiques personnelles. Sans aucun programme d'études structuré ou cours pré-requis, chaque étudiant est encouragé à suivre sa propre voie d'exploration, sinueuse et changeante.

L'Académie des arts de Cranbrook est devenue célèbre dans les années 1990 lorsque, sous l'égide du post-modernisme, des questions de fond comme le style, l'esthétique, la lisibilité et le rôle du designer ont été exhumées et réexaminées. Paratonnerre pour le débat, Cranbrook a été souvent accusée d'être gratuitement "transgressive", "laide" ou simplement de faire du "mauvais design". ED Fella, Jeff Keedy, Scott et Laurie Makela, Elliott Earls, Andrew Blauvelt et Matt Owens sont quelques-uns des grands designers à émerger de Cranbrook ; ils ont disséminé leurs travaux tant au plan universitaire que commercial, national qu'international. Katherine McCoy a été la première graphiste en résidence au département de design 2D ; c'est elle qui a introduit durant ses vingt années en poste l'idée d'une recherche théorique incluse dans la pratique. Inspirée par les idées foisonnantes de la déconstruction française, elle va, avec ses étudiants, donner l'assaut aux propriétés formelles du graphisme. La période se caractérise par un design réfléchi qui utilise le canon moderniste du graphisme comme point de départ. Tout commence vraiment en 1991 par une exposition et un livre, *Cranbrook Design: The New Discourse*, qui restituent dix ans de polémiques et de design critique.

58 : 8.2004

10.10 Elliott Earls, *Presenting Cranbrook*, p. 58. Pamphlet. Courtesy Ali Madad.

10.11 Stefan Sagmeister, *Set the Twilight Reeling*, 1996. Poster for album cover. Courtesy Sagmeister, Inc.

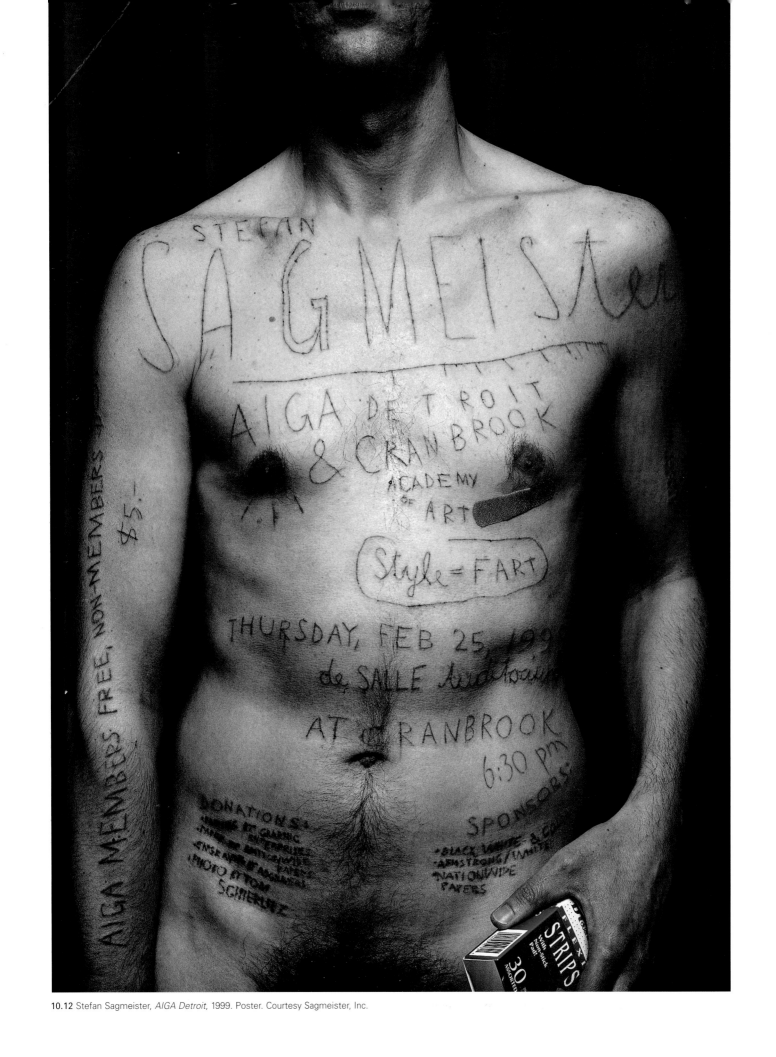

10.12 Stefan Sagmeister, *AIGA Detroit*, 1999. Poster. Courtesy Sagmeister, Inc.

body with a knife. There is an element of Kalman-like humor in the way in which Sagmeister's hand is shown clutching a box of bandaids, as if anything could cover the broad slashes across his body. The spirit of Kalman is also evident in the elements of sensationalism and sexuality that the work contains. Like his mentor, Sagmeister has been disillusioned by the commercialism of design, and at this point is able to be selective in choosing what projects to take on. The slogan that appears on the poster, "Style=fart," was one he had posted on a sign in his studio, there to remind everyone that graphic design must be more than just a trendy style that sells. In some ways, Sagmeister's philosophy is directly counter to that of David Carson, who has been attacked, perhaps unfairly, for turning graphic design into nothing more than a stylish commercial endeavor. In 2001, Sagmeister, like so many young high-profile designers, published a book that gives an overview of his career to date. Written with Peter Hall, the book is titled *Sagmeister: Made You Look,* and simultaneously celebrates his work while satirizing it. The subtitle, *Another self-indulgent design monograph (practically everything we have ever designed including the bad stuff),* is typical of Sagmeister's self-reflexive sense of humor.

MTV

During the past decade, the time between when a new design style appears in art schools or in small, self-published printed ephemera or on the web, and when it appears in the corporate world, has diminished to the point where a distinction can often no longer be made. In fact, it is arguable that large commercial design firms and in-house corporate departments have co-opted the anti-authoritarian attitude so effectively that the age-old process whereby art on the margins gradually joins the mainstream has ceased to exist. A fine example of this phenomenon is the work of the in-house design department of the MTV networks. MTV was originally founded in 1981 with a fairly simple concept of presenting music videos. From the first, the producers of the network wanted to establish a unique, hip design identity. For this reason, the original rather staid logo was created as only a touchstone, as the animator Fred Seibert (b. 1951) developed the now familiar process whereby it is constantly in flux, transforming into an eclectic set of shapes (*fig. 10.13*). Using cell animation, Seibert would have the logo shift from its original form into any manner of person, place, or thing, often including witty references to popular culture.

In 1985, MTV was bought by the Viacom Corporation, which has since grown into a "Fortune 100" company that owns a stable of media properties, including CBS Television, Paramount Pictures, and Infinity Broadcasting. In the 1990s, MTV gradually shifted away from the music business and turned into a series of lifestyle channels that, because of its clout with desirable young consumers, wields enormous influence on the music, television, movie, advertising, and retail industries. Today, MTV maintains design departments headed by Jeffrey Keaton that consist of about forty designers of various types. Under Keaton, MTV has made a practice of hiring young designers fresh out of art schools in New York City such as the Pratt Institute and the School of the

Visual Arts. These young employees are charged with the task of creating a continuous stream of graphics for both the on-air programs and the T-shirts, coffee mugs, publications, and print advertisements produced by the network. Essentially, young creative people who would formerly have been trying out unconventional styles and concepts in their own time as they built a career are instead making lively, "experimental" designs for a division of one of the largest media conglomerates in the world. Because corporate entities such as MTV have so effectively absorbed and marketed the counterculture impulse of the young, designers who want to stay on the fringe, such as Earls or Sagmeister, have to go to greater extremes in order to maintain some sort of non-commercial credibility. But still, companies such as MTV are employing the young, talented admirers of "radical designers" as fast as they can identify and hire them.

On any typical day, MTV's designers churn out compelling new graphics that make use of the most advanced trends. For example, when the network relaunched its channel, MTV2, in 2004, a series of teaser advertisements featuring a two-headed dog appeared on television, the web, and in print (*fig. 10.14*). One of the earliest teasers did not mention the network but used fractured words and an austere silhouette style to grab the viewer's attention. Later versions of the advertisement gradually filled in the information missing from the original. The MTV2 campaign and logo were designed to make a blunt statement, complete with a mutant junkyard dog, in order to appeal to the young men who were the

left: **10.13** Fred Seibert, *MTV* Logo, 1985. Courtesy MTV.

below: **10.14** Stacy Drummond, *MTV2* Logo, 2004. Look Here, Inc. Courtesy MTV.

bottom: **10.15** Nancy Mazzei, *MTV* Logo channel, 2005. Courtesy MTV.

sm
the new lesbian & gay channel
from MTV Networks, LOGOonline.com

above and below: **10.16a,b,c** MTV, Video Music Awards (VMA) Program Book, *Communication Arts*, May/June 2005, p. 77.

target audience of the channel. In contrast, the 2005 launch of MTV's Logo channel, devoted to the gay and lesbian community, has been greatly understated (*fig. 10.15*). The logo for the new channel makes use of custom-drawn lettering that is reminiscent of the pure geometric type of the 1920s, as each "O" forms a perfect circle while the bowl of the "G" does likewise. In turn, what could have been an unwieldy "L" is carved out of the negative space of yet another circle. The "L" is also matched symmetrically by the descender of the "G." This clean corporate shape is colored with a muted green. Overall, this logo is nearly invisible, as the designer went to great lengths to create something that could serve equally for a television network or an automobile parts company. Because of the nature of the Logo network, and the possibility that it might attract negative publicity, it would seem that Viacom has opted for the least expressive style imaginable.

The Comic Book Aesthetic

The designers at MTV have created a lot of buzz in recent years with the program books that are printed to accompany the network's annual Video Music Awards (VMA). The 2004 version of this publication showed how effectively the network picks up on

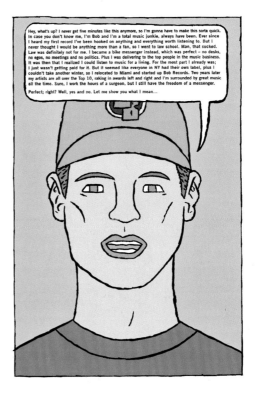

current trends, in this case the popular resurgence of comic books and especially their longer, more sophisticated cousin, the graphic novel (*fig. 10.16a,b,c*). In a clever send-up of the long-winded, pontificating speeches sometimes made by characters in these "novels," as well as their plain, textureless style, MTV's version featured Bob, a fictional music lover turned record label owner. Today, this sort of appropriation of vernacular culture, which has radical roots in the postmodern work of the 1970s, is just another amusing way of designing corporate publications.

Chip Kidd

Book cover design in the United States has been influenced by the work of one graphic designer more than any other, Chip Kidd (b. 1964). Kidd's reputation as a wunderkind owes partly to his immediate success in the 1980s, when he landed a prestigious position at the Knopf Publishing Group directly after completing his B.A in graphic design. Working in concert with another Knopf designer, Carol Carson, Kidd proceeded to revolutionize the design of the covers of fiction books, giving photography a more prominent role. Although not the originator of the use of photographic, as opposed to illustrative, covers of fiction books, Kidd proved to have a sophisticated eye for choosing an image that was both visually and conceptually intriguing. Often utilizing Futura, of which he is something of a devotee, as well as his trademark composition made up of two vertically-stacked rectangular elements, Kidd has produced over 1,000 book covers during the last decade and a half. As Veronique Vienne explained in her monograph on Kidd, his selection of photographs is so effective because they create a conceptual gap between text and cover for readers and viewers, allowing them to sort out this ambiguous terrain for themselves.

Considering his penchant for innovative photographic solutions for his covers, Kidd's other professional persona, as an editor of graphic novels—the more complex cousins of comics that feature sophisticated characters and narratives—for Knopf's Pantheon division comes as a surprise to many people. In fact, the art of the comic, with its carnivalesque aesthetic and tendency to devour and regurgitate aspects of popular culture, is in many ways at the heart of Kidd's photographic work. A childhood love of Batman initially drove Kidd's work in this area, and over the last few years he has produced more and more designs related to comics and graphic narratives. He has edited the works of both Ben Katchor and Chris Ware, while also overseeing the production of a number of comic anthologies.

Kidd's cover for George Saunders's *Pastoralia* (2000; *fig. 10.17*), a collection of short stories, represents a fine example of his more recent comic-based aesthetic. It displays his fascination with odd, ambiguous imagery, as the bewigged monkey is suggestive of playful silliness while the cropped face of a glaring man floats above the horizontal rule, bringing up issues of surveillance, judgment, and even the threat of violence. In this example, Kidd used comic-based imagery in the same manner that he used photography on hundreds of earlier covers, as a vaguely poetic device that challenges the reader to investigate how the cover and the text relate. For some viewers, there is an additional layer of

10.17 George Saunders, *Pastoralia*, 2000. Book cover. Courtesy Bloomsbury Publishing, London.

meaning as the oversized Benday dots will recall for them the Pop Art paintings of Roy Lichtenstein (1923–1997), many of which were made before Kidd was even born. In typical postmodern fashion, Kidd devised a rectangular, geometric scheme for *Pastoralia* that recalls the elegant use of rules that was a defining part of the international style—while subverting the sense of clarity, order, and even seriousness of purpose with his employment of images that have an obvious lowbrow, pop culture pedigree. Likewise, his use of type involves a carefully calibrated mixture of sizes and weights, cropped letters like the E at the end of George, and an S in the title that drops perilously into the yellow rule. In a way, Kidd's use of ostensibly hand-drawn comic art brings the design of fiction book covers back full circle to where he began, as Kidd had played a significant role in the rejection of illustration that had rocked the field twenty years before.

Work for Hire

Kidd's career has benefited from a relationship with his employer that is unique to the book cover design niche; he is allowed to offer his services on a freelance basis to anyone willing to hire him, including Knopf's major competitors in the fiction market.

Kidd's fame as one of the cadre of iconic, celebrity designers that have dominated the pages of design books and periodicals in recent years, as well as the relatively unrestrictive terms of his employment at Knopf, contrasts starkly with the other, darker side of contemporary freelance graphic design, the controversial "work-for-hire" policies of many corporate design clients. Traditionally, staff designers for a company employed under what is called a "work-for-hire" basis have no economic or artistic rights over their creations, which are the sole property of the company that employs them. In recent years, it has become more common for clients also to insist on "work-for-hire" agreements, which state that the client will be the exclusive owner of all rights to the work. A work-for-hire agreement essentially grants to the client copyright control over every aspect of a design, including preliminary ideas that do not form part of the final work. Under this form of agreement, the client can, for example, alter the work in such a way that the original artist feels it has been ruined, or can sell the work or use it in a new format without paying royalties, and can prevent the artist from creating something else that shares a similar design. Many freelance graphic designers object to the loss of artistic control that this imposes on them, especially as one of the joys of their independent practice is the presumed autonomy that they have in contrast to staff designers. The argument can be made that work-for-hire agreements sometimes stifle the creative process, as designers worry about irrevocably losing an original idea.

Illustration in a Digital Age

The pervasiveness of digital technology in graphic design has hastened the decline of illustration, which began in the immediate post-war era. The New York-based designer and illustrator Laurie Rosenwald (b.1955) summarized this situation in 2002 in an article, "Illustration: Graphic Design's Poor Relation," published in *Communication Arts*. This article points out how illustrators have been increasingly marginalized in the graphic design profession, where the digital collaging of text and photo has become the standard, and drawing skills are viewed as quaint and passé. Illustrators are rarely seen in positions of authority, and most have been relegated to doing piecework for magazines and advertising agencies. Gender seems to have played a role in this situation, as the majority of illustrators today are women. Despite these challenges, Rosenwald and other illustrators have managed to carve a reliable niche out of the commercial market. In the last few years, in fact, there has been a resurgence in the popularity of illustration in graphic design as part of the postmodern nostalgia for past styles. For example, Rosenwald's advertisements for Neiman Marcus, which combine a delicate line with spare compositions, have been widely acclaimed.

Another trend in contemporary graphic design that has helped to keep the art of illustration alive has been the absorption of the comic book aesthetic into other aspects of visual culture. This resurgence has partly been fueled by a series of blockbuster movies that feature comic heroes, as well as by the American fascination with Japanese Manga. "Comic book style" refers to the glossy hyperrealism, vivid colors, and strong contours that are

Graffiti

Graffiti is another example of a popular, anti-authoritarian culture that has been widely co-opted by corporations in order to give their advertisements a raw, authentic look—one that has an element of much sought-after "street credibility." The modern era of graffiti began in New York City during the early 1970s, when the introduction of aerosol spray paint in cans combined with a burgeoning hip hop culture to create a critical mass of new artists and aficionados. Centered mainly in the outlying boroughs of Brooklyn and the Bronx, graffiti artists tended to be self-taught young men with limited access to formal artistic education; their work was often both an outlet for creative expression as well as a form of social protest.

The most famous graffiti works from this pioneering era were painted in the expressionist, free-form mode known as "wildstyle," and the compositions often covered the entire side of a subway car. The New York City transit system was an intrinsic part of the movement; artists sought to have their images shown to a wide public as the cars traveled throughout the city on elevated tracks. Talented graffiti artists such as Lee Quinones (b. 1960) and Fab Five Freddie (an alias for Fred Brathwaite, b. 1959) actually entered the mainstream art world for a number of years as their work caught the broader public's imagination. A debate ensued as to whether graffiti represented a legitimate form of art or was merely a kind of vandalism. Eventually, the city government declared graffiti art to be a public nuisance that promoted an image of lawlessness, and by the middle of the 1980s a crackdown had essentially eliminated the presence of graffiti in the transit system.

In the 1990s, graffiti experienced something of a revival, celebrated as a prime example of what is now called "outsider art". Although graffiti artists had broken into the fine art mainstream in the 1980s, only quite recently have designers expressed interest in graffiti and, just as importantly, so have their clients. Nowadays some companies, in their unending quest for an advertising strategy that will reflect popular culture and appear non-commercial, have hired graffiti artists to produce murals for them. This tactic has sometimes led to popular backlashes, however, as activists have resented being upstaged and co-opted by urban street culture; in an ironic twist, commercial graffiti art masquerading as street art has at times been defaced by activists with more graffiti.

In the design field, recognizable stylistic elements of graffiti, such as its expressive brushstrokes, clever use of symbols, and "allover" style, have been thoroughly absorbed into the mainstream. It is arguable that the chaos and overprinting that characterized the grunge aesthetic, for example, has roots in urban graffiti. Wildstyle graffiti was influential because of its near illegibility, its interlocking, abstract letters flowing chaotically across the compositions. In addition, it is now commonplace to see urban trains and buses festooned with advertisements that cover the entire vehicle, an "allover" strategy that was originally used by street artists to emblazon whole train cars with their graffiti.

a staple of the genre. For example, the popular comic book illustrator Greg Horn has garnered a great deal of corporate work the last few years, including the creation early in 2004 of a three-story billboard in New York City that shows basketball star Lebron James (*fig. 10.18*). With its airbrushed smoothness and hand-drawn lettering, which replicates the verve and energy of

10.18 Greg Horn, *The Chosen One*, 2004. Billboard.
Courtesy Greg Horn.

comics, the billboard makes James into a larger-than-life hero, his arms a blur of superhuman motion. Horn emphasized the comic book angle even more in a small poster of the same image, but with the addition of a silhouette of the basketball player that Horn drew as a homage to 1970s comic classics such as *The Avengers*.

The Technology Aesthetic

Digital Idealism

Another strong trend in graphic design of the 1990s was the embrace of a hybrid style inspired by references to science fiction, video games, and technology. In stark contrast to the expressively distorted work of grunge designers, artists who pursue a technology-informed style tend to imagine a world where forms and surfaces are smooth and unbroken. While glimpses of a futuristic world first appeared in the work of Wolfgang Weingart and April Greiman in the 1980s, the focus on a "technology aesthetic"— akin to the machine aesthetic of earlier decades—greatly increased in the early 1990s. This new crop of designers have completely rejected the awkward "primitive" look that had appeared in the 1980s at *Emigre* in favor of a reductive, and notably textureless, aesthetic that is partly derived from the virtual worlds depicted in video games. For a time, this technological look proved to be absolutely intoxicating to graphic designers.

Conceptually, the acceptance of technologically influenced design was driven by what was thought to be the infinite potential of digital technology. Designers became caught up in a frenzy of speculation about the enormous social changes that were soon to be wrought in the digital age. In a parallel to the embrace of the machine that had characterized the 1920s in Europe and Russia, people believed that the digital age would utterly transform society for the better; overblown speculation as to the spread of peace and justice throughout a new world driven by digital information was rampant for several years. A 1993 statement by Mitchell Kapor (b. 1950), software designer and founder of Lotus Development Corporation, sums up people's faith in technologically spurred social change. "Life in cyberspace is more egalitarian than elitist, more decentralized than hierarchical … we might think of life in cyberspace as shaping up exactly like Thomas Jefferson would have wanted it: founded on the primacy of individual liberty and a commitment to pluralism, diversity, and community." The reference to Jefferson encapsulates how deeply held was the belief that technology was leading to the founding of a better society. Artists and other thinkers expected to welcome this new age— which never quite arrived—with open arms, and many people were overjoyed at the prospect of a coming "technotopia."

Wired Magazine

One of the major publications that encapsulated the belief in a coming technological utopia was *Wired* magazine, founded in 1993 in San Francisco, near the heart of America's "Silicon Valley." The editorial team at *Wired*, led by publisher Louis Rossetto (b. 1949) and art director John Plunkett (b. 1974), sought from the first to use a visual style that would signify the magnificence of the coming age of technological wonders, justice, and prosperity. Rossetto wrote in 1993 that he foresaw "social changes so profound their only parallel is probably the discovery of fire." Rossetto and Plunkett's most famous innovation at *Wired* was the "mind grenade," which consisted of one or more double-page spreads that took the place of the conventional "editor's note" in many magazines. Each "mind grenade" consisted of a quote from that month's issue, chosen by Rossetto, matched with lively graphics, overseen by Plunkett. The very first issue of *Wired* featured a mind grenade that combined a quote by Marshall McLuhan (1911–1980), the innovative theorist who had predicted, long before the digital age had begun, that evolving technology was going to have a tremendous impact on modern society. The text that accompanies McLuhan's words is designed not so much as an illustration of them as a visual accompaniment (*fig. 10.19*). Plunkett had an enviable budget in planning the images, as the magazine was printed using a six-color process that far surpassed even the most glossy commercial publications of the day. Using a synthesis of scanned photographs, Adobe Illustrator, and QuarkXpress, the dominant layout software of the decade, Erik Adigard of M.A.D. created a richly chaotic image that grabs the viewer with its fluorescent colors, a palette that would become the standard at *Wired*. A greenish solarized image of a father and son watching television anchors the spread. It has been layered with a collage of red and orange fragments of faces, computer and television equipment, and lettering. The kinetic visual punch of this image is stunning, while the frenzied blend of fragmented

10.19 John Plunkett, *Wired*, No. 1.01, 1993. Magazine collage. Courtesy Wired Magazine.

10.20 Johan Vipper, *Wired*, No. 3.02, 1995. © Johan Vipper.

forms shows how the grunge and technological aesthetics overlapped in their embrace of frenetic layered designs.

Wired issue 3.02 (a numbering system that affected that used by software developers) featured a mind grenade that delved into computer viruses. The quote by Julian Dibbell, a well-known journalist, states that computer viruses are "a carrier for the purest and strongest signal a human being can send." Of course, the euphoria of the early 1990s allowed a statement like this to be made completely without irony. The design by Johan Vipper (b. 1955), a Swedish expatriate based in New York, is a dense fluorescent web of abstract shapes hurtling horizontally across the spread (*fig. 10.20*). The cool palette of the image contrasts with the warmer colors and vertical emphasis of the letters, which seem to float on top of it. A strong red line, perhaps suggesting the path of a computer virus, shoots under the middle row of text, giving the page a clearly divided structure. Fractured bits of red type as well as graffiti-like scrawls become visible when the image is studied closely. This image is typical of technological utopianists beginning with the author William Gibson (b. 1948), many of whom focused on depictions of the "net" or the "matrix," the immaterial world of cyberspace.

Techno Type

Dirk Uhlenbrock (b. 1964), a typographer and graphic designer based in Cologne, Germany, publishes his work through his firm Signalgrau Designbureau. Many of his fonts display the sleek, stylized shapes that would be at home in a video game spaceship. For example, **Electrance**, a sans serif with unstressed letters, features horizontally proportioned forms and smooth regular curves (*fig. 10.21*). Most notable is the way the "U" and the "V" are almost identical except for the addition of a squared corner on the latter. This sort of typography brings up a more general facet

of technology-inspired graphic design; it imagines the world of science and technology as a stylish one, where information flows freely across impeccably designed interfaces. Electrance and other fonts like it are a far cry from the chaotic disorder shown in *Wired*; here there is nothing expressed that is outside of the control of the designer.

Carlos Segura (b. 1956), a Cuban-born designer now based in Chicago, has released a number of fascinating typefaces through his [T-26] Digital Type Foundry, which he founded in 1994. Tim Marcus's **Taser** face, released by T-26 in 1999, uses regular dots that appear futuristic, just as the name is borrowed from a high-technology weapon, the taser stun gun. Taser also invoked the recent past, in this case the bit-mapped fonts of Zuzana Licko from the mid-1980s (*fig. 10.22*). The tendency for styles to come and go and then be revived as historicist, or retro, only a few years later is an important development in recent design. Formerly, historicism implied the revival of something that was at the very least a few decades, if not a few centuries, old. In current culture this process has speeded up tremendously, so that a revival of the 1980s has already come and gone early in the twenty-first century.

Like the digital world itself, the technological aesthetic of the 1990s was quickly adopted by commercial forces that wanted to appear futuristic to consumers. In 1995, the Me Company, based in London, made a series of posters for Nike that demonstrated how effectively the technological style could be applied to sports advertising (*fig. 10.23*). Featuring a cryptic blue background that could easily be the inside of a space station or even the core of a computer, the foreground of the poster shows a cyborg soccer/football player, part man and part machine, shooting missile-like balls at the viewer. Cyborgs, a name given to technologically enhanced humans, had become a staple of video game culture by the mid-1990s, and this madly grinning creature would be familiar to a young audience. The smooth, textureless surfaces of the being, including its face, are also reminiscent of video

10.21 Dirk Uhlenbrock, Electrance Typeface, 2002. Courtesy D. Uhlenbrock.

10.22 Tim Marcus, Taser Typeface, 1999. Courtesy Carlos Segura.

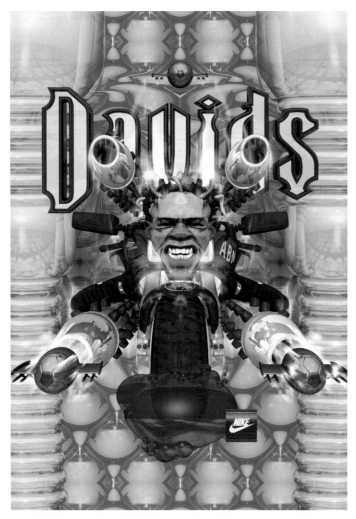

10.23 Me Company, Advertisement for Nike, The Netherlands, 1995. Poster.

games, in which varying surfaces—metal, flesh, earth—all have the same indistinguishable, flat, featureless quality. Many games are based on fantasies of space warfare, so the heavily armed cyborg in the poster would meet many Nike consumers' taste for virtual blood sport. The lettering near the bottom of the image is also designed to replicate the type of graphical menu that is common in video games. Interestingly, the conventional "Nike" and the swoosh logo that appear next to this technologically styled text seem sorely out of place, its inexpressive sans serif and simple form starkly contrasting with the dense color and kinetic energy of the rest of the poster.

Web Design 1.0: Beginnings

While graphic designers throughout the 1990s made use of new digital tools and pursued a technologically informed aesthetic, around the middle of the decade a new field arose because of further innovations: web design. While the first web browsers were introduced as early as 1990, it was not until the middle of the decade that design started to become an integral part of the World Wide Web. A key question is as follows: Is web design simply another part of graphic design, or does it constitute a

separate field altogether? While on the one hand, many websites look exactly like print media and would seem to require the same set of design skills, on the other hand the complex software programs in use today to make print media are totally different from the software used for web design. In addition, as web design technology constantly evolves and offers more opportunities for motion graphics, it would seem that the two disciplines may diverge more in the future. While some individual graphic designers—and most design firms—work in both print and web media, for the most part there is still some separation between the two design spheres. Perhaps a new generation of design software will integrate print and web design more seamlessly in the future.

For better or for worse, web design has come of age over the last decade, during an era when there is no overarching movement, such as the International Style, to guide its aesthetic development. Also, inexpensive software programs have allowed literally hundreds of millions of amateurish pages to clutter the web, creating a chaotic visual environment where one rarely knows what to expect. (It is as if in the late nineteenth century half the population had had the ability to print posters and the hoardings of European cities were filled with the result.) This has led to a situation where it is extremely hard to identify specific stylistic trends in web design. Additionally, as the internet has rapidly become the province of market forces, many websites have been designed with functionality in mind.

Generally, the success of a website is determined outside the design community and the most important criterion is its ability to generate sales. For this reason, web design has developed an arcane subspecialty that is devoted to maximizing sales, and large retail clients such as Amazon are intent more on grabbing and holding customers and leading them by the hand through the checkout process than they are on aesthetics. In contrast, arts institutions, which have provided a forum for so much in the way of adventurous design over the last century, also commissioned some of the first daring websites. Another issue that substantially impacts the design of websites versus print media is the way in which the sites often evolve over time according to the exigencies of the marketplace.

Many corporate websites feature designs that are derived from previously existing print media. For example, the site maintained by the Fedex Corporation is simple and unassuming, its most dominant feature being a logo that had been designed in

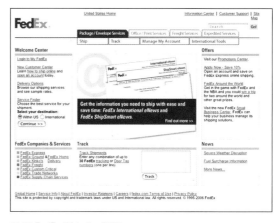

10.24 FedEx Website, 2002.

1994 by Lindon Leader of Landor Associates (see fig. 8.41). Because of the Fedex designers' desire to maintain a strong corporate identity, the website is simply an extension of its other graphic output: the envelopes, trucks, and retail stores, which already had a clean, functional look (*fig. 10.24*). The use of Times New Roman is equally understated, as that type was not created to call attention to itself in any way. It is likely that this typeface was also selected because of its universal availability, so that computers around the world could correctly display the website without the aid of embedded font technology. The modest design of the site belies its incredible technological complexity, as it allows consumers in over one hundred countries to access and manage their Fedex accounts. The multitude of international sites connected to the main page uses the same basic graphics as the American one, with the substitution of text in the appropriate language and photos that show employees of a different ethnicity.

While web design overall lacks a definitive set of styles, that is not to say that a number of sites in recent years have not been exceedingly stylish. For example, the site created by Perimetre-Flux for the San Francisco Museum of Modern Art's 010101 exhibition stands out because of its exquisite design (*fig. 10.25*). Particularly noticeable is the way in which the text is integrated into the graphic elements, and startling devices, such as the way in which the justified text is pinched by a vertical gray column underlying it, pull the viewer in. The most compelling element in

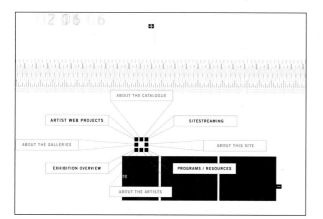

10.25 Perimetre-Flux, *010101*, 2001. Museum of Modern Art, San Francisco, CA.

10.26 Fuel, Website, 2004.

the site is the vertical strip of abstract lines that flow through the page when the cursor crosses them, allowing the name of each of the exhibition's seven themes to alternately appear and disappear.

The viewer who tries to peruse the website of an arts institution such as the San Francisco Museum of Modern Art as opposed to a retail site will immediately notice the tremendous difference in terms of both aesthetics and ease of navigation. While the Fedex site is far from enchanting in a visual sense, its tabs and links clearly indicate to the user how to proceed with their business. In contrast, the floating, scrolling text fields of the 010101 site are difficult to manage, and there is actually a user's guide on the site to help the uninitiated make sense of it. Of course, from an aesthetic standpoint, the colors and patterns flow across the screen with an ethereal beauty that is wholly lacking on most commercial sites and a far cry from the bold, boisterous purple and orange of the Fedex pages.

In more recent years, a new appreciation of minimalist graphics has pushed aside the baroque complexity characteristic of sites such as 010101 in favor of simple elegance. While the omnipresent search engine Google helped to pioneer this trend, there have been a number of attempts to balance visual impact with clarity. London's Fuel design group (see fig. 10.8) maintains a self-promotional website that eschews motion graphics and the like for its initial pages in favor of a straightforward list of available information on their work, with headings such as "books," "magazines," and "Film & TV" (*fig. 10.26*). However, in order to keep the page interesting as well as to remind the viewer that this is a design firm after all, the subsequent links on the page lead to a variety of pop-up windows that are organized visually in a number of ways—some are clear, some are obscure in intent.

Web 2.0: Interactivity

The buzzword "Web 2.0"—a term that imitates the numbers used to describe new releases of software—refers to the central role that interactivity plays in the latest incarnation of the internet. Over the last few years, a tremendous wave of change has permeated the world of web design, as corporate clients who had until recently refrained from creating so-called "rich media" websites now clamor for them. The companies' initial reluctance had resulted from a fear of losing customers who lacked high-speed internet access and so would be loath to wait as complicated graphics and interactive elements slowly loaded. However, the continuing surge in broadband access combined with the wide availability of Adobe Flash as an interactive web platform has revolutionized the field. Flash is a web-authoring tool that has the advantage of storing graphics not as pixels, a technique that consumes memory while putting limits on the kind of screen that can view the result, but through the vector process. The latter technology works by creating a mathematical description of an image—rather than the image itself—that can adapt itself to the specifications of just about any individual desktop computer. Flash works with many applications, and is the technology behind everything from showing video on websites like Youtube.com to the animated banner advertisements and

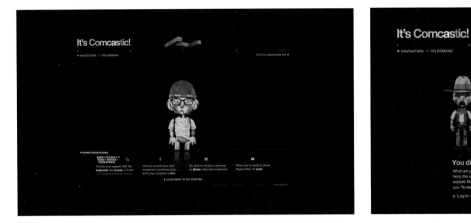

10.27a,b Comcastic.com website. The Barbarian Group, 2006.

interactive games that dominate today's internet. The Flash player was originally released in 1996, and it is estimated that today it has been installed on over ninety percent of computers worldwide, some 600 million.

In a 2006 article titled "Web Design 2.0" published on AIGA's Design Forum website, graphic designer Craig Elimeliah wrote "So now we seem to be embarking on a new kind of web, one that demands more interaction, more design, better video, clearer audio. . . . the web demands that the story come alive, that it move and morph and twist and turn and open up video windows and audio players left and right. The public is now getting used to an interactive experience that has never before existed." Elimeliah neatly summarizes the situation that confronts any designer who works in web-based media; many viewers today expect to have a rich, highly interactive and, most importantly, entertaining experience if they are going to commit time to a given website. There is a balancing act at work here for the advertiser. Viewers will resist a site that appears too commercial or seems manipulative; yet, it is of course senseless to create an expensive interactive experience that does not at least increase brand recognition.

A good example of the recent push toward amusing, interactive websites that limit the degree of direct commercial appeal can be found in the website created by The Barbarian Group (TBG) for the Comcast Corporation, a purveyor of cable television and broadband internet service (*fig. 10.27a,b*). This Flash-based site, Comcastic.com, uses extended animation sequences to create a number of interactive elements, including a series of games of skill in which visitors must manipulate the computer mouse, take part in a trivia contest, and, for the less competitive, more whimsical visitors, create their own digital puppets. In the latter experience, the viewer selects one of the five available puppets that appear floating in an indefinite space, after which the puppet appears alone and accompanied by music that matches its character; for example the "science fiction" puppet is paired with a softly haunting melody. In fact, each of the puppets has a distinct visual appeal designed to correlate with different kinds of television entertainment such as westerns, science fiction, or sports. After selecting a puppet, users can add their voices to it via computer or telephone as well as choreograph its movement. Finally, an element of viral marketing is introduced (see below), as the recorded

puppet performance can be sent as a link via email to a friend. According to one of the producers, Amanda Kelso, there is also a conceptual link between the user's ability to manipulate a puppet and the cable company's "on demand" television offerings, which are intended to offer a greater degree of interactivity and control. The most observable commercial message of the site, however, is Comcast's new brand identity, which is anchored by colorful graphics.

The Flash-based website Free-soil.org/fruit provides a different example to the commercial-driven agenda of sites like Comcastic.com. At Fruit, interactivity acts as a compelling element in its own right while simultaneously educating and, the creators hope, even enlisting the viewer in a social cause. A protest designed as an outgrowth of the Free Soil artist-activist group, the overall goal of the Fruit project is to "elevat[e] the ecological knowledge of consumers and encourage[e] a way of life that is friendly to the environment." Using many strategies, including exhibitions, websites, and a variety of art and design projects, Free Soil hopes to engage people in finding ways to participate in reforming society in a positive way. This activist intention aligns it with the "citizen designer" movement, which is discussed in more detail later in the chapter.

The online part of the Fruit project uses interactive elements not to sell viewers something or to create general brand awareness but rather to inveigle them into joining forces with the site's creators. Visitors to Fruit can read the contributions of other visitors that appear as the speech bubbles of little people who are planted in pots (*fig. 10.28a,b*). This fanciful visual device, which was designed by Free Soil founder Amy Franceschini, also illustrates the group's purpose, which is to plant the seeds of ecological activism. The artwork for the site was originally created in Adobe Illustrator and then animated in Flash. Visitors can interact with the site by joining the digital protest and adding their own thoughts; they can even identify their specific interests such as urban gardening. The compiled information is tied to a database through the open source scripting language PHP, which allows users to sort the database by different categories, for example, urban, rural, or suburban. The creators of Fruit hope to raise awareness of what is going on in a given city's activist community while encouraging the creation of additional networks devoted to social change. There is also a viral component to the Fruit project,

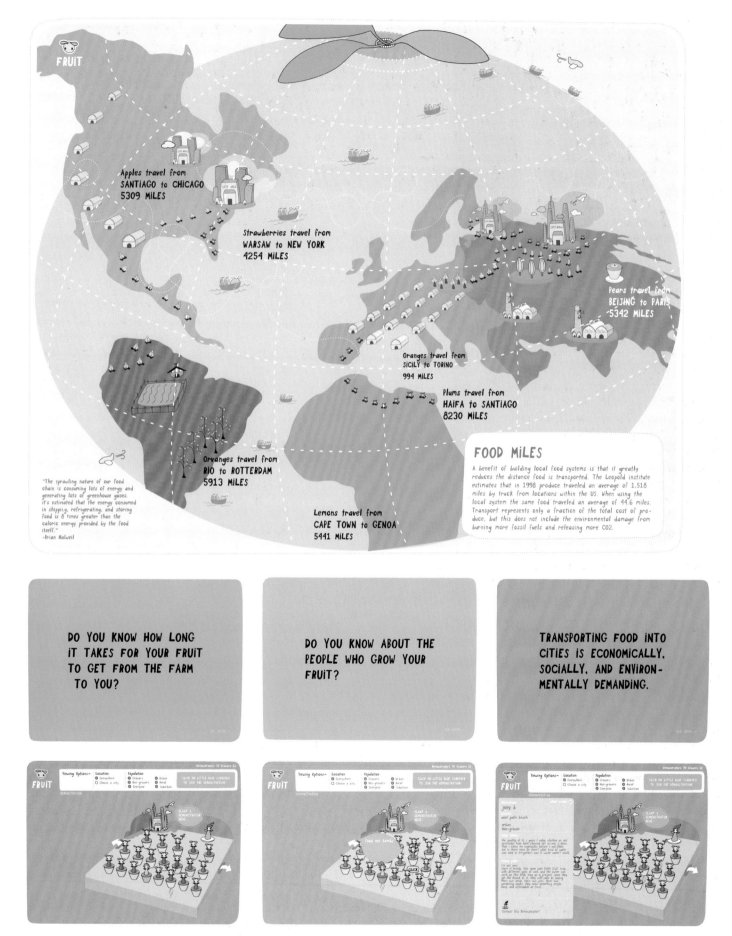

10.28a,b Amy Franceschini, F.R.U.I.T website, 2005.

10.29a,b Heavenspot, web-based banner ad generator for *Snakes on a Plane*, 2005.

contemporary phenomenon is discussed at length below) and develop their own graphics, Myspace pages, and audio tracks. It was hoped that the enormous buzz created by the film's web presence would lead to greater success at the box office. Perhaps the most innovative part of the internet campaign was the banner generator that Heavenspot designed as part of the DIY package. With this feature, viewers could create their own banner advertisement for the movie, either using the official graphics or uploading their own original ones, while also choosing a tagline for the banner. Viewers could even add their own face to the banner, coalescing individual identity with that of the product (*fig. 10.29a,b*). They could then cut and paste the resulting html into their own website, creating a custom advertisement for themselves and their social circle. Users could also add a "ticket widget" that would direct people who inputed their "zip code" (area code) to a local theater where the film was playing.

When the movie *Snakes on a Plane* was released to theaters in August 2006, its success was closely tracked in the industry because few films had ever generated such an enormous pre-release web presence. For better or for worse, the internet buzz failed to translate into ticket sales, as the film proved to be only modestly attended. This situation points to one of the major questions regarding interactive websites. Will the entertainment elements on the internet become simply an end in themselves rather than fulfilling their creator's purpose? It would seem that consumers, at least in this case, were willing to immerse themselves in a marketing campaign without actually ever buying the product.

Viral Advertising

The banner generator for *Snakes on a Plane* and the Comcastic puppet show both represent examples of the prevalence in digital culture of so-called "viral advertising." This term refers to advertising campaigns that are designed to take advantage of pre-existing communities, relying on consumers themselves to spread the commercial message. Some viral campaigns work without the active participation of the consumer. Probably the original example of this type of viral marketing arose in the late 1990s: the free email system Hotmail, which spread its name throughout the digital universe by appending its name to the bottom of each email message sent by its users. In this manner, knowledge of the service spread like a virus, jumping from person to person even though individual users had no interest in furthering Hotmail's corporate fortunes. This sort of self-replicating system is now widely in place as otherwise free services generate new business and increased brand recognition in an organic fashion.

The Comcastic and *Snakes on a Plane* campaigns are examples of the more sophisticated second wave of viral advertising, whereby consumers actively promote a commercial message because they find the content to be funny or otherwise noteworthy. Also, because many consumers invest some portion of their personal identity in the movies, television shows, music, and internet sites that they consume, they may want to create a personal link to a given media product and spread it to their friends. Viral campaigns often make use of DIY elements to

as visitors can print out and distribute Fruit "wrappers," which could in theory be attached to fruit at the local grocery, spreading the message in a more personal, non-digital manner.

In some ways, the use of interactive web design is reminiscent of the late nineteenth century, when the field of graphic design was experiencing its first flowering, and segments of the entertainment industry—especially the cafés, nightclubs, and theaters of Paris—were most willing to experiment with innovative, provocative styles and content. Not surprisingly, the entertainment industry today has again proved to be willing aggressively to try new, experimental marketing strategies. The unusual, internet-based marketing campaign for the comedy-horror movie *Snakes on a Plane* combined traditional print and television advertisements with a variety of internet-based interactive elements, including a feature whereby users could arrange for the voice of the movie's star, Samuel L. Jackson, to call a friend and encourage that person to see the film. *Snakes on a Plane* developed an enormous internet presence, as the filmmakers actively solicited advice from bloggers and other fans while finishing the movie's production.

A key part of the film's internet promotion was its official website, designed by the Heavenspot studio. Sharing the same postmodern, kitsch sensibility of the film itself, the website features cartoonish graphics as well as many interactive features. Much of the website was devoted to different types of "customizer" elements, allowing fans to "design it yourself" (DIY; this

drive consumer interest. Regardless of one's stance on the commercialization of contemporary culture, it is hard to deny that it is fun to send someone a Comcastic puppet message or to show-off the DIY banner that was made to publicize a new movie. Graphic designers working on this type of campaign find themselves in an interesting position; they are creating compelling websites that are intended to seduce consumers into creating a DIY product. Also, because professional designers usually create the templates used for banner generators, the resulting DIY works are to some extent already professionally designed.

Advertising Transformed

The sheer complexity as well as the interactive and viral elements of the campaign for *Snakes on a Plane* is indicative of the dramatic changes that are at present transforming the advertising industry and, by extension, the field of graphic design. A range of recent articles in trade magazines and websites popular with advertising and design professionals have attempted to make sense of the new situation, a difficult task considering that one of the fundamental facts of the contemporary advertising business is that it is in a perennial state of flux. One thing that is clear is that there has been a broad fracturing of the standard television-based advertising campaign into multiple digital elements; there is often a tendency to throw a bunch of different elements at the digital wall and see what sticks. Along these lines, the release of a new car model will involve traditional television and print advertisements; professionally-made "spoofs" of said advertisements posted anonymously on Youtube; behind-the-scenes agency photographs released on the photo-sharing site Flickr; a layered, interactive website featuring elaborate motion graphics, the opportunity to create collaged, or "mashed-up" content, as well as a car customizer and ordering system; even logos that can be downloaded and spread virally by cell phone or email. The chief creative director of the J. Walter Thompson advertising agency was quoted in the design magazine *Creative Review* as saying that all this content needs above all to engage the consumer: "The challenge for us is to stop interrupting what people are interested in and be what people are interested in."

In past decades a modernist designer like Paul Rand could create an entire range of corporate identity products simply by transferring a single, static print design from package to letterhead to product. All of these media were easily interchangeable. Today, designers need to work in a much more complex environment where they must seamlessly transfer text and graphics across diverse platforms, often altering the aesthetic of the piece along the way to meet consumers' expectations. For example, viewers of television graphics expect a high degree of polish, but content uploaded to Youtube with the same high production values would stand out in a negative way, blaring "commercial and artificial." In the Youtube context the designer has to work to create content that appears authentically raw, even amateurish, in order to fit into the stream of non-commercial work. Ideally, these different manifestations of the same campaign will still share an aesthetic despite their divergent platforms.

Motion Graphics

Probably the most striking transformation in the graphic design profession over the last few years has been the increased importance placed on mastering the technology behind motion graphics. Motion graphics is a broad term used to describe any context in which text or image appears to move, but more often refers to digital work that involves dramatic changes in form, color, and composition. While there are still many opportunities for the designer who specializes in static print media or web design, it would seem that knowledge of motion graphics will gradually become even more central to the profession. This situation is evident from any perusal of contemporary graphic design magazines such as *Print*, *Communication Arts*, or *Creative Review*, as these publications feature minimal content that is devoted to static media and conventional typography. Rather, they demonstrate the expanded field of graphic design as it grapples with the internet, animation, film, viral advertising, and the like.
The motion graphics area is complicated because it is a hybrid field that combines skills common to the graphic designer with those of the animator, and its practitioners have entered the field through both avenues. Graphic designers' knowledge of typography and general compositional rules are essential to making motion graphics visually effective. However, the skills of the traditional animator play perhaps a more significant role in motion graphics because they include the ability to conceptualize how a sequence of transformations will appear over time, how to effectively pace the motion, and how to relate the graphics to sound—as music is playing an increasingly vital role in this field. Animators also benefit from their familiarity with working on a project made up of a sequence of static frames.

A graphic designer needs to devote considerable effort to acquire the extra skills needed for motion graphics, yet there is little doubt that the enhanced value of these skills in today's rapidly changing business world makes the additional training worthwhile. Fortunately, it is becoming more and more common for design schools to offer instruction in the complex software that lies behind digital motion. In fact, another reason for the rapid expansion of this field in recent years is due to the availability of a number of inexpensive desktop software programs, making the need to own and maintain exorbitantly expensive custom workstations obsolete. Although a number of programs serve this market, including Apple Motion and Autodesk Combustion, one program, Adobe's After Effects, has come to dominate the field. After Effects and its competitors are powerful programs that provide the highest possible production values and are suitable for a range of applications, from editing a commercial film to creating simple animated sequences for a web page. While After Effects can usefully make original digital animations, it is in the role of "compositor" that this type of program truly shines. A compositor allows the designer to layer together a variety of raw source materials—photos, videos, hand-drawn elements, and music clips—into a unified whole while editing it in a time-based format.

Although the term "motion graphics" first appeared in the context of graphic design during the 1990s, graphic designers had been creating animated graphics for several decades using the techniques of traditional animation. The best example of an

10.30 Robert Brownjohn (director) & Trevor Bond (animator), Film title sequence for *From Russia with Love*, 1963.

earlier graphic designer working in this field is Saul Bass, who made a number of compelling sets of animated film titles in the 1950s (see Chapter 8). Perhaps Bass's finest foray into animated graphics was his design for Otto Preminger's 1954 movie *The Man with the Golden Arm* (see fig. 8.21), in which abstract geometric shapes come together to form a man's arm, symbolizing the heroin addiction that is the focus of the film. However, it was unusual at this time for graphic designers to involve themselves in animation, and it was essentially fortuitous that Bass—who lived in the heart of the American film industry in Los Angeles—struck out in this direction. Even though Bass's work had an enormous impact on the field and he is viewed reverently as the originator of sophisticated film titles, motion graphics never became an acknowledged part of graphic design but remained the province of conventional animators who were associated with the film industry. In the United States geography also played a role, as the graphic design community was principally located in New York City, while animated graphics were mainly created in and around Hollywood.

Robert Brownjohn (1925–1970) was another prominent graphic designer who dabbled in animated graphics long before the digital revolution. An American who attended the "Chicago Bauhaus" where he was taught by László Moholy-Nagy, Brownjohn later moved to New York where he collaborated with Ivan Chermayeff and Tom Geismar in founding the legendary graphic design firm of Brownjohn, Chermayeff, & Geismar (see Chapter 8). In 1960, Brownjohn left the firm and emigrated to England where he soon established himself as London's hottest new design talent, a precursor of the celebrity designers familiar from recent years. In 1963, Brownjohn used his fame to launch into the production of animated film titles (*fig. 10.30*), about

which he had little experience. According to a now legendary anecdote, Brownjohn sold his concept to the producers of *From Russia with Love*, the newest James Bond film, by dancing shirtless in front of a slide projector while explaining that the actual title sequence would be better because it would feature attractive women. The resulting work stands even today as one of the most memorable examples of motion graphics, as the text of the titles seems to flow on and around the dancers' writhing bodies. This kinetic element is further enhanced by the palette, as a judicious use of paired complementary colors (red and green as well as orange and blue) causes the viewer's eye to bounce from one line of text to another. While the vibrant polychromatic nature of the work is suggestive of the "psychedelic sixties," in many other ways this set of titles strongly suggests roots in the International Style; Moholy-Nagy had experimented with projected light at the Bauhaus in the 1920s, while the cropped, close-up photography resonates with his experiments in that medium both in Germany and later in Chicago. Brownjohn, who often worked impulsively, eschewing a great deal of preplanning and structure, also fortuitously hit upon the importance of music in motion graphics, which provides a visceral complement that amplifies the power of the visual elements.

Kyle Cooper (b. 1963) is perhaps the most influential graphic designer working today in the field of motion graphics, having created over 150 film title sequences over the last decade (*fig. 10.31*). After receiving his Master of Fine Arts in graphic design from Yale University, Cooper worked for several years at the New York-based design firm R/GA, before joining a few colleagues to form first a new branch of R/GA and then their own firm, Imaginary Forces, in Los Angeles in 1996. As had been Saul Bass's case decades earlier, proximity to Hollywood provided a

10.31 Kyle Cooper (titles) & Brian De Palma (director), Film title sequence for *Spider-Man*, 2002.

10.32 Mark Bohman & Troika Design Group,
ESPN—SportsCenter, 2004.
Courtesy ESPN Network.

10.33 Mathematics, "My Army of Birds and Gulls," Betchadupa, 2005. Video. Courtesy Liberation Music.

significant impetus that drove Cooper into the film title business. In 2002, soon before he left Imaginary Forces to form a solo practice called Prologue Films, Cooper completed the title sequence for *Spider-Man*, that summer's blockbuster entertainment. The opening credits feature two distinct sequences. First, a dizzyingly fast, almost strobe light-like set of comics flash by the viewer's eyes in a matter of seconds. The sequence has a flip-book effect that nimbly connects the frame-by-frame narration typical of the comics medium that is the original format of *Spider-Man* with the frame-by-frame animation of the film medium; in other words, the titles suggest that the film is essentially an animated comic flip book. This type of simultaneously visual and conceptual conceit lies at the heart of Cooper's success. The second, longer sequence of titles appears as if animated in the style of a cartoon with large flat areas of color, introducing yet another comic/film hybrid; in this series of images the letters that fashion the credits form and reform, seeming to leap from web to web like the protagonist of the film. These powerfully kinetic forms were created using a variety of software, including After Effects and Maxon's Cinema 4D, a program that facilitates three-dimensional digital modeling and animation. In addition, rousing symphonic music has been smoothly integrated with the motion of the credits, so that the music swells as the letters catch hold of a web, and then flows forward again as the letters tumble and spin in space.

The technological aesthetic that has been so prevalent in recent years first emerged in video game graphics, which have had an enormous impact on the field of graphic design by popularizing a smooth, exuberantly colorful, and futuristic texture-less

style. Cooper himself has also expanded his practice to include the design of titles for video games. For example, his titles for the 2004 video game *Metal Gear Solid 3 Snake Eater* (MGS3) demonstrate how well his style transfers across these different platforms.

Television networks are one of the most important sources of commissions for designers of motion graphics. Founded in 2001, the Troika Design group based in Hollywood is responsible for one of the most familiar set of television motion graphics of the twenty-first century. Displaying a technological aesthetic that is clearly informed by video game imagery, Troika's graphics package for the ESPN network's signature sports information show, SportsCenter, combines powerful kineticism with sleek, texture-less surfaces (*fig. 10.32*). Likewise, the lettering in the credits is decisively geometric in structure, with the flattened curves and orthogonal forms typical of the genre. One of the first graphics packages designed for high-definition television, the graphics have an almost vertiginous effect on the viewer as text and image spin while simultaneously plunging into deep space. The central image of the piece—which may or may not be recognized as such by the viewer because of the abstract nature of the work—is a huge turbine, a power generator that resonates with the symbolism of the man-machine hybrid often seen in technology-inspired graphics. The original graphics package has since been expanded to encompass a variety of implementations across the network.

Some credit for the success of this graphics package must go to the composer of the theme music, a frenetic, triumphalist piece that is beloved by sports aficionados across the globe. The music was composed by Annie Roboff, a country music writer who originally composed it for a news channel, after which it was sold to

ESPN. Of course, the key to the graphics is the way in which Troika designed them to complement the theme music seamlessly. As is often the case, the Sportscenter graphics were produced using a mixture of software programs, including After Effects, the 3D modeling program Autodesk Maya, and Apple's video editing software Final Cut Pro. The complexity of these different programs is one factor that has led to a great degree of collaboration in motion graphics, as it requires a team of designers, each of whom has their own software specialty, to complete such a work.

In a music video more than in any other type of motion graphics, the audio track takes precedence and the graphic elements play something of a supportive role. Additionally, because many music videos are intended to introduce the musicians to their audience, perhaps for the first time, it is common to see live action video and digital animation blended together. This was the case with the video that the design studio Mathematics, based in Sydney, Australia, produced in 2005 for the rock band Betchadupa (*fig. 10.33*). The first step in the creative process was to listen to the song "My Army of Birds and Gulls," after which the designers at Mathematics formulated their aesthetic approach and devised a needed list of live action footage. Betchadupa next played the song as well as some reaction shots on digital video, after which the video and original animation were merged using the compositing software After Effects.

The Betchadupa video shows the band amidst an eerie, wintry landscape populated by birds. This digital landscape nicely complements the haunting quality of the song itself, which portrays birds as a symbol of escape through a natural, nomadic

existence. Perhaps the strongest shot shows an animated feather that floats softly into the filmed hand of Liam Finn, the lead singer of Betchadupa, while an animated hummingbird hovers in the near background. The scene then dissolves through an increasing close-up of the singer's arm as it fills with black.

The design of music videos such as this one and film titles has resulted in a blurring between the graphic design and film-making fields. The software programs used by motion graphics professionals are the same ones used in movie post-production. Also, the use of a "storyboarding" process to plot the animated sequences is a strategy borrowed from filmmakers. Unsurprisingly, a number of graphic designers who specialize in motion graphics, such as Kyle Cooper, have sought out opportunities in the design and direction of motion pictures. In fact, Cooper's current studio has a name befitting a movie production company, Prologue Films.

Another hybrid format common in today's design world are complex, Flash-based websites with motion graphics sequences. Technically speaking, it is possible to include animated graphics either as separate elements that can be displayed on a media player such as Quicktime or as video segments that can be formatted for the Flash player, for example, in the case of the popular Youtube.com website. A fine example of the former strategy can be found in Foreign Office's 2004 website for the fashionable clothing company Blue Guru. Foreign Office, based in London, was originally founded in 1999 by three young designers, Sonia Ortiz Alcón, Matteo Manzini, and Fredrik Nordbeck. The Flash-based site provides all of the usual information that a visiting consumer would want to know about the company in a readable

10.34 Foreign Office, "The Story of Blue Guru," Blue Guru, 2004. Website animation. Courtesy Levi-Strauss.

format punctuated by funky, ornamental graphic elements; this straightforward approach is neatly integrated with a whimsical three-minute animated short that opens on the Quicktime player. This piece, titled "The Story of Blue Guru," purports to tell the story of the Indian origins of blue denim. It is a fascinating and sometimes confoundingly surreal pastiche—at one point poodles run across the screen—of hand-drawn graphics, archival photos, and film clips that have been composited together with After Effects (*fig. 10.34*). Foreign Office clearly adheres to a conceptual approach to design, as odd juxtapositions and poetic associations dominate the short. The animation is visually tied to the broader website by the occasional appearance of the abstract graphics that adorn the latter's pages. However, the graphics in the animation move with greater freedom, approaching the hallucinatory effect of psychedelic graphic design.

Foreign Office's own website offers a view into the sophisticated software skills that must now complement traditional visual and conceptual abilities in order to thrive in today's interactive and motion graphics-dominated design culture: "[W]e have extensive capabilities in the following computer programs: Adobe After Effects 5.5, Apple Final Cut Pro 3, Macromedia Flash 5.0, Adobe Photoshop 6, Adobe Illustrator 10, Quark Xpress 5.0, Strata Studio Pro, Adobe Premiere 5.1, Macromedia Sound Edit 2, Steinberg Cubase VST 4.0. In addition, our close collaborator Mikhail Goldgaber provides expertise in Dynamic HTML, JavaScript 1.2, Cascading Style Sheets/CSS) and HTML 4.0." Such a daunting list needs constant updating, as each year software companies release new, more powerful programs that enhance designers' aesthetic flexibility while simultaneously demanding continuing education; this is worlds' away from the pre-digital era, when designers could master a lifetime of technical skills at the outset of their career.

Contemporary Typography

This section examines some developments in typography since 1990, during which time the field has been shaken by the opportunities and problems caused by the emergence of inexpensive, powerful design software. In terms of typography, many designers feel that there has been a cheapening of the quality of type, especially as metal type has been transformed into digital sets that do not make allowances for the subtle changes in proportion and shape for different sizes and weights of type. Paradoxically, the profession of graphic design is now facing the same challenge that beset it in the nineteenth century, in that desktop publishing software has allowed many amateur "Do It Yourself" (DIY) designers to publish works of poor quality.

Arial for Everyone

The stranglehold that Adobe had on the market for high-quality, so-called "Type 1" Postscript fonts in the late 1980s led indirectly to the creation of one of the most ubiquitous typefaces of the present day, **Arial**. Arial was designed in 1989 (*fig. 10.35*) for

ABCDEFGHIJKL
MNOPQRSTVWX
YZabcdefghijklm
nopqrstuvwxyz
1234567890?!*&

"Arial was designed in 1988 for Monotype as a cheap clone that closely resembled Adobe's Type 1 Postscript Helvetica."

10.35 Arial Typeface, 1989. Monotype Corporation.

ABCDEFGHIJKL
MNOPQRSTVWX
YZabcdefghijkl
mnopqrstuvwxyz
1234567890?!*&

"Another bête noire of the typographic community is Comic Sans, which was released by Microsoft in 1995."

10.36 Comic Sans Typeface, 1995. Microsoft Corporation.

Monotype as a cheap clone that closely resembled Adobe's Type 1 Postscript Helvetica. Arial's dubious parentage—it is not exactly like Helvetica, and lacks the elegant proportions of the original—did not prevent it from being adopted in the early 1990s by Microsoft as the default font for its Windows brand of system software. Because of the success of Microsoft in dominating the desktop computer software business since the 1990s, Arial has become so commonplace as to be almost invisible. Each day, tens of millions of e-mails, memos, and PowerPoint presentations are produced with this unremarkable type. In 1996, Microsoft made available **Verdana**, by the esteemed typographer Mathew Carter (b. 1937), a type that was specifically created in order to look good on computer monitors. Verdana was released into the public domain without charge, and typographers hope it will eventually displace the hated Arial.

ABCDEFGHIJKLMNOPQRST UVWXYZabcdefghijklmnop qrstuvwxyz1234567890?!*&

"Brody himself designed a number of fonts for FSI, including FF Blur, which represented a sort of rejoinder to the clear structure of Helvetica [...]"

10.37 Neville Brody, FF Blur Typeface, 1990.

ABCDEFGHIJKLMNOPQRSTUVWXYZabcdefghijklnopq rstuvwxyz1234567890?!*&%()@£<>?$

"Garage Gothic is a fine example of the postmodern adoption of the vernacular [..]"

10.38 Tobias Frere-Jones, Garage Gothic Typeface, 1992.

10.39 Paul Elliman, Bits Typeface, 1997. Courtesy FontShop International.

10.40 Mark Andresen, Not Caslon Typeface, 1991. Courtesy MoMA.

ABCDEFGHIJKLMNOPQRSTUVWXYZabcdef ghijklmnopqrstuvwxyz 1234567890?!

"In the case of Kosmik, each letter has three versions which are sequentially employed by the program."

10.41 Erik van Blokland, FF Kosmik Typeface, 1993. Courtesy Erik van Blokland.

Although many users have found it to be truly functional, Arial has been derided by graphic designer Mark Simonson (b. 1955) as a "scourge" that is exemplary of the manner in which the digital age has led to a degradation of typography. Another *bête noire* of the typographic community is **Comic Sans**, which was released by Microsoft in 1995 (*fig. 10.36*). Originally intended to resemble the text used in the little speech bubbles placed above characters' heads in comic books, Comic Sans somehow caught the public's (as well as the design community's) imagination and became widespread in an enormous variety of publications. Somewhat histrionically, and perhaps ironically, the website BanComicSans.com claims that the spread of this font "threaten(s) to erode the very foundations upon which centuries of typographic history are built." From this perspective, the age of desktop publishing has resulted in a situation where there are no longer gatekeepers to the world of typography, and with Comic Sans the inmates have taken over the asylum.

Typography Transformed

In the 1990s, the entry cost of becoming a designer of typefaces plunged as inexpensive computer equipment and powerful programs such as Macromedia's Fontographer allowed just about anyone with the inclination to take up typography. Fontographer and Adobe Illustrator—Adobe bought Macromedia in 2005— were introduced in the second half of the 1980s, and for the first time allowed designers to create fonts from scratch as well as to make subtle changes to existing fonts. This development has resulted in some stunning new work, as artists who probably would never have been introduced to the field found that they could borrow or buy a complete system and begin exploring. Over the last decade, there has been a veritable explosion in the quantity of novel typeface designs. In addition, new digital type firms have arisen that act as clearing-houses for newly designed fonts. In 1990, Neville Brody and the German typographer Erik Spiekermann (b. 1947) founded FontShop International (FSI), whose faces are designated by the prefix FF. Like Emigre and Bitstream, FSI is a publisher of new fonts, not a type design firm. Brody himself designed a number of fonts for FSI, including FF Blur, which represented a sort of rejoinder to the clear structure of Helvetica, the ultimate International Style type. Brody created FF Blur in 1990 (*fig. 10.37*) by transforming Helvetica into a hazy form by manipulating it with the newly released program, Adobe Photoshop.

Brody also collaborated with Jon Wozencroft in the early 1990s to create *Fuse*, a series of publications that both celebrated and at times denounced the wild excesses of the new digital "experimental" fonts. "Excess" is the right word, as it seems probable that there are more books on new type—each featuring more than a hundred new designs—published each year than there were new typefaces created in any given decade during the middle of the twentieth century.

One of the success stories of the 1990s is Tobias Frere-Jones (b. 1970), who gravitated toward typography while he was a student at the Rhode Island School of Design (RISD) between 1988 and 1992. Frere-Jones had enjoyed experimenting with letters from the time he was in high school, but he discovered that American art schools such as RISD generally do not offer degree programs in type design, so he had to find his own way outside a traditional curriculum. Fortunately, the accessibility conferred on the field by digital equipment has somewhat ameliorated the lack of high-profile academic programs and helped artists like Frere-Jones break into the field.

While at RISD, Frere-Jones designed **Garage Gothic** (1992; *fig. 10.38*), which was based on the idea of making a set of letters to match the numerals commonly found on the stamped tickets at parking garages. Garage Gothic is a fine example of the postmodern adoption of the vernacular; it is essential to recognize that Frere-Jones did not simply appropriate his typeface from the stamped tickets of the world, but, in line with Robert Venturi's conceptualization, he used a commonplace set of numbers as the jumping-off point for his art.

The London-based typographer Paul Elliman (b. 1961) makes startling use of found objects in the construction of letters for his **Bits** typeface, first released in 1997 (*fig. 10.39*). Originally featured in Brody's *Fuse* #15, it was also given a prominent place as a display face in an issue of the *New York Times Magazine* of 2003. Bits is perhaps the best example of a new breed of conceptual type that shares the approach of Tibor Kalman or Stefan Sagmeister. Bits relies on the witty disjunctions that occur when fragments of urban detritus appear together to create words. It also has a human element, in that the recognizable objects can remind the reader of past experiences, while the forlorn scraps of material also have a suggestion of memento mori about them.

The taste for historicism was an important part of typography during this time, as Adobe began reviving a series of historical faces such as Garamond and Caslon in the early 1990s. Emigre released an amusing anti-historicist font, **Not Caslon**, in 1991, designed by Mark Andresen (*fig. 10.40*). Because of their commitment to exploring new technology, the thought that Adobe would make the digital world a hotbed of centuries-old roman types was especially anathema to Zuzana Licko and Rudy VanderLans. The Typeface Not Caslon is an ironic Frankenstein's monster of a font; it is made up of various parts of Caslon Swash Italic that have been stitched together into something altogether different.

A number of typeface designers have embraced the idea that digital type must innately demonstrate its unique quality of changeability. For example, Dutch typographer Erik van Blokland (b. 1967) released his "flipper font" FF **Kosmik** in 1993 (*fig. 10.41*). (A flipper font is one that changes designs on a letter by letter basis.) In the case of Kosmik, each letter has three versions which are sequentially employed by the program. The result is a casual, hand-drawn look that offers a less regimented feel than most type of this sort. Kosmik solves the problem through which *faux* hand-drawn type can look stylized and unconvincing if each letter is the same. The flexibility offered by digital technology was also exploited by Matthew Carter in his typeface **Walker**, created in 1995 for the Walker Art (b. 1937) Center in Minneapolis (*fig. 10.43*). Walker features five kinds of what Carter calls "snap-on" serifs in different styles, allowing the museum's designers to choose the best version of the typeface for a given application.

Jonathan Hoefler

Another prominent typographer, Jonathan Hoefler (b. 1971), had founded his own type foundry in 1988 in order to market his work directly to the public. Hoefler's fame in the design community came less from the creation of flashy "experimental" fonts than through his consistent work for hundreds of corporate clients. Since the release of Macintosh System 7.5 in 1994, his **Hoefler Text**, an all-inclusive family of twenty-seven conventional faces created as part of Macintosh's GX project, has been included with the Macintosh operating system (*fig. 10.42*). GX technology preceded the more successful **OpenType** system, although it enabled many of the same functions, such as large character sets, which permitted substitutions.

Hoefler's typeface **Fetish No. 338** is essentially a satire of the postmodern adulation of pastiche (*fig. 10.44*). Hoefler claimed the font to be an amalgam of historical references to everything from Victorian eclecticism to Byzantium; all of these sources were then customized by him into something stylish and new. By the later 1990s, the helter-skelter "no more rules" world of postmodern typography was ripe for satire. As a seemingly endless stream of often trite historicist designs was being released each month, many typographers such as Hoefler began to assert that the field was drowning under a wave of amateurish theatrics. The name of Hoefler's face, Fetish No. 338, gently mocks both the obsession with digitally driven pastiches and the sheer quantity of new faces, the name suggesting that there are 337 earlier versions. It seems possible that future generations will look back on the experimental typefaces of the 1990s in much the same way that current typographers view the Purist geometrics of the 1920s, as typifying a certain era and mindset.

In 2004, Hoefler teamed up with Frere-Jones, and the foundry is now known as Hoefler & Frere-Jones (HTF). In its current incarnation HTF is a major player in the publishing industry and its high-quality work, such as Gotham and Mercury, are the mainstay of the business. In 2005, Gotham Rounded was chosen as the official sans serif of *Print*, the graphic design magazine. Of course, the term "foundry" has become nothing more than a quaint historical reference itself, as one is unlikely to find molten metal in the typography companies that have prevailed in the digital age. The standard in today's typographic workplace is the OpenType format, which was developed by Adobe and Microsoft. Since the release in 2000 of several OpenType fonts, this format has come to dominate the design field because of its flexibility.

The End of Type

While inexpensive technology has enabled a number of inventive new types to come to light and make it in the mainstream, the situation has also led to what most typographers see as a precipitous decline in the quality of new faces. When almost anyone with access to a computer and software can declare themselves a part of the profession, the result has been an endless stream of incoherent novelty, as poorly designed faces followed by uninspired copies of poorly designed faces quickly spread through a design community

that has few gatekeepers. In contrast to the pre-digital era, when the adoption of a new typeface for the Linotype or Monotype systems required a significant financial outlay that resulted in substantial peer review, nowadays there are no such barriers and consequently no review of new work. Additionally, the internet has allowed for the proliferation of literally tens of thousands of typefaces that are available for sale online, so that it is almost impossible to make sense of new directions in the field. It is all too easy to take someone else's work, upload it to a computer, make some arbitrary and meaningless changes, and declare it the birth of a new typeface. Sadly, the internet has also made the outright theft of copyrighted typefaces a simple process, further damaging the ongoing viability of typographic practice. As mainstream culture has adopted a postmodern sensibility that embraces eclectic novelty, it is much harder to find a consensus about what constitutes a serious achievement in design. The digitization of typography has therefore been both a blessing and a curse, as it has opened up the field to many exciting new designs while simultaneously leading to the degradation of standards of quality.

A fascinating example of what can go wrong in the new digital age of typography is provided by the case of New York's Museum of Modern Art. In 1964, Ivan Chermayeff (b. 1932) of the corporate identity firm Chermayeff & Geismar had overseen a switch away from a purist geometric style of lettering that was reminiscent of Herbert Bayer's work at the Bauhaus. Chermayeff replaced the old lettering with Morris Fuller Benton's sans serif Franklin Gothic no. 2 (*fig. 10.45*). Like the Akzidenz Grotesk favored by Swiss designers, Franklin Gothic was popular with followers of the International Style because it had more of a humanist structure than the 1920s' geometric sans serifs, and the stresses in the letters made them less cold and forbidding than the previous type. Another development began in the 1980s, when the administration of the Museum of Modern Art recognized that the quasi-word "MoMA" formed by the museum's acronym was a better substitute for the older preferred abbreviation "MOMA," because MoMA with the lower case "o" had developed a pronunciation and a visual identity that had the impact of a corporate logo in the public's mind.

In 2002, MoMA's designers began planning an updated look to correspond with the 2005 opening of a new building with greatly expanded exhibition space. While Franklin Gothic survived the process, it was noted that the current incarnation of the type had imperfect proportions. The fault was traced back to the use of digital versions of Franklin Gothic, which had been originally scanned into the computer from only one set of smallish type. Designers had then created an entire typeface in a variety of weights and sizes from this one original set, resulting in distorted proportions for many of the letters, especially at large sizes. While this is the sort of typography problem that few people outside the profession were aware of, MoMA's administration decided to order a new, better copy of Franklin Gothic from the typographer Matthew Carter. Carter had to tweak the proportions of many of the letters in order to return the face to its original, elegant balanced state (*fig. 10.46*). Carter's work creating the new **MoMA Gothic** was facilitated by the discovery of a number of sets of Franklin Gothic metal type in museum storage. After scanning this type into his computer,

ABCDEFGHIJKLMNOPQRSTUV
WXYZabcdefghijklmnopqrstuvwxyz
1234567890

Since the release of Macintosh System 7.5 in 1994, his Hoefler Text, an all-inclusive family of twenty-seven conventional faces ...

10.42 Jonathan Hoefler, Hoefler Text Typeface, 1994.

ABCDEFGHIJKLMNO
PQRSTUVWXYZ
1234567890

10.43 Matthew Carter, Walker Typeface, Walker Art Center, Minneapolis, 1995.

HOMEWARD

10.44 Jonathan Hoefler, Fetish No. 338 Typeface, 1996. Courtesy Jonathan Hoefler.

ABCDEFGHIJKLMNOPQRSTUV
WXYZabcdefghijklmnopqrstuvw
xyz 1234567890?!&%£*

"Franklin Gothic was popular with followers of the International Style because it had more of a humanist structure than the 1920s' geometric sans serifs."

10.45 Morris Fuller Benton, Franklin Gothic Typeface no. 2, 1920.

10.46 Matthew Carter, MoMA Gothic Typeface Logo, 2003.

Carter was able to get a better sense of the correct proportions of the letters and how they needed to be scaled in order to serve the myriad functions demanded by MoMA's design and publicity needs.

This episode points out one of the pitfalls related to the proliferation of inexpensive digital type in the last two decades; type that had been carelessly transformed into a digital commodity was able to insinuate itself even into one of the bastions of design history, where one would expect discerning eyes to have noted the problem in a more timely fashion. The fact that MoMA chose to remedy the situation is unusual in itself, and it is unlikely that other, non-art institutions would have been willing to spend the time, money, and energy entailed by such a project. While this is a situation that is vexing to typographers and other connoisseurs of quality typesetting, it is clear that the spread of tens of thousands of eclectic postmodern typefaces has erased whatever awareness of good typography had ever existed among the general public. While early in the twentieth century, there was at least some mainstream awareness of quality typography, particularly in books, today even the designers at the preeminent modern art museum in the world had been blithely using poorly designed lettering for years. Sadly, it seems possible that the general state of obliviousness with regard to typography is here to stay, and the field could become nothing more than the rarefied province of a small group of professionals and eccentrics.

Global Graphics?

Pick up almost any contemporary graphic design publication, and there will be a reference to the global nature of contemporary practice. The argument has been made time and again that digital as well as transportation technology has created a situation where the world is interconnected across national and ethnic lines in a way that it never was before. It is not at all uncommon, for example, to see design elements culled from non-Western traditions in the contemporary graphics of Europe and the United States. However, the question remains: has there truly been a "globalization" of graphic design, or has there actually been mainly a "Westernization" of the field, whereby American and European practices have become a global standard? It is arguable that the co-opting of elements from non-Western cultures, for example the way the Japanese Manga comics have been quite popular with Western designers for the last few years, is not truly representative of globalism, but simply the continuation of a long-standing trend whereby Western artists have adopted fashionable, "exotic"-looking foreign styles. When nineteenth-century designers in Europe made consistent use of Japanese woodblock prints over several decades, for example (see Chapter 1), no one spoke of this representing a global movement.

An American or European person who travels to Asia, Africa, or Latin America would likely recognize the styles of sophisticated graphics, even if they could not read the language. This is because Western graphic design has been exported all around the world. One factor that drives the "Westernization" of graphic design is the global reach of corporations whose home is the United States.

For example, the document services company Fedex, among many others, brought the clean look of Western corporate identity and spread it across the globe. A screenshot of Fedex's site (see fig. 10.24) shows how, as noted earlier in this chapter, the company can simply take its clear, functional design and change the text and photograph in order to improve its appeal to its customers anywhere in the world. Another factor in promoting a homogeneous, Western-derived style of graphic design the world over is digital technology. The majority of designers the world over work on desktop platforms, using software that has been adapted from American versions, leading not unexpectedly to work that retains a resemblance to that produced in the West, regardless of its country of origin.

The influence of Western graphic design on the wider world stage is quite evident in many contexts, and the graphic art of India well illustrates this phenomenon. India, an Asian country of over 1 billion people, has been experiencing enormous economic growth over the past decade, much of it fueled by its thriving information technology industries that have developed close ties to Europe and the United States. Sprawling cities like Mumbai (formerly Bombay), home to over 20 million people, are saturated with print advertising, as billboards, hoardings, and murals dazzle the eye along almost every commercial street. Many of the most important buyers of commercial graphics in Mumbai are companies involved in the Hindi film industry, nicknamed Bollywood. A significant part of what is the largest film industry in the world, Bollywood movie studios have typically plastered Indian cities with hand-painted billboards. Films are not commonly advertised through a conceptual approach but rather through the star system, so these billboards generally consist mainly of the faces of famous actors (*fig. 10.47*).

Bollywood movie posters are for the most part made by artisans referred to as "graphicswallah," a Hindi-English term that suggests a fairly low professional status. Their traditional painted illustrations are gradually conceding some ground to Western design styles, as more and more film studios opt for photographic-based work that has been designed with the help of print media programs such as Adobe's Photoshop and InDesign. In fact, an

10.47 Jeeva, *Run*, 2004. Film poster.

10.48 Mourad Boutros, "Apple Magazine of the Arab World, " 2005. Magazine cover. Courtesy Mourad Boutros.

10.49 Phunk Studio, *Electricity*, Tiger Beer "Translate" project, 2006. Silkscreen on canvas, 12 ft (4 m) wide.

important part of these programs' success worldwide has been the multilingual capabilities built into the software. The poster shown here for the 2004 feature titled *Run* replicates the convention of relying on the star power of the lead actor, in this case Abhishek Bachchan, to promote the film (see fig. 10.47). However, rather than just showing his face, a still from the film shows him racing away on a motorcycle from a pursuing truck. The title of the film has been layered in transparent letters across the top of the photo in such a way that it is clear the image was produced through digital means. Of course, it is in some ways only natural that a film with substantial Western influence would be publicized through a visual matrix that first arose in the United States.

One of the greatest challenges facing designers who work for corporations with a global reach is the need to integrate Western styles within a diverse set of cultural traditions. A whole new set of design problems appears when one has not only to balance different styles but also different alphabets. Mourad Boutros, a London-based designer who specializes in this area, has often been called to create works that blend the Latin alphabet, with its left to right reading style and mix of upper- and lower-case letters, with the Arabic alphabet, which is read right to left and does not use uppercase. These differences represent just two of the contrasting elements that need to be reconciled for a successful design. In the example shown here (*fig. 10.48*) from the "Apple Magazine of the Arab World," Boutros has smoothly integrated the Apple Computer logo as well as the symmetry and horizontal

rules typical of the International Style with the curvilinear forms of the areas of Arabic text. Note how the name Apple in Arabic sinuously wraps around the English name at the top of the page. This issue of the magazine dealt with the history of Arabic calligraphy, and Boutros himself penned the expressive forms contained in the oval at the bottom of the page.

Instances of truly global graphic design can be found most often in countries that are not defined solely by adherence to a national tradition. For example, the Singapore-based designer Jackson Tan, who established the Phunk Studio in 1994, has explained to Geoffrey Caban that in his personal experience Singapore's culture is a hybrid one: "Our ancestors were migrants from China. We speak English as a first language, eat Asian food,

read American magazines, and watch Kung Fu movies from Hong Kong and dig Japanese anime." Corporations with a global business, such as MTV and Nike, have sought out Phunk in order to broaden their appeal internationally.

In 2006 the Malaysian-based brewer Tiger Beer commissioned Phunk Studio to create a huge (4 meters wide) silkscreen on canvas titled *Electricity* as part of Tiger's "Translate" project (*fig. 10.49*). The Translate project involves the sponsorship of artists and designers who are invited to contribute works that thematically address life in contemporary Asia. Typical of the low-key branding/lifestyle campaigns that have multiplied in today's marketplace, Tiger has arranged a number of exhibitions around the world, and *Electricity* was originally produced for the Translate show in Dublin, Ireland. *Electricity* is a celebration of Asia's global-ized culture, a pastiche of skyscrapers and superhighways that pulse with life while together representing a vision of urban utopia. Symbolically, the anonymous character of the cityscape, which could be from either East or West, rejects national identity in favor of global culture and commerce. This theme fit the client perfectly as Tiger is itself an example of globalization; a European company owns a large share of it and its main product is brewed in Asia with European and Australian ingredients.

The most commonplace producers of "global" graphics are the major advertising agencies based in Europe and the United States, who plan and execute corporate publicity campaigns intended to appeal to consumers across different continents. A good example of this type of agency is Weiden + Kennedy, which has its home base in Portland, Oregon—the location of its first and foremost client, Nike—and additional offices in New York, London, Tokyo, and Shanghai. Multinational corporations such as Nike hire Weiden + Kennedy to create marketing strategies with a global reach; the "Chamber of Fear" campaign from the fall of 2004 is a fine example of one recent project of this type. Originating in Weiden's Tokyo office, the Chamber of Fear cam-paign was built around the young American basketball star Lebron James. James is one of Nike's most important spokesper-sons, and generates more of his own income selling shoes than playing basketball. While initially intended for Nike's Asian mar-kets, the campaign gained so much favorable publicity that it was extended to American and European markets.

The Chamber of Fear campaign was centered on a group of television commercials that featured James in a series of battles with epic themes; the basketball player must defeat hype, tempta-tion, envy, complacency, and self-doubt. The commercials mixed together a voiceover in various languages with visual elements derived from Hong Kong martial arts films, video games, and Japanese anime. This type of pan-Asian pastiche is commonplace in advertisements both in the United States and Asia itself.

The television commercials were complemented by a wide selection of additional media, including a website and many types of print, billboards and posters. The basis for most of the print media, such as the poster shown here, was a series of paintings by the team of Boris Vallejo (b. 1941) and Julie Bell (b. 1972), who specialize in over-the-top images of virile heroes and strong, buxom heroines (*fig. 10.51*). These illustrations were devised to mimic the style of Asian film posters in their use of brilliant color and a strong kinetic element. Also, the disembodied heads that float above James's body are typical of kung fu publicity cam-paigns. Vallejo and Bell painted the image, which was then tweaked slightly, and the text was added by the in-house team at Weiden + Kennedy. The manner in which the different parts of the image seem to be awkwardly pasted together, lacking the seamless, smooth transitions that are characteristic of contemporary digital art, is also borrowed from Asian examples.

Yet another part of the Chamber of Fear campaign consisted of a comic book designed by the Korean artist Kim Young-heon. Kim is well known in Korea as the creator of the comic series called *Pacheonilgeom* (literally, "The one sword that breaks heaven"), which depicts heroic adventures with a martial arts theme. For Nike, Kim was hired to make three issues of a comic

above: **10.50** Kim Young-heon, *Chamber of Fear*, 2004. Comic book. Courtesy W+K and Nike.

that was then given away as a promotion in Korean stores (*fig. 10.50*). Additional translations of the comic were given away in a variety of Asian countries as well as the United States. This type of marketing represents a literal absorption of the comic book genre into graphic design.

Nike learned of some of the perils of global marketing when China's State Administration for Radio, Film, and Television (SARFT) attacked the Chamber of Fear commercials for displaying Chinese culture in what was deemed a humiliating light. SARFT issued a statement contending that the images "violate regulations that mandate that all advertisements in China should uphold national dignity and interest and respect the motherland's culture." The manner in which James's defeated adversaries were represented by Asian characters, including a Shaolin priest and a pair of dragons—which are sacred in Chinese culture—was thought to imply American domination of China. In addition, the Chamber of Fear campaign ran into another sort of trouble in Singapore, where the hip graffiti style of the print advertising was criticized for glorifying a type of vandalism that is harshly proscribed in that country.

Design It Yourself

One of the most striking graphic design trends in the early twenty-first century has been the new attention devoted to the "do it yourself" movement, a term that has become interchangeable with the term "design it yourself." The acronym DIY is used as a shorthand for either definition. Of course, the essence of DIY, the impulse to design and build projects on an amateur basis—from assembling a radio kit to weaving a textile to remodeling a kitchen—has been a part of society for centuries. However, the expansion of the internet and the availability of powerful desktop computers have fueled a tremendous increase in the amount of time and energy that the average person devotes to

DIY projects. As the movement has gathered steam, designers have been forced to grapple with the implications that it has for their profession as well as for society at large.

Supporters of DIY in the design community see it as a democratizing force akin to the internet itself, one that empowers people to do creative work, entering a realm from which they were previously excluded. In her 2006 collaborative book *D.I.Y. Design it Yourself*, graphic designer Ellen Lupton (b. 1963) asserts that DIY projects represent an attempt by people to resist the corporate culture saturating the Western world, oppressively narrowing design choices and restricting personal expression. Along these lines, DIY can be seen as a part of the "citizen designer" movement (see p.417), members of which also espouse the idea that "everyone is a designer," although their goal is not to inspire creativity for its own sake but to motivate social activism. Another aspect of the DIY debate questions why people would want to advertise the products of a major corporation on their T-shirts when they can create their own whimsical or poetic message. Tens of millions of people have taken up this call to arms, creating posters, T-shirts, and websites that showcase their personal interests. Clearly, DIY graphics may well serve to broaden visual culture, allowing a modicum of autonomy from the visual mainstream.

Some of the most inventive DIY graphics in recent years have evolved from the music industry. Paul Grushkin and Dennis King's book *Art of Modern Rock: The Poster Explosion* touches on this theme and demonstrates how a generation of young people currently participate in a new golden age of the music poster. The wide availability of digital tools and the economy of xerographic and silkscreen reproduction have helped to facilitate this development, while a plethora of small, independent bands wanting to publicize their shows—most often without being able to pay for professional designers—has created a demand for anyone willing to make a poster. In this area, DIY has helped to spread design awareness outside of major urban centers, and often produces the

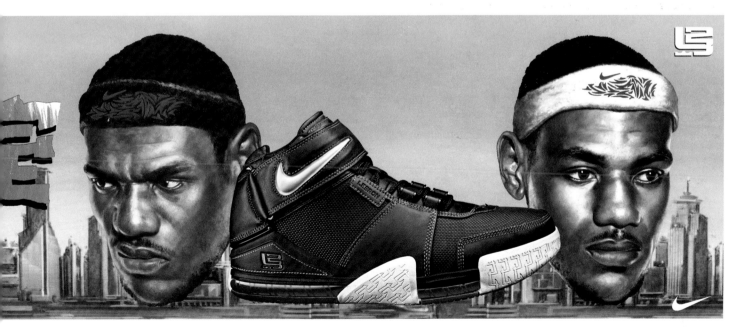

10.51 Boris Vallejo and Julie Bell, *Chamber of Fear*, W+K, 2004. Billboard. Courtesy W+K and Nike.

10.52 Leia Bell, "Reggie and the Full Effect..." 2006. Courtesy DIY Music.

most visible images in small towns and on university campuses.

A wonderful example can be found in the posters made by Leia Bell for Kilby Court, a tiny musical venue in Salt Lake City, Utah, that caters to the independent music scene. Bell, who studied printmaking in college, got involved in making posters because she was personally immersed in the local indie rock scene and felt that most posters she saw seemed uninspired. Like a number of other DIY artists, Bell does not use digital technology, but rather has combined her interests in drawing, photography, and silkscreen to create a series of stunning works. The poster shown here exemplifies her style in its flat, albeit textured, planes of color and spare, quirky drawing style (*fig. 10.52*). It is notable that the DIY movement, which at times can seem completely beholden to digital technology, has also provided a refuge of sorts for the art of illustration that has become increasingly excluded from the professional design world.

While some designers celebrate DIY as a liberating, creative force, others decry the degradation of design standards that they say has occurred as more and more internet content is derived from the work of amateurs working with standardized templates. This is one of the major differences between pre- and post-digital DIY; DIY projects designed for the internet are clearly much more widely viewed than DIY projects of the past. This phenomenon has been accelerated by social networking websites and blogs which, when combined with the trend of advertisers to provide opportunities for consumers to create content, have become a ubiquitous feature of the internet.

The harnessing of DIY opportunities by advertisers and other commercial interests has somewhat undermined the movement's attempt to free people from homogenous, corporate culture. In practice, a great deal of DIY, especially on the internet, directs personal expression towards a commercial goal that may be implicit or explicit. For example, in the United States social networking websites such as MySpace and Facebook have become hugely popular, channeling the desire of people to create a web presence into a set format. Notably, the templates that help users design their homepages on these networks lead to aesthetic homogeneity, and the vast majority of pages lack any clearly decipherable personal expression. Additionally, by joining these networks and stating their interests and demographic groups, users are exposing themselves to targeted advertising, which of course is the true aim of the corporate parents providing the server space. As it is now commonplace for any newly launched corporate product—from a blockbuster movie to a new brand of perfume to a new car—to establish its presence with a "personal" page, it has become harder and harder to think of this type of digital DIY representing an act of resistance against the mainstream.

Another kind of commercialized DIY that has been immensely successful in recent years relies on the interactive capabilities of the latest websites. So-called "customizer" sites such as the one that R/GA designed for Nike iD allow consumers to express themselves by choosing some aspects of the design of athletic shoes, notably the specific colors. While this does not represent a pure form of self-expression, it is nonetheless a satisfying experience to be given even a small amount of control over the design of such a well-known product. Many customizer sites allow the user to add personalized text to the product. In the Nike example, for instance, a consumer can add words to the tongues of the shoes. This again brings up the question as to whether DIY has had a degrading effect on design; are consumers really that likely to come up with text that is more compelling than the words scripted by advertising professionals? The current author was reminded of this while trying to improve on the "run fast run long" text that adorns a pair of shoes in his possession. As is the case with DIY typography, it is arguable that some aspects of design culture are better left to professionals. Perhaps the most uproarious satire of DIY amateurism was the one produced by artist Joe Scanlan, who has devised a set of plans showing potential DIYers how to build their own coffin using only inexpensive materials from Ikea.

The "Citizen Designer"

In recent years, numerous designers have publicly grappled with the question of pursuing an expanded role for the profession in society. Rather than confining themselves to working within the narrow parameters of client/designer relationships focused on solving aesthetic problems such as creating a new logo, reconfiguring the shape of a coffee pot, or launching a new e-commerce website, a subset of designers believe that the field must confront the most pressing problems of contemporary society, from global warming to treating and preventing HIV/AIDS. The concept behind these various ideas is that of the "citizen designer," a professional who attempts to address societal issues either through or in addition to his or her commercial work.

This concept of the responsible citizen designer can actually be traced back to one of the first artists discussed in this book, the British leader of the Arts and Crafts movement William Morris (see pp. 32–35). In the late nineteenth century, at the time of the origins of professional design culture, Morris asserted that high-quality design could serve as a beneficent social force to reform the ills of the industrial age. Versions of this conceptualization of design resurfaced throughout the twentieth century, and in the counterculture-driven 1970s it was reconceived so as to suggest that commercial work, which for Morris had had the potential to exert a reforming influence, was in fact itself a distraction from designers' commitment to social change. In 1976 Brian Smith offered a typical call to arms: "So what happens to our ideals? How do design students with radical ideas seem to end up a few years later designing hotel interiors, lighting, chairs and so on?"

In the current decade, thinkers such as Samina Quraeshi argue in favor of citizen designers in a post-industrial age as public intellectuals who use their skills in collaboration with people from government, industry, and private life to benefit the world at large. Quraeshi and others assert that the multidisciplinary approach common in all fields of design makes designers perfectly positioned to see how social change can only be wrought through consensus and connections. A flurry of essays, conferences, and

anthologies have welcomed in the new millennium, as esteemed designers including Katherine McCoy criticize the apolitical direction followed by many of her peers. She laments, "We have trained a profession that feels political or social concerns are either extraneous to our work, or inappropriate."

Advocates of the citizen designer approach often define the term "design" in its broadest possible sense, including all of the traditional design arts as well as disparate forces ranging from engineers who run the world's power grids to captains of industry, with a special emphasis often placed on the designers and promoters of information technology. In this manner, proponents of the citizen designer such as design historian Victor Margolin stray quite far from the design arts in an effort to redefine "design" in such a way that it lies at the core not just of aesthetics but of social life in general, as well as its material infrastructure. The case can be made that many of the practices called "design" by citizen designers are in fact better understood as engineering, activism, or even administration; but a central idea of the movement is to use terminology that emphasizes open-ended interconnectedness at every turn. This philosophy of inclusiveness also aligns the movement with some of the ideas behind DIY projects, emphasizing that everyone in society can make a contribution to repairing the world's problems.

Thus Bruce Mau (b. 1959) writes in regards to his vision of what an informed practice of design can accomplish: "Massive Change is an ambitious project that humbly attempts to chart the bewildering complexity of our increasingly interconnected (and designed) world. . . . Massive Change is not about the world of design; it's about the design of the world." Mau has been one of the most high-profile proponents of the citizen designer movement over the last few years. Based in Toronto, Canada, where he has directed a thriving practice since 1985, Mau has never constrained himself by working in only one design field, having pursued graphic design and industrial design projects with equal vigor. In 2002 Mau found a new calling when, acting upon separate requests from a curator at the Vancouver Art Gallery and a Toronto university, he founded a multidisciplinary internship program in which students worked to create an exhibition devoted to the future of design. The educational component of the project, later called the Institute without Boundaries, served as a think tank of sorts where Mau's vision of the goal of the citizen designer, "Massive Change", could be fleshed out amidst an environment of youthful conviction and collaboration. The original "Massive Change" exhibition opened at the Vancouver Art Gallery on October 2, 2004, and closed on January 3, 2005.

The essence of "Massive Change" is an old chestnut of postmodernism: the breakdown of categories and disciplines combined with a new commitment to cross-pollination and collaboration (*figs. 10.53, 10.54*). What separates it from other citizen designer formulations is its commitment to optimistic bravado, a refusal to sound the call to arms with a negative assessment of humanity but rather with a positive outlook. In tune with the democratic principles of DIY, Mau does not advocate a future led by designers-as-prophets, but instead opines that people from all works of life can participate in cultural transformation. Mau hopes to harness the synergistic energy that is so often espoused as the key to a successful corporate strategy and redirect it towards positive social change. It is important to recognize how he has shifted the terms of the discussion, no longer decrying the realm of commerce as an evil that must be avoided. In addition, there is arguably something uniquely Canadian in Mau's outlook, as he espouses a harmonious blend of capitalism and socialism that resonates with that country's attempts at finding a middle ground in such areas.

Mau views traditional graphic design as an example of a restrictive discipline, writing "Instead of isolating graphic design, we considered the economies of information." The "Information Economies" section of the "Massive Change" exhibition in Vancouver and its accompanying catalog, however, had little to say about the place of graphic design in Mau's larger vision, as it dealt solely with technological issues such as grid computing and open source software. Reflecting the free-spirited tone of much of the project, text devoted to the latter topic predicted the imminent demise of the Microsoft Corporation, perhaps underestimating the resilience of this bête noir of anti-capitalists. Notwithstanding its failure to locate graphic design practice in terms of the goals espoused by what is, after all, a design exhibi-

Above: **10.53** Bruce Mau, "Massive Change", Art Gallery of Ontario, 2005. Bruce Mau Design, Inc.
Below: **10.54** Bruce Mau, "Massive Change", Vancouver Art Gallery, 2006. Bruce Mau Design, Inc.

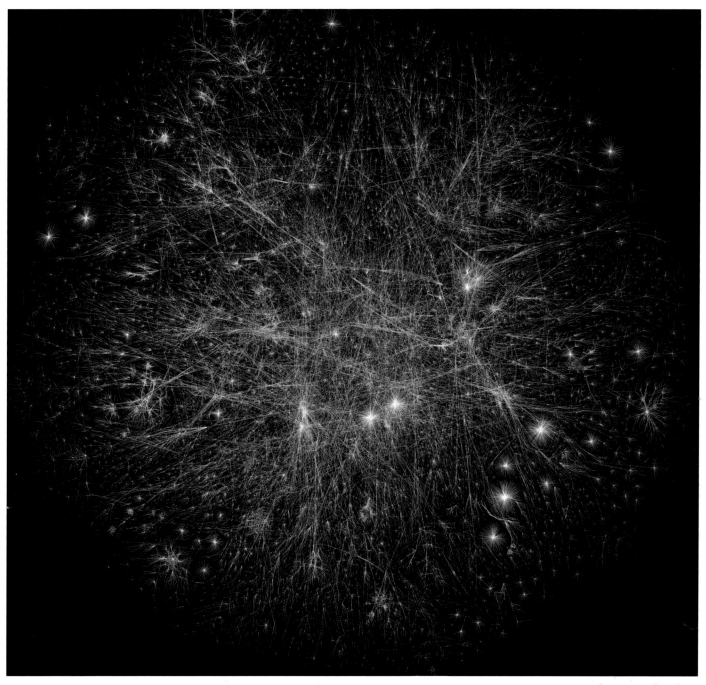

10.55 Bruce Mau & the Opte Project, Map of the internet, 2003, for "Massive Change" catalog, 2004.

tion, this section of the exhibition featured what was by far the strongest visual element, a 2003 snapshot of the internet produced by the Opte Project. While not strictly speaking an example of graphic design, the image recalls the elegance of some of the best instances of information design such as Harry Beck's 1933 map of the London underground (see fig. 4.14). Both images allow the viewer to understand better a system that is otherwise daunting in its vastness and irregularity. The Opte Project's map of the internet at one specific moment (*fig. 10.55*), which was also utilized for the cover of the "Massive Change" catalog, demonstrates how effective images can harness a visceral power that is often missing in text alone, as the viewer for the first time can feel what Mau means when he touts abstractions regarding the "global accumulation of knowledge."

Mau brought "Massive Change" to the public's attention through relatively traditional media, the museum exhibition in Vancouver—which has since traveled to the United States—an accompanying book, and a website. The teaching potential of each of these three media contains both strengths and weaknesses. The exhibition itself features an almost cacophonous selection of wall texts covering most available surfaces; as in the politically motivated exhibitions of Barbara Kruger, the exhibition's text is presented in a sturdy sans serif, with major themes announced by letters almost two feet high. Interactivity is provided by the introduction of challenging questions—such as the pros and cons of genetically modified food—that the viewer may answer through depositing a slip of paper in a Plexiglas box. The exhibition catalog, which Mau devised in collaboration with former student

Jennifer Leonard, features the same tone of breathless enthusiasm that defined the first few volumes of *Wired* magazine, as each new topic is treated with a frenetic dose of rhetoric. Curiously, the website associated with the project does not attempt to demonstrate the potential of the internet as a communication medium, but rather offers a straightforward recounting of the exhibition, the book, and related events. After the exhibition has run its course, the website will need to carry more of the load, and it will be interesting to track how it develops.

Of course, projects devoted to the citizen designer concept such as "Massive Change" have strong parallels with Europe's historic avant-garde and its commitment to the transformative effects of technology; the artists of De Stijl, the Bauhaus, and the Russian Constructivists all hoped in varying degrees to remake society based on new technologies (see Chapters 5 and 6). While Mau and others vehemently reject the notion that theirs is a utopian project, one cannot help but think back to the discarded ideals of the Constructivists, for example, and wonder whether "Massive Change" and its like will end up being viewed as ultimately ineffective and naive. One sincerely hopes not. Whatever its limitations, Mau's optimistic call for designers to see themselves as public intellectuals with profound responsibilities to shape society is a welcome counter to the narrow focus that defines so much of the profession.

Jonathan Barnbrook

There is another subset of graphic designers mindful of the need for social change who see less reason for optimism than Bruce Mau and who have taken a more antagonistic stance towards modern society and its leaders. These designers have, somewhat paradoxically, set aside their own commercial work in order to produce images that attack commerce in general and the Western domination wreaked by "globalization" in particular. The London designer Jonathan Barnbrook (b. 1966), founder of Barnbrook Design as well as Virus Fonts, has pursued a number of works along these lines including his recent set of images gathered under the title "Globanalization," a reference to the homogeniz-ing force of Western corporations that dominate the world with their banal graphics. For example, Barnbrook has made facsimiles of Tibetan Buddhist mandalas, circular images that show the structure of the heavens. Barnbrook's versions appear conven-tional at first glance, but further study reveals that the abstract symbols are made out of the logos of American companies.

This sort of demonization of the United States has become something of a marketing device for Barnbrook. For example, when he introduced his Virus font collection in Japan in 1999, the publicity poster featured the slogan "Virus says stop American cultural imperialism" (*fig. 10.56*). Barnbrook's profession and political commitments present him with a dilemma. It is unclear how one can reconcile political issues with the quest to market type. The complex design, a melding of Art Chantry-like dense horror vacui style with a layered technological aesthetic, is in many ways indistinguishable from the sort of graphic conventions used daily by Barnbrook's antagonists.

10.56 Jonathan Barnbrook, *Virus says stop American cultural imperialism*, 1999. Courtesy Jonathan Barnbrook.

Conclusion

One question that is constantly raised in regard to contemporary graphic design and typography is: what is the raison d'être, the conceptual core, of current practice? Throughout this book, disparate design groups have been surveyed, all of whom had a commitment of one sort or another, be it aesthetic or ideological: nineteenth-century designers wanted to raise the quality of industrial goods; the Dadaists wanted to subvert Western society; the practitioners of the New Typography wanted to create a universal language of the machine; followers of the International Style wanted to create modern design solutions for their clients; and the postmodernists of the 1970s and 1980s wanted to reject the orthodoxy of the International Style and experiment with new technology. The questions remains: what is the purpose, other than the obvious day-to-day work of meeting deadlines and serving commercial clients, of contemporary graphic design? The first generation of postmodernists was united by the thrill of breaking the rules of the International Style, but this iconoclasm played itself out in the 1990s. Are there really any rules left to break?

If postmodernism has ended, then what has replaced it? Some designers have found a sense of purpose in political activism. Following in the footsteps of Tibor Kalman or Jonathan Barnbrook, they have found themselves in the uncomfortable position of attacking the very profession that supports them. This type of self-loathing is not in itself a solution. The quest for meaning in graphic design is partly a product of its artistic side. While accountants or engineers are not usually beset with finding larger meaning in their work, graphic designers often have asked abstract questions along these lines. Perhaps in future decades their broader mission will again become clear.

Glossary

A

Aesthetic movement A British corollary to the French Symbolist movement in literature and the arts. Artists such as Oscar Wilde reveled in sensuality, mysticism, and beauty; it was sometimes disparagingly referred to as the Decadent movement.

Agitprop Short for "agitation propaganda," this term originated with the Russian Communist campaign to spread their ideology.

Akzidenz Grotesk One of the first high-quality sans serif typefaces, it was released by the German foundry Berthold in 1896.

Appropriation To borrow; this term refers to the way in which postmodern artists often borrow imagery from outside the art and design worlds and include them in their work.

Arabesque The term denotes the geometric patterns that were a popular part of Art Nouveau style.

Arbeitsrat für Kunst Founded in 1918, the activist group of artists and architects who called themselves the "Workers for Art" sought to participate in the restructuring of German society after the collapse of the government upon its defeat in the First World War.

Arcadia Neville Brody designed Arcadia in 1986 based on his earlier work for *Arena* magazine.

Architectonic A composition structured in such a way that its forms are suggestive of the elements of architecture.

Arial A typeface designed in 1988 as an inexpensive copy of Adobe's Postscript Helvetica.

Art Deco An English-language term derived from the name of the 1925 exposition of the decorative arts held in Paris; Art Deco is a style characterized by geometric regularity, planar surfaces, rectilinear compositions, and an overall elegant machine aesthetic.

Art Nouveau Literally "new art," a late nineteenth-century decorative arts movement in Europe and the United States that favored a unified design style based on organic forms, and featured a significant Asian, particularly Japanese, formal influence.

Arts and Crafts A late nineteenth-century decorative arts movement in Europe and the United States that rejected industrial production in favor of handcrafted goods with simple, often geometric, designs.

Auriol An Art Nouveau typeface designed in 1901 by Georges Auriol that displayed an Asian influence.

Avant-Garde From a French military term, avant-garde refers to artists who are at the revolutionary edge of stylistic and conceptual experimentation.

Avant-Garde Gothic Herb Lubalin designed this stylish sans serif typeface in 1967 for the masthead of the magazine *Avant Garde.*

B

Baskerville Eighteenth-century Transitional type designed in England by John Baskerville.

Bauhaus The "House of Building," a state-sponsored school of the arts founded by Walter Gropius in Weimar, Germany, in 1919. The Bauhaus was closed by the Nazis in 1933.

Behrens-Antiqua A roman typeface designed by Peter Behrens in 1908 for the AEG corporation.

Behrens-Fraktur A decorative typeface designed by Peter Behrens in the early 1900s as a compromise between the blackletter and Art Nouveau styles.

Behrens-Schrift A typeface designed by Peter Behrens in 1901 that combined elements of blackletter script and roman structure.

Bembo A fifteenth-century Old Style type designed in Venice by Aldus Manutius.

Bernhard Antiqua A bold roman display typeface designed in 1912 by Lucian Bernhard and based on the style of lettering in his earlier hand-drawn posters.

Bifur A decorative typeface designed by Cassandre in 1929 as part of the Art Deco movement.

Bijin-ga A subset of *Ukiyo-e* woodblock prints that showcase images of beautiful young women, mainly courtesans.

Bit-mapped Bit-mapped letters are made up of an array of pixels (tiny dots), which drastically limit their scalability because of their extremely low resolution.

Bits Paul Elliman released the first version of his decorative Bits typeface in 1997.

Blackletter The general term for typefaces that resemble the forms of medieval script; the positive space formed by black ink overwhelms the negative white space of the paper.

Bocklin A German Art Nouveau typeface designed by Otto Weisert in 1904.

Bodoni Eighteenth-century Modern type designed in Italy by Giambattista Bodoni.

Bolshevik Literally a member of the "majority," the Marxist-inspired Bolshevik party led by Vladimir Lenin seized control of Russia in 1917, later forming the Communist Party that controlled the USSR for most of the twentieth century.

Broadway An influential Art Deco typeface designed in 1929 by Morris Fuller Benton.

C

Cabaret Voltaire A modest nightclub in the back room of a restaurant in Zurich made famous by the Dada gatherings held there in 1916.

Caslon Eighteenth-century Transitional type designed in England by William Caslon.

Chromolithography Color lithography; the process whereby a color image is reproduced using flat stones that have been drawn on with greasy ink or crayons. A separate stone is used for each color.

Cochin A roman typeface designed in 1914 for the Monotype letterpress machine by the French artist and foundry owner Dominique Peignet.

Comic Sans A decorative typeface released by Microsoft in 1995.

Commedia dell'Arte A kind of vernacular, often improvisational, folk theater that originated in Italy in the sixteenth century and soon spread to Britain and France.

Commercial Modern Almost a synonym for Art Deco, "Commercial Modern" refers to designs that borrow from the modern movement in the fine arts, especially Cubism and Futurism.

Constructivist Congress A gathering of Constructivist artists held in Weimar, Germany, in 1922 at the behest of Theo van Doesburg. It was partially disrupted by the arrival of a number of Dadaists.

Cubism An art movement focusing on painting that originated in Paris in the early twentieth century. Georges Braque and Pablo Picasso were the key figures who developed a new type of abstraction that would influence generations of future artists.

Curvilinear A design characterized by fluid, curving lines.

D

Dada A constellation of social protest and art movements that originated in Zurich, Switzerland, which was a protest against World War I as well as the European culture that had fomented it.

De Stijl Literally "The Style," a Dutch art movement from the post-World War I era influenced by Neoplatonism. De Stijl promoted a distinct type of reductive geometric abstract art.

Deutscher Werkbund A German organization founded in Munich in 1907 with the intent of raising the quality, both aesthetic and functional, of the nation's industrial production.

Deutschland A blackletter typeface produced under the Nazis in 1934, it mixes calligraphic strokes with the simplified structure of contemporary sans serifs.

Didot Eighteenth-century Modern type designed in France by Firmin Didot.

E

Eckmann A German typeface devised by Otto Eckmann in 1900 to reconcile Art Nouveau and blackletter elements.

Electrance A typeface with a technological aesthetic designed by Dirk Uhlenbrock, a typographer and graphic designer based in Cologne, Germany.

Elliott's Blue Eyeshadow Part of the "Apollo Program Font Set," this is a typeface designed by Elliott Earls in the 1990s that partakes of a grunge aesthetic.

Em box A unit of measurement in typography that corresponds to the size of the frame around a letter.

Emperor 8 An early 1980s bit-mapped typeface by Zuzana Licko, it utilized a ratio of a two-pixel stem to a one-pixel counter.

Entartete Kunst Literally "Degenerate Art," a term used in Nazi Germany to denigrate modern art, which the regime asserted had a corrupting influence on the national culture.

Expressionism Generally speaking, any artistic style that focuses more on reproducing the way the world feels, as opposed to how it looks.

F

Fetish No. 338 Jonathan Hoefler's typeface represented an ironic commentary on the postmodern love of historical pastiche.

FF Dax A popular, stylish sans serif typeface designed in 1997 by Hans Reichel.

Foreshortened The result of a drawing technique that allows for the accurate representation of elements perpendicular to the picture plane, such as a finger pointing at the viewer.

Fraktur Blackletter type characterized by "fractured" forms that originated in Germany in the early sixteenth century; also used as a general synonym for blackletter type.

Franklin Gothic A high-quality sans serif typeface designed in 1902 by the American Morris Fuller Benton.

Full-bleed photograph A photograph that completely covers the page of a magazine or book, all the way to the edges.

Futura An influential sans serif typeface designed by Paul Renner in 1927.

Futurism An Italian art and political protest

movement led by Filippo Marinetti. The Futurists hoped to revolutionize Italian culture, returning it to its historical position as a dominant force in Europe.

G

Garage Gothic Tobias Frere-Jones designed the typeface Garage Gothic, which features vernacular references, in 1992.

Garamond Fifteenth-century Old Style type designed in France by Claude Garamond.

Gesamtkunstwerk A "total work of art," meaning a piece—originating with the music dramas of Richard Wagner—that collapses every possible aesthetic experience into a unified whole.

Gill Sans An influential sans serif typeface designed in 1928 by Eric Gill for the Monotype Corporation.

Gothic An alternative name for blackletter type that imitates medieval script; alternatively, in the United States it can refer to sans serif type.

Grotesque A synonym for sans serif type commonly used in Britain and Europe.

Grunge An unofficial category describing contemporary graphic design that appears in a holistic sense to be unpolished, grungy, and scruffy.

Gutter The inner margins of two facing pages of a magazine or book.

H

Halftone A commercial method for printing images so as to preserve their tonal scale.

Hamburger Druckschrift A typeface designed in 1914 by Friedrich Bauer in the hope of reconciling the blackletter and roman traditions.

Heimatschutz A term used in Nazi Germany to refer to the "preservation of regional tradition" as opposed to the cosmopolitan, urban culture of greater Europe.

Helvetica A key component of the International Style, and perhaps the most influential sans serif typeface of the twentieth century, Helvetica, originally called Neue Haas Grotesk, was designed in 1953 by Max Meidinger.

Historicist A work that references styles from the past.

Hoarding Akin to a billboard, a hoarding is an exterior space (such as a wall) intended for the presentation of posters.

Hoefler Text A family of twenty-seven elegant, traditional typefaces released by Jonathan Hoefler as part of Macintosh's GX project in 1994.

Horror vacui Literally, a fear of empty space, it refers to a composition that completely fills the frame.

I

Incunabula A book printed before 1501.

International Constructivism Distinct from, although strongly influenced by, Russian Constructivism, this term refers to the very broad group of designers and artists interested in geometric abstract art in Europe during the 1920s and after.

International Style A term coined in 1931 by Museum of Modern Art curators Philip Johnson and Henry-Russell Hitchcock to explain the new geometric style in architecture. In graphic design, "International Style" refers to work that operates under the same aesthetic and ideological principles; also called the Swiss Style.

Isotype An acronym meaning "International System of Typographic Picture Education," devised by Otto Neurath, an Austrian sociologist, in the 1920s.

Italics Type that slants elegantly upward and to the right.

J

Japonisme The European, especially French, adoption of Japanese art and fashion during the late nineteenth century.

Jenson-Eusebius A fifteenth-century Old Style type designed in Venice by the typographer Nicolas Jenson.

Job printer A general term for a printing house and its employees that work "job to job" without apparent specialization or design training.

Johnston Sans A sans serif typeface designed by Edward Johnston for the London Underground in 1916.

Jugendstil A German synonym for Art Nouveau meaning "young art," derived from the magazine *Jugend.*

Justified The spacing of text so that the ends of lines are even.

K

Kosmik A "flipper" typeface designed in 1993 by Dutch typographer Erik van Blokland.

Kunstgewerbeschule A Viennese school dedicated to the theory and practice of the decorative arts.

Kunstschule A German school devoted to the theory and practice of the fine arts, as opposed to the decorative arts.

L

Letterpress Printing technique whereby the ink is supported on a raised surface, such as the letters of metal type.

Linotype An industrial machine, developed in 1886, that facilitated mechanical typesetting by setting an entire line of type.

Logotype A visual symbol that identifies a given company or institution, such as a trademark.

Lubok A kind of Russian folk art print, many of which featured religious stories.

M

Machine Aesthetic Most often used in reference to the art of the 1920s, this term refers to works that reproduce the sleek, shiny surfaces and geometric regularity of actual industrial machines.

Modern type Eighteenth-century roman type that is characterized by extreme contrast in stroke thickness, staunchly vertical stress, and hairline serifs.

Modula Zuzana Licko's 1986 typeface utilized Postscript technology in order to create a high-resolution version of her earlier bit-mapped font Emperor.

MoMA Gothic In 2005 Mathew Carter created MOMA Gothic (for the Museum of Modern Art in New York City), a bespoke version of Morris Fuller Benton's Franklin Gothic, as part of the museum's renewal of its corporate identity.

Monotype An industrial machine, developed in 1889, that facilitated mechanical typesetting by producing type character by character, thereby revolutionizing the field.

N

Neo-Plasticism A term used by Piet Mondrian to denote his universal aesthetic, and especially his rejection of contemporary Expressionism.

Neoplatonism A loosely defined philosophy popular with artists in the 1910s and 1920s that posits a transcendent world of universal harmony best represented in the arts through mathematically structured forms.

New Typography A term coined in 1923 and soon made popular by Jan Tschichold, it denotes the progressive changes in typography that occurred during this era; some of the stylistic attributes of the New Typography include orthogonal compositions, bold rules, asymmetry, and sans serif lettering.

Nieuwe beelding Literally "new imagery," this term was used by the members of De Stijl to indicate their plan for revolutionary change in the visual arts.

Non-objective A non-objective artwork bears no direct relationship to the natural world; it is totally abstract.

Not Caslon An ironic decorative typeface designed by Mark Andresen in 1991.

O

Old Style Roman type of the fifteenth and sixteenth centuries that is characterized by understated contrast, bracketed serifs, and oblique stress.

OpenType A font format that allows for cross-platform utilization and increased flexibility versus Postscript and TrueType; it was developed by Adobe and Microsoft, and released in 2000.

Optima Designed for the Linotype machine in 1958 by Hermann Zapf, Optima was one of the more successful Humanist sans serif typefaces, meaning it combined sans serif forms with traditional roman proportions.

Organic form A form in art that is derived from the natural world through its shape, which is often curving, irregular, and plant-like.

Orphism A name coined by the poet Guillaume Apollinaire in response to the artwork of Robert and Sonia Delaunay.

Orthogonal A design that is structured mostly with right angles, such as a grid.

P

Peignot Cassandre's sans serif typeface from 1937 became an icon of the stylish Art Deco era.

Photomontage A composite work made up of photographs that have been combined through any number of ways, including cut and paste as well as multiple exposures.

Phototypesetting A technique developed in the 1950s whereby type was reproduced from photographic negatives as opposed to the metal type used in the Monotype and Linotype machines.

Planar A design dominated by flat planes.

Pop art An art movement that rose to prominence in the 1960s in Britain and the United States, focusing on aspects of popular culture that had traditionally been ignored by fine artists, such as consumerism, comic books, and celebrity.

Postmodern Literally "after modern," this contested term refers to a constellation of design practices, styles, and ideologies that arose in the 1960s through to the present.

Purism An art movement led by Amedée Ozenfant and Charles Edouard Jeanneret that sought to create a new artistic style based upon Cubist principles combined with a classical aesthetic.

R

Rayonism A French-influenced art movement in Russia during the 1910s led by two Moscow artists, Natalya Goncharova and Mikhail Larionov.

Rebus The representation of a word by a picture that creates the same sound; for example, when the famous American designer Paul Rand used a drawing of a bee in place of the letter "B" in a version of the classic IBM logo.

Rectilinear A design characterized by straight lines.

Ring Neue Werbegestalter The "Circle of New Advertising Designers" was co-founded by Kurt Schwitters and others in 1928 to promote their common interest in the New Typography.

Rococo An eighteenth-century unified design style that featured exuberant color, sinuous forms, and an overall emphasis on a sensual atmosphere.

Roman A typeface style dating from the Renaissance, originally derived from Carolingian Minuscule; roman letters feature serifs.

Rubrication The process of highlighting words through the utilization of colored inks.

Russian Constructivism Arising out of the work of the artist Vladimir Tatlin, the artists of this movement from the 1920s develop ed an abstract, geometric style that was designed to serve the needs of the powerful, new Soviet state.

S

Sachplakat The work of a group of poster artists during the early twentieth century noted for their simple, direct mode of expression, led by Lucian Bernhard in Germany.

Sans serif A roman letter or typeface that does not feature serifs.

Schaftstiefelgrotesk An ironic term that mocks the typefaces promulgated under the Nazi regime (such as Deutschland), comparing the strokes of the letters to the black jackboots worn by members of the military and paramilitary forces.

Schwabacher Blackletter type that originated in Germany in about the fifteenth century.

Secessionstil Literally "Secession Style," a synonym for Art Nouveau as it was practiced in Vienna.

Semiotics The academic study and interpretation of signs in the broadest sense, such as languages, and their ability to produce meaning as well as act as arbiters of social power.

Silkscreen A commercial printing technique later adopted by artists whereby ink is forced through a screen made of fabric framed by a hard stencil.

Slab serif A typeface that features heavy rectangular serifs.

Small capitals Uppercase letters that are sized equal to the "x height" of a given typeface and therefore smaller than the standard uppercase letters.

Socialist Realism Conventionally styled, heavily didactic artworks favored by the Russian Communist leader Josef Stalin, who rejected the abstract strategies favored by the Russian Constructivists.

Souvenir Designed by Ed Benguiat in 1970, this sans serif typeface featured subtly fluid, rounded forms.

Stencil A stylized geometric sans serif typeface designed at the Bauhaus by Josef Albers in 1925.

Streamlining A characteristic element of the Art Deco style, streamlining refers to the shape of objects that have been modified to appear as if they could smoothly flow through space, like the bow of a ship.

Stress In a typeface, this denotes the angle of the major axis around which the strokes of a letter are structured (not the angle of the strokes themselves).

Stylized Designs that appear to be structured around a set style or group of compositional rules.

Suprematism The term used by Kasimir Malevich to indicate the spiritual, Neoplatonist underpinnings of his abstract paintings of the 1910s.

Surrealism A movement in art, literature, and politics led by André Breton in the 1920s. Arising out of the Dada movement and inspired by the work of Sigmund Freud, the Paris-based Surrealists exalted and explored the terrain of the unconscious mind.

Symbolism A late nineteenth-century movement in literature and the other arts based in France, which focused on themes of spirituality, sensuality, and the artist's subjective experience of the world.

T

Taser A font family with a technological aesthetic designed by Jim Marcus in 1998.

Template Gothic A typeface designed by Barry Deck in the early 1990s, which combined hand-drawn characteristics with the firm structure of International Style typography.

Textura A kind of early blackletter type that was utilized in the Gutenberg Bible.

Times New Roman Stanley Morison designed this narrowly proportioned roman for *The Times* of London in 1932.

Transitional type Seventeenth-century roman type that is characterized by vertical stress, significant contrast, wide proportions, and thin, elegant serifs.

Typophoto A term coined by László Moholy-Nagy in 1925 to denote the set of aesthetic principles that would govern the integration of typography and photography as the new basis for graphic design.

U

Ukiyo-e Literally "pictures of the floating world," it generally refers to Japanese woodblock prints that feature images of actors, courtesans, and landscape views.

Unger-Fraktur Blackletter type introduced in 1793 by Johann Friedrich Unger, who attempted to adopt the geometric structure of Modern style roman type.

Univers A geometric sans serif typeface designed in 1957 by Adrian Frutiger as part of the International Style.

Universal A staunchly geometric sans serif typeface designed by Herbert Bayer at the Bauhaus, beginning in 1923.

V

Verdana An elegant typeface designed by Mathew Carter for Microsoft in 1996, it is hoped that it will eventually displace the ubiquitous Arial.

Vienna Secession A group of young artists in late nineteenth-century Vienna who rejected the conservative artistic conventions of the era.

Vorticism A British offshoot of the Futurist movement, founded by Wyndham Lewis in 1913.

W

Walker Matthew Carter created this typeface, featuring a variety of "snap-on" serifs, for the Walker Art Center in Minneapolis.

Weimar Republic The liberal democratic government based in the city of Weimar that governed Germany from soon after the end of the First World War (1914–1918) until the rise of the Nazis in 1933.

Westinghouse Gothic A bespoke sans serif typeface designed by Paul Rand for the Westinghouse Corporation in 1968.

Whiplash curve A defining stylistic element of Art Nouveau, it is an S curve that is suggestive of the pent-up energy of a whip suspended in mid-air.

Wiener Werkstätte The "Viennese Workshops," a group of artists spun off from the Vienna Secession who wanted to raise the quality of Austrian decorative arts.

Woodcut Relief printing in which the image is carved into a block of wood to facilitate reproduction.

X

X height A standardized type measurement based on the size of a lowercase letter (excluding any ascenders or descenders) such as the letter x.

Bibliography

Ades, Dawn, *Posters: The 20th-century Poster: Design of the Avant-garde* (New York: Abbeville Press, 1990).

Ades, Dawn, *The Dada Reader: A Critical Anthology* (Chicago: University of Chicago Press, 2006).

Aicher, Otl, *Typographie* (Berlin: Ernst Lüdenscheid: Maack, 1989).

Anderson, Stanford, *Peter Behrens and a New Architecture for the Twentieth Century* (Cambridge, MA: MIT Press, 2000).

Arwas, Victor, *Art Deco* (New York: St. Martin's Press, 1976).

Arwas, Victor, *Berthon and Grasset* (New York: Rizzoli, 1978).

Aynsley, Jeremy, *Graphic Design in Germany: 1890–1945* (Berkeley: California University Press, 2000).

Bain, Eric K., *The Theory and Practice of Typographic Design* (New York: Hastings House, 1970).

Bain, Peter, and Shaw, Paul, eds., *Blackletter: Type and National Identity* (New York: Princeton Architectural Press, 1998).

Baines, Phil, and Haslam, Andrew, *Type and Typography* (London: Laurence King, 2005).

Barr, Alfred H. Jr., *Cubism and Abstract Art* (New York: Museum of Modern Art, 1936).

Barr, Alfred H. Jr., ed., *Fantastic Art, Dada, Surrealism* (New York: Museum of Modern Art, 1936).

Barron, Stephanie, ed., *Degenerate Art: The Fate of the Avant-garde in Nazi Germany* (New York: Abrams, 1991).

Barthes, Roland, *Mythologies* (New York: Hill and Wang, 1972).

Bartram, Alan, *Five Hundred Years of Book Design* (New Haven, CT: Yale University Press, 2001).

Bartram, Alan, *Bauhaus, Modernism, and the Illustrated Book* (New Haven, CT: Yale University Press, 2004).

Bayer, Herbert, ed. (with Walter Gropius and Ise Gropius), *Bauhaus, 1919–1928* (New York, Museum of Modern Art, 1938).

Beardsley, Aubrey, *Le Morte d'Arthur: Selected Illustrations* (Mineola, NY: Dover Publications, 2001).

Bellantoni, Jeff, and Woolman, Matt, *Type in Motion: Innovations in Digital Graphics* (New York: Rizzoli, 1999).

Benson, Timothy O., *Expressionist Utopias: Paradise, Metropolis, Architectural Fantasy* (Los Angeles: Los Angeles County Museum of Art, 1993).

Benton, Josiah H., *John Baskerville: Type-founder and Printer, 1706–1775* (Bristol: Nico Editions, 1998).

Berry, W. Turner, *The Encyclopaedia of Type Faces* (Poole, Dorset: Blandford Press, 1953).

Bicknell, Julian, and McQuiston, Liz, eds., *Design for Need: The Social Contribution of Design: An Anthology of Papers Presented to the Symposium at the Royal College of Art, London, April, 1976* (Oxford: Pergamon Press, 1976).

Birdsall, Derek, *Notes on Book Design* (New Haven, CT: Yale University Press, 2004).

Blackwell, Lewis, *20th-century Type* (New Haven, CT: Yale University Press, 2004).

Blotkamp, Carel, *De Stijl: The Formative Years, 1917–1922* (Cambridge, MA: MIT Press, 1986).

Bojko, Szymon, *New Graphic Design in Revolutionary Russia* (New York: Praeger, 1972).

Brandstätter, Christian, *Wiener Werkstätte: Design in Vienna, 1903–1932: Architecture, Furniture, Commercial Art, Postcards, Bookbinding, Posters, Glass, Ceramics, Metal, Fashion, Textiles, Accessories, Jewelry* (New York: Abrams, 2003).

Bringhurst, Robert, *The Elements of Typographic Style* (Point Roberts, WA: Hartley & Marks, 2004).

Burke, Christopher, *Paul Renner: The Art of Typography* (New York: Princeton Architectural Press, 1998).

Byars, Mel, and Riley, Terrence, *The Design Encyclopedia* (New York: Museum of Modern Art, 2004).

Caban, Geoffrey, *World Graphic Design: Contemporary Graphics from Africa, the Far East, Latin America, and the Middle East* (New York: Merrell, 2004).

Calloway, Stephen, *Aubrey Beardsley* (New York: Abrams, 1998).

Calloway, Stephen, ed., *The House of Liberty: Masters of Style and Decoration* (London: Thames and Hudson, 1992).

Campbell, Colin, *Beggarstaff Posters: The Work of James Pryde and William Nicholson* (New York: Abbeville Press, 1993).

Carson, David, *The End of Print: The Graphic Design of David Carson* (San Francisco: Chronicle Books, 1995).

Carter, Rob, *Typographic Design: Form and Communication* (Hoboken, NJ: John Wiley & Sons, 2006).

Cassandre, A.M., *The Poster Art of A. M. Cassandre* (New York: Dutton, 1979).

Chanzit, Gwen Finkel, *From Bauhaus to Aspen: Herbert Bayer and Modernist Design in America* (Boulder, CO: Johnson Books, 2005).

Chappell, Warren, *Short History of the Printed Word* (New York: Knopf, 1970).

Chipp, Herschel, *Jugendstil and Expressionism in German Posters* (Berkeley: California University Press, 1965).

Chwast, Seymour, *Left-handed Designer* (New York: Abrams, 1985).

Chwast, Seymour, *Push Pin Graphic: A Quarter Century of Innovative Design and Illustration* (San Francisco: Chronicle Books, 2004).

Cohen, Arthur Allen, *Herbert Bayer: The Complete Work* (Cambridge, MA: MIT Press, 1984).

Cooke, Catherine, ed., *Russian Avant-garde Art and Architecture* (New York: St. Martin's Press, 1983).

Coote, Stephen, *William Morris: His Life and Work* (Stroud: Alan Sutton, 1996).

Copley, Frederick S., *Art Deco Alphabets: A Treasury of Original Alphabets from the 1920s and 1930s* (Pittstown, NJ: Main Street Press, 1985).

Craig, James, *Thirty Centuries of Graphic Design: An Illustrated Survey* (New York: Watson-Guptill Publications, 1987).

Crawford, Alan, *Charles Rennie Mackintosh* (New York: Thames and Hudson, 1995).

Dabrowski, Magdalena, Dickerman, Leah, and Galassi, Peter, *Aleksandr Rodchenko* (New York: Museum of Modern Art, 1998).

Dachy, Marc, *Dada: The Revolt of Art* (New York: Abrams, 2006).

Delhaye, Jean, *Art Deco Posters and Graphics* (London: Academy Editions, 1977).

DeNoon, Christopher, *Posters of the WPA* (Los Angeles: Wheatley Press, with the University of Washington Press, 1987).

Denscher, Bernhard, *Österreichische Plakatkunst, 1898–1938* (Vienna: Brandstätter, 1992).

D'Harnoncourt, Anne, *Futurism and the International Avant-garde* (Philadelphia: Philadelphia Museum of Art, 1980).

Doig, Allan, *Theo Van Doesburg: Painting into Architecture, Theory into Practice* (Cambridge: Cambridge University Press, 1986).

Drate, Spencer, and Salavetz, Jutka, *Extreme Fonts: Digital Faces of the Future* (New York: Madison Square Press, 1999).

Drucker, Johanna, *Visible Word: Experimental Typography and Modern Art, 1909–1923* (Chicago: University of Chicago Press, 1994).

Duncan, Alastair, *Art Nouveau* (New York: Thames and Hudson, 1994).

Duncan, Alastair, *Modernism: Modernist Design, 1880–1940: The Norwest Collection*, (Woodbridge, Suffolk: Antique Collectors' Club, 1998).

Ehrlich, Frederic, *The New Typography and Modern Layouts* (New York: Frederick A. Stokes, 1934).

El Lissitzky, *Monuments of the Future: Designs by El Lissitzky* (Los Angeles: Getty Research Institute, 1998).

Elam, Kimberly, *Grid Systems: Principles of Organizing Type* (New York: Princeton Architectural Press, 2004).

Fiell, Charlotte, and Fiell, Peter, *Graphic Design for the 21st Century/Grafikdesign im 21. Jahrhundert/Le design graphique au 21e siécle: 100 of the World's Best Graphic Designers* (Cologne: Taschen, 2003).

Forster-Hahn, Françoise, ed., *Imagining Modern German Culture, 1889–1910* (Washington, DC: National Gallery of Art, 1996).

Friedman, Dan, *Dan Friedman: Radical Modernism* (New Haven, CT: Yale University Press, 1994).

Friedman, Mildred S., ed., *De Stijl, 1917–1931: Visions of Utopia* (New York: Abbeville Press, 1989).

Gatta, Kevin, *Foundations of Graphic Design* (Worcester, MA: Davis Publications, 1991).

Gillon, Edmund Vincent, *Art Nouveau: An Anthology of Design and Illustration from the Studio* (New York: Dover Publications, 1969).

Glaser, Milton, *Graphic Design* (New York: Overlook Press, 1976).

Green, Oliver, *Underground Art: London Transport Posters 1908 to the Present* (London: Laurence King, 2001).

Greenberg, Allan C., *Artists and Revolution: Dada and the Bauhaus, 1917–1925* (Ann Arbor, MI: UMI Research Press, 1979).

Greenhalgh, Paul, *Essential Art Nouveau* (London: V & A Publications, 2000).

Greiman, April, *Hybrid Imagery: The Fusion of Technology and Graphic Design* (New York: Watson-Guptill, 1990).

Hall, Peter, *Sagmeister: Made You Look* (London: Booth-Clibborn Editions Press, 2001).

Hall, Peter, and Bierut, Michael, eds., *Tibor Kalman, Perverse Optimist* (New York: Princeton Architectural Press, 1998).

Harris, Robert L., *Information Graphics: A Comprehensive Illustrated Reference* (London: Oxford University Press, 1999).

Haworth-Booth, Mark, *Edward McKnight Kauffer: A Designer and His Public* (New York: Abrams, 2005).

Helfand, Jessica, *Screen: Essays on Graphic Design, New Media, and Visual Culture* (New York: Princeton Architectural Press, 2001).

Heller, Steven, *Design Literacy (Continued): Understanding Graphic Design* (New York: Allworth Press, 1999).

Heller, Steven, *Paul Rand* (London and New York: Phaidon, 1999).

Heller, Steven, *Graphic Design Time Line: A Century of Design Milestones* (New York: Allworth Press, 2000).

Heller, Steven, *Merz to Emigré and Beyond: Avant-garde Magazine Design of the Twentieth Century* (New York and London: Phaidon, 2003).

Heller, Steven, and Fili, Louise, *Cover Story: The Art of American Magazine Covers, 1900–1950* (San Francisco: Chronicle Books, 1996).

Heller, Steven, and Fili, Louise, *Typology: Type Design from the Victorian Era to the Digital Age* (San Francisco: Chronicle Books, 1999).

Heller, Steven, and Finamore, Marie, eds., *Design Culture: An Anthology of Writing from the AIGA Journal of Graphic Design* (New York: Allworth Press: American Institute of Graphic Arts, 1997).

Heller, Steven, and Meggs, Philip, *Texts on Type: Critical Writings on Typography* (New York: Allworth Press, 2001).

Heller, Steven, and Thompson, Christine, *Letterforms Bawdy, Bad and Beautiful: The Evolution of Hand-drawn, Humorous, Vernacular, and Experimental Type* (New York: Watson-Guptill, 2000).

Heller, Steven, and Vienne, Véronique, eds., *Citizen Designer: Perspectives on Design Responsibility* (New York: Allworth Press, 2003).

Heyman, Therese Thau, *Posters American Style* (Washington, DC: National Museum of American Art, Smithsonian Institution, 1998).

Hiesinger, Kathryn Bloom, *Art Nouveau in Munich: Masters of the Jugendstil from the Stadtmuseum, Munich, and other Public and Private Collections* (Philadelphia: Philadelphia Museum of Art, 1988).

Hitchcock, Henry-Russell, and Johnson, Philip, *The International Style* (New York: W.W. Norton, 1966).

Holland, D.K., Helfand, Jessica, and Kidd, Chip, *Graphic Design: America 2* (Rockport, MA: Rockport/Allworth Editions, 1997).

Hollis, Richard, *Graphic Design: A Concise History* (New York: Thames and Hudson, 1993).

Hollis, Richard, *Swiss Graphic Design: The Origins and Growth of an International Style 1920–1965* (New Haven, CT: Yale University Press, 2006).

Huelsenbeck, Richard, *Memoirs of a Dada Drummer* (Berkeley: California University Press, 1991).

Huelsenbeck, Richard, ed., *The Dada Almanac* (London: Atlas Press, 1993).

Humphreys, Richard, *Futurism* (Cambridge and New York: Cambridge University Press, 1999).

Hutchings, Frederick, *The Impact of William Morris* (Toronto: Copp Clark, 1968).

Ing, Janet Thompson, *Johann Gutenberg and his Bible: A Historical Study* (New York: Typophiles, 1988).

Jackson, Anna, *Japanese Textiles in the Victoria and Albert Museum* (London: V & A Publications, 2000).

Jaffé, Hans L.C., *De Stijl: Extracts from the Magazine* (London, Thames & Hudson, 1970).

James-Chakraborty, Kathleen, ed., *Bauhaus Culture: from Weimar to the Cold War* (Minneapolis: Minnesota University Press, 2006).

Jobling, Paul, and Crowley, David, *Graphic Design: Reproduction and Representation since 1800* (Manchester: Manchester University Press, 1996).

Kaplan, Wendy, ed., *Charles Rennie Mackintosh* (New York: Abbeville Press, 1996).

Kery, Patricia Frantz, *Art Deco Graphics* (New York: Abrams, 1986).

King, Emily, *Robert Brownjohn: Sex and Typography: 1925–1970, Life and Work* (New York: Princeton Architectural Press, 2005).

Kinross, Robin, *Modern Typography: An Essay in Critical History* (London and New York: Hyphen Press, 1994).

Kirkham, Pat, *Saul Bass* (New Haven, CT: Yale University Press, 2007).

Kirkham, Pat, ed., *Women Designers in the USA, 1900–2000: Diversity and Difference* (New Haven, CT: Yale University Press, 2000).

Kostelanetz, Richard, ed., *Moholy-Nagy: An Anthology* (New York: Da Capo Press, 1991).

Kozloff, Max, *Cubism/Futurism* (New York: Charterhouse, 1973).

Lambourne, Lionel, *Japonisme: Cultural Crossings between Japan and the West* (New York: Phaidon, 2005).

Lavin, Maud, *Clean New World: Culture, Politics and Graphic Design* (Cambridge, MA: MIT Press, 2001).

Lavin, Maud, ed., *Business of Holidays* (New York: Monacelli, 2004).

Lesser, Robert, *Pulp Art: Original Cover Paintings for the Great American Pulp Magazines* (Edison, NJ: Castle Books, 2003).

Lissitzky-Kuppers, Sophie, *El Lissitzky: Life, Letters, Texts* (London: Thames and Hudson, 1980).

Livingston, Alan, and Livingston, Isabella, *The Thames and Hudson Dictionary of Graphic Design* (New York: Thames and Hudson, 1992).

Lodder, Christina, *Russian Constructivism* (New Haven, CT: Yale University Press, 1983).

Lovegrove, Keith, *Railroad: Identity, Design, and Culture* (New York: Rizzoli, 2005).

Lowry, Martin, *Nicholas Jenson and the Rise of Venetian Publishing in Renaissance Europe* (Oxford: Blackwell, 1991).

Loxley, Simon, *Type: The Secret History of Letters* (London: I.B. Tauris, 2004).

Lupton, Ellen, *Mixing Messages: Contemporary Graphic Design in America* (New York: Cooper-Hewitt National Design Museum, Smithsonian Institution, and Thames and Hudson, 1996).

Lupton, Ellen, *Thinking with Type: A Critical Guide for Designers, Writers, and Editors* (New York: Princeton Architectural Press, 2004).

Lupton, Ellen, and Cohen, Elaine Lustig, *Letters from the Avant-garde: Modern Graphic Design* (New York: Princeton Architectural Press, 1996).

Lupton, Ellen, and Miller, J. Abbott, eds., *The ABC's of [Triangle Square Circle]: The Bauhaus and Design Theory* (New York: Princeton Architectural Press, 1991).

Lupton, Ellen, and Miller, J. Abbot, *Design, Writing, Research: Writing on Graphic Design* (New York: Kiosk: Distributed by Princeton Architectural Press, 1996).

Mackintosh, Alastair, *Symbolism and Art Nouveau* (London: Thames and Hudson, 1975).

Mansbach, Steven A., *Visions of Totality: Laszlo Moholy-Nagy, Theo Van Doesburg, and El Lissitzky* (Ann Arbor, MI: UMI Research Press, 1980).

Marcus, George H., *Masters of Modern Design: A Critical Assessment* (New York: Monacelli, 2005).

Margolin, Victor, *The Struggle for Utopia: Rodchenko, Lissitzky, Moholy-Nagy, 1917–1946* (Chicago: University of Chicago Press, 1997).

Margolin, Victor, ed., *Design Discourse: History, Theory, Criticism* (Chicago: University of Chicago Press, 1989).

Massin, *Letter and Image,* translated by Caroline Hillier and Vivienne Menkes (New York: Van Nostrand Reinhold, 1970).

Mau, Bruce, *Massive Change* (London and New York: Phaidon, 2004).

McLean, Ruari, *Jan Tschichold: A Life in Typography* (New York: Princeton Architectural Press, 1997).

McLuhan, Marshall, *The Medium is the Message* (New York: Random House, 1967).

McQuiston, Liz, *Graphic Agitation: Social and Political Graphics since the Sixties* (London: Phaidon, 1995).

McQuiston, Liz, *Graphic Agitation 2: Social and Political Graphics in the Digital Age* (London: Phaidon, 2004).

Meggs, Philip B., *Six Chapters in Design: Saul Bass, Ivan Chermayeff, Milton Glaser, Paul Rand, Ikko Tanaka, Henryk Tomaszewski* (San Francisco: Chronicle Books 1997).

Meggs, Philip, and McKelvey, Roy, eds., *Revival of the Fittest: Digital Versions of Classic Typefaces* (New York: RC Publications, 2000).

Milner, John, *Vladimir Tatlin and the Russian Avant-garde* (New Haven, CT: Yale University Press, 1983).

Moholy-Nagy, László, *Painting, Photography, Film* (Cambridge, MA: MIT Press, 1969).

Moholy-Nagy, Sibyl, *Moholy-Nagy: Experiment in Totality* (Cambridge, MA: MIT Press, 1969).

Morison, Stanley, *The Typographic Book, 1450–1935* (Chicago: University of Chicago Press, 1963).

Moscoso, Victor, *Sex, Rock, and Optical Illusions* (Woodacre, CA: Electric City, 2002).

Motherwell, Robert, *The Dada Painters and Poets: An Anthology,* 2nd ed. (Boston, MA: G.K. Hall, 1981).

Mount, Christopher, *Stenberg Brothers: Constructing a Revolution in Soviet Design* (New York: Museum of Modern Art and Abrams, 1997).

Müller-Brockmann, Josef, *Grid Systems* (New York: Hastings House Publishers, 1981).

Müller-Brockmann, Josef, *Josef Müller-Brockmann, Designer: A Pioneer of Swiss Graphic Design* (Baden, Switzerland: Lars Müller, 1995).

Murray-Robertson, Anne, *Grasset: Pionnier de l'Art Nouveau* (Paris: Bibliothèque des Arts, 1981).

Museen der Stadt Wien, *Ver Sacrum: die Zeitschrift der Wiener Secession, 1898–1903* (Vienna: Museen der Stadt Wien, 1982).

Needham, Paul, *William Morris and the Art of the Book* (New York: Pierpont Morgan Library, 1976).

Nunoo-Quarcoo, Franc, *Paul Rand: Modernist Design* (New York: Distributed Art Publishers, 2003).

Paret, Peter, Lewis, Irwin, Beth, and Paret, Paul, *Persuasive Images: Posters of War and Revolution from the Hoover Institution Archives* (Princeton, NJ: Princeton University Press, 1992).

Passuth, Krisztina, *Moholy-Nagy* (London: Thames and Hudson, 1987).

Paul, Ned, and Sternberger, Drew, *By its Cover: Modern American Book Cover Design* (New York: Princeton Architectural Press, 2005).

Pentagram Design, *The Compendium: Thoughts, Essays and Work from the Pentagram Partners in London, New York and San Francisco* (London: Phaidon, 1993).

Pentagram Design, *Living by Design: The Partners of Pentagram* (New York: Whitney Library of Design, 1979).

Perfect, Christopher, *Rookledge's Classic International Type Finder: The Essential Handbook of Typeface Recognition* (London: Laurence King, 2004).

Perloff, Marjorie, *The Futurist Moment: Avant-Garde, Avant Guerre, and the Language of Rupture* (Chicago: University of Chicago Press, 2003).

Perloff, Nancy, and Reed, Brian, eds., *Situating El Lissitzky: Vitebsk, Berlin, Moscow* (Los Angeles: Getty Research Institute, 2003).

Petric, Vlada, *Constructivism in Film: The Man with the Movie Camera: A Cinematic Analysis* (Cambridge: Cambridge University Press, 1987).

Pevsner, Nikolaus, *Pioneers of the Modern Movement from William Morris to Walter Gropius* (London: Faber & Faber, 1936).

Plunkett, John, and Rossetto, Louis, eds., *Mind Grenades: Manifestos from the Future* (San Francisco: HardWired, 1996).

Poynor, Rick, *Typographica* (New York: Princeton Architectural Press, 2002).

Poynor, Rick, *No More Rules: Graphic Design and Postmodernism* (New Haven, CT: Yale University Press, 2003).

Poynor, Rick, ed., *Communicate: Independent British Graphic Design since the Sixties* (New Haven, CT: Yale University Press, 2004).

Purvis, Alston W., *H.N. Werkman* (New Haven, CT: Yale University Press, 2004).

Purvis, Alston W., and Le Coultre, Martijn F., *Graphic Design 20th Century* (New York: Princeton Architectural Press, 2003).

Rand, Paul, *Paul Rand: A Designer's Art* (New Haven, CT: Yale University Press, 2001).

Reade, Brian, *Art Nouveau and Alphonse Mucha*, 2nd ed. (London: HMSO, 1967).

Remington, R. Roger, *American Modernism: Graphic Design, 1920–1960* (London: Laurence King, 2003).

Remington, R. Roger, *Lester Beall: Space, Time, and Content* (Rochester, NY: RIT, Cary Graphic Arts Press, 2003).

Remington, Roger, and Hodik, Barbara, *Nine Pioneers in American Graphic Design* (Cambridge, MA: The MIT Press, 1989).

Rennhofer, Maria, *Koloman Moser: Master of Viennese Modernism* (New York: Thames and Hudson, 2002).

Reyes, Jesse Marinoff, *Next: The New Generation in Graphic Design* (Cincinnati, OH: North Light Books, 2000).

Rickards, Maurice, *Banned Posters* (Park Ridge, NJ: Noyes Press, 1972).

Rothschild, Deborah, Lupton, Ellen, and Goldstein, Darra, *Graphic Design in the Mechanical Age: Selections from the Merrill C. Berman Collection* (New Haven, CT: Yale University Press, 1998).

Rowland, Anna, *Bauhaus Source Book* (New York: Van Nostrand Reinhold, 1990).

Ruder, Emil, *Typographie* (New York: Hastings House, 1981).

Scheidig, Walther, *Crafts of the Weimar Bauhaus, 1919–1924; An Early Experiment in Industrial Design* (New York: Van Nostrand Reinhold, 1967).

Scher, Paula, *Make It Bigger* (New York: Princeton Architectural Press, 2005).

Schwartz, Frederick J., *The Werkbund: Design Theory and Mass Culture before the First World War* (New Haven, CT: Yale University Press, 1996)

Scotford, Martha, *Cipe Pineles: A Life of Design* (New York: W.W. Norton, 1998).

Selz, Peter, and Constantine, Mildred, eds., *Art Nouveau; Art and Design at the Turn of the Century* (New York: Museum of Modern Art, by Arno Press, 1972).

Sharp, Dennis, *Bauhaus, Dessau: Walter Gropius* (London: Phaidon, 1993).

Shaughnessy, Adrian, *How to Be a Graphic Designer, without Losing your Soul* (New York: Princeton Architectural Press, 2005).

Silver, Kenneth E., *Esprit de Corps: The Art of the Parisian Avant-garde and the First World War, 1914–1925* (Princeton, NJ: Princeton University Press, 1989).

Spencer, Herbert, *Pioneers of Modern Typography* (New York, Hastings House, 1970).

Spencer, Herbert, *The Liberated Page: A 'Typographica' Anthology* (San Francisco: Bedford Press, 1987).

Sturgis, Matthew, *Aubrey Beardsley: A Biography* (Woodstock, NY: Overlook Press, 1998).

Swanson, Gunnar, ed., *Graphic Design and Reading: Explorations of an Uneasy Relationship* (New York: Allworth Press, 2000).

Thompson, Bradbury, *The Art of Graphic Design* (New Haven, CT: Yale University Press, 1988).

Thomson, Ellen Mazur, *Origins of Graphic Design in America, 1870–1920* (New Haven, CT: Yale University Press, 1997).

Thorpe, James Ernest, *The Gutenberg Bible: Landmark in Learning* (San Marino, CA: Huntington Library, 1999).

Timmers, Margaret, ed., *The Power of the Poster* (London: V & A Publications, 2003).

Tomato, *Bareback: A Tomato Project* (Corte Madera, CA: Gingko Press, 1999).

Tschichold, Jan, *Asymmetric Typography* (London: Faber & Faber, 1967).

Tschichold, Jan, *New Typography: A Handbook for Modern Designers*, translated by Ruari McLean, with an introduction by Robin Kinross (Berkeley: California University Press, 1995).

Tufte, Edward, *The Visual Display of Quantitative Information* (Cheshire, CT: Graphic Press, 1983).

Tufte, Edward, *Envisioning Information* (Cheshire, CT: Graphics Press, 1990).

Tufte, Edward, *Visual Explanations. Images and Quantities, Evidence and Narrative* (Cheshire, CT: Graphics Press, 1997).

Typitsyn, Margarita, with contributions by Matthew Drutt and Ulrich Pohlmann, *El Lissitzky: Beyond the Abstract Cabinet: Photography, Design, Collaboration* (New Haven, CT: Yale University Press, 1999).

VanderLans, Rudy, and Licko, Zuzana, *Emigré: Graphic Design into the Digital Realm* (New York: Van Nostrand Reinhold, 1993).

VanderLans, Rudy, et al., *If We're Standing on the Shoulders of Giants, What Are We Reaching For?* (Sacramento, CA: Emigré; and New York: Princeton Architectural Press, 2003).

Varnedoe, Kirk, *Vienna 1900: Art, Architecture, and Design* (New York: Museum of Modern Art, 1986).

Vienne, Véronique, *Chip Kidd* (New Haven, CT: Yale University Press, 2003).

Waggoner , Diane, ed., *'The Beauty of Life': William Morris and the Art of Design* (New York: Thames and Hudson, 2003).

Walker Art Center, *Graphic Design in America: A Visual Language History* (New York: Abrams, 1989).

Ware, Colin, *Information Visualization, Perception for Design* (San Francisco: Morgan Kaufmann, 2000).

Weingart, Wolfgang, *Typography* (New York: Princeton Architectural Press, 2000).

Weisberg, Gabriel P., *Art Nouveau Bing: Paris Style 1900* (New York: Abrams, 1996).

White, Stephen, *Bolshevik Poster* (New Haven, CT: Yale University Press, 1988).

Windsor, Alan Peter, *Behrens, Architect and Designer* (New York: Whitney Library of Design, 1981).

Wingler, Hans Maria, *Das Bauhaus: 1919–1933: Weimar, Dessau, Berlin und die Nachfolge in Chicago seit 1937* (Bramsche: Gebr. Rasch Publishers, 1962).

Wozencroft, Jon, *Brody: The Graphic Language of Neville Brody* (Eastbourne, East Sussex: Gardners Books, 1988).

Wrede, Stuart, *Modern Poster* (New York: Museum of Modern Art, 1988).

Wye, Deborah, and Rowell, Margit, *Russian Avant-garde Books, 1910–1934* (New York: Museum of Modern Art, 2002).

Index

Picture Credits

0.1. 0.2, 0.3, 0.4, 0.6, 0.11, 0.22 The British Library, London; 0.7, 0.8, 0.10, 0.16 St Bride Printing Library, London; 0.19, 0.20 V&A Picture Library, Courtesy of the Trustees of the Victoria & Albert Museum, London; 0.21 Library of Congress, Washington, DC.; 1.1, 1.2 William Morris Gallery, The London Borough of Waltham Forest; 1.3 The British Library, London; 1.4, 1.7 St Bride Printing Library, London; 1.5 Reproduced by permission of the Trustees of the Wallace Collection, London; 1.6 Les Arts Décoratifs, Musée de Publicité, Paris; 1.8 © Photo SCALA, Florence, The Museum of Modern Art, New York, 2006; 1.9 © The Trustees of the British Museum, London; 1.10 V&A Picture Library, Victoria & Albert Museum, London; 1.11, 1.12 Museum für Gestaltung, Zurich, Poster Collection; 1.13 © ADAGP, Paris and DACS, London. Photo: St Bride Printing Library, London; 1.14 © ADAGP, Paris and DACS, London. Photo: St Bride Printing Library, London; 1.15, 1.16 St Bride Printing Library, London; 1.17, 1.18 V&A Picture Library, Victoria & Albert Museum, London; 1.20 Rue des Archives, Paris; 1.21, 1.22 St Bride Printing Library, London; 1.23 V&A Picture Library, Victoria & Albert Museum, London; 1.24 © ADAGP, Paris and DACS, London. Photo: St Bride Printing Library, London; 1.25 Cincinnati Art Museum, Reproduced by permission of Ringling Bros—Barnum & Bailey Combined Shows, Inc.; 1.26 Les Arts Décoratifs, Musée de la Publicité, Paris; 1.27 V&A Picture Library, Victoria & Albert Museum, London; 1.28 Art & Architecture Collection, Miriam & Ira D Wallach Division of Art, Prints & Photographs, The New York Public Library, Astor, Lenox & Tilden Foundations; 1.29 © ADAGP, Paris and DACS, London/The Bridgeman Art Library; 1.30, 1.31 Library of Congress, Prints & Photographs Division; 1.32, 1.33, 1.34, 1.35 St Bride Printing Library, London; 1.36, 1.37, 1.38, 1.39, 1.40, 1.41, 1.42, 1.43, 1.44 V&A Picture Library, Victoria & Albert Museum, London; 1.45 St Bride Printing Library, London; 1.46 St Bride Printing Library, London. Reproduced by permission of Elizabeth Banks; 2.1 Glasgow School of Art Collection; 2.2, 2.3, 2.4 © Hunterian Museum & Art Gallery, University of Glasgow, Mackintosh Collection; 2.5, 2.6 Glasgow School of Art Collection; 2.7 The Burrell Collection, Glasgow, Glasgow City Council (Museums); 2.8 © Photo SCALA, Florence, The Museum of Modern Art, New York, 2006; 2.9 Photo: akg-images, London; 2.11, 2.12, 2.13 MAK–Austrian Museum of Applied Arts/Contemporary Art, Vienna; 2.14 Private Collection. Museum für Gestaltung, Zurich, Poster Collection; 2.15 V&A Picture Library, Victoria & Albert Museum, London; 2.17 Albertina Museum, Vienna; 2.18, 2.19, 2.20, 2.21, 2.22 MAK – Austrian Museum of Applied Arts / Contemporary Art, Vienna; 2.20 Photo: akg-images, London; 2.23 © Oskar Kokoschka. Licensed by DACS 2006, Photo: V&A Picture Library; 2.24 Photo: akg-images, London; 2.25, 2.26 MAK–Austrian Museum of Applied Arts/Contemporary Art, Vienna; 2.27 Wien Museum, Berlin; 2.28 St Bride Printing Library, London; 2.29 Bayerische Staatsbibliotek, Munich; 2.32 Museum für Gestaltung Zurich, Poster Collection; 2.33, 2.34 Stadtmuseum, Munich; 2.35 Brohan-Museum, Berlin; 3.1 Institut für Auslandsbeziehungen, Berlin; 2.36 Private Collection; 2.37 By permission of The British Library, London; 2.38 © Peter Behrens. Licensed by DACS 2006, Photo: Museum fur Gestaltung, Zurich; 2.39 © Peter Behrens. Licensed by DACS 2006, Photo: akg-images, London; 2.40, 2.41 © Peter Behrens. Licensed by DACS 2006; 2.42 © Peter Behrens. Licensed by DACS 2006, Photo: The Minneapolis Institute of Arts, The Modernism Collection, gift of Norwest Bank Minnesota; 2.43 © Peter Behrens. Licensed by DACS 2006, Photo: Merril C. Berman Collection; 2.44 © Peter Behrens. Licensed by DACS 2006, Photo: Museum für Gestaltung, Zurich; 2.45 © Peter Behrens. Licensed by DACS 2006, Photo: V&A Picture Library; 3.2 Gift of the Lauder Foundation, Acc no. 236.1987. © 2006 The Museum of Modern Art, New York/Scala, Florence; 3.3 Museum für Kunst und Gewerbe, Hamburg; 3.4 Deutsches Historisches Museum, Berlin; 3.5 V&A Images/Victoria and Albert Museum; 3.6 Gift of Peter Müller Munk, Acc no. 560.1943. © 2006 The Museum of Modern Art, New York/Scala, Florence; 3.8 V&A Images/Victoria and Albert Museum; 3.10 Imperial War Museum, London; 3.11 Imperial War Museum, London; 3.12 Imperial War Museum, London; 3.13 Imperial War Museum, London; 3.14 Imperial War Museum, London; 3.16 Imperial War Museum, London; 3.16 Imperial War Museum, London; 3.17 Imperial War Museum, London; 3.18 Beaverbrook Collection of War Art © Canadian War Museum (CWM); 3.19 Imperial War Museum, London; 3.20 Imperial War Museum, London; 3.21 Princeton University Poster Collection, Archives, Center, National Museum of American History, Behring Center, Smithsonian Institution; 3.23 Courtesy of P.E.T.A.; 3.24 Library of Congress, Willard and Dorothy Straight Collection; 3.25 Imperial War Museum, London; 3.26 Imperial War Museum, London; 3.28 Imperial War Museum, London; 3.29 Imperial War Museum, London; 3.30 Imperial War Museum, London; 3.31 Imperial War Museum, London; 3.32 Deutsches Historisches Museum, Berlin; 3.33 V&A Images/Victoria and Albert Museum; 3.34 Imperial War Museum, London; 3.35 © Kunsthaus Zurich. All rights reserved; 3.36 Purchase, Acc no. 457.1937. © 2006 The Museum of Modern Art, New York/Scala, Florence; 3.37 International Dada Archive, University of Iowa Libraries; 3.39 University College London, Special Collections; 3.40 International Dada Archive, University of Iowa Libraries; 3.41 University College London, Special Collections; 3.42 International Dada Archive, University of Iowa Libraries; 3.43

Merrill C. Berman Collection. Photo by Jim Frank; 3.44 Bildarchiv Preussischer Kulturbesitz; 3.45 Bildarchiv Preussischer Kulturbesitz; 3.46 University College London, Special Collections; 3.47 Solomon R. Guggenheim Museum, New York 52.1325; 3.48 Cambridge University Library; 4.1 Acc no. 176.1945 © 2006 The Museum of Modern Art, New York/Scala, Florence; 4.2 Washington University Gallery of Art, St. Louis, MO, University purchase, Kende Sale Fund, 1946; 4.4 Private Collection; 4.5 L&M Services B.V. Amsterdam 20060103; 4.6 L&M Services B.V. Amsterdam 20060207; 4.7 London's Transport Museum © Transport for London; 4.8 London's Transport Museum © Transport for London; 4.9 Gift of the Artist, Acc no. 376.1939 © 2006 The Museum of Modern Art, New York/Scala, Florence; 4.10 London's Transport Museum © Transport for London; 4.11 London's Transport Museum © Transport for London; 4.12 London's Transport Museum © Transport for London; 4.13 London's Transport Museum © Transport for London; 4.14 London's Transport Museum © Transport for London; 4.15a,b London's Transport Museum © Transport for London; 4.16 City Archives/Stadsarchief, Ghent; 4.17 ACRPP; 4.18 Private Collection; 4.19 Collection Elaine Lustig Cohen; 4.20 © 1990 Photo Scala, Florence; 4.21 University College London, Special Collections; 4.22 Acc no. 580.1967. © 2006 The Museum of Modern Art, New York/Scala, Florence; 4.23 Depero Archive, Rovereto; 4.24 University College London, Special Collections; 4.25 University College London, Special Collections; 4.26 Gift of the Artist, Acc no. 401.1939. © 2006 The Museum of Modern Art, New York/Scala, Florence; 4.27 V&A Images/Victoria and Albert Museum. © Simon Rendall; 4.28 The British Library; 4.29 St Bride Printing Library, London; 4.30 Solomon R. Guggenheim Foundation, Peggy Guggenheim Collection, 1976. 76.2553.24; 4.31 Photo Musée des Arts Décoratifs, Editions A. Lévy, Paris/© FLC/ADAGP, Paris and DACS, London; 4.32 V&A Images/Victoria and Albert Museum; 4.33 The Minneapolis Institute of Arts, The Modernism Collection. Gift of Norwest Bank Minnesota; 4.34 Given anonymously, Acc no. 280.1935. © 2006 The Museum of Modern Art, New York/Scala, Florence; 4.35 Bibliothèque Forney, France; 4.36 Gift of Bernhard Davis, Acc no. 158.1950. © 2006 The Museum of Modern Art, New York/Scala, Florence; 4.37 Shiseido Corporate Museum; 4.38 © Schenectady Museum; Hall of Electrical History Foundation/Corbis; 4.39 Les Arts Décoratifs, Musée de la Publicité, Paris. Photo Laurent Sully Jaulmes. All rights reserved; 4.40 St. Bride Printing Library; 4.42 St. Bride Printing Library; 4.43 Cary Graphic Arts Collection, RIT, Rochester, New York; 4.44 Bibliothèque Littéraire Jacques Doucet; 4.46 Library of Congress Rare Book and Special Collections Division; 4.46 National Archives Picture Library; 4.47 National Archives Picture Library; 4.48 National Archives Picture Library; 4.49 Bibliothèque Historique de la Ville de Paris/Bridgeman Art Library; 4.50 Photo RMN/© Thierry Ollivier; 4.51 Les Arts Décoratifs, Musée de la Publicité, Paris. Photo Laurent Sully Jaulmes. All rights reserved; 5.1 Solomon R. Guggenheim Museum. © 2006 Mondrian/Holtzman Trust c/o HCR International, Warrenton VA; 5.2a Purchase 227.1948.1 © 2006 The Museum of Modern Art, New York/Scala, Florence; 5.2b Purchase 227.1948.6 © 2006 The Museum of Modern Art, New York/Scala, Florence; 5.3 University College London, Special Collections; 5.4 St Bride Printing Library, London; 5.5 University College London, Special Collections; 5.6 Collection Elaine Lustig Cohen; 5.7 Private Collection; 5.8 Netherlands Architecture Institute; 5.9 Het Utrechts Archief; 5.10 Merrill C. Berman Collection. Photo by Jim Frank; 5.11 Merrill C. Berman Collection. Photo by Jim Frank; 5.12 photo Tim Koster, Institut Collectie Nederland, Rijswijk, Amsterdam; 5.13 Gift of Philip Johnson, Acc no. 178.1945. © 2006 The Museum of Modern Art, New York/Scala, Florence; 5.14 International Dada Archive, University of Iowa Libraries; 5.15 Professor Stephen White, Glasgow University; 5.16 Professor Stephen White, Glasgow University; 5.17 Uppsala University Library, Sweden; 5.18 Professor Stephen White, Glasgow University; 5.19 Professor Stephen White, Glasgow University; 5.20 Solomon R. Guggenheim Museum, New York 57.1484; 5.21 Purchase. Acquisition confirmed in 1999 by agreement with the Estate of Kazimir Malevich and made possible with funds from the Mrs. John Hay Whitney Bequest (by exchange). Acc no. 248.1935. © 2006 The Museum of Modern Art, New York/Scala, Florence; 5.22 © Vladimir Tatlin. Licensed by RAO, Moscow and VISCOPY, Australia. National Gallery of Australia; 5.23 © Vladimir Tatlin. Licensed by DACS 2006; 5.24 © 2006 The Museum of Modern Art, New York/Scala, Florence; 5.25 Van Abbemuseum, Eindhoven, The Netherlands; 5.26 Given anonymously, Acc no. 497.1987. © 2006 The Museum of Modern Art, New York/Scala, Florence; 5.27 Rodchenko Archives; 5.28 Nationalgalerie Staatliche Museen Preussischer Kulturbesitz, Berlin. Bildarchiv Preussischer Kulturbesitz, Berlin; 5.29 Rodchenko Archives; 5.30 Museum of Modern Art, New York. Given anonymously. Acc no. 498.1987. © 2006 The Museum of Modern Art, New York/Scala, Florence; 5.31 Rodchenko Archives; 5.32 Merrill C. Berman Collection. Photo by Jim Frank; 5.33 Merrill C. Berman Collection. Photo by Jim Frank; 5.34 V&A Images/Victoria and Albert Museum; 5.35 Merrill C. Berman Collection. Photo by Jim Frank; 5.36 Bridgeman Art Library; 5.37 Research Library, Getty Research Institute, Los Angeles (930030)/© DACS; 5.38 V&A Images/Victoria and Albert Museum; 5.39 Merrill C. Berman Collection. Photo by Jim Frank; 5.40 Merrill C. Berman Collection. Photo by Jim Frank; 5.41 The Metropolitan Museum of Art, Ford Motor Company Collection, Gift of Ford Motor Company and John C. Waddell, 1987 (1987.1100.47) Photograph © 1989 The Metropolitan Museum of Art; 5.42 Purchase, Acc no. 353.1937. © 2006 The Museum of Modern Art, New York/Scala, Florence; 6.1 © ADAGP, Paris & DACS, London; 6.2 Decla-Bioscop/The Kobal Collection; 6.3 photo Tim Koster, Institut Collectie